WILKINSON'S

ROAD TRAFFIC
OFFENCES

WILKINSON'S
ROAD TRAFFIC OFFENCES

Twelfth Edition

VOLUME 2

Prepared by PAUL H. NIEKIRK MA
of Grays' Inn, Barrister

PATRICK HALNAN
Metropolitan Stipendiary Magistrate

JOHN SPENCER
of the Inner Temple, Barrister
Clerk to the Bridport, Dorchester, Sherborne, and Weymouth
and Portland Justices

Longman Professional

© Longman Group Limited 1985

ISBN 2 Vols: 0 85121 073 2
Vol 1: 0 85120 980 7
Vol 2: 0 85121 101 1

First published   1953
Twelfth edition   1985

Published by:
Longman Professional and Business Communications Division
21–27 Lamb's Conduit Street
London WC1N 3NJ
ENGLAND

Associated offices:

Longman Professional Publishing (Pty) Limited
130 Phillip Street
Sydney
NSW 2000
AUSTRALIA

Longman Group (USA)
500 North Dearborn Street
Chicago, Illinois 60610
USA

Longman Group (Far East) Limited
Cornwall House, 18th Floor
Tai Koo Trading Estate
Tong Chong Street
Quarry Bay
HONG KONG

Longman Singapore Publishers (PTE) Limited
25 First Lok Yang Road
SINGAPORE 2262

Longman Malaysia Sdn Bhd
Wisma Damansara/Tingkat 2
5 Jalan Semantan
Peti Surat 63
Kuala Lumpur 01–02
MALAYSIA

Printed in Great Britain by
Butler & Tanner Ltd, Frome and London

Contents

Table of Statutes

Table of Statutory Instruments

Table of European Provisions

International Agreements

Levels of Fines on the Standard Scale

The standard scale of fines is set out in the Criminal Justice Act 1982, s 37, as amended. The levels on the standard scale were increased in respect of offences committed after 30 April 1984 by the Criminal Penalties etc (Increase) Order 1984 (SI 1984 No 447). For convenience, the former levels and the current levels are set out below:

Level on the standard scale	Amount before 1 May 1984	Amount after 30 April 1984
1	£25	£50
2	£50	£100
3	£200	£400
4	£500	£1000
5	£1000	£2000

Article 1 (2) of SI 1984 No 447 reads: 'This Order shall not affect the amount of any fine imposed, nor the amount of any compensation order made, in respect of any offence committed before 1st May 1984 nor the amount of any fine imposed in respect of any act or omission taking place before that date.'

The same instrument increased the amount of the prescribed sum (see the Magistrates' Courts Act 1980, s 32 (9)) payable on conviction of any offence triable either way from £1000 to £2000.

General Note

Volume 2 of this book contains only a selection of statutory provisions and the omission of any provision does not necessarily imply that it is not operative.

Section A

Statutes

The Criminal Attempts Act 1981

(1981 c 47)

An Act to amend the law of England and Wales . . . and . . . to repeal the provisions of section 4 of the Vagrancy Act 1824 which apply to suspected persons and reputed thiefs; to make provision against unauthorised interference with vehicles . . .

[27th July 1981]

*　　*　　*

PART II

Suspected Persons etc

8. Abolition of offence of loitering etc with intent

The provisions of section 4 of the Vagrancy Act 1824 which apply to suspected persons and reputed thieves frequenting or loitering about the places described in that section with the intent there specified shall cease to have effect.

[In the Vagrancy Act 1824, s 4, the words from 'every suspected person' to 'arrestable offence' were formally repealed by s 10 of and Part II of the Schedule to this Act.]

9. Interference with vehicles

(1) A person is guilty of the offence of vehicle interference if he interferes with a motor vehicle or trailer or with anything carried in or on a motor vehicle or trailer with the intention that an offence specified in subsection (2) below shall be committed by himself or some other person.

(2) The offences mentioned in subsection (1) above are—

(*a*) theft of the motor vehicle or trailer or part of it;

(*b*) theft of anything carried in or on the motor vehicle or trailer; and

(*c*) an offence under section 12 (1) of the Theft Act 1968 (taking and driving away without consent);

and, if it is shown that a person accused of an offence under this section intended that one of those offences should be committed, it is immaterial that it cannot be shown which it was.

(3) A person guilty of an offence under this section shall be liable on summary conviction to imprisonment for a term not exceeding three months or to a fine not exceeding [level 4 in the standard scale] or to both.

(4) *A constable may arrest without warrant anyone who is or whom he with reasonable cause suspects to be guilty of an offence under this section.*

(5) In this section 'motor vehicle' and 'trailer' have the meanings assigned to them be section 190 (1) of the Road Traffic Act 1972.

3

[Section 9 is printed as amended by the Criminal Justice Act 1982, s 46 (1).
Section 9 (4) is repealed by the Police and Criminal Evidence Act 1984, s 119 (2) and Sched 7,
Part I (with effect from a date to be announced).]

*   *   *

The Criminal Justice Act 1982

(1982 c 48)

An Act to make further provision as to the sentencing and treatment of offenders (including provision as to . . . the standardisation of fines and of certain other sums specified in enactments relating to the powers of criminal courts) . . .

[28th October 1982]

*   *   *

Introduction of standard scale of fines

37. The standard scale of fines for summary offences

(1) There shall be a standard scale of fines for summary offences, which shall be known as 'the standard scale'.

(2) The scale *at the commencement of this section* is shown below.

Level on the scale	Amount of fine
1	[£50]
2	[£100]
3	[£400]
4	[£1000]
5	[£2000]

(3) Where any enactment (whether contained in an Act passed before or after this Act) provides—

(*a*) that a person convicted of a summary offence shall be liable on conviction to a fine or a maximum fine by reference to a specified level on the standard scale; or

(*b*) confers power by subordinate instrument to make a person liable on conviction of a summary offence (whether or not created by the instrument) to a fine or maximum fine by reference to a specified level on the standard scale,

it is to be construed as referring to the standard scale for which this section provides as that standard scale has effect from time to time by virtue either of this section or of an order under section 143 of the Magistrates' Courts Act 1980.

[Section 37 is printed as amended by the Criminal Penalties etc (Increase) Order 1984 (SI 1984 No 447) so far as it relates to offences committed after 30 April 1984. On the substitution of the new rates the words in italics have in effect lapsed.]

The Highways Act 1980

(1980 c 66)

An Act to consolidate the Highways Acts 1959 to 1971 and related enactments, with amendments to give effect to recommendations of the Law Commission.

[13th November 1980]

*   *   *

137. Penalty for wilful obstruction

(1) If a person, without lawful authority or excuse, in any way wilfully obstructs the free passage along a highway he is guilty of an offence and liable to a fine not exceeding [level 3 on the standard scale].

(2) A constable may arrest without warrant any person whom he sees committing an offence against this section.

[Section 137 is printed as amended by the Criminal Justice Act 1982, ss 38, 46 (1).

As to the application of the fixed penalty procedure to offences under s 137, see the Transport Act 1982, Part III and Sched 1.]

*   *   *

SCHEDULE 4

CLASSES OF TRAFFIC FOR PURPOSES OF SPECIAL ROADS

Class I:

Heavy and light locomotives, motor tractors, heavy motor cars, motor cars and motor cycles whereof the cylinder capacity of the engine is not less than 50 cubic centimetres, and trailers drawn thereby, which comply with general regulations as to construction and use made, or having effect as if made, under section 40 of the Road Traffic Act 1972 and in the case of which the following conditions are satisfied:—

  (i) that the whole weight of the vehicle is transmitted to the road surface by bans of wheels;
 (ii) that all wheels of the vehicle are equipped with pneumatic tyres;
(iii) that the vehicle is not controlled by a pedestrian;
 (iv) that the vehicle is not a vehicle chargeable with duty under paragraph 2 of Part I of Schedule 3 to the Vehicles (Excise) Act 1971; and
  (v) in the case of a motor vehicle, that it is so constructed as to be capable of attaining a speed of 25 miles per hour on the level under its own power, when unladen and not drawing a trailer.

Class II:

Motor vehicles and trailers the use of which for or in connection with the conveyance of abnormal indivisible loads is authorised by order made, or having effect as if made, by the Minister under section 42 (1) of the Road Traffic Act 1972.

Motor vehicles and trailers constructed for naval, military, air force or other defence purposes, the use of which is authorised by order made, or having effect as if made, by the Minister under section 42 (1) of the Road Traffic Act 1972.

Motor vehicles and trailers, to which any of the following Articles of the Motor Vehicles (Authorisation of Special Types) General Order 1973 namely, Article 16 (which relates to vehicles for moving excavated material), Article 17 (which relates inter alia to vehicles constructed for use outside the United Kingdom) and Article 21 (which relates to engineering plant) relate and which are authorised to be used by any of those Articles of the said order or by any other order under section 42 (1) of the Road Traffic Act 1972, the said motor vehicles being vehicles in respect of which the following condition is satisfied, that is to say, that the vehicle is so constructed as to be capable of attaining a speed of 25 miles per hour on the level under its own power, when unladen and not drawing a trailer.

Class III:
Motor vehicles controlled by pedestrians.

Class IV:
All motor vehicles (other than invalid carriages and motor cycles whereof the cylinder capacity of the engine is less than 50 cubic centimetres) not comprised in Class I, Class II or Class III.

Class V:
Vehicles drawn by animals.

Class VI:
Vehicles (other than pedal cycles, perambulators, push-chairs and other forms of baby carriages) drawn or propelled by pedestrians.

Class VII:
Pedal cycles.

Class VIII:
Animals ridden, led or driven.

Class IX:
Pedestrians, perambulators, push-chairs and other forms of baby carriages and dogs held on a lead.

Class X:
Motor cycles whereof the cylinder capacity of the engine is less than 50 cubic centimetres.

Class XI:
Invalid carriages.

In this Schedule any expression defined for the purposes of the Road Traffic Act 1972 has the same meaning as in that Act and the expression 'abnormal indivisible load' has the same meaning as in the Motor Vehicles (Authorisation of Special Types) General Order 1973.

[Schedule 4 refers to the Motor Vehicles (Authorisation of Special Types) General Order 1973 (SI 1973 No 1101). This order was, however, revoked and replaced on 1 November 1979 by the Motor Vehicles (Authorisation of Special Types) General Order 1979 (SI 1979 No 1198). The provisions in the 1979 Order which relate to vehicles for moving excavated material, vehicles constructed for use outside the United Kingdom, and engineering plant, are arts 15, 16 and 19 respectively.

In the Highways Act 1980, the term 'the Minister' originally referred, in relation to England, to the Minister of Transport and, in relation to Wales, to the Secretary of State; see s 329 (1) of that Act. The functions of the Minister of Transport were transferred to the Secretary of State for Transport by the Transfer of Functions (Transport) Order 1981 (SI 1981 No 238).]

The Police and Criminal Evidence Act 1984

(1984 c 60)

An Act to make further provision in relation to the powers and duties of the police . . .

[31st October 1984]

ARRANGEMENT OF SECTIONS

PART I

POWERS TO STOP AND SEARCH

*   *   *

PART 1

POWERS TO STOP AND SEARCH

1. Power of constable to stop and search persons, vehicles etc

(1) A constable may exercise any power conferred by this section—

(a) in any place to which at the time when he proposes to exercise the power the public or any section of the public has access, on payment or otherwise, as of right or by virtue of express or implied permission; or

(b) in any other place to which people have ready access at the time when he proposes to exercise the power but which is not a dwelling.

(2) Subject to subsection (3) to (5) below, a constable—

(a) may search—
    (i) any person or vehicle;
    (ii) anything which is in or on a vehicle,

for stolen or prohibited articles; and

(b) may detain a person or vehicle for the purpose of such a search.

(3) This section does not give a constable power to search a person or vehicle or anything in or on a vehicle unless he has reasonable grounds for suspecting that he will find stolen or prohibited articles.

9

(4) *[Omitted]*

(5) If a vehicle is in a garden or yard occupied with and used for the purposes of a dwelling or on other land so occupied and used, a constable may not search the vehicle or anything in or on it in the exercise of the power conferred by this section unless he has reasonable grounds for believing—

 (a) that the person in charge of the vehicle does not reside in the dwelling; and

 (b) that the vehicle is not in the place in question with the express or implied permission of a person who resides in the dwelling.

(6) If in the course of such a search a constable discovers an article which he has reasonable grounds for suspecting to be a stolen or prohibited article, he may seize it.

(7) An article is prohibited for the purposes of this Part of this Act if it is—

 (a) an offensive weapon; or

 (b) an article—
   (i) made or adapted for use in the course of or in connection with an offence to which this sub-paragraph applies; or
   (ii) intended by the person having it with him for such use by him or by some other person.

(8) The offences to which subsection (7)(b)(i) above applies are—

 (a) burglary;

 (b) theft;

 (c) offences under section 12 of the Theft Act 1968 (taking motor vehicle or other conveyance without authority); and

 (d) offences under section 15 of that Act (obtaining property by deception).

(9) In this Part of this Act 'offensive weapon' means any article—

 (a) made or adapted for use for causing injury to persons; or

 (b) intended by the person having it with him for such use by him or by some other person.

[So much of this section as relates to a search for stolen articles came into force on 1 January 1985 for the purpose of conferring powers on constables in localities in which there was in force on 31 December 1984 an enactment conferring power on a constable to search for stolen or unlawfully obtained goods (other than an enactment contained in a public general Act or an enactment relating to statutory undertakers); see the Police and Criminal Evidence Act 1984 (Commencement No 1) Order 1984, SI 1984 No 2002, art 2.]

2. Provisions relating to search under section 1 and other powers

(1) A constable who detains a person or vehicle in the exercise—

 (a) of the power conferred by section 1 above; or

 (b) of any other power—
   (i) to search a person without first arresting him; or
   (ii) to search a vehicle without making an arrest,

need not conduct a search if it appears to him subsequently—

 (i) that no search is required; or

 (ii) that a search is impracticable.

(2) If a constable contemplates a search, other than a search of an unattended vehicle, in the exercise—

(*a*) of the power conferred by section 1 above; or

(*b*) of any other power, except the power conferred by section 6 below and the power conferred by section 27(2) of the Aviation Security Act 1982—

    (i) to search a person without first arresting him; or

    (ii) to search a vehicle without making an arrest,

it shall be his duty, subject to subsection (4) below, to take reasonable steps before he commences the search to bring to the attention of the appropriate person—

    (i) if the constable is not in uniform, documentary evidence that he is a constable; and

    (ii) whether he is in uniform or not, the matters specified in subsection (3) below;

and the constable shall not commence the search until he has performed that duty.

(3) The matters referred to in subsection (2)(ii) above are—

(*a*) the constable's name and the name of the police station to which he is attached;

(*b*) the object of the proposed search;

(*c*) the constable's grounds for proposing to make it; and

(*d*) the effect of section 3(7) or (8) below, as may be appropriate.

(4) A constable need not bring the effect of section 3(7) or (8) below to the attention of the appropriate person if it appears to the constable that it will not be practicable to make the record in section 3(1) below.

(5) In this section 'the appropriate person' means—

(*a*) if the constable proposes to search a person, that person; and

(*b*) if he proposes to search a vehicle, or anything in or on a vehicle, the person in charge of the vehicle.

(6) On completing a search of an unattended vehicle or anything in or on such a vehicle in the exercise of any such power as is mentioned in subsection (2) above a constable shall leave a notice—

(*a*) stating that he has searched it;

(*b*) giving the name of the police station to which he is attached;

(*c*) stating that an application for compensation for any damage caused by the search may be made to that police station; and

(*d*) stating the effect of section 3(8) below.

(7) The constable shall leave the notice inside the vehicle unless it is not reasonably practicable to do so without damaging the vehicle.

(8) The time for which a person or vehicle may be detained for the purposes of such a search is such time as is reasonably required to permit a search to be carried out either at the place where the person or vehicle was first detained or nearby.

(9) Neither the power conferred by section 1 above nor any other power to detain and search a person without first arresting him or to detain and search a vehicle without making an arrest is to be construed—

(*a*) as authorising a constable to require a person to remove any of his clothing in public other than an outer coat, jacket or gloves; or

(*b*) as authorising a constable not in uniform to stop a vehicle.

(10) This section and section 1 above apply to vessels, aircraft and hovercraft as they apply to vehicles.

3. Duty to make records concerning searches

(1) Where a constable has carried out a search in the exercise of any such power as is mentioned in section 2(1) above, other than a search—

(a) under section 6 below; or

(b) under section 27(2) of the Aviation Security Act 1982,

he shall make a record of it in writing unless it is not practicable to do so.

(2)–(6) *[Omitted]*

(7) If a constable who conducted a search of a person made a record of it, the person who was searched shall be entitled to a copy of the record if he asks for one before the end of the period specified in subsection (9) below.

(8) If—

(a) the owner of a vehicle which has been searched or the person who was in charge of the vehicle at the time when it was searched asks for a copy of the record of the search before the end of the period specified in subsection (9) below; and

(b) the constable who conducted the search made a record of it,

the person who made the request shall be entitled to a copy.

(9) The period mentioned in subsections (7) and (8) above is the period of 12 months beginning with the date on which the search was made.

(10) The requirements imposed by this section with regard to records of searches of vehicles shall apply also to records of searches of vessels, aircraft and hovercraft.

4. Road checks

(1) This section shall have effect in relation to the conduct of road checks by police officers for the purpose of ascertaining whether a vehicle is carrying—

(a) a person who has committed an offence other than a road traffic offence or a vehicles excise offence;

(b) a person who is a witness to such an offence;

(c) a person intending to commit such an offence; or

(d) a person who is unlawfully at large.

(2) For the purposes of this section a road check consists of the exercise in a locality of the power conferred by section 159 of the Road Traffic Act 1972 in such a way as to stop during the period for which its exercise in that way in that locality continues all vehicles or vehicles selected by any criterion.

(3) Subject to subsection (5) below, there may only be such a road check if a police officer of the rank of superintendent or above authorises it in writing.

(4) An officer may only authorise a road check under subsection (3) above—

(a) for the purpose specified in subsection (1)(a) above, if he has reasonable grounds—

   (i) for believing that the offence is a serious arrestable offence; and

   (ii) for suspecting that the person is, or is about to be, in the locality in which vehicles would be stopped if the road check were authorised;

(b) for the purpose specified in subsection (1)(b) above, if he has reasonable grounds for believing that the offence is a serious arrestable offence;

(c) for the purpose specified in subsection (1)(c) above, if he has reasonable grounds—

    (i) for believing that the offence would be a serious arrestable offence; and

    (ii) for suspecting that the person is, or is about to be, in the locality in which vehicles would be stopped if the road check were authorised;

(d) for the purpose specified in subsection (1)(d) above, if he has reasonable grounds for suspecting that the person is, or is about to be, in that locality.

(5) An officer below the rank of superintendent may authorise such a road check if it appears to him that it is required as a matter of urgency for one of the purposes specified in subsection (1) above.

(6) If an authorisation is given under subsection (5) above, it shall be the duty of the officer who gives it—

(a) to make a written record of the time at which he gives it; and

(b) to cause an officer of the rank of superintendent or above to be informed that it has been given.

(7) The duties imposed by subsection (6) above shall be performed as soon as it is practicable to do so.

(8) An officer to whom a report is made under subsection (6) above may, in writing, authorise the road check to continue.

(9) If such an officer considers that the road check should not continue, he shall record in writing—

(a) the fact that it took place; and

(b) the purpose for which it took place.

(10) An officer giving an authorisation under this section shall specify the locality in which vehicles are to be stopped.

(11) An officer giving an authorisation under this section, other than an authorisation under subsection (5) above—

(a) shall specify a period, not exceeding seven days, during which the road check may continue; and

(b) may direct that the road check—

    (i) shall be continuous; or

    (ii) shall be conducted at specified times,

during that period.

(12) If it appears to an officer of the rank of superintendent or above that a road check ought to continue beyond the period for which it has been authorised he may, from time to time, in writing specify a further period, not exceeding seven days, during which it may continue.

(13) Every written authorisation shall specify—

(a) the name of the officer giving it;

(b) the purpose of the road check; and

(c) the locality in which vehicles are to be stopped.

(14) The duties to specify the purposes of a road check imposed by subsections (9) and (13) above include duties to specify any relevant serious arrestable offence.

(15) Where a vehicle is stopped in a road check, the person in charge of the vehicle

at the time when it is stopped shall be entitled to obtain a written statement of the purpose of the road check if he applies for such a statement not later than the end of the period of twelve months from the day on which the vehicle was stopped.

(16) Nothing in this section affects the exercise by police officers of any power to stop vehicles for purposes other than those specified in subsection (1) above.

['Serious arrestable offences' are described in s 116 of and Sched 5 to this Act.]

* * *

6. Statutory undertakers etc.

(1) A constable employed by statutory undertakers may stop, detain and search any vehicle before it leaves a goods area included in the premises of the statutory undertakers.

(2) In this section 'goods area' means any area used wholly or mainly for the storage or handling of goods.

(3), (4) *[Omitted]*

7. Part I—supplementary

(1), (2) *[Omitted]*

(3) In this Part of this Act 'statutory undertakers' means persons authorised by any enactment to carry on any railway, light railway, road transport, water transport, canal, inland navigation, dock or harbour undertaking.

* * *

The Powers of Criminal Courts Act 1973

(1973 c 62)

An Act to consolidate certain enactments relating to the powers of courts to deal with offenders and defaulters, to the treatment of offenders and to arrangements for persons on bail.   [25th October 1973]

* * *

43. Power to deprive offender of property used, or intended for use, for purposes of crime

(1) Where a person is convicted of an offence punishable on indictment with imprisonment for a term of two years or more and the court by or before which he is convicted is satisfied that any property which was in his possession or under his control at the time of his apprehension—

(*a*) has been used for the purpose of committing, or facilitating the commission of, any offence; or

(*b*) was intended by him to be used for that purpose;

the court may make an order under this section in respect of that property.

(2) Facilitating the commission of an offence shall be taken for the purposes of this section and section 44 of this Act to include the taking of any steps after it has been committed for the purpose of disposing of any property to which it relates or of avoiding apprehension or detection, and references in this or that section to an offence punishable with imprisonment shall be construed without regard to any prohibition or restriction imposed by or under any enactment on the imprisonment of young offenders.

(3) An order under this section shall operate to deprive the offender of his rights, if any, in the property to which it relates, and the property shall (if not already in their possession) be taken into the possession of the police.

(4) The Police (Property) Act 1897 shall apply, with the following modifications, to property which is in the possession of the police by virtue of this section—

(*a*) no application shall be made under section 1 (1) of that Act by any claimant of the property after the expiration of six months from the date on which the order in respect of the property was made under this section; and

(*b*) no such application shall succeed unless the claimant satisfies the court either that he had not consented to the offender having possession of the property or that he did not know, and had no reason to suspect, that the property was likely to be used for the purpose mentioned in subsection (1) above.

(5) In relation to property which is in the possession of the police by virtue of this section, the power to make regulations under section 2 (1) of the Police (Property) Act 1897 (disposal of property in cases where the owner of the property has not been

ascertained and no order of a competent court has been made with respect thereto) shall include power to make regulations for disposal in cases where no application by a claimant of the property has been made within the period specified in subsection (4) (*a*) above or no such application has succeeded.

44. Driving disqualification where vehicle used for purposes of crime

(1) This section applies where a person is convicted before the Crown Court of an offence punishable on indictment with imprisonment for a term of two years or more or, having been convicted by a magistrates' court of such an offence, is committed under [section 38 of the Magistrates' Courts Act 1980] to the Crown Court for sentence.

(2) If in a case to which this section applies the Crown Court is satisfied that a motor vehicle was used (by the person convicted or by anyone else) for the purpose of committing, or facilitating the commission of, the offence in question (within the meaning of section 43 of this Act), the court may order the person convicted to be disqualified, for such period as the court thinks fit, for holding or obtaining a licence to drive a motor vehicle granted under Part III of the Road Traffic Act 1972.

(3) A court which makes an order under this section disqualifying a person for holding or obtaining any such licence as is mentioned in subsection (2) above shall require him to produce any such licence held by him; and—

(*a*) if he does not produce the licence as required he shall be guilty of an offence under section 101 (4) of the Road Traffic Act 1972 (failure to produce licence for endorsement); and

(*b*) if he applies under section 95 of that Act for the disqualification to be removed and the court so orders, subsection (4) of that section shall not have effect so as to require particulars of the order to be endorsed on the licence, but the court shall send notice of the order to the [Secretary of State for Transport] and section 105 (5) of that Act (procedure for sending notice to [Secretary of State for Transport]) shall apply to the notice.

[Section 44 is printed as amended by the Minister of Transport Order 1979 (SI 1979 No 571); the Magistrates' Courts Act 1980, s 154 (1) and Sched 7, para 122; and the Transfer of Functions (Transport) Order 1981 (SI 1981 No 238).]

*   *   *

The Public Passenger Vehicles Act 1981

(1981 c 14)

An Act to consolidate certain enactments relating to public passenger vehicles.

[15th April 1981]

PART I

PRELIMINARY

Definition and classification of public service vehicles

1. Definition of 'public service vehicle'

(1) Subject to the provisions of this section, in this Act 'public service vehicle' means a motor vehicle (other than a tramcar) which—

(*a*) being a vehicle adapted to carry more than eight passengers, is used for carrying passengers for hire or reward; or

(*b*) being a vehicle not so adapted, is used for carrying passengers for hire or reward at separate fares in the course of a business of carrying passengers.

(2) For the purposes of subsection (1) above a vehicle 'is used' as mentioned in paragraph (*a*) or (*b*) of that subsection if it is being so used or if it has been used as mentioned in that paragraph and that use has not been permanently discontinued.

(3) A vehicle carrying passengers at separate fares in the course of a business of carrying passengers, but doing so in circumstances in which the conditions set out in Part I, II or III of Schedule 1 to this Act are fulfilled, shall be treated as not being a public service vehicle unless it is adapted to carry more than eight passengers.

(4) For the purposes of this section a journey made by a vehicle in the course of which one or more passengers are carried at separate fares shall not be treated as made in the course of a business of carrying passengers if—

(*a*) the fare or aggregate of the fares paid in respect of the journey does not exceed the amount of the running costs of the vehicle for the journey; and

(*b*) the arrangements for the payment of fares by the passenger or passengers so carried were made before the journey began;

and for the purposes of paragraph (*a*) above the running costs of a vehicle for a journey shall be taken to include an appropriate amount in respect of depreciation and general wear.

(5) For the purposes of this section, section 2 and Schedule 1 to this Act—

(*a*) a vehicle is to be treated as carrying passengers for hire or reward if payment is made for, or for matters which include, the carrying of passengers, irrespective of the person to whom the payment is made and, in the case of a transaction effected by or on behalf of a member of any association of persons (whether

17

incorporated or not) on the one hand and the association or another member thereof on the other hand, notwithstanding any rule of law as to such transactions;

(*b*) a payment made for the carrying of a passenger shall be treated as a fare notwithstanding that it is made in consideration of other matters in addition to the journey and irrespective of the person by or to whom it is made;

(*c*) a payment shall be treated as made for the carrying of a passenger if made in consideration of a person's being given a right to be carried, whether for one or more journeys and whether or not the right is exercised.

(6) Where a fare is paid for the carriage of a passenger on a journey by air, no part of that fare shall be treated for the purposes of subsection (5) above as paid in consideration of the carriage of the passenger by road by reason of the fact that, in case of mechanical failure, bad weather or other circumstances outside the operator's control, part of that journey may be made by road.

2. Classification of public service vehicles as stage, express or contract carriages

(1) For the purposes of this Act—

(*a*) a 'stage carriage' is a public service vehicle being used in the operation of a local service;

(*b*) an 'express carriage' is a public service vehicle being used in the operation of an express service; and

(*c*) a 'contract carriage' is a public service vehicle being used to carry passengers otherwise than at separate fares;

and references in this Act to use as a stage, express or contract carriage shall be construed accordingly.

(2) In this section—

(*a*) 'local service' means a service for the carriage of passengers by road at separate fares, not being an express service;

(*b*) 'express service' means a service for the carriage of passengers by road at separate fares, being a service as regards which the conditions specified in subsection (3) below are satisfied.

(3) The conditions referred to in subsection (2) (*b*) above are—

(*a*) except in the case of an emergency, either of the following requirements as to length of journey is satisfied in respect of every passenger using the service, namely—

    (i) the place where he is set down is thirty miles or more, measured in a straight line, from the place where he was taken up; or

    (ii) some point on the route between those places is thirty miles or more, measured in a straight line, from either of those places; and

(*b*) either—

    (i) the service is an excursion or tour; or

    (ii) the prescribed particulars of the service (including the route and the timetable) and of every change of any prescribed kind made in the service have, not later than the prescribed time for doing so, been notified in the prescribed manner to the traffic commissioners within whose area the place specified in the notification as the beginning of the route is situated.

(4) Where, in the case of any service for the carriage of passengers by road at separate fares, the condition specified in subsection (3)(*a*) above is satisfied as regards any part of the service taken in isolation, but not as regards the service as a whole—

(*a*) that part of the service shall be treated for the purposes of subsections (2)(*b*) and (3) above as a separate service (and will accordingly be an express service if the condition specified in subsection (3)(*b*) is satisfied as regards it); and

(*b*) any part of the service which is not an express service by virtue of the preceding paragraph shall be treated for the purposes of this section as a separate local service.

(5) A public service vehicle carrying passengers at separate fares shall be treated as a contract carriage, and not as a stage carriage or an express carriage, when used in circumstances in which the conditions set out in Part II or III of Schedule 1 to this Act are fulfilled.

*   *   *

SCHEDULE 1

Public Service Vehicles: Conditions Affecting Status for Classification

PART I

Sharing of Taxis and Hire-Cars

1. The making of the agreement for the payment of separate fares must not have been initiated by the driver or by the owner of the vehicle, by any person who has made the vehicle available under any arrangement, or by any person who receives any remuneration in respect of the arrangements for the journey.

2.—(1) The journey must be made without previous advertisement to the public of facilities for its being made by passengers to be carried at separate fares, except where the local authorities concerned have approved the arrangements under which the journey is made as designed to meet the social and welfare needs of one or more communities, and their approvals remain in force.

(2) In relation to a journey the local authorities concerned for the purposes of this paragraph are those in whose area any part of the journey is to be made; and in this sub-paragraph 'local authority' means—

(*a*) in relation to England and Wales, the Greater London Council or a county council;

(*b*) in relation to Scotland, a regional or islands council.

3. The journey must not be made in conjunction with, or in extension of, a service provided under a road service licence if the vehicle is owned by, or made available under any arrangement with, the holder of the licence or any person who receives any remuneration in respect of the service provided under it or in respect of arrangements for that service.

PART II

Parties of Overseas Visitors

4. Each of the passengers making the journey must have been outside Great Britain at the time of concluding his arrangements to make the journey.

PART III

ALTERNATIVE CONDITIONS AFFECTING STATUS FOR CLASSIFICATION

5. Arrangements for the bringing together of all the passengers for the purpose of making the journey must have been made otherwise than by, or by a person acting on behalf of—

(a) the holder of the PSV operator's licence under which the vehicle is to be used, if such a licence is in force.

(b) the driver or the owner of the vehicle or any person who has made the vehicle available under any arrangement, if no such licence is in force,

and otherwise than by any person who receives any remuneration in respect of the arrangements.

6. The journey must be made without previous advertisement to the public of the arrangements therefor.

7. All passengers must, in the case of a journey to a particular destination, be carried to, or to the vicinity of, that destination, or, in the case of a tour, be carried for the greater part of the journey.

8. No differentiation of fares for the journey on the basis of distance or of time must be made.

PART IV

SUPPLEMENTARY

9. For the purposes of paragraphs 2 and 6 above no account shall be taken of any such advertisement as follows, that is to say—

(a) a notice displayed or announcement made—
   (i) at or in any place of worship for the information of persons attending that place of worship;
   (ii) at or in any place of work for the information of persons who work there; or
   (iii) by any club or other voluntary association at or in any premises occupied or used by the club or association;

(b) a notice contained in any periodical published for the information of, and circulating wholly or mainly among—
   (i) persons who attend or might reasonably be expected to attend a particular place of worship or a place of worship in a particular place; or
   (ii) persons who work at a particular place of work or at any of two or more particular places of work; or
   (iii) the members of a club or other voluntary association.

*   *   *

The Road Traffic Act 1972

(1972 c 20)

An Act to consolidate certain enactments relating to road traffic with amendments to give effect to recommendations of the Law Commission and the Scottish Law Commission. [30th March 1972]

ARRANGEMENT OF SECTIONS

PART I

PRINCIPAL ROAD SAFETY PROVISIONS

Offences connected with driving of motor vehicles

21

PART II

Construction and Use of Vehicles and Equipment

General provisions

*   *   *

SCHEDULES

*   *   *

PART I

PRINCIPAL ROAD SAFETY PROVISIONS

Offences connected with driving of motor vehicles

[1. Causing death by reckless driving

A person who causes the death of another person by driving a motor vehicle on a road recklessly shall be guilty of an offence.]

[Section 1 was substituted by the Criminal Law Act 1977, s 50.

The offence under s 1 is expressly excluded from the application of the Criminal Justice Act 1982, s 32 (early release of prisoners); see Part II of Sched 1 to that Act.

An offence under s 1 is designated as a 'serious arrestable offence' by the Police and Criminal Evidence Act 1984, s 116 (2), and Sched 5, Part II (with effect from a date to be announced).]

[2. Reckless driving

A person who drives a motor vehicle on a road recklessly shall be guilty of an offence.]

[Section 2 was substituted by the Criminal Law Act 1977, s 50.]

3. Careless, and inconsiderate, driving

If a person drives a motor vehicle on a road without due care and attention, or without reasonable consideration for other persons using the road, he shall be guilty of an offence.

*   *   *

5. Driving, or being in charge, when under the influence of drink or drugs

(1) A person who, when driving or attempting to drive a motor vehicle on a road or [other public place, is unfit to drive through drink or drugs shall be guilty of an offence.

(2) Without prejudice to subsection (1) above, a person who, when in charge of a motor vehicle which is on a road or other public place, is unfit to drive through drink or drugs shall be guilty of an offence.

(3) For the purposes of subsection (2) above a person shall be deemed not to have been in charge of a motor vehicle if he proves that at the material time the circumstances were such that there was no likelihood of his driving it so long as he remained unfit to drive through drink or drugs [but in determining whether there was such a likelihood the court may disregard any injury to him and any damage to the vehicle.]

(4) For the purposes of this section a person shall be taken to be unfit to drive if his ability to drive properly is for the time being impaired.

[(5) A constable may arrest a person without warrant if he has reasonable cause to suspect that that person is or has been committing an offence under this section.]

[(6) For the purpose of arresting a person under the power conferred by subsection (5) above a constable may enter (if need be by force) any place where that person is or where the constable, with reasonable cause, suspects him to be.]

[(7) Subsection (6) above does not extend to Scotland and nothing in that subsection shall affect any rule of law in Scotland concerning the right of a constable to enter any premises for any purpose.]

[Section 5 is printed as amended by the Transport Act 1981, s 25.
The power of arrest under subs (5) is expressly preserved by the Police and Criminal Evidence Act 1984, s 26 (2), and Sched 2.]

[6. Driving or being in charge of a motor vehicle with alcohol concentration above prescribed limit

(1) If a person—

(*a*) drives or attempts to drive a motor vehicle on a road or other public place; or

(*b*) is in charge of a motor vehicle on a road or other public place;

after consuming so much alcohol that the proportion of it in his breath, blood or urine exceeds the prescribed limit he shall be guilty of an offence.

(2) It is a defence for a person charged with an offence under subsection (1) (*b*) above to prove that at the time he is alleged to have committed the offence the circumstances were such that there was no likelihood of his driving the vehicle whilst the proportion of alcohol in his breath, blood or urine remained likely to exceed the prescribed limit; but in determining whether there was such a likelihood the court may disregard any injury to him and any damage to the vehicle.]

[Section 6 was substituted by the Transport Act 1981, s 25 (3), and Sched 8.]

[7. Breath tests

(1) Where a constable in uniform has reasonable cause to suspect—

(*a*) that a person driving or attempting to drive or in charge of a motor vehicle on a road or other public place has alcohol in his body or has committed a traffic offence whilst the vehicle was in motion; or

(*b*) that a person has been driving or attempting to drive or been in charge of a motor vehicle on a road or other public place with alcohol in his body and that that person still has alcohol in his body; or

(*c*) that a person has been driving or attempting to drive or been in charge of a motor vehicle on a road or other public place and has committed a traffic offence whilst the vehicle was in motion;

he may, subject to section 9 below, require him to provide a specimen of breath for a breath test.

(2) If an accident occurs owing to the presence of a motor vehicle on a road or other public place a constable may require any person who he has reasonable cause to believe was driving or attempting to drive or in charge of the vehicle at the time of the accident to provide a specimen of breath for a breath test, but subject to section 9 below.

(3) A person may be required under subsection (1) or subsection (2) of this section to provide a specimen either at or near the place where the requirement is made or, if the requirement is made under subsection (2) and the constable making the requirement thinks fit, at a police station specified by the constable.

(4) A person who, without reasonable excuse, fails to provide a specimen of breath when required to do so in pursuance of this section shall be guilty of an offence.

(5) A constable may arrest a person without warrant if—

(a) as a result of a breath test he has reasonable cause to suspect that the proportion of alcohol in that person's breath or blood exceeds the prescribed limit; or

(b) that person has failed to provide a specimen of breath for a breath test when required to do so in pursuance of this section and the constable has reasonable cause to suspect that he has alcohol in his body;

but a person shall not be arrested by virtue of this subsection when he is at a hospital as a patient.

(6) For the purpose of requiring a person to provide a specimen of breath under subsection (2) above in a case where he has reasonable cause to suspect that the accident involved injury to another person or of arresting him in such a case under subsection (5) above a constable may enter (if need be by force) any place where that person is or where the constable, with reasonable cause, suspects him to be.

(7) Subsection (6) above does not extend to Scotland and nothing in that subsection shall affect any rule of law in Scotland concerning the right of a constable to enter any premises for any purpose.

(8) In this section 'traffic offence' means an offence under any provision of this Act except Part V, or under any provision of Part III of the Road Traffic Act 1960, the Road Traffic Regulation Act [1984] or Part I of the Transport Act 1980.]

[Section 7 was substituted by the Transport Act 1981, s 25 (3) and Sched 8, and is printed as amended by the Road Traffic Regulation Act 1984, s 146, and Sched 13, para 13.

Part III of the Road Traffic Act 1960 and most of the provisions in Part I of the Transport Act 1980 were repealed and replaced by the Public Passenger Vehicles Act 1981 with effect from 30 October 1981. Section 88 (2) of, and Sched 7, para 12 to, the 1981 Act expressly amended the corresponding provision in the previous legislation by deleting the reference to Part III of the Road Traffic Act 1960 and by adding a reference to 'Part II or III of the Public Passenger Vehicles Act 1981 (including an offence under section 30 (7) of that Act as applied by section 45 (6) thereof)'.

An offence under subs (4) above is an offence involving discretionary disqualification; see the Transport Act 1981, s 25 (4).

The power of arrest under this section is expressly preserved by the Police and Criminal Evidence Act 1984, s 26 (2), and Sched 2.]

[8. Provision of specimens for analysis

(1) In the course of an investigation whether a person has committed an offence under section 5 or section 6 of this Act a constable may, subject to the following provisions of this section and section 9 below, require him—

(a) to provide two specimens of breath for analysis by means of a device of a type approved by the Secretary of State; or

(b) to provide a specimen of blood or urine for a laboratory test.

(2) A requirement under this section to provide specimens of breath can only be made at a police station.

(3) A requirement under this section to provide a specimen of blood or urine can only be made at a police station or at a hospital; and it cannot be made at a police station unless—

(a) the constable making the requirement has reasonable cause to believe that for medical reasons a specimen of breath cannot be provided or should not be required; or

(b) at the time the requirement is made a device or a reliable device of the type mentioned in subsection (1) (a) is not available at the police station or it is then for any other reason not practicable to use such a device there; or

(c) the suspected offence is one under section 5 of this Act and the constable making the requirement has been advised by a medical practitioner that the condition of the person required to provide the specimen might be due to some drug;

but may then be made notwithstanding that the person required to provide the specimen has already provided or been required to provide two specimens of breath.

(4) If the provision of a specimen other than a specimen of breath may be required in pursuance of this section the question whether it is to be a specimen of blood or a specimen of urine shall be decided by the constable making the requirement, except that if a medical practitioner is of the opinion that for medical reasons a specimen of blood cannot or should not be taken the specimen shall be a specimen of urine.

(5) A specimen of urine shall be provided within one hour of the requirement for its provision being made and after the provision of a previous specimen of urine.

(6) Of any two specimens of breath provided by any person in pursuance of this section that with the lower proportion of alcohol in the breath shall be used and the other shall be disregarded; but if the specimen with the lower proportion of alcohol contains no more than 50 microgrammes of alcohol in 100 millilitres of breath the person who provided it may claim that it should be replaced by such a specimen as may be required under subsection (4), and if he then provides such a specimen neither specimen of breath shall be used.

(7) A person who, without reasonable excuse, fails to provide a specimen when required to do so in pursuance of this section shall be guilty of an offence.

(8) On requiring any person to provide a specimen in pursuance of this section a constable shall warn him that a failure to provide it may render him liable to prosecution.

(9) The Secretary of State may by regulations substitute another proportion of alcohol in the breath for that specified in subsection (6).]

[Section 8 was substituted by the Transport Act 1981, s 25 (3), and Sched 8.

The device comprising the 'Camic Simulator' and the 'Camic Breath Analyser' and the device comprising the 'Lion Breath Simulator' and the 'Lion Intoximeter 3000' have been approved for use in England and Wales (see the Breath Analysis Devices (Approval) Order 1983 dated 18 April 1983).]

[9. Protection for hospital patients

(1) While a person is at a hospital as a patient he shall not be required to provide a specimen of breath for a breath test or to provide a specimen for a laboratory test unless the medical practitioner in immediate charge of his case has been notified of the proposal to make the requirement; and—

(*a*) if the requirement is then made it shall be for the provision of a specimen at the hospital; but

(*b*) if the medical practitioner objects on the ground specified in subsection (2) below the requirement shall not be made.

(2) The ground on which the medical practitioner may object is that the requirement or the provision of a specimen or, in the case of a specimen of blood or urine, the warning required under section 8 (8) above, would be prejudicial to the proper care and treatment of the patient.]

[Section 9 was substituted by the Transport Act 1981, s 25 (3), and Sched 8.]

[10. Evidence in proceedings for an offence under s 5 or s 6

(1) The following provisions apply with respect to proceedings for an offence under section 5 or section 6 of this Act.

(2) Evidence of the proportion of alcohol or any drug in a specimen of breath, blood or urine provided by the accused shall, in all cases, be taken into account, and it shall be assumed that the proportion of alcohol in the accused's breath, blood or urine at the time of the alleged offence was not less than in the specimen; but if the proceedings are for an offence under section 6 of this Act, or for an offence under section 5 of this Act in a case where the accused is alleged to have been unfit through drink, the assumption shall not be made if the accused proves—

(*a*) that he consumed alcohol after he had ceased to drive, attempt to drive or be in charge of a motor vehicle on a road or other public place and before he provided the specimen; and

(*b*) that had he not done so the proportion of alcohol in his breath, blood or urine would not have exceeded the prescribed limit and, if the proceedings are for an offence under section 5 of this Act, would not have been such as to impair his ability to drive properly.

(3) Evidence of the proportion of alcohol or a drug in a specimen of breath, blood or urine may, subject to subsections (5) and (6) below, be given by the production of a document or documents purporting to be whichever of the following is appropriate, that is to say—

(*a*) a statement automatically produced by the device by which the proportion of alcohol in a specimen of breath was measured and a certificate signed by a constable (which may but need not be contained in the same document as the statement) that the statement relates to a specimen provided by the accused at the date and time shown in the statement; and

(*b*) a certificate signed by an authorised analyst as to the proportion of alcohol or any drug found in a specimen of blood or urine identified in the certificate.

(4) A specimen of blood shall be disregarded unless it was taken from the accused with his consent by a medical practitioner; but evidence that a specimen of blood was so taken may be given by the production of a document purporting to certify that fact and to be signed by a medical practitioner.

(5) A document purporting to be such a statement or such a certificate, or both such a statement and such a certificate, as is mentioned in subsection (3) (*a*) above is admissible in evidence on behalf of the prosecution in pursuance of this section only if a copy of it either has been handed to the accused when the document was produced or has been served on him not later than seven days before the hearing, and any other document is so admissible only if a copy of it has been served on the accused not later

than seven days before the hearing; but a document purporting to be a certificate (or so much of a document as purports to be a certificate) is not so admissible if the accused, not later than three days before the hearing or within such further time as the court may in special circumstances allow, has served notice on the prosecutor requiring the attendance at the hearing of the person by whom the document purports to be signed.

(6) Where, at the time a specimen of blood or urine was provided by the accused, he asked to be supplied with such a specimen, evidence of the proportion of alcohol or any drug found in the specimen is not admissible on behalf of the prosecution unless—

(a) the specimen in which the alcohol or drug was found is one of two parts into which the specimen provided by the accused was divided at the time it was provided; and

(b) the other part was supplied to the accused.

(7) In Scotland—

(a) a document produced in evidence on behalf of the prosecution in pursuance of subsection (3) or (4) above and, where the person by whom the document was signed is called as a witness, the evidence of that person, shall be sufficient evidence of the facts stated in the document; and

(b) a written execution purporting to be signed by the person who handed to or served on the accused or the prosecutor a copy of the document or of the notice in terms of subsection (5) above, together with, where appropriate, a post office receipt for the relative registered or recorded delivery letter shall be sufficient evidence of the handing or service of such a copy or notice.

(8) A copy of a certificate required by this section to be served on the accused or a notice required by this section to be served on the prosecutor may be served personally or sent by registered post or recorded delivery service.

(9) In this section 'authorised analyst' means any person possessing the qualifications prescribed by regulations made under section 89 of the Food and Drugs Act 1955 or section 27 of the Food and Drugs (Scotland) Act 1956 as qualifying persons for appointment as public analysts under those Acts, and any other person authorised by the Secretary of State to make analyses for the purposes of this section.]

[Section 10 was substituted by the Transport Act 1981, s 25 (3), and Sched 8.]

[11. Detention of persons affected by alcohol or a drug

A person required to provide a specimen of breath, blood or urine may thereafter be detained at a police station until it appears to a constable that, were that person then driving or attempting to drive a motor vehicle on a road, he would not be committing an offence under section 5 or section 6 of this Act; but—

(a) a person shall not be detained in pursuance of this section if it appears to a constable that there is no likelihood of his driving or attempting to drive a motor vehicle whilst his ability to drive properly is impaired or whilst the proportion of alcohol in his breath, blood or urine exceeds the prescribed limit; and

(b) a constable shall consult a medical practitioner on any question arising under this section whether a person's ability to drive properly is or might be impaired through drugs and shall act on the medical practitioner's advice.]

[Section 11 was substituted by the Transport Act 1981, s 25 (3), and Sched 8.]

[12. Interpretation of sections 5 to 11

(1) The following provisions apply for the interpretation of sections 5 to 11 of this Act.

(2) In those sections—

'breath test' means a preliminary test for the purpose of obtaining, by means of a device of a type approved by the Secretary of State, an indication whether the proportion of alcohol in a person's breath or blood is likely to exceed the prescribed limit;

'drug' includes any intoxicant other than alcohol;

'fail' includes refuse;

'hospital' means an institution which provides medical or surgical treatment for in-patients or out-patients;

'the prescribed limit' means, as the case may require—

   (a) 35 microgrammes of alcohol in 100 millilitres of breath;

   (b) 80 milligrammes of alcohol in 100 millilitres of blood; or

   (c) 107 milligrammes of alcohol in 100 millilitres of urine;

or such other proportion as may be prescribed by regulations made by the Secretary of State.

[(3) A person does not provide a specimen of breath for a breath test or for analysis unless the specimen is sufficient to enable the test or the analysis to be carried out [and provided in such a way as to enable the objective of the test or analysis to be satisfactorily achieved].

(4) A person provides a specimen of blood if and only if he consents to its being taken by a medical practitioner and it is so taken.]

[Section 12 was substituted by the Transport Act 1981, s 25 (3), and Sched 8. Subsection (3) is printed as amended by the Transport Act 1982, s 59.]

13. Person liable to be charged with offence under s 5, 6 or 8 not liable to be charged with certain other offences

A person liable to be charged with an offence under section 5, 6 or 8 of this Act shall not be liable to be charged—

   (a) under section 12 of the Licensing Act 1872 with the offence of being drunk while in charge, on a highway or other public place, of a carriage, or

   (b) under section 70 of the Licensing (Scotland) Act 1903 with the offence of being drunk while in charge, in a street or other place, of a carriage.

[Section 13 is printed as amended by the Transport Act 1981, s 30 (3), and Sched 9, para 1.]

14. Motor racing on highways

A person who promotes or takes part in a race or trial of speed between motor vehicles on a public highway shall be guilty of an offence.

15. Regulation of motoring events on highways

(1) A person who promotes or takes part in a competition or trial (other than a race or trial of speed) involving the use of motor vehicles on a public highway shall be guilty of an offence unless the competition or trial is authorised, and is conducted in accordance with any conditions imposed, by or under regulations under this section.

(2) The [Secretary of State for Transport] may by regulations authorise, or provide for authorising, the holding of such competitions and trials as aforesaid, either generally, or as regards any area, or as regards any class or description of competition or trial or any particular competition or trial, subject to such conditions, including conditions requiring the payment of fees, as may be imposed by or under the regulations.

(3) Regulations under this section may—

(a) prescribe the procedure to be followed, and the particulars to be given, in connection with applications for authorisation under the regulations, and

(b) make different provision for different classes or descriptions of competition or trial.

[Section 15 is printed as amended by the Minister of Transport Order 1979 (SI 1979 No 571) and the Transfer of Functions (Transport) Order 1981 (SI 1981 No 238).]

16. Restriction on carriage of persons on motor cycles

It shall not be lawful for more than one person in addition to the driver to be carried on a two-wheeled motor cycle, nor shall it be lawful for any such one person to be so carried otherwise than sitting astride the cycle and on a proper seat securely fixed to the cycle behind the driver's seat; and if a person is carried on a cycle in contravention of this section, the driver of the cycle shall be guilty of an offence.

[As to the application of the fixed penalty procedure to offences under s 16, see the Transport Act 1982, Part III, and Sched 1.]

Offences connected with riding of pedal cycles

[17. Reckless cycling

A person who rides a cycle, not being a motor vehicle, on a road recklessly shall be guilty of an offence.
In this section 'road' includes a bridleway.]

[Section 17 was substituted by the Criminal Law Act 1977, s 50.]

18. Careless, and inconsiderate, cycling

If a person rides a cycle, not being a motor vehicle, on a road without due care and attention, or without reasonable consideration for other persons using the road, he shall be guilty of an offence.
In this section 'road' includes a bridleway.

19. Cycling when under influence of drink or drugs

(1) A person who, when riding a cycle, not being a motor vehicle, on a road or other public place, is unfit to ride through drink or drugs shall be guilty of an offence.

(2) A person liable to be charged with an offence under this section shall not be liable to be charged—

(a) under section 12 of the Licensing Act 1872, with the offence of being drunk while in charge, on a highway or other public place, of a carriage, or

(b) under section 70 of the Licensing (Scotland) Act 1903, with the offence of being drunk while in charge, in a street or other placte, of a carriage.

(3) *A constable may arrest without warrant a person committing an offence under this section.*

(4) In this section 'unfit to ride through drink or drugs' means, as regards a person riding a cycle, under the influence of drink or a drug to such an extent as to be incapable of having proper control of it.

(5) In this section 'road' includes a bridleway.

[Section 19 (3) is repealed by the Police and Criminal Evidence Act 1984, s 119 (2), and Sched 7, Part I (with effect from a date to be announced).]

* * *

Offences connected with traffic generally

22. Drivers to comply with traffic directions

(1) Where a constable is for the time being engaged in the regulation of traffic in a road, or where a traffic sign, being a sign of the prescribed size, colour and type, or of another character authorised by the Secretary of State under the provisions in that behalf of the Road Traffic Regulation Act [1984] has been lawfully placed on or near a road, a person driving or propelling a vehicle who—

(a) neglects or refuses to stop the vehicle or to make it proceed in, or keep to, a particular line of traffic when directed so to do by the constable in the execution of his duty, or

(b) fails to comply with the indication given by the sign,

shall be guilty of an offence.

(2) A traffic sign shall not be treated for the purposes of this section as having been lawfully placed unless either—

(a) the indication given by the sign is an indication of a statutory prohibition, restriction or requirement, or

(b) it is expressly provided by or under any provision of this Act or of the Road Traffic Regulation Act [1984] that this section shall apply to the sign or to signs of a type of which the sign is one;

and where the indication mentioned in paragraph (a) of this subsection is of the general nature only of the prohibition, restriction or requirement to which the sign relates a person shall not be convicted of failure to comply with the indication unless he has failed to comply with the said prohibition, restriction or requirement.

(3) For the purposes of this section a traffic sign placed on or near a road shall be deemed to be of the prescribed size, colour and type, or of another character authorised as mentioned in subsection (1) above, and (subject to subsection (2) above) to have been lawfully so placed, unless the contrary is proved.

(4) It shall be lawful in Scotland to convict a person of a contravention of this section on the evidence of one witness.

[Section 22 is printed as amended by the Road Traffic Regulation Act 1984, s 146, and Sched 13, para 14.

As to the application of the fixed penalty procedure to offences under s 22, see the Transport Act 1982, Part III, and Sched 1.]

[22A. Traffic directions for purposes of traffic surveys

(1) If a traffic survey of any description is carried out on or in the vicinity of a road, then—

(a) for the purposes of section 22 of this Act, a traffic direction given by a constable to a person driving or propelling a vehicle, being a direction given for the purposes of the survey, shall be treated as a direction given by him in the execution of his duty and at a time when he is engaged in the regulation of traffic; and

(*b*) section 22 of this Act shall apply to a traffic sign by which a traffic direction is given for the purpose of the survey.

(2) In this section 'traffic direction' means a direction to stop a vehicle, to make it proceed in, or keep to, a particular line of traffic or to proceed to a particular point on or near the road on which the vehicle is being driven or propelled, but does not include a direction requiring any person to furnish any information for the purposes of a traffic survey.

(3) In relation to a traffic direction given by a constable by virtue of this section and requiring a vehicle to proceed to a particular point, paragraph (*a*) of subsection (1) of section 22 of this Act shall have effect as if, after the words 'line of traffic' there were inserted the words 'or to proceed to a particular point'.

(4) The power to give a traffic direction for the purposes of a traffic survey shall be so exercised as not to cause any unreasonable delay to a person who indicates that he is unwilling to furnish any information for the purposes of the survey.]

[Section 22A was inserted by the Road Traffic Act 1974, s 6.]

23. Pedestrians to comply with directions to stop given by constable regulating vehicular traffic

Where a constable in uniform is for the time being engaged in the regulation of vehicular traffic in a road, a person on foot who proceeds across or along the carriageway in contravention of a direction to stop given by the constable, in the execution of his duty, either to persons on foot or to persons on foot and other traffic, shall be guilty of an offence.

24. Leaving vehicles in dangerous positions

If a person in charge of a vehicle causes or permits the vehicle or a trailer drawn thereby to remain at rest on a road in such a position or in such condition or in such circumstances as to be likely to cause danger to other persons using the road, he shall be guilty of an offence.

[As to the application of the fixed penalty procedure to offences under s 24, see the Transport Act 1982, Part III, and Sched 1.]

Accidents

25. Duty to stop, and furnish particulars, in case of accident

(1) If in any case, owing to the presence of a motor vehicle on a road, an accident occurs whereby personal injury is caused to a person other than the driver of that motor vehicle or damage is caused to a vehicle other than that motor vehicle or a trailer drawn thereby or to an animal other than an animal in or on that motor vehicle or a trailer drawn thereby [or to any other property constructed on, fixed to, growing in or otherwise forming part of the land on which the road in question is situated or land adjacent thereto] the driver of the motor vehicle shall stop and, if required so to do by any person having reasonable grounds for so requiring, give his name and address, and also the name and address of the owner and the identification marks of the vehicle.

(2) If in the case of any such accident as aforesaid the driver of the motor vehicle

for any reason does not give his name and address to any such person as aforesaid, he shall report the accident at a police station or to a constable as soon as reasonably practicable, and in any case within twenty-four hours of the occurrence thereof.

(3) In this section 'animal' means any horse, cattle, ass, mule, sheep, pig, goat or dog.

(4) A person who fails to comply with this section shall be guilty of an offence.

[Section 25 (1) is printed as amended by the Road Traffic Act 1974, Sched 6, para 12.]

*   *   *

Ancillary provisions for preventing, or mitigating effects of, accidents

29. Penalisation of tampering with motor vehicles

If, while a motor vehicle is on a road or on a parking place provided by a local authority, a person otherwise than with lawful authority or reasonable cause gets on to the vehicle or tampers with the brake or other part of its mechanism, he shall be guilty of an offence.

30. Penalisation of holding or getting on to vehicle in order to be towed or carried

(1) If a person otherwise than with lawful authority or reasonable cause takes or retains hold of, or gets on to, a motor vehicle or trailer while in motion on a road, for the purpose of being carried, he shall be guilty of an offence.

(2) If a person takes or retains hold of a motor vehicle or trailer while in motion on a road for the purpose of being drawn he shall be guilty of an offence.

*   *   *

32. Wearing of protective headgear

(1) The [Secretary of State for Transport] may make regulations requiring, subject to such exceptions as may be specified in the regulations, persons driving or riding (otherwise than in side-cars) on motor cycles of any class specified in the regulations to wear protective headgear of such description as may be so specified.

(2) Regulations under this section may make different provision in relation to different circumstances.

[(2A) A requirement imposed by regulations under this section (whenever made) shall not apply to any follower of the Sikh religion while he is wearing a turban.]

(3) Any person who drives or rides on a motor cycle in contravention of regulations under this section shall be guilty of an offence.

[Section 32 is printed as amended by the Motor-Cycle Crash Helmets (Religious Exemption) Act 1976, s 1, the Minister of Transport Order 1979 (SI 1979 No 571), and the Transfer of Functions (Transport) Order 1981 (SI 1981 No 238).

As to the application of the fixed penalty procedure to offences under s 32 (3), see the Transport Act 1982, Part III, and Sched 1.

The Motor Cycles (Protective Helmets) Regulations 1980 (SI 1980 No 1279) were made partly under this section.]

*   *   *

[33AA. Authorisation of head-worn appliances for use on motor cycles

(1) The Secretary of State may make regulations prescribing (by reference to shape, construction or any other quality) types of appliance of any description to which this section applies as authorised for use by persons driving or riding (otherwise than in sidecars) on motor cycles of any class specified in the regulations.

(2) Regulations under this section—

(a) may impose restrictions or requirements with respect to the circumstances in which appliances of any type prescribed by the regulations may be used; and

(b) may make different provision in relation to different circumstances.

(3) If a person driving or riding on a motor cycle on a road uses an appliance of any description for which a type is prescribed under this section he shall be guilty of an offence if that appliance is not of a type so prescribed or is otherwise used in contravention of regulations under this section.

(4) If a person sells, or offers for sale, an appliance of any such description as authorised for use by persons on or in motor cycles, or motor cycles of any class, and that appliance is not of a type prescribed under this section as authorised for such use, he shall, subject to subsection (5) below, be guilty of an offence.

(5) A person shall not be convicted of an offence under this section in respect of the sale or offer for sale of an appliance if he proves that it was sold or, as the case may be, offered for sale for export from Great Britain.

(6) In England or Wales the council of a county or of a London borough, the Greater London Council or the Common Council of the City of London may institute proceedings for an offence under this section.

(7) The provisions of Schedule 1 to this Act shall have effect in relation to contraventions of subsection (4) of this section as they have effect in relation to contraventions of section 33 of this Act; and in that Schedule, as it has effect by virtue of this subsection—

(a) references to helmets shall be read as references to appliances to which this section applies; and

(b) the reference in paragraph 4 (1) (a) to a type which under the principal section could be lawfully sold or offered for sale shall be read as a reference to a type which under this section could be lawfully sold or offered for sale as authorised for use in the manner in question.

(8) This section applies to appliances of any description designed or adapted for use—

(a) with any headgear; or

(b) by being attached to or placed upon the head;

(as, for example, eye protectors or earphones).

(9) References in this section to selling or offering for sale include respectively references to letting on hire and offering to let on hire.]

[Section 33AA was inserted in to the Road Traffic Act 1972 immediately before s 33A by the Transport Act 1982, s 57 (1).]

[33A. Wearing of seat belts

(1) The Secretary of State may make regulations requiring, subject to such excep-

tions as may be prescribed, persons who are driving or riding in motor vehicles on a road to wear seat belts of such description as may be prescribed.

(2) Regulations under this section—

(*a*) may make different provision in relation to different classes of vehicles, different descriptions of persons and different circumstances;

(*b*) shall include exceptions for—

    (i) the users of vehicles constructed or adapted for the delivery of goods or mail to consumers or addressees, as the case may be, while engaged in making local rounds of deliveries;

    (ii) the drivers of vehicles while performing a manoeuvre which includes reversing;

    (iii) any person holding a valid certificate signed by a medical practitioner to the effect that is inadvisable on medical grounds for him to wear a seat belt;

(*c*) may make any prescribed exceptions subject to such conditions as may be prescribed; and

(*d*) may prescribe cases in which a fee of a prescribed amount may be charged on an application for any certificate required as a condition of any prescribed exception.

(3) Any person who drives or rides in a motor vehicle in contravention of regulations under this section shall be guilty of an offence; but notwithstanding any enactment or rule of law no person other than the person actually committing the contravention shall be guilty of an offence by reason of the contravention.

(4) If the holder of any such certificate as is referred to in subsection (2) (*b*) above is informed by a constable that he may be prosecuted for an offence under subsection (3) above, he shall not, in proceedings for that offence, be entitled to rely on the exception afforded to him by the certificate unless—

(*a*) it is produced to the constable at the time he is so informed; or

(*b*) within five days after the date on which he is so informed, it is produced at such police station as he may have specified to the constable.

(5) Regulations under this section requiring the wearing of seat belts by persons riding in motor vehicles shall not apply to children under the age of fourteen years (to whom the next following section applies).]

[Section 33A was inserted by the Transport Act 1981, s 27 (1).

As to the application of the fixed penalty procedure to offences under s 33A (3), see the Transport Act 1982, Part III, Sched 1.

The Motor Vehicles (Wearing of Seat Belts) Regulations 1982 (SI 1982 No 1203) have been made under this section.]

[33B. Restriction on carrying children in the front of motor vehicles

(1) Except as provided by regulations a person shall not, without reasonable excuse, drive a motor vehicle on a road when there is in the front of the vehicle a child under the age of fourteen years who is not wearing a seat belt in conformity with regulations.

(2) It is an offence for a person to drive a motor vehicle in contravention of subsection (1) above.

(3) Provision may be made by regulations—

(a) excepting from the prohibition in subsection (1) above children of any pre-scribed description, vehicles of a prescribed class or the driving of vehicles in such circumstances as may be prescribed;

(b) defining in relation to any class of vehicle what part of the vehicle is to be regarded as the front of the vehicle for the purposes of that subsection;

(c) prescribing for the purposes of that subsection the descriptions of seat belt to be worn by children of any prescribed description and the manner in which such a belt is to be fixed and used.

(4) In this section—

'regulations' means regulations made by the Secretary of State under this section; and

'seat belt' includes any description of restraining device for a child and any reference to wearing a seat belt shall be construed accordingly.]

[Section 33B was inserted by the Transport Act 1981, s 28 (1).

As to the application of the fixed penalty procedure to offences under s 338 (2), see the Transport Act 1982, Part III, and Sched 1.

The Motor Vehicles (Wearing of Seat Belts by Children) Regulations 1982 (SI 1982 No 1342) have been made under this section.]

*　　　　*　　　　*

Restrictions on use of motor vehicles off roadway

*　　　　*　　　　*

36. Prohibition of driving motor vehicles elsewhere than on roads

(1) Subject to the provisions of this section, if without lawful authority a person drives a motor vehicle on to or upon any common land, moorland or other land of whatsoever description, not being land forming part of a road, or on any road being a footpath or bridleway, he shall be guilty of an offence.

(2) It shall not be an offence under this section to drive a motor vehicle on any land within fifteen yards of a road, being a road on which a motor vehicle may lawfully be driven, for the purpose only of parking the vehicle on that land.

(3) *[No offence in emergencies such as fire and rescue.]*

(4) *[Saving for s 193 of the Law of Property Act 1925 and byelaws and for law of trespass.]*

[As to the application of the fixed penalty procedure to offences under s 36, see the Transport Act 1982, Part III, and Sched 1.]

[36A. Prohibition of parking of heavy commercial vehicles on verges and footways

(1) Subject to subsection (2) below, a person who parks a heavy commercial vehicle wholly or partly—

(a) on the verge of a road; or

(b) on any land situated between two carriageways and which is not a footway; or

(c) on a footway;

shall be guilty of an offence.

(2) A person shall not be convicted of an offence under this section with respect to a vehicle if he proves to the satisfaction of the court—

(a) that it was parked in accordance with permission given by a constable in uniform; or

(b) that it was parked in contravention of this section for the purpose of saving life or extinguishing fire or meeting any other like emergency; or

(c) that it was parked in contravention of this section but the conditions specified in subsection (3) below were satisfied.

(3) The conditions mentioned in subsection (2) (c) above are—

(a) that the vehicle was parked on the verge of a road or on a footway for the purpose of loading or unloading; and

(b) that the loading or unloading of the vehicle could not have been satisfactorily performed if it had not been parked on the footway or verge; and

(c) that the vehicle was not left unattended at any time while it was so parked.

[(3A) The [Secretary of State for Transport] may by regulations provide that, in relation to vehicles of such classes as may be specified in the regulations, subsection (1) above shall not apply or shall apply subject to such conditions as may be so specified.

(3B) In England and Wales a local authority may institute proceedings for an offence under this section committed with respect to the verge of a road, land or a footway in their area; and in this section 'local authority' means the council of a county, district or London borough, the Greater London Council or the Common Council of the City of London.]

(4) In this section 'carriageway' and 'footway' have the same meanings respectively in [the Highways Act 1980] or, as respects Scotland, the [Roads (Scotland) Act 1984].

[(5) In this section 'heavy commercial vehicle' means any goods vehicle which has an operating weight exceeding 7·5 tonnes.]

[(6) The operating weight of a goods vehicle for the purposes of this section is—

(a) in the case of a motor vehicle not drawing a trailer or in the case of a trailer, its maximum laden weight;

(b) in the case of an articulated vehicle, its maximum laden weight (if it has one) and otherwise the aggregate maximum laden weight of all the individual vehicles forming part of that articulated vehicle; and

(c) in the case of a motor vehicle (other than an articulated vehicle) drawing one or more trailers, the aggregate maximum laden weight of the motor vehicle and the trailer or trailers attached to it.]

[(7) In this section 'articulated vehicle' means a motor vehicle with a trailer so attached to it as to be partially superimposed upon it; and references to the maximum laden weight of a vehicle are references to the total laden weight which must not be exceeded in the case of that vehicle if it is to be used in Great Britain without contravening any regulations for the time being in force under section 40 of this Act.]

[(8) In this section, and in the definition of 'goods vehicle' in section 196(1) of this Act as it applies for the purposes of this section, 'trailer' means any vehicle other than a motor vehicle.]

[(9) The Secretary of State may by regulations amend subsections (5) and (6) above (whether as originally enacted or as previously amended under this subsection)—

(*a*) by substituting weights of a different description for any of the weights there mentioned; or

(*b*) in the case of subsection (5) above, by substituting a weight of a different description or amount, or a weight different both in description and amount, for the weight there mentioned.]

[(10) Different regulations may be made under subsection (9) above as respects different classes of vehicles or as respects the same class of vehicles in different circumstances and as respects different times of the day or night and as respects different localities.]

[(11) Regulations under subsection (9) above shall not so amend subsection (5) above that there is any case in which a goods vehicle whose operating weight (ascertained in accordance with subsection (6) above as originally enacted) does not exceed 7·5 tonnes is a heavy commercial vehicle for any of the purposes of this section.]

[Section 36A was inserted by the Heavy Commercial Vehicles (Controls and Regulations) Act 1973, s 2, and is printed as amended by the Road Traffic Act 1974, s 24 (2), and Sched 6, para 13; the Minister of Transport Order 1979 (SI 1979 No 571); the Highways Act 1980, s 343 (2), and Sched 24, para 21; the Transfer of Functions (Transport) Order 1981 (SI 1981 No 238); the Road Traffic Acts 1960 and 1972, Road Traffic Regulation Act 1967 (Metrication) (No 2) Regulations 1981 (SI 1981 No 1374); the Transport Act 1982, s 56 (2); and the Roads (Scotland) Act 1984, s 156 (2), and Sched 10, para 2.

Subsections (3A) and (3B) are to be brought into force on a date to be announced.

In the Highways Act 1980, 'carriageway' is defined as 'a way constituting or comprised in a highway, being a way (other than a cycle track) over which the public have a right of way for the passage of vehicles', and 'footway' is defined as 'a way comprised in a highway which also comprises a carriageway, being a way over which the public have a right of way on foot only': ibid, s 329 (1).

As to the application of the fixed penalty procedure to offences under s 36A (1), see the Transport Act 1982, Part III, and Sched 1.]

[36B. Prohibition of parking of vehicles on verges, central reservations and footways

(1) Subject to the provisions of this section, a person who parks a vehicle, other than a heavy commercial vehicle, within the meaning of section 36A of this Act, wholly or partly—

(*a*) on the verge of an urban road, or

(*b*) on any land which is situated between two carriageways of an urban road and which is not a footway, or

(*c*) on a footway comprised in an urban road,

shall be guilty of an offence.

(2) A person shall not be convicted of an offence under this section with respect to a vehicle if he proves to the satisfaction of the court—

(*a*) that it was parked in accordance with permission given by a constable in uniform; or

(*b*) that it was parked in contravention of this section for the purpose of saving life or extinguishing fire or meeting any other like emergency; or

(*c*) that it was parked in contravention of this section but the conditions specified in subsection (3) below were satisfied.

(3) The conditions mentioned in subsection (2) (*c*) above are:—

(*a*) that the vehicle was parked on a verge or footway for the purpose of loading or unloading; and

(*b*) that the loading or unloading of the vehicle could not have been satisfactorily performed if it had not been parked on the footway or verge; and

(*c*) that the vehicle was not left unattended at any time while it was so parked.

(4) The [Secretary of State for Transport] may by regulations provide that, in relation to vehicles of such classes as may be specified in the regulations, subsection (1) above shall not apply or shall apply subject to such conditions as may be so specified.

(5) The authority having power, otherwise than by virtue of [Part I of Schedule 9 (reserve powers of Secretary of State) to the Road Traffic Regulation Act 1984], to make an order under section 1 or section 6 of that Act in relation to a road may by order specifying that road provide that the provisions of subsection (1) above shall not apply in relation to it or to any part of it specified in the order, either at all times or during periods so specified.

(6) In England and Wales a local authority, within the meaning of section 36A of this Act, may institute proceedings for an offence under this section committed with respect to a road in their area.

(7) In the Road Traffic Regulation Act [1984]—

(*a*) [section 125 (boundary roads)] shall apply for the purpose of subsection (5) above as it applies for the purposes of sections 1 (1) and 6 (1) of that Act;

(*b*) [section 122 (exercise of functions by local authorities)] shall apply as if subsections (1) and (5) above were contained in that Act; and

(*c*) [Part I (reserve powers of Secretary of State), Part III (procedure as to certain orders), Part IV (variation or revocation of certain orders) and Part VI (validity of certain orders) of Schedule 9] shall apply in relation to orders under subsection (5) above as they apply in relation to orders under any provision of section 1 or section 6 of that Act.

(8) In this section 'footway' has the same meaning as in [the Highways Act 1980] or, as respects Scotland, the [Roads (Scotland) Act 1984] and 'urban road' means a road which—

(*a*) is a restricted road for the purposes of [section 81] of the [Road Traffic Regulation Act 1984] (30 mph speed limit); or

(*b*) is subject to an order under [section 84] of that Act imposing a speed limit not exceeding 40 mph; or

(*c*) is subject to a speed limit not exceeding 40 mph which is imposed by or under any local Act.]

[Section 36B was inserted by the Road Traffic Act 1974, s 7, and is printed as amended by the Minister of Transport Order 1979 (SI 1979 No 571); the Highways Act 1980, s 343 (2), and Sched 24, para 21; the Transfer of Functions (Transport) Order 1981 (SI 1981 No 238); the Road Traffic Regulation Act 1984, ss 144 (1), 146, and Sched 10, para 2, Sched 13, para 15; and the Roads (Scotland) Act 1984, s 156 (2), and Sched 10, para 2.

Subsections (1)–(4) are to be brought into force on a date to be announced.

As to the application of the fixed penalty procedure to offences under s 36B (1), see the Transport Act 1982, Part III, and Sched 1.

For definition of 'footway' in the Highways Act 1980, see the note to s 36A.]

Road safety information and road training

[37. The Highway Code

(1)–(6) *[Omitted.]*

[(7) A failure on the part of a person to observe a provision of the Highway Code shall not of itself render that person liable to criminal proceedings of any kind but any such failure may in any proceedings (whether civil or criminal, and including proceedings for an offence under this Act, the Road Traffic Regulation Act [1984] or the Public Passenger Vehicles Act 1981) be relied upon by any party to the proceedings as tending to establish or to negative any liability which is in question in those proceedings.]

[(8) In this section 'the Highway Code' means the code comprising directions for the guidance of persons using roads issued under section 45 of the Road Traffic Act 1930, as from time to time revised under this section or under any previous enactment.]

(9) *[Omitted.]*]

[Section 37 which had previously been amended by the Public Passenger Vehicles Act 1981, s 88 (2), and Sched 7, para 13) was substituted by the Transport Act 1982, s 60. Subsection (7) is printed as amended by the Road Traffic Regulation Act 1984, s 146, and Sched 13, para 16.]

*　　　*　　　*

PART II

Construction and Use of Vehicles and Equipment

General provisions

40. Regulation of construction, weight, equipment and use of vehicles

(1)–(4) *[Omitted.]*

(5) Subject to the provisions of this section and sections 41 and 42 of this Act, a person—

(*a*) who contravenes or fails to comply with any regulations under this section; or

(*b*) who uses on a road a motor vehicle or trailer which does not comply with any such regulations or causes or permits a vehicle to be so used,

shall be guilty of an offence.

(6) In any proceedings for an offence under subsection (5) above in which there is alleged a contravention of or failure to comply with a construction and use requirement relating to any description of weight applicable to a goods vehicle, it shall be a defence to prove either—

(*a*) that at the time when the vehicle was being used on the road it was proceeding to a weighbridge which was the nearest available one to the place where the loading of the vehicle was completed for the purpose of being weighed, or was proceeding from a weighbridge after being weighed to the nearest point at which it was reasonably practicable to reduce the weight to the relevant limit, without causing an obstruction on any road; or

(*b*) in a case where the limit of that weight was not exceeded by more than five per cent, that that limit was not exceeded at the time the loading of the vehicle was originally completed and that since that time no person has made any addition to the load.

(7) In this Part of this Act—

'construction and use requirements' means requirements, whether applicable
generally or at specified times or in specified circumstances, imposed under this
section *or by or under sections 68 to 79 of this Act;*

'plated particulars' means such particulars as are required to be marked on a goods
vehicle in pursuance of regulations under this section by means of a plate;

'plated weights' means such weights as are required to be so marked.

*[In subs (7), the words 'or by or under sections 68 to 79 of this Act' have been repealed, with
effect from a date to be announced, by the Road Traffic Act 1974, s 24 (3) and Sched 7.*

*Sections 41 and 42 of this Act relate to the temporary exemption from regulations made under this
section and the authorisation of special vehicles for use of roads notwithstanding their non-com-
pliance with regulations under this section.*

*As to the application of the fixed penalty procedure to offences under s 40(5), see the Transport
Act 1982, Part III, and Sched 1.*

*The regulations in force under this section include the Motor Vehicles (Construction and Use)
(Track Laying Vehicles) Regulations 1955 (SI 1955 No 990), the Minibus (Conditions of Fitness,
Equipment and Use) Regulations 1977 (SI 1977 No 2103), the Motor Vehicles (Construction and
Use) Regulations 1978 (SI 1978 No 1017), the Community Bus Regulations 1978 (SI 1978 No
1313), the Public Service Vehicles (Conditions of Fitness, Equipment, Use and Certification)
Regulations 1981 (SI 1981 No 257), the Road Transport (International Passenger Services) Regu-
lations 1984 (SI 1984 No 748), and the Road Vehicles Lighting Regulations 1984 (SI 1984 No
812).]*

*   *   *

43. Tests of satisfactory condition of vehicles other than goods vehicles to which s 45 applies

(1) The provisions of this section and of sections 44 and 52 (1) of this Act shall
have effect in relation to motor vehicles other than goods vehicles which are required
by regulations under section 45 of this Act to be submitted for a goods vehicle test
under that section and for the purpose of ascertaining whether the prescribed statutory requirements relating to the construction and condition of motor vehicles or their
accessories or equipment are complied with.

(2) The [Secretary of State for Transport] may by regulations make provision for
the examination of vehicles submitted for examination under this section and for the
issue, where it is found on such an examination that the said requirements are complied with, of a certificate (hereafter in this Act referred to as a 'test certificate') that
at the date of the examination the requirements were complied with in relation to the
vehicle.

(3)–(6) *[Omitted.]*

[(7) In its application to vehicles in which recording equipment is required by
article 3 of the Community Recording Equipment Regulation to be installed and
used, this section shall have effect as if any reference to prescribed statutory requirements included a reference to the prescribed requirements of so much of that Regulation as relates to the installation of recording equipment and the seals to be affixed to
such equipment.]

*[Section 43 is printed as amended by the Minister of Transport Order 1979 (SI 1979 No 571),
the Transfer of Functions (Transport) Order 1981 (SI 1981 No 238) and the Passenger and Goods
Vehicles (Recording Equipment) Regulations 1981 (SI 1981 No 1692).*

*The Motor Vehicles (Tests) Regulations 1981 (SI 1981 No 1694) were made (in part) under
this section.]*

44. Obligatory test certificates for vehicles other than goods vehicles to which s 45 applies

(1) A person who uses on a road at any time, or causes or permits to be so used, a motor vehicle to which this section applies, and as respects which no test certificate has been issued within the appropriate period before the said time, shall be guilty of an offence.

(2) Subject to section 43 (1) of this Act and to subsection (4) below, the motor vehicles to which this section applies at any time are—

(a) those first registered under the Vehicles (Excise) Act 1971, the Vehicles (Excise) Act 1962, the Vehicles (Excise) Act 1949 or the Roads Act 1920, not less than ten years before that time, and

(b) those which, having a date of manufacture not less than the specified period before that time, have been used on roads (whether in Great Britain or elsewhere) before being registered under the Vehicles (Excise) Act 1971 or the Vehicles (Excise) Act 1962.

(3) For the purposes of paragraph (b) above there shall be disregarded the use of a vehicle—

(a) before it is sold or supplied by retail; or

(b) before it is registered by the [Secretary of State for Transport] under paragraph (b) of section 19 (1) of the Vehicles (Excise) Act 1971 (registration when [Secretary of State for Transport] receives from a motor dealer particulars of a vehicle to which the dealer has assigned a mark under section 20 thereof) and after a mark is so assigned to it.

(4) This section shall not apply to . . . vehicles of such classes as may be prescribed . . .

(5) The [Secretary of State for Transport] may by order made by statutory instrument direct that subsection (2)(a) above shall have effect with the substitution, for ten years, of such shorter period as may be specified in the order.

An order under this subsection shall not have effect unless approved by resolution of each House of Parliament.

(6) The [Secretary of State for Transport] may by regulations exempt from subsection (1) above the use of vehicles for such purposes as may be prescribed.

(7) The [Secretary of State for Transport] may by regulations exempt from subsection (1) above the use of vehicles in any such area as may be prescribed.

(8)–(12) *[Omitted.]*

(13) In this section—

'appropriate period' means a period of twelve months or such shorter period as may be prescribed;

'specified period' means a period of ten years or such shorter period as may be specified in an order under subsection (5) above.

[Section 44 is printed as amended by the Transport Act 1978, s 5 (10); the Minister of Transport Order 1979 (SI 1979 No 571); the Transport Act 1980, ss 34, 43 (1), 69, Sched 5, Part II, and Sched 9, Part I; and the Transfer of Functions (Transport) Order 1981 (SI 1981 No 238). (Cf the Public Passenger Vehicles Act 1981, s 88 (2), and Sched 7, para 14.)

The Motor Vehicles (Tests) (Extension) Order 1966 (SI 1966 No 973) extended the application of subs (1) by substituting 'three' for 'ten' in subs (2) (a). The 1966 Order has been revoked and, with effect from 1 January 1983, 'one year' was substituted for 'ten years' in subs (2)(a) by the Motor Vehicles (Tests) (Extension) Order 1982 (SI 1982 No 1550) in respect of a vehicle being—

    (i) a motor vehicle used for the carriage of passengers and with more than 8 seats, excluding the driver's seat, or

    (ii) a taxi (as defined in section 64 (3) of the Transport Act 1980), being a vehicle licensed to ply for hire, or

    (iii) an ambulance, that is to say a motor vehicle which is constructed or adapted, and primarily used, for the carriage of persons to a place where they will receive, or from a place where they have received, medical or dental treatment, and which, by reason of design, marking or equipment is readily identifiable as a vehicle so constructed or adapted.

The 1982 Order also provides that subs (2)(a) has effect with the substitution of 'three years' for 'ten years' as respects a vehicle other than one of a kind specified above.

The Motor Vehicles (Tests) Regulations 1981 (SI 1981 No 1694) were made (in part) under subss (4), (6) and (7).]

45. Tests of satisfactory condition of certain classes of goods vehicles and determination of plated weights and other particulars therefor

(1) The [Secretary of State for Transport] may by regulations make provision for the examination of goods vehicles of any prescribed class for the purpose of selecting or otherwise determining plated weights or other plated particulars for goods vehicles of that class or for the purpose of ascertaining whether any prescribed construction and use requirements (whether relating to plated particulars or not) are complied with in the case of goods vehicles of that class, or for both purposes, and in particular—

    (*a*) for the determination, according to criteria or by methods prescribed by or determined under the regulations, of the plated particulars for a goods vehicle (including its plated weights), on an examination of the vehicle for the purpose, and for the issue on such an examination, except as provided by regulations made by virtue of paragraph (*c*) of this subsection, of a certificate (hereafter in this Act referred to as a 'plating certificate') specifying those particulars;

    (*b*) for the issue, for a goods vehicle which has been found on examination for the purpose to comply with the prescribed construction and use requirements, of a certificate (hereafter in this Act referred to as a 'goods vehicle test certificate') stating that the vehicle has been found so to comply; and

    (*c*) for the refusal of a goods vehicle test certificate for a goods vehicle which is so found not to comply with those requirements and for requiring a written notification to be given of any such refusal and of the grounds of the refusal, and for the refusal of a plating certificate where a goods vehicle test certificate is refused.

References in the foregoing provisions of this subsection to construction and use requirements shall be construed, in relation to an examination of a vehicle solely for the purpose of ascertaining whether it complies with any such requirements, as references to such of those requirements as are applicable to the vehicle at the time of the test and, in relation to an examination of a vehicle both for that purpose and for the purpose of determining its plated particulars, as references to such of those requirements as will be applicable to the vehicle if a plating certificate is issued for it.

(2)–(9) *[Omitted.]*

[(9A) In its application to vehicles in which recording equipment is required by article 3 of the Community Recording Equipment Regulation to be installed and used, this section shall have effect as if any reference to prescribed construction and use requirements included a reference to prescribed requirements of so much of that Regulation as relates to the installation of recording equipment and the seals to be affixed to such equipment.]

(10) *[Omitted.]*

[Section 45 is printed as amended by the Minister of Transport Order 1979 (SI 1979 No 571); the Transfer of Functions (Transport) Order 1981 (SI 1981 No 238); and the Passenger and Goods Vehicles (Recording Equipment) Regulations 1981 (SI 1981 No 1692).

The Goods Vehicles (Plating and Testing) Regulations 1982 (SI 1982 No 1478) have been made under this section.]

46. Obligatory test certificates for goods vehicles to which s 45 applies

(1) If any person at any time on or after the relevant date uses on a road, or causes or permits to be so used, a goods vehicle of a class required by regulations under section 45 of this Act to have been submitted for examination for plating and at that time there is no plating certificate in force for the vehicle, he shall be guilty of an offence.

In this subsection 'relevant date', in relation to any goods vehicle, means the date by which it is so required to be submitted for examination for plating.

(2) If any person at any time on or after the relevant date uses on a road, or causes or permits to be so used, a goods vehicle of a class required by regulations under the said section 45 to have been submitted for a goods vehicle test and at that time there is no goods vehicle test certificate in force for the vehicle, he shall be guilty of an offence.

In this subsection 'relevant date', in relation to any goods vehicle, means the date by which it is so required to be submitted for its first goods vehicle test.

(3) Any person who uses on a road, or causes or permits to be so used, a goods vehicle when an alteration has been made to the vehicle or its equipment which is required by regulations under the said section 45 to be, but has not been, notified to the [Secretary of State for Transport] [or the prescribed testing authority] shall be guilty of an offence.

(4) In any proceedings for an offence under subsection (3) above, it shall be 'a defence to prove that the alteration was not specified in the relevant plating certificate in accordance with regulations under the said section 45.

(5) The [Secretary of State for Transport] may by regulations—

(*a*) exempt from all or any of the foregoing provisions of this section the use of goods vehicles for such purposes or in such an area as may be prescribed; and

(*b*) make provision for the issue in respect of a vehicle in such circumstances as may be prescribed of a certificate of temporary exemption exempting that vehicle from the provisions of subsection (1) or (2) above for such period as may be specified in the certificate.

[Section 46 is printed as amended by the Minister of Transport Order 1979 (SI 1979 No 571); the Transfer of Functions (Transport) Order 1981 (SI 1981 No 238); and the Transport Act 1982, s 10(7)(b).

The words ('or the prescribed testing authority') inserted in subs (3) by the Transport Act 1982 will take effect on a date to be announced.

Regulations containing exemptions from the requirements of this section are contained in Part VIII of the Goods Vehicles (Plating and Testing) Regulations 1982 (SI 1982 No 1478), as amended.]

47. Approval of design, construction, etc, of . . . vehicles

(1)–(3) *[Omitted.]*

(4) Where the [Secretary of State for Transport] is satisfied on application made to him by the manufacturer of a . . . vehicle of a class to which regulations under this section apply and after examination of the vehicle—

(a) that the vehicle complies with the relevant type approval requirements; and

(b) that adequate arrangements have been made to secure that other vehicles purporting to conform with that vehicle in the relevant aspects of design, construction, equipment and marking will so conform in all respects or with such variations as may be permitted;

he may approve that vehicle as a type vehicle and, if so, shall issue a certificate (hereafter in this Part of this Act referred to as a 'type approval certificate') stating that the vehicle complies with the relevant type approval requirements and specifying the permitted variations from the type vehicle and the design weights for vehicles so conforming in all respects and for vehicles so conforming with any such variations.

In the following provisions of this section and in section 48 of this Act 'conform' means conform in all respects or with any permitted variation.

(5) A manufacturer of a type vehicle in respect of which a type approval certificate is in force may issue, in respect of each . . . vehicle manufactured by him which conforms with the type vehicle in such of the relevant aspects of design, construction, equipment and marking as are mentioned in the type approval certificate, a certificate (hereafter in this Part of this Act referred to as a ['certificate of conformity']) stating that it does so conform and specifying the design weights for the vehicle, and shall [in the case of goods vehicles of such classes] as may be prescribed specify in the certificate one or more of the plated weights for the vehicle.

(6), (7) *[Omitted.]*

(8) Where the [Secretary of State for Transport] is satisfied, on application made to him by any person in respect of a . . . vehicle of a class to which regulations under this section apply and after examination of the vehicle, that the vehicle complies with the relevant type approval requirements and [in the case of a goods vehicle] the [Secretary of State for Transport] has sufficient information to enable the plated weights to be ascertained for the vehicle he may issue a certificate (hereafter in this Part of this Act referred to as a 'Minister's approval certificate') stating that the vehicle complies with those requirements and specifying its design weights and [in the case of a goods vehicle] plated weights and, where he issues such a certificate [in respect of a goods vehicle], shall secure that the plated weights are marked on the vehicle by means of a plate fixed to it.

(9)–(13) *[Omitted.]*

[Section 47 is printed as amended by the Road Traffic Act 1974, ss 10 (1), 24 (3), and Sched 7, the Minister of Transport Order 1979 (SI 1979 No 571), and the Transfer of Functions (Transport) Order 1981 (SI 1981 No 238).]

*   *   *

51. Obligatory type approval [certificates, certificates of conformity], and Minister's approval certificates

(1) If any person at any time on or after the day appointed by regulations made by the [Secretary of State for Transport] in relation to . . . vehicles [or vehicle parts] of a prescribed class, being vehicles [or vehicle parts] to which type approval require-

ments prescribed by those regulations apply, uses on a road, or causes or permits to be so used, a . . . vehicle of that class [or a vehicle to which is fitted a vehicle part of that class] and it does not appear from one or more certificates then in force under section 47 of this Act that the vehicle [or vehicle part] complies with those requirements, he shall be guilty of an offence.

Different days may be appointed under this subsection in relation to different classes of vehicles [or vehicle parts].

(2) If a plating certificate has been issued for a goods vehicle to which section 46 (1) of this Act or subsection (1) above applies, but does not specify a maximum laden weight for the vehicle together with any trailer which may be drawn by it, any person who on or after the relevant date within the meaning of the said section 46 (1) or, as the case may be, the day appointed under the said subsection (1) uses the vehicle on a road for drawing a trailer, or causes or permits it to be so used, shall be guilty of an offence.

(3) Any person who uses on a road, or causes or permits to be so used, a . . . vehicle when an alteration has been made to the vehicle or its equipment which is required by regulations or directions under section 48 of this Act to be but has not been, notified to the [Secretary of State for Transport] [or the prescribed testing authority] shall be guilty of an offence.

(4) In any proceedings for an offence under subsection (3) above, it shall be a defence to prove that the regulations were not, or, as the case may be, the alteration was not, specified in the relevant [certificate of conformity] or Minister's approval certificate in accordance with regulations under section 48 (4) of this Act.

(5) The [Secretary of State for Transport] may by regulations—

(a) exempt from all or any of the foregoing provisions of this section the use of . . . vehicles for such purposes or in such an area as may be prescribed;

(b) exempt any class of goods vehicles from the provisions of subsection (2) above; and

(c) make provision for the issue in respect of a vehicle [or vehicle part] in such circumstances as may be prescribed of a certificate of temporary exemption exempting that vehicle [or vehicle part] from the provisions of subsection (1) above for such period as may be specified in the certificate.

[Section 51 is printed as amended by the Road Traffic Act 1974, ss 10 (7), 24 (3), Sched 2, paras 7 and 9, and Sched 7, the Minister of Transport Order 1979 (SI 1979 No 571), the Transfer of Functions (Transport) Order 1981 (SI 1981 No 238) and the Transport Act 1982, s 10 (7) (c).

The words ('or the prescribed testing authority') inserted in subs (3) by the Transport Act 1982 will take effect on a date to be announced.

The Motor Vehicles (Type Approval for Goods Vehicles) (Great Britain) Regulations 1982 (SI 1982 No 1271) and the Motor Vehicles (Type Approval) (Great Britain) Regulations 1984 (SI 1984 No 981) were made (in part) under subs (1). For exemptions from the application of subs (2), see the Goods Vehicles (Plating and Testing) Regulations 1982 (SI 1982 No 1478), Part VIII.]

*   *   *

60. Vehicles not to be sold in unroadworthy condition or altered so as to be unroadworthy

(1) Subject to the provisions of this section it shall not be lawful to sell, or to supply, or to offer to sell or supply [or expose for sale], a motor vehicle or trailer for delivery in such a condition that the use thereof on a road in that condition would be unlawful by virtue of any provision made by regulations under section 40 of this Act

as respects brakes, steering gear or tyres or as respects the construction, weight or equipment of vehicles [or as respects the maintenance of vehicles, their parts and accessories in such a condition that no danger is or is likely to be caused], or in such a condition, as respects lighting equipment or reflectors or the maintenance thereof, that it is not capable of being used on a road during the hours of darkness without contravention of the requirements imposed by law as to obligatory lamps or reflectors.

(2) Subject to the provisions of this section it shall not be lawful to alter a motor vehicle or trailer so as to render its condition such that the use thereof on a road in that condition would be unlawful by virtue of any provision made as respects the construction, weight or equipment of vehicles by regulations under the said section 40.

(3) If a motor vehicle or trailer is sold, supplied, offered [exposed for sale] or altered in contravention of the provisions of this section, any person who so sells, supplies, [or offers it, exposes it for sale] or alters it, or causes or permits it to be so sold, supplied, offered [exposed for sale] or altered, shall be guilty of an offence.

(4) A person shall not be convicted of an offence under this section in respect of the sale, supply, offer [exposure for sale] or alteration of a motor vehicle or trailer if he proves—

(a) that it was sold, supplied, offered [exposed for sale] or altered, as the case may be, for export from Great Britain, or

(b) that he had reasonable cause to believe that the vehicle or trailer would not be used on a road in Great Britain, or would not be so used until it had been put into a condition in which it might lawfully be so used, or

(c) in the case of a vehicle or trailer the sale, supply [offer or exposure for sale] of which is alleged to be unlawful by reason of its condition as respects lighting equipment or reflectors or the maintenance thereof, that he had reasonable cause to believe that the vehicle or trailer would not be used on a road in Great Britain during the hours of darkness until it had been put into a condition in which it might be so used during those hours without contravention of the requirements imposed by law as to obligatory lamps or reflectors.

(5) Nothing in the foregoing provisions of this section shall affect the validity of a contract or any rights arising under a contract.

(6) In this section 'obligatory lamps or reflectors' means, in relation to a motor vehicle or trailer, the lamps or reflectors required by law to be carried thereon while it is on a road during the hours of darkness and when it is neither drawing nor being drawn by another vehicle, except that the said expression does not, in the case of a motor vehicle, include any lamps or reflectors required to be carried by virtue of section 79 of this Act, or, in the case of a trailer, include any lamps or reflectors so required to be carried or any lamps showing a white light to the front.

[Section 60 is printed as amended by the Road Traffic Act 1974, s 11 (2)–(4).]

*   *   *

62. Goods vehicles not to be sold without required [certificate of conformity] or Minister's approval certificate

(1) If any person at any time on or after the day appointed by regulations under section 51(1) of this Act sells, supplies or offers to sell or supply [or exposes for sale a vehicle or vehicle part] of a class to which those regulations apply and it does not

appear from one or more certificates in force at that time under section 47 of this Act that the vehicle [or vehicle part] complies with all the relevant type approval requirements prescribed by those regulations, he shall be guilty of an offence.

(2) A person shall not be convicted of an offence under this section in respect of the sale, supply [offer or exposure for sale] of a vehicle [or vehicle part] if he proves—

(a) that it was sold, supplied [offered or exposed for sale], as the case may be, for export from Great Britain;

(b) that he had reasonable cause to believe that it would not be used on a road in Great Britain [or, in the case of a vehicle part, that it would not be fitted to a vehicle used on a road in Great Britain] or would not be so used [or fitted] until it had been certified as aforesaid; or

(c) that he had reasonable cause to believe that it would only be used for purposes or in any area prescribed by the [Secretary of State for Transport] under section. . . 51 (5) of this Act [or, in the case of a goods vehicle, under section 46 (5) of this Act].

(3) Nothing in subsection (1) above shall affect the validity of a contract or any rights arising under or in relation to a contract.

[Section 62 is printed as amended by t he Road Traffic Act 1974, s 10 (7), and Sched 2, para 11, the Minister of Transport Order 1979 (SI 1979 No 571) and the Transfer of Functions (Transport) Order 1981 (SI 1981 No 238).]

63. Approval marks

(1) Where any international agreement to which the United Kingdom is a party [or a Community obligation] provides—

(a) for markings to be applied—
(i) to motor vehicle parts of any description to indicate conformity with a type approved by any country; or
(ii) to a motor vehicle to indicate that the vehicle is fitted with motor vehicle parts of any description and either that the parts conform with a type approved by any country or that the vehicle is such that as so fitted it conforms with a type so approved; and

(b) for motor vehicle parts or, as the case may be, motor vehicles, bearing those markings to be recognised as complying with the requirements imposed by the law of another country;

the [Secretary of State for Transport] may by regulations designate the markings as approval marks, and any markings so designated shall be deemed for the purposes of the Trade Descriptions Act 1968 to be a trade description, whether or not the markings fall within the definition of that expression in section 2 of that Act.

(2) Any person who, without being authorised by the competent authority to apply any approval mark, applies that mark or a mark so nearly resembling it as to be calculated to deceive shall be guilty of an offence under the Trade Descriptions Act 1968, whether or not he would be guilty of such an offence apart from this subsection.

(3) The conditions subject to which approval of any type may be given on behalf of the United Kingdom or the use of approval marks indicating conformity with a type approved by the United Kingdom may be authorised may include such conditions as to testing or inspection and the payment of fees as the [Secretary of State for Transport] may impose.

(4) In this section—

'motor vehicle' means a mechanically propelled vehicle or a vehicle designed or adapted for towing by a mechanically propelled vehicle,

'motor vehicle part' means any article made or adapted for use as part of a mechanically propelled vehicle, or a vehicle drawn by a mechanically propelled vehicle, or for use as part of the equipment of any such vehicle, and shall be treated as including any equipment for the protection of drivers or passengers in or on a motor vehicle notwithstanding that it does not form part of, or of the equipment of, that vehicle; and

'the competent authority' means,—

(a) as respects any approval mark indicating conformity with a type approved by the United Kingdom, the [Secretary of State for Transport]; and

(b) as respects any approval mark indicating conformity with a type approved by any other country, the authority having power under the law of that country to authorise the use of that mark.

[Section 63 is printed as amended by the Designation of Approval Marks (European Communities) Regulations 1973 (SI 1973 No 1193); the Minister of Transport Order 1979 (SI 1979 No 571); and the Transfer of Functions (Transport) Order 1981 (SI 1981 No 238).

The Trade Descriptions Act 1968, s 1, makes it an offence for any person in the course of a trade or business to (a) apply a false trade description to any goods, or (b) supply or offer to supply any goods to which a false trade description is applied. Under ibid, s 18, the penalty, on summary conviction, is a fine at level 5 on the standard scale and, on conviction on indictment, a fine, imprisonment for up to two years (s 18 has been amended by the Magistrates' Courts Act 1980, s 32 (2), and the Criminal Justice Act 1982, s 46 (1)). For the statutory defences to charges under the Trade Descriptions Act 1968, see ss 24 and 25 of that Act.]

64. Provisions as to proceedings for certain offences in connection with goods vehicles

(1) If in any proceedings for an offence under section 40 (5) of this Act any question arises as to a weight of any description specified in the plating certificate for a goods vehicle, and a weight of that description is marked on the vehicle, it shall be assumed, unless the contrary is proved, that the weight marked on the vehicle is the weight so specified.

(2) If in any proceedings for an offence under this Part of this Act except sections 44 and 60 any question arises as to the date of manufacture of a . . . vehicle, a date purporting to be such a date and marked on the vehicle in pursuance of regulations under this Part of this Act shall be evidence (and in Scotland sufficient evidence) that the vehicle was manufactured on the date so marked.

(3) If in any proceedings for the offence of driving a goods vehicle on a road, or causing or permitting a goods vehicle to be so driven, in contravention of a prohibition under section 57 (7) of this Act any question arises whether a weight of any description has been reduced to a limit imposed by construction and use requirements, the burden of proof shall lie on the accused.

(4) If in any proceedings in Scotland for an offence under the Road Traffic Regulation Act [1984] or this Act any question arises as to a weight of any description in relation to a . . . vehicle, a certificate purporting to be signed by an inspector of weights and measures and certifying the accuracy of a weighbridge or other machine for weighing vehicles shall be sufficient evidence of the facts stated therein, and where

the inspector is called as a witness his evidence shall be sufficient evidence of the aforesaid facts.

In this subsection 'inspector of weights and measures' has the same meaning as in the Weights and Measures Act 1963, except that it includes a chief inspector within the meaning of that Act.

[Section 64 is printed as amended by the Road Traffic Act 1974, ss 10 (7), 24 (3), Sched 2, para 12, and Sched 7, and the Road Traffic Regulation Act 1984, s 146, and Sched 13, para 17.

The prohibition under s 57 (7) of this Act is a written notice prohibiting the driving of a vehicle on any road until its excessive weight is reduced.

Subject to transitional provisions relating to persons appointed before the commencement of the Weights and Measures Act 1963, an 'inspector of weights and measures' in that Act means a person duly appointed as such by a weights and measures authority under s 41 of that Act: ibid, s 58 (1).]

*   *   *

Provisions as to lighting of vehicles

81. Offences

(1) . . .

(2) If any person sells, or offers or exposes for sale, any appliance adapted for use as a reflector or tail lamp to be carried on a vehicle in accordance with the provisions of this Act or of any regulations made thereunder, not being an appliance which complies with the [construction and use requirements applicable to] a class of vehicles for which the appliance is adapted, he shall be guilty of an offence.

[Section 81 is printed as amended by the Road Traffic Act 1974, ss 9(3), (4), 24(3), and Sched 7.]

Supplementary

82. Interpretation of Part II

[(1)] In this Part of this Act, unless the context otherwise requires, the following expressions have the meanings hereby assigned to them respectively, that is to say—

['the Community Recording Equipment Regulation' means Council Regulation (EEC) No 1463/60 of 20th July 1970 on the introduction of recording equipment in road transport *[OJ L 164, 27.7.70, p 1]*, as amended by Council Regulations (EEC) Nos 1787/73 *[OJ L 181, 4.7.73, p 1]* and 2828/77 *[OJ L 334, 24.12.77, p 5]*, and as read with the Community Road Transport Rules (Exemption) Regulations 1978 *[SI 1978 No 1158]* and the Community Road Transport Rules (Exemptions) (Amendment) Regulations 1980 *[SI 1980 No 266]*;

'construction and use requirement' has the meaning assigned to it in section 40 (7) of this Act;

['certificate of conformity'] has the meaning assigned to it in section 47 (5) of this Act;

'Minister's approval certificate' has the meaning assigned to it in section 47 (8) of this Act;

'plating certificate' has the meaning assigned to it in section 45 (1) of this Act;

'prescribed' means prescribed by regulations made by the [Secretary of State for Transport];

'type approval certificate' has the meaning assigned to it in section 47 (4) of this Act;

['vehicle part' means any article which is a motor vehicle part, within the meaning of section 63 of this Act, and any other article which is made or adapted for use as part of, or as part of the equipment of, a vehicle which is intended or adapted to be used on roads but which is not a motor vehicle within the meaning of that section].

[(2) References in any provision of this Part of this Act to an authorised inspector are references to a person authorised by the Secretary of State under section 8 of the Transport Act 1982 to exercise the function to which that provision relates.]

[Section 82 (including selected definitions only) is printed as amended by the Road Traffic Act 1974, ss 10 (7), 24 (3), and Sched 2, paras 7 and 13, and Sched 7; the Minister of Transport Order 1979 (SI 1979 No 571); the Transfer of Functions (Transport) Order 1981 (SI 1981 No 238); the Passenger and Goods Vehicles (Recording Equipment) Regulations 1981 (SI 1981 No 1692); and the Transport 1982, s 74 (1), and Sched 5, para 11 (2).

The addition of subs (2) to this section (and the necessary implication that the preceding provisions should be designated as subs (1)) which was effected by the Transport Act 1982 will take effect on a date to be announced.

Section 8 of the Transport Act 1982, inter alia, empowers the Secretary of State to authorise individuals (referred to as 'authorised inspectors') to exercise testing and surveillance functions in the course of a vehicle testing business in relation to goods vehicles, etc.]

*   *   *

PART III

LICENSING OF DRIVERS OF VEHICLES

Driving licences

84. Drivers of motor vehicles to have driving licences

(1) It shall be an offence for a person to drive on a road a motor vehicle of any class if he is not the holder of a licence authorising him to drive a motor vehicle of that class.

(2) It shall be an offence for a person to [cause or permit another person] to drive on a road a motor vehicle of any class [if that other person] is not the holder of a licence authorising him to drive a motor vehicle of that class.

(3) Notwithstanding the foregoing provisions of this section [it shall be lawful for a person who is not the holder of a licence, to] act as steersman of a motor vehicle, being a vehicle on which a speed limit of five miles per hour or less is imposed by or under [section 86 of the Road Traffic Regulation Act 1984], under the orders of another person engaged in the driving of the vehicle who is licensed in that behalf in accordance with the requirements of this Part of this Act and Part IV of this Act, and [for a person to cause or permit] another person who is not the holder of a licence so to act.

(4) Notwithstanding the foregoing provisions of this section [it shall be lawful for a person to drive or cause or permit] another person to drive a vehicle of any class if—

(a) the driver has held [a licence to drive vehicles of that class or [an exchangeable licence] to drive vehicles of a category corresponding to that class and (in either case)] is entitled to obtain a licence to drive vehicles of that class; and

(b) an application by the driver for the grant of such a licence for a period which includes that time has been received by the [Secretary of State for Transport] or such a licence granted to him has been revoked or surrendered in pursuance of section 89 of this Act; and

(c) any conditions which by virtue of section 88 (2) or (4) of this Act apply to the driving under the authority of the licence of vehicles of that class are complied with;

but the benefit of the foregoing provisions of this subsection shall not extend beyond the date when a licence is granted in pursuance of the application mentioned in paragraph (b) above or, as the case may be, in pursuance of subsection (4) of the said section 89 in consequence of the revocation or surrender so mentioned nor (in a case where a licence is not in fact so granted) beyond the expiration of the period [of one year or such shorter period as may be prescribed, beginning on the date of the application or, as the case may be, the revocation or surrender mentioned in paragraph (b) above].

[(4A) The Secretary of State may by regulations provide that subsection (4) above shall also apply (where the requirements of that subsection are otherwise met) in the case of a person who has not previously held a licence to drive vehicles of the relevant class.

Regulations under this subsection shall, if not previously revoked, expire at the end of the period of one year beginning with the day on which they came into operation.]

(5) Regulations may provide that a person who becomes resident in Great Britain shall, during the prescribed period after he becomes so resident, be treated for the purposes of subsections (1) and (2) above as the holder of a licence authorising him to drive motor vehicles of the prescribed classes if he satisfies the prescribed conditions and is the holder of a permit of the prescribed description authorising him to drive vehicles under the law of a country outside the United Kingdom; and the regulations may provide for the application of any enactment relating to licences or licence holders, with or without modifications, in relation to any such permit and its holder respectively.

[Section 84 is printed as amended by the Road Traffic Act 1974, Sched 3, para 1; the Road Traffic (Driver's Age and Hours of Work) Act 1976, s 1 (2), and Sched 1, para 1; the Minister of Transport Order 1979 (SI 1979 No 571); the Transfer of Functions (Transport) Order 1981 (SI 1981 No 238); the Transport Act 1981, s 29 (1); the Driving Licences (Community Driving Licence) Regulations 1982 (SI 1982 No 1555); the Road Traffic (Driving Licences) Act 1983, s 1 (3)(a); and the Road Traffic Regulation Act 1984, s 184, and Sched 13, para 18.

For the meaning of 'exchangeable licence', see the notes to s 85.

In relation to a person who becomes normally resident in the United Kingdom and holds a Community licence, the reference to 'Great Britain' in s 84 (5) has effect as if it were a reference to 'Great Britain, Northern Ireland or Gibraltar'; see SI 1982 No 1555, reg 4 (1)(a).

The term 'Community licence' is defined in s 110 (1) of the Act as amended by SI 1982 No 1555. The following definition is taken from s 110 (1):

'Community licence' means a document issued in respect of a member State other than the United Kingdom by an authority of that or another member State (including the United Kingdom) authorising the holder to drive a motor vehicle, not being—

(a) a document containing a statement to the effect that that or a previous document was issued in exchange for a document issued in respect of a State other than a member State, or

(b) a document in any of the forms for an international driving permit annexed to the Paris Convention on Motor Traffic of 1926 *[Cmnd 3510]*, the Geneva

Convention on Road Traffic of 1949 *[Cmnd 7997]* or the Vienna Convention on Road Traffic of 1968 *[Cmnd 4032]*.

As to the application of the fixed penalty procedure to offences under s 84 (1), see the Transport Act 1982, Part III, and Sched 1.]

85. Tests of competence to drive

(1) Subject to the provisions of this Part of this Act as to provisional licences [and to the provisions of any regulations made by virtue of section 107 (1)(*f*) of this Act], a licence authorising the driving of motor vehicles of any class shall not be granted to a person unless he satisfies the [Secretary of State for Transport]—

(*a*) that at some time during the period of ten years ending on the date of coming into force of the licence applied for he has passed the test of competence to drive prescribed by virtue of subsection (2) below or a test of competence which under subsection (4) below is a sufficient test, or

(*b*) that within the said period of ten years he has held a licence authorising the driving of vehicles of that class, not being a provisional licence or a licence granted by virtue of section 99 (4) of the Road Traffic Act 1960, or

[(*bb*) that, at the time of application for the licence—
  (i) he holds [an exchangeable licence] authorising the driving of vehicles of a category corresponding to that class, and
  (ii) he is normally resident in [Great Britain or (where the exchangeable licence is a Community licence)] the United Kingdom but has not been so resident for more than one year, or]

(*c*) that within the said period of ten years he has held a licence granted under a relevant external law to drive vehicles of that class, not being a licence corresponding to a provisional licence or a licence granted under any provision of that law corresponding to the said section 99 (4), and is not, at the time of application for the licence, disqualified under that law for holding or obtaining a licence thereunder to drive vehicles of any class.

For the purposes of paragraph (*c*) above 'relevant external law'. means the law for the time being in force in Northern Ireland, that for the time being in force in the Isle of Man or that for the time being in force in any of the Channel Islands that corresponds to this Part of this Act.

(2) *[Power to make regulations regarding driving tests.]*

(3) A magistrates' court acting for the petty sessions area in which a person who has submitted himself for a test of competence to drive resides, or if he resides in Scotland, the sheriff within whose jurisdiction he resides, shall have power on the application of that person to determine whether the test was properly conducted in accordance with the regulations and, if it appears to the court or sheriff that the test was not so conducted, the court or sheriff may order that the applicant shall be eligible to submit himself to another test before the expiration of the period specified for the purposes of subsection (2) (*c*) above and may order that any fee payable by the applicant in respect of the test shall not be paid or, if it has been paid, shall be repaid.

(4) For the purposes of paragraph (*a*) of subsection (1) above a test of competence shall be sufficient for the granting of a licence authorising the driving of—

(*a*) vehicles of any class, if at the time the test was passed it authorised the granting of a licence to drive vehicles of that class:

(*b*) vehicles of any classes which are designated by regulations as a group for the purposes of the said paragraph (*a*), if at the said time the test authorised the granting of a licence to drive vehicles of any class included in the group;

and if vehicles of any classes are designated by regulations as a group for the purposes of paragraph (*b*) of subsection (1) above, a licence authorising the driving of vehicles of a class included in the group shall be deemed for the purposes of the said paragraph (*b*) to authorise the driving of vehicles of all classes included in the group.

(5) The last reference in subsection (4) above and the first reference in paragraph (*b*) of subsection (1) above to a licence do not include a licence which has been revoked in pursuance of section 89 (2) of this Act.

[(6) For the purposes of this section and section 84(4) of this Act, [an exchangeable licence] issued in respect of a member State [, country or territory] shall not be treated as authorising a person to drive a vehicle of any category if—

(*a*) the licence is not for the time being valid for that purpose, or

(*b*) it was issued in respect of that category for a purpose corresponding to that mentioned in section 88(2) of this Act.]

[(7) Where [an exchangeable licence] authorises the driving of vehicles of any category and any vehicle falling within that category falls also within any of the classes designated as a group for the purposes of subsection (1)(*a*) above—

(*a*) that category shall be treated for the purposes of subsection (1)(*bb*) above as corresponding to all classes included in the group; and

(*b*) where, by virtue of regulations under subsection (2) above, a person who passes a test of competence authorising the granting of a licence to drive vehicles of any class included in the group is treated as competent also to drive vehicles of a class included in another group, that category shall be treated for the purposes of subsection (1)(*bb*) above as corresponding to all categories included in that other group.]

[Section 85 is printed as amended by the Road Traffic (Drivers' Ages and Hours of Work) Act 1979, s 1 (3), and Sched 1, para 2; the Minister of Transport Order 1979 (SI 1979 No 571); the Transfer of Functions (Transport) Order 1981 (SI 1981 No 238); the Driving Licences (Community Driving Licence) Regulations 1982 (SI 1982 No 1555); and the Road Traffic (Driving Licences) Act 1983, s 1(3), (a)–(c).

Section 99 (4) of the Road Traffic Act 1960 empowered the making of regulations dispensing with requirements corresponding to those contained in subs (1) above in the case of persons not resident in Great Britain.

Subsection (2) (c) above (not reproduced) specifically empowers regulations to be made ensuring that an unsuccessful candidate at a driving test may not take the test again until after a specified time has elapsed. (See further the Motor Vehicles (Driving Licences) Regulations 1981 (SI 1981 No 952), reg 22.)

Regulations having been made under subs (2) providing for a test of competence to drive to be in separate parts (see the Motor Vehicles (Driving Licences) Regulations 1981 (SI 1981 No 952), reg 18, as amended), subs (3) applies in relation to each part as well as in relation to the whole of the test; see the Transport Act 1981, s 23 (6).

The term 'exchangeable licence' is defined in s 110(1) of the Act, as amended by the Road Traffic (Driving Licences) Act 1983, s 1(1), in the following terms:

'exchangeable licence' means a Community licence or a document which would be a Community licence if—

(*a*) Gibraltar; and

(*b*) each country or territory within this paragraph by virtue of an order under subsection (2) below, were or formed part of a member State other than the United Kingdom.

The countries designated in accordance with para (b) above and Australia, Kenya, New Zealand, Norway, Singapore, Spain, Sweden, Switzerland and the territory of Hong Kong; see the Driving Licences (Exchangeable Licences) Order 1984 (SI 1984 No 672).]

*   *   *

87. Requirements as to physical fitness of drivers

(1) An application for the grant of a licence shall include a declaration by the applicant, in such form as the [Secretary of State for Transport] may require, stating whether he is suffering or has at any time (or, if a period is prescribed for the purposes of this subsection, has during that period) suffered—

[(a)] from any prescribed disability or from any other disability likely to cause the driving of a vehicle by him in pursuance of the licence to be a source of danger to the public (such prescribed or other disability being hereafter in this section referred to as a 'a relevant disability') [or

(b) from any other disability which at the time of the application is not of such a kind that it is a relevant disability but which, by virtue of the intermittent or progressive nature of the disability or otherwise, may become a relevant disability in the course of time (such disability hereafter in this section referred to as a 'prospective disability')].

(2)–(7) *[Omitted.]*

[Section 87 is printed as amended by the Road Traffic Act 1974, s 13 (1), and Sched 3, para 2 (1), the Minister of Transport Order 1979 (SI 1979 No 571) and the Transfer of Functions (Transport) Order 1981 (SI 1981 No 238).

For the disabilities prescribed for the purpose of s 87 (1) (a), see the Motor Vehicles (Driving Licences) Regulations 1981 (SI 1981 No 952), reg 22.]

88. Grant of licences

(1) Subject to section 87 of this Act, the [Secretary of State for Transport] shall, on [payment of such fee, if any, as may be prescribed], grant a licence to a person who—

(a) makes an application for it in such manner and containing such particulars as the [Secretary of State for Transport] may specify; and

(b) furnishes the [Secretary of State for Transport] with such evidence or further evidence in support of the application as the [Secretary of State for Transport] may require; and

[(bb) may, in the case of a person appearing to the [Secretary of State for Transport] to be suffering from a relevant disability or a prospective disability, within the meaning of section 87 of this Act, be restricted so as to authorise only the driving [of vehicles of a particular construction or design specified in the licence; and]

(c) surrenders to the [Secretary of State for Transport] any previous licence granted to him after 1st June 1970 or furnishes the [Secretary of State for Transport] with an explanation for not surrendering it which the [Secretary of State for Transport] considers adequate [and, where the application is made by virtue of section 85 (1) (bb) of this Act, surrenders to the Secretary of State his [exchangeable licence]]; and

(d) is not disqualified by reason of age or otherwise from obtaining the licence for which he makes the application and is not prevented from obtaining it by the provisions of section 85 of this Act.

[but regulations may authorise or require the Secretary of State to refuse a provisional licence authorising the driving of a motor cycle of a prescribed class if the applicant has held such a provisional licence and the licence applied for would come into force within the prescribed period beginning at the end of the period for which the previous licence authorised (or would, if not surrendered or revoked, have authorised) the driving of such a motor cycle or beginning at such other time as may be prescribed.]

(2) If the application aforesaid states that it is made for the purpose of enabling the applicant to drive a motor vehicle with a view to passing a test of competence to drive, any licence granted in pursuance of the application shall be a provisional licence for that purpose, and nothing in section 85 of this Act shall apply to such a licence; but a provisional licence—

(a) shall be granted subject to prescribed conditions;

(b) shall, in any cases prescribed for the purposes of this paragraph, be restricted so as to authorise only the driving of vehicles of the classes so prescribed; and

[(c) shall not authorise a person, before he has passed the test of competence to drive prescribed under section 85 of this Act, to drive a motor cycle having two wheels only, unless it is a learner motor cycle as defined in subsection (2A) below or its first use (as defined in regulations) occurred before 1st January 1982 and the cylinder capacity of its engine does not exceed 125 cubic centimetres;]

[(2A) A learner motor cycle is a motor cycle which either is propelled by electric power or has the following characteristics—

(a) the cylinder capacity of its engine does not exceed 125 cubic centimetres;

(b) the maximum power output of its engine does not exceed 9 kilowatts (as measured in accordance with International Standards Organisation standard 4106–1978.09.01); and

(c) its power to weight ratio does not exceed 100 kilowatts per metric tonne, the power being the maximum power output mentioned in paragraph (b) above and the weight that mentioned in subsection (2B) below.]

[(2B) The weight referred to in subsection (2A) above is the weight of the motor cycle with a full supply of fuel in its tank, an adequate supply of other liquids needed for its propulsion and no load other than its normal equipment, including loose tools.]

(3) A licence shall be in such form as the [Secretary of State for Transport] may determine and shall—

(a) state whether, apart from subsection (4) below, it authorises its holder to drive motor vehicles of all classes or of certain classes only and, in the latter case, specify those classes:

[(b) specify the restrictions on the driving of vehicles of any class in pursuance of the licence to which its holder is subject by virtue of the provisions of section 96 of this Act;]

(c) in the case of a provisional licence, specify the conditions subject to which it is granted; and

(d) where by virtue of subsection (4) below the licence authorises its holder to drive vehicles of classes other than those specified in the licence in pursuance of paragraph (a) above, contain such statements as the [Secretary of State for Transport] considers appropriate for indicating the effect of that subsection.

(4) [subject to subsection (4A) below] a licence which, apart from this subsection authorises its holder to drive motor vehicles of certain classes only shall also authorise him to drive motor vehicles of all other classes subject to the same conditions as if he were authorised by a provisional licence to drive the last-mentioned vehicles; but a licence shall not by virtue of this subsection authorise a person to drive—

[(a) a vehicle of a class for the driving of which he could not, by reason of the provisions of section 96 of this Act, lawfully hold a licence, or]

[(b) unless he has passed the test there mentioned, a motor cycle which, by virtue of subsection (2) (c) above, a provisional licence would not authorise him to drive before he had passed that test.]

[(4A) In such cases as the [Secretary of State for Transport] may prescribe, the provisions of subsection (4) above shall not apply or shall apply subject to such limitations as he may prescribe.]

(5) In subsection (4) above the first reference to a licence does not include a reference to a licence granted before 1st June 1970 or a provisional licence granted thereafter . . .

(6) A person who fails to comply with any condition applicable to him by virtue of subsection (2) or (4) above shall be guilty of an offence.

[Section 88 is printed as amended by the Road Traffic Act 1974, ss 13 (1), 24 (3), Sched 3, para 4, and Sched 7; the Road Traffic (Drivers' Ages and Hours of Work) Act 1976, s 1 (2), and Sched 1, para 3; the Minister of Transport Order 1979 (SI 1979 No 571); the Transfer of Functions (Transport) Order 1981 (SI 1981 No 238); the Transport Act 1981, s 23; the Driving Licences (Community Driving Licence) Regulations 1982 (SI 1982 No 1555); and the Road Traffic (Driving Licences) Act 1983, s 1 (3) (d).

For the meaning of 'exchangeable licence', see the notes to s 85.

As to the application of the fixed penalty procedure to offences under s 88 (6), see the Transport Act 1982, Part III, and Sched 1.]

89. Duration of licences

(1) A licence shall, unless previously revoked or surrendered, remain in force [subject to subsection 1A below]—

[(a) except in a case falling within paragraph (aa), [or (b)] of this subsection, for the period ending on the seventieth anniversary of the applicant's date of birth or for a period of three years, whichever is the longer;

(aa) except in a case falling within paragraph (b) . . . of this subsection if the [Secretary of State for Transport] so determines in the case of a licence to be granted to a person appearing to him to be suffering from a relevant or prospective disability within the meaning of section 87 of this Act, for such [period of not more than three years and not less than one year as the [Secretary of State for Transport] may determine [and]]

(b) in the case of a licence granted in exchange for a subsisting licence and in pursuance of an application requesting a licence for the period authorised by this paragraph, for a period equal to the remainder of that for which the subsisting licence was granted;

(c) . . .

and any such period shall begin with the date on which the licence in question is expressed to come into force.

[(1A) To the extent that a provisional licence authorises the driving of a motor cycle of a prescribed class it shall, unless previously surrendered or revoked, remain in force for such period as may be prescribed or, if the licence is granted to the holder of a previous licence which was surrendered, revoked or treated as being revoked, for the remainder of the period for which the previous licence would have authorised the driving of such a motor cycle, or, in such circumstances as may be prescribed, for a period equal to that remainder at the time of surrender or revocation.]

(2) Where it appears to the [Secretary of State for Transport]—

[(a)] that a licence granted by him to any person is required to be endorsed in pursuance of any enactment or was granted in error or with an error or omission in the particulars specified in the licence or required to be so endorsed on it, [or

(b) that the particulars specified in a licence granted by him to any person do not comply with any requirement imposed since the licence was granted by any provision made by or having effect under any enactment,]

the [Secretary of State for Transport] may serve notice in writing on that person revoking the licence and requiring him to deliver up the licence forthwith to the [Secretary of State for Transport].

(3) Where the name or address of the licence holder as specified in a licence ceases to be correct, its holder shall forthwith surrender the licence to the [Secretary of State for Transport] and furnish to him particulars of the alterations falling to be made in the name or address and, in the case of a provisional licence as respects which the prescribed conditions are satisfied, with a statement of his sex and date of birth; and a person who fails to comply with the provisions of this subsection shall be guilty of an offence.

(4) On the surrender of a licence by any person in pursuance of subsection (2) or (3) above, the [Secretary of State for Transport]

(a) shall, except where the licence was granted in error or is surrendered in pursuance of the said subsection (2) in consequence of an error or omission appearing to the [Secretary of State for Transport] to be attributable to that person's fault or in consequence of a current disqualification, and

(b) may in such an excepted case which does not involve a current disqualification,

grant to that person free of charge a new licence [for such a period that it expires on the date on which the surrendered licence would have expired had it not been surrendered, except that, where the period for which the surrendered licence was granted was based on an error with respect to the licence holder's date of birth such that, if that error had not been made, that licence would have been expressed to expire on a different date, the period of the new licence shall be such that it expires on that different date].

[Section 89 is printed as amended by the Road Traffic Act 1974, s 13 (1), and Sched 3, para 5; the Minister of Transport Order 1979 (SI 1979 No 571); the Transfer of Functions (Transport) Order 1981 (SI 1981 No 238); and the Transport Act 1981, ss 23, 40 (1), and Sched 12, Part III.

As to breach of any duty under this section to deliver a licence to the Secretary of State when the licence has been surrendered on the receipt of a fixed penalty notice, see the Transport Act 1982, s 35 (7).]

90. Appeals relating to licences

(1) a person who is aggrieved by the [Secretary of State for Transport's]

(a) refusal to grant or revocation of a licence in pursuance of section 87 of this Act, or [(*b*) determination under section 89 (1) (*aa*) of this Act to grant a licence for three years or less, or]

[(*bb*) . . .]

(*c*) revocation of a licence in pursuance of section 89 (2) of this Act, or by a notice served on him in pursuance of section 87 (4) of this Act may, after giving to the [Secretary of State for Transport] notice of his intention to do so, appeal to a magistrates' court acting for the petty sessions area in which he resides or, if he resides in Scotland, to the sheriff within whose jurisdiction he resides; and on any such appeal the court or sheriff may make such order as it or he thinks fit and the order shall be binding on the [Secretary of State for Transport].

(2) It is hereby declared that, without prejudice to section 85 (3) of this Act, in any proceedings under this section the court or sheriff is not entitled to entertain any question as to whether the appellant passed a test of competence to drive if he was declared by the person who conducted it to have failed it.

[Section 90 is printed as amended by the Road Traffic Act 1974, s 13 (1), Sched 3, para 6; the Minister of Transport Order 1979 (SI 1979 No 571); the Transfer of Functions (Transport) Order 1981 (SI 1981 No 238); and the Transport Act 1981, s 40 (1), Sched 12 (Part III).]

91. Driving with uncorrected defective eyesight

(1) If a person drives a motor vehicle on a road while his eyesight is such (whether through a defect which cannot be or one which is not for the time being sufficiently corrected) that he cannot comply with any requirement as to eyesight prescribed under this Part of this Act for the purposes of tests of competence to drive, he shall be guilty of an offence.

(2) A constable having reason to suspect that a person driving a motor vehicle may be guilty of an offence under subsection (1) above may require him to submit to a test for the purpose of ascertaining whether, using no other means of correction than he used at the time of driving, he can comply with the said requirement as to eyesight; and if that person refuses to submit to the test he shall be guilty of an offence.

92. Notification of disease or disability

[(1)] If, in any proceedings for an offence committed in respect of a motor vehicle, it appears to the court that the accused may be suffering from any [relevant disability or prospective disability within the meaning of the section 87 of this Act], the court shall notify the [Secretary of State for Transport].

A notice sent by a court to the [Secretary of State for Transport] in pursuance of this section shall be sent in such manner and to such address and contain such particulars as the [Secretary of State for Transport] may determine.

[(2) If an authorised insurer refuses to issue to any person a policy of insurance as complies with the requirements of Part VI of this Act on the ground that the state of health of that person is not satisfactory or on grounds which include that ground, the insurer shall as soon as practicable notify the [Secretary of State] for Transport of that refusal and of the full name, address, sex and date of birth of that person as disclosed by him to the insurer.

(3) In subsection (2) above 'authorised insurer' has the same meaning as in section 145 (2) of this Act.]

[Section 92 is printed as amended by the Road Traffic Act 1974, s 13 (1), and Sched 3, para 7, and the Minister of Transport Order 1979 (SI 1979 No 571) and the Transfer of Functions (Transport) Order 1981 (SI 1981 No 238).]

Disqualification and endorsement of licences

93. Disqualification on conviction of certain offences

(1) Where a person is convicted of an offence—

(*a*) under a provision of this Act specified in column 1 of Part I of Schedule 4 to this Act in relation to which there appears in column 5 of that Part the word 'obligatory' or the word 'obligatory' qualified by conditions or circumstances relating to the offence; and

(*b*) where the said word 'obligatory' is so qualified, the conditions or circumstances are satisfied or obtain in the case of the offence of which he is convicted;

or where a person is convicted of the offence specified in Part II of that Schedule (any such offence being in this Part of this Act referred to as an 'offence involving obligatory disqualification') the court shall order him to be disqualified for such period not less than twelve months as the court thinks fit unless the court for special reasons thinks fit to order him to be disqualified for a shorter period or not to order him to be disqualified.

(2) Where a person is convicted of an offence—

(*a*) under a provision of this Act specified in column 1 of Part I of Schedule 4 to this Act [or under a provision of the Road Traffic Regulation Act 1984 specified in column 1 of Schedule 7 to that Act in relation to which there appears in column 5 of the said Part I or Schedule 7, as the case may be] the word 'discretionary' or the word 'discretionary' qualified by conditions or circumstances relating to the offence; and

(*b*) where the said word 'discretionary' is so qualified, the conditions or circumstances are satisfied or obtain in the case of the offence of which he is convicted; or where a person is convicted of an offence specified in Part III of [Schedule 4 to this Act] (any such offence being in this Part of this Act referred to as an 'offence involving discretionary disqualification'), the court may order him to be disqualified for such period as the court thinks fit.

(3) *[Repealed.]*

(4) Where a person convicted of an offence under any of the following provisions of this Act, namely sections 5 (1), [6 (1) (*a*)] or [8 (7)] (where the latter is an offence involving obligatory disqualification), has within the ten years immediately preceding the commission of the offence been convicted of any such offence, subsection (1) above shall apply in relation to him with the substitution of three years for twelve months.

(5) *[Repealed.]*

(6) The foregoing provisions of this section shall apply in relation to a conviction of an offence committed by aiding, abetting, counselling or procuring, or inciting to the commission of an offence involving obligatory disqualification as if the offence were an offence involving discretionary disqualification.

(7) Where a person is convicted of an offence involving obligatory or discretionary disqualification the court may, whether or not he has previously passed the test of competence to drive prescribed under this Act, and whether or not the court makes an order under the foregoing provisions of this section [or under section 19 of the Transport Act 1981], order him to be disqualified until he has, since the date of the order, passed that test; and a disqualification by virtue of an order under this subsection shall be deemed to have expired on production to the [Secretary of State for Transport] of evidence, in such form as may be prescribed by regulations under section 107

of this Act, that the person disqualified has, since the order was made, passed that test.

(8) *[Omitted.]*

[Section 93 is printed as amended by the Minister of Transport Order 1979 (SI 1979 No 571); the Transfer of Functions (Transport) Order 1981 (SI 1981 No 238); the Transport Act 1981, ss 30 (3), 40 (1), Sched 9, paras 2 to 4, and Sched 12, Part III; the Transport Act 1982, s 74 (1), and Sched 5, para 13 (1); and the Road Traffic Regulation Act 1984, s 146 and Sched 13, para 19.

For the purposes of subs (4) as amended, a previous conviction of an offence under the corresponding provision of the old law is treated as a conviction under the new provision; Transport Act 1982, Sched 5, para 13 (2). For these purposes s 6 (1) of the 1972 Act (before it was substituted by the Transport Act 1981) is the provison of the old law which corresponds to s 6 (1) (a) of the 1972 (as so substituted) and the former s 9 (3) corresponds to s 8 (7) (as so substituted); see the Transport Act 1982, Sched 5, para 13 (3) and (4).]

* * *

95. Removal of disqualification

(1) Subject to the provisions of this section, a person who by an order of a court is disqualified may apply to the court by which the order was made to remove the disqualification, and on any such application the court may, as it thinks proper, having regard to the character of the person disqualified and his conduct subsequent to the order, the nature of the offence, and any other circumstances of the case, either by order remove the disqualification as from such date as may be specified in the order or refuse the application.

(2) No application shall be made under subsection (1) above for the removal of a disqualification before the expiration of whichever is relevant of the following periods from the date of the order by which the disqualification was imposed, that is to say—

(*a*) two years, if the disqualification is for less than four years,

(*b*) one half of the period of the disqualification, if it is for less than ten years but not less than four years,

(*c*) five years in any other case;

and in determining the expiration of the period after which under this subsection a person may apply for the removal of a disqualification, any time after the conviction during which the disqualification was suspended or he was not disqualified shall be disregarded.

(3) Where an application under subsection (1) above is refused, a further application thereunder shall not be entertained if made within three months after the date of the refusal.

(4) If under this section a court orders a disqualification to be removed, the court shall cause particulars of the order to be endorsed on the licence, if any, previously held by the applicant and the court shall in any case have power to order the applicant to pay the whole or any part of the costs of the application.

(5) The foregoing provisions of this section shall not apply where the disqualification was imposed by order under section 93 (7) of this Act, section 5 (7) of the Road Traffic Act 1962 or section 104 (3) of the Road Traffic Act 1960.

[As to the application of subs (4) to domestic driving permits, Convention driving permits and British Forces (BFG) driving licences, see the Motor Vehicles (Driving Licences) Regulations 1981 (SI 1981 No 952), reg 23 (3) (c), (4).]

[96. Disqualification of persons under age

(1) A person is disqualified for holding or obtaining a licence to drive a motor vehicle of a class specified in the following Table if he is under the age specified in relation thereto in the second column of that Table.

TABLE

Class of motor vehicle	Age (in years)
1. Invalid carriage	16
2. Motor cycle	16
3. Small passenger vehicle or small goods vehicle	17
4. Agricultural tractor	17
5. Medium-sized goods vehicle	18
6. Other motor vehicles	21

(2) The [Secretary of State for Transport] may by regulations provide that subsection (1) above shall have effect as if for the classes of vehicles and the ages specified in the Table thereto there were substituted different classes of vehicles and ages or different classes of vehicles or different ages.

(3) Subject to sub-paragraph (4) below, regulations under subsection (2) above may—

(a) apply to persons of a class specified in or under the regulations;

(b) apply in circumstances so specified;

(c) impose conditions or create exemptions or provide for the imposition of conditions or the creation of exemptions;

(d) contain such transitional and supplemental provisions (including provisions amending section 110, 124 or 188 (3) of this Act as the [Secretary of State for Transport] considers necessary or expedient.

(4) For the purpose of defining the class of persons to whom, the class of vehicles to which, the circumstances in which or the conditions subject to which regulations under subsection (2) above are to apply where an approved training scheme for drivers is in force, it shall be sufficient for the regulations to refer to a document which embodies the terms (or any of the terms) of the scheme or to a document which is in force in pursuance of the scheme.

(5) In subsection (4) above—

'approved' means approved for the time being by the [Secretary of State for Transport] for the purpose of regulations under subsection (2) above;

'training scheme for drivers' means a scheme for training persons to drive vehicles of a class in relation to which the age which is in force under this section but apart from any such scheme is 21 years;

but no approved training scheme for drivers shall be amended without the approval of the [Secretary of State for Transport.]]

[Section 96 was substituted by the Road Traffic (Drivers' Ages and Hours of Work) Act 1976, s 1 (1), and is printed as amended by the Minister of Transport Order 1979 (SI 1979 No 571) and the Transfer of Functions (Transport) Order 1981 (SI 1981 No 238).

In relation to items 2, 4 and 6 in s 96 (1), see further the Motor Vehicles (Driving Licences) Regulations 1981 (SI 1981 No 952), reg 4, as amended.]

*   *   *

98. Effect of disqualification

(1) Where the holder of a licence is disqualified by an order of a court, the licence shall be [treated as being revoked with effect from the beginning of the period of disqualification; and for this purpose, if the holder of the licence appeals against the order and the disqualification is suspended under section 94 of this Act, the period of disqualification shall be treated as beginning on the day on which the disqualification ceases to be suspended].

(2) A licence obtained by any person who is disqualified shall be of no effect.

(3) Notwithstanding anything in this Part of this Act, a person disqualified by order of a court under section 93 (7) of this Act, section 5 (7) of the Road Traffic Act 1962 or section 104 (3) of the Road Traffic Act 1960 shall (unless he is disqualified otherwise than by virtue of such an order) be entitled to obtain and to hold a provisional licence and to drive a motor vehicle in accordance with the conditions subject to which the provisional licence is granted.

[Section 98 is printed as amended by the Road Traffic Act 1974, s 13 (1), and Sched 3, para 9.
Section 94 of this Act empowers a court which makes an order for disqualification to suspend, if it thinks fit, the disqualification pending an appeal.]

99. Offence of obtaining licence, or driving, while disqualified

If a person disqualified for holding or obtaining a licence—

(a) obtains a licence while he is so disqualified, or

(b) while he is so disqualified drives on a road a motor vehicle, or if the disqualification is limited to the driving of a motor vehicle of a particular class, a motor vehicle of that class,

he shall be guilty of an offence.

*　　　*　　　*

101. Endorsement of licences

(1) Subject to subsection (2) below, where a person is convicted of an offence—

(a) under a provision of this Act specified in column 1 of Part I of Schedule 4 to this Act [or under a provision of the Road Traffic Regulation Act 1984 in relation to which there appears in column 6 of the said Part I or Schedule 7, as the case may be] and the word 'obligatory' or the word 'obligatory' qualified by conditions relating to the offence; and

(b) where the said word 'obligatory' is so qualified, the conditions are satisfied in the case of the offence of which he is convicted;

or where a person is convicted of an offence specified in Part II or Part III of [Schedule 4 to this Act] (any such offence being in this section referred to as an 'offence involving obligatory endorsement'), [the court shall order that there shall be endorsed on any licence held by him particulars of the conviction and, if the court orders him to be disqualified, particulars of the disqualification, and, if the court does not order him to be disqualified, the particulars and penalty points required by section 19 (1) of the Transport Act 1981; and the endorsement may be produced as prima facie evidence of the matters endorsed.]

(2) If the court does not order the said person to be disqualified, the court [need not make an order under subsection (1) above] if for special reasons it thinks fit not to do so.

(3) [An order that any particulars or penalty points are to be endorsed on any licence held by the convicted person] shall, whether he is at the time the holder of a licence or not, operate as an order that any licence he may then hold or may subsequently obtain shall be so endorsed until he becomes entitled under subsection (7) below to have a licence issued to him free from the particulars [or penalty points].

(4) A person who is prosecuted for an offence involving obligatory endorsement and who is the holder of a licence, shall either—

(a) cause it to be delivered to the clerk of the court not later than the day before the date appointed for the hearing, or

(b) post it, at such a time that in the ordinary course of post it would be delivered not later than that day, in a letter duly addressed to the clerk and either registered or sent by the recorded delivery service, or

(c) have it with him at the hearing;

and if he is convicted of the offence [the court shall, before making any order under subsection (1) above, require the licence to be produced to it]; and if the offender has not posted the licence or caused it to be delivered as aforesaid and does not produce it as required then, unless he satisfies the court that he has applied for a new licence and has not received it, he shall be guilty of an offence and the licence shall be suspended from the time when its production was required until it is produced to the court and shall, while suspended, be of no effect.

[(4A) Where a person is convicted of an offence involving obligatory endorsement and his licence is produced to the court, then in determining what order to make in pursuance of the conviction the court may take into consideration particulars of any previous conviction or disqualification endorsed on the licence [and any penalty points endorsed on it which are to be taken into account under section 19(3) of the Transport Act 1981].]

(5) On the issue of a new licence to a person any particulars [or penalty points] ordered to be endorsed on any licence held by him shall be entered on the licence unless he has become entitled under subsection (7) below to have a licence issued to him free from those particulars [or penalty points].

(6) If a person whose licence has been ordered to be endorsed with any particulars [or penalty points] and who has not previously become entitled under subsection (7) below to have a licence issued to him free from those particulars [or penalty points] applies for or obtains a licence without giving particulars of the order, he shall be guilty of an offence and any licence so obtained shall be of no effect.

[(7) A person whose licence has been ordered to be endorsed (whether under this section or a previous enactment) shall be entitled to have a new licence issued to him free from the endorsement if, after the end of the period for which the endorsement remains effective, he applies for a new licence in pursuance of subsection (1) of section 88 of this Act, surrenders any subsisting licence, pays the prescribed fee and satisfies the other requirements of that subsection.]

[(7A) An endorsement ordered on a person's conviction of an offence remains effective—

(a) if an order is made for the disqualification of the offender, until four years have elapsed since the conviction; and

(b) if no such order is made, until either four years have elapsed since the commission of the offence or such an order is made;

but if the offence was one under section 1 or 2 of this Act the endorsement remains in any case effective until four years have elapsed since the conviction, and if it was one under section 5 (1) or 6 (1) (a) of this Act or was one under section 8 (7) of this Act involving obligatory disqualification, the endorsement remains effective until eleven years have elapsed since the conviction.]

[(8)], [9] *[Omitted.]*

[Section 101 is printed as amended by the Road Traffic Act 1974, s 13 (1), and Sched 3, para 10, the Transport Act 1981, s 30 (3), and Sched 9, paras 6 to 12, and the Road Traffic Regulation Act 1984, s 146, and Sched 13, para 20.

As to the application of subs (4) to domestic driving permits, Convention driving permits and British Forces (BFG) driving licences, see the Motor Vehicles (Driving Licences) Regulations 1981 (SI 1981 No 952), reg 23 (3) (b), (4).

In relation to endorsements made under Part III of the Transport Act 1982 (fixed penalty procedure), see generally s 34 (7) and (8) of that Act.

As to offences under subs (4) where a licence has been surrendered on receipt of a fixed penalty notice, see the Transport Act 1982, s 35 (4).]

* * *

104. Information as to date of birth and sex

(1) If on convicting a person of an offence involving obligatory or discretionary disqualification or of such other offence as may be prescribed, the court . . . does not know his date of birth, the court shall order him to state that date in writing.

(2) It shall be the duty of a person giving a notification to the clerk of a court in pursuance of [section 12 (2) of the Magistrates' Courts Act 1980] (which relates to pleas of guilty in the absence of the accused) in respect of an offence mentioned in subsection (1) above to include in the notification a statement of the date of birth and the sex of the accused; and in a case where the foregoing provisions of this subsection are not complied with the court shall, if on convicting the accused it . . . does not know his date of birth or sex, order him to furnish that information in writing to the court.

(3) Nothing in section 56 (5) of the Criminal Justice Act 1967 (which provides that where a magistrates' court commits a person to another court under subsection (1) of that section, certain of its powers and duties are transferred to that other court) shall apply to any duty imposed upon a magistrates' court by the foregoing provisions of this section. . . .

(4) A person who knowingly fails to comply with an order under subsection (1) or (2) above shall be guilty of an offence.

(5) Where in accordance with this section a person has stated his date of birth to a court or in such a notification as aforesaid, the [Secretary of State for Transport] may serve on that person a notice in writing requiring him to furnish the [Secretary of State for Transport]—

(a) with such evidence in that person's possession or obtainable by him as the [Secretary of State for Transport] may specify for the purpose of verifying that date; and

(b) if his name differs from his name at the time of his birth, with a statement in writing specifying his name at that time;

and a person who knowingly fails to comply with a notice under this subsection shall be guilty of an offence.

(6) *[Omitted.]*

[Section 104 is printed as amended by the Road Traffic Act 1974, ss 13 (1), 24 (3), Sched 3, para 11, and Sched 7, the Minister of Transport Order 1979 (SI 1979 No 571), the Magistrates' Courts Act 1980, s 154 (1), and Sched 7, para 111, and the Transfer of Functions (Transport) Order 1981 (SI 1981 No 238).]

* * *

PART IV

LICENSING OF DRIVERS OF HEAVY GOODS VEHICLES

112. Drivers of heavy goods vehicles to be licensed

(1) It shall be an offence for a person to drive a heavy goods vehicle of any class on a road if he is not licensed under this Part of this Act to drive a heavy goods vehicle of that class.

(2) It shall be an offence for a person to [cause or permit] another person to drive a heavy goods vehicle of any class on a road if that other person is not so licensed to drive a heavy goods vehicle of that class.

(3) Nothing in subsection (1) or (2) above, [shall make it unlawful for a person who is not so licensed to act or, as the case may be, for a person to cause or permit such a person] to act, as steersman of a heavy goods vehicle (being a vehicle on which a speed limit of five miles per hour or less is imposed by or under [section 86 of the Road Traffic Regulation Act 1984] under the orders of another person engaged in the driving of the vehicle who is licensed in that behalf in accordance with the requirements of Part III of this Act and this section.

(4) Neither subsection (1) nor subsection (2) above shall apply to the driving of, or the [causing or permitting] of a person to drive, a vehicle in any case where the excise duty in respect of the vehicle under the Vehicles (Excise) Act 1971 is chargeable at the rate applicable to vehicles specified in paragraph 2 (1) of Schedule 3 to that Act and the vehicle is being driven for one of the purposes for which it must be solely used if the duty is to remain chargeable at that rate.

[Section 112 is printed as amended by the Road Traffic (Drivers' Ages and Hours of Work) Act 1976, s 1 (2), and Sched 1, para 7, and the Road Traffic Regulation Act 1984, s 146, and Sched 13, para 21.

The Road Traffic Regulation Act 1984, s 86, prescribes (by reference to Sched 6 to that Act, as amended) maximum speed limits for specific classes of vehicles.]

* * *

123. Restriction on institution of proceedings for certain offences

Proceedings for an offence under section 112 or 114 (3) of this Act shall not, in England or Wales, be instituted except by or on behalf of the Director of Public Prosecutions or by a person authorised in that behalf by the traffic commissioners, a chief officer of police or the council of a county . . . or county district.

[Section 123 is printed as amended by the Local Government Act 1972, s 272 (1), and Sched 30.]

PART VI

THIRD-PARTY LIABILITIES

Compulsory insurance or security against third-party risks

143. Users of motor vehicles to be insured or secured against third-party risks

(1) Subject to the provisions of this Part of this Act, it shall not be lawful for a person to use, or to cause or permit any other person to use, a motor vehicle on a road unless there is in force in relation to the use of the vehicle by that person or that other person, as the case may be, such a policy of insurance or such a security in respect of third-party risks as complies with the requirements of this Part of this Act; and if a person acts in contravention of this section he shall be guilty of an offence.

(2) A person charged with using a motor vehicle in contravention of this section shall not be convicted if he proves that the vehicle did not belong to him and was not in his possession under a contract of hiring or of loan, that he was using the vehicle in the course of his employment and that he neither knew nor had reason to believe that there was not in force in relation to the vehicle such a policy of insurance or security as is mentioned in subsection (1) above.

(3) This Part of this Act shall not apply to invalid carriages.

*   *   *

145. Requirements in respect of policies of insurance

(1) In order to comply with the requirements of this Part of this Act, a policy of insurance must satisfy the following conditions.

(2) The policy must be issued by an authorised insurer, that is to say, a person or body of persons carrying on [insurance business within Group 2 in Part II of Schedule 2 to the Insurance Companies Act [1982]] [and being a member of the Motor Insurers' Bureau, a company limited by guarantee and incorporated under the Companies Act 1929 on 14th June 1946].

(3) Subject to subsection (4) below, the policy—

(*a*) must insure such person, persons or classes of persons as may be specified in the policy in respect of any liability which may be incurred byhim or them in respect of the death of or bodily injury to any person caused by, or arising out of, the use of the vehicle on a road [in Great Britain]; and

[(*aa*) must insure him or them in respect of any liability which may be incurred by him or them in respect of the use of the vehicle and of any trailer, whether or not coupled, in the territory other than Great Britain and Gibraltar of each of the member states of the Communities according to the law on compulsory insurance against civil liability in respect of the use of vehicles of the state where the liability may be incurred; and]

(*b*) must also insure him or them in respect of any liability which may be incurred by him or them under the provisions of this Part of this Act relating to payment for emergency treatment.

(4) The policy shall not, by virtue of subsection (3) (*a*) above, be required to cover—

(*a*) liability in respect of the death, arising out of and in the course of his employment, of a person in the employment of a person insured by the policy or of bodily injury sustained by such a person arising out of and in the course of his employment; or

(*b*) any contractual liability.

[Section 145 is printed as amended by the Motor Vehicles (Compulsory Insurance) (No 2) Regulations 1973 (SI 1973 No 2143), the Road Traffic Act 1974, s 20 (1), Insurance Companies Act 1981, s 36 (1) and Sched 4, para 22, and the Insurance Companies Act 1982, s 99 (2), and Sched 5, para 12.

Group 2 in Part II of Sched 2 to the Insurance Companies Act 1982 refers to motor insurance; this category groups together the following classes of insurance from Part I of that Schedule: class 1 (to the extent that the relevant risks are risks of the person insured sustaining injury, or dying, as the result of travelling as a passenger) and classes 3, 7 and 10. The nature of business under those classes is defined in Part I of Sched 2 as follows:

Number	Description	Nature of Business
1	*Accident*	*Effecting and carrying out contracts of insurance providing fixed pecuniary benefits or benefits in the nature of indemnity (or a combination of both) against risks of the person insured or, in the case of a contract made by virtue of section 140, 140A or 140B of the Local Government Act 1972, a person for whose benefit the contract is made—*
		(a) sustaining injury as the result of an accident or of an accident of a specified class, or
		(b) dying as the result of an accident or of an accident of a specified class, or
		(c) becoming incapacitated in consequence of disease or of disease of a specified class,
		inclusive of contracts relating to industrial injury and occupational disease but exclusive of contracts falling within class 2 below or within class IV in Schedule I to this Act (permanent health).
*	* * *	* * *
3	*Land vehicles*	*Effecting and carrying out contracts of insurance against loss or damage to vehicles used on land, including motor vehicles but excluding railway rolling stock.*
*	* * *	* * *
7	*Goods in transit*	*Effecting and carrying out contracts of insurance against loss of or damage to merchandise, baggage and all other goods in transit, irrespective of the form of transport*
*	* * *	* * *
10	*Motor vehicle liability*	*Effecting and carrying out contracts of insurance against damage arising out of or in connection with the use of motor vehicles on land, including third-party risks and carrier's liability.*
*	* * *	* * *

The Local Government Act 1972, ss 140, 140A and 140B (referred to in class 1 in the above table) deal with the following subject-matter: s 140 (as amended), contracts of insurance within class 1 entered into by a local authority in respect of members of the authority while engaged on business of the authority; s 140A (together with s 140B, added by the Local Government (Miscellaneous Provisions) Act 1982), contracts of insurance entered into by a local authority in respect of (inter alia) personal accidents suffered by voluntary assistants of the authority while engaged as such; and s 140B, contracts of insurance entered into by county councils or the Greater London Council in respect of (inter alia) personal accidents suffered by voluntary assistants of relevant probation committees while engaged as such.

Class 2 of Part I of Sched 2 (also referred to in class 1 in the above table), is sickness insurance (ie loss attributable to sickness or infirmity).

The term 'policy of insurance' includes a covering note (s 158 (1)).]

* * *

148. Avoidance of certain exceptions to policies or securities and of certain agreements, etc., as to risks required to be covered thereby

(1) Where a certificate of insurance or certificate of security has been delivered under section 147 of this Act to the person by whom a policy has been effected or to whom a security has been given, so much of the policy or security as purports to restrict, as the case may be, the insurance of the persons insured by the policy or the operation of the security by reference to any of the following matters, that is to say,—

(a) the age or physical or mental condition of persons driving the vehicle, or

(b) the condition of the vehicle, or

(c) the number of persons that the vehicle carries, or

(d) the weight or physical characteristics of the goods that the vehicle carries, or

(e) the times at which or the areas within which the vehicle is used, or

(f) the horsepower or cylinder capacity or value of the vehicle, or

(g) the carrying on the vehicle of any particular apparatus, or

(h) the carrying on the vehicle of any particular means of identification other than any means of identification required to be carried by or under the Vehicles (Excise) Act 1971,

shall, as respect such liabilities as are required to be covered by a policy under section 145 of this Act, be of no effect:

Provided that nothing in this subsection shall require an insurer or the giver of a security to pay any sum in respect of the liability of any person otherwise than in or towards the discharge of that liability, and any sum paid by an insurer or the giver of a security in or towards the discharge of any liability of any person which is covered by the policy or security by virtue only of this subsection shall be recoverable by the insurer or giver of the security from that person.

(2) A condition in a policy or security issued or given for the purposes of this Part of this Act providing that no liability shall arise under the policy or security, or that any liability so arising shall cease, in the event of some specified thing being done or omitted to be done after the happening of the event giving rise to a claim under the policy or security, shall be of no effect in connection with such liabilities as are required to be covered by a policy under section 145 of this Act:

Provided that nothing in this subsection shall be taken to render void any provision in a policy or security requiring the person insured or secured to pay to the insurer or the giver of the security any sums which the latter may have become liable to pay under the policy or security and which have been applied to the satisfaction of the claims of third parties.

(3) Where a person uses a motor vehicle in circumstances such that under section 143 of this Act there is required to be in force in relation to his use of it such a policy of insurance or security as is mentioned in subsection (1) of that section, then, if any other person is carried in or upon the vehicle while the user is so using it, any antecedent agreement or understanding between them (whether intended to be legally binding or not) shall be of no effect so far as it purports or might be held—

(a) to negative or restrict any such liability of the user in respect of persons carried in or upon the vehicle as is required by section 145 of this Act to be covered by a policy of insurance; or

(b) to impose any conditions with respect to the enforcement of any such liability of the user;

and the fact that a person so carried has willingly accepted as his the risk of negligence on the part of the user shall not be treated as negativing any such liability of the user.

For the purposes of this subsection references to a person being carried in or upon a vehicle include references to a person entering or getting on to, or alighting from, the vehicle, and the reference to an antecedent agreement is to one made at any time before the liability arose.

(4) Notwithstanding anything in any enactment, a person issuing a policy of insurance under section 145 of this Act shall be liable to indemnify the persons or classes of persons specified in the policy in respect of any liability which the policy purports to cover in the case of those persons or classes of persons.

[(5) To the extent that a policy or security issued or given for the purposes of this Part of this Act—

(a) restricts, as the case may be, the insurance of the persons insured by the policy or the operation of the security to use of the vehicle for specified purposes (for example, social, domestic and pleasure purposes) of a non-commercial character; or

(b) excludes from, as the case may be, that insurance or the operation of the secu. ity—

    (i) use of the vehicle for hire or reward; or

    (ii) business or commercial use of the vehicle; or

    (iii) use of the vehicle for specified purposes of a business or commercial character,

then, for the purposes of that policy or security so far as it relates to such liabilities as are required to be covered by a policy under section 145 of this Act, the use of a vehicle on a journey in the course of which one or more passengers are carried at separate fares shall, if the conditions specified in subsection (6) below are satisfied, be treated as falling within that restriction or as not falling within that exclusion, as the case may be.]

[(6) The conditions referred to in subsection (5) above are—

(a) the vehicle is not adapted to carry more than eight passengers and is not a motor cycle;

(b) the fare or aggregate of the fares paid in respect of the journey does not exceed the amount of the running costs of the vehicle for the journey (which for the purposes of this paragraph shall be taken to include an appropriate amount in respect of depreciation and general wear); and

(c) the arrangements for the payment of fares by the passenger or passengers carried at separate fares were made before the journey began.]

[(7) Subsections (5) and (6) above apply however the restrictions or exclusions described in subsection (5) are framed or worded; and in those subsections 'fare' and 'separate fares' have the same meaning as in [section 1 (4) of the Public Passenger Vehicles Act 1981.]

[Section 148 is printed as amended by the Interpretation Act 1978, s 17 (2) (a), and the Transport Act 1980, s 61.]

* * *

PART VII

MISCELLANEOUS AND GENERAL

Furnishing of information and production of documents

159. Power of police to stop vehicles

A person driving a motor vehicle on a road and a person riding a cycle, not being a motor vehicle, on a road shall stop the same on being so required by a constable in uniform, and if he fails to do so he shall be guilty of an offence.

[As to the application of the fixed penalty procedure to offences under s 159, see the Transport Act 1982, Part III, and Sched 1.]

* * *

161. Power of constables to require production of driving licences and in certain cases statement of date of birth

(1) Any such person as follows, that is to say,—

(a) a person driving a motor vehicle on a road, or

(b) a person whom a constable has reasonable cause to believe to have been the driver of a motor vehicle at a time when an accident occurred owing to its presence on a road, or

(c) a person whom a constable has reasonable cause to believe to have committed an offence in relation to the use of a motor vehicle on a road, or

(d) a person who supervises the holder of a provisional licence granted under Part III of this Act while the holder is driving a motor vehicle on a road or whom a constable has reasonable cause to believe was supervising the holder of such a licence while driving at a time when an accident occurred owing to the presence of the vehicle on a road or at a time when an offence is suspected of having been committed by the said holder in relation to the use of the vehicle on a road,

shall, on being so required by a constable, produce for examination his licence to drive a motor vehicle granted under Part III of this Act, so as to enable the constable to ascertain the name and address of the holder of the licence, the date of issue, and the authority by which it was issued; and shall in prescribed circumstances, on being so required by the constable, state his date of birth.

(2) Where a licence to drive a motor vehicle granted under Part III of this Act has been revoked by the [Secretary of State for Transport] under section 87 or 89 thereof then if the holder of the licence fails to deliver it to the [Secretary of State for Transport] in pursuance of that section a constable may require him to produce it, and upon its being produced may seize it and deliver it to the [Secretary of State for Transport].

(3) Where a constable has reasonable cause to believe that the person to whom a licence to drive a motor vehicle has been granted under Part III of this Act, or any other person, has knowingly made a false statement for the purpose of obtaining the grant of the licence the constable may require the holder of the licence to produce it to him.

[(3A) Where a person has been required under section 101 (4) of this Act to produce a licence to the court and fails to do so a constable may require him to produce it and, upon its being produced, may seize it and deliver it to the court.]

(4) If a person required under the foregoing provisions of this section to produce a licence or state his date of birth to a constable fails to do so he shall be guilty of an offence; but if within five days after the production of his licence was so required he produces the licence in person at such police station as may have been specified by him at the time its production was required, he shall not be convicted of an offence under this subsection [in respect of a failure to produce his licence].

(5) Where in accordance with this section a person has stated his date of birth to a constable, the [Secretary of State for Transport] may serve on that person a notice in writing requiring him to furnish the [Secretary of State for Transport]—

(a) with such evidence in that person's possession or obtainable by him as the [Secretary of State for Transport] may specify for the purposes of verifying that date; and

(b) if his name differs from his name at the time of his birth, with a statement in writing specifying his name at that time;

and a person who knowingly fails to comply with a notice under this subsection shall be guilty of an offence.

(6) A notice authorised to be served on any person by subsection (5) above may be served on him by delivering it to him or by leaving it at his proper address or by sending it to him by post; and for the purposes of this subsection and [section 7 of the Interpretation Act 1978] in its application to this subsection the proper address of any person shall be his latest address as known to the person giving the notice.

[*Section 161 is printed as amended by the Road Traffic Act 1974, s 24 (6), and Sched 6, para 19; the Interpretation Act 1978, s 25 (2); the Minister of Transport Order 1979 (SI 1979 No 571); the Transfer of Functions (Transport) Order 1981 (SI 1981 No 238); and the Transport Act 1981, s 22.*

As to the application of subss (1) and (4) to domestic driving permits, Convention driving permits and British Forces (BFG) driving licences, see the Motor Vehicles (Driving Licences) Regulations 1981 (SI 1981 No 952), reg 23 (3) (d), (4); and see also the Motor Vehicles (International Circulation) Order 1975 (SI 1975 No 1208), Sched 3, para 5.

As to offences under subs (4) where a licence has been surrendered following the receipt of a fixed penalty notice, see the Transport Act 1982, s 35 (6).]

162. Power of constables to obtain names and addresses of drivers and others, and to require production of evidence of insurance or security and test certificates

(1) Any such person as follows, that is to say,—

(a) a person driving on a road a motor vehicle (other than an invalid carriage), or

(b) a person whom a constable has reasonable cause to believe to have been the driver of a motor vehicle (other than an invalid carriage) at a time when an accident occurred owing to its presence on a road, or

(c) a person whom a constable has reasonable cause to believe to have committed an offence in relation to the use on a road of a motor vehicle (other than an invalid carriage),

shall, on being so required by a constable, give his name and address and the name and addess of the owner of the vehicle and produce for examination—

    (i) the relevant certificate of insurance or certificate of security within the meaning of Part VI of this Act, or such other evidence that the vehicle is not or was not being driven in contravention of section 143 thereof as may be prescribed by regulations made by the [Secretary of State for Transport],

    (ii) in relation to a vehicle to which section 44 of this Act applies, a test certificate issued in respect thereof as mentioned in subsection (1) of that section, and

    (iii) in relation to a goods vehicle the use of which on a road without a plating certificate [or] goods vehicle test certificate . . . is an offence under section 46 (1) or (2) . . . of this Act, any such certificate issued in respect of that vehicle or any trailer drawn by it,

and if he fails to do so he shall, subject to subsection (2) below, be guilty of an offence.

(2) A person shall not be convicted of an offence under subsection (1) above by reason only of failure to produce any certificate or other evidence to a constable if, within five days after the date on which the production of the certificate or other evidence was required, it is produced at such police station as may have been specified by him at the time when its production was required.

(3) A person who supervises the holder of a provisional licence granted under Part III of this Act while the holder is driving on a road a motor vehicle (other than an invalid carriage) or whom a constable has reasonable cause to believe was supervising the holder of such a licence while driving at a time when an accident occurred owing to the presence of the vehicle on a road or at a time when an offence is suspected of having been committed by the said holder in relation to the use of the vehicle on a road shall, on being so required by a constable, give his name and address and the name and address of the owner of the vehicle, and if he fails to do so he shall be guilty of an offence

(4) In this section 'owner', in relation to a vehicle which is the subject of a hiring agreement, includes each party to the agreement.

[Section 162 is printed as amended by the Road Traffic Act 1974, ss 10 (6), 24 (3), and Sched 7, the Minister of Transport Order 1979 (SI 1979 No 571) and the Transfer of Functions (Transport) Order 1981 (SI 1981 No 238).]

*   *   *

164. Penalisation of failure to give name and address, and power of arrest, in case of dangerous or careless driving or cycling, etc

(1) Any such person as the following, namely—

(a) the driver of a motor vehicle who is alleged to have committed an offence against section 2 or 3 of this Act, or

(b) the rider of a cycle who is alleged to have committed an offence against section 17 or 18 of this Act,

who refuses, on being so required by any person having reasonable ground for so requiring, to give his name and address, or gives a false name or address, shall be guilty of an offence.

(2) A constable may—

(a) arrest without warrant the driver of a motor vehicle who within his view commits an offence against section 2 or 3 of this Act unless the driver either gives his name and address or produces for examination his licence to drive a motor vehicle granted under Part III of this Act;

(b) arrest without warrant the rider of a cycle who within his view commits an offence against section 17 or 18 of this Act unless the rider gives his name and address.

[Section 164 (2) is repealed by the Police and Criminal Evidence Act 1984, s 119 (2), and Sched 7, Part I (with effect from a date to be announced).

[As to the application of subs (2) to domestic driving permits, Convention driving permits and British Forces (BFG) driving licences, see the Motor Vehicles (Driving Licences) Regulations 1981 (SI 1981 No 952), reg 23 (3) (e), (4); see also the Motor Vehicles (International Circulation) Order 1975 (SI 1975 No 1208), Sched 3, para 5.]

*   *   *

166. Duty of driver, in case of accident involving injury to another, to produce evidence of insurance or security or to report accident

(1) If in a case where, owing to the presence on a road of a motor vehicle (other than an invalid carriage) an accident occurs involving personal injury to another person, the driver of the vehicle does not at the time produce to a constable or some person who, having reasonable grounds for so doing, has required its production, such a certificate of insurance or security or other evidence, as is mentioned in paragraph (i) of section 162 (1) of this Act, the driver shall as soon as possible, and in any case within twenty-four hours of the occurrence of the accident, report the accident at a police station or to a constable and thereupon produce such a certificate or other evidence as aforesaid, and if he fails to do so he shall, subject to subsection (2) below, be guilty of an offence.

(2) A person shall not be convicted of an offence under subsection (1) above by reason only of a failure to produce a certificate or other evidence if, within five days after the occurrence of the accident, [the certificate or other evidence is produced] at such police station as may be specified by him at the time when the accident was reported.

[Section 166 is printed as amended by the Road Traffic Act 1974, s 24 (2), and Sched 6, para 20.]

*   *   *

168. Duty to give information as to identity of driver, etc, in certain cases

(1) This section applies—

(a) to any offence under the foregoing provisions of this Act and to an offence under section 175 of this Act except an offence under Part V thereof or under section 15, 32, 45 (7), 50 (5), 53 (4), 55 (5), 56 (3), 91 or 119, and

(b) to offences against any other enactment relating to the use of vehicles on roads.

(2) Where the driver of a vehicle is alleged to be guilty of an offence to which this section applies—

(a) the person keeping the vehicle shall give such information as to the identity of the driver as he may be required to give by or on behalf of a chief officer of police, and

(b) any other person shall if required as aforesaid give any information which it is in his power to give and may lead to the identification of the driver.

In this subsection references to the driver of a vehicle include references to the person riding a cycle, not being a motor vehicle.

(3) A person who fails to comply with the requirement of subsection (2) (*a*) above shall be guilty of an offence unless he shows to the satisfaction of the court that he did not know and could not with reasonable diligence have ascertained who the driver of the vehicle, or, as the case may be, the rider of the cycle, was; and a person who fails to comply with the requirement of subsection (2) (*b*) above shall be guilty of an offence.

[Section 168 (2) (a) has been amended by the Road Traffic Act 1974, s 24 (2), and Sched 6, para 21, with effect from a date to be announced. From that date, after the word 'police' in subs (2) (a) the following words will be inserted—[or, in the case of an offence under section 36A or section 36B of this Act, by or on behalf of a local authority within the meaning of the said section 35A].

Part V of this Act (ie ss 126–142) concerns driving instruction.

Section 175 of this Act relates to the taking, by a person in Scotland, of a motor vehicle without authority, etc.]

Forgery, false statements, etc

169. Forgery of documents, etc

(1) A person shall be guilty of an offence who, with intent to deceive—

(*a*) forges, or alters, or uses or lends to, or allows to be used by, any other person, a document or other thing to which this section applies, or

(*b*) makes or has in his possession any document or other thing so closely resembling a document or other thing to which this section applies as to be calculated to deceive.

(2) This section applies to the following documents and other things, namely—

(*a*) any licence under any Part of this Act;

(*b*) any test certificate, goods vehicle test certificate, plating certificate, [certificate of conformity] or Minister's approval certificate;

[(*bb*) any certificate required as a condition of any exception prescribed under section 33A of this Act;]

(*c*) any plate containing plated particulars or containing other particulars required to be marked on a goods vehicle by section 47 of this Act or regulations thereunder;

[(*cc*) any notice removing a prohibition under section 57 of this Act;]

(*d*) any records required to be kept by virtue of section 59 of this Act;

(*e*) any document which, in pursuance of section 85 (2) or 119 (1) of this Act, is issued as evidence of the result of a test of competence to drive;

(*f*) any badge or certificate prescribed by regulations under section 135 of this Act;

(*g*) any certificate of insurance or certificate of security under Part VI of this Act;

[(*gg*) any document produced as evidence of insurance in pursuance of regulation 6 of the Motor Vehicles (Compulsory Insurance) (No 2) Regulations 1973;]

(*h*) any document issued under regulations made by the [Secretary of State for Transport] in pursuance of his power under paragraph (i) of section 162(1) of this Act to prescribe evidence which may be produced in lieu of a certificate of insurance or a certificate of security;

[(*i*) any international road haulage permit].

(3) In this section 'plated particulars', '[certificate of conformity]' and 'Minister's approval certificate' have the same meanings as they respectively have for the purposes of Part II of this Act; and in the application of this section to England and Wales ['forges' means makes a false document or other thing in order that it may be used as genuine].

[Section 169 is printed as amended by the Motor Vehicles (Compulsory Insurance) (No 2) Regulations 1973 (SI 1973 No 2143); the Road Traffic Act 1974, s 10 (7), and Sched 2, para 14; the International Road Haulage Permits Act 1975, s 3 (2); the Minister of Transport Order 1979 (SI 1979 No 571); the Transfer of Functions (Transport) Order 1981 (SI 1981 No 238); the Forgery and Counterfeiting Act 1981, s 12; the Transport Act 1981, s 27 (2); and the Transport Act 1982, s 23(3).

Paragraph (cc) in subs (2) (inserted by the Transport Act 1982) does not take effect until a date to be announced.

Section 57 of the Road Traffic Act 1972 contains a power to prohibit the driving of an unfit goods vehicle on a road.

Section 59 of this Act requires operators of goods vehicles to keep records of inspections.

Section 135 of this Act empowers the making of regulations prescribing the form of certificate of registration, etc, of driving instructors.

For the interpretation section to Part II, see s 82.

As to the application of this section to domestic driving permits, Convention driving permits and British Forces (BFG) driving licences, see the Motor Vehicles (Driving Licences) Regulations 1981 (SI 1981 No 952), reg 23 (3) (f), (4); see also the Motor Vehicles (International Circulation) Order 1975 (SI 1975 No 1208), Sched 3, para 5, and the Motor Vehicles (International Circulation) (Amendment) Order 1980 (SI 1980 No 1095), art 8 (1), (3).]

170. False statements and withholding material information

(1) A person shall be guilty of an offence who knowingly makes a false statement for the purpose—

(a) of obtaining the grant of a licence under any Part of this Act to himself or any other person, or

(b) of preventing the grant of any such licence, or

(c) of procuring the imposition of a condition or limitation in relation to any such licence, or

(d) of securing the entry or retention of the name of any person in the register of approved instructors maintained under Part V of this Act [or

(e) of obtaining the grant of an international road haulage permit to himself or any other person].

(2) A person shall be guilty of an offence who in supplying information or producing documents for the purposes either of section 46, 47, 48, [49, 49A or 51] of this Act or of regulations made under section 45, 50 or 52 (2) thereof makes a statement which he knows to be false in a material particular or recklessly makes a statement which is false in a material particular, or produces, furnishes, sends or otherwise makes use of a document which he knows to be false in a material particular or recklessly produces, furnishes, sends or otherwise makes use of a document which is false in a material particular.

(3) A person shall be guilty of an offence who knowingly produces false evidence for the purposes of regulations under section 52 (1) of this Act or knowingly makes a false statement in a declaration required to be made by the regulations.

(4) A person shall be guilty of an offence who knowingly makes a false statement in

a certificate or declaration under section 54 of this Act (including that section as applied by section 55 (3) thereof).

(5) A person shall be guilty of an offence who wilfully makes a false entry in any record required to be made or kept by regulations under section 59 of this Act or, with intent to deceive, makes use of any such entry which he knows to be false.

[(5A) A person shall be guilty of an offence who fails without reasonable excuse to notify the [Secretary of State for Transport] as required by section 87A (1) of this Act, but no proceedings for an offence under this subsection shall be instituted in England and Wales except by the [Secretary of State for Transport] or by a constable acting with the approval of the [Secretary of State for Transport.]

(6) A person shall be guilty of an offence who makes a false statement or withholds any material information for the purpose of obtaining the issue—

(a) of a certificate of insurance or certificate of security under Part VI of this Act, or

(b) of any document issued under regulations made by the [Secretary of State for Transport] in pursuance of his power under paragraph (i) of section 162 (1) of this Act to prescribe evidence which may be produced in lieu of a certificate of insurance or a certificate of security.

(7) Section 64 (2) of this Act shall apply for the purposes of proceedings under subsections (2) and (5) above as it applies for the purposes of the proceedings mentioned in that subsection.

[Section 170 is printed as amended by the Road Traffic Act 1974, ss 10 (7), 13 (2), and Sched 2, para 15; the International Road Haulage Permits Act 1975, s 3 (3); the Minister of Transport Order 1979 (SI 1979 No 571); and the Transfer of Functions (Transport) Order 1981 (SI 1981 No 238).

Sections 48, 49, 49A and 50 of this Act relate to type-approval certificates, certificates of conformity and Minister's approval certificates; s 52 relates to excise licences; ss 54 and 55 concern roadside tests of vehicles; s 59 relates to operators' duty to inspect goods vehicles; and s 87A relates to the provision of information, etc, relating to disabilities.

As to the application of this section to Convention driving permits, see the Motor Vehicles (International Circulation) (Amendment) Order 1980 (SI 1980 No 1095), art 8 (1), (3).]

Prosecution and punishment of offences
and other provisions relating to legal proceedings, etc

*   *   *

179. Restrictions on prosecutions for certain offences

(1) This section applies to—

(a) any offence under this Act to which it is applied by column 7 of Part I of Schedule 4 to this Act; and

[(aa) any offence under subsection (4) of [section 17 of the Road Traffic Regulation Act 1984] (traffic regulation on special roads) consisting of failure to observe a speed limit imposed by regulations under that section; and]

(b) any offence under [section 88 (7) of the Road Traffic Regulation Act 1984], or punishable by virtue of section 89 of that Act.

(2) Subject to the following provisions of this section and to the provisions of paragraphs 5, 6 and 7 of Part IV of the said Schedule 4 where a person is prosecuted for an offence to which this section applies he shall not be convicted unless either—

(a) he was warned at the time the offence was committed that the question of prosecuting him for some one or other of the offences to which this section applies would be taken into consideration; or

(b) within fourteen days of the commission of the offence a summons (or, in Scotland, a complaint) for the offence was served on him; or

(c) within the said fourteen days a notice of the intended prosecution specifying the nature of the alleged offence and the time and place where it is alleged to have been committed, was—

    (i) in the case of an offence against section 17 or 18 of this Act, served on him;

    (ii) in the case of any other offence served on him or on the person, if any, registered as the keeper of the vehicle at the time of the commission of the offence;

and the notice shall be deemed for the purposes of paragraph (c) above to have been served on any person if it was sent by registered post or recorded delivery service addressed to him at his last known address, notwithstanding that the notice was returned as undelivered or was for any other reason not received by him.

(3) The requirement of subsection (2) above shall in every case be deemed to have been complied with unless and until the contrary is proved.

[(3A) The requirement of subsection (2) above shall not apply in relation to an offence if, at the time of the offence or immediately thereafter, an accident occurs owing to the presence on a road of the vehicle in respect of which the offence was committed.]

(4) Failure to comply with the requirement of subsection (2) above shall not be a bar to the conviction of the accused in a case where the court is satisfied—

(a) that neither the name and address of the accused nor the name and address of the registered owner, if any, could with reasonable diligence have been ascertained in time for a summons or, as the case may be, a complaint to be served or for a notice to be served or sent in compliance with the said requirement; or

(b) that the accused by his own conduct contributed to the failure.'

[Section 179 is printed as amended by the Road Traffic Act 1974, s 24 (2), and Sched 6, para 22; the Criminal Law Act 1977, s 65 and Sched 12; and the Road Traffic Regulation Act 1984, s 146, Sched 13, para 23.

Section 88 (7) of the Road Traffic Regulation Act 1984 relates to driving at a speed below a minimum speed limit; and s 89 relates to speeding offences under that Act (except s 17 (2)), under the Parks Regulation (Amendment) Act 1926, s 2, and under any enactment not contained in the 1984 Act but passed after 1 September 1960.

This section does not apply to any offence in respect of which a fixed penalty notice has been given or affixed under Part III of the Transport Act 1982, or in respect of which a notice is given under s 28 (1) of that Act (inviting the recipient to present himself at an appointed police station to receive a fixed penalty notice); see s 49 (12) of that Act.]

180. Time within which summary proceedings for certain offences must be commenced

Summary proceedings for an offence under this Act to which this section is applied by column 7 of Part I of Schedule 4 to this Act may be brought within a period of six months from the date on which evidence sufficient in the opinion of the prosecutor to warrant the proceedings came to his knowledge; but no such proceedings shall be brought by virtue of this section more than three years after the commission of the offence.

For the purposes of this section a certificate signed by or on behalf of the prosecutor and stating the date on which such evidence as aforesaid came to his knowledge shall be conclusive evidence of that fact; and a certificate stating that matter and purporting to be so signed shall be deemed to be so signed unless the contrary is proved.

*   *   *

182. Admissibility of records in evidence

(1) A statement contained in a document purporting to be—

(a) a part of the records maintained by the [Secretary of State for Transport] in connection with any functions exercisable by him by virtue of Part III of this Act or a part of any other records maintained by the [Secretary of State for Transport] with respect to vehicles [or of any records maintained with respect to vehicles by an approved testing authority in connection with the exercise by that authority of any functions conferred on such authorities, or on that authority as such an authority, by or under any enactment]; or

(b) a copy of a document forming part of those records; or

(c) a note of any information contained in those records,

and to be authenticated by a person authorised in that behalf by the [Secretary of State for Transport] [or (as the case may be) by the approved testing authority] shall be admissible in any proceedings as evidence of any fact stated therein to the same extent as oral evidence of that fact is admissible in those proceedings.

(2) In subsection (1) above 'document' and 'statement' have the same meanings as subsection (1) of section 10 of the Civil Evidence Act 1968 and the reference to a copy of a document shall be construed in accordance with subsection (2) of that section; but nothing in this subsection shall be construed as limiting to civil proceedings the references to proceedings in subsection (1) above.

[(2A) In any case where—

(a) any such statement as is referred to in subsection (1) above is produced to a magistrates' court in any proceedings for an offence involving obligatory or discretionary disqualification, within the meaning of Part III of this Act, and

(b) the statement specifies an alleged previous conviction of an accused person of any such offence [or any order made on the conviction], and

(c) it is proved to the satisfaction of the court, on oath or in such manner as may be prescribed by rules under [section 144 of the Magistrates' Courts Act 1980], that not less than 7 days before the statement is so produced a notice was served on the accused, in such form and manner as may be so prescribed, specifying the previous conviction [or order] and stating that it is proposed to bring it to the notice of the court in the event of, or, as the case may be, in view of his conviction, and

(d) the accused is not present in person before the court when the statement is so produced,

the court may take account of the previous conviction [or order] as if the accused had appeared and admitted it.]

(3) Nothing in the foregoing provisions of this section shall enable evidence to be given with respect to any matter other than a matter of the prescribed description.

(4) *[Omitted.]*

[Section 182 is printed as amended by the Road Traffic Act 1974, s 13 (3); the Minister of Transport Order 1979 (SI 1979 No 571); the Magistrates' Courts Act 1980, s 154 (2), and Sched 8, para 5; the Transfer of Functions (Transport) Order 1981 (SI 1981 No 238); the Transport Act 1981, s 30 (3), and Sched 9, para 15; and the Transport Act 1982, s 74(1), and Sched 5, para 14.

The words inside square brackets in subs (1) (a) ('[or of any records . . . any enactment]') and after subs (1) (c) ('[or . . . testing authority]') inserted by the Transport Act 1982 will take effect from a date to be announced.

For selected sections of Part III of this Act, see ss 84 et seq.

Section 10 (1) of the Civil Evidence Act 1968 provides that:

. . .

'document' includes, in addition to a document in writing—

(a) any map, plan, graph or drawing;

(b) any photograph;

(c) any disc, tape, sound track or other device in which sounds or other data (not being visual images) are embodied so as to be capable (with or without the aid of some other equipment) of being reproduced therefrom; and

(d) any film, negative, tape or other device in which one or more visual images are embodied so as to be capable (as aforesaid) of being reproduced therefrom;

. . .

'statement' includes any representation of fact, whether made in words or otherwise.

For these purposes s 10 (2) provides that:
any reference to a copy of a document includes—

(a) in the case of a document falling within paragraph (c) but not (d) of the definition of 'document' in the foregoing subsection, a transcript of the sounds or other data embodied therein;

(b) in the case of a document falling within paragraph (d) but not (c) of that definition, a reproduction or still reproduction of the image or images embodied therein, whether enlarged or not;

(c) in the case of a document falling within both those paragraphs, such a transcript together with such a still reproduction; and

(d) in the case of a document not falling within the said paragraph (d) of which a visual image is embodied in a document falling within that paragraph, a reproduction of that image, whether enlarged or not,

and any reference to a copy of the material part of a document shall be construed accordingly.

[For the purposes of subs (2A) in relation to endorsements under the fixed penalty procedure (Transport Act 1982, Part III), see s 34 (7), (8) of the 1982 Act.

As to the application of this section to records maintained for the purpose of the Motor Vehicles (International Circulation) Order 1975 (SI 1975 No 1208), art 1, see the Motor Vehicles (International Circulation) (Amendment) Order 1980 (SI 1980 No 1095), art 8 (2).]

*   *   *

Interpretation

190. Interpretation of expressions relating to motor vehicles and classes thereof

(1) In this Act 'motor vehicle' means a mechanically propelled vehicle intended or adapted for use on roads, and 'trailer' means a vehicle drawn by a motor vehicle:

Provided 'that a side-car attached to a motor cycle shall, if it complies with such conditions as may be specified in regulations made by the [Secretary of State for Transport], be regarded as forming part of the vehicle to which it is attached and not as being a trailer.

(2) In this Act 'motor car' means a mechanically propelled vehicle, not being a motor cycle or an invalid carriage, which is constructed itself to carry a load or passengers and the weight of which unladen—

(a) if it is constructed solely for the carriage of passengers and their effects, is adapted to carry not more than seven passengers exclusive of the driver, and is fitted with tyres of such type as may be specified in regulations made by the [Secretary of State for Transport], does not exceed [3050 kilograms];

(b) if it is constructed or adapted for use for the conveyance of goods or burden of any description, does not exceed [3050 kilograms], or [3500 kilograms] if the vehicle carries a container or containers for holding for the purpose of its propulsion any fuel which is wholly gaseous at [17.5 degrees Celsius] under a pressure of [1.013 bar] or plant and materials for producing such fuel;

(c) does not exceed [2540 kilograms] in a case falling within neither of the foregoing paragraphs.

(3) In this Act 'heavy motor car' means a mechanically propelled vehicle, not being a motor car, which is constructed itself to carry a load or passengers and the weight of which unladen exceeds [2540 kilograms].

(4) In this Act 'motor cycle' means a mechanically propelled vehicle, not being an invalid carriage, with less than four wheels and the weight of which unladen does not exceed [410 kilograms].

(5) In this Act 'invalid carriage' means a mechanically propelled vehicle the weight of which unladen does not exceed [254 kilograms] and which is specially designed and constructed, and not merely adapted, for the use of a person suffering from some physical defect or disability and is used solely by such a person.

(6) In this Act 'motor tractor' means a mechanically propelled vehicle which is not constructed itself to carry a load, other than the following articles, that is to say, water, fuel, accumulators and other equipment used for the purpose of propulsion, loose tools and loose equipment, and the weight of which unladen does not exceed [7370 kilograms].

(7) In this Act 'light locomotive' means a mechanically propelled vehicle which is not constructed itself to carry a load, other than any of the articles aforesaid, and the weight of which unladen does not exceed [11690 kilograms] but does exceed [7370 kilograms].

(8) In this Act 'heavy locomotive' means a mechanically propelled vehicle which is not constructed itself to carry a load, other than any of the articles aforesaid, and the weight of which unladen exceeds [11690 kilograms].

(9) For the purposes of this section, in a case where a motor vehicle is so

constructed that a trailer may by partial super-imposition be attached to the vehicle in such a manner as to cause a substantial part of the weight of the trailer to be borne by the vehicle, that vehicle shall be deemed to be a vehicle itself constructed to carry a load.

(10) For the purposes of this section, in the case of a motor vehicle fitted with a crane, dynamo, welding plant or other special appliance or apparatus which is a permanent or essentially permanent fixture, the appliance or apparatus shall not be deemed to constitute a load or goods or burden of any description, but shall be deemed to form part of the vehicle.

(11) *[Empowers the maximum and minimum weights to be varied by regulations.]*

[Section 190 is printed as amended by the Minister of Transport Order 1979 (SI 1979 No 571); the Transfer of Functions (Transport) Order 1981 (SI 1981 No 238); the Road Traffic Acts 1960 and 1972, Road Traffic Regulations Act 1967, and Transport Act 1968 (Metrication) Regulations 1981 (SI 1981 No 1373); and the Road Traffic Acts 1960 and 1972, and Road Traffic Regulation Act 1967 (Metrication) (No 2) Regulations 1981 (SI 1981 No 1374).

(Subsection (11), which is not reproduced, has been amended by the Road Traffic Regulation Act 1984, s 146, and Sched 13, para 24.)]

191. Articulated vehicles

[(1) Unless it falls within subsection (2) below, a vehicle so constructed that it can be divided into two parts both of which are vehicles and one of which is a motor vehicle shall (when not so divided) be treated for the purposes of the enactments mentioned in subsection (3) below as that motor vehicle with the other part attached as a trailer.

(2) A passenger vehicle so constructed that—

(*a*) it can be divided into two parts, both of which are vehicles and one of which is a motor vehicle, but cannot be so divided without the use of facilities normally available only at a workshop; and

(*b*) passengers carried by it when not so divided can at all times pass from either part to the other,

shall (when not so divided) be treated for the purposes of the enactments mentioned in subsection (3) below as a single motor vehicle.

(3) The enactments referred to in subsections (1) and (2) above are the Road Traffic Act 1960, the Road Traffic Regulation Act [1984], this Act and Part I of the Transport Act 1980.

(4) In this section 'passenger vehicle' means a vehicle constructed or adapted for use solely or principally for the carriage of passengers.]

[Section 191 was substituted by the Transport Act 1980, s 63, and is printed as amended by the Road Traffic Regulation Act 1984, s 146, and Sched 13, para 25.

The Transport Act 1980, Part I, has been largely repealed by the Public Passenger Vehicles Act 1981.]

* * *

194. Method of calculating weight of motor vehicles and trailers

For the purposes of this Act and of the Road Traffic Regulation Act [1984], and of any other enactment relating to the use of motor vehicles or trailers on roads, the weight unladen of a vehicle or trailer shall be taken to be the weight of the vehicle or trailer inclusive of the body and all parts (the heavier being taken where alternative bodies or parts are used) which are necessary to or ordinarily used with the vehicle or trailer when working on a road, but exclusive of the weight of water, fuel or accumulators used for the purpose of the supply of power for the propulsion of the vehicle, or, as the case may be, of any vehicle by which the trailer is drawn, and of loose tools and loose equipment.

[Section 194 is printed as amended by the Road Traffic Regulation Act 1984, s 146, and Sched 13, para 27.]

*   *   *

196. General interpretation provisions

(1) In this Act, unless the context otherwise requires, the following expressions have the meanings hereby assigned to them respectively, that is to say—

['approved testing authority' means a person authorised by the Secretary of State under section 8 of the Transport Act 1982 to carry on a vehicle testing business within the meaning of Part II of that Act;]

'bridleway' means a way over which the public have the following, but no other, rights of way, that is to say, a right of way on foot and a right of way on horseback or leading a horse, with or without a right to drive animals of any description along the way;

'carriage of goods' includes the haulage of goods;

'cycle' means a bicycle, tricycle, or cycle having four or more wheels, not being in any case a motor vehicle;

except for the purposes of section 1, 'driver', where a separate person acts as steersman of a motor vehicle, includes that person as well as any other person engaged in the driving of the vehicle, and 'drive' shall be construed accordingly;

'footpath' means a way over which the public have a right of way on foot only;

'goods' includes goods or burden of any description;

'goods vehicle' means a motor vehicle constructed or adapted for use for the carriage of goods, or a trailer so constructed or adapted;

'goods vehicle test certificate' has the meaning assigned to it by section 45 (1) of this Act;

'highway authority' means—

(a) for the purposes of the application of this Act to England or Wales, in relation to a road other than a trunk road, the authority (being either the council of a county, . . . the Common Council of the City of London, the council of a London borough or the Greater London Council) which is responsible for the maintenance of the road, and in relation to a trunk road, the [Secretary of State for Transport];

(b) *[Omitted.]*

['international road haulage permit' means a licence, permit authorisation or other document issued in pursuance of a Community instrument relating to the carriage of goods by road between member States or an internationalagreement to which the United Kingdom is a party and which relates to the international carriage of goods by road;]

'magistrates' court' and 'petty sessions area' have the same meanings as in [the Magistrates' Courts Act 1980];

'owner', in relation to a vehicle which is the subject of a hiring agreement or hire-purchase agreement, means the person in possession of the vehicle under that agreement;

'plating certificate' has the meaning assigned to it by section 45 (1) of this Act;

'prescribed' means prescribed by regulations made by the [Secretary of State for Transport];

'road' means any highway and any other road to which the public has access, and includes bridges over which a road passes;

'statutory', in relation to any prohibition, restriction, requirement or provision, means contained in, or having effect under, any enactment (including any enactment contained in this Act);

'test certificate' has the meaning assigned to it by section 43 (2) of this Act;

'traffic sign' has the meaning assigned to it by [section 64 (1) of the Road Traffic Regulation Act 1984];

'tramcar' includes any carriage used on any road by virtue of an order made under the Light Railways Act 1896;

'trolley vehicle' means a mechanically propelled vehicle adapted for use upon roads without rails and moved by power transmitted thereto from some external source.

(2) References in this Act to a class of vehicles shall be construed as references to a class defined [or described] by reference to any characteristics of the vehicles or to any other circumstances whatsoever.

(3) References in this Act to any enactment shall be construed, except where the context otherwise requires, as references to that enactment as amended by or under any subsequent enactment.

[Section 196 is printed as amended by the Local Government Act 1972, ss 186 (1), 272 (1), Sched 19, para 6, and Sched 30; the International Road Haulage Act 1975, s 3 (5); the Road Traffic (Drivers' Ages and Hours of Work) Act 1976, s 1 (2), and Sched 1, para 13; the Minister of Transport Order 1979 (SI 1979 No 571); the Magistrates' Courts Act 1980, s 154 (2), and Sched 8, para 5; the Transfer of Functions (Transport) Order 1981 (SI 1981 No 238); the Transport Act 1982, s 74 (1), and Sched 5, para 16; and the Road Traffic Regulation Act 1984, s 146, and Sched 13, para 28.

The definition of 'approved testing authority' (inserted by the Transport Act 1982) will take effect from a date to be announced.

In Part II (ss 8 to 26) of the Transport Act 1982, a 'vehicle testing business' is a business which consists of or includes the exercise by any person in the course of that business of any of the functions specified in s 9 of the 1982 Act (ie the testing of goods vehicles and other vehicles and related matters; these are referred to in Part II as the 'testing and surveillance' functions); see ss 8 (1) and 26 of the 1982 Act.

The Magistrates' Courts Act 1980, s 148 (1), defines 'magistrates' court' as 'any justice or justices of the peace acting under any enactment or by virtue of his or their commission or under the common law', and s 150 (1) of that Act, defines 'petty sessions area' as 'any of the following areas, that is to say, a non-metropolitan county which is not divided into petty sessional divisions, a petty sessional division of a non-metropolitan county, a metropolitan district which is not divided into petty sessional divisions, a petty sessional division of a metropolitan district, a London commission area which is not divided into petty sessional divisions, a petty sessional division of a London commission area and the City of London'.]

*   *   *

SCHEDULE 1

Supplementary Provisions in connection with Proceedings for Offences under Section 33

1.—(1) A person against whom proceedings are brought in England or Wales for an offence under section 33 of this Act (hereinafter referred to as 'the principal section') shall, upon information duly laid by him and on giving to the prosecution not less than three clear days' notice of his intention, be entitled to have any person to whose act or default he alleges that the contravention of that section was due brought before the court in the proceedings; and if, after the contravention has been proved, the original accused proves that the contravention was due to the act or default of that other person, that other person may be convicted of the offence, and, if the original accused further proves that he has used all due diligence to secure that that section was complied with, he shall be acquitted of the offence.

(2) Where an accused seeks to avail himself of the provisions of sub-paragraph (1) above—

(a) the prosecution, as well as the person whom the accused charges with the offence, shall have the right to cross-examine him, if he gives evidence, and any witness called by him in support of his pleas, and to call rebutting evidence;

(b) the court may make such orders as it thinks fit for the payment of costs by any party to the proceedings to any other party thereto.

(3) Where it appears that an offence under the principal section has been committed in respect of which proceedings might be taken in England or Wales against some person (hereinafter referred to as 'the original offender'), and a person proposing to take proceedings in respect of the offence is reasonably satisfied that the offence of which complaint is made was due to an act or default of some other person, being an act or default which took place in England or Wales, and that the original offender could establish a defence under sub-paragraph (1) above, the proceedings may be taken against that other person without proceedings first being taken against the original offender.

In any such proceedings the accused may be charged with, and on proof that the contravention was due to his act or default be convicted of, the offence with which the original offender might have been charged.

2.—(1) Where proceedings are brought in England or Wales against a person (hereafter in this paragraph referred to as 'the accused') in respect of a contravention of the principal section, and it is proved—

(a) that the contravention was due to the act or default of some other person, being an act or default which took place in Scotland, and

(b) that the accused used all due diligence to secure compliance with that section,

the accused shall, subject to the provisions of this paragraph, be acquitted of the offence.

(2) The accused shall not be entitled to be acquitted under this paragraph unless within seven days from the date of the service of the summons on him he has given notice in writing to the prosecution of his intention to rely upon the provisions of this paragraph, specifying the name and address of the person to whose act or default he alleges that the contravention was due, and has sent a like notice to that person.

(3) The person specified in a notice served under this paragraph shall be entitled

to appear at the hearing and to give evidence, and the court may, if it thinks fit, adjourn the hearing to enable him to so do.

(4) Where it is proved that the contravention of the principal section was due to the act or default of some person other than the accused, being an act or default which took place in Scotland, the court shall (whether or not the accused is acquitted) cause notice of the proceedings to be sent to the Secretary of State.

3.—(1) Where a contravention of the principal section committed by a person in Scotland was due to an act or default of any other person, being an act or default which took place in Scotland, then, whether proceedings are or are not taken against the first-mentioned person, that other person may be charged with and convicted of the contravention and shall be liable on conviction to the same punishment as might have been inflicted on the first-mentioned person if he had been convicted of the contravention.

(2) Where a person who is charged in Scotland with a contravention of the principal section proves to the satisfaction of the court that he has used all due diligence to secure that the provision in question was complied with and that the contravention was due to the act or default of some other person, the first-mentioned person shall be acquitted of the contravention.

4.—(1) Subject to the provisions of this paragraph, in any proceedings (whether in England or Wales or Scotland) for an offence under the principal section it shall be a defence for the accused to prove—

(a) that he purchased the helmet in question as being of a type which under the principal section could be lawfully sold or offered for sale, and with a written warranty to that effect, and

(b) that he had no reason to believe at the time of the commission of the alleged offence that it was not of such a type, and

(c) that it was then in the same state as when he purchased it.

(2) A warranty shall only be a defence in any such proceedings if—

(a) the accused—
    (i) has, not later than three clear days before the date of the hearing, sent to the prosecutor a copy of the warranty with a notice stating that he intends to rely on it and specifying the name and address of the person from whom he received it, and
    (ii) has also sent a like notice of his intention to that person, and

(b) in the case of a warranty given by a person resident outside the United Kingdom, the accused proves that he had taken reasonable steps to ascertain, and did in fact believe in, the accuracy of the statement contained therein.

(3) Where the accused is a servant of the person who purchased the helmet in question under a warranty, he shall be entitled to rely on the provisions of this paragraph in the same way as his employer would have been entitled to do if he had been the accused.

(4) The person by whom the warranty is alleged to have been given shall be entitled to appear at the hearing and to give evidence, and the court may, if it thinks fit, adjourn the hearing to enable him to do so.

5.—(1) An accused who in any proceedings for an offence under the principal section wilfully applies to a helmet a warranty not given in relation to that helmet shall be guilty of an offence.

(2) A person who, in respect of a helmet sold by him, being a helmet in respect of which a warranty might be pleaded under paragraph 4 above, gives to the purchaser a false warranty in writing, shall be guilty of an offence, unless he proves that when he gave the warranty he had reason to believe that the statements or description contained therein were accurate.

(3) Where the accused in a prosecution for an offence under the principal section relies successfully on a warranty given to him or to his employer, any proceedings under sub-paragraph (2) above in respect of the warranty may, at the option of the prosecutor, be taken either before a court having jurisdiction in the place where the helmet, or any of the helmets, to which the warranty relates was procured, or before a court having jurisdiction in the place where the warranty was given.

[Schedule 1 is applied to contraventions of s 33AA(4) by s 33AA(7), subject to the modifications in s 33AA(7)(a) and (b).]

* * *

SCHEDULE 4

PROSECUTION AND PUNISHMENT OF OFFENCES

PART I

OFFENCES UNDER THIS ACT

1 Provision creating offence	2 General nature of offence	3 Mode of prosecution	4 Punishment	5 Disqualification	6 Endorsement	7 Additional provisions
1	[Causing death by reckless driving.]	On indictment.	5 years or, in the case of a conviction by a court in Scotland other than the High Court of Justiciary, 2 years.	Obligatory.	Obligatory.	Section 181 and paragraph 3 of Part IV of this Schedule apply.
2	[Reckless driving.]	(a) Summarily.	[6 months or the prescribed sum (within the meaning of [section 32 of the Magistrates' Courts Act 1980] or, in Scotland, of section 289B of the Criminal Procedure (Scotland) Act 1975) or both.]	(a) Obligatory, if committed within 3 years after a previous conviction of an offence under section 1 or 2. (b) Discretionary if committed otherwise than as mentioned in paragraph (a) above.	Obligatory.	Sections 179, 181 and 183 and paragraphs 1, 2, 3, 5 and 6 of Part IV of this Schedule apply.
		(b) On indictment.	2 years or a fine or both.			
3	Careless, and inconsiderate, driving.	Summarily.	[Level 4].	Discretionary.	Obligatory.	Sections 179, 181 and 183 and paragraphs [3A, 4, 5] and 7 of Part IV of this Schedule apply.

5(1)	Driving or attempting to drive when unfit to drive through drink or drugs.	[Summarily].	[6 months or [level 5] or both.]	Obligatory.	Obligatory.	Sections 181 and 183 and paragraph 3 of Part IV of this Schedule apply.
5(2)	Being in charge of a motor vehicle when unfit to drive through drink or drugs.	[Summarily].	[3 months or [level 4] or both.]	Discretionary.	Obligatory.	Sections 181 and 183 and paragraph 3 of Part IV of this Schedule apply.
[6(1)(a)]	Driving or attempting to drive with excess alcohol in breath, blood or urine.]	[Summarily].	[6 months or [level 5] or both.]	Obligatory.	Obligatory.	Sections 181 and 183 and paragraph 3 of Part IV of this Schedule apply.
[6(1)(b)]	Being in charge of a motor vehicle with excess alcohol in breath, blood or urine.]	[Summarily].	[3 months or [level 4] or both.]	Discretionary.	Obligatory.	Sections 181 and 183 and paragraph 3 of Part IV of this Schedule apply.
[7(4)]	Failing to provide a specimen of breath for a breath test.	Summarily	[Level 3].	[Discretionary.]	[Obligatory.]	Sections 181 and 183 apply.
[8(7)]	Failing to provide specimen for analysis or laboratory test.	Summarily	(a) Where the specimen was required to ascertain ability to drive or proportion of alcohol at the time offender was driving or attempting to drive, six months or [level 5] or both. (b) In any other case three months or [level 4] or both.	(a) Obligatory in case mentioned in paragraph (a) of column 4. (b) Discretionary in any other case.]	Obligatory.	Sections 181 and 183 and paragraph 3 of Part IV of this Schedule apply.

1 Provision creating offence	2 General nature of offence	3 Mode of prosecution	4 Punishment	5 Disqualification	6 Endorsement	7 Additional provisions
14	Motor racing and speed trials on highways.	Summarily.	[Level 4].	Obligatory.	Obligatory.	Sections 181 and 183 apply.
15	Other unauthorised or irregular competitions or trials on highways.	Summarily.	[Level 3].	—	—	—
16	Carrying passenger on motor-cycle contrary to section 16.	Summarily.	[Level 3].	Discretionary.	Obligatory.	Sections 181 and 183 apply.
17	[Reckless cycling.]	Summarily.	[Level 3].	—	—	Sections 179, 181 and 183 apply.
18	Careless, and inconsiderate, cycling.	Summarily.	[Level 1].	—	—	Sections 179, 181 and 183 and paragraphs [3A] 4 and 7 of Part IV of this Schedule apply.
19	Cycling when unfit through drink or drugs.	Summarily.	[Level 3].	—	—	Sections 181 and 183 apply.
20	Unauthorised or irregular cycle racing or trials of speed on highways.	Summarily.	[Level 1].	—	—	Sections 181 and 183 apply.

21	Carrying passenger on bicycle contrary to section 21.	Summarily.	[Level 1].	—	—	Sections 181 and 183 apply.
22	Failing to comply with traffic directions.	Summarily.	[Level 3].	Discretionary, if committed in respect of a motor vehicle by a failure to comply with a direction of a constable [or traffic warden] or an indication given by a sign specified for the purposes of this paragraph in regulations made by the [[Secretary of State for Transport], the Secretary of State for Wales] and the Secretary of State for Scotland acting jointly.	Obligatory, if committed as described in the entry in column 5 relating to this offence.	Sections 179, 181 and 183 apply.
23	Pedestrian failing to stop when directed by constable regulating traffic.	Summarily.	[Level 3].	—	—	—
24	Leaving vehicles in dangerous positions.	Summarily.	[Level 3].	Discretionary, if committed in respect of a motor vehicle.	Obligatory, if committed in respect of a motor vehicle.	Sections 179, 181 and 183 apply.
25(4)	Failing to stop after accident and give particulars or report accident.	Summarily.	[Level 5].	Discretionary.	Obligatory.	Sections 181 and 183 apply.

1 Provision creating offence	2 General nature of offence	3 Mode of prosecution	4 Punishment	5 Disqualification	6 Endorsement	7 Additional provisions
26(2)	Obstructing inspection of vehicles after accident.	Summarily.	[Level 3].	—	—	—
29	Tampering with motor vehicles.	Summarily.	[Level 3].	—	—	Section 181 applies.
30(1)	Holding or getting on to vehicle in order to be carried.	Summarily.	[Level 1].	—	—	Section 181 applies.
30(2)	Holding on to vehicle in order to be towed.	Summarily.	[Level 1].	—	—	Sections 181 and 183 apply.
31(1)	Dogs on designated roads without being held on lead.	Summarily.	[Level 1].	—	—	—
32(3)	Driving or riding motor cycles in contravention of regulations requiring wearing of protective headgear.	Summarily.	[Level 2].	—	—	—
33	Selling, etc, helmet not of prescribed type as helmet for affording protection for motor cyclists.	Summarily.	[Level 3].	—	—	—

[33A	Driving or riding in a motor vehicle in contravention of regulations requiring the wearing of seat belts.	Summarily.	[Level 2].	—	—	Sections 181 and 183 apply.]
[33AA(3)	Contravention of regulations with respect to use of head-worn-appliances on motor cycles.	Summarily.	[Level 2].	—	—	—]
[33AA(4)	Selling, etc, appliance not of prescribed type as approved for use on motor cycles.	Summarily.	[Level 3].	—	—	—]
[33B	Driving motor vehicle with child in the front seat wearing seat belt.	Summarily.	[Level 2].	—	—	Sections 181 and 183 apply.]
34(4)	Causing, etc, heavy motor vehicles to be driven or to haul without proper crew.	Summarily.	[Level 3].	—	—	Section 181 applies.
35(3)	Unauthorised motor vehicle trial on footpaths or bridleways.	Summarily.	[Level 3].	—	—	Sections 181 and 183 apply.
36	Driving motor vehicles elsewhere than on roads.	Summarily.	[Level 3].	—	—	Sections 181 and 183 apply.

1 Provision creating offence	2 General nature of offence	3 Mode of prosecution	4 Punishment	5 Disqualification	6 Endorsement	7 Additional provisions
[36A	Prohibition of parking of heavy commercial vehicles on verges and footways.	Summarily.	[Level 3].	—	—	Sections 181 and 183 apply.]
[36B	Prohibition of parking of vehicles on verges, central reservations and footways.	Summarily.	[Level 3].	—	—	Sections 181 and 183 apply.]
40(5)	Contravention of construction and use regulations.	Summarily.	[[Level 5] in the case of an offence of using, or causing or permitting the use of, a goods vehicle [or a vehicle adapted to carry more than eight passengers]— (a) so as to cause, or to be likely to cause, danger by the condition of the vehicle or its parts or accessories, the number of passengers carried by it, or the weight, distribution, packing, or adjustment of its load; or (b) in breach of a construction and use requirement as to brakes, steering gear, tyres or any description of weight; or	Discretionary if committed by using, or causing or permitting the use of, any motor vehicle or trailer— (a) as described in paragraph (a) [or paragraph (c)] in the entry in column 4 relating to this offence; or (b) in breach of a construction and use requirement as to brakes, steering-gear, or tyres; except where the offender proves that he did not know and had no reasonable	Obligatory if committed as described in the entry in column 5 relating to this offence, but subject to the exception there mentioned.	Sections 181 and 183 apply.

Section	General nature of offence	Mode of prosecution	Punishment	Disqualification			Special provisions
			(c) for any purpose for which it is so unsuitable as to cause or to be likely to cause danger; [Level 5] in the case of an offence of carrying on a goods vehicle a load which, by reason of its insecurity or position, is likely to cause danger; [level 4] in any other case.] (The levels of fines in respect of offences under s 40(5) are those applicable to offences committed after 11 April 1983.)	cause to suspect that the facts of the case were such that the offence would be committed. [Discretionary if committed by carrying on a motor vehicle or trailer a load which, by reason of its insecurity or position is likely to cause danger, but subject to the exception above.]	—	—	Sections 181 and 183 apply.
44(1)	Using, etc, vehicle without required test certificate being in force.	Summarily.	[In relation to offences committed after 11 April 1983— (a) [level 4], in the case of a vehicle adapted to carry more than eight passengers; and (b) [level 3] in any other case].				
Regulations under 45(7)	Contravention of requirement of regulations that driver of goods vehicle being tested be present throughout test or drive vehicle, etc, which is declared by regulations to be an offence.	Summarily.	[Level 3].				

1 Provision creating offence	2 General nature of offence	3 Mode of prosecution	4 Punishment	5 Disqualification	6 Endorsement	7 Additional provisions
46(1)	Using, etc, goods vehicle without required plating certificate being in force.	Summarily.	[Level 3].	—	—	Sections 181 and 183 apply.
46(2)	Using, etc, goods vehicle without required goods vehicle test certificate being in force.	Summarily.	[Level 4].	—	—	Sections 181 and 183 apply.
46(3)	Using, etc, goods vehicle with alteration thereto required to be but not notified to Secretary of State under regulations under section 45.	Summarily.	[Level 3].	—	—	Sections 181 and 183 apply.
Regulations under 50(5)	Contravention of requirement of regulations that driver of goods vehicle being tested after notifiable alteration be present throughout test and drive vehicle, etc, which is declared by regulations to be an offence.	Summarily.	[Level 3].	—	—	—

51(1)	Using, etc, ... vehicle without required certificate being in force showing that it complies with type approval requirements applicable to it.	Summarily.	[Level 4].	—	—	Sections 181 and 183 apply.
51(2)	Using, etc, certain ... vehicles for drawing trailer when plating certificate does not specify maximum laden weight for vehicle and trailer.	Summarily.	[Level 3].	—	—	Sections 181 and 183 apply.
51(3)	Using, etc, ... vehicle with alteration thereto required to be but not notified to [Secretary of State for Transport] under regulations under section 48.	Summarily.	[Level 3].	—	—	Sections 181 and 183 apply.
53(4)	Obstructing testing of vehicle by examiner on road or failing to comply with requirements of section 53 or Schedule 3.	Summarily.	[Level 3].	—	—	—
54(5) (including application by 55(3))	Failure of owner of vehicle discovered to be defective on roadside test or further test to give required certificate or declaration.	Summarily.	[Level 3].	—	—	—

1 Provision creating offence	2 General nature of offence	3 Mode of prosecution	4 Punishment	5 Disqualification	6 Endorsement	7 Additional provisions
54(6) (including application by 55(3))	Failure of person in charge of vehicle on roadside test or further test to give particulars of owner.	Summarily.	[Level 3].	—	—	—
55(5)	Obstructing further testing of vehicle by [Secretary of State for Transport's] officer or failing to comply with requirements of section 55 or paragraph 3 or 4 of Schedule 3.	Summarily.	[Level 3].	—	—	—
56(3)	Obstructing goods vehicle examiner inspecting goods vehicle or entering premises where such vehicle believed to be.	Summarily.	[Level 3].	—	—	—
56(5)	Person in charge of stationary goods vehicle refusing etc, to proceed to nearby place of inspection.	Summarily.	[Level 3].	—	—	—

Section	General nature of offence	Mode of prosecution	Punishment			Sections 181 and 183 apply.
57(9)	Driving, etc, goods vehicle in contravention of prohibition on driving it as being unfit for service [or refusing, neglecting or otherwise failing to comply with a direction to remove a goods vehicle found over-loaded].	Summarily.	[Level 5].	—	—	
59(3)	Contravention of regulations requiring goods vehicle operator to inspect, and keep records of inspections of, goods vehicles.	Summarily.	[Level 3].	—	—	—
60(3)	Selling, etc, unroad-worthy vehicle or trailer or altering vehicle or trailer so as to make it unroadworthy.	Summarily.	[Level 5].	—	—	—
[60A (1)	Fitting of defective or unsuitable vehicle parts.	Summarily.	[Level 5].	—	—	—]
[60A (3)	Selling defective or unsuitable vehicle parts.	Summarily.	[Level 4].	—	—	—]

1 Provision creating offence	2 General nature of offence	3 Mode of prosecution	4 Punishment	5 Disqualification	6 Endorsement	7 Additional provisions
[60A (6)]	Obstructing examiner testing vehicles to ascertain whether defective or unsuitable part has been fitted, etc.	Summarily.	[Level 3].	—	—	—]
61(2)	Obstructing examiner testing condition of used vehicles at sale rooms, etc.	Summarily.	[Level 3].	—	—	—
62	Selling, etc, goods vehicle without required certificate being in force showing that it complies with type approval requirements applicable to it.	Summarily.	[Level 5].	—	—	—
66(5)	Selling, etc, pedal cycle in contravention of regulations as to brakes, bells, etc.	Summarily.	[Level 3].	—	—	—

81(1)	Causing, etc, vehicle to be on road in contravention of provisions as to lighting, etc, of vehicles.	Summarily.	[Level 3].	—	—	Sections 181 and 183 apply.
81(2)	Selling, etc, wrongly made tail lamps or reflectors.	Summarily.	[Level 5].	—	—	—
84(1)	Driving without a licence.	Summarily.	[Level 3].	Discretionary, if the offence is committed by driving a motor vehicle in a case where either no licence authorising the driving of that vehicle could have been granted to the offender or, if a provisional (but no other) licence to drive it could have been granted to him, the driving would not have complied with the conditions thereof.	Obligatory, if committed as described in the entry in column 5 relating to this offence.	Sections 181 and 183 apply.
84(2)	[Causing or permitting] a person to drive without a licence.	Summarily.	[Level 3].	—	—	Section 181 applies.
88(6)	Failing to comply with any conditions prescribed for driving under provisional licence or full licence treated as provisional licence.	Summarily.	[Level 3].	Discretionary.	Obligatory.	Sections 181 and 183 apply.

1 Provision creating offence	2 General nature of offence	3 Mode of prosecution	4 Punishment	5 Disqualification	6 Endorsement	7 Additional provisions
89(3)	Driving licence holder failing, when his particulars become incorrect, to surrender licence and give particulars.	Summarily.	[Level 3].	—	—	Section 180 applies.
91(1)	Driving with uncorrected defective eyesight.	Summarily.	[Level 3].	Discretionary.	Obligatory.	—
91(2)	Refusing to submit to test of eyesight.	Summarily.	[Level 3].	Discretionary.	Obligatory.	—
99(a)	Obtaining driving licence while disqualified.	Summarily.	[Level 3].	—	—	Section 180 applies.
99(b)	Driving while disqualified.	(a) Summarily.	[6 months or the prescribed sum (within the meaning of [section 32 of the Magistrates' Courts Act 1980] or, in Scotland, of section 289B of the Criminal Procedure (Scotland) Act 1975) or both.]	Discretionary.	Obligatory.	Sections 180, 181 and 183 apply.
		(b) On indictment	[12 months or a fine or both.]			

101(4) (including application by 103(4))	Failing to produce licence to court for endorsement on conviction of offence involving obligatory endorsement or on committal for sentence, etc, for offence involving obligatory or discretionary disqualification when no interim disqualification ordered.	Summarily.	[Level 3].
101(6)	Applying for or obtaining licence without giving particulars of current endorsement.	Summarily.	[Level 3].
103(2)	Failing to produce driving licence to court making order for interim disqualification on committal for sentence, etc.	Summarily.	[Level 3].
104(4)	Failing to state to court or give information as to date of birth or sex.	Summarily.	[Level 3].
104(5)	Failing to furnish Secretary of State with evidence of date of birth etc.	Summarily.	[Level 3].

1 Provision creating offence	2 General nature of offence	3 Mode of prosecution	4 Punishment	5 Disqualification	6 Endorsement	7 Additional provisions
111(2)	Failing to produce to court Northern Ireland driving licence.	Summarily.	[Level 3].	—	—	—
112(1)	Driving heavy goods vehicle without heavy goods driver's licence.	Summarily.	[Level 4].	—	—	Sections 181 and 183 apply.
112(2)	[Causing or permitting] a person to drive heavy goods vehicle without heavy goods vehicle driver's licence.	Summarily.	[Level 4].	—	—	Section 181 applies.
114(3)	Failing to comply with conditions of heavy goods vehicle driver's licence.	Summarily.	[Level 3].	—	—	Sections 181 and 183 apply.
[114(4)	[Causing or permitting] a person under 21 to drive heavy goods vehicle in contravention of conditions of heavy goods vehicle/driver's licence.	Summarily.	[Level 3].	—	—	Section 181 applies.]

Regulations under 119(2)	Contravention of regulations about heavy goods vehicle drivers' licences which is declared by regulation to be an offence.	Summarily.	[Level 3].	—	—	—
126(3)	Giving of paid driving instruction by unregistered and unlicensed persons or their employers.	Summarily.	[Level 4].	—	—	—
[126(4A)	Giving of paid instruction without there being exhibited in the motor car a certificate of registration or a licence under Part V.	Summarily.	[Level 3].	—	⌐	—
135(2)	Unregistered instructor using title or displaying badge, etc, prescribed for registered instructor, and employers using such title, etc, in relation to his unregistered instructor or issuing misleading advertisement, etc.	Summarily.	[Level 4].	—	—	—
136	Failure of instructor to surrender to Registrar certificate or licence.	Summarily.	[Level 3].	—	—	—

1 Provision creating offence	2 General nature of offence	3 Mode of prosecution	4 Punishment	5 Disqualification	6 Endorsement	7 Additional provisions
137(3)	Failing to produce certificate of registration or licence as driving instructor.	Summarily.	[Level 3].	—	—	—
143	Using motor vehicle while uninsured or unsecured against third-party risks.	Summarily.	[Level 4].	Discretionary.	Obligatory.	Sections 180, 181 and 183 apply.
147(4)	Failing to surrender certificate of insurance or security to insurer on cancellation or make statutory declaration of loss or destruction.	Summarily.	[Level 3].	—	—	—
151(2)	Failing to give information, or wilfully making false statement, as to insurance or security when claim made.	Summarily.	[Level 4].	—	—	—
159	Failing to stop vehicle when required by constable.	Summarily.	[Level 3].	—	—	Sections 181 and 183 apply.
160(1)	Refusing or neglecting to allow motor vehicle or trailer to be weighed, etc.	Summarily.	[Level 5].	—	—	Sections 181 and 183 apply.

161(4)	Failing to produce driving licence to constable or to state date of birth.	Summarily.	[Level 3].	—	—	Sections 181 and 183 apply.
161(5)	Failing to furnish Secretary of State with evidence of date of birth, etc.	Summarily.	[Level 3].	—	—	—
162(1)	Failing to give constable certain names and addresses or to produce certificate of insurance or certain test and other like certificates.	Summarily.	[Level 3].	—	—	Sections 181 and 183 apply.
162(3)	Supervisor of learner-driver failing to give constable certain names and addresses.	Summarily.	[Level 3].	—	—	Section 181 applies.
164(1)	Refusing to give, or giving false, name and address in case of reckless, dangerous, careless or inconsiderate driving or cycling.	Summarily.	[Level 3].	—	—	Sections 181 and 183 apply.
165	Pedestrian failing to give constable his name and address after failing to stop when directed by constable controlling traffic.	Summarily.	[Level 1].	—	—	—

1 Provision creating offence	2 General nature of offence	3 Mode of prosecution	4 Punishment	5 Disqualification	6 Endorsement	7 Additional provisions
166(1)	Failure by driver, in case of accident involving injury to another, to produce evidence of insurance or security or to report accident.	Summarily.	[Level 3].	—	—	Sections 181 and 183 apply.
167	Failure by owner of motor vehicle to give police information for verifying compliance with requirement of compulsory insurance or security.	Summarily.	[Level 4].	—	—	Sections 181 and 183 apply.
168(3)	Failure of person keeping vehicle and others to give police information as to identity of driver, etc, in the case of certain offences.	Summarily.	[Level 3].	—	—	—
169(1)	Forgery, etc, of licences, test certificates, certificates of insurance and other documents and things.	(a) Summarily.	[The prescribed sum].	—	—	Section 180 applies.
		(b) On indictment	2 years.			

							Section 180 applies.
170(1)	Making false statements in connection with licences under this Act and with registration as an approved driving instructor.	Summarily.	[Level 4].		—	—	—
170(2)	Making, or making use of, false statements relating to goods vehicles.	Summarily.	[Level 4].		—	—	—
170(3)	Producing false evidence or making false declaration in connection with applications for vehicle excise licences for vehicles required to have test certificates.	Summarily.	[Level 4].		—	—	—
170(4)	Making false statements as to the remedying of defects discovered in vehicles on roadside tests.	Summarily.	[Level 4].		—	—	—
170(5)	Making, or making use of, false entry in records required to be kept of condition of goods vehicles.	Summarily.	[Level 4].				

1 Provision creating offence	2 General nature of offence	3 Mode of prosecution	4 Punishment	5 Disqualification	6 Endorsement	7 Additional provisions
[170(5A)]	Failure to notify [Secretary of State for Transport] of onset of, or deterioration in, relevant or prospective disease.	Summarily.	[Level 3].	—	—	Section 180 applies.]
170(6)	Making false statement or withholding material information in order to obtain the issue of insurance certificates, etc.	Summarily.	[Level 4].	—	—	Section 180 applies.
171[(1)]	Issuing false insurance certificates, etc, or false test certificates.	Summarily.	[Level 4].	—	—	Section 180 applies.
[171(2)]	Falsely amending certificate of conformity.	Summarily.	[Level 4].	—	—	Section 180 applies.]
172	Using goods vehicle with unauthorised weights as well as authorised weights marked thereon.	Summarily.	[Level 3].	—	—	—
174	Personation of, or of person employed by, authorised examiner.	Summarily.	[Level 3].	—	—	—

	General nature of offence	Mode of prosecution	Punishment	Discretionary.	Obligatory.	
175	Taking, etc, in Scotland a motor vehicle without authority or, knowing that it has been so taken, driving it or allowing oneself to be carried in it without authority.	(a) Summarily.	3 months or [the prescribed sum].			Sections 181 and 183 and paragraph 8 of Part IV of this Schedule apply.
		(b) On indictment.	12 months or a fine or both.	—	—	—
187(2)	Failing to attend, give evidence or produce documents to, inquiry held by Secretary of State, etc.	Summarily.	[Level 3].	—	—	—
Schedule 1 para 5(1)	Applying warranty to protective helmet in defending proceedings under section 33 where no warranty given.	Summarily.	[Level 3].	—	—	—
para 5(2)	Giving to purchaser of protective helmet a false warranty in case where warranty might be defence in proceedings under section 33.	Summarily.	[Level 3].			

[Schedule 4, Part I, is printed as amended by the Heavy Commercial Vehicles (Controls and Regulations) Act 1973, ss 2 (2) and 3 (2); the Road Traffic Act 1974, ss 7 (2), 12 (2), 13 (4), 15 (5), 21, 24 (2) and (3), Sched 5, Parts III and IV, Sched 6, para 24, and Sched 7; the Road Traffic (Drivers' Ages and Hours of Work) Act 1976, s 1 (2) and (5), Sched 1, para 15, and Sched 3, Part I; the Secretary of State for Transport Order 1976 (SI 1976 No 1775), art 6 (1), and Sched 3, para 9;the Criminal Law Act 1977, ss 15, 28, 30, 31, 65, Sched 1, Sched 5, para 2, and Scheds 6, 12 and 13; the Transport Act 1978, s 9 (1), and Sched 3, para 7; the Minister of Transport Order 1979 (SI 1979 No 571); the Magistrates' Courts Act 1980, s 154 (1), and Sched 7, para 112; the Transfer of Functions (Transport) Order 1981 (SI 1981 No 238); the Transport Act 1981, ss 26 (1), 27 (4), 28 (2), 30 (3), and Sched 9, paras 19 to 22; the Criminal Justice Act 1982, ss 38, 39, 46 and Scheds 2, 3; the Transport Act 1982, ss 24 (3), 57, 63; and the Road Traffic (Driving Instruction) Act 1984, s 1 (5).

The entry relating to s 36B (which was inserted by the Road Traffic Act 1974, s 7 (2)) has not yet been brought into operation.

The entry relating to s 126 (4A) (which was inserted by the Road Traffic (Driving Instruction) Act 1984, s 1 (5)) has not yet been brought into operation.

The entry relating to s 171 (2) (which was inserted by the Transport Act 1982, s 24 (3)) has also not yet been brought into operation. Until this entry is operative, the immediately preceding entry relates to s 171 (see s 24 (3) of the 1982 Act).

The references to levels in column 4 of the table are references to levels of fines on the standard scale; see 'Levels of fines on the standard scale' opposite page 1 of this volume.

In relation to the entries relating to ss 2, and 99 (b), 169 (1) and 175, for the purposes of s 32 of the Magistrates' Courts Act 1980, the 'prescribed sum' is £2,000; see the Criminal Penalties etc (Increase) Order 1984 (SI 1984 No 447).]

PART II

OTHER OFFENCE INVOLVING OBLIGATORY DISQUALIFICATION AND ENDORSEMENT

Manslaughter or, in Scotland, culpable homicide by the driver of a motor vehicle.

PART III

OTHER OFFENCES INVOLVING DISCRETIONARY DISQUALIFICATION AND OBLIGATORY ENDORSEMENT

1. Stealing or attempting to steal a motor vehicle.

2. An offence, or attempt to commit an offence, in respect of a motor vehicle under section 12 of the Theft Act 1968 (taking conveyance without consent of owner etc. or, knowing it has been so taken, driving it or allowing oneself to be carried in it).

3. An offence under section 25 of the Theft Act 1968 (going equipped for stealing, etc.) committed with reference to the theft or taking of motor vehicles.

4–8. *[Repealed.]*

[Paragraphs 4 to 8 of Part III of Sched 4 were repealed by the Road Traffic Regulation Act 1984, s 146, and Sched 14.]

PART IV

SUPPLEMENTARY PROVISIONS AS TO PROSECUTION, TRIAL AND PUNISHMENT
OF OFFENCES

*   *   *

[3A—(1) Where on a person's trial on indictment in England or Wales for an offence under section 1, 2, or 17 the jury find him not guilty of the offence specifically charged in the indictment, they may (without prejudice to section 6 (3) of the Criminal Law Act 1967) find him guilty—

(a) if the offence so charged is an offence under section 1 or 2, of an offence under section 3; or

(b) if the offence so charged is an offence under section 17, of an offence under section 18.

(2) The Crown Court shall have the like powers and duties in the case of a person who is by virtue of this paragraph convicted before it of an offence under section 3 or 18 as a magistrates' court would have had on convicting him of that offence.]

[Paragraph 3A was inserted by the Criminal Law Act 1977, s 65, and Sched 12.
The Criminal Law Act 1967, s 6 (3), contains a power enabling juries in specified circumstances to bring in a verdict of guilty other than to the offence charged.]

4. Where a person is charged in England or Wales before a magistrates' court with an offence under section 2 or with an offence under section 17, and the court is of opinion that the offence is not proved, then, at any time during the hearing or immediately thereafter the court may, without prejudice to any other powers possessed by the court, direct or allow a charge for an offence under section 3 or, as the case may be, section 18 to be preferred forthwith against the defendant and may thereupon proceed with that charge, so however that he or his solicitor or counsel shall be informed of the new charge and be given an opportunity, whether by way of cross-examining any witness whose evidence has already been given against the defendant or otherwise, of answering the new charge, and the court shall, if it considers that the defendant is prejudiced in his defence by reason of the new charge's being so preferred, adjourn the hearing.

5. Where a person is prosecuted on indictment in England or Wales for an offence to which section 179 does not apply [or (if that section does not apply) as regards which the requirement of section 179 (2) has been satisfied, or does not apply], section 179 (2) shall not be taken to prejudice any power of the jury on the charge for that offence, if they find him not guilty of it, to find him guilty of an offence against section 2 [or 3].

[Paragraph 5 is printed as amended by the Criminal Law Act 1977, s 65, and Sched 12.]

*   *   *

7. A person may be convicted of an offence against section 3 or 18 notwithstanding that the requirement of section 179(2) has not been satisfied as respects that offence where—

(a) the charge for the offence has been preferred against him by virtue of paragraph 4 above, and

(b) the said requirement has been satisfied, or does not apply, as respects the alleged offence against section 2 or, as the case may be, section 17.

*   *   *

PART V

INTERPRETATION

1. *[Repealed.]*

2. 'Construction and use requirement' has the same meaning for the purposes of this Schedule as it has for the purposes of Part II of this Act.

[Paragraph 1 in Part V of this Schedule was repealed by the Transport Act 1981, ss 30 (3), 40 (1), Sched 9, para 23, and Sched 12, Part III.

For the interpretation section of Part II of this Act, see s 82.]

*   *   *

The Road Traffic Regulation Act 1984

(1984 c 27)

An Act to consolidate the Road Traffic Regulation Act 1967 and certain related enactments, with amendments to give effect to recommendations of the Law Commission and the Scottish Law Commission. [26th June 1984]

ARRANGEMENT OF SECTIONS

* * *

117

*   *   *

PART VIII

CONTROL AND ENFORCEMENT

*   *   *

Enforcement of excess parking charges

*   *   *

PART IX

FURTHER PROVISIONS AS TO ENFORCEMENT

General provisions

*   *   *

PART X

GENERAL AND SUPPLEMENTARY PROVISIONS

*   *   *

*   *   *

SCHEDULES

*   *   *

PART II

TRAFFIC REGULATION IN SPECIAL CASES

*   *   *

17. Traffic regulation on special roads

(1) A special road shall not, except as provided by or under regulations made under subsection (2) below, be used—

(a) by any traffic other than traffic of a class authorised in that behalf by a scheme made, or having effect as if made, under section 16 of the Highways Act 1980, or in Scotland, under [section 7 of the Roads (Scotland) Act 1984], or

(b) if the road is one to which certain provisions of the Highways Act 1980 apply by virtue of paragraph 3 of Schedule 23 to that Act, by any traffic other than traffic of a class for the time being authorised by virtue of that paragraph.

(2) The Secretary of State may make regulations with respect to the use of special roads, and such regulations may in particular—

(a) regulate the manner in which and the conditions subject to which special roads may be used by traffic of the class authorised in that behalf by such a scheme as is mentioned in subsection (1) (a) above or, as the case may be, by virtue of the said paragraph 3;

(b) authorise, or enable such authority as may be specified in the regulations to authorise, the use of special roads on occasion or in an emergency or for the purpose of crossing, or for the purpose of securing access to premises abutting on or adjacent to the roads, by traffic other than that described in paragraph (a) above; or

(c) relax, or enable any authority so specified to relax, any prohibition or restriction imposed by the regulations.

(3) Regulations made under subsection (2) above may make provision with respect to special roads generally, or may make different provision with respect to special roads provided for the use of different classes of traffic, or may make provision with respect to any particular special road.

(4) If a person uses a special road in contravention of this section or of regulations under subsection (2) above, he shall be guilty of an offence.

(5) Where, in the case of any part of a special road, the date of opening is a date after the commencement of this Act, the provisions of this section and of any regulations made under subsection (2) above shall not apply to that part of the road until the date of opening; but nothing in this subsection shall be construed as preventing the making of regulations under subsection (2) above so as to come into force, in relation to that part of the road, on the date of opening.

(6) In this section 'use', in relation to a road, includes crossing, and 'the date of opening', in relation to a part of a special road, means the date declared, by a notice

published as mentioned in section 1(4) of this Act, to be the date on which it is open for use as a special road.

[Section 17 is printed as amended by the Roads (Scotland) Act 1984, s 156(1), and Sched 9, para 93(7).

The Motorways Traffic (England and Wales) Regulations 1982 (SI 1982 No 1163), as amended, have effect as if made under this section.

For the application of the fixed penalty procedure to offences under subs (4), see the Transport Act 1982, Part III, and Sched 1 (as amended by s 146 of and Sched 15, para 55, to this Act).]

*　　　*　　　*

PART III

CROSSINGS AND PLAYGROUNDS

*　　　*　　　*

25. Pedestrian crossing regulations

(1) The Secretary of State may make regulations with respect to the precedence of vehicles and pedestrians respectively, and generally with respect to the movement of traffic (including pedestrians), at and in the vicinity of crossings.

(2)–(4). *[Omitted.]*

(5) A person who contravenes any regulations made under this section shall be guilty of an offence.

(6) In this section 'crossing' means a crossing for pedestrians established—

(*a*) by a local authority under section 23 of this Act, or

(*b*) by the Secretary of State in the discharge of the duty imposed on him by section 24 of this Act,

and (in either case) indicated in accordance with the regulations having effect as respects that crossing; and, for the purposes of a prosecution for a contravention of the provisions of a regulation having effect as respects a crossing, the crossing shall be deemed to be so established and indicated unless the contrary is proved.

[Sections 23 and 24 of this Act provide for the establishment of pedestrian crossings by local authorities on roads in their areas (other than trunk roads) and the establishment of pedestrian crossings by the Secretary of State on trunk roads, respectively.

The 'Pelican' Pedestrian Crossings Regulations and General Directions 1969 (SI 1969 No 888) and the 'Zebra' Pedestrian Crossings Regulations 1971 (SI 1971 No 1524) have effect (in part) as if made under this section.

Paragraph 9(2) of Sched 10 to this Act provides as follows:

Section 25(6) of this Act shall apply in relation to a crossing established, or having effect as if established—

(*a*) by a local authority under section 21 of the 1967 Act (whether as that section had effect at any time before the commencement of the said Act of 1980 or as it had effect by virtue of that Act), or

(*b*) by a Minister under section 22 of the 1967 Act,

as it applies in relation to a crossing established by a local authority under section 23 or by the Secretary of State under section 24 of this Act.

For the application of the fixed penalty procedure to offences under subs (5) (except offences in respect of moving motor vehicles), see the Transport Act 1982, Part III, and Sched 1 (as amended by s 146 of and Sched 13, para 55, to this Act).]

*   *   *

28. Stopping of vehicles at school crossings

(1) When between the hours of eight in the morning and half-past five in the afternoon a vehicle is approaching a place in a road where children on their way to or from school, or from one part of a school to another, are crossing or seeking to cross the road, a school crossing patrol wearing a uniform approved by the Secretary of State shall have power, by exhibiting a prescribed sign, to require the person driving or propelling the vehicle to stop it.

(2) When a person has been required under subsection (1) above to stop a vehicle—

(a) he shall cause the vehicle to stop before reaching the place where the children are crossing or seeking to cross and so as not to stop or impede their crossing, and

(b) the vehicle shall not be put in motion again so as to reach the place in question so long as the sign continues to be exhibited.

(3) A person who fails to comply with paragraph (a) of subsection (2) above, or who causes a vehicle to be put in motion in contravention of paragraph (b) of that subsection, shall be guilty of an offence.

(4) In this section—

(a) 'prescribed sign' means a sign of a size, colour and type prescribed by regulations made by the Secretary of State or, if authorisation is given by the Secretary of State for the use of signs of a description not so prescribed, a sign of that description;

(b) 'school crossing patrol' means a person authorised to patrol in accordance with arrangements under section 26 of this Act;

and regulations under paragraph (a) above may provide for the attachment of reflectors to signs or for the illumination of signs.

(5) For the purposes of this section—

(a) where it is proved that a sign was exhibited by a school crossing patrol, it shall be presumed, unless the contrary is proved, to be of a size, colour and type prescribed, or of a description authorised, under subsection (4)(b) above, and, if it was exhibited in circumstances in which it was required by the regulations to be illuminated, to have been illuminated in the prescribed manner;

(b) where it is proved that a school crossing patrol was wearing a uniform, the uniform shall be presumed, unless the contrary is proved, to be a uniform approved by the Secretary of State; and

(c) where it is proved that a prescribed sign was exhibited by a school crossing patrol at a place in a road where children were crossing or seeking to cross the road, it shall be presumed, unless the contrary is proved, that those children were on their way to or from school or from one part of a school to another.

[The Traffic Signs Regulations and General Directions 1981 (SI 1981 No 859) have effect (in part) as if made under this section.]

*   *   *

PART V

Traffic Signs

64. General provisions as to traffic signs

(1) In this Act 'traffic sign' means any object or device (whether fixed or portable) for conveying, to traffic on roads or any specified class of traffic, warnings, information, requirements, restrictions or prohibitions of any description—

(a) specified by regulations made by the Ministers acting jointly, or

(b) authorised by the Secretary of State,

and any line or mark on a road for so conveying such warnings, information, requirements, restrictions or prohibitions.

(2) Traffic signs shall be of the size, colour and type prescribed by regulations made as mentioned in subsection (1)(a) above except where the Secretary of State authorises the erection or retention of a sign of another character; and for the purposes of this subsection illumination, whether by lighting or by the use of reflectors or reflecting material, or the absence of such illumination, shall be part of the type or character of a sign.

(3) Regulations under this section may be made so as to apply either generally or in such circumstances only as may be specified in the regulations.

(4) Except as provided by this Act, no traffic sign shall be placed on or near a road except—

(a) a notice in respect of the use of a bridge;

(b) a traffic sign placed, in pursuance of powers conferred by a special Act of Parliament or order having the force of an Act, by the owners or operators of a tramway, light railway or trolley vehicle undertaking, a dock undertaking or a harbour undertaking; or

(c) a traffic sign placed on any land—

    (i) by a person authorised under the following provisions of this Act to place the sign on a highway, and

    (ii) for a purpose for which he is authorised to place it on a highway.

(5) Regulations under this section, or any authorisation under subsection (2) above, may provide that section 22 of the Road Traffic Act 1972 (drivers to comply with traffic directions) shall apply to signs of a type specified in that behalf by the regulations or, as the case may be, to the sign to which the authorisation relates.

(6) References in any enactment (including any enactment contained in this Act) to the erection or placing of traffic signs shall include references to the display of traffic signs in any manner, whether or not involving fixing or placing.

[The Traffic Signs Regulations and General Directions 1981 (SI 1981 No 859) have effect, in part, as if made under this section.]

*   *   *

PART VI

Speed Limits

81. General speed limit for restricted roads

(1) It shall not be lawful for a person to drive a motor vehicle on a restricted road at a speed exceeding 30 miles per hour.

(2) The Ministers acting jointly may by order made by statutory instrument and approved by a resolution of each House of Parliament increase or reduce the rate of speed fixed by subsection (1) above, either as originally enacted or as varied under this subsection.

[Paragraph 14 of Sched 10 to this Act provides as follows:

(1) A direction in an order made under section 1 of the Road Traffic Act 1934 that a length of road is to be deemed to be, or not to be, a road in a built-up area, if—

(a) by virtue of paragraph 10 of Schedule 8 to the 1967 Act it had effect as a direction that that length of road was to become, or (as the case may be) was to cease to be, a restricted road for the purposes of section 71 of that Act, and

(b) the direction continues so to have effect immediately before the commencement of this Act,

shall have the like effect for the purposes of section 81 of this Act.

(2) Any reference in any provision of an Act, or of any instrument (other than such an order as is mentioned in sub-paragraph (1) above) made under an enactment repealed by the Road Traffic Act 1960, to a road in a built-up area, if the provision is in force immediately before the commencement of this Act, shall be construed as a reference to a restricted road for the purposes of section 81 of this Act.]

82. What roads are restricted roads

(1) Subject to the provisions of this section and of section 84(3) of this Act, a road is a restricted road for the purposes of section 81 of this Act if there is provided on it a system of street lighting furnished by means of lamps placed not more than 200 yards apart.

(2) A direction may be given—

(a) that a specified road which is a restricted road for the purposes of section 81 of this Act shall cease to be a restricted road for those purposes, or

(b) that a specified road which is not a restricted road for those purposes shall become a restricted road for those purposes.

(3) Where, by a notice published as mentioned in section 1(4) of this Act, a date has been or is declared to be the date on which a part of a special road is open for use as a special road, that part of the road shall not be a restricted road for the purposes of section 81 of this Act or (if the date so declared is a date after the commencement of this section) shall not be a restricted road for those purposes on or after that date.

[Paragraph 16 of Sched 10 to this Act provides as follows:

(1) This paragraph applies to any road which—

(a) would have become a restricted road for the purposes of section 71 of the 1967 Act on 1st November 1982 as a result of the repeal of section 72(2) of the 1967 Act by section 61 of the Transport Act 1982; but

(b) by reason of section 61(2) of that Act was taken to have ceased to be a restricted road before that day by virtue of a direction duly given under section 72(3) of the 1967 Act and still in force at the beginning of that day; and

(c) did not become a restricted road at any time between the beginning of that day and the commencement of this Act.

(2) At the commencement of this Act, any road to which this paragraph applies shall be treated as if it were the subject of a direction duly given under section 82(2)(*a*) of this Act.

(3) Nothing in sub-paragraph (2) above prevents a direction under section 82(2)(*b*) of this Act being given in respect of any road to which this paragraph applies.]

83. Provisions as to directions under s 82(2)

(1) Any direction under section 82(2) of this Act in respect of a trunk road shall be given by means of an order made by the Secretary of State after giving public notice of his intention to make an order.

(2) Any such direction in respect of a road which is not a trunk road shall, subject to Parts I to III of Schedule 9 to this Act, be given by means of an order made by the local authority.

(3) Section 68(1)(*c*) of this Act shall apply to any order made under subsection (2) above.

84. Speed limits on roads other than restricted roads

(1) An order made under this subsection as respects any road may prohibit, either generally or during periods specified in the order, the driving of motor vehicles on that road at a speed exceeding that specified in the order.

(2) The power to make an order under subsection (1) above shall be exercisable by an authority after giving public notice of their intention to make an order under that subsection; and the authority having that power—

(*a*) as respects a trunk road, shall be the Secretary of State, and

(*b*) as respects any other road, subject to Parts I to III of Schedule 9 to this Act, shall be the local authority.

(3) While an order under subsection (1) above is in force as respects a road, that road shall not be a restricted road for the purposes of section 81 of this Act.

(4) This section does not apply to any part of a special road which is open for use as a special road.

(5) Section 68(1)(*c*) of this Act shall apply to any order made under subsection (1) above.

[*Paragraph 15 of Sched 10 to this Act provides as follows:*

Any limit of speed which was in force on 1st November 1962 by virtue of any direction, order or regulation given or made by an authority under section 19(2), 26 or 34 of the Road Traffic Act 1960, if—

(*a*) by virtue of paragraph 12 of Schedule 8 to the 1967 Act it was deemed to have been imposed by an order made by that authority under section 74(1) of the 1967 Act, and

(*b*) it continues to be in force immediately before the commencement of this Act

shall be deemed to have been imposed by an order made by that authority under section 84(1) of this Act and may be revoked or varied accordingly.]

85. Traffic signs for indicating speed restrictions

(1) For the purpose of securing that adequate guidance is given to drivers of motor

vehicles as to whether any, and if so what, limit of speed is to be observed on any road, it shall be the duty of the Secretary of State, in the case of a trunk road, to erect and maintain the prescribed traffic signs in such positions as may be requisite for that purpose.

(2) In the case of any road which is not a trunk road, it shall be the duty of the local authority—

(a) to erect and maintain the prescribed traffic signs in such positions as may be requisite in order to give effect to general or other directions given by the Secretary of State for the purpose mentioned in subsection (1) above, and

(b) to alter or remove traffic signs as may be requisite in order to give effect to such directions, either in consequence of the making of an order by the Secretary of State or otherwise.

(3) If a local authority makes default in executing any works required for the performance of the duty imposed on them by subsection (2) above, the Secretary of State may himself execute the works; and the expense incurred by him in doing so shall be recoverable by him from the local authority and, in England or Wales, shall be so recoverable summarily as a civil debt.

(4) Where no system of street lighting furnished by means of lamps placed not more than 200 yards apart is provided on a road, but a limit of speed is to be observed on the road, a person shall not be convicted of driving a motor vehicle on the road at a speed exceeding the limit unless the limit is indicated by means of such traffic signs as are mentioned in subsection (1) or subsection (2) above.

(5) In any proceedings for a contravention of section 81 of this Act, where the proceedings relate to driving on a road provided with such a system of street lighting as is specified in subsection (4) above, evidence of the absence of traffic signs displayed in pursuance of this section to indicate that the road is not a restricted road for the purposes of that section shall be evidence that the road is a restricted road for those purposes.

(6) Where by regulations made under section 17(2) of this Act a limit of speed is to be observed then, if it is to be observed—

(a) on all special roads, or

(b) on all special roads provided for the use of particular classes of traffic, or

(c) on all special roads other than special roads of such description as may be specified in the regulations, or

(d) as mentioned in paragraph (a), (b) or (c) above except for such lengths of special road as may be so specified,

this section shall not apply in relation to that limit (but without prejudice to its application in relation to any lower limit of maximum speed or, as the case may be, any higher limit of minimum speed, required by any such regulations to be observed on any specified length of any specified special road).

(7) The power to give general directions under subsection (2) above shall be exercisable by statutory instrument.

86. Speed limits for particular classes of vehicles

(1) It shall not be lawful for a person to drive a motor vehicle of any class on a road at a speed greater than the speed specified in Schedule 6 to this Act as the maximum speed in relation to a vehicle of that class.

(2)–(6) [Omitted.]

87. Exemption of fire brigade, ambulance and police vehicles for speed limits

No statutory provision imposing a speed limit on motor vehicles shall apply to any vehicle on an occasion when it is being used for fire brigade, ambulance or police purposes, if the observance of that provision would be likely to hinder the use of the vehicle for the purpose for which it is being used on that occasion.

88. Temporary speed limits

(1) Where it appears to the Secretary of State desirable to do so in the interests of safety or for the purpose of facilitating the movement of traffic, he may, after giving public notice of his intention to do so, by order prohibit, for a period not exceeding 18 months, the driving of motor vehicles—

(*a*) on all roads, or on all roads in any area specified in the order, or on all roads of any class so specified, or on all roads other than roads of any class so specified, or on any road so specified, at a speed greater than that specified in the order, or

(*b*) on any road specified in the order, at a speed less than the speed specified in the order, subject to such exceptions as may be so specified.

(2) Any prohibition imposed by an order under subsection (1) above may be so imposed either generally, or at times, on days or during periods specified in the order; but the provisions of any such order shall not, except in so far as may be provided by the order, affect the provisions of sections 81 to 84 of this Act.

(3) For the purposes of an order under subsection (1)(*a*) above, roads may be classified by reference to any circumstances appearing to the Secretary of State to be suitable for the purpose, including their character, the nature of the traffic to which they are suited or the traffic signs provided on them.

(4) The provisions of any order under subsection (1) above may be continued, either indefinitely or for a specified period, by an order of the Secretary of State made by statutory instrument, which shall be subject to annulment in pursuance of a resolution of either House of Parliament.

(5) Where by virtue of an order under this section a speed limit is to be observed, then—

(*a*) if it is to be observed on all roads, on all roads of any class specified in the order or on all roads other than roads of any class so specified, section 85 of this Act shall not apply in relation to that limit;

(*b*) if it is to be observed on all roads in any area and, at all points where roads lead into the area, is indicated as respects the area as a whole by means of such traffic signs as are mentioned in subsection (1) or subsection (2) of section 85 of this Act, the limit shall, for the purposes of subsection (4) of that section, be taken as so indicated with respect to all roads in the area.

(6) This section does not apply to any part of a special road which is open for use as a special road.

(7) If a person drives a motor vehicle on a road in contravention of an order under subsection (1)(*b*) above, he shall be guilty of an offence; but a person shall not be liable to be convicted of so driving solely on the evidence of one witness to the effect that, in the opinion of the witness, he was driving the vehicle at a speed less than that specified in the order.

[For the application of the fixed penalty procedure to offences under subs (7), see the Transport Act 1982, Part III, and Sched 1 (as amended by s 146 of and Sched 13, para 55, to this Act).]

89. Speeding offences generally

(1) A person who drives a motor vehicle on a road at a speed exceeding a limit imposed by or under any enactment to which this section applies shall be guilty of an offence.

(2) A person prosecuted for such an offence shall not be liable to be convicted solely on the evidence of one witness to the effect that, in the opinion of the witness, the person prosecuted was driving the vehicle at a speed exceeding a specified limit.

(3) The enactments to which this section applies are—

(a) any enactment contained in this Act except section 17(2);

(b) section 2 of the Parks Regulation (Amendment) Act 1926; and

(c) any enactment not contained in this Act, but passed after 1st September 1960, whether before or after the passing of this Act.

(4) If a person who employs other persons to drive motor vehicles on roads publishes or issues any time-table or schedule, or gives any directions, under which any journey, or any stage or part of any journey, is to be completed within some specified time, and it is not practicable in the circumstances of the case for that journey (or that stage or part of it) to be completed in the specified time without the commission of such an offence as is mentioned in subsection (1) above, the publication or issue of the time-table or schedule, or the giving of the directions, may be produced as prima facie evidence that the employer procured or (as the case may be) incited the persons employed by him to drive the vehicles to commit such an offence.

[For the application of the fixed penalty procedure to offences under subs (1), see the Transport Act 1982, Part III, and Sched 1 (as amended by s 146 of and Sched 13, para 55, to this Act).]

90. Approval of radar speed measuring devices

On the prosecution of a person for any speeding offence, evidence of the measurement of any speed by a device designed or adapted for measuring by radar the speed of motor vehicles shall not be admissible unless the device is of a type approved by the Secretary of State.

[Section 90 will come into force on a date to be announced; see s 145(2).]

91. Interpretation of Part VI

In sections 83 to 85 of this Act 'local authority'—

(a) in relation to a road in Greater London, means the Greater London Council;

(b) in relation to a road elsewhere in England and Wales, means the council of the county; and

(c) in relation to Scotland, means the local highway authority.

*   *   *

PART VIII

CONTROL AND ENFORCEMENT

*   *   *

98. Prosecution of offences and maximum penalties on conviction

(1) Schedule 7 to this Act shall have effect with respect to the prosecution and punishment of offences under the provisions of this Act specified in column 1 of that Schedule (of which the general nature is indicated in column 2 of the Schedule).

(2) In relation to each of those offences (in this section referred to as 'the specified offences')—

(a) column 3 of that Schedule shows whether the offence is punishable on summary conviction or on indictment or either in one way or the other;

(b) column 4 of that Schedule shows the maximum punishment by way of fine or imprisonment which (either generally or in circumstances specified in that column in relation to the offence) may be imposed on a person convicted of the offence in the way specified in relation to it in column 3 (that is to say, summarily or on indictment);

(c) column 5 of that Schedule shows in relation to which of the specified offences the court is empowered by section 93 (2) of the Road Traffic Act 1972 to order the person convicted to be disqualified for holding or obtaining a licence to drive a motor vehicle under Part III of that Act (whether or not the court is also required to disqualify him for a period by section 19(2) of the Transport Act 1981);

(d) column 6 of that Schedule shows in relation to which of the specified offences the court is required by section 101 (1) of the Road Traffic Act 1972 to order that particulars of the conviction, and, if it orders the person convicted to be disqualified, particulars of the disqualification, are to be endorsed on any licence held by him; and

(e) column 7 of that Schedule indicates, in relation to the specified offences, additional provisions of this Act (relating to the prosecution and trial of offences) which apply to those offences respectively.

(3) Any reference in that Schedule to a numbered section is a reference to the section bearing that number in this Act.

(4) Any reference in column 4 of that Schedule to a period of years shall be construed as a reference to a term of imprisonment of that duration; and any reference in that column to a level followed by a number shall be construed as a reference to a fine at the level bearing that number on the standard scale as defined by section 75 of the Criminal Justice Act 1982.

*   *   *

104. Immobilisation of vehicles illegally parked

(1) Subject to sections 105 and 106 of this Act, where a constable finds on a road a vehicle which has been permitted to remain at rest there in contravention of any prohibition or restriction imposed by or under any enactment, he may—

(a) fix an immobilisation device to the vehicle while it remains in the place in which he finds it; or

(b) move it from that place to another place on the same or another road and fix an immobilisation device to it in that other place;

or authorise another person to take under his direction any action he could himself take by virtue of paragraph (a) or (b) above.

(2) On any occasion when an immobilisation device is fixed to a vehicle in accordance with this section the constable or other person fixing the device shall also affix to the vehicle a notice—

(a) indicating that such a device has been fixed to the vehicle and warning that no attempt should be made to drive it or otherwise put it in motion until it has been released from that device;

(*b*) specifying the steps to be taken in order to secure its release; and

(*c*) giving such other information as may be prescribed.

(3) A vehicle to which an immobilisation device has been fixed in accordance with this section may only be released from that device by or under the direction of a constable.

(4) Subject to subsection (3) above, a vehicle to which an immobilisation device has been fixed in accordance with this section shall be released from that device on payment in any manner specified in the notice affixed to the vehicle under subsection (2) above of such charge in respect of the release as may be prescribed.

(5) A notice affixed to a vehicle under this section shall not be removed or interfered with except by or under the authority of the person in charge of the vehicle or the person by whom it was put in the place where it was found by the constable; and any person contravening this subsection shall be guilty of an offence.

(6) Any person who, without being authorised to do so in accordance with this section, removes or attempts to remove an immobilisation device fixed to a vehicle in accordance with this section shall be guilty of an offence.

(7) Where a vehicle is moved in accordance with this section before an immobilisation device is fixed to it, any power of removal under regulations for the time being in force under section 99 of this Act which was exercisable in relation to that vehicle immediately before it was so moved shall continue to be exercisable in relation to that vehicle while it remains in the place to which it was so moved.

(8) In relation to any vehicle which is removed in pursuance of any such regulations or under section 3 of the Refuse Disposal (Amenity) Act 1978 (duty of local authority to remove abandoned vehicles) from a place to which it was moved in accordance with this section, references in the definition of 'person responsible' in section 102(8) of this Act and section 5 of the said Act of 1978 mentioned above (recovery from person responsible of charges and expenses in respect of vehicles removed) to the place from which the vehicle was removed shall be read as references to the place in which it was immediately before it was moved in accordance with this section.

(9) In this section 'immobilisation device' means any device or appliance designed or adapted to be fixed to a vehicle for the purpose of preventing it from being driven or otherwise put in motion, being a device or appliance of a type approved by the Secretary of State for use for that purpose in accordance with this section.

(10)–(12) *[Omitted.]*

[Section 106 (to which this section is subject) states that ss 104 and 105 only extend to such areas as the Secretary of State specifies. At 1 January 1985, the only Order having effect under s 106 was the Immobilisation of Vehicles Illegally Parked (London Boroughs of Westminster, and Kensington and Chelsea) (Experimental) Order 1983 (SI 1983 No 218).

The term 'road' is defined by s 142(1) as 'any length of highway or of any other road to which the public has access, and includes bridges over which a road passes'.

Two immobilisation devices, the 'Wheelock "P" ' and the 'Bulldog Model II T' have been approved; see the Immobilisation Devices (Approval) Order 1983, dated 22 April 1983.]

105. Exemptions from s 104

(1) Subject to the following provisions of this section, section 104(1) of this Act shall not apply in relation to a vehicle found by a constable in the circumstances mentioned in that subsection if either—

(a) a current disabled person's badge is displayed on the vehicle; or

(b) the vehicle is in a meter bay within a parking place designated by a designation order.

(2) The exemption under subsection (1)(b) above shall not apply in the case of any vehicle if—

(a) the meter bay in which it was found was not authorised for use as such at the time when it was left there (referred to below in this section as the time of parking); or

(b) an initial charge was not duly paid at the time of parking; or

(c) there has been since that time any contravention in relation to the relevant parking meter of any provision made by virtue of section 46(2)(c) of this Act; or

(d) more than two hours have elapsed since the end of any period for which an initial charge was duly paid at the time of parking or (as the case may be) since the end of any unexpired time in respect of another vehicle available on the relevant parking meter at the time of parking.

(3) For the purposes of subsection (2)(a) above, a meter bay in a parking place designated by a designation order is not authorised for use as such at any time when—

(a) by virtue of section 49(1)(a) of this Act the parking place is treated for the purposes of sections 46 and 47 of this Act as if it were not designated by that order; or

(b) the use of the parking place or of any part of it that consists of or includes that particular meter bay is suspended under section 49(4) of this Act.

(4) In relation to any vehicle found in a meter bay within a parking place designated by a designation order, references in subsection (2) above to an initial charge are references to an initial charge payable in respect of that vehicle under section 45 or 50 of this Act.

(5) In any case where section 104(1) of this Act would apply in relation to a vehicle but for subsection (1)(a) above, the person guilty of contravening the prohibition or restriction mentioned in section 104(1) is also guilty of an offence under this subsection if the conditions mentioned in subsection (6) below are met.

(6) Those conditions are that at the time when the contravention occurred—

(a) the vehicle was not being used either by the person to whom the disabled person's badge was issued or under subsection (4) (institutional use) of section 21 of the Chronically Sick and Disabled Persons Act 1970 (badges for display on motor vehicles used by disabled persons); and

(b) he was not using the vehicle in circumstances falling within section 117(2)(b) of this Act.

(7) In this section, 'meter bay' means a parking space equipped with a parking meter; and the references in subsection (2) above to the relevant parking meter are references to the parking meter relating to the meter bay in which the vehicle in question was found.

[The term 'initial charge' is defined by ss 46(1), 142(1) as an amount payable in respect of an initial period in respect of a vehicle left in a parking place designated by order. The term 'parking meter' is defined by ss 46(2), 142(1), as apparatus of such type or design as may be approved either generally or specifically by the Secretary of State, being apparatus designed either (i) to indicate whether any charge has been paid and whether the period for which it has been paid or any further

period has elapsed, or (ii) to indicate the time and to issue tickets indicating the payment of a charge and the period in respect of which it has been paid.]

*   *   *

Enforcement of excess parking charges

107. Liability of vehicle owner in respect of excess parking charge

(1) This section applies where—

(*a*) an excess charge has been incurred in pursuance of an order under sections 45 and 46 of this Act;

(*b*) notice of the incurring of the excess charge has been given or affixed as provided in the order; and

(*c*) the excess charge has not been duly paid in accordance with the order;

and in the following provisions of this Part of this Act "the excess charge offence" means the offence under section 47 of this Act of failing duly to pay the excess charge.

(2) Subject to the following provisions of this section—

(*a*) for the purposes of the institution of proceedings in respect of the excess charge offence against any person as being the owner of the vehicle at the relevant time, and

(*b*) in any proceedings in respect of the excess charge offence brought against any person as being the owner of the vehicle at the relevant time,

it shall be conclusively presumed (notwithstanding that that person may not be an individual) that he was the driver of the vehicle at the time and, accordingly, that acts or omissions of the driver of the vehicle at that time were his acts or omissions.

(3) Subsection (2) above shall not apply in relation to any person unless, within the period of 6 months beginning on the day on which the notice of the incurring of the excess charge was given or affixed as mentioned in subsection (1)(*b*) above, a notice under section 108 of this Act has been served on him—

(*a*) by or on behalf of the authority which is the local authority for the purposes of sections 45 and 46 of this Act in relation to the parking place concerned, or

(*b*) by or on behalf of the chief officer of police.

(4) If the person on whom a notice under section 108 of this Act is served in accordance with subsection (3) above was not the owner of the vehicle at the relevant time, subsection (2) above shall not apply in relation to him if he furnishes a statutory statement of ownership to that effect in compliance with the notice.

(5) The presumption in subsection (2) above shall not apply in any proceedings brought against any person as being the owner of the vehicle at the relevant time if, in those proceedings, it is proved—

(*a*) that at the relevant time the vehicle was in the possession of some other person without the consent of the accused, or

(*b*) that the accused was not the owner of the vehicle at the relevant time and that he has a reasonable excuse for failing to comply with the notice under section 108 of this Act served on him in accordance with subsection (3) above.

[Modifications apply to this section and to s 108 where a notice under s 108 is served on a vehicle-hire firm and the vehicle to which the notice relates was let (at the relevant time) to another person under a hiring agreement (but not a hire-purchase agreement) for a fixed period of less than 6 months; see s 109.]

108. Notice in respect of excess parking

(1) A notice under this section shall be in the prescribed form, shall give particulars of the excess charge and shall provide that, unless the excess charge is paid before the expiry of the appropriate period, the person on whom the notice is served—

(a) is required, before the expiry of that period, to furnish to the authority or chief officer of police by or on behalf of whom the notice was served a statutory statement of ownership (as defined in Part I of Schedule 8 to this Act), and

(b) is invited, before the expiry of that period, to furnish to that authority or chief officer of police a statutory statement of facts (as defined in Part II of that Schedule).

(2) If, in any case where—

(a) a notice under this section has been served on any person, and

(b) the excess charge specified in the notice is not paid within the appropriate period,

the person so served fails without reasonable excuse to comply with the notice by furnishing a statutory statement of ownership he shall be guilty of an offence.

(3) If, in compliance with or in response to a notice under this section any person furnishes a statement which is false in a material particular, and does so recklessly or knowing it to be false in that particular, he shall be guilty of an offence.

(4) Where a notice under this section has been served on any person in respect of any excess charge—

(a) payment of the charge by any person before the date on which proceedings are begun for the excess charge offence, or, as the case may be, for an offence under subsection (2) above in respect of a failure to comply with the notice, shall discharge the liability of that or any other person (under this or any other enactment) for the excess charge offence or, as the case may be, for the offence under subsection (2) above;

(b) conviction of any person of the excess charge offence shall discharge the liability of any other person (under this or any other enactment) for that offence and the liability of any person for an offence under subsection (2) above in respect of a failure to comply with the notice; and

(c) conviction of the person so served of an offence under subsection (2) above in respect of a failure to comply with the notice shall discharge the liability of any person for the excess charge offence;

but, except as provided by this subsection, nothing in section 107 of this Act or this section shall affect the liability of any person for the excess charge offence.

[As to the liability of vehicle-hire firms, see the note to s 107.]

*   *   *

110. Time for bringing, and evidence in, proceedings for certain offences

(1) Proceedings in England or Wales for an offence under section 108(3) of this Act may be brought within a period of six months from the date on which evidence sufficient in the opinion of the prosecutor to warrant the proceedings came to his knowledge; but no such proceedings shall be brought by virtue of this section more than 3 years after the commission of the offence.

(2) *[Omitted.]*

(3) For the purposes of subsections (1) and (2) above a certificate signed by or on behalf of the prosecutor or, as the case may be, the Lord Advocate or the local authority, and stating the date on which evidence such as is mentioned in the subsection in question came to his or their knowledge, shall be conclusive evidence of that fact; and a certificate stating that matter and purporting to be so signed shall be deemed to be so signed unless the contrary is proved.

(4) Where any person is charged with the offence of failing to pay an excess charge, and the prosecutor produces to the court any of the statutory statements in Schedule 8 to this Act or a copy of a statement of liability (within the meaning of section 109 of this Act) purporting—

(a) to have been furnished in compliance with or in response to a notice under section 108 of this Act, and

(b) to have been signed by the accused,

the statement shall be presumed, unless the contrary is proved, to have been signed by the accused and shall be evidence (and, in Scotland, sufficient evidence) in the proceedings of any facts stated in it tending to show that the accused was the owner, the hirer or the driver of the vehicle concerned at a particular time.

111. Supplementary provisions as to excess charges

(1) The provisions of Schedule 8 to this Act shall have effect for the purposes of sections 107 to 109 of this Act (in this section referred to as 'the specified sections').

(2) In the specified sections—

'appropriate period', in relation to a notice under section 108 of this Act, means the period of 14 days from the date on which the notice is served, or such longer period as may be specified in the notice or as may be allowed by the chief officer of police or authority by or on behalf of whom the notice is served;

'driver', in relation to an excess charge and in relation to an offence of failing duly to pay such a charge, means the person driving the vehicle at the time when it is alleged to have been left in the parking place concerned;

'relevant time', in relation to an excess charge, means the time when the vehicle was left in the parking place concerned, notwithstanding that the period in respect of which the excess charge was incurred did not begin at that time.

(3) For the purposes of the specified sections the owner of a vehicle shall be taken to be the person by whom the vehicle is kept; and for the purpose of determining, in the course of any proceedings brought by virtue of the specified sections, who was the owner of the vehicle at any time, it shall be presumed that the owner was the person who was the registered keeper of the vehicle at that time.

(4) Notwithstanding the presumption in subsection (3) above, it shall be open to the defence in any proceedings to prove that the person who was the registered keeper of a vehicle at a particular time was not the person by whom the vehicle was kept at that time, and it shall be open to the prosecution to prove that the vehicle was kept by some other person at that time.

(5) A notice under section 108 of this Act may be served on any person—

(a) by delivering it to him or by leaving it at his proper address, or

(b) by sending it to him by post;

and, where the person on whom such a notice is to be served is a body corporate, it shall be duly served if it is served on the secretary or clerk of that body.

(6) For the purposes of subsection (5) above and of section 7 of the Interpretation Act 1978 (references to service by post) in its application to that subsection, the proper address of any person on whom such a notice is to be served—

(a) shall, in the case of the secretary or clerk of a body corporate, be that of the registered or principal office of that body or the registered address of the person who is the registered keeper of the vehicle concerned at the time of service, and

(b) shall in any other case be the last known address of the person to be served.

(7) References in this section to the person who was or is the registered keeper of a vehicle at any time are references to the person in whose name the vehicle was or is at that time registered under the Vehicles (Excise) Act 1971; and, in relation to any such person, the reference in subsection (6)(a) above to that person's registered address is a reference to the address recorded in the record kept under that Act with respect to that vehicle as being that person's address.

(8) For the purposes of sections 1(2) and 2(1) of the Magistrates' Courts Act 1980 (power to issue summons or warrant and jurisdiction to try offences), any offence under subsection (2) of section 108 of this Act shall be treated as committed at any address which at the time of service of the notice under that section to which the offence relates was the accused's proper address (in accordance with subsection (6) above) for the service of any such notice as well as at the address to which any statutory statement furnished in response to that notice is required to be returned in accordance with the notice.

PART IX

FURTHER PROVISIONS AS TO ENFORCEMENT

General provisions

112. Information as to identity of driver or rider

(1) This section applies to any offence under any of the foregoing provisions of this Act except—

(a) sections 43, 52, 88(7), 104, 105 and 108;

(b) the provisions of subsection (2) or (3) of section 108 as modified by subsections (2) and (3) of section 109; and

(c) section 35(7) in its application to England and Wales.

(2) Where the driver of a vehicle is alleged to be guilty of an offence to which this section applies—

(a) the person keeping the vehicle shall give such information as to the identity of the driver as he may be required to give—
(i) by or on behalf of a chief officer of police, or
(ii) in the case of an offence under section 35(4) or against section 47 of this Act, by or on behalf of a chief officer of police or, in writing, by or on behalf of the local authority for the parking place in question; and

(b) any other person shall, if required as mentioned in paragraph (a) above, give any information which it is in his power to give and which may lead to the identification of the driver.

(3) In subsection (2) above, references to the driver of a vehicle include references to the person riding a bicycle or tricycle (not being a motor vehicle); and—

(a) in relation to parking places designated by virtue of section 50(1) of this Act by an order of the Greater London Council, the reference in subsection (2) above to the local authority shall be construed as a reference to that Council, and

(b) in relation to an offence under section 61(5) of this Act, subsection (2)(a) above shall have effect as if, for subparagraphs (i) and (ii), there were substituted the words 'by a notice in writing given to him by a local authority in whose area the loading area in question is situated',

and in subsection (2)(a) above, as modified by paragraph (b) of this subsection, 'local authority' means any of the following, that is to say, a county council, the Greater London Council, a district council, a London borough council and the Common Council of the City of London.

(4) Except as provided by subsection (5) below, a person who fails to comply with the requirements of subsection (2)(a) above shall be guilty of an offence unless he shows to the satisfaction of the court that he did not know, and could not with reasonable diligence have ascertained, who was the driver of the vehicle or, as the case may be, the rider of the bicycle or tricycle; and a person who fails to comply with the requirements of subsection (2)(b) above shall be guilty of an offence.

(5) As regards Scotland, subsection (4) above shall not apply where the offence of which the driver of the vehicle is alleged to be guilty is an offence under section 61(5) of this Act.

113. Evidence by certificate

(1) In any proceedings in England or Wales for an offence to which section 112 of this Act applies (other than an offence under section 61(5)) a certificate in the prescribed form, purporting to be signed by a constable, and certifying that a person specified in the certificate stated to the constable—

(a) that a particular motor vehicle was being driven or used by, or belonged to, that person on a particular occasion, or

(b) that a particular motor vehicle on a particular occasion was used by, or belonged to, a firm, and that the person making the statement was, at the time of making it, a partner in that firm, or

(c) that a particular motor vehicle on a particular occasion was used by, or belonged to, a corporation, and that the person making the statement was, at the time of making it, a director, officer or employee of that corporation,

shall be admissible as evidence for the purpose of determining by whom the vehicle was being driven or used, or to whom it belonged, as the case may be, on that occasion.

(2) Nothing in subsection (1) above shall be deemed to make a certificate admissible as evidence in proceedings for an offence except in a case where, and to the like extent to which, oral evidence to the like effect would have been admissible in those proceedings.

(3) Nothing in subsection (1) above shall be deemed to make a certificate admissible as evidence in proceedings for an offence—

(a) unless a copy of the certificate has, not less than 7 days before the hearing or trial, been served in the prescribed manner on the person charged with the offence, or

(b) if that person, not later than 3 days before the hearing or trial or within such further time as the court may in special circumstances allow, serves a notice in the prescribed form and manner on the prosecutor requiring attendance at the trial of the person who signed the certificate.

(4) In this section 'prescribed' means prescribed by rules made by the Secretary of State under section 242 of the Road Traffic Act 1960 or section 181 of the Road Traffic Act 1972.

114. Proof of identity of driver

Where on the summary trial in England or Wales of an information for an offence to which section 112 of this Act applies—

(a) it is proved to the satisfaction of the court, on oath or in manner prescribed by rules made under section 144 of the Magistrates' Courts Act 1980, that a requirement under section 112(2) of this Act to give information as to the identity of the driver of a particular vehicle on the particular occasion to which the information relates has been served on the accused by post, and

(b) a statement in writing is produced to the court, purporting to be signed by the accused, that the accused was the driver of that vehicle on that occasion,

the court may accept that statement as evidence that the accused was the driver of that vehicle on that occasion.

115. Mishandling of parking documents and related offences

(1) A person shall be guilty of an offence who, with intent to deceive,—

(a) uses, or lends to, or allows to be used by, any other person, any ticket issued by a parking meter, or any authorisation by way of such a certificate, other means of identification or device as is referred to in any of sections 4(2), 4(3), 7(2), and 7(3) or any such permit or token as is referred to in section 46(2)(i) of this Act, or

(b) makes or has in his possession any document so closely resembling any such ticket or authorisation as to be calculated to deceive; or

(c) in Scotland, forges or alters any such ticket or authorisation.

(2) A person who knowingly makes a false statement for the purpose of procuring the grant or issue to himself or any other person of any such authorisation as is mentioned in subsection (1) above shall be guilty of an offence.

(3) *[Applies to Scotland.]*

116. Provisions supplementary to s 115

(1) If any person authorised in that behalf by or under a designation order has reasonable cause to believe that a document or article carried on a vehicle, or by the driver or person in charge of a vehicle, is a document or article in relation to which an offence has been committed under subsection (1) of section 115 of this Act (so far as that subsection relates to such authorisations as are referred to in it) or under subsection (2) of that section, he may detain that document or article, and may for that purpose require the driver or person in charge of the vehicle to deliver up the document or article; and if the driver or person in charge of the vehicle fails to comply with that requirement, he shall be guilty of an offence.

(2) When a document or article has been detained under subsection (1) above and—

(a) at any time after the expiry of 6 months from the date when that detention began no person has been charged since that date with an offence in relation to the document or article under subsection (1) or (2) of section 115 of this Act, and

(b) the document or article has not been returned to the person to whom the authorisation in question was issued or to the person who at that date was the driver or person in charge of the vehicle,

then, on an application made for the purpose to a magistrates' court (or, in Scotland, on a summary application made for the purpose to the sheriff court), the court shall make such order respecting disposal of the document or article and award such costs (or, in Scotland, expenses) as the justice of the case may require.

(3) Any of the following, but no other, persons shall be entitled to make an application under subsection (2) above with respect to a document or article, that is to say—

(a) the person to whom the authorisation was issued;

(b) the person who, at the date when the detention of the document or article began, was the driver or person in charge of the vehicle; and

(c) the person for the time being having possession of the document or article.

117. Wrongful use of disabled person's badge

(1) A person who is guilty of an offence in relation to a motor vehicle under a provision of this Act other than this section ('the first offence') is also guilty of an offence under this section if the conditions specified in subsection (2) below are satisfied.

(2) The conditions mentioned in subsection (1) above are that at the time of the commission of the first offence—

(a) a disabled person's badge was displayed on the motor vehicle;

(b) he was using the motor vehicle in circumstances where a disabled person's concession would be available to a disabled person's vehicle; and

(c) the vehicle was not being used either by the person to whom the badge was issued or under section 21(4) (institutional use) of the Chronically Sick and Disabled Persons Act 1970.

(3) In this section—

'disabled person's badge' means a badge of a form prescribed under section 21(1) of the Chronically Sick and Disabled Persons Act 1970; and

'disabled person's concession' means—

(a) an exemption from an order under this Act given by reference to disabled persons' vehicles; or

(b) a provision made in any order under this Act for the use of a parking place by disabled persons' vehicles.

[Disabled persons' badges are in the form prescribed in the Schedule to the Disabled Persons (Badges for Motor Vehicles) Regulations 1982 (SI 1982 No 1740) which were made under the Chronically Sick and Disabled Persons Act 1970, s 21.]

118. Contravention of regulations

If a person acts in contravention of, or fails to comply with, any regulations made by the Secretary of State under this Act (other than regulations made under section 28, Schedule 4, Part III of Schedule 9 or Schedule 12) and contravention of, or failure to comply with, the regulations is not made an offence under any other provision of this Act, he shall be guilty of an offence under this section.

[Schedule 4 to this Act relates to the control of off-street parking. Part III of Sched 9 relates to procedure as to certain orders. Schedule 12 makes temporary provision as to fixed penalties. For the text of s 28, see above.]

*   *   *

PART X

General and Supplementary Provisions

*   *   *

130. Application of Act to Crown

(1) Subject to the provisions of this section and section 132 of this Act, the provisions of this Act specified in subsection (2) below shall apply to vehicles and persons in the public service of the Crown.

(2) The provisions referred to in subsection (1) above are—

(a) sections 1 to 5, 9 to 16, 21 to 26, 38, 42, 45 to 51, 52(2) and (3), 58 to 60, 62 to 67, 69 to 71, 76 to 91, 99, 100, 104, 105, 125 and 126;

(b) except in relation to vehicles and persons in the armed forces of the Crown when on duty, sections 6 to 8; and

(c) Schedule 7, so far as it relates to offences under any of the provisions mentioned in paragraphs (a) and (b) above.

(3) In relation to vehicles used for naval, military or air force purposes, while being driven by persons for the time being subject to the orders of a member of the armed forces of the Crown, the Secretary of State may by regulations vary the provisions of any statutory provision imposing a speed limit on motor vehicles; but regulations under this subsection may provide that any variation made by the regulations shall have effect subject to such conditions as may be specified in the regulations.

(4) Where an offence under this Act is alleged to have been committed in connection with a vehicle in the public service of the Crown, proceedings may be brought in respect of the offence against a person nominated for the purpose on behalf of the Crown; and subject to subsection (5) below, where any such offence is committed any person so nominated shall also be guilty of an offence as well as any person actually responsible for the offence (but without prejudice to proceedings against any person so responsible).

(5) Where a person is convicted of an offence by virtue of subsection (4) above—

(a) no order may be made on his conviction save an order imposing a fine;

(b) payment of any fine imposed on him in respect of that offence may not be enforced against him; and

(c) apart from the imposition of any such fine, the conviction shall be disregarded for all purposes other than any appeal (whether by way of case stated or otherwise).

[Section 132 of this Act (to which this section is subject) makes special provision regarding certain Crown roads.]

*   *   *

SCHEDULE 6

Speed Limits for Vehicles of Certain Classes

PART I

Vehicles Fitted with Pneumatic Tyres on all Wheels
(see application provisions below the following Table)

Table

1	2	3		
Item No	Class of Vehicle	Maximum speed (in miles per hour) while vehicle is being driven on:		
		(a) Motorway	(b) Dual carriage-way road not being a motorway	(c) Other road
1	A passenger vehicle, motor caravan or dual-purpose vehicle not drawing a trailer being a vehicle with an unladen weight exceeding 3·05 tonnes or adapted to carry more than 8 passengers: (i) if not exceeding 12 metres in overall length (ii) if exceeding 12 metres in overall length	70 60	60 60	50 50
2	An invalid carriage	not applicable	20	20
3	A passenger vehicle, motor caravan, car-derived van or dual-purpose vehicle drawing one trailer	50	50	50
4	A passenger vehicle, motor caravan, car-derived van or dual-purpose vehicle drawing more than one trailer	40	20	20
5	(1) A goods vehicle having a maximum laden weight not exceeding 7·5 tonnes and which is not— (a) an articulated vehicle, or (b) drawing a trailer, or (c) a car-derived van (2) A goods vehicle which is— (a) (i) an articulated vehicle having a maximum laden weight not exceeding 7·5 tonnes, or (ii) a motor vehicle, other than a car-derived van, which is drawing one trailer where the aggregate maximum laden weight of the motor vehicle and the trailer does not exceed 7·5 tonnes	70 60	60 50	50 50

1	2	3		
Item No	Class of Vehicle	Maximum speed (in miles per hour) while vehicle is being driven on:		
		(a) Motorway	(b) Dual carriage-way road not being a motorway	(c) Other road
	(b) (i) an articulated vehicle having a maximum laden weight exceeding 7·5 tonnes, (ii) a motor vehicle having a maximum laden weight exceeding 7·5 tonnes and not drawing a trailer, or (iii) a motor vehicle drawing one trailer where the aggregate maximum laden weight of the motor vehicle and the trailer exceeds 7·5 tonnes	60	50	40
	(c) a motor vehicle, other than a car-derived van, drawing more than one trailer	40	20	20
6	A motor tractor (other than an industrial tractor), a light locomotive or a heavy locomotive—			
	(a) if the provisions about springs and wings as specified in paragraph 3 of Part IV of this Schedule are complied with and the vehicle is not drawing a trailer, or if those provisions are complied with and the vehicle is drawing one trailer which also complies with those provisions	40	30	30
	(b) in any other case	20	20	20
7	A works truck	18	18	18
8	An industrial tractor	not applicable	18	18

Application

This Part applies only to motor vehicles, not being track-laying vehicles, every wheel of which is fitted with a pneumatic tyre and to such vehicles drawing one or more trailers, not being track-laying vehicles, every wheel of which is fitted with a pneumatic tyre.

PART II

Vehicles (Other than Track-Laying Vehicles)
not Fitted with Pneumatic Tyres on all Wheels
(see application provisions below the following Table)

TABLE

1	2	3
Item No	Class of Vehicle	Maximum Speed (in miles per hour) while vehicle is being driven on a road
1	A motor vehicle, or in the case of a motor vehicle drawing one or more trailers, the combination, where— (a) every wheel is fitted with a resilient tyre, or (b) at least one wheel is fitted with a resilient tyre and every wheel which is not fitted with a resilient tyre is fitted with a pneumatic tyre	20
2	A motor vehicle, or in the case of a motor vehicle drawing one or more trailers, the combination, where any wheel is not fitted with either a pneumatic tyre or a resilient tyre	5

Application

This Part does not apply to—

(*a*) a motor vehicle which is a track-laying vehicle; or

(*b*) a motor vehicle which is not a track-laying vehicle but which is drawing one or more trailers any one of which is a track-laying vehicle.

PART III

TRACK-LAYING VEHICLES
(see application provisions below the following Table)

TABLE

1	2	3
Item No	Class of Vehicle	Maximum Speed (in miles per hour) while vehicle is being driven on a road
1	A motor vehicle, being a track-laying vehicle which is fitted with— (a) springs between its frame and its weight-carrying rollers, and (b) resilient material between the rim of its weight-carrying rollers and the surface of the road, and which is not drawing a trailer	20
2	A vehicle specified in item 1 above drawing one or more trailers each one of which is either— (a) a track-laying vehicle fitted with springs and resilient material as mentioned in that item, or (b) not a track-laying vehicle and each wheel of which is fitted with either a pneumatic tyre or a resilient tyre	20
3	A vehicle specified in item 1 above drawing one or more trailers any one of which is either— (a) a track-laying vehicle not fitted with springs and resilient material as mentioned in that item, or (b) not a track-laying vehicle and at least one wheel of which is not fitted with either a pneumatic tyre or a resilient tyre	5
4	A motor vehicle being a track-laying vehicle which is not fitted with springs and resilient material as mentioned in item 1 above, whether drawing a trailer or not	5
5	A motor vehicle not being a track-laying vehicle, which is drawing one or more trailers any one or more of which is a track-laying vehicle— (a) if every wheel of the motor vehicle and of any non-track-laying trailer is fitted with a pneumatic tyre or with a resilient tyre, and every trailer which is a track-laying vehicle is fitted with springs and resilient material as mentioned in item 1 (b) in any other case	20 5

Application

This Part applies to—

(a) a motor vehicle which is a track-laying vehicle, and

(b) a motor vehicle of any description which is drawing one or more trailers any one or more of which is a track-laying vehicle.

PART IV

APPLICATION AND INTERPRETATION

1. This Schedule does not apply to a vehicle which is being used for the purpose of experiments or trials under section 6 of the Road Improvements Act 1925 or section 283 of the Highways Act 1980.

2. In this Schedule—

'articulated vehicle', 'dual-purpose vehicle', 'industrial tractor', 'passenger vehicle', 'pneumatic tyre', 'track-laying', 'wheel' and 'works truck' have the same meanings as are respectively given to those expressions in Regulation 3(1) of the Motor Vehicles (Construction and Use) Regulations 1978 [SI 1978 No 1017];

'car-derived van' means a goods vehicle which is constructed or adapted as a derivative of a passenger vehicle and which has a maximum laden weight not exceeding 2 tonnes;

'construction and use requirements' has the same meaning as in section 40(7) of the Road Traffic Act 1972;

'dual-carriageway road' means a road part of which consists of a central reservation to separate a carriageway to be used by vehicles proceeding in one direction from a carriageway to be used by vehicles proceeding in the opposite direction;

'goods vehicle' has the same meaning as in section 196(1) of the Road Traffic Act 1972;

'maximum laden weight' in relation to a vehicle or a combination of vehicles means—

    (*a*) in the case of a vehicle, or combination of vehicles, in respect of which a gross weight not to be exceeded in Great Britain is specified in construction and use requirements, that weight;

    (*b*) in the case of any vehicle, or combination of vehicles, in respect of which no such weight is specified in construction and use requirements, the weight which the vehicle, or combination of vehicles, is designed or adapted not to exceed when in normal use and travelling on a road laden;

'motor caravan' has the same meaning as in Regulation 2(1) of the Motor Vehicles (Type Approval) (Great Britain) Regulations 1979 [SI 1979 No 1092];

'motorway' has the same meaning as in Regulation 3(1) of the Motorways Traffic (England and Wales) Regulations 1982 [SI 1982 No 1163], as regards England and Wales, and Regulation 2(2) of the Motorways Traffic (Scotland) Regulations 1964 [SI 1964 No 1002], as regards Scotland; and

'resilient tyre' means a tyre, not being a pneumatic tyre, which is soft or elastic.

3. The specification as regards springs and wings mentioned in item 6 of Part I of this Schedule is that the vehicle—

    (i) is equipped with suitable and sufficient springs between each wheel and the frame of the vehicle, and

    (ii) unless adequate protection is afforded by the body of the vehicle, is provided with wings or other similar fittings to catch, so far as practicable, mud or water thrown up by the rotation of the wheels.

4. A vehicle falling in two or more classes specified in Part I, II or III of this

Schedule shall be treated as falling within the class for which the lower or lowest speed limit is specified.

[The term 'motor caravan' is defined in reg 2(1) of the Motor Vehicles (Type Approval) (Great Britain) Regulations 1984 (SI 1984 No 981, which revoked and replaced SI 1979 No 1092), as follows: 'a motor vehicle which is constructed or adapted for the carriage of passengers and their effects and which contains, as permanently installed equipment, the facilities which are reasonably necessary for enabling the vehicle to provide mobile living accommodation for its users'.

Section 144(2) of this Act provides that the enactment of this Schedule (being a re-enactment, with or without modifications, of provisions contained in the Motor Vehicles (Variation of Speed Limits) Regulations 1984 (SI 1984 No 325) is without prejudice to the validity of the re-enacted provisions; and any question as to their validity should be determined as if the re-enacted provisions were contained in instruments made in the exercise of statutory powers.]

SCHEDULE 7

PROSECUTION FOR OFFENCES AND MAXIMUM PENALTIES ON CONVICTION

Section 98

1 Provision creating offence	2 General nature of offence	3 Mode of prosecution	4 Maximum penalty	5 Disqualification	6 Endorsement	7 Additional provisions
5	Contravention of traffic regulation order	Summarily	Level 3	—	—	Sections 112 to 114 apply
8	Contravention of order regulating traffic in Greater London	Summarily	Level 3	—	—	Sections 112 to 114 apply
11	Contravention of experimental traffic order	Summarily	Level 3	—	—	Sections 90 and 112 to 114 apply
13	Contravention of experimental traffic scheme in Greater London	Summarily	Level 3	—	—	Sections 112 to 114 apply
16(1)	Contravention of temporary prohibition or restriction	Summarily	Level 3	—	—	Sections 90 and 112 to 114 apply

1 Provision creating offence	2 General nature of offence	3 Mode of prosecution	4 Maximum penalty	5 Disqualification	6 Endorsement	7 Additional provisions
17(4)	Use of special road contrary to scheme or regulations	Summarily	Level 4	(a) Discretionary if committed in respect of a motor vehicle otherwise than by unlawfully stopping or allowing the vehicle to remain at rest on a part of a special road on which vehicles are in certain circumstances permitted to remain at rest (b) None in other cases	Obligatory if committed as mentioned in entry (a) in column 5 relating to this offence	Sections 90 and 112 to 114 apply
18(3)	Wrongful use of trunk road	Summarily	Level 3	—	—	Sections 112 to 114 apply
20(5)	Contravention of prohibition or restriction for roads of certain classes	Summarily	Level 3	—	—	Sections 112 to 114 apply
25(5)	Contravention of pedestrian crossing regulations	Summarily	Level 3	(a) Discretionary if committed in respect of a motor vehicle (b) None in other cases	Obligatory if committed in respect of a motor vehicle	Sections 112 to 114 apply
28(3)	Not stopping at school crossing	Summarily	Level 3	(a) Discretionary if committed in respect of a motor vehicle (b) None in other cases	Obligatory if committed in respect of a motor vehicle —	Sections 112 to 114 apply

29(3)	Contravention of order relating to street playground	Summarily	Level 3	(*a*) Discretionary if committed in respect of a motor vehicle (*b*) None in other cases	Obligatory if committed in respect of a motor vehicle —	Sections 112 to 114 apply
30(5)	As above (Greater London)	Summarily	Level 3	(*a*) Discretionary if committed in respect of a motor vehicle (*b*) None in other cases	Obligatory if committed in respect of a motor vehicle —	Sections 112 to 114 apply
35(4)	Contravention of order as to use of parking place	Summarily	(*a*) Level 3 in the case of an offence committed by a person in a street parking place reserved for disabled persons' vehicles or in an off-street parking place reserved for such vehicles, where that person would not be guilty of that offence if the motor vehicle in respect of which it is committed had been a disabled person's vehicle (*b*) Level 2 in any other case	—	—	Sections 35(8) and 112 to 114 apply
35(5)	Interference with apparatus for collecting charges	Summarily	Level 3	—	—	Sections 35(8) and 112 to 114 apply
35(7)	Plying for hire in parking place	Summarily	Level 2	—	—	Section 35(8) applies. Section 112 applies in Scotland

1 Provision creating offence	2 General nature of offence	3 Mode of prosecution	4 Maximum penalty	5 Disqualification	6 Endorsement	7 Additional provisions
43(5)	Unauthorised disclosure of information in respect of licensed parking place	Summarily	Level 3	—	—	—
43(10)	Failure to comply with term or conditions of licence to operate parking place	Summarily	Level 3	—	—	—
43(12)	Operation of public off-street parking place without a licence	Summarily	Level 5	—	—	—
47(1)	Contraventions relating to designated parking places	Summarily	(a) Level 3 in the case of an offence committed by a person in a street parking place reserved for disabled persons' vehicles where that person would not have been guilty of that offence if the motor vehicle in respect of which it was committed had been a disabled person's vehicle (b) Level 2 in any other case	—	—	Sections 47(4)–(7), 48, 52(3) and 112 to 114 apply
47(3)	Tampering with parking meter	Summarily	Level 3	—	—	Sections 47(5) and (7) and 112 to 114 apply

52(1) . . .	Misuse of parking device	Summarily	Level 2	—	—	Section 47(5) and (7) (as applied by section 52(2)) applies
53(5) . . .	Contravention of certain provisions of designation orders	Summarily	Level 3	—	—	Sections 112 to 114 apply
53(6) . . .	Other contraventions of designation orders	Summarily	Level 2	—	—	Sections 53(7) and 112 to 114 apply
61(5) . . .	Unauthorised use of loading area	Summarily	Level 3	—	—	Sections 112 and 114 apply
88(7) . . .	Contravention of minimum speed limit	Summarily	Level 3	—	—	—
89(1) . . .	Exceeding speed limit	Summarily	Level 3	Discretionary	Obligatory	Sections 89(2), 90 and 112 to 114 apply
104(5) . . .	Interference with notice as to immobilisation device	Summarily	Level 2	—	—	—
104(6) . . .	Interference with immobilisation device.	Summarily	Level 3	—	—	—
105(5) . . .	Misuse of disabled person's badge (immobilisation devices)	Summarily	Level 3	—	—	—
108(2) (or 108(2) as modified by 109(2) and (3)).	Non-compliance with notice (excess charge)	Summarily	Level 3	—	—	—

1 Provision creating offence	2 General nature of offence	3 Mode of prosecution	4 Maximum penalty	5 Disqualification	6 Endorsement	7 Additional provisions
108(3) (or 108(3) as modified by 109(2) and (3)).	False response to notice (excess charge)	Summarily	Level 5	—	—	Section 110 applies
112(4) ...	Failure to give information as to identity of driver	Summarily	Level 3	—	—	—
115(1) ...	Mishandling or faking parking documents	(a) On indictment (b) Summarily	(a) 2 years (b) The statutory maximum	—	—	Section 115(3) applies
115(2) ...	False statement for procuring authorisation	Summarily	Level 4	—	—	Section 115(3) applies
116(1) ...	Non-delivery of suspect document or article	Summarily	Level 3	—	—	—
117 ...	Wrongful use of disabled person's badge	Summarily	Level 3	—	—	—
118 ...	Contravention of regulations	Summarily	Level 3	—	—	—
129(3) ...	Failure to give evidence at inquiry	Summarily	Level 3	—	—	—

Sched 12 para 3(5)	Interference with fixed penalty notice	Summarily	Level 2	—	—	Paragraph 8 of Schedule 12 applies
para 6(2)	Non-compliance with notice to owner (fixed penalty)	Summarily	Level 3	—	—	
para 6(3)	False response to notice as above	Summarily	Level 5	—	—	

SCHEDULE 8

Statutory Statements (Excess Charges)

PART I

Statutory Statement of Ownership or Hiring

1. For the purposes of the specified sections, a statutory statement of ownership is a statement in the prescribed form, signed by the person furnishing it and stating—

   (*a*) whether he was the owner of the vehicle at the relevant time; and

   (*b*) if he was not the owner of the vehicle at the relevant time, whether he ceased to be the owner before, or became the owner after, the relevant time, and, if the information is in his possession, the name and address of the person to whom, and the date on which, he disposed of the vehicle or, as the case may be, the name and address of the person from whom, and the date on which, he acquired it.

2. For the purposes of the specified sections, a statutory statement of hiring is a statement in the prescribed form, signed by the person furnishing it, being the person by whom a statement of liability was signed and stating—

   (*a*) whether at the relevant time the vehicle was let to him under the hiring agreement to which the statement of liability refers; and

   (*b*) if it was not, the date on which he returned the vehicle to the possession of the vehicle-hire firm concerned.

PART II

Statutory Statement of Facts

3. For the purposes of the specified sections, a statutory statement of facts is a statement which is in the prescribed form and which—

   (*a*) states that the person furnishing it was not the driver of the vehicle at the relevant time;

   (*b*) states the name and address at the time when the statement is furnished of the person who was the driver of the vehicle at the relevant time; and

   (*c*) is signed both by the person furnishing it and by the person stated to be the driver of the vehicle at the relevant time.

PART III

Interpretation

4. In this Schedule 'the specified sections' has the meaning assigned to it by sub-section (1) of section 111 of this Act.

5. Subsections (2) to (4) of that section shall have effect for the purposes of Parts I and II of this Schedule as they have effect for the purposes of the specified sections.

6. In paragraph 2 above 'statement of liability', 'hiring agreement' and 'vehicle-hire firm' have the same meanings as in section 109 of this Act.

[Paragraph 3 of Sched 8 will come into operation on a date to be appointed under s 145(2). Until such date, para 20(2) of Sched 10 has effect: para 20(1). Paragraph 20(2) reads as follows:

   For the purposes of sections 107 to 109 of this Act, a statutory statement of facts is a statement which is in the prescribed form and which either—

(*a*) states that the person furnishing it was the driver of the vehicle at the relevant time and is signed by him; or

(*b*) states that that person was not the driver of the vehicle at the relevant time, states the name and address at the time the statement is furnished of the person who was the driver of the vehicle at the relevant time and is signed both by the person furnishing it and by the person stated to be the driver of the vehicle at the relevant time.

The expression 'statement of liability' is defined in s 109(6) as: 'a statement made by the hirer under a hiring agreement to which this section applies to the effect that the hirer acknowledges that he will be liable, as the owner of the vehicle, in respect of any excess charge which, during the currency of the hiring agreement, may be incurred with respect to the vehicle in pursuance of an order under sections 45 and 46 of this Act'.

Subsection (7) of s 109 states that the expression ' "hiring agreement" refers only to an agreement which contains such particulars as may be prescribed and does not include a hire-purchase agreement within the meaning of the Consumer Credit Act 1974', and the expression ' "vehicle-hire firm" means any person engaged in hiring vehicles in the course of a business'.]

The Theft Act 1968

(1968 c 60)

An Act to revise the law of England and Wales as to theft and similar or associated offences . . .   [26th July 1968]

*   *   *

12. Taking motor vehicle or other conveyance without authority

(1) Subject to subsections (5) and (6) below, a person shall be guilty of an offence if, without having the consent of the owner or other lawful authority, he takes any conveyance for his own or another's use or, knowing that any conveyance has been taken without such authority, drives it or allows himself to be carried in or on it.

(2) A person guilty of an offence under subsection (1) above shall on conviction on indictment be liable to imprisonment for a term not exceeding three years.

(3) Offences under subsection (1) above and attempts to commit them shall be deemed for all purposes to be arrestable offences within the meaning of section 2 of the Criminal Law Act 1967.

(4) If on the trial of an indictment for theft the jury are not satisfied that the accused committed theft, but it is proved that the accused committed an offence under subsection (1) above, the jury may find him guilty of the offence under subsection (1).

(5) Subsection (1) above shall not apply in relation to pedal cycles; but, subject to subsection (6) below, a person who, without having the consent of the owner or other lawful authority, takes a pedal cycle for his own or another's use, or rides a pedal cycle knowing it to have been taken without such authority, shall on summary conviction be liable to a fine not exceeding [level 3 on the standard scale].

(6) A person does not commit an offence under this section by anything done in the belief that he has lawful authority to do it or that he would have the owner's consent if the owner knew of his doing it and the circumstances of it.

(7) For the purposes of this section—

(a) 'conveyance' means any conveyance constructed or adapted for the carriage of a person or persons whether by land, water or air, except that it does not include a conveyance constructed or adapted for use only under the control of a person not carried in or on it, and 'drive' shall be construed accordingly; and

(b) 'owner', in relation to a conveyance which is the subject of a hiring agreement or hire-purchase agreement, means the person in possession of the conveyance under that agreement.

[Section 12 is printed as amended by the Criminal Justice Act 1982, ss 38, 46.]

*   *   *

25. Going equipped for stealing, etc

(1) A person shall be guilty of an offence if, when not at his place of abode, he has with him any article for use in the course of or in connection with any burglary, theft or cheat.

(2) A person guilty of an offence under this section shall on conviction on indictment be liable to a term of imprisonment for a term not exceeding three years.

(3) Where a person is charged with an offence under this section, proof that he had with him any article made or adapted for use in committing a burglary, theft or cheat shall be evidence that he had it with him for such use.

(4) Any person may arrest without warrant anyone who is or whom he, with reasonable cause, suspects to be, committing an offence under this section.

(5) For purposes of this section an offence under section 12 (1) of this Act of taking a conveyance shall be treated as theft and 'cheat' means an offence under section 15 of this Act.

The Transport Act 1968

(1968 c 73)

An Act to make further provision with respect to transport and related matters.

[25th October 1968]

ARRANGEMENT OF SECTIONS

*   *   *

PART V

REGULATION OF CARRIAGE OF GOODS BY ROAD

*   *   *

Operators' licences

*   *   *

Control of operating centres for goods vehicles on environmental grounds

*   *   *

Supplementary

*   *   *

PART VI

DRIVERS' HOURS

*   *   *

PART V

REGULATION OF CARRIAGE OF GOODS BY ROAD

*   *   *

Operators' licences

60. Users of certain goods vehicles to hold operators' licences

(1) Subject to subsection (2) of this section and to the other provisions of this Part of this Act, no person shall, after the appointed day for the purposes of this section, use a goods vehicle on a road for the carriage of goods—

(*a*) for hire or reward; or

(*b*) for or in connection with any trade or business carried on by him,

except under a licence granted under this Part of this Act (hereafter in this Part of this Act referred to as an 'operator's licence').

(2) Subsection (1) of this section shall not apply—

(*a*) to the use of a small goods vehicle as defined in subsection (4) of this section; or

(*b*) to the use of a vehicle of any class specified in regulations.

(3) It is hereby declared that, for the purposes of this Part of this Act, the performance by a local or public authority of their functions constitutes the carrying on of a business.

(4) For the purposes of subsection (2) (*a*) of this section a small goods vehicle is a goods vehicle which—

(*a*) does not form part of a vehicle combination and has a relevant plated weight not exceeding [3.5 tonnes] or (not having a relevant plated weight) has an unladen weight not exceeding [1525 kilograms]; or

(*b*) forms part of a vehicle combination (not being an articulated combination) which is such that—

   (i) if all the vehicles comprised in the combination (or all of them except any small trailer) have relevant plated weights, the aggregate of the relevant plated weights of the vehicles comprised in the combination (exclusive of any such trailer) does not exceed [3.5 tonnes];

   (ii) in any other case, the aggregate of the unladen weights of those vehicles (exclusive of any such trailer) does not exceed [1525 kilograms]; or

(*c*) forms part of an articulated combination which is such that—

   (i) if the trailer comprised in the combination has a relevant plated weight, the aggregate of the unladen weight of the motor vehicle comprised in the combination and the relevant plated weight of that trailer does not exceed [3.5 tonnes];

   (ii) in any other case, the aggregate of the unladen weights of the motor vehicle and the trailer comprised in the combination does not exceed [1525 kilograms].

In any provision of this subsection 'relevant plated weights' means a plated weight of the description specified in relation to that provision by regulations; and in paragraph (*b*) of this subsection 'small trailer' means a trailer having an unladen weight not exceeding [1020 kilograms].

(5) A person who uses a vehicle in contravention of this section shall be liable on summary conviction to a fine not exceeding [level 4 on the standard scale].

[Section 60 is printed as amended by the Road Traffic Acts 1960 and 1972, Road Traffic Regulation Act 1967, Transport Act 1968 (Metrication) (Regulations) 1981 (SI 1981 No 1371), Transport Act 1968 (Metrication) (Amendment) Regulations 1984 (SI 1984 No 177), and the Criminal Justice Act 1982, ss 38 and 46 (1).

The reference in s 60 (2) (b) to any class specified in regulations is a reference to any class specified in Sched 5 to the Goods Vehicles (Operators' Licences, Qualifications and Fees) Regulations 1984 (SI 1984 No 176); see reg 34 of those regulations.]

61. Authorised vehicles

(1) Subject to subsection (2) of this section, the vehicles authorised to be used under an operator's licence shall be—

(*a*) such motor vehicles, being vehicles belonging to the holder of the licence or in his possession under an agreement for hire-purchase, hire or loan, as are specified in the licence;

(*b*) trailers from time to time belonging to the holder of the licence or in his possession under an agreement for hire-purchase, hire or loan, not exceeding at any time such maximum number as is specified in the licence;

(*c*) unless the licence does not permit the addition of authorised vehicles under this paragraph and subject to subsection (3) of this section, motor vehicles not exceeding such maximum number as is specified in the licence, being vehicles belonging to the holder of the licence or in his possession under an agreement for hire-purchase, hire or loan, but acquired by him, or coming into his possession under such an agreement, only after the grant of the licence.

For the purposes of paragraphs (*b*) and (*c*) of this subsection different types of trailers or different types of motor vehicles, as the case may be, may be distinguished in a licence and a maximum number may be specified in the licence for trailers or vehicles of each type.

(2) An operator's licence shall not authorise the use of any vehicle unless the place which is for the time being its operating centre—

(*a*) is in the area of the licensing authority by whom the licence was granted; or

(*b*) is outside that area and has not been the operating centre of that vehicle for a period of more than three months.

For the purposes of paragraph (*b*) of this subsection, two or more successive periods which are not separated from each other by an interval of at least three months shall be treated as a single period having a duration equal to the total duration of those periods.

(3) A motor vehicle which, after the grant of an operator's licence, is acquired by the holder of the licence, or comes into his possession under an agreement for hire-purchase, hire or loan, and thereupon becomes an authorised vehicle by virtue of subsection (1) (*c*) of this section, shall cease to be an authorised vehicle on the expiration of one month from the date on which it was acquired by him or came into his possession unless before the expiration of that period he delivers to the licensing auth-

ority a notice in such form as the authority may require to the effect that the vehicle has been acquired by him, or has come into his possession, as the case may be.

(4) *[Licensing authority to vary licence on receipt of such notice.]*

(5) A motor vehicle specified in an operator's licence shall not, while it remains so specified, be capable of being effectively specified in any other operator's licence.

(6) *[Power to vary licence by removing vehicle therefrom.]*

* * *

Control of operating centres for goods vehicles on environmental grounds

[69A. Operating centres for authorised vehicles to be specified in operators' licences

(1) A person may not use a place in the area of any licensing authority as an operating centre for authorised vehicles under any operator's licence granted to him by that authority unless it is specified in that licence.

(2) *[Applicant for operator's licence to provide particulars.]*

(3) *[Licensing authority may require additional particulars.]*

(4) Any person who contravenes subsection (1) of this section shall be liable on summary conviction to a fine not exceeding [level 4 on the standard scale]].

[Section 69A was added by the Transport Act 1982, s 52 (2) and Sched 4, Part I, and is printed as amended by the Criminal Justice Act 1982, s 46 (1).]

* * *

[69C. Conditions as to the use of operating centres

(1) Subject to the following provisions of this section, a licensing authority may attach such conditions to an operator's licence as appear to him to be appropriate for the purpose of preventing or minimising any adverse effects on environmental conditions arising from the use for authorised vehicles under the licence of any operating centre of the holder of the licence in the area of the authority.

(2) The conditions which may be attached to a licence under this section shall be of such description as may be prescribed; and, without prejudice to the generality of the preceding provision, the descriptions which may be prescribed include conditions regulating—

(a) the number, type and size of motor vehicles or trailers which may at any one time be at any operating centre of the holder of the licence in the area of the authority for any prescribed purpose;

(b) the parking arrangements to be provided at or in the vicinity of any such centre; and

(c) the hours at which operations of any prescribed description may be carried on at any such centre.

(3) *[Power to vary or remove conditions.]*

(4) *[Time when conditions may be granted, etc.]*

(5) *[When condition may not be attached unless applicant first given opportunity to make representations.]*

(6) Any person who contravenes any condition attached under this section to a

licence of which he is the holder shall be liable on summary conviction to a fine not exceeding [level 4 on the standard scale]].

[Section 69C was added by the Transport Act 1982, s 52 (2) and Sched 4, Part I and is printed as amended by the Criminal Justice Act 1982, s 46 (1).]

Supplementary

*　　*　　*

92. Interpretation of Part V

(1) In this Part of this Act . . . , unless the context otherwise requires—

'articulated combination' means a combination made up of—

(*a*) a motor vehicle which is so constructed that a trailer may by partial superimposition be attached to the vehicle in such a manner as to cause a substantial part of the weight of the trailer to be borne by the vehicle, and

(*b*) a trailer attached to it as aforesaid;

'authorised vehicle' means, in relation to an operator's licence, a vehicle authorised to be used thereunder, whether or not it is for the time being in use for a purpose for which an operator's licence is required and whether it is specified therein as so authorised or, being of a type so authorised subject to a maximum number, belongs to the holder of the licence or is in his possession under an agreement for hire-purchase, hire or loan;

'carriage of goods' includes haulage of goods;

'carrier's licence' means a licence granted under Part IV of the Act of 1960;

'contravention', in relation to any condition or provision, includes a failure to comply with the condition or provision, and 'contravenes' shall be construed accordingly;

'driver' means, in relation to a trailer, the driver of the vehicle by which the trailer is drawn and 'drive' shall be construed accordingly;

'goods' includes goods or burden of any description;

'goods vehicle' means, subject to subsection (5) of this section, a motor vehicle constructed or adapted for use for the carriage of goods, or a trailer so constructed or adapted;

'large goods vehicle' shall be construed in accordance with section 71 of this Act;

['operating centre', in relation to any vehicles, means the base or centre at which the vehicle is normally kept, and references to an operating centre of the holder of an operator's licence are references to any place which is an operating centre for authorised vehicles under the licence;]

['owner', in relation to any land in England and Wales, means a person, other than a mortgagee not in possession, who, whether in his own right or as trustee for any other person, is entitled to receive the rack rent of the land or, where the land is not let at a rack rent, would be so entitled if it were so let;]

'prescribed' means prescribed by regulations;

'regulations' means regulations made by the [Secretary of State for Transport] under this Part of this Act;

'subsidiary' means a subsidiary as defined by section 154 of the Companies Act 1948;

'vehicle combination' means a combination of goods vehicles made up of one or more motor vehicles and one or more trailers all of which are linked together when travelling;

and any expression not defined above which is also used in the Act of 1960 has the same meaning as in that Act.

(2) For the purposes of this Part of this Act, the driver of a vehicle, if it belongs to him or is in his possession under an agreement for hire, hire-purchase or loan, and in any other case the person whose servant or agent the driver is, shall be deemed to be the person using the vehicle; and references to using a vehicle shall be construed accordingly.

(3) In this Part of this Act references to directing that an operator's licence be curtailed are references to directing (with effect for the remainder of the duration of the licence or for any shorter period) all or any of the following, that is to say—

(a) that any one or more of the vehicles specified in the licence be removed therefrom;

(b) that the maximum number of trailers or of motor vehicles specified in the licence in pursuance of section 61 (1) (b) or (c) of this Act be reduced;

(c) that the addition of authorised vehicles under the said section 61 (1) (c) be no longer permitted.

[(d) that any one or more of the places specified in the licence as operating centres be removed therefrom.]

(4) [Bankruptcy includes sequestration in Scotland.]

(5) In this Part of this Act . . . , references to goods vehicles do not include references to tramcars or trolley vehicles operated under statutory powers within the meaning of [section 198 of the Road Traffic Act 1972].

(6) Anything required or authorised by this Part of this Act to be done to or by a licensing authority by whom a licence . . . was granted may be done to or by any person for the time being acting as licensing authority for the area for which the first-mentioned authority was acting at the time of the granting of the licence . . .

[Section 92 is printed as amended by the Secretary of State for the Environment Order 1970 (SI 1970 No 1681); the Road Traffic Act 1972, s 203 (1), and Sched 7; the Secretary of State for Transport Order 1976 (SI 1976 No 1775); the Minister of Transport Order 1979 (SI 1979 No 571); the Transport Act 1980, s 69, and Sched 12, Part II; the Transfer of Functions (Transport) Order 1981 (SI 1981 No 238); and the Transport Act 1982, ss 52 (1), (3), 74 (2), Sched 4, Part II, and Sched 6.

Part V of this Act and regulations under that part have effect in relation to standard licences subject to the provisions of the Goods Vehicles (Operators' Licences, Qualifications and Fees) Regulations 1984 (SI 1984 No 176); see ibid, reg 36 (7). But, except as provided in reg 36, those regulations do not affect the application of Part V or of any regulations under that part to restricted licences; see reg 36 (8).]

*   *   *

PART VI

DRIVERS' HOURS

95. Vehicles and drivers subject to control under Part VI

(1), (1A) *[Omitted.]*

(2) This Part of this Act applies to—

(*a*) passenger vehicles, that is to say—
  (i) public service vehicles; and
  (ii) motor vehicles (other than public service vehicles) constructed or adapted to carry more than twelve passengers;

(*b*) goods vehicles, that is to say—
  (i) heavy locomotives, light locomotives, motor tractors and any motor vehicle so constructed that a trailer may by partial superimposition be attached to the vehicle in such a manner as to cause a substantial part of the weight of the trailer to be borne by the vehicle; and
  (ii) motor vehicles (except those mentioned in paragraph (*a*) of this subsection) constructed or adapted to carry goods other than the effects of passengers.

(3) This Part of this Act applies to any such person as follows (in this Part of this Act referred to as 'a driver'), that is to say—

(*a*) a person who drives a vehicle to which this Part of this Act applies in the course of his employment (in this Part of this Act referred to as 'an employee-driver'); and

(*b*) a person who drives such a vehicle for the purposes of a trade or business carried on by him (in this Part of this Act referred to as 'an owner-driver');

and in this Part of this Act references to driving by any person are references to his driving as aforesaid.

96. Permitted driving time and periods of duty

(1) Subject to the provisions of this section, a driver shall not on any working day drive a vehicle or vehicles to which this Part of this Act applies for periods amounting in the aggregate to more than ten hours.

(2) Subject to the provisions of this section, if on any working day a driver has been on duty for a period of, or for periods amounting in the aggregate to, five and a half hours and—

(*a*) there has not been during that period, or during or between any of those periods, an interval of not less than half an hour in which he was able to obtain rest and refreshment; and

(*b*) the end of that period, or of the last of those periods, does not mark the end of that working day,

there shall at the end of that period, or of the last of those periods, be such an interval as aforesaid.

(3) Subject to the provisions of this section, the working day of a driver—

(*a*) except where paragraph (*b*) or (*c*) of this subsection applies, shall not exceed eleven hours;

(*b*) if during that day he is off duty for a period which is, or periods which taken together are, not less than the time by which his working day exceeds eleven hours, shall not exceed twelve and a half hours;

(c) if during that day—

    (i) all the time when he is driving vehicles to which this Part of this Act applies is spent in driving one or more express carriages or contract carriages; and

    (ii) he is able for a period of not less than four hours to obtain rest and refreshment,

shall not exceed fourteen hours.

(4) Subject to the provisions of this section, there shall be, between any two successive working days of a driver, an interval for rest which—

(a) subject to paragraph (b) of this subsection, shall not be of less than eleven hours;

(b) if during both those days all or the greater part of the time when he is driving vehicles to which this Part of this Act applies is spent in driving one or more passenger vehicles, may, on one occasion in each working week, be of less than eleven hours but not of less than nine and a half hours;

and for the purposes of this Part of this Act a period of time shall not be treated, in the case of an employee-driver, as not being an interval for rest by reason only that he may be called upon to report for duty if required.

(5) Subject to the provisions of this section a driver shall not be on duty in any working week for periods amounting in the aggregate to more than sixty hours.

(6) Subject to the provisions of this section, there shall be, in the case of each working week of a driver, a period of not less than twenty-four hours for which he is off duty, being a period either falling wholly in that week or beginning in that week and ending in the next week; but—

(a) where the requirements of the foregoing provisions of this subsection have been satisfied in the case of any week by reference to a period ending in the next week, no part of that period (except any part after the expiration of the first twenty-four hours of it) shall be taken into account for the purpose of satisfying those requirements in the case of the next week; and

(b) those requirements need not be satisfied in the case of any working week of a driver who on each working day falling wholly or partly in that week drives one or more stage carriages if that week is immediately preceded by a week in the case of which those requirements have been satisfied as respects that driver or during which he has not at any time been on duty.

(7) If in the case of the working week of any driver the following requirement is satisfied, that is to say, that, in each of the periods of twenty-four hours beginning at midnight which make up that week, the driver does not drive a vehicle to which this Part of this Act applies for a period of, or periods amounting in the aggregate to, more than four hours, the foregoing provisions of this section shall not apply to him in that week, except that the provisions of subsections (1), (2) and (3) shall nevertheless have effect in relation to the whole of any working day falling partly in that week and partly in a working week in the case of which that requirement is not satisfied.

(8) If on any working day a driver does not drive any vehicle to which this Part of this Act applies—

(a) subsections (2) and (3) of this section shall not apply to that day, and

(b) the period or periods of duty attributable to that day for the purposes of subsection (5) of this section shall, if amounting to more than eleven hours, be treated as amounting to eleven hours only.

(9) For the purposes of subsections (1) and (7) of this section no account shall be taken of any time spent driving a vehicle elsewhere than on a road if the vehicle is being so driven in the course of operations of agriculture or forestry.

(10) For the purpose of enabling drivers to deal with cases of emergency or otherwise to meet a special need, the [Secretary of State for Transport] may by regulations—

(a) create exemptions from all or any of the requirements of subsections (1) to (6) of this section in such cases and subject to such conditions as may be specified in the regulations;

(b) empower the traffic commissioners or licensing authority for any area, subject to the provisions of the regulations—

(i) to dispense with the observance of all or any of those requirements (either generally or in such circumstances or to such extent as the commissioners or authority think fit) in any particular case for which provision is not made under paragraph (a) of this subsection;

(ii) to grant a certificate (which, for the purposes of any proceedings under this Part of this Act, shall be conclusive evidence of the facts therein stated) that any particular case falls or fell within any exemption created under the said paragraph (a)

and regulations under this subsection may enable any dispensation under paragraph (b) (i) of this subsection to be granted retrospectively and provide for a document purporting to be a certificate granted by virtue of paragraph (b) (ii) of this subsection to be accepted in evidence without further proof.

(11) If any of the requirements of [the domestic drivers' hours code] is contravened in the case of any driver—

(a) that driver; and

(b) any other person (being that driver's employer or a person to whose orders that driver was subject) who caused or permitted the contravention,

shall be liable on summary conviction to a fine not exceeding [level 4 on the standard scale]; but a person shall not be liable to be convicted under this subsection if he proves to the court—

(i) that the contravention was due to unavoidable delay in the completion of a journey arising out of circumstances which he could not reasonably have foreseen; or

(ii) in the case of a person charged under paragraph (b) of this subsection, that the contravention was due to the fact that the driver had for any particular period or periods driven or been on duty otherwise than in the employment of that person or, as the case may be, otherwise than in the employment in which he is subject to the orders of that person, and that the person charged was not, and could not reasonably have become, aware of that fact.

[(11A) Where, in the case of a driver member of the crew of a motor vehicle, there is in Great Britain a contravention of any requirement of the applicable community rules as to period of driving, or distance driven, or periods on or off duty, then the offender and any other person (being the offender's employer or a person to whose orders the offender was subject) who caused or permitted the contravention shall be liable on summary conviction to a fine not exceeding [level 4 on the standard scale].]

[(11B) But a person shall not be liable to be convicted under subsection (11A) if—

(a) he proves the matters specified in paragraph (i) of subsection (11); or

(b) being charged as the offender's employer or a person to whose orders the offender was subject, he proves the matters specified in paragraph (ii) of that subsection.]

(12) The [Secretary of State for Transport] may by order—

(a) direct that subsection (1) of this section shall have effect with the substitution for the reference to ten hours of a reference to nine hours, either generally or with such exceptions as may be specified in the order;

(b) direct that paragraph (a) of subsection (3) of this section shall have effect with the substitution for the reference to eleven hours of a reference to any shorter period, or remove, modify or add to the provisions of that subsection containing exceptions to the said paragraph (a);

(c) remove, modify or add to any of the requirements of subsections (2), (4), (5) or (6) of this section or any of the exemptions provided for by subsections (7), (8) and (9) thereof;

and any order under this subsection may contain such transitional and supplementary provisions as the [Secretary of State for Transport] thinks necessary or expedient, including provisions amending any definition in section 103 of this Act which is relevant to any of the provisions affected by the order.

[(13) In this Part of this Act 'the domestic drivers' hours code' means the provisions of subsection (1) to (6) of this section as for the time being in force (and, in particular, as modified, added to or substituted by or under any instrument in force under section 95 (1) of this Act or subsection (10) or (12) of this section).]

[Section 96 is printed as amended by the Secretary of State for the Environment Order 1970 (SI 1970 No 1681); the European Communities Act 1972, s 4, and Sched 4, para 9 (2); the Road Traffic (Drivers' Ages and Hours of Work) Act 1976, s 2 (1); the Secretary of State for Transport Order 1976 (SI 1976 No 1775); the Transport Act 1978, s 10; the Minister of Transport Order 1979 (SI 1979 No 571); the Transfer of Functions (Transport) Order 1981 (SI 1981 No 238) and the Criminal Justice Act 1982, ss 38 and 46(1). For the modification etc of the provisions of s 96 in particular circumstances, see 14.17–24 and 14.31–45 in Volume 1 of this book.

Section 95 (1) of this Act, as amended, inter alia, empowers the Secretary of State for Transport to make regulations substituting, adapting, etc, the provisions of this Part of this Act to take account of the operation of any Community provision.]

[97. Installation and use of recording equipment

[(1) No person shall use, or cause or permit to be used, a vehicle to which this section applies unless there is in the vehicle recording equipment which—

(a) has been installed in accordance with the Community Recording Equipment Regulations;

(b) complies with Annexes I and II to that Regulation; and

(c) is being used as provided by Articles 15 to 17 of that Regulation

and any person who contravenes this subsection shall be liable on summary conviction to a fine not exceeding level 4 on the standard scale.]

(2) A person shall not be liable to be convicted under subsection (1) of this section if he proves to the court that the vehicle in question was proceeding to a place where recording equipment which would comply with the requirements of Annexes I and II

of the Community Recording Equipment Regulation was to be installed in the vehicle in accordance with that Regulation.

(3) A person shall not be liable to be convicted under subsection (1) of this section by reason of the recording equipment installed in the vehicle in question not being in working order if he proves to the court that—

(*a*) it had not become reasonably practicable for the equipment to be repaired by an approved fitter or workshop; and

(*b*) the requirements of Article 18 (2) of the Community Recording Equipment Regulation were being complied with.

(4) A person shall not be liable to be convicted under subsection (1) of this section by reason of any seal on the recording equipment installed in the vehicle in question not being intact if he proves to the court that—

(*a*) the breaking or removal of the seal could not have been avoided;

(*b*) it had not become reasonably practicable for the seal to be replaced by an proved fitter or workshop; and

(*c*) in all other respects the equipment was being used as provided by Articles 15 to 17 of the Community Recording Equipment Regulation.

(5) For the purposes of this section recording equipment is used as provided by Articles 15 to 17 of the Community Recording Equipment Regulation if, and only if, the circumstances of its use are such that each requirement of those Articles is complied with.

(6) This section applies at any time to any vehicle to which this Part of this Act applies if, at that time, Article 3 of the Community Recording Equipment Regulation requires recording equipment to be installed and used in that vehicle; and in this section and sections 97A and 97B of this Act any expression which is also used in that Regulation has the same meaning as in that Regulation.

(7) In this Part of this Act—

'the Community Recording Equipment Regulation' means Council Regulation (EEC) No 1463/70 of 20th July 1970 on the introduction of recording equipment in road transport, as amended by Council Regulations (EEC) Nos 1787/73 and 2828/77, and as read with the Community Road Transport Rules (Exemptions) Regulations 1978 [and the Passenger and Goods Vehicles (Recording Equipment) (Amendment) Regulations 1984 *[SI 1984 No 144]*];

'recording equipment' means equipment for recording information as to the use of a vehicle.]

[Section 97 was substituted by the Passenger and Goods Vehicles (Recording Equipment) Regulations 1979 (SI 1979 No 1746) and was subsequently amended by the Passenger and Goods Vehicles (Recording Equipment) (Amendment) Regulations 1984 (SI 1984 No 144), reg 2 (2), and the Criminal Justice Act 1982, ss 39 (2), 46 (1) and Sched 3.]

[97A. Provisions supplementary to section 97

(1) If an employed crew member of a vehicle to which secton 97 of this Act applies fails—

(*a*) without reasonable excuse to return any record sheet which relates to him to his employer within twenty-one days of completing it; or

(*b*) where he has two or more employers by whom he is employed as a crew member of such a vehicle, to notify each of them of the name and address of the other or others of them,

he shall be liable on summary conviction to a fine not exceeding [level 4 on the standard scale].

(2) If the employer of crew members of a vehicle to which section 97 of this Act applies fails without reasonable excuse to secure that they comply with subsection (1) (*a*) of this section, he shall be liable on summary conviction to a fine not exceeding [level 4 on the standard scale].

(3) Where a crew member of a vehicle to which section 97 of this Act applies has two or more employers by whom he is employed as a crew member of such a vehicle, subsection (1) (*a*) and subsection (2) of this section shall apply as if any reference to his employer, or any reference which is to be construed as such a reference, were a reference to such of those employers as was the first to employ him in that capacity.]

[Section 97A was inserted by the Passenger and Goods Vehicles (Recording Equipment) Regulations 1979 (SI 1979 No 1746) and was subsequently amended by the Criminal Justice Act 1982, ss 39 (2), 46 (1), and Sched 3.]

[97B. Records etc produced by equipment may be used in evidence

(1) Where recording equipment is installed in a vehicle to which this Part of this Act applies, any record produced by means of the equipment shall, in any proceedings under this Part of this Act, be evidence, and in Scotland sufficient evidence, of the matters appearing from the record.

(2) Any entry made on a record sheet by a crew member for the purposes of Article 17 (2) or (3) or 18 (2) of the Community Recording Equipment Regulation shall, in any proceedings under this Part of this Act, be evidence, and in Scotland sufficient evidence, of the matters appearing from that entry.]

[Section 97B was inserted by the Passenger and Goods Vehicles (Recording Equipment) Regulations 1979 (SI 1979 No 1746).]

98. Written records

(1) *[Power to make regulations regarding keeping records and maintaining registers.]*

(2) *[Power to include supplementary and incidental provisions in regulations.]*

(2A) The requirements of regulations made under this section shall not apply as respects the driving of a vehicle to which section 97 of this Act applies and in relation which subsection (1) (*b*) of that section has come into force.)

(3) *[Dispensations from requirements imposed by this section.]*

(4) Any person who contravenes any regulations made under this section [or any requirement as to books, records or documents] of [the applicable Community rules]] shall be liable on summary conviction to a fine not exceeding [level 4 on the standard scale]; but the employer of an employee-driver shall not be liable to be convicted under this subsection by reason of contravening any such regulation whereby he is required to cause any records to be kept if he proves to the court that he has given proper instructions to his employees with respect to the keeping of the records and has from time to time taken reasonable steps to secure that those instructions are being carried out.

[(4A) A person shall not be liable to be convicted under subsection (4) of this section by reason of contravening any regulation made under this section if he proves to the court that, if the vehicle in question had been such a vehicle as is mentioned in subsection (2A) of this section, there would have been no contravention of the provisions of this Part of this Act so far as they relate to the use of such vehicles.]

(5) Any entry made by an employee-driver for the purposes of regulations under this section [or of [the applicable Community rules]] shall, in any proceedings under this Part of this Act, be admissible in evidence against his employer.

[Section 98 is printed as amended by the European Communities Act 1972, s 4, and Sched 4, para 9, the Road Traffic (Drivers' Ages and Hours of Work) Act 1976, s 2 (1), the Passenger and Goods Vehicles (Recording Equipment) Regulations 1979 (SI 1979 No 1746), and the Criminal Justice Act 1982, ss 38, 46 (1).

The Drivers' Hours (Keeping of Records) Regulations 1976 (SI 1976 No 1447), as amended, were made under s 98.]

99. Inspection of records and other documents

(1) An officer may, on production if so required of his authority, require any person to produce, and permit him to inspect and copy—

(a) any book or register which that person is required by regulations under section 98 of this Act to carry or have in his possession for the purpose of making in it any entry required by those regulations or which is required under those regulations to be carried on any vehicle of which that person is the driver;

(b) any . . . , book or register which that person is required by regulations under section . . . 98 of this Act to preserve;

[(bb) any record sheet which that person is required by Article 16 (2) of the Community Recording Equipment Regulation to retain or by Article 17 (5) of that Regulation to be able to produce;]

(c) if that person is the owner of a vehicle to which this Part of this Act applies, any other document of that person which the officer may reasonably require to inspect for the purpose of ascertaining whether the provisions of this Part of this Act or of regulations made thereunder have been complied with;

[(d) any . . . book, register or document required by [the applicable Community rules] or which the officer may reasonably require to inspect for the purpose of ascertaining whether the requirements of [the applicable Community rules] have been complied with;]

and that record [sheet], book, register or document shall, if the officer so requires by notice in writing served on that person, be produced at the office of the traffic commissioners or licensing authority specified in the notice within such time (not being less than ten days) from the service of the notice as may be so specified.

(2) An officer may, on production if so required of his authority—

[(a) at any time, enter any vehicle to which this Part of this Act applies and inspect that vehicle and any recording equipment installed in it and inspect and copy any record sheet on the vehicle on which a record has been produced by means of the equipment or an entry has been made;]

(b) at any time which is reasonable having regard to the circumstances of the case, enter any premises on which he has reason to believe that such a vehicle is kept or that any such [record sheets], books, registers or other documents as are mentioned in subsection (1) of this section are to be found, and inspect any such vehicle, and inspect and copy any such record [sheet], book, register or document which he finds there.

(3) For the purpose of exercising his powers under subsection (2) (*a*) and, in respect of a document carried on, or by the driver of, a vehicle, under subsection (1) (*a*) [or (*d*)] of this section, an officer may detain the vehicle in question during such time as is required for the exercise of that power.

(4) Any person who—

(*a*) fails to comply with any requirement under subsection (1) of this section; or

(*b*) obstructs an officer in the exercise of his powers under subsection (2) or (3) of this section,

shall be liable on summary conviction to a fine not exceeding [level 3 on the standard scale].

[(4A) A person shall not be liable to be convicted under subsection (4) of this section by reason of failing to comply with any requirement under subsection 6(1) (*a*) or (*b*) of this section if he proves to the court that, if the vehicle in question had been such a vehicle as is mentioned in section 98 (2A) of this Act, there would have been no contravention of the provisions of this Part of this Act so far as they relate to the use of such vehicles.]

(5) Any person who makes, or causes to be made, [any record or entry on a record sheet kept or carried for the purposes of the Community Recording Equipment Regulation or] section 97 of this Act or any entry in a [book, register or document kept or carried] for the purposes of regulations under section 98 thereof [or the applicable Community rules] which he knows to be false or, with intent to deceive, alters or causes to be altered any such record or entry shall be liable—

(*a*) on summary conviction, to a fine not exceeding [the prescribed sum];

(*b*) on conviction on indictment, to imprisonment for a term not exceeding two years.

(6) If an officer has reason to believe that an offence under subsection (5) of this section has been committed in respect of any record or document inspected by him under this section, he may seize that record or document; and where a record or document is seized as aforesaid and within six months of the date on which it was seized no person has been charged since that date with an offence in relation to that record or document under that subsection and the record or document has not been returned to the person from whom it was taken, a magistrates' court shall, on an application made for the purpose by that person or by an officer, make such order respecting the disposal of the record or document and award such costs as the justice of the case may require.

(7) *[Application to Scotland.]*

(8) In this section 'officer' means a certifying officer appointed under [section 56 of the Road Traffic Act 1972] a public service vehicle examiner, an examiner appointed under Part IV of that Act and any person authorised for the purposes of this section by the traffic commissioners or licensing authority for any area.

(9) The powers conferred by this section on an officer as defined in subsection (8) of this section shall be exercisable also by a police constable, who shall not, if wearing uniform, be required to produce any authority.

(10) In this section references to the inspection and copying of any record produced by means of equipment installed for the purposes of section 97 of this Act in a vehicle include references to the application to the record of any process for eliciting the information recorded thereby and to taking down the information elicited from it.

[Section 99 is printed as amended by the European Communities Act 1972, s 4, and Sched 4, para 9; the Road Traffic Act 1972, s 203 (1), and Sched 7; the Road Traffic (Drivers' Ages and Hours of Work) Act 1976, s 2 (1); the Passenger and Goods Vehicles (Recording Equipment) Regulations 1979 (SI 1979 No 1746); the Magistrates' Courts Act 1980, s 32 (2); and the Criminal Justice Act 1982, ss 38, 46 (1).

Officers are appointed under the Road Traffic Act 1972, s 56, to inspect goods vehicles. Part IV of that Act (ss 112–125) relates to the licensing of drivers of heavy goods vehicles.

The 'prescribed sum' is £2000 (Magistrates' Courts Act 1980, s 32 (9), as amended by the Criminal Penalties etc (Increase) Order 1984 (SI 1984 No 447).]

*　　　*　　　*

102. Application to the Crown and exemption for police and fire brigade

(1) Subject to subsection (2) of this section, this Part of this Act shall apply to vehicles and persons in the public service of the Crown.

(2) This Part of this Act shall not apply in the case of motor vehicles owned by the Secretary of State for Defence and used for naval, military or air force purposes or in the case of vehicles so used while being driven by persons for the time being subject to the orders of a member of the armed forces of the Crown.

[(3) Where an offence under this Part of this Act is alleged to have been committed in connection with a vehicle in the public service of the Crown, proceedings may be brought in respect of the offence against a person nominated for the purpose on behalf of the Crown; and subject to subsection (3A) below, where any such offence is committed any person so nominated shall also be guilty of the offence as well as any person actually responsible for the offence (but without prejudice to proceedings against any person so responsible).]

[(3A) Where a person is convicted of an offence by virtue of subsection (3) above—

(*a*) no order may be made on his conviction save an order imposing a fine;

(*b*) payment of any fine imposed on him in respect of that offence may not be enforced against him; and

(*c*) apart from the imposition of any such fine, the conviction shall be disregarded for all purposes other than any appeal (whether by way of case stated or otherwise).]

(4) This Part of this Act shall not apply in the case of motor vehicles while being used for police or fire brigade purposes.

[Section 102 is printed as amended by the Transport Act 1982, s 64.]

103. Interpretation, supplementary provisions, etc, for Part VI

(1) In this Part of this Act—

'agriculture' has the meaning assigned by section 109 (3) of the Agriculture Act 1947 or, in relation to Scotland, section 86 (3) of the Agriculture (Scotland) Act 1948;

['the applicable Community rules' means any directly applicable Community provision for the time being in force about the driving of road vehicles;]

['the Community Recording Equipment Regulation' has the meaning given by section 97 (7) of this Act;]

['the domestic drivers' hours code' has the meaning given by section 96 (13) of this Act;]

'driver', 'employee-driver' and 'owner-driver' have the meaning assigned by section 95 (3) of this Act;

'employer', in relation to an employee-driver, means the employer of that driver in the employment by virtue of which that driver is an employee-driver;

'licensing authority' has the same meaning as in Part V of this Act;

'prescribed' means prescribed by regulations made by the [Secretary of State for Transport];

['recording equipment' has the meaning given by section 97 (7) of this Act;]

['record sheet' includes a temporary sheet attached to a record sheet in accordance with Article 18 (2) of the Community Recording Equipment Regulation;]

['relevant Community provision' means any Community provision for the time being in force about the driving of road vehicles, whether directly applicable or not;]

'working day' in relation to any driver, means—

(a) any period during which he is on duty and which does not fall to be aggregated with any other such period by virtue of paragraph (b) of this definition; and

(b) where a period during which he is on duty is not followed by an interval for rest of not less than eleven hours or (where permitted by virtue of section 96 (4) (b) of this Act) of not less than nine and a half hours, the aggregate of that period and each successive such period until there is such an interval as aforesaid, together with any interval or intervals between periods so aggregated;

'working week' means, subject to subsection (5) of this section, a week beginning at midnight between Saturday and Sunday;

and any expression not defined above which is also used in the [Act of 1972] has the same meaning as in that Act,

(2) For the purposes of this Part of this Act a director of a company shall be deemed to be employed by it.

(3) In this Part of this Act references to a person driving a vehicle are references to his being at the driving controls of the vehicle for the purpose of controlling its movement, whether it is in motion or is stationary with the engine running.

(4) In this Part of this Act references to a driver being on duty are references—

(a) in the case of an employee-driver, to his being on duty (whether for the purpose of driving a vehicle to which this Part of this Act applies or for other purposes) in the employment by virtue of which he is an employee-driver, or in any other employment under the person who is his employer in the first-mentioned employment; and

(b) in the case of an owner-driver, to his driving a vehicle to which this Part of this Act applies for the purposes of a trade or business carried on by him or being otherwise engaged in work for the purposes of that trade or business, being work in connection with such a vehicle or the load carried thereby.

(5) The traffic commissioners or licensing authority for any area may, on the application of an owner-driver or of the employer of an employee-driver, from time to time direct that a week beginning at midnight between two days other than Saturday and Sunday shall be, or be deemed to have been, a working week in relation to that owner-driver or employee-driver; but where by virtue of any such direction a new working week begins before the expiration of a previous working week then, without prejudice to the application of the provisions of this Part of this Act in relation to the new work-

ing week, those provisions shall continue to apply in relation to the previous working week until its expiration.

(6) In [section] 98 (2) (*e*) of this Act 'a small goods vehicle' means a goods vehicle which has a plated weight of the prescribed description not exceeding [3500 kilograms] or (not having a plated weight) has an unladen weight not exceeding [1525 kilograms]; but the [Secretary of State for Transport] may by regulations direct that the foregoing provisions of this subsection shall have effect, in relation to either or both of those sections—

(*a*) with the substitution for either of the weights there specified of such other weight as may be specified in the regulations;

(*b*) with the substitution for either of those weights or for any other weight for the time being specified as aforesaid of a weight expressed in terms of the metric system, being a weight which is equivalent to that for which it is substituted or does not differ from it by more than 5 per cent thereof.

[(7) An offence under this Part of this Act may be treated for the purpose of conferring jurisdiction on a court (but without prejudice to any jurisdiction it may have apart from this subsection) as having been committed in any of the following places, that is to say—

(*a*) the place where the person charged with the offence was driving when evidence the offence first came to the attention of a constable or vehicle examiner;

(*b*) the place where that person resides or is or is believed to reside or be at the time when the proceedings are commenced; or

(*c*) the place where at that time that person or, in the case of an employee-driver, that person's employer or, in the case of an owner-driver, the person for whom he was driving, has his place or principal place of business or his operating centre for the vehicle in question.

In this subsection 'vehicle examiner' means an officer within the meaning of section 99 of this Act.]

(8) The enactments specified in Schedule 11 to this Act shall have effect subject to the amendments there specified.

(9) Any order made under section 166 (2) of this Act appointing a day for the purposes of any of the provisions of this Part of this Act may contain such transitional provisions as the [Secretary of State for Transport] thinks necessary or expedient as respects the application of any particular provision of this Part of this Act to a working week or working day falling partly before and partly after the date on which that provision comes into operation.

[Section 103 is printed as amended by the Road Traffic (Drivers' Ages and Hours of Work) Act 1976, ss 2 (1) and 3; the Minister of Transport Order 1979 (SI 1979 No 571); the Passenger antd Goods Vehicles (Recording Equipment) Regulations 1979 (SI 1979 No 1746); the Transfer of Functions (Transport) Order 1981 (SI 1981 No 238); and the Road Traffic Acts 1960 and 1972, Road Traffic Regulation Act 1967, and Transport Act 1968 (Metrication) Regulations 1981 (SI 1981 No 1373).

For the modification etc of the provisions of s 103 in particular circumstances, see Volume 1, 14.22.

The amendments to subs (6) effected by the Road Traffic Acts 1960 and 1972, Road Traffic Regulation Act 1967, and Transport Act 1968 (Metrication) Regulations 1981 (SI 1981 No 1373) (namely '3500 kilograms' for '3½ tons' and '1525 kilograms' for '30 hundredweight') were expressed specifically to apply to s 98 (2) of this Act.

The term 'agriculture' is stated by the Agriculture Act 1947, s 109 (3), to include 'horticulture, fruit growing, seed growing, dairy farming and livestock breeding and keeping, the use of land as grazing land, meadow land, river land, market gardens and nursery grounds, and the use of land for woodlands where that use is ancillary to the farming land for other agricultural purposes. . .'.

For the purposes of Part V of this Act (ie ss 59–94), the chairman of the traffic commissioners in each traffic area is the licensing authority (s 59 (1)).]

The Transport Act 1980

(1980 c 34)

An Act to . . . prohibit the display of certain roof-signs on vehicles other than taxis; . . . and for connected purposes. [30th June 1980]

* * *

64. Roof-signs on vehicles other than taxis

(1) There shall not, in any part of England and Wales outside the metropolitan police district and the City of London, be displayed on or above the roof of any vehicle which is used for carrying passengers for hire or reward but which is not a taxi—

    (*a*) any sign which consists of or includes the word 'taxi' or 'cab', whether in the singular or plural, or 'hire', or any word of similar meaning or appearance to any of those words, whether alone or as part of another word; or

    (*b*) any sign, notice, mark, illumination or other feature which may suggest that the vehicle is a taxi.

(2) Any person who knowingly—

    (*a*) drives a vehicle in respect of which subsection (1) is contravened; or

    (*b*) causes or permits that subsection to be contravened in respect of any vehicle,

shall be liable on summary conviction to a fine not exceeding [level 3 on the standard scale].

(3) In this section 'taxi' means a vehicle licensed under section 37 of the Town Police Clauses Act 1847, section 6 of the Metropolitan Carriage Act 1869, section 270 of the Burgh Police (Scotland) Act 1892 or any similar local enactment.

[Section 64 is printed as amended by the Criminal Justice Act 1982, s 46 (1).]

* * *

The Transport Act 1981

(1981 c 56)

An Act to make . . . further provision for promoting road safety   [31st July 1981]

ARRANGEMENT OF SECTIONS

*   *   *

PART IV

ROAD SAFETY

*   *   *

SCHEDULES

*   *   *

19. Disqualification for repeated offences

(1) Where a person is convicted of an offence involving obligatory or discretionary disqualificaton and the court does not order him to be disqualified (whether on that or any other conviction) but orders particulars of the conviction to be endorsed under section 101 of the 1972 Act, the endorsement ordered shall include—

(a) particulars of the offence, including the date when it was committed; and

(b) the number of penalty points shown in respect of the offence in Schedule 7 to this Act (or, where a range of numbers is so shown, a number falling within the range);

but if a person is convicted of two or more such offences the number of penalty points to be endorsed in respect of those of them that were committed on the same occasion shall be the number or highest number that would be endorsed on a conviction of one of those offences.

(2) Where a person is convicted of an offence involving obligatory or discretionary disqualification and the penalty points to be taken into account under subsection (3)

175

number twelve or more, the court shall order him to be disqualified for not less than the minimum period defined in subsection (4) unless the court is satisfied, having regard to all the circumstances not excluded by subsection (6), that there are grounds for mitigating the normal consequences of the conviction and thinks fit to order him to be disqualified for a shorter period or not to order him to be disqualified.

(3) The penalty points to be taken into account on the occasion of a person's conviction are—

(a) any that on that occasion will be ordered to be endorsed on any licence held by him or would be so ordered if he were not then ordered to be disqualified; and

(b) any that were on a previonus occasion ordered to be so endorsed, unless the offender has since that occasion and before the conviction been disqualified, whether under subsection (2) or under section 93 of the 1972 Act;

but if any of the offences was committed more than three years before another the penalty points in respect of that offence shall not be added to those in respect of the other.

(4) The minimum period referred to in subsection (2) is—

(a) six months if no previous disqualification imposed on the offender is to be taken into account; and

(b) one year if one, and two years if more than one, such disqualification is to be taken into account;

and a previous disqualification imposed on an offender is to be taken into account if it was imposed within the three years immediately preceding the commission of the latest offence in respect of which penalty points are taken into account under subsection (3).

(5) Where an offender is convicted on the same occasion of more than one offence involving obligatory or discretionary disqualification—

(a) not more than one disqualification shall be imposed on him under subsection (2); and

(b) in determining the period of the disqualification the court shall take into account all the offences; and

(c) for the purposes of any appeal any disqualification imposed under subsection (2) shall be treated as an order made on the conviction of each of the offences.

(6) No account is to be taken under subsection (2) of—

(a) any circumstances that are alleged to make the offence or any of the offences not a serious one;

(b) hardship, other than exceptional hardship; or

(c) any circumstances which, within the three years immediately preceding the conviction, have been taken into account under that subsection in ordering the offender to be disqualified for a shorter period or not ordering him to be disqualified.

(7) For the purposes of this section—

(a) an order for endorsement which was made before the commencement of this section counts as an order made in pursuance of subsection (1) for the endorsement of 3 penalty points, unless a disqualification was imposed on the offender on that or any subsequent occasion; and

(b) circumstances which have been taken into account under section 93 (3) of the

1972 Act in ordering an offender to be disqualified for a shorter period or not ordering him to be disqualified shall be treated as having been so taken into account under subsection (2) of this section.

(8) The Secretary of State may by order made by statutory instrument—

(a) alter the number of penalty points shown in Schedule 7 in respect of an offence (or, where a range of numbers is shown, alter that range); and

(b) provide for different numbers to be shown in respect of the same offence committed in different circumstances;

but no such order shall be made unless a draft of it has been laid before Parliament and approved by resolution of each House of Parliament.

(9) References in this section to disqualification do not include a disqualification imposed under section 103 of the 1972 Act (interim disqualification on committal to Crown Court) or section 44 of the Powers of Criminal Courts Act 1973 (disqualification by Crown Court where vehicle was used for commission of offence).

[In relation to endorsements made under Part III of the Transport Act 1982 (fixed penalty procedure), see generally s 34 (7) and (9) (a) of that Act.

The penalty points to be endorsed by a court on a conviction may have to be reduced to take into account an offence committed on the same occasion for which penalty points have been (or are liable to be) endorsed under Part III of the 1982 Act; subss 19 (1) (b) and (3) (a) have to be construed accordingly; see s 44 of the 1982 Act.]

20. Removal of disqualification

Where, in pursuance of section 93 (5) of the 1972 Act, a period of disqualification was imposed on an offender in addition to any other period or periods then, for the purpose of determining whether an application may be made under section 95 of that Act for the removal of either or any of the disqualifications the periods shall be treated as one continuous period of disqualification.

21. Offender escaping consequences of endorseable offence by deception

(1) Where—

(a) in dealing with a person convicted of an endorseable offence a court was deceived regarding any circumstances that were or might have been taken into account in deciding whether or for how long to disqualify him; and

(b) the deception constituted or was due to an offence committed by that person;

then, if he is convicted of that offence, the court by or before which he is convicted shall have the same powers and duties regarding an order for disqualification as had the court which dealt with him for the endorseable offence but shall in dealing with him take into account any order made on his conviction of the endorseable offence.

(2) In this section 'endorseable offence' means an offence involving obligatory or discretionary disqualification.

24. Electrically assisted pedal cycles

(1) *[Omitted.]*

(2) An electrically assisted pedal cycle of a class specified in regulations made for the purposes of section 193 of the 1972 Act and [section 140 of the Road Traffic Regulation Act 1984] shall not be driven on a road by a person under the age of fourteen; and if any person—

(a) drives such a pedal cycle; or

(*b*) knowing or suspecting that another person is under the age of fourteen, causes or permits him to drive such a pedal cycle;

in contravention of this subsection he shall be guilty of an offence.

(3) An offence under section (2) above shall be punishable on summary conviction with a fine not exceeding [level 2 on the standard scale].

[Section 24 is printed as amended by the Criminal Justice Act 1982, s 46 (1), and the Road Traffic Regulation Act 1984, s 146, and Sched 13, para 50.]

* * *

30. Interpretation of Part IV and consequential and minor amendments

(1) *[Omitted.]*

(2) Sections 19 to 21 shall be construed as if they were contained in Part III of the 1972 Act [and (without prejudice to the effect of the preceding provision) those sections shall apply to vehicles and persons in the public service of the Crown].

(3) *[Omitted.]*

[Section 30 is printed as amended by the Transport Act 1982, s 74 (1), Sched 5, para 25.

The reference in s 30 (2) to the '1972 Act' is a reference to the Road Traffic Act 1972 (see s 30 (1)). Part III of that Act relates to the licensing of drivers of vehicles.]

SCHEDULE 7

PENALTY POINTS

[PART I

OFFENCES WHERE DISQUALIFICATION OBLIGATORY FOR PRINCIPAL OFFENDERS EXCEPT FOR SPECIAL REASONS

Description of offence	Number of penalty points
Any offence involving obligatory disqualification (within the meaning of Part III of the Road Traffic Act 1972)—	
(*a*) in the case of an offence which is treated as an offence involving discretionary disqualification for the purposes of section 93 of that Act by virtue of subsection (6) of that section (offences committed by aiding, etc., the commission of an offence involving obligatory disqualification)	10
(*b*) in any other case	4]

PART II

OFFENCES WHERE DISQUALIFICATION DISCRETIONARY

A—Offences under Road Traffic Act 1972

Section of 1972 Act creating offence	Description	Number of penalty points
2	Reckless driving	10
3	Careless or inconsiderate driving	2—5
5 (2)	Being in charge of motor vehicle when unfit through drink or drugs	10
6 (1) (*b*)	Being in charge of motor vehicle with alcohol above prescribed limit	10
7 (4)	Failing to provide specimen for breath test	4
8 (7)	Failing to provide specimen for analysis	10
16	Carrying passenger on motor cycle contrary to section 16	1
22	Failing to comply with traffic directions	3
24	Leaving vehicle in dangerous position	3
25 (4)	Failing to stop after accident	5—9
25 (4)	Failing to give particulars or report accident	4—9
40 (5)	Contravention of construction and use regulations	3
84 (1)	Driving without licence	2
88 (6)	Failing to comply with conditions of licence	2
91 (1)	Driving with uncorrected defective eyesight	2

Section of 1972 Act creating offence	Description	Number of penalty points
91 (2)	Refusing to submit to test of eyesight	2
99 (b)	Driving while disqualified as under age	2
99 (b)	Driving while disqualified by order of court	6
143	Using, or causing or permitting use of, motor vehicle uninsured and unsecured against third-party risks	4—8
175	Taking in Scotland a motor vehicle without consent or lawful authority or driving, or allowing oneself to be carried in, a motor vehicle so taken	8

B—Offences under other Acts
(or, where stated, attempts)

Act and section creating offence or providing for its punishment	Description	Number of penalty points
[Road Traffic Regulation Act 1984 s 17 (4)]	Contravention of traffic regulations on special roads	3
[Road Traffic Regulation Act 1984 s 25 (5)]	Contravention of pedestrian crossing regulations	3
[Road Traffic Regulation Act 1984 s 28 (3)]	Failure to obey sign exhibited by school crossing patrol	3
[Road Traffic Regulation Act 1984 s 29 (3), s 30 (5)]	Contravention of order prohibiting or restricting use of street playground by vehicles	2
[Road Traffic Regulation Act 1984 s 89]	Exceeding a speed limit	3
Theft Act 1968 s 12	Taking or attempting to take conveyance without consent or lawful authority or driving or attempting to drive a motor vehicle so taken or allowing oneself to be carried in a motor vehicle so taken.	8
Theft Act 1968 s 25	Going equipped for stealing with reference to theft or taking of motor vehicle	8

C—Thefts and attempted thefts

Description of offence	Number of penalty points
Stealing or attempting to steal motor vehicle	8

Note: The descriptions of offences under A and B above indicate only their general nature.

[Schedule 7 is printed as amended by the Transport Act 1982, s 58, and the Road Traffic Regulation Act 1984, s 146, and Sched 13, para 51. (An amendment effected by the Transport Act 1982, s 74 (1), and Sched 5, para 26, related only to the period before ss 6 to 12 of the Road Traffic Act 1972 (as substituted by the Transport Act 1981) came into operation.)]

The Transport Act 1982

(1982 c 49)

An Act . . . to make new provisions extending and amending the law with respect to fixed penalties for certain road traffic offences and the procedure to be followed and the punishments available in cases where fixed penalties apply . . . and to make further miscellaneous amendments of the law relating to road traffic (including provisions relating to the testing and fitness of vehicles).

[28th October 1982]

ARRANGEMENT OF SECTIONS

* * *

PART III

FIXED PENALTIES

Fixed penalty offences and fixed penalty notices

Miscellaneous and supplemental

*   *   *

SCHEDULES

*   *   *

PART III

FIXED PENALTIES

Fixed penalty offences and fixed penalty notices

27. Fixed penalty offences and fixed penalty notices

(1) Subject to subsection (3) below, where a constable in uniform finds a person on any occasion and has reason to believe that on that occasion he is committing or has committed a fixed penalty offence, he may give him a fixed penalty notice in respect of the offence.

(2) Subject to subsection (4) below, where on any occasion a constable has reason to believe in the case of any stationary vehicle that a fixed penalty offence is being or has been committed in respect of it on that occasion, he may affix a fixed penalty notice in respect of the offence to that vehicle.

(3) A constable may not give a fixed penalty notice to any person under subsection (1) above in respect of an offence which appears to the constable to be an offence involving obligatory endorsement unless—

(a) he produces his driving licence for inspection by the constable; and

(b) the constable is satisfied, on inspecting the licence, that he would not be liable to be disqualified under section 19(2) of the Transport Act 1981 (disqualification where penalty points number twelve or more) if he were convicted of that offence; and

(c) he surrenders his driving licence to the constable to be retained and dealt with in accordance with this Part of this Act.

(4) A constable may not affix a fixed penalty notice to a vehicle under subsection (2) above in any case where the offence in question appears to the constable to be an offence involving obligatory endorsement.

(5) Subject to subsection (6) below and any limitation or exception mentioned in the entry relating to any enactment in column 2 of Schedule 1 to this Act, any offence in respect of a vehicle committed or punishable under an enactment specified in column 1 of that Schedule is a fixed penalty offence for the purposes of this Part of this Act.

(6) An offence committed under an enactment so specified is not a fixed penalty offence for those purposes if it is committed by causing or permitting a vehicle to be

used by another person in contravention of any provision made or restriction or pro-hibition imposed by or under any enactment.

(7) In relation to any enactment specified in column 1 of Schedule 1 to this Act—

(a) the enactment is contained in the Act referred to in the heading under which that enactment appears;

(b) the entry in column 2 of that Schedule broadly describes offences under that enactment, indicating any limitation or exception with respect to the offences under that enactment which are fixed penalty offences for the purposes of this Part of this Act; and

(c) the entry in column 3 of that Schedule indicates whether a person's driving licence is subject to endorsement on conviction of any such offence.

(8) In this Part of this Act, 'fixed penalty notice' means a notice offering the oppor-tunity of the discharge of any liability to conviction of the offence to which the notice relates by payment of a fixed penalty in accordance with this Part of this Act.

(9) For the purposes of this Part of this Act an offence is an offence involving obligatory endorsement if—

(a) it is an offence under an enactment specified in column 1 of Schedule 1 to this Act in relation to which there appears in column 3 of that Schedule the word 'obligatory' or the word 'obligatory' qualified by conditions relating to the offence; and

(b) where the word 'obligatory' is so qualified, the conditions are satisfied in the case of that offence.

[Section 27 will come into operation on a date to be announced; see s 76(2).]

28. Fixed penalty notices given at a police station

(1) In any case where—

(a) a constable in uniform finds a person on any occasion and has reason to believe that on that occasion he is committing or has committed a fixed penalty offence;

(b) the offence appears to the constable to be an offence involving obligatory endorsement; and

(c) the person concerned does not produce his driving licence for inspection by the constable;

the constable may give him a notice stating that if, within five days after the notice is given, he produces the notice together with his driving licence in person to a constable at the police station specified in the notice (being a police station chosen by the person concerned) and the requirements of subsection (2)(a) and (b) below are met he will then be given a fixed penalty notice in respect of the offence.

(2) If a person to whom a notice has been given under subsection (1) above pro-duces the notice together with his driving licence in person to a constable at the police station specified in the notice within five days after the notice was so given to him and the following requirements are met, that is—

(a) the constable is satisfied, on inspecting the licence, that he would not be liable to be disqualified under section 19(2) of the Transport Act 1981 (disquali-fication where penalty points number twelve or more) if he were convicted of that offence; and (*b*) he surrenders his driving licence to the constable to be retained and dealt with in accordance with this Part of this Act;

the constable shall give him a fixed penalty notice in respect of the offence to which the notice under subsection (1) above relates.

(3) A notice under subsection (1) above shall give such particulars of the circumstances alleged to constitute the offence to which it relates as are necessary for giving reasonable information about the alleged offence.

(4) This section does not apply in respect of offences committed in Scotland and a notice under this section may not specify a police station in Scotland.

[Section 28 will come into operation on a date to be announced; see s 76(2).]

29. Further provisions with respect to fixed penalty offences and notices

(1) Proceedings shall not be brought against any person for the offence to which a fixed penalty notice relates until the end of the period of twenty-one days following the date of the notice or such longer period (if any) as may be specified in the notice (referred to below in this Part of this Act as the suspended enforcement period in respect of the offence).

(2) The Secretary of State may by order provide for offences to become or (as the case may be) to cease to be fixed penalty offences for the purposes of this Part of this Act, and may make such modifications of the provisions of this Part of this Act as appear to him to be necessary for the purpose.

(3) The fixed penalty for a fixed penalty offence shall be—

(*a*) the amount appropriate in accordance with subsection (4) below in the case of that offence; or

(*b*) one-half of the maximum amount of the fine to which a person committing that offence would be liable on summary conviction

whichever is the less.

(4) Subject to subsection (5) below, the amount appropriate in the case of a fixed penalty offence is—

(*a*) £20 in the case of any offence involving obligatory endorsement; and

(*b*) £10 in any other case.

(5) The Secretary of State may by order substitute a different amount or amounts for either or both of the amounts for the time being specified in subsection (4) above.

(6) A fixed penalty notice—

(*a*) shall give such particulars of the circumstances alleged to constitute the offence to which it relates as are necessary for giving reasonable information about the alleged offence;

(*b*) shall state the period which, by virtue of subsecton (1) above, is the suspended enforcement period in respect of the offence, the amount of the fixed penalty and the justices' clerk or, in Scotland, the clerk of court to whom and the address at which the fixed penalty may be paid; and

(*c*) shall, when it is given under section 27(1) of this Act in respect of an offence committed in Scotland, be in the prescribed form.

(7) A notice affixed to a vehicle under section 27(2) of this Act shall not be removed or interfered with except by or under the authority of the driver or person in

charge of the vehicle or the person liable for the offence in question; and any person contravening this subsection shall be liable on summary conviction to a fine not exceeding [level 2 on the standard scale].

[Section 29 will come into operation on a date to be announced; see s 76(2).]

30. Effect where fixed penalty notice is given to the alleged offender

(1) This section applies where a fixed penalty notice relating to an offence has been given to any person under section 27(1) or 28(2) of this Act; and references below in this section to the recipient are references to the person to whom that notice was given.

(2) No proceedings shall be brought against the recipient for the offence to which the fixed penalty notice relates unless before the end of the suspended enforcement period he has given notice requesting a hearing in respect of that offence in the manner specified in the fixed penalty notice.

(3) Where—

(a) the recipient has not given notice requesting a hearing in respect of the offence to which the fixed penalty notice relates in the manner to specified; and

(b) the fixed penalty has not been paid in accordance with this Part of this Act before the end of the suspended enforcement period;

a sum equal to the fixed penalty plus one-half of the amount of that penalty may be registered under section 36 of this Act for enforcement against the recipient as a fine.

[Section 30 will come into operation on a date to be announced; see s 76(2).]

31. Effect where fixed penalty notice is affixed to the vehicle

(1) This section applies where a fixed penalty notice relating to an offence has been affixed to a vehicle under section 27(2) of this Act.

(2) Subject to subsection (3) below, where the fixed penalty has not been paid in accordance with this Part of this Act within the suspended enforcement period, a notice under this section (referred to below in this Part of this Act as a notice to owner) may be served by or on behalf of the chief officer of police on any person who appears to him (or to any person authorised to act on his behalf for the purposes of this section) to be the owner of the vehicle.

(3) Subsection (2) above does not apply where before the end of the suspended enforcement period any person has given notice requesting a hearing in respect of the offence in the manner specified in the fixed penalty notice, and the notice so given contains a statement by that person to the effect that he was the driver of the vehicle at the time when the offence is alleged to have been committed (referred to below in this Part of this Act as the time of the alleged offence).

(4) A notice to owner—

(a) shall give particulars of the alleged offence and of the fixed penalty concerned;

(b) shall state the period which, by virtue of subsection (9) below, is the period allowed for response to the notice; and

(c) shall indicate that, if the fixed penalty is not paid before the end of that period, the person on whom the notice is served is asked to furnish before the end of that period to the chief officer of police by or on whose behalf the notice was served a statutory statement of ownership (as defined in Part I of Schedule 3 to this Act).

(5) A person on whom a notice to owner relating to the offence is served under subsection (2) above shall not be liable in respect of the offence by virtue of this section if—

(a) he was not the owner of the vehicle at the time of the alleged offence; and

(b) he furnishes a statutory statement of ownership to that effect in response to the notice before the end of the period mentioned in subsection (4) above.

(6) Except as provided by subsection (5) above, and subject to section 32 of this Act, where—

(a) a notice to owner relating to the offence has been served on any person under subsection (2) above before the end of the period of six months beginning with the day on which the fixed penalty notice was affixed to the vehicle; and

(b) the fixed penalty has not been paid in accordance with this Part of this Act before the end of the period allowed under this section for response to the notice to owner;

proceedings may be brought in respect of the offence against the person on whom the notice to owner was served.

(7) Subject to subsection (8) below—

(a) for the purposes of the institution of proceedings by virtue of subsection (6) above against any person on whom a notice to owner has been served; and

(b) in any proceedings brought by virtue of that subsection against any such person;

it shall be conclusively presumed (notwithstanding that that person may not be an individual) that he was the driver of the vehicle at the time of the alleged offence and, accordingly, that acts or omissions of the driver of the vehicle at that time were his acts or omissions.

(8) That presumption shall not apply in any proceedings brought against any person by virtue of subsection (6) above if, in those proceedings, it is proved that at the time of the alleged offence the vehicle was in the possession of some other person without the consent of the accused.

(9) The period allowed for response to a notice to owner is the period of twenty-one days from the date on which the notice is served, or such longer period (if any) as may be specified in the notice.

[Section 31 will come into operation on a date to be announced; see s 76(2).]

32. Punishment without prosecution in cases within section 31

(1) Proceedings in respect of an offence to which a notice to owner relates shall not be brought against the person on whom the notice to owner was served unless he has given notice requesting a hearing in respect of that offence in the manner indicated by the notice to owner, before the end of the period allowed under section 31 of this Act for response to the notice to owner.

(2) Subject to subsection (5)(b) below, where apart from this section proceedings in respect of an offence to which a notice to owner relates would lie by virtue of section 31(6) of this Act against the person on whom that notice was served, a sum equal to the fixed penalty plus one-half of the amount of that penalty may be registered under section 36 of this Act for enforcement against that person as a fine.

(3) A notice to owner relating to any offence shall indicate that the person on

whom it is served may, before the end of the period allowed under section 31 of this Act for response to the notice, either—

    (*a*) give notice requesting a hearing in respect of the offence in the manner indicated by the notice; or

    (*b*) if he was not the driver of the vehicle at the time of the alleged offence and a person purporting to be the driver wishes to give notice requesting a hearing in respect of the offence, furnish together with a statutory statement of ownership furnished as requested in that notice a statutory statement of facts (as defined by Part II of Schedule 3 to this Act) which has effect by virtue of that Schedule as a notice requesting a hearing in respect of the offence given by the driver.

(4) In any case where a notice to owner relating to an offence may be served under section 31 of this Act, no proceedings shall be brought in respect of the offence against any person other than a person on whom such a notice has been served, unless he is identified as the driver of the vehicle at the time of the alleged offence in a statutory statement of facts furnished in pursuance of subsection (3)(*b*) above by a person on whom such a notice has been served.

(5) In any case where a person on whom a notice to owner relating to any offence has been served furnishes a statutory statement of facts in pursuance of subsection (3)(*b*) above—

    (*a*) any notice requesting a hearing in respect of the offence he purports to give on his own account shall be of no effect; and

    (*b*) the sum mentioned in subsection (2) above may not be registered for enforcement against him as a fine unless no summons or, in Scotland, complaint in respect of the offence in question is served on the person identified in that statement as the driver within the period of two months immediately following the period allowed under section 31 of this Act for response to the notice to owner.

(6) Once any sum determined by reference to the fixed penalty for an offence has been registered by virtue of this section under section 36 of this Act for enforcement as a fine against a person on whom a notice to owner relating to that offence has been served, no proceedings shall be brought against any other person in respect of that offence.

[Section 32 will come into operation on a date to be announced; see s 76(2).]

33. Payment of fixed penalties, effect of payment and supplementary provisions

(1) Payment of a fixed penalty under this Part of this Act shall be made to such justices' clerk or, in Scotland, clerk of court as may be specified in the fixed penalty notice relating to that penalty and, in England and Wales, sums paid by way of fixed penalty for an offence shall be treated for the purposes of section 61 of the Justices of the Peace Act 1979 (application of fines and fees) as if they were fines imposed on summary conviction for that offence.

(2) References below in this Part of this Act, in relation to any fixed penalty or fixed penalty notice, to the fixed penalty clerk are references to the clerk specified in accordance with subsection (1) above in the fixed penalty notice relating to that penalty or (as the case may be) in that fixed penalty notice.

(3) Without prejudice to payment by any other method, payment of a fixed penalty under this Part of this Act may be made by properly addressing, prepaying and posting a letter containing the amount of the penalty (in cash or otherwise) and,

unless the contrary is proved, shall be regarded as having been made at the time at which the letter would be delivered in the ordinary course of post.

A letter is properly addressed for the purposes of this subsection if it is addressed to the fixed penalty clerk at the address specified in the fixed penalty notice relating to the fixed penalty as the address at which the fixed penalty may be paid.

(4) In any proceedings a certificate—

(a) that payment of a fixed penalty was or was not received, by a date specified in the certificate, by the fixed penalty clerk; or

(b) that a letter containing an amount sent by post in payment of a fixed penalty was marked as posted on a date so specified;

shall, if the certificate purports to be signed by the fixed penalty clerk, be evidence (and, in Scotland, sufficient evidence) of the facts stated.

(5) Proceedings may not be brought against any person in respect of an offence to which a fixed penalty notice relates if the fixed penalty is paid in accordance with this Part of this Act before the end of the suspended enforcement period.

(6) Proceedings in respect of an offence to which a notice to owner relates may not be brought against any person identified as the driver of the vehicle in a statutory statement of facts furnished in response to the notice if the fixed penalty is paid in accordance with this Part of this Act before the end of the period allowed for response to that notice to owner under section 31 of this Act.

(7) Where, in England and Wales, a justices' clerk for a petty sessions area comprised in the area of one responsible authority (within the meaning of section 59 of the Justices of the Peace Act 1979) discharges functions in connection with a fixed penalty for an offence alleged to have been committed in a petty sessions area comprised in the area of another such authority—

(a) that other authority shall make to the first-mentioned authority such payment in connection with the discharge of those functions as may be agreed between them or, in default of such agreement, as may be determined by the Secretary of State; and

(b) any such payment between responsible authorities shall be taken into account in determining for the purposes of subsection (4) of section 59 of that Act the net cost to those authorities respectively of the functions referred to in subsection (1) of that section.

(8) Subsection (7) above does not apply to functions discharged in connection with a fixed penalty on or after the registration of a sum determined by reference to the penalty under section 36 of this Act.

[Section 33 will come into operation on a date to be announced; see s 76(2).]

34. Endorsement of licences without hearings

(1) Subject to subsection (2) below, where a person ('the licence holder') has surrendered his driving licence to a constable on the occasion when he was given a fixed penalty notice under section 27(1) or 28(2) of this Act, his licence may be endorsed in accordance with this section without any order of a court.

(2) A person's licence may not be endorsed under this section if before the end of the suspended enforcement period he gives notice requesting a hearing in respect of the offence to which the fixed penalty notice relates in the manner specified in the fixed penalty notice, unless proceedings against him in respect of the offence are

nevertheless excluded by section 33(5) of this Act by payment of the fixed penalty before the end of that period.

(3) A licence surrendered in accordance with section 27 or 28 of this Act shall be sent to the fixed penalty clerk.

(4) Where the fixed penalty is paid before the end of the suspended enforcement period, the fixed penalty clerk shall thereupon endorse the relevant particulars on the licence and return it to the licence holder.

(5) Where any sum determined by reference to the fixed penalty is registered under section 36 of this Act for enforcement against the licence holder as a fine, the fixed penalty clerk shall endorse the relevant particulars on the licence and return it to the licence holder—

    (a) if he is himself the clerk who registers that sum, on registration of that sum; and

    (b) in any other case, on being notified of the registration by the clerk who registers that sum.

(6) References above in this section to the relevant particulars are references to—

    (a) particulars of the offence, including the date when it was committed; and

    (b) the number of penalty points shown in respect of the offence in Schedule 7 to the Transport Act 1981 (points to be taken into account in determining disqualification for repeated offences).

(7) On the endorsement of a person's licence under this section he shall be treated for the purposes of—

    (a) the provisions of section 101(1) of the 1972 Act (power of court to order endorsement) with respect to evidence of any conviction ordered to be endorsed under that section;

    (b) subsections (5) to (8) of that section (effect and removal of endorsement);

    (c) section 182(2A) of that Act (admissibility in evidence of records maintained by the Secretary of State);

    (d) section 19 of the Transport Act 1981 (disqualification for repeated offences); and

    (e) the Rehabilitation of Offenders Act 1974;

as if he had been convicted of the offence and the endorsement had been made in pursuance of an order made on his conviction by a court under section 101(1) of the 1972 Act, and as if the particulars of the offence by virtue of subsection (6)(a) above were particulars of his conviction of that offence.

(8) In relation to any endorsement of a person's licence under this section—

    (a) the reference in section 101(6) of the 1972 Act to the order for endorsement; and

    (b) the references in section 182(2A) of that Act to any order made on a person's conviction;

shall be read as references to the endorsement itself.

(9) Where—

    (a) in endorsing any person's licence under this section the fixed penalty clerk is deceived as to whether endorsement under this section is excluded by section 41(2) of this Act by virtue of the fact that the licence holder would be liable to be disqualified under section 19(2) of the Transport Act 1981 if he were convicted of the offence; and (*b*) the deception constituted or was due to an offence committed by the licence holder;

then, if he is convicted of that offence, the court by or before which he is convicted shall have the same powers and duties as it would have had if it had convicted him of the offence of which particulars were endorsed under this section.

(10) On endorsing a person's licence under this section the fixed penalty clerk shall send notice of the endorsement and of the particulars endorsed to the Secretary of State.

[Section 34 will come into operation on a date to be announced; see s 76(2).]

35. Licence receipts

(1) Where a person surrenders his driving licence to a constable on receiving a fixed penalty notice given to him under section 27(1) or 28(2) of this Act, the constable shall issue a receipt for the licence under this section.

(2) In any case within subsection (1) above the fixed penalty clerk may issue a new receipt for the licence on the application of the licence holder.

(3) A receipt issued under this section shall cease to have effect—

(*a*) if issued by a constable, on the expiration of the period of one month beginning with the date of issue or such longer period as may be prescribed; and

(*b*) if issued by the fixed penalty clerk, on such date as he may specify in the receipt;

or, if earlier, on the return of the licence to the licence holder.

(4) A person shall not be guilty of an offence under section 101(4) of the 1972 Act by virtue of not having posted his licence or caused it to be delivered as mentioned in that subsection or by virtue of not producing it to the court for endorsement if—

(*a*) he has instead posted or caused to be delivered as so mentioned a current receipt for the licence issued under this section or surrenders any such receipt to the court at the hearing; and

(*b*) he produces the licence to the court immediately on its return.

(5) A person shall not be guilty of an offence under section 103(2) of that Act by virtue of not producing his licence to the court as required under that subsection if instead—

(*a*) he surrenders to the court a current receipt for the licence issued under this section; and

(*b*) he produces the licence to the court immediately on its return.

(6) A person shall not be guilty of an offence under section 161(4) of that Act by virtue of not producing his licence on being required to do so by a constable under any provision of that section if either—

(*a*) on the occasion when the production of his licence is so required he produces a current receipt for the licence issued under this section; or

(*b*) within five days after the production of his licence was so required he produces any such receipt in person at such police station as may have been specified by him on that occasion;

and in either case, if required to do so, he produces the licence in person, immediately on its return, at such police station as may have been so specified.

(7) Where a person is not in possession of his driving licence in consequence of the

fact that he has surrendered the licence as mentioned in subsection (1) above, he shall not be taken to be in breach of any duty under section 87 or 89 of that Act (revocation on disability and in certain other circumstances) to deliver his licence forthwith to the Secretary of State if he delivers his licence to the Secretary of State immediately on its return.

[Section 35 will come into operation on a date to be announced; see s 76(2).]

36. Registration of sums payable in default for enforcement as fines

(1) The following provisions of this section apply where by virtue of section 30(3) or 32(2) of this Act a sum determined by reference to the fixed penalty for any offence (referred to below in this section as a sum payable in default) may be registered under this section for enforcement against any person (referred to below in this section as the defaulter) as a fine.

(2) Subject to subsection (3) below, the chief officer of police may issue a certificate in respect of any sum payable in default stating that the sum is registrable under this section for enforcement against the defaulter as a fine (referred to below in this section as a registration certificate).

(3) Subsection (2) above shall not apply where the fixed penalty notice in question was given to the defaulter under section 27(1) of this Act in respect of an offence committed in Scotland; but in any such case the fixed penalty clerk—

(*a*) if the defaulter appears to him to reside within the jurisdiction of the court of summary jurisdiction of which he is himself the clerk, shall register the sum payable in default for enforcement as a fine by that court;

(*b*) in any other case, shall issue a registration certificate in respect of that sum.

(4) Where the chief officer of police or the fixed penalty clerk issues a registration certificate under this section, he shall cause it to be sent—

(*a*) if the defaulter appears to him to reside in England and Wales, to the clerk to the justices for the petty sessions area in which the defaulter appears to him to reside; and

(*b*) if the defaulter appears to him to reside in Scotland, to the clerk of a court of summary jurisdiction for the area in which the defaulter appears to him to reside.

(5) A registration certificate issued under this section in respect of any sum payable in default shall—

(*a*) give particulars of the offence to which the fixed penalty notice relates;

(*b*) indicate whether registration is authorised under section 30(3) or 32(2) of this Act; and

(*c*) state the name and last known address of the defaulter and the amount of the sum payable in default.

(6) Subject to subsection (7) below—

(*a*) where the clerk to the justices for a petty sessions area receives a registration certificate issued under this section in respect of any sum payable in default, he shall register that sum for enforcement as a fine in that area by entering it in the register of a magistrates' court acting for that area;

(*b*) where the clerk of a court of summary jurisdiction receives a registration certificate so issued he shall register the sum payable in default for enforcement as a fine by that court.

(7) The clerk receiving a registration certificate so issued shall not be required by subsection (6) above to register the sum payable in default if it appears to him that the defaulter does not reside in the petty sessions area or (as the case may be) within the jurisdiction of the court of summary jurisdiction in question; but in any such case he shall cause the certificate to be sent—

(a) if the defaulter appears to him to reside in England and Wales, to the clerk to the justices for the petty sessions area in which the defaulter appears to him to reside; and

(b) if the defaulter appears to him to reside in Scotland, to the clerk of a court of summary jurisdiction for the area in which the defaulter appears to him to reside;

and that subsection shall apply accordingly on receipt by that clerk of the certificate as it applies on receipt by the clerk to whom it was originally sent.

(8) Where the clerk to the justices for a petty sessions area or the clerk of a court of summary jurisdiction registers any sum under this section for enforcement as a fine, he shall thereupon give notice of registration to the defaulter, specifying the amount of that sum and giving the information with respect to the offence and the authority for registration included in the registration certificate by virtue of subsection (5)(a) and (b) above or (in a case within subsection (3)(a) above) the corresponding information.

(9) For the purposes of this section, where the defaulter is a body corporate, the place where that body resides and the address of that body shall be either of the following—

(a) the registered or principal office of that body; and

(b) the address which, with respect to the vehicle concerned, is the address recorded in the record kept under the Vehicles (Excise) Act 1971 as being that body's address.

(10) On the registration of any sum in a magistrates' court or a court of summary jurisdiction by virtue of this section any enactment referring (in whatever terms) to a fine imposed or other sum adjudged to be paid on the conviction of such a court shall have effect in the case in question as if the sum so registered were a fine imposed by that court on the conviction of the defaulter on the date of the registration.

(11) Accordingly, in the application by virtue of this section of the provisions of the Magistrates' Courts Act 1980 relating to the satisfaction and enforcement of sums adjudged to be paid on the conviction of a magistrates' court, section 85 of that Act (power to remit a fine in whole or in part) is not excluded by subsection (2) of that section (references in that section to a fine not to include any other sum adjudged to be paid on a conviction) from applying to a sum registered in a magistrates' court by virtue of this section.

[Section 36 will come into operation on a date to be announced; see s 76(2).]

37. Registration and endorsement invalid in certain circumstances

(1) This section applies where—

(a) a person who has received notice of the registration of a sum under section 36 of this Act for enforcement against him as a fine makes a statutory declaration to the effect mentioned in subsection (2) or (3) below (as the case may require); and

(b) that declaration is served within twenty-one days of the date on which the person making it received notice of the registration on the clerk of the relevant court.

(2) In a case where the registration was made by virtue of section 30(3) of this Act, the statutory declaration must state either—

(*a*) that the person making the declaration was not the person to whom the relevant fixed penalty notice was given; or

(*b*) that he gave notice requesting a hearing in respect of the alleged offence as permitted by the fixed penalty notice before the end of the suspended enforcement period.

(3) In a case where the registration was made by virtue of section 32(2) of this Act, the statutory declaration must state either—

(*a*) that the person making the declaration did not know of the fixed penalty concerned or of any fixed penalty notice or notice to owner relating to that penalty until he received notice of the registration; or

(*b*) that he was not the owner of the vehicle at the time of the alleged offence of which particulars are given in the relevant notice to owner and that he has a reasonable excuse for failing to comply with that notice; or

(*c*) that he gave notice requesting a hearing in respect of that offence as permitted by the relevant notice to owner before the end of the period allowed under section 31 of this Act for response to that notice.

(4) In any case within subsection (2)(*a*) above the relevant fixed penalty notice, the registration and any proceedings taken before the declaration was served for enforcing payment of the sum registered shall be void.

(5) Where in any such case the person to whom the relevant fixed penalty notice was given surrendered a driving licence held by the person making the declaration, any endorsement of that licence made under section 34 of this Act in respect of the offence in respect of which that notice was given shall be void.

(6) In any case within subsection (2)(*b*) above—

(*a*) the registration, any proceedings taken before the declaration was served for enforcing payment of the sum registered, and any endorsements, in respect of the offence in respect of which the relevant fixed penalty notice was given, made under section 34 of this Act before the declaration was served, shall be void; and

(*b*) the case shall be treated after the declaration is served as if the person making the declaration had given notice requesting a hearing in respect of the alleged offence as stated in the declaration.

(7) In any case within subsection (3)(*a*) or (*b*) above, the relevant notice to owner, the registration and any proceedings taken before the declaration was served for enforcing payment of the sum registered shall be void, but without prejudice, in a case within paragraph (*a*) of that subsection, to the service of a further notice to owner under section 31 of this Act on the person making the declaration.

This subsection applies whether or not the relevant notice to owner was duly served in accordance with that section on the person making the declaration.

(8) In any case within subsection (3)(*c*) above, no proceedings for enforcing payment of the sum registered shall be taken after the statutory declaration is served until the end of the period of twenty-one days following the date of that declaration; and where before the end of that period a notice is served by or on behalf of the chief officer of police on the person making the declaration asking him to furnish a new statutory statement of ownership to that chief officer of police before the end of the period

of twenty-one days from the date on which the notice is served, no such proceedings shall be taken until the end of the period allowed for response to that notice.

(9) Where in any case within subsection (3)(c) above—

(a) no notice is served by or on behalf of the chief officer of police in accordance with subsection (8) above; or

(b) such a notice is so served and the person making the declaration furnishes a new statutory statement of ownership in accordance with the notice;

the registration and any proceedings taken before the declaration was served for enforcing payment of the sum registered shall be void, and the case shall be treated after the time mentioned in subsection (10) below as if the person making the declaration had given notice requesting a hearing in respect of the alleged offence as stated in the declaration.

(10) The time referred to in subsection (9) above is—

(a) in a case within paragraph (a) of that subsection, the end of the period of twenty-one days following the date of the statutory declaration;

(b) in a case within paragraph (b) of that subsection, the time when the statement is furnished.

[Section 37 will come into operation on a date to be announced; see s 76(2).]

38. Provisions supplementary to section 37

(1) It shall be the duty of the clerk of the relevant court to cancel an endorsement of a licence under section 34 of this Act that is void by virtue of section 37(5) or (6)(a) of this Act on production of the licence to him for that purpose, and to send notice of the cancellation to the Secretary of State.

(2) In any case where notice is served by or on behalf of the chief officer of police in accordance with section 37(8), the chief officer of police shall cause the clerk of the relevant court to be notified of that fact immediately on service of the notice.

(3) In any case within section 37(2)(b) or (3), section 127(1) of the Magistrates' Courts Act 1980 (limitation of time) and section 331(1) of the Criminal Procedure (Scotland) Act 1975 (statutory offences time limit) shall have effect as if for the reference to the time when the offence was committed or (as the case may be) the time when the contravention occurred there were substituted a reference to the date of the statutory declaration made for the purposes of section 37(1).

(4) For the purposes of section 37(1) a statutory declaration shall be taken to be duly served on the clerk of the relevant court if it is delivered to him, left at his office, or sent in a registered letter or by the recorded delivery service addressed to him at his office.

(5) If on the application of a person who has received notice as mentioned in section 37(1)(a) it appears to the relevant court (which for this purpose may be composed of a single justice) that it was not reasonable to expect him to serve a statutory declaration to the effect there mentioned within the period allowed by that subsection, the court may accept service of such a declaration by that person after that period has expired; and a statutory declaration accepted under this subsection shall be taken to have been served as required by that subsection.

(6) References in section 37 to the relevant fixed penalty notice or the relevant notice to owner are references to the fixed penalty notice or notice to owner relating to the fixed penalty concerned.

(7) In this section—

(a) references to the relevant court are references—

    (i) in the case of a sum registered under section 36 of this Act for enforcement as a fine in a petty sessions area in England and Wales, to any magistrates' court acting for that area; and

    (ii) in the case of a sum registered under that section for enforcement as a fine by a court of summary jurisdiction in Scotland, to that court;

(b) references to the clerk of the relevant court, where that court is a magistrates' court, are references to a clerk to the justices for the petty sessions area for which that court is acting; and

(c) references to proceedings for enforcing payment of the sum registered are references to any process issued or other proceedings taken for or in connection with enforcing payment of that sum;

and for the purposes of that section and this section a person shall be taken as receiving notice of the registration of a sum under section 36 of this Act for enforcement against him as a fine when he receives notice either of the registration as such or of any proceedings for enforcing payment of the sum registered.

(8) Nothing in the provisions of section 37 shall be read as prejudicing any rights a person may have apart from those provisions by virtue of the invalidity of any action purportedly taken in pursuance of this Part of this Act which is not in fact authorised by this Part of this Act in the circumstances of the case (and accordingly references in those provisions to the registration of any sum or to any other action taken under or by virtue of any provision of this Part of this Act shall not be read as implying that the registration or action was validly made or taken in accordance with that provision).

[Section 38 will come into operation on a date to be announced; see s 76(2).]

39. Notification of court and date of trial

(1) On an occasion when a person is given a fixed penalty notice under section 27(1) or 28(2) of this Act in respect of an offence, he may be given written notification specifying the magistrates' court by which and the date on which the offence will be tried if that person gives notice requesting a hearing in respect of the offence as permitted by the fixed penalty notice.

(2) Subject to subsections (4) and (5) below, where—

(a) a person has been notified in accordance with this section of the court and date of trial of an offence in respect of which he has been given a fixed penalty notice; and

(b) that person has given notice requesting a hearing in respect of the offence as permitted by the fixed penalty notice;

the provisions of the Magistrates' Courts Act 1980 shall apply as mentioned in subsection (3) below.

(3) Those provisions shall have effect for the purpose of any proceedings in respect of that offence as if—

(a) the allegation in the fixed penalty notice with respect to that offence were an information duly laid in accordance with section 1 of that Act; and

(b) the notification of court and date of trial were a summons duly issued on that information by a justice of the peace for the area for which the magistrates' court notified as the court of trial acts, requiring the person notified to appear before that court to answer to that information and duly served on him on the date on which the notification was given.

(4) If, in the case within subsection (2) above, notice is served by or on behalf of the chief officer of police on the person who gave notice requesting a hearing stating that no proceedings are to be brought in respect of the offence concerned, that subsection shall not apply and no such proceedings may be brought against the person who gave notice requesting a hearing.

(5) Section 14 of that Act (proceedings invalid where accused did not know of them) is not applied by subsection (2) above in a case where a person has been notified in accordance with this section of the court and date of trial of an offence.

(6) This section does not apply to Scotland.

[Section 39 will come into operation on a date to be announced; see s 76(2).]

40. *[Court procedure in Scotland.]*

41. Provision for exclusion of fixed penalty procedures where fixed penalty notice mistakenly given

(1) This section applies where on inspection of any driving licence sent to him under section 34(3) of this Act after being surrendered by the licence holder on the occasion when he was given a fixed penalty notice in respect of an offence under section 27(1) or 28(2) of this Act it appears to the fixed penalty clerk that the licence holder would be liable to be disqualified under section 19(2) of the Transport Act 1981 (disqualification where penalty points number twelve or more) if he were convicted of that offence.

(2) The fixed penalty clerk may not endorse the licence under section 34 of this Act, but shall instead send it to the chief officer of police.

(3) Nothing in this Part of this Act shall prevent proceedings being brought in respect of the offence for which the fixed penalty notice was given, provided that those proceedings are commenced before the end of the period of six months beginning with the date on which that notice was given.

(4) If proceedings in respect of that offence are commenced before the end of that period, the case shall thereupon be treated in all respects as if no fixed penalty notice had been given in respect of the offence; and accordingly, any action taken in pursuance of any provision of this Part of this Act by reference to that fixed penalty notice shall be void (including, but without prejudice to the generality of the preceding provision, the registration under section 36 of this Act of any sum determined by reference to the fixed penalty for the offence for enforcement against the licence holder as a fine and any proceedings for enforcing payment of any such sum within the meaning of section 38 of this Act).

[Section 41 will come into operation on a date to be announced; see s 76(2).]

42, 43. *[Fixed penalties in Scotland.]*

Miscellaneous and supplemental

44. Treatment of other offences committed on the same occasion

(1) Section 19 of the Transport Act 1981 (disqualification for repeated offences) shall have effect subject to this section in any case where—

(*a*) a person is convicted of an offence involving obligatory or discretionary disqualification; and

(*b*) the court is satisfied that his driving licence has been or is liable to be endorsed under section 34 or 43 of this Act in respect of an offence committed on the same occasion as the offence of which he is convicted (referred to below in this section as the connected offence).

(2) The appropriate number of penalty points for the offence of which he is convicted shall be treated for the purposes of section 19 of that Act as reduced by the number of penalty points required to be endorsed on his licence under section 34 or 43 of this Act in respect of the connected offence.

(3) References in this section, in relation to any offence, to the appropriate number of penalty points for that offence are references—

(a) to the number of penalty points shown in respect of that offence in Schedule 7 to that Act, where only one number is so shown; and

(b) where a range of numbers is so shown, to a number falling within that range determined by the court as the appropriate number of penalty points in respect of that offence apart from the provisions of this section.

(4) In any case within subsection (1) above—

(a) the reference in section 19(1)(b) of that Act to the number of penalty points shown in respect of an offence in Schedule 7 to that Act or to a number falling within a range of numbers so shown shall be read in relation to the offence mentioned in subsection (1) above as referring to the number so shown in respect of that offence or (as the case may be) to a number within the range so shown, reduced in either case in accordance with subsection (2) above; and

(b) the reference in section 19(3)(a) to any penalty points that on the occasion of a person's conviction will be ordered to be endorsed on any licence held by him or would be so ordered if he were not then ordered to be disqualified shall be read as referring to any such points that will or would be so ordered after reduction in accordance with subsection (2) above of the appropriate number of penalty points for any offence of which he is then convicted.

[Section 44 will come into operation on a date to be announced; see s 76(2).]

45. Hired vehicles

(1) This section applies where—

(a) a notice to owner has been served on a vehicle-hire firm;

(b) at the time of the alleged offence the vehicle in respect of which the notice was served was let to another person by the vehicle-hire firm under a hiring agreement to which this section applies; and

(c) within the period allowed under section 31 of this Act for response to the notice the firm furnishes to the chief officer of police by or on whose behalf the notice was served the documents mentioned in subsection (2) below.

(2) Those documents are a statement on an official form, signed by or on behalf of the firm, stating that at the time of the alleged offence the vehicle concerned was hired under a hiring agreement to which this section applies, together with—

(a) a copy of that hiring agreement; and

(b) a copy of a statement of liability signed by the hirer under that hiring agreement.

(3) In this section a 'statement of liability' means a statement made by the hirer under a hiring agreement to which this section applies to the effect that the hirer acknowledges that he will be liable, as the owner of the vehicle, in respect of any fixed

penalty offence which may be committed with respect to the vehicle during the currency of the hiring agreement and giving such information as may be prescribed.

(4) In any case where this section applies sections 31 and 32 of this Act shall have effect as if—

(a) any reference to the owner of the vehicle were a reference to the hirer under the hiring agreement; and

(b) any reference to a statutory statement of ownership were a reference to a statutory statement of hiring;

and accordingly references in this Part of this Act (with the exceptions mentioned below) to a notice to owner shall include references to a notice served under section 31 of this Act as it applies by virtue of this section.

This subsection does not apply to references to a notice to owner in this section or in section 47(7)(b) of or Part I of Schedule 3 to this Act.

(5) In any case where this section applies a person authorised in that behalf by the chief officer of police to whom the documents mentioned in subsection (2) above are furnished may, at any reasonable time within six months after service of the notice to owner (and on production of his authority) require the firm to produce the originals of the hiring agreement and statement of liability in question.

(6) If a vehicle-hire firm fails to produce the original of a document when required to do so under subsection (5) above, this section shall thereupon cease to apply (and section 31 shall apply accordingly in any such case after that time as it applies in a case where the person on whom the notice to owner was served has failed to furnish a statutory statement of ownership in response to the notice within the period allowed).

(7) This section applies to a hiring agreement under the terms of which the vehicle concerned is let to the hirer for a fixed period of less than six months (whether or not that period is capable of extension by agreement between the parties or otherwise); and any reference in this section to the currency of the hiring agreement includes a reference to any period during which, with the consent of the vehicle-hire firm, the hirer continues in possession of the vehicle as hirer, after the expiry of the fixed period specified in the agreement, but otherwise on terms and conditions so specified.

(8) In this section—

'hiring agreement' refers only to an agreement which contains such particulars as may be prescribed and does not include a hire-purchase agreement within the meaning of Consumer Credit Act 1974; and

'vehicle-hire firm' means any person engaged in hiring vehicles in the course of business.

[Section 45 will come into operation on a date to be announced; see s 76(2).]

46. False statements in response to notices to owner

(1) If, in response to a notice to owner, any person furnishes a statement which is false in a material particular and does so recklessly or knowing it to be false in that particular, he shall be liable on summary conviction to a fine not exceeding [level 5 on the standard scale].

(2) Proceedings for an offence in England and Wales under subsection (1) above may be brought within a period of six months from the date on which evidence sufficient in the opinion of the prosecutor to warrant the proceedings came to his knowledge, but no such proceedings shall be brought by virtue of this section more than three years after the commission of the offence.

(3), (4) *[Proceedings in Scotland.]*

(5) For the purposes of subsections (2) and (3) above, a certificate signed by or on behalf of the prosecutor or, as the case may be, the procurator fiscal and stating the date on which such evidence as is there mentioned came to his knowledge shall be conclusive evidence of that fact; and a certificate stating that matter and purporting to be so signed shall be taken to be so signed unless the contrary is proved.

[Section 46 will come into operation on a date to be announced; see s 76(2).
Section 46(1) is printed as amended by the Criminal Justice Act 1982, s 46(1).]

47. Evidence in fixed penalty notice cases

(1) In any proceedings a certificate that a copy of a statement by a constable with respect to the alleged offence (referred to below in this section as a constable's witness statement) was included in or given with a fixed penalty notice or a notice under section 28(1) of this Act given to the accused on a date specified in the certificate shall, if the certificate purports to be signed by the constable who gave the accused the notice, be evidence of service of a copy of that statement by delivery to the accused on that date.

(2) In any proceedings a certificate that a copy of a constable's witness statement was included in or served with a notice to owner served on the accused in a manner and on a date specified in the certificate shall, if the certificate purports to be signed by any person employed by the police authority for the police area in which the offence to which the proceedings relate is alleged to have been committed, be evidence of service in the manner and on the date so specified both of a copy of that statement and of the notice to owner.

(3) Any address specified in any such certificate as is mentioned in subsection (2) above as being the address at which service of the notice to owner was effected shall be taken for the purposes of any proceedings in which the certificate is tendered in evidence to be the accused's proper address, unless the contrary is proved.

(4) Where a copy of a constable's witness statement is included in or served with a notice to owner served in any manner in which the notice is authorised to be served under this Part of this Act, the statement shall be treated as duly served for the purposes of section 9 of the Criminal Justice Act 1967 (proof by written statement) notwithstanding that the manner of service is not authorised by subsection (8) of that section.

(5) In relation to any proceedings in which service of a constable's witness statement is proved by certificate under this section—

(*a*) that service shall be taken for the purposes of subsection (2)(*c*) of that section (copy of statement to be tendered in evidence to be served before hearing on other parties to the proceedings by or on behalf of the party proposing to tender it) to have been effected by or on behalf of the prosecutor; and

(*b*) subsection (2)(*d*) of that section (time for objection) shall have effect with the substitution, for the reference to seven days from the service of the copy of the statement, of a reference to seven days from the relevant date.

In paragraph (*b*) of this subsection, 'relevant date' means—

(i) where the accused gives notice requesting a hearing in respect of the offence in accordance with any provision of this Part of this Act, the date on which he gives that notice; and

(ii) where a notice in respect of the offence was given to the accused under section 28(1) of this Act but no fixed penalty notice is given in respect of it, the last day for production of the first-mentioned notice at a police station in accordance with that section.

(6) Where any person is charged with a fixed penalty offence and the prosecutor produces to the court a document to which this subsection applies purporting to have been signed by the accused, the document shall be presumed, unless the contrary is proved, to have been signed by the accused and shall be evidence (and, in Scotland, sufficient evidence) in the proceedings of any facts stated in it tending to show that the accused was the owner, the hirer or the driver of the vehicle concerned at a particular time.

(7) Subsection (6) above applies to any document purporting to be—

(a) a notice requesting a hearing in respect of the offence charged given in accordance with a fixed penalty notice relating to that offence; or

(b) a statutory statement of any description defined in Schedule 3 to this Act or a copy of a statement of liability within the meaning of section 45 of this Act furnished in response to a notice to owner.

(8) Subsections (1) to (5) above do not apply to Scotland.

[Section 47 will come into operation on a date to be announced; see s 76(2).]

48. *[Jurisdiction in Scotland.]*

49. Supplementary provisions

(1) The Secretary of State may by regulations make provision as to any matter incidental to the operation of this Part of this Act, and in particular—

(a) for prescribing any information or further information to be provided in any notice, notification, certificate or receipt under section 27, 28, 31, 35, 36(2) or (3), 37(8), 39(1), 40(1) or 42 of this Act or in any official form for a statutory statement mentioned in Schedule 3 to, or a statement under section 45(2) of, this Act;

(b) for requiring any such official form to be served with any notice served under section 31 or 37(8) of this Act; and

(c) for prescribing the duties of justices' clerks or (as the case may be) clerks of courts of summary jurisdiction and the information to be supplied to them.

(2) For the purposes of this Part of this Act, the owner of a vehicle shall be taken to be the person by whom the vehicle is kept; and for the purposes of determining, in the course of any proceedings brought by virtue of section 31 of this Act, who was the owner of a vehicle at any time, it shall be presumed that the owner was the person who was the registered keeper of the vehicle at that time.

(3) Notwithstanding the presumption in subsection (2) above, it shall be open to the defence in any proceedings to prove that the person who was the registered keeper of a vehicle at a particular time was not the person by whom the vehicle was kept at that time and to the prosecution to prove that the vehicle was kept by some other person at that time.

(4) Subject to any requirement of this Part of this Act with respect to the manner in which any such document may be furnished, the following documents may be furnished by post (but without prejudice to any other method of furnishing), that is to say—

(*a*) any of the statutory statements mentioned in Schedule 3 to this Act; and

(*b*) any of the documents mentioned in section 45(2) of this Act.

(5) Where a notice requesting a hearing in respect of an offence is permitted by a fixed penalty notice or notice to owner relating to that offence to be given by post, section 7 of the Interpretation Act 1978 (service of documents by post) shall apply as if that notice were permitted to be so given by this Act.

(6) A notice to owner may be served on any person—

(*a*) by delivering it to him or by leaving it at his proper address; or

(*b*) by sending it to him by post;

and where the person on whom such a notice is to be served is a body corporate it shall be duly served if it is served on the secretary or clerk of that body.

(7) For the purposes of this Part of this Act and of section 7 of the Interpretation Act 1978 as it applies for the purposes of subsection (6) above the proper address of any person in relation to service on him of a notice to owner shall be—

(*a*) in the case of the secretary or clerk of a body corporate, that of the registered or principal office of that body or the registered address of the person who is or was the registered keeper of the vehicle concerned at the time of service; and

(*b*) in any other case, his last known address at the time of service.

(8) References in this section to the person who was or is the registered keeper of a vehicle at any time are references to the person in whose name the vehicle was or is at that time registered under the Vehicles (Excise) Act 1971; and, in relation to any such person, the reference in subsection (7)(*a*) above to that person's registered address is a reference to the address recorded in the record kept under that Act with respect to that vehicle as being that person's address.

(9) References in this Part of this Act to statutory statements of any description are references to the statutory statements of that description defined in Schedule 3 to this Act; and that Schedule shall have effect also for the purpose of requiring certain information to be provided in official forms for the statutory statements so defined to assist persons in completing those forms and generally in determining what action to take in response to a notice to owner.

(10) In this Part of this Act, 'official form', in relation to a statutory statement mentioned in Schedule 3 to, or a statement under section 45(2) of this Act, means a document supplied by or on behalf of a chief officer of police for use in making that statement.

(11) An order under [section 95(5) of the Road Traffic Regulation Act 1984] may not authorise the employment of a traffic warden to discharge any function under this Part of this Act in respect of an offence if the offence appears to the traffic warden to be an offence involving obligatory endorsement.

(12) Section 179 of the 1972 Act (restrictions on prosecutions for certain offences) shall not apply to any offence in respect of which a fixed penalty notice has been given or affixed under any provisions of this Part of this Act or in respect of which a notice has been given under section 28(1) of this Act.

(13) In any case where—

(*a*) by virtue of section 31(6) of this Act proceedings may be brought in respect of an offence against a person on whom a notice to owner was served; and

(*b*) section 38(3) of this Act does not apply;

section 127(1) of the Magistrates' Courts Act 1980 (information must be laid within six months of time offence committed) and section 331(1) of the Criminal Procedure (Scotland) Act 1975 (proceedings must be commenced within six months of that time) shall have effect as if for the reference to six months there were substituted a reference to twelve months.

[Section 49 will come into operation on a date to be announced; see s 76(2).

The section is printed as amended by the Road Traffic Regulation Act 1984, s 146, and Sched 13, para 54.]

50. Interpretation of Part III

(1) In this Part of this Act—

'chief officer of police' means, in relation to any fixed penalty notice or notice to owner, the chief officer of police for the police area in which the fixed penalty offence in question is alleged to have been committed;

'court of summary jurisdiction' has the same meaning as in section 462(1) of the Criminal Procedure (Scotland) Act 1975;

'driving licence' means any licence to drive a motor vehicle granted under Part III of the 1972 Act;

'justices clerk' means a clerk to the justices for a petty sessions area;

'magistrates' court' and 'petty sessions area' have the same meanings as in the Magistrates' Courts Act 1980; and

'proceedings', except in relation to proceedings for enforcing payment of a sum registered under section 36 of this Act, means criminal proceedings.

(2) In this Part of this Act—

(a) references to a notice requesting a hearing in respect of an offence are references to a notice indicating that the person giving the notice wishes to contest liability for the offence or seeks a determination by a court with respect to the appropriate punishment for the offence; and

(b) references to an offence include an alleged offence.

(3) In so far as an order under [section 95(5) of the Road Traffic Regulation Act 1984] authorises the employment of traffic wardens for the purposes of this Part of this Act references in this Part of this Act to a constable or, as the case may be, to a constable in uniform shall include a traffic warden.

(4) In sections 31, 32 and 47(6) of this Act and in Schedule 3 to this Act 'driver', in relation to an alleged fixed penalty offence, means the person by whom, assuming the offence to have been committed, it was committed.

(5) Subject to any express exceptions references in this Part of this Act to this Part of this Act include Schedules 1 to 3.

(6) The expressions listed in the left-hand column below are respectively defined or (as the case may be) fall to be construed in accordance with the provisions of this Part of this Act listed in the right-hand column in relation to those expressions.

Expression	*Relevant provisions*
Fixed penalty	Section 29(3)
Fixed penalty clerk	Section 33(2)
Fixed penalty notice	Section 27(8)
Fixed penalty offence	Sections 27(5) and 42(3)

Expression	*Relevant provisions*
Notice to owner	Sections 31(2) and 45(4)
Offence involving obligatory endorsement	Sections 27(9) and 42(3)
Official form	Section 49(10)
Owner	Section 49(2)
Statutory statement of facts	Part II of Schedule 3
Statutory statement of hiring	Part I of Schedule 3
Statutory statement of ownership	Part I of Schedule 3
Suspended enforcement period	Section 29(1)
Time of the alleged offence	Section 31(3)

[Section 50 will come into operation on a date to be announced; see s 76(2).

The section is printed as amended by the Road Traffic Regulation Act 1984, s 146 and Sched 13, para 54.]

51. Guidance on application of Part III

The Secretary of State shall issue guidance to chief officers of police for police areas in respect of the operation of this Part of this Act with the objective so far as possible of working towards uniformity.

[Section 51 will come into operation on a date to be announced; see s 76(2).]

*   *   *

SCHEDULE 1

Fixed Penalty Offences

Offences under [the Road Traffic Regulation Act 1984]

Relevant enactment	Description of offence	Endorsement
[Section 5(1)]	Using a vehicle in contravention of traffic regulation order outside Greater London.	—
[Section 8(1)]	Breach of traffic regulation order in Greater London.	—
[Section 11]	Breach of experimental traffic order.	—
[Section 13]	Breach of experimental traffic scheme regulations in Greater London.	—
[Section 16(1)]	Using a vehicle in contravention of temporary prohibition or restriction of traffic in case of execution of works, etc.	
[Section 17(4)]	Wrongful use of special road.	Obligatory, if committed as described in paragraph 4 of Part III of Schedule 4 to the 1972 Act.
[Section 18(3)]	Using a vehicle in contravention of provision for one-way traffic on trunk road.	—
[Section 20(5)]	Driving a vehicle in contravention of order prohibiting or restricting driving vehicles on certain classes of roads.	
[Section 25(5)]	Breach of pedestrian crossing regulations, except an offence in respect of a moving motor vehicle.	Obligatory, if committed as described in paragraph 5 of Part III of Schedule 4 to the 1972 Act.
[Section 29(3)]	Using a vehicle in contravention of a street playground order outside Greater London.	Obligatory, if committed as described in paragraph 7 of Part III of Schedule 4 to the 1972 Act.
[Section 30(5)]	Using a vehicle in contravention of a street playground order in Greater London.	Obligatory, if committed as described in paragraph 7 of Part III of Schedule 4 to the 1972 Act.

Offences under [the Road Traffic Regulation Act 1984] *continued*

Relevant enactment	Description of offence	Endorsement
[Section 35(4)]	Breach of an order regulating the use, etc., of a parking place provided by a local authority, but only where the offence is committed in relation to a parking place provided on a road.	—
[Section 47(1)]	Breach of a provision of a parking place designation order and other offences committed in relation to a parking place designated by any such order, except any offence of failing to pay an excess charge within the meaning of [section 46 of the Road Traffic Regulation Act 1984]	—
[Section 53(5)]	Using a vehicle in contravention of any provision of a parking place designation order having effect by virtue of [section 53(1)(*a*) of the Road Traffic Regulation Act 1984] (inclusion of certain traffic regulation provisions).	—
[Section 53(6)]	Breach of a provision of a parking place designation order having effect by virtue of [section 53(1)(*b*) of the Road Traffic Regulation Act 1984] (use of any part of a road for parking without charge).	—
[Section 88(7)]	Driving a motor vehicle in contravention of an order imposing a minimum speed limit under [section 88 (1)(*b*)].	—
[Section 89(1)]	Speeding offences under [the Road Traffic Regulation Act 1984] and other Acts.	Obligatory.

Offences under the Vehicles (Excise) Act 1971

Relevant enactment	Description of offence	Endorsement
Section 12(4)	Using or keeping a vehicle on a public road without licence being exhibited in the prescribed manner.	—
Section 22(1)	Driving or keeping a vehicle without required registration mark or hackney carriage sign.	—
Section 22(2)	Driving or keeping a vehicle with registration mark or hackney carriage sign obscured, etc.	—

Offences under the 1972 Act

Relevant enactment	Description of offence	Endorsement
Section 16	Unlawful carrying of passengers on motor cycles.	Obligatory.
Section 22	Failure to comply with traffic directions or signs.	Obligatory, if committed as described in the entry in column 5 of Part I of Schedule 4 to the 1972 Act relating to this offence.
Section 24	Leaving vehicle in dangerous position.	Obligatory, if committed as described in the entry in column 6 of Part I of Schedule 4 to the 1972 Act relating to this offence.
Section 32(3)	Breach of regulations relating to protective headgear for motor cycle drivers and passengers.	—
Section 33A(3)	Breach of regulations requiring wearing of seat belts.	—
Section 33B(2)	Breach of restriction on carrying children in the front of vehicles.	—
Section 36	Driving motor vehicle elsewhere than on a road.	—
Section 36A(1)	Parking a heavy commercial vehicle on verge or footway.	—

OFFENCES UNDER THE 1972 ACT *continued*

Relevant enactment	Description of offence	Endorsement
Section 36B(1)	Parking a vehicle other than a heavy commercial vehicle on verge or footway.	—
Section 40(5)(a)	Breach of construction and use regulations.	Obligatory, if committed as described in the entry in column 5 of Part I of Schedule 4 to the 1972 Act relating to an offence under section 40(5), but subject to the exception there mentioned.
Section 40(5)(b)	Using on a road a motor vehicle or trailer which does not comply with construction and use regulations.	Obligatory, if committed as described in the entry in column 5 of Part I of Schedule 4 to the 1972 Act relating to an offence under section 40(5), but subject to the exception there mentioned.
Section 81(1)	Contravention of any provisions of sections 68 to 79 of the 1972 Act or regulations under any of those provisions (requirements with respect to lights, reflectors, etc.).	—
Section 84(1)	Driving vehicle without requisite licence.	Obligatory, if committed as described in the entry in column 5 of Part I of Schedule 4 to the 1972 Act relating to this offence.
Section 88(6)	Breach of provisional licence conditions.	Obligatory.
Section 159	Failure to stop vehicle on being so required by constable in uniform.	—

OFFENCE UNDER THE GREATER LONDON COUNCIL (GENERAL POWERS) ACT 1974 (c xxiv)

Relevant enactment	Description of offence	Endorsement
Section 15	Parking a vehicle on footways, verges etc.	—

Offence under the Highways Act 1980

Relevant enactment	Description of offence	Endorsement
Section 137	Obstructing a highway, but only where the offence is committed in respect of a vehicle.	—

[Schedule 1 will come into operation on a date to be announced; see s 76(2).
Schedule 1 is printed as amended by the Road Traffic Regulation Act 1984, s 146, and Sched 13, para 55.
The reference to the '1972 Act' is a reference to the Road Traffic Act 1972; see s 75.]

*   *   *

SCHEDULE 3

STATUTORY STATEMENTS

PART I

STATUTORY STATEMENT OF OWNERSHIP OR HIRING

1.—(1) For the purposes of Part III of this Act, a statutory statement of ownership is a statement on an official form signed by the person furnishing it and stating whether he was the owner of the vehicle at the time of the alleged offence and, if he was not the owner of the vehicle at that time, whether—

(a) he was never the owner; or

(b) he ceased to be the owner before, or became the owner after, that time;

and in a case within paragraph (b) above, stating, if the information is in his possession, the name and address of the person to whom, and the date on which, he disposed of the vehicle or (as the case may be) the name and address of the person from whom, and the date on which, he acquired it.

(2) An official form for a statutory statement of ownership shall—

(a) indicate that the person furnishing the statement in response to a notice to owner relating to an offence may give notice requesting a hearing in respect of the offence in the manner specified in the form; and

(b) direct the attention of any person proposing to complete the form to the information provided in accordance with paragraph 3(3) below in any official form for a statutory statement of facts.

2.—(1) For the purposes of Part III of this Act, a statutory statement of hiring is a statement on an official form, signed by the person furnishing it, being the person by whom a statement of liability was signed, and stating—

(a) whether at the time of the alleged offence the vehicle was let to him under the hiring agreement to which the statement of liability refers; and

(b) if it was not, the date on which he returned the vehicle to the possession of the vehicle-hire firm concerned.

(2) An official form for a statutory statement of hiring shall—

(a) indicate that the person furnishing the statement in pursuance of a notice relating to an offence served under section 31 of this Act by virtue of section 45 of this Act may give notice requesting a hearing in respect of the offence in the manner specified in the form; and

(b) direct the attention of any person proposing to complete the form to the information provided in accordance with paragraph 3(3) below in any official form for a statutory statement of facts.

(3) In sub-paragraph (1) above 'statement of liability', 'hiring agreement' and 'vehicle-hire firm' have the same meanings as in section 45 of this Act.

PART II

Statutory Statement of Facts

3.—(1) For the purposes of Part III of this Act, a statutory statement of facts is a statement on an official form, signed by the person furnishing it, which—

(a) states that the person furnishing it was not the driver of the vehicle at the time of the alleged offence; and

(b) states the name and address at the time when the statement is furnished of the person who was the driver of the vehicle at the time of the alleged offence.

(2) A statutory statement of facts has effect as a notice given by the driver requesting a hearing in respect of the offence if it is signed by the person identified in the statement as the driver of the vehicle at the time of the alleged offence.

(3) An official form for a statutory statement of facts shall indicate—

(a) that if a person identified in the statement as the driver of the vehicle at the time of the alleged offence signs the statement he will be regarded as having given notice requesting a hearing in respect of the offence;

(b) that the person on whom the notice to owner relating to the offence is served may not give notice requesting a hearing in respect of the offence on his own account if he furnishes a statutory statement of facts signed by a person so identified; and

(c) that if the fixed penalty is not paid before the end of the period stated in the notice to owner as the period for response to the notice, a sum determined by reference to that fixed penalty may be registered without any court hearing for enforcement as a fine against the person on whom the notice to owner is served, unless he has given notice requesting a hearing in respect of the offence;

but that, in a case within paragraph (c) above, the sum in question may not be so registered if the person on whom the notice to owner is served furnishes a statutory statement of facts as mentioned in paragraph (b) above until two months have elapsed from the end of the period so stated without service of a summons or, in Scotland, complaint in respect of the offence on the person identified in that statement as the driver of the vehicle.

[Schedule 3 will come into operation on a date to be announced; see s 76(2).]

*　　　*　　　*

The Vehicles (Excise) Act 1971

(1971 c 10)

An Act to consolidate certain enactments relating to excise duties on mechanically propelled vehicles, and to the licensing and registration of such vehicles with amendments to give effect to recommendations of the Law Commission and the Scottish Law Commission. [16th March 1971]

ARRANGEMENT OF SECTIONS

* * *

* * *

212

Miscellaneous

Legal proceedings, etc

*　　　*　　　*

SCHEDULES

*　　　*　　　*

Exemptions from duty

4. Exemptions from duty of certain descriptions of vehicle

(1) No duty shall be chargeable under this Act in respect of mechanically propelled vehicles of any of the following descriptions, that is to say—

[(*aa*) electrically propelled vehicles;]

(*a*) fire engines;

(*b*) vehicles kept by a local authority while they are used or kept on a road for the purposes of their fire brigade service;

(*c*) ambulances;

(*d*) road rollers;

(*e*) vehicles used on tram lines . . .;

(*f*) vehicles used or kept on a road for no purpose other than the haulage of lifeboats and the conveyance of the necessary gear of the lifeboats which are being hauled;

(*g*) vehicles (including cycles with an attachment for propelling them by mechanical power) which do not exceed [ten] hundredweight in weight unladen and are adapted, and used or kept on a road, for invalids;

(*h*) road construction vehicles used or kept on a road solely for the conveyance of built-in road construction machinery (with or without articles or material used for the purposes of that machinery);

(*i*) vehicles constructed or adapted, and used, solely for the conveyance of machinery for spreading material on roads to deal with frost, ice or snow or for the conveyance of such machinery and articles and material used for the purposes of that machinery;

(*j*) local authority's watering vehicles;

(*k*) tower wagons used solely by a street lighting authority, or by any person acting in pursuance of a contract with such an authority, for the purpose of installing or maintaining materials or apparatus for lighting streets, roads or public places;

[(*l*) vehicles which are made available by the Secretary of State to any person, body or local authority in pursuance of [section 23 or section 26 of the National Health Service Act 1977] and which are used in accordance with the terms on which they are so made available].

(2) In this section—

'road construction vehicle' means a vehicle constructed or adapted for use for the conveyance of built-in road construction machinery and not constructed or adapted for the conveyance of any other load except articles and material used for the purposes of that machinery;

'road construction machinery' means a machine or contrivance suitable for use for the construction or repair of roads and used for no purpose other than the construction or repair of roads at the public expense;

'built-in road construction machinery', in relation to a vehicle, means road construction machinery built in as part of the vehicle or permanently attached thereto;

'local authority's watering vehicle' means a vehicle used solely within the area of a local authority by that local authority, or by any person acting in pursuance of a contract with that local authority, for the purpose of cleansing or watering roads or cleansing gulleys;

'tower wagon' has the same meaning as in Schedule 4 to this Act;

'street lighting authority' means any local authority or Minister having power under any enactment to provide or maintain materials or apparatus for lighting streets, roads or public places.

[Section 4 is printed as amended by the Finance Act 1972, s 128 (3), the National Health Service (Vehicles) Order 1974 (SI 1974 No 168), the Finance Act 1975, ss 5 (5), 75 (5), and Sched 14, Part II, and the National Health Service Act 1977, Sched 14, para 2, and the Finance Act 1980, s 4 (4).

'Tower wagon' is defined in Sched 4 to this Act (para 15 (1), as substituted by the Finance Act 1982, s 5 (4), and Sched 5, Part A) as 'a goods vehicle—(a) into which there is built, as part of the vehicle, any expanding or extensible contrivance designed for facilitating the erection, inspection, repair or maintenance of overhead structures or equipment; and (b) which is neither constructed nor adapted for use nor used for the conveyance of any load, except such a contrivance and articles used in connection therewith'.]

5. Exemptions from duty in connection with vehicle testing, etc

(1) A mechanically propelled vehicle shall not be chargeable with any duty under this Act by reason of its use on public roads—

(*a*) solely for the purpose of submitting it by previous arrangement for a specified time on a specified date for, or bringing it away from, a compulsory test; or

(*b*) in the course of a compulsory test, solely for the purpose of taking it to, or bringing it away from, any place where a part of the test is to be or, as the case may be, has been carried out, or of carrying out any part of the test, the person so using it being an authorised person; or

(*c*) where the relevant certificate is refused on a compulsory test, solely for the purpose of delivering it by previous arrangement for a specified time on a specified date at a place where work is to be done on it to remedy the defects on the ground of which the certificate was refused, or bringing it away from a place where work has been done on it to remedy such defects.

(2) In paragraph (c) above the reference to work done or to be done on the vehicle to remedy the defects there mentioned is, in a case where the relevant certificate which is refused is a test certificate, a reference to work done or to be done to remedy those defects for a further compulsory test and includes, in a case where the relevant certificate which is refused is a goods vehicle test certificate, type approval certificate or Minister's approval certificate, a reference to work done or to be done to alter the vehicle in some aspect of design, construction, equipment or marking on account of which the certificate was refused.

(3) In this section—

'compulsory test' means an examination under [section 43 of the Road Traffic Act 1972] with a view to obtaining a test certificate without which a vehicle licence cannot be granted for the vehicle under this Act or, in the case of a goods vehicle for which by virtue of [section 52 (2) of that Act] a vehicle licence cannot be so granted an examination under regulations under [section 45 or for the purposes of section 47] of that Act (examinations as to a goods vehicle's compliance with construction and use or type approval requirements respectively) or an examin-ation under regulations under [section 50 (1) (a)] of that Act (in connection with alterations to goods vehicles subject to type approval requirements) or for the purposes of [section 49] of that Act (appeals);

'the relevant certificate' means a test certificate as defined in subsection (2) of the said [section 43], a goods vehicle test certificate as defined in the said [section 45], a type approval certificate or a Minister's approval certificate as defined in the said [section 47];

'authorised person' in the case of a compulsory test under the said [section 43] means a person authorised as an examiner or appointed as an inspector under that section or acting on behalf of a person so authorised, or a person acting under the personal direction of such a person as aforesaid; and in the case of any other compulsory test means a goods vehicle examiner or a person carrying out the test under his direction or a person driving the vehicle in pursuance of a requirement to do so under regulations under which the compulsory test is car-ried out;

'goods vehicle examiner' means an examiner appointed under section [56 of the Road Traffic Act 1972] or a certifying officer appointed under [the Public Pas-senger Vehicles Act 1981].

[Section 5 is printed as amended by the Road Traffic Act 1972, s 203 (1), and Sched 7, and the Interpretation Act 1978, s 17 (2) (a).]

6. Exemptions from duty in respect of vehicles acquired by overseas residents

[(1) A mechanically propelled vehicle shall not be chargeable with any duty under this Act if it has been supplied to the person keeping it by a taxable person within the meaning of [section 2 (2) of the Value Added Tax Act 1983] and the supply has been zero-rated in pursuance of [subsection (7) of section 16] of that Act; but if, at any time, the value added tax that would have been chargeable on the supply but for the zero-rating becomes payable under [subsection (9)] of that section, or would have become so payable but for any authorisation or waiver under that subsection, then the provisions of subsection (3) below shall apply in relation to that vehicle.]

(2) [Repealed.]

(3) Where under subsection (1) . . . above the provisions of this subsection are to apply in relation to a vehicle, the vehicle shall be deemed never to have been exempted from duty under the said subsection (1) . . . and, without prejudice to the provisions of section 9 of this Act, unless, or except to the extent that, the [Secretary of State for Transport] sees fit to waive payment of the whole or part of the duty, there shall be recoverable by the [Secretary of State for Transport] as a debt due to him—

(a) from the person by whom the vehicle was acquired from its manufacturer, the duty in respect of the whole period since the registration of the vehicle; or

(b) from any other person who is for the time being the keeper of the vehicle, the duty in respect of the period since the vehicle was first kept by that other person.

other than any part of that period by reference to which there was calculated an amount ordered to be paid by the person in question in respect of the vehicle in pursuance of section 9 (1) of this Act.

[Section 6 is printed as amended by the Finance Act 1972, ss 54 (8), 55 (6), 134, and Sched 28, Part II; the Secretary of State for Transport Order 1976 (SI 1976 No 1775); the Minister of Transport Order 1979 (SI 1979 No 571); the Transfer of Functions (Transport) Order 1981 (SI 1981 No 238); and the Value Added Tax Act 1983, ss 50 (1), 51 (2), and Sched 9, para 2.

Section 2 (2) of the Value Added Tax Act 1983 defines a 'taxable person' as a 'person who makes or intends to make taxable supplies . . . while he is or is required to be registered under this Part of this Act'.]

7. Miscellaneous exemptions from duty

(1) If an applicant for a vehicle licence satisfies the [Secretary of State for Transport] that the vehicle is intended to be used on public roads—

(a) only in passing from land in his occupation to other land in his occupation, and

(b) for distances not exceeding in the aggregate six miles in any calendar week,

then, with the consent of the Treasury, the [Secretary of State for Transport] may exempt the vehicle from the duty chargeable under this Act in respect of the use of the vehicle on roads; but if a vehicle so exempted is used on public roads otherwise than for the purpose or to the extent specified above, the vehicle shall cease to be exempted.

[(2) A mechanically propelled vehicle shall not be chargeable with any duty under this Act by reason of its use by or for the purposes of a person ('a disabled person') suffering from a physical defect or disability or by reason of its being kept for such use if

(a) it is registered under this Act in the name of that person; and

(b) he has obtained, or is eligible for, a grant under paragraph 2 of Schedule 2 to the National Health Service Act 1977 [or section 46 (3) of the National Health Service (Scotland) Act 1978] in relation to that vehicle or is in receipt of a mobility allowance; and

(c) no other vehicle registered in his name under this Act is exempted from duty under this subsection or section 7 of the Finance Act 1971.

and for the purposes of this subsection a vehicle shall be deemed to be registered in the name of a disabled person in receipt of a mobility allowance if it is registered in the name of a person appointed pursuant to regulations under the Social Security Act 1975 to exercise any of his rights or powers or in the name of a person nominated for the purposes of this subsection by the disabled person or by a person so appointed.]

(3) A mechanically propelled vehicle shall not be chargeable with any duty under this Act by reason of its use for clearing snow from public roads by means of a snow plough or similar contrivance, whether forming part of the vehicle or not, or by reason of its being kept for such use or by reason of its use for the purpose of going to or from the place where it is to be used for clearing snow from public roads by those means.

(4) Regulations under this Act may provide that, in such cases and subject to such conditions as may be prescribed, a mechanically propelled vehicle shall not be chargeable with any duty under this Act by reason of any use made of it for the purpose of a public or local authority's functions in connection with civil defence as defined in the Civil Defence Act 1948, or by reason of its being kept on a road for any such use, or both.

(5) Regulations under this Act may provide for the total or partial exemption for a limited period from the duty chargeable under this Act of any mechanically propelled vehicles for the time being licensed under section 1 or 10 of the Vehicles (Excise) Act (Northern Ireland) 1954; and, without prejudice to section 37 (1) of this Act, regulations made under this subsection may—

(a) make different provision in relation to vehicles of different descriptions;

(b) provide that any exemption conferred by the regulations in respect of any vehicle shall have effect subject to such conditions as may be prescribed.

[Section 7 is printed as amended by the Secretary of State for Transport Order 1976 (SI 1976 No 1775); the Finance Act 1978, s 8 (1); the Minister of Transport Order 1979 (SI 1979 No 571); the Finance Act 1980, s 4 (6); and the Transfer of Functions (Transport) Order 1981.

The application of sub-s (2) to a person in receipt of mobility allowance has been extended to include a person in receipt of mobility supplement (as defined) by the Finance Act 1984; see further ibid, s 5.

The Civil Defence Act 1948, s 9 (1), states that 'civil defence does not include the provision or maintenance of a shelter which is used or intended to be used wholly or mainly by naval, military, or air forces but, save as aforesaid, includes any measures not amounting to actual combat for affording defence against any form of hostile attack by a foreign power or for depriving any form of hostile attack by a foreign power of the whole or part of its effect, whether the measures are taken before, at or after the time of the attack'.]

Liability to pay duty and consequences of non-payment thereof

8. Using and keeping vehicles without a licence

(1) If any person uses or keeps on a public road any mechanically propelled vehicle for which a licence is not in force, not being a vehicle exempted from duty under this Act by virtue of any enactment (including any provision of this Act), he shall be liable to the greater of the following penalties, namely—

(a) an excise penalty of [level 3 on the standard scale]; or

(b) an excise penalty equal to five times the amount of the duty chargeable in respect of the vehicle.

(2) . . .

(3) For the purposes of this section—

(a) where a vehicle for which a licence is in force is transferred by the holder of the licence to another person, the licence shall be treated as no longer in force unless it is delivered to that other person with the vehicle;

(b) the amount of the duty chargeable in respect of a vehicle shall be taken to be an amount equal to the annual rate of duty applicable to the vehicle at the date on which the offence was committed or, where in the case of a vehicle kept on a public road that rate differs from the annual rate by reference to which the vehicle was at that date chargeable under section 1 of this Act in respect of the keeping thereof, equal to the last mentioned rate.

For the purposes of paragraph (b) above the offence shall, in the case of a conviction for a continuing offence, be taken to have been committed on the date or latest date to which the conviction relates.

[Section 8 is printed as amended by s 39 and Sched 7, para 6. Subsection (2) is accordingly omitted until such date as the Secretary of State for Transport may order. Section 8 is printed as further amended by the Criminal Justice Act 1982, ss 38, 46(1).

Section 1 of this Act relates to the charge to excise duty.]

9. Additional liability for keeping unlicensed vehicle

(1) Where a person convicted of an offence under section 8 of this Act is the person by whom the vehicle in respect of which the offence was committed was kept at the time it was committed, the court shall, in addition to any penalty which it may impose under that section, order him to pay an amount calculated in accordance with subsections (2) to (4) below.

(2) The said amount shall, subject to subsection (3) below, be an amount equal to one three-hundred-and-sixty-fifth of the annual rate of duty appropriate to the vehicle in question for each day in the relevant period, and the relevant period shall be one ending with the date of the offence and beginning—

(a) if the person convicted has before that date notified the [Secretary of State for Transport] of his acquisition of the vehicle in accordance with regulations under this Act, with the date on which the notification was received by the [Secretary of State for Transport] or, if later, with the expiry of the vehicle licence last in force for the vehicle, or

(b) in any other case, with the expiry of the vehicle licence last in force for the vehicle before the date of the offence or, if there has not at any time before that date been a vehicle licence in force for the vehicle, with the date on which the vehicle was first kept by that person:

Provided that, where the person convicted has been ordered to pay an amount under this section on the occasion of a previous conviction in respect of the same vehicle, and the offence then charged was committed after the date specified above for the beginning of the relevant period, that period shall begin instead with the day following that on which the former offence was committed.

(3) Where the person convicted proves—

(a) that throughout any day comprised in the relevant period the vehicle in question was not kept by him, or

(b) that throughout any such day the vehicle in question was neither used nor kept by him on a public road and that he was exempt by virtue of section 10 (2) (b) or (c) of this Act from liability under subsection (1) of that section in respect of that day, or

(c) that throughout any such day the vehicle in question was not chargeable with duty, or

(d) that he has paid duty in respect of the vehicle for any such day, whether or not on a licence,

the said amount shall be calculated as if that day were not comprised in the relevant period.

(4) In relation to any day comprised in the relevant period, the reference in subsection (2) above to the annual rate of duty appropriate to the vehicle in question is a reference to the annual rate applicable to it on that day; and, except so far as it is proved to have fallen within some other description for the whole of any such day, a vehicle shall be taken for the purposes of this section to have belonged throughout the relevant period to that description of vehicle to which it belonged for the purposes of duty at the date of the offence or, if the prosecution so elect, the date when a vehicle licence for it was last issued.

(5) Where, on a person's conviction of an offence under section 8 of this Act, an order is made under Part I of the Criminal Justice Act 1948 placing him on probation or discharging him absolutely or conditionally, the foregoing provisions of this section shall apply as if the conviction were deemed to be a conviction for all purposes.

(6) In the foregoing provisions of this section any reference to the expiry of a vehicle licence includes a reference to its surrender, and to its being treated as no longer in force for the purposes of section 8 of this Act by virtue of subsection (3) (a) of that section; and in the case of a conviction for a continuing offence, the offence shall be taken for the purposes of those provisions to have been committed on the date or latest date to which the conviction relates.

(7) The foregoing provisions of this section shall have effect subject to the provisions (applying with the necessary modifications) of any enactment relating to the imposition of fines by magistrates' courts, other than one conferring a discretion as to their amount; and any sum payable by virtue of an order under this section shall be treated as a fine, and the order as a conviction, for the purposes of [Part III of the Magistrates' Courts Act 1980] (including any enactment having effect as if contained in that Part) and of any other enactment relating to the recovery or application of sums ordered to be paid by magistrates' courts.

(8) *[Application to Scotland.]*

[Section 9 is printed as amended by the Secretary of State for Transport Order 1976 (SI 1976 No 1775); the Minister of Transport Order 1979 (SI 1979 No 571); the Magistrates' Courts Act 1980, s 154, and Sched 8, para 5; and the Transfer of Functions (Transport) Order 1981 (SI 1981 No 238)

Several of the provisions in Part I of the Criminal Justice Act 1948 have been repealed by the Powers of Criminal Courts Act 1973. As to orders of probation and discharge under the 1973 Act, see (by virtue of Sched 4, para 1 (b), to that Act) ss 2 to 13.

Section 10 (1) provides (subject to the provisions of that section and of s 11) that a person who for any period keeps a vehicle in respect of which duty under the Act has at any time become chargeable is liable to pay duty in respect of that vehicle for that period. Section 10 (2) provides exemptions from the liability under s 10 (1) for, inter alia, (b) any period in respect of which he has given notice in proper form to the Secretary of State for Transport that the vehicle will not be used or kept on a public road; and (c) any period when the vehicle is not a mechanically propelled vehicle and a notice stating that it has ceased to be such a vehicle has been given in proper form to the Secretary of State for Transport and has not been revoked.]

*   *   *

Issue, exhibition, exchange, surrender, etc of licences

12. Issue and exhibition of licences

(1)—(3) *[Omitted.]*

(4) Subject to the provisions of regulations under this Act, and without prejudice to section 8 thereof, any person who uses or keeps on a public road any mechanically

propelled vehicle on which duty under this Act is chargeable without there being fixed to and exhibited on that vehicle in the prescribed manner a licence for, or in respect of the use of, that vehicle issued under this Act and for the time being in force shall be liable on summary conviction to a fine not exceeding [level 1 on the standard scale].

(5) . . .

(6)–(7) [Omitted.]

[Section 12 is printed as amended by s 39 and Sched 7, para 9. Subsection (5) is accordingly omitted until such date as the Secretary of State for Transport may order. Section 12 is printed as further amended by the Criminal Justice Act 1982, ss 38, 46(1).

The amending provisions of the Criminal Justice Act 1982 referred to above would not have been applicable to s 12 (4) if the penalty had been amended by the Criminal Law Act 1977, s 30 or s 31. (Section 30 of that Act relates to specified provisions of which s 12(4) is not one.) Section 31 of the 1977 Act provides (inter alia) for an increase in the penalty for any summary offence created under a pre-1949 enactment (which is defined as including enactments passed after 1 January 1949 which re-enact with or without modification pre-1949 enactments) in respect of which no 'alteration' had otherwise been made since the end of 1948. It is believed that s 31 of the 1977 Act did not affect the penalty enacted in s 12 (4) of the Vehicles (Excise) Act 1971, since s 12 (4) of the 1971 Act (not-withstanding the fact that it is a consolidation Act) does not re-enact with modification an enactment passed before 1 January 1949.

For the application of the fixed penalty procedure to offences under s 12 (4), see the Transport Act 1982, Part III, and Sched 1.]

* * *

16. Trade licences

(1)—If a motor trader or a vehicle tester applies in the prescribed manner to the [Secretary of State for Transport] to take out a licence under this section (in this Act referred to as a 'trade licence')—

 (i) in the case of a motor trader, for all mechanically propelled vehicles which are from time to time temporarily in his possession in the course of his business as a motor trader and all recovery vehicles kept by him for the purpose of dealing with disabled vehicles in the course of that business; or

 (ii) in the case of a vehicle tester, for all mechanically propelled vehicles which are from time to time submitted to him for testing in the course of his business as a vehicle tester; or

 (iii) in the case of a motor trader who is a manufacturer of mechanically propelled vehicles, for all vehicles kept and used by him solely for purposes of conducting research and development in the course of his business as such a manufacturer,

the [Secretary of State for Transport] may, subject to the prescribed conditions, issue to him a trade licence on payment of duty at the rate applicable to the licence in accordance with the following provisions of this section:

Provided that the holder of a trade licence shall not be entitled by virtue of that licence—

 (a) to use more than one mechanically propelled vehicle at any one time, except in the case of a recovery vehicle drawing a disabled vehicle; or

 (b) to use any vehicle for any purpose other than such purposes as may be prescribed; or

(c) to keep any vehicle on a road if it is not being used thereon.

(2) Regulations shall be made under this section prescribing the conditions subject to which trade licences are to be issued and the purposes for which the holder of a trade licence may use a vehicle under the licence.

(3) The purposes which may be prescribed as those for which the holder of a trade licence may use a vehicle under the licence shall not include the conveyance of goods or burden of any description other than—

(a) a load which is carried solely for the purpose of testing or demonstrating the vehicle or any of its accessories or equipment and which is returned to the place of loading without having been removed from the vehicle except for such purpose or in the case of accident; or

(b) in the case of a recovery vehicle, any such load as is referred to in the definition of such a vehicle contained in subsection (8) below or a load consisting of a disabled vehicle; or

(c) any load built in as part of the vehicle or permanently attached thereto; or

(d) a load consisting of parts, accessories or equipment designed to be fitted to the vehicle and of tools for so fitting them; or

(e) a load consisting of a trailer;

and, for the purposes of this subsection, where a vehicle is so constructed that a trailer may by partial superimposition be attached to the vehicle in such a manner as to cause a substantial part of the weight of the trailer to be borne by the vehicle, the vehicle and the trailer shall be deemed to constitute a single vehicle.

[(4) A trade licence may be taken out either for one calendar year or, except in the case of a licence which is to be used only for vehicles to which Schedule 1 to this Act relates, for a period of three months beginning with the first day of January, of April, of July or of October.]

[(5) The rate of duty applicable to a trade licence taken out for a calendar year shall be [£44] or, if the licence is to be used only for vehicles to which Schedule 1 to this Act relates, [£9]; and the rate of duty applicable to a licence taken out for a period of three months shall be eleven fortieths of the rate applicable to the corresponding trade licence taken out for a calendar year, any fraction of 5p being treated as 5p if it exceeds 2·5p but otherwise being disregarded.]

(6) Nothing in this section shall operate to prevent a person entitled to take out a trade licence from holding two or more trade licences.

(7) If any person holding a trade licence or trade licences issued under this section uses on a public road by virtue of that licence or those licences—

(i) a greater number of vehicles at any one time than he is authorised to use by virtue of that licence or those licences; or

(ii) any vehicle for any purpose other than such purposes as may have been prescribed under subsection (2) above;

or if that person uses that licence or any of those licences for the purpose of keeping on a road a vehicle which is not being used on that road, he shall be liable to the greater of the following penalties, namely—

(a) an excise penalty of [level 3 on the standard scale]; or

(b) an excise penalty equal to five times the amount of the duty chargeable in respect of the vehicle or vehicles.

The amount of the duty chargeable in respect of a vehicle shall be calculated for the purposes of this subsection in the same manner as it is calculated for the purposes of section 8 of this Act by virtue of subsection (3) thereof.

(8) In this section—

['disabled vehicle' includes a vehicle which has been abandoned or is scrap;]

'motor trader' means a manufacturer or repairer of, or dealer in, mechanically propelled vehicles; and a person shall be treated for the purposes of this section as a dealer in such vehicles if he carries on a business consisting wholly or mainly of collecting and delivering mechanically propelled vehicles, and not including any other activities except activities as a manufacturer or repairer of, or dealer in, such vehicles;

'vehicle tester' means a person, other than a motor trader, who regularly in the course of his business engages in the testing on roads of mechanically propelled vehicles belonging to other persons; and

'recovery vehicle' means a vehicle on which there is mounted, or which is drawing, or which is carrying as part of its equipment, apparatus designed for raising a disabled vehicle wholly or partly from the ground or for drawing a disabled vehicle when so raised, and which is not used for the conveyance of goods other than a disabled vehicle wholly raised by that apparatus, and which carries no other load than articles required for the operation of, or in connection with, that apparatus or otherwise for dealing with disabled vehicles.

[Section 16 is printed as amended by s 39 and Sched 7, para 12; the Secretary of State for Transport Order 1976 (SI 1976 No 1775); the Finance Act 1977, s 5 (3); the Minister of Transport Order 1979 (SI 1979 No 571); the Finance Act 1980, s 4 (3); the Transfer of Functions (Transport) Order 1981 (SI 1981 No 238); the Criminal Justice Act 1982, ss 38, 46 (1), 47 (1); and the Finance Act 1984, s 4 (4).

Subsections (4) and (5) as so amended have effect until such date as the Secretary of State for Transport may order, whereupon subss (4) and (5) as originally enacted take effect (s 39 and Sched 7, para 6).]

* * *

18. Alteration of vehicle or of its use

(1) Subject to the provisions of this section, where a vehicle licence has been taken out for a vehicle at any rate under this Act and the vehicle is at any time while the licence is in force used in an altered condition or in a manner or for a purpose which brings it within, or which if it was used solely in that condition or in that manner or for that purpose would bring it within, a description of vehicle to which a higher rate of duty is applicable under this Act, duty at that higher rate shall become chargeable in respect of the licence for the vehicle.

(2), (3) *[Omitted.]*

(4) Where a vehicle licence has been taken out for a vehicle, and by reason of the vehicle being used as mentioned in subsection (1) above, a higher rate of duty becomes chargeable and duty at the higher rate was not paid before the vehicle was so used, the person so using the vehicle shall be liable to the greater of the following penalties, namely—

(a) an excise penalty of [level 3 on the standard scale]; or

(b) an excise penalty of an amount equal to five times the difference between the duty actually paid on the licence and the amount of the duty at that higher rate.

(5)—(9) [Omitted.]

[Section 18 is printed as amended by the Criminal Justice Act 1982, ss 38, 46 (1), 47 (1).]

[18A. Additional liability in relation to alteration of vehicle or its use

(1) Where a person convicted of an offence under section 18 of this Act is the person by whom the vehicle in respect of which the offence was committed was kept at the time it was committed, the court shall, in addition to any penalty which it may impose under that section, order him to pay an amount (the 'additional duty') calculated in accordance with this section.

(2) The additional duty shall, subject to subsections (7) and (8) below, be an amount equal to [one-twelfth] of the appropriate annual rate of duty for each [calendar month or part of a calendar month in the relevant period].

(3) The following Cases are referred to in subsections (5) and (6) below—

CASE A

Where—

(a) at the time of the offence the vehicle in question had a plated weight (the 'higher plated weight') which exceeds the plated weight (the 'previous plated weight') which it had when the current licence was taken out; and

(b) the current licence was taken out at the rate of duty applicable to the previous plated weight.

CASE B

Where—

(a) the vehicle in question is a tractor unit (within the meaning of paragraph 15 of Schedule 4 to this Act);

(b) the current licence was taken out at a rate of duty applicable to the use of the vehicle only with semi-trailers having not less than two axles or, as the case may be, only with semi-trailers having not less than three axles; and

(c) the offence consisted in using the vehicle with a semi-trailer with a smaller number of axles than that mentioned in paragraph (b) above, in circumstances in which it was not treated by virtue of paragraph 14(2) of Schedule 4 to this Act as being licensed in accordance with the requirements of this Act.

CASE C

Where—

(a) the current licence was taken out at the rate of duty applicable, by virtue of paragraph 8 of Schedule 4 to this Act, to a weight lower than the plated weight of the vehicle in question; and

(b) the offence consisted in using the vehicle in contravention of a condition imposed by virtue of paragraph 8(3) of Schedule 4.

CASE D

Where the current licence was taken out at a rate of duty lower than that applicable to the vehicle in question by reference to its plated weight and the circumstances of the case do not bring it within Case A, B or C.

CASE E

Where the current licence was taken out at a rate of duty lower than that at which duty was chargeable in respect of that condition or manner of use of the vehicle which constituted the offence and the circumstances of the case do not bring it within Case A, B, C or D.

(4) In this section 'current licence' means the licence in relation to which the offence was committed.

(5) In this section 'appropriate annual rate of duty' means the difference between the rate of duty at which the current licence was taken out and—

(a) in Case A, the rate which would have been applicable had the current licence been taken out by reference to the higher plated weight;

(b) in Case B, the rate which would have been applicable had the current licence been taken out by reference to that use of the vehicle which constituted the offence;

(c) in Case C, the rate which would have been applicable had the current licence been taken out by reference to the plated weight of the vehicle;

(d) in Case D, the rate which would have been applicable had the current licence been taken out by reference to the plated weight of the vehicle; and

(e) in Case E, the rate which would have been applicable had the current licence been taken out by reference to that condition or use of the vehicle which constituted the offence.

(6) In this section 'relevant period' means the period ending with the day on which the offence was committed and beginning—

(a) in relation to Case A, with the day on which the vehicle in question was plated with the higher plated weight; and

(b) in relation to each of the other Cases, with the day on which the current licence first took effect.

(7) Where the person convicted proves—

(a) that throughout any [month or part of a month] comprised in the relevant period he was not the keeper of the vehicle in question;

(b) that throughout any such [month or part] the vehicle in question was neither used nor kept by him on a public road . . .;

(c) that he had, before his conviction, paid the higher of the two rates of duty referred to in the relevant paragraph of subsection (5) above in respect of the vehicle for any such [month or part], whether or not on a licence; or

(d) that throughout any such [month or part] the vehicle was not chargeable with duty;

the additional duty shall be calculated as if that [month or part] were not comprised in the relevant period.

(8) Where a person is convicted of more than one contravention of section 18 of this Act in respect of the same vehicle (whether or not in the same proceedings) the court shall, in calculating the additional duty payable in respect of any one of those offences, reduce the amount calculated in accordance with the preceding provisions of this section in relation to a particular period by the amount of the additional duty ordered to be paid under this section in relation to that period in respect of the other offence or, as that case may be, offences.

(9) Except so far as it is proved to have fallen within some other description for the whole of [any month or part of a month comprised in the relevant period], the vehicle in question shall be taken for the purposes of this section to have belonged throughout

the relevant period to that description of vehicle to which it belonged for the purposes of duty at the date of the offence.

(10) Where, on a person's conviction of an offence under section 18 of this Act, an order is made under Part I of the Powers of Criminal Courts Act 1973 placing him on probation or discharging him absolutely or conditionally, this section shall apply as if the conviction were deemed to be a conviction for all purposes.

(11) This section shall have effect subject to the provisions (applying with the necessary modifications) of any enactment relating to the imposition of fines by magistrates' courts, other than one conferring a discretion as to their amount; and any sum payable by virtue of an order under this section shall be treated as a fine, and the order as a conviction, for the purposes of Part III of the Magistrates' Courts Act 1980 (including any enactment having effect as if contained in that Part) and of any other enactment relating to the recovery or application of sums ordered to be paid by magistrates' courts.

(12) *[Application to Scotland.]*

(13) This section is subject to Schedule 7 to this Act.]

[Section 18A was inserted by the Finance Act 1982, s 7 (1), and is printed as amended by Sched 7, para 17A, to the Vehicles (Excise) Act 1971 (para 17A having been inserted into Sched 7 by the Finance Act 1982, s 7 (3)).]

Registration and registration marks, etc

* * *

22. Failure to fix, and obstruction of, marks and signs

(1) If any mark to be fixed or sign to be exhibited on a vehicle in accordance with section 19 or 21 of this Act is not so fixed or exhibited, the person driving the vehicle, or, where the vehicle is not being driven, the person keeping the vehicle, shall be guilty of an offence:
Provided that it shall be a defence for a person charged under this subsection with failing to fix a mark on a vehicle to prove—

(a) that he had no reasonable opportunity of registering the vehicle under this Act and that the vehicle was being driven on a public road for the purpose of being so registered; or

(b) in a case where the charge relates to a vehicle to which [section 44 of the Road-Traffic Act 1972 applies by virtue of subsection (2) (b) thereof (vehicles manufactured before the prescribed period and used before registration)], that he had no reasonable opportunity of so registering the vehicle and that the vehicle was being driven on a road for the purposes of or in connection with its examination under [section 43 of the said Act of 1972 (examinations for test certificates) in circumstances in which its use is exempted from the said section 44 (1) by regulations under section 44 (6) thereof].

(2) If any mark fixed or sign exhibited on a vehicle as aforesaid is in any way obscured or rendered or allowed to become not easily distinguishable, the person driving the vehicle, or, where the vehicle is not being driven, the person keeping the vehicle, shall be guilty of an offence:
Provided that it shall be a defence for a person charged with such an offence to prove that he took all steps reasonably practicable to prevent the mark or sign being obscured or rendered not easily distinguishable.

(3) Any person guilty of an offence under this section shall be liable on summary conviction . . . to a fine not exceeding [level 3 on the standard scale].

[Section 22 is printed as amended by the Road Traffic Act 1972, s 203 (1), and Sched 7, and the Criminal Justice Act 1982, ss 38 (4), 46 (1) (this section fell within the term 'pre-1949 enactment' in the Criminal Law Act 1977, s 31 (9), its pedigree being traceable back to the Roads Act 1920, ss 6 (2), 11 (1); accordingly, the '£20' in subs (3)(a) was increased to '£50' under s 31(5)(a), (6)(a) and (7) of the 1977 Act, notwithstanding the fact that this resulted in the same penalty being applicable under subs (3)(a) (first conviction) and (3)(b) (subsequent conviction)).

For the application of the fixed penalty procedure to offences under subss (1) and (2), see the Transport Act 1982, Part III, and Sched 1.

Sections 19 and 21 of this Act relate to registration marks and distinctive signs for hackney carriages.]

* * *

Miscellaneous

* * *

26. Forgery and false information

(1) If any person forges or fraudulently alters or uses, or fraudulently lends or allows to be used by any other person—

(a) any mark to be fixed or sign to be exhibited on a mechanically propelled vehicle in accordance with section 19 or 21 of this Act; or

(b) any trade plates or replacements such as are mentioned in [section 23 (2) (c)] of this Act; or

(c) any licence or registration document under this Act,

he shall be liable on summary conviction to a fine not exceeding [the prescribed sum] or on conviction on indictment to imprisonment for a term not exceeding two years.

(2) Any person who—

(a) in connection with an application for a licence . . . makes a declaration which to his knowledge is false or in any material respect misleading; or

(b) being required by virtue of this Act to furnish particulars relating to, or to the keeper of, any vehicle, furnishes any particulars which to his knowledge are false or in any material respect misleading,

shall be liable on summary conviction to a fine not exceeding [the prescribed sum] or on conviction on indictment to imprisonment for a term not exceeding two years.

[Section 26 is printed as amended by s 39 and Sched 7, para 23, and the Criminal Law Act 1977, s 28 (2). Subsections (1) (b) and (2) (a) as so amended have effect until such date as the Secretary of State for Transport may order, whereupon subss (1) (b) and (2) (a) as originally enacted take effect (s 39 and Sched 7, para 6).

Sections 19 and 21 of this Act relate to registration marks and distinctive marks for hackney carriages.

The 'prescribed sum' is £2000 (Magistrates' Courts Act 1980, s 32 (9), as amended by the Criminal Penalties etc (Increase) Order 1984 (SI 1984 No 447)).]

27. Duty to give information

(1) Where it is alleged that a mechanically propelled vehicle has been used or kept in contravention of section 8, 16 (7) or 18 (4) of this Act—

(a) the person keeping the vehicle shall give such information as he may be required by or on behalf of a chief officer of police or the [Secretary of State for Transport] to give as to the identity of the person or persons concerned and, if he fails to do so, shall be guilty of an offence unless he shows to the satisfaction of the court that he did not know and could not with reasonable diligence have ascertained the identity of the person or persons concerned;

(b) any other person shall, if required as aforesaid, give such information as it is in his power to give and which may lead to the identification of any of the persons concerned and, if he fails to do so, shall be guilty of an offence; and

(c) in a case where it is alleged that the vehicle has been used at any time in contravention of the said section 8, the person who is alleged to have so used the vehicle shall, if required as aforesaid, give such information as it is in his power to give as to the identity of the person by whom the vehicle was kept at that time and, if he fails to do so, shall be guilty of an offence.

(2) The following persons shall be treated for the purposes of subsection (1) (a) and (b) above as persons concerned, that is to say—

(a) in relation to an alleged offence of using a vehicle in contravention of section 8, 16 (7) or 18 (4) of this Act, both the driver and any person using the vehicle;

(b) in relation to an alleged offence of keeping the vehicle in contravention of the said section 8, the person keeping the vehicle.

(3) A person guilty of an offence under subsection (1) of this section shall be liable on summary conviction to a fine not exceeding [level 3 on the standard scale].

[Section 27 is printed as amended by the Secretary of State for Transport Order 1976 (SI 1976 No 1775); the Minister of Transport Order 1979 (SI 1979 No 571); the Transfer of Functions (Transport) Order 1981 (SI 1981 No 238); and the Criminal Justice Act 1982, ss 38, 46 (1).]

Legal proceedings, etc

28. Institution and conduct of proceedings in England and Wales

(1) Subject to the provisions of this section, summary proceedings for an offence under section 8, 11 (2), 16 (7), 18 (4) or 26 (1) or (2) of this Act or under regulations made in pursuance of this Act may be instituted in England and Wales by the [Secretary of State for Transport] or a constable (in this section severally referred to as 'the authorised prosecutor') at any time within six months from the date on which evidence sufficient in the opinion of the authorised prosecutor to warrant the proceedings came to his knowledge; but no proceedings for any offence shall be instituted by virtue of this subsection more than three years after the commission of the offence.

(2) No proceedings for an offence under section 8, 16 (7) or 18 (4) of this Act shall be instituted in England and Wales except by the authorised prosecutor; and no proceedings for such an offence shall be so instituted by a constable except with the approval of the [Secretary of State for Transport]

(3) A certificate stating—

(a) the date on which such evidence as is mentioned in subsection (1) above came to the knowledge of the authorised prosecutor; or

(b) that the [Secretary of State for Transport's] approval is given for the institution by a constable of any proceedings specified in the certificate,

and signed by or on behalf of the authorised prosecutor or, as the case may be, the [Secretary of State for Transport] shall for the purposes of this section be conclusive evidence of the date or approval in question; and a certificate purporting to be given in pursuance of this subsection and to be signed as aforesaid shall be deemed to be so signed unless the contrary is proved.

(4) In a magistrates' court or before the registrar of a county court any proceedings by or against the [Secretary of State for Transport] under this Act may be conducted on behalf of the [Secretary of State for Transport] by a person authorised by him for the purposes of this subsection.

(5) [Section 145 of the Customs and Excise Management Act 1979] (which restricts the bringing of proceedings under that Act) and [section 147 (1)] of that Act (which extends the time for bringing such proceedings) shall not apply to proceedings in England or Wales for offences under this Act.

[Section 28 is printed as amended by the Secretary of State for Transport Order 1976 (SI 1976 No 1775); the Customs and Excise Management Act 1979, s 177 (1); and Sched 4, para 12; the Minister of Transport Order 1979 (SI 1979 No 571); and the Transfer of Functions (Transport) Order 1981 (SI 1981 No 238).
Section 11 of this Act relates to the continuous liability for duty.]

*   *   *

31. Admissibility of records as evidence

(1) A statement contained in a document purporting to be—

(a) a part of the records maintained by the [Secretary of State for Transport] in connection with any functions exercisable by the [Secretary of State for Transport] by virtue of this Act; or

(b) a copy of a document forming part of those records; or

(c) a note of any information contained in those records,

and to be authenticated by a person authorised in that behalf by the [Secretary of State for Transport] shall be admissible in any proceedings as evidence of any fact stated therein to the same extent as oral evidence of that fact is admissible in those proceedings.

(2) In subsection (1) above 'document' and 'statement' have the same meanings as in subsection (1) of section 10 of the Civil Evidence Act 1968, and the reference to a copy of a document shall be construed in accordance with subsection (2) of that section; but nothing in this subsection shall be construed as limiting to civil proceedings the references to proceedings in subsection (1) above.

(3) Nothing in the foregoing provisions of this section shall enable evidence to be given with respect to any matter other than a matter of the prescribed description.

(4) *[Application to Scotland.]*

[Section 31 is printed as amended by the Secretary of State for Transport Order 1976 (SI 1976 No 1775); the Minister of Transport Order 1979 (SI 1979 No 571); and the Transfer of Functions (Transport) Order 1981 (SI 1981 No 238).
For the meanings of the terms 'document' and 'statement' as defined in the Civil Evidence Act 1968, s 10, see the notes to the Road Traffic Act 1972, s 182.]

32. Evidence of admissions in certain proceedings

Where in any proceedings in England and Wales for an offence under section 8 or section 16 (7) of this Act—

(a) it is proved to the satisfaction of the court, on oath or in manner prescribed by rules made under section 15 of the Justices of the Peace Act 1949, that a requirement under section 27 (1) (*a*) or (*b*) of this Act to give information as to the identity of the driver of, or the person using or keeping, a particular vehicle on the particular occasion on which the offence is alleged to have been committed has been served on the accused by post; and

(*b*) a statement in writing is produced to the court purporting to be signed by the accused that the accused was the driver of, or the person using or keeping, that vehicle on that occasion,

the court may accept the statement as evidence that the accused was the driver of, or the person using or keeping, that vehicle on that occasion.

33. Burden of proof in certain proceedings

If in any proceedings under section 8, 16 (7) or 26 (2) of this Act any question arises—

(*a*) as to the number of mechanically propelled vehicles used, or

(*b*) as to the character, weight, horse-power or cylinder capacity of any mechanically propelled vehicle, or

(*c*) as to the number of persons for which a mechanically propelled vehicle has seating capacity, or

(*d*) as to the purpose for which any mechanically propelled vehicle has been used,

the burden of proof in respect of the matter in question shall lie on the defendant.

34. Fixing of amount payable under s 9 on plea of guilty by absent accused

Where in pursuance of [section 12 (2) of the Magistrates' Courts Act 1980] a person is convicted in his absence of an offence under section 8 of this Act and it is proved to the satisfaction of the court, on oath or in the manner prescribed by rules made under [section 144 of the Magistrates' Courts Act 1980], that there was served on the accused with the summons a notice stating that, in the event of his being convicted of the offence, it will be alleged that an order requiring him to pay an amount specified in the notice falls to be made by the court in pursuance of section 9 (1) of this Act then, unless in the notification purporting to be given by or on behalf of the accused in pursuance of [the said section 12 (2)] it is stated that the amount so specified is inappropriate, the court shall proceed in pursuance of the said section 9 (1) as if that amount had been calculated as required by that subsection.

[Section 34 is printed as amended by the Magistrates' Courts Act 1980, s 154 (1), and Sched 7, para 93.

Section 9 (1) of this Act provides that where a person convicted of an offence under s 8 is the person by whom the vehicle in respect of which the offence was committed was kept at the time it was committed, the court shall, in addition to any penalty under s 8, order him to pay an amount calculated in accordance with s 9 (2)–(4).]

* * *

SCHEDULE 3

ANNUAL RATES OF DUTY ON TRACTORS, ETC

PART I

1. The annual rate of duty applicable to a mechanically propelled vehicle of a description specified in the first column of Part II of this Schedule shall, according to the

unladen weight of the vehicle as set out in the second and third columns of that Table, be the initial rate specified in relation to vehicles of that description and that weight in the fourth column of that Table together with any additional rate so specified in the fifth column of that Table.

2.—(1) In this Schedule 'agricultural machine' means a locomotive ploughing engine, tractor, agricultural tractor or other agricultural engine which is not used on public roads for hauling any objects, except as follows, that is to say—

(a) for hauling its own necessary gear, threshing appliances, farming implements, a living van for the accommodation of persons employed in connection with the vehicle, or supplies of water or fuel required for the purposes of the vehicle or for agricultural purposes;

(b) for hauling, from one part of a farm to another part of that farm, agricultural or woodland produce of, or articles required for, the farm;

(c) for hauling, within 15 miles of a farm in the occupation of the person in whose name the vehicle is registered under this Act, agricultural or woodland produce of that farm, or agricultural or woodland produce of land occupied with that farm, or fuel required for any purpose on that farm or for domestic purposes by persons employed on that farm by the occupier of the farm;

(d) for hauling articles required for a farm by the person in whose name the vehicle is registered as aforesaid, being either the owner or occupier of the farm or a contractor engaged to do agricultural work on the farm by the owner or occupier of the farm, or for hauling articles required by that person for land occupied by him with a farm;

(e) for hauling, within 15 miles of a forestry estate in the occupation of the person in whose name the vehicle is registered as aforesaid, agricultural or woodland produce of that estate or fuel required for any purpose on that estate or for domestic purposes by persons employed on that estate by the occupier of the estate, or for hauling articles required for such a forestry estate by the occupier of the estate:

(f) for hauling, within 15 miles of a farm in the occupation of the person in whose name the vehicle is registered as aforesaid, material to be spread on roads to deal with frost, ice or snow;

(g) for hauling, for the purpose of clearing snow, a snow plough or similar contrivance.

(2) In this paragraph—

(a) any reference to a farm includes a market garden;

(b) any reference to woodland produce includes the wood and other produce of trees which are not woodland trees;

(c) any reference to articles required for a farm, forestry estate or other land includes articles which are or have been required for doing work on and for the purposes of the farm, forestry estate or other land, except that—

(i) the reference to articles required for a farm by a contractor engaged to do agricultural work on the farm shall include only articles required for the farm in connection with that work, and

(ii) the reference to articles required for land occupied with a farm shall include only articles required for the land in connection with the doing on the land of any agricultural or forestry work (including the getting and carrying away of any woodland produce);

(*d*) any reference to the owner of a farm includes any person having any estate or interest in land comprised in the farm.

3. In this Schedule 'digging machine' means a vehicle designed, constructed and used for the purpose of trench digging or any kind of excavating or shovelling work which—

(*a*) is used on public roads only for that purpose or for the purpose of proceeding to and from the place where it is to be used for that purpose; and

(*b*) when so proceeding, neither carries nor hauls any load than such as is necessary for its propulsion or equipment.

4. In this Schedule 'mobile crane' means a vehicle designed and constructed as a mobile crane which—

(*a*) is used on public roads only either as a crane in connection with work being carried on on a site in the immediate vicinity or for the purpose of proceeding to and from a place where it is to be used as a crane; and

(*b*) when so proceeding neither carries nor hauls any load than such as is necessary for its propulsion or equipment.

5. In this Schedule 'works truck' means a goods vehicle (within the meaning of Schedule 4 to this Act) designed for use in private premises and used on public roads only for carrying goods between such premises and a vehicle on a road in the immediate vicinity, or in passing from one part of any such premises to another or to other private premises in the immediate vicinity, or in connection with road works while at or in the immediate vicinity of the site of such works.

[5A. In this Schedule 'fisherman's tractor' means a tractor registered under this Act in the name of a person engaged in the business of sea fishing for food and not used on public roads for hauling anything except—

(*a*) a fishing boat and anything (including the catch) carried in it, which belongs to that person or to him and other persons engaged in that business in the same locality;

(*b*) fishing tackle or other equipment required by the crew, or for the operation, of any such boat;

(*c*) fishing tackle or other equipment required for and the catch from, fishing operations carried out with the tractor.]

[Paragraph 5A was inserted by the Finance Act 1976, s 14 (2).]

6. In this Schedule 'haulage vehicle' means a vehicle (other than one described in any of the foregoing paragraphs) which is constructed and used on public roads for haulage solely and not for the purpose of carrying or having superimposed upon it any load except such as is necessary for its propulsion or equipment.

7. In this Schedule 'showman's vehicle' means a vehicle registered under this Act in the name of a person following the business of a travelling showman and used solely by him for the purposes of his business and for no other purpose.

[PART II

1.	Weight unladen of vehicle		Rate of duty	
	2.	3.	4.	5. Additional for each ton or part of a ton in excess of the weight in column 2
Description of vehicle	Exceeding	Not exceeding	Initial	
			£	£
1. Agricultural machines; digging machines; mobile cranes; works trucks; mowing machines; fishermen's tractors.	—	—	15.00	—
2. Haulage vehicles, being show-men's vehicles.	—	7¼ tons	144.00	—
	7¼ tons	8 tons	172.00	—
	8 tons	10 tons	203.00	—
	10 tons	—	203.00	31.00
3. Haulage vehicles, not being showmen's vehicles.	—	2 tons	171.00	—
	2 tons	4 tons	308.00	—
	4 tons	6 tons	445.00	—
	6 tons	7¼ tons	581.00	—
	7¼ tons	8 tons	710.00	—
	8 tons	9 tons	831.00	—
	9 tons	10 tons	951.00	—
	10 tons	11 tons	1088.00	—
	11 tons	—	1088.00	—]

[Part II was substituted by the Finance Act 1984, s 4 (2), and Sched 2, Part I.]

Section B

Statutory Instruments

The Community Road Transport Rules (Exemptions) Regulations 1978

(SI 1978 No 1158)

[The text of these regulations is printed as amended by:
> *the Community Road Transport Rules (Exemptions) (Amendment) Regulations 1980 (SI 1980 No 266) (31 March 1980);*
> *the Community Road Transport Rules (Exemptions) (Amendment) Regulations 1980 (SI 1980 No 2018) (31 December 1980); and*
> *the Community Road Transport Rules (Exemptions) (Amendment) Regulations 1981 (SI 1981 No 1855) (31 December 1981).*

The amending regulations are referred to in the notes to the main regulations only by their year and number. The dates referred to above are the dates on which the regulations came into force.]

1. Citation, commencement and interpretation

(1) *[Omitted.]*

(2) In these Regulations—

'the Community Drivers' Ages and Hours of Work Regulation' means Council Regulation (EEC) No 543/69 on the harmonisation of certain social legislation relating to road transport, as amended by Council Regulations (EEC) Nos 514/72, 515/72, and 2827/77;

'the Community Recording Equipment Regulation' means Council Regulation (EEC) No 1463/70 on the introduction of recording equipment in road transport, as amended by Council Regulations (EEC) Nos 1787/73 and 2828/77.

(3) [The Interpretation Act 1978] shall apply for the interpretation of these Regulations as it applies for the interpretation of an Act of Parliament.

[Regulation 1 is printed as amended by the Interpretation Act 1978, s 17 (2).]

2. Limited exemptions for short distance freight transport operations

Pursuant to Article 14a (1) (power to grant exemption for short distance freight-transport) of the Community Drivers' Ages and Hours of Work Regulation exemption granted in the case of internal goods transport operations carried out within a radius of 50 kilometres from the place where the vehicle is based (including municipalities the centre of which is situated within that radius)—

(*a*) from Article 7 (1) (continuous driving periods) and Article 8 (breaks in driving periods) of that Regulation, provided that the daily driving period includes sufficient breaks to ensure that the periods laid down in paragraphs (1) and (2) of the said Article 8 are observed and that, in each case, there is a break of at least 30 minutes or two breaks of not less than 15 minutes each;

(*b*) as regards the transport of harvest produce and in respect of not more than 30 days in any year, from Article 11 (1) (daily rest period) of that Regulation, pro-

236

vided that a daily rest period of not less than 10 consecutive hours is observed and that the reduction in the daily rest period is made good by a corresponding additional rest period to be taken immediately before or after the weekly rest period; and

(c) until the compulsory installation of the recording equipment provided for in Article 1 of the Community Recording Equipment Regulation, from Article 14 (keeping of individual control books) of the Community Drivers' Ages and Hours of Work Regulation, provided that time spent in driving in the course of any day does not exceed 4 hours.

3. General exemptions for small passenger vehicles, for vehicles undergoing road tests and for vehicles used for transport of animals, animal carcases and waste unfit for human consumption

(1) Pursuant to Article 14a (2) (a), (b) and (c) (power to grant exemptions for certain national transport operations) of the Community Drivers' Ages and Hours of Work Regulation exemption is granted from that Regulation for the national transport operations mentioned in paragraph (3) below.

(2) Pursuant to Article 3 (2) (power to grant exemptions for certain vehicles) of the Community Recording Equipment Regulation exemption is granted from the application of that Regulation for vehicles when being used for the national transport operations mentioned in paragraph (3) . . . below.

(3) The national transport operations referred to in [paragraphs (1) and (2)] above are—

(a) operations involving the use of vehicles which are constructed and equipped to carry not more than 15 persons, including the driver,

(b) operations involving the use of vehicles undergoing local road tests for purposes of repair or maintenance, and

(c) operations for the transport of live animals from farms to local markets or vice-versa, or for the transport of animal carcases or waste not intended for human consumption,

. . .

[Regulation 3 is printed as amended by SI 1980 No 266.]

4. General exemptions for certain specialised vehicles

(1) Pursuant to Article 14a (3) (a) (power to grant exemptions in certain specialised cases) of the Community Drivers' Ages and Hours of Work Regulation exemption is granted from that Regulation for the national transport operations mentioned in paragraph (3) below.

(2) Pursuant to Article 3 (3) (power to grant exemptions for certain vehicles) of the Community Recording Equipment Regulation exemption is granted from the application of that Regulation for vehicles when being used for the national transport operations mentioned in paragraph (3) below.

(3) The national transport operations referred to in paragraphs (1) and (2) above are operations involving the use of specialised vehicles—

(a) at local markets,

(b) for door-to-door selling,

(c) for mobile banking, exchange or savings transactions,

(d) for purposes of worship,

(e) for the lending of books, records or cassettes, or

(f) for cultural events or mobile exhibitions.

5. Conditional exemption for certain operations for the transport of milk

[(1) Pursuant to Article 14a(3)(b) (power to grant exemptions in relation to the transport of milk) of the Community Drivers' Ages and Hours of Work Regulation exemption is granted, subject to paragraph (2) below, from that Regulation for national transport operations—

(a) for the transport of milk directly from farms to a dairy or to a reload point, which involves the collection of milk from farms, or

(b) until 31st December 1984, for the transport of untreated milk between reload points and dairies.]

(2) The exemption granted by paragraph (1) above is granted subject to the following conditions:—

(a) no period of continuous driving by a person engaged in the operations mentioned in paragraph (1) above shall exceed 5 hours,

(b) the total driving period for such a person in any two consecutive weeks shall not exceed 108 hours,

(c) such a person shall have—
  (i) in any week a continuous rest period of at least 24 hours, or
  (ii) in any period of two consecutive weeks a continuous rest period of at least 48 hours, and

(d) [Revoked.]

[Regulation 5 is printed as amended by SI 1980 No 2018 and SI 1981 No 1855.]

6. Consultation with or authorisation by the Commission

(1) The exemptions granted by Regulations 2 and 3 above are granted after consultation with the Commission of the European Communities as required by the provisions of the Community Regulations respectively mentioned in Regulations 2 and 3 above.

(2) The exemptions granted by Regulations 4 and 5 above are granted after the authorisation of the Commission given in their decision [OJ L 203 27.7.78, p 39] which has been taken under the relevant provisions of the Community Regulations mentioned above on 30th June 1978 on an application by the United Kingdom Government.

The Disabled Persons (Badges for Motor Vehicles) Regulations 1982

(SI 1982 No 1740)

ARRANGEMENT OF REGULATIONS

1. *[Omitted.]*

2. Revocation

(1) The Disabled Persons (Badges for Motor Vehicles) Regulations 1975 *[SI 1975 No 266]* are hereby revoked.

(2) Any application made, any badge issued or anything else done under and in accordance with the Regulations hereby revoked or having effect as if so made, issued or done shall not be invalidated by the revocation thereof but shall have effect as if made, issued or done under and in accordance with the corresponding provision of these Regulations.

3. Interpretation

(1) In these Regulations—

'the Act' means the [Road Traffic Regulation Act 1984];

'disabled person' means a person who is over two years of age and who is of a description prescribed by Regulation 5;

'disabled person's badge' means a badge in the form prescribed by Regulation 4 issued by a local authority for display on a motor vehicle driven by a disabled person, or used for the carriage of a disabled person or of several disabled persons, and includes a duplicate badge issued pursuant to Regulation 8;

'holder', in relation to a disabled person's badge means the person to whom the badge was issued;

'institution' means an institution concerned with the care of the disabled;

'local authority' means an authority referred to in section 21(8) of the Chronically Sick and Disabled Persons Act 1970;

'relevant conviction', means

(a) the conviction of either—
   (i) the holder of a disabled person's badge; or
   (ii) any other person using a disabled person's badge with holder's consent.

of an offence of using or causing or permitting a vehicle to be used arising—
   (A) under section 1(8), 6(9), 9(9) or 12(9) of the Act if the offence consisted of the unlawful parking of the vehicle, or
   (B) under section 31(3), 31(3A), 42(1) or 42(1A) of the Act; and

(b) the conviction of any person other than the holder of a disabled person's badge of an offence under [section 117] of the Act where the badge was displayed on the vehicle with the consent of the holder at any time during which the offence was being committed;

and the expression 'relevant conviction' includes the liability of any person who would be liable to the conviction of an offence as mentioned above but who is liable, instead, to pay a fixed penalty pursuant to [sections 107 to 111 of and Schedule 12 to the Act].

(2) *[Omitted.]*

[Regulation 3 is printed as amended by the Road Traffic Regulation Act 1984, s 144(1), and Sched 10, para 2.

The Chronically Sick and Disabled Persons Act 1970, s 21(8) (referred to in the definition of 'local authority'), as amended by the Local Government Act 1972, Sched 30, and the Local Government (Scotland) Act 1973, Sched 14, defines local authorities as 'the common council of the City of London, the council of a county . . . in England and Wales or of a London borough and the council of a [region or islands area] in Scotland.']

4. *[Form of badge.]*

5. Descriptions of disabled persons

The prescribed descriptions of disabled person to whom a local authority may issue a disabled person's badge are a person who—

(a) receives a mobility allowance pursuant to section 37A of the Social Security Act 1975;

(b) uses a motor vehicle supplied by the Department of Health and Social Security, the Scottish Home and Health Department or the Welsh Office or is in receipt of a grant pursuant to section 5(2)(a) of the National Health Service Act 1977 or section 46 of the National Health Service (Scotland) Act 1978;

(c) is registered as blind under section 29 of the National Assistance Act 1948, or, in Scotland, is a blind person within the meaning of section 64(1) of that Act; or

(d) has a permanent and substantial disability which causes inability to walk or very considerable difficulty in walking.

[Section 37A was inserted into the Social Security Act 1975 by the Social Security Pension Act 1975, s 22(1). A footnote in the regulations draws attention, in the context of s 37A, to the Social Security (Miscellaneous Provisions) Act 1977, s 13.]

6. Badges for institutions

An institution is eligible to apply for the issue to it of a disabled person's badge for any motor vehicle or, as the case may be, for each motor vehicle used by or on behalf of the institution to carry disabled persons.

7. Period of issue of badge

Subject to the provisions of Regulation 11, a disabled person's badge shall be issued for a period of three years beginning with the date upon which it is issued.

8. *[Duplicate badge.]*

9. *[Fee for badge.]*

10. Grounds for refusing to issue badge

(1) The cases in which a local authority may refuse to issue a disabled person's badge are cases where—

(a) the applicant for the badge holds or has held a disabled person's badge, either under the provisions of these Regulations or under any of the provisions mentioned in Regulation 13, and in respect of that badge there has occurred on at least three occasions misuse which has led to a relevant conviction or which would give grounds for a relevant conviction; or

(b) the applicant fails to provide the authority with adequate evidence that he is a person to whom one or more of the descriptions of disabled person prescribed in Regulation 5 applies; or

(c) the applicant fails to pay the fee (if any) chargeable for the issue of the badge.

(2) In a case where a local authority refuses to issue a disabled person's badge in response to an application for one, it shall issue to the applicant a notice stating the grounds for refusal.

11. Return of badge to issuing authority

(1) A disabled person's badge shall be returned to the local authority by whom it was issued immediately on the occurrence of any of the following events, namely—

(a) if the badge ceases to be required for the motor vehicle or all the motor vehicles in respect of which it was issued;

(b) on the expiry of the period for which the badge was issued;

(c) on the death of the person to whom the badge was issued or, where the badge was issued to an institution, on the institution ceasing to exist;

(d) if the holder of the badge ceases to be a disabled person or, in the case of an institution, ceases to be eligible under Regulation 6;

(e) if the badge has been obtained by false representation;

(f) where a duplicate badge has been issued to replace a badge lost or stolen, and the duplicated badge is subsequently found or recovered.

(2) Subject to the provisions of Regulation 12, a disabled person's badge shall, within the time prescribed in paragraph (3), be returned to the local authority by whom it was issued in the event of that authority issuing a notice stating—

(a) that the authority refuses to allow the issue of the badge to continue in consequence of the misuse on at least three occasions of the badge which has either led to a relevant conviction or would give grounds for a relevant conviction; and (*b*) particulars of that misuse.

(3) The prescribed time for the return of a disabled person's badge in a case where a notice is issued as mentioned in paragraph (2) is—

(*a*) where no appeal is made as mentioned in Regulation 12, 28 days from the date of the issue of the notice;

(*b*) where an appeal is made as mentioned in Regulation 12, and the appeal is not allowed, 28 days from the date on which the Secretary of State issues a notice of his determination of the appeal.

(4) A local authority by whom a disabled person's badge is issued may take such action as may be appropriate to recover a badge which the holder is liable to return in accordance with paragraph (1) or (2).

12. Appeals

(1) A person to whom a notice has been issued as provided in Regulation 10(2) stating as the grounds for refusal the grounds mentioned in Regulation 10(1)(*a*) or as provided in Regulation 11(2) may appeal, against the decision in respect of which the notice is issued, to the Secretary of State within 28 days of the date on which the notice is issued, and in relation to any such appeal the procedure specified in paragraph (2) shall, subject to paragraph (3), be followed.

(2) The procedure mentioned in paragraph (1) is as follows:—

(*a*) every appeal shall be written, dated, signed by the appellant or by another person authorised to sign on the appellant's behalf, and shall state the ground on which the appeal is made;

(*b*) the appellant shall serve the appeal on the Secretary of State either by post or otherwise by delivery—

    (i) if the local authority against whose decision the appeal is made is in England, to the Department of Transport, 2 Marsham Street, London SW1P 3EB,

    (ii) if the local authority against whose decision the appeal is made is in Scotland, to the Scottish Development Department, New St. Andrew's House, Edinburgh EH1 3SZ,

    (iii) if the local authority against whose decision the appeal is made is in Wales, to the Welsh Office, Cathays Park, Cardiff CP1 3NQ;

(*c*) on receipt of an appeal made as provided above, the Secretary of State shall send a copy of it to the local authority against whose decision the appeal is made;

(*d*) within 28 days of the date on which a local authority receives a copy of an appeal as mentioned in sub-paragraph (*c*), it shall send to the Secretary of State—

    (i) a copy of the notice mentioned in Regulation 10(2) or, as the case may be, Regulation 11(2), and

    (ii) any comments it may wish the Secretary of State to take into account in determining the appeal;

(*e*) when the Secretary of State determines an appeal made as mentioned in paragraph (1) he shall issue a notice to the appellant stating whether he confirms or reverses the decision of the local authority, and such notice shall state the reasons for the determination; and

(*f*) the Secretary of State shall send a copy of the notice mentioned in sub-paragraph (*e*) to the local authority against whose decision the appeal was made.

(3) The Secretary of State may in his discretion determine an appeal made under paragraph (1) even if the provisions specified in paragraph (2)(*a*) to (*d*) have not been fully complied with.

(4) If the Secretary of State confirms the decision of the local authority the appellant shall return the disabled person's badge in question to the local authority within the time prescribed in Regulation 11(3).

13. Transitional provisions

(1) Any order made before the coming into operation of these Regulations, being an order made or having effect as if made under [section 1, 6, 9, 35, 45 or 46] of the Act and containing a provision operating with reference to—

(*a*) badges issued by a local authority in pursuance of any scheme having effect under section 29 of the National Assistance Act 1948, or any similar scheme having effect in Scotland, and borne by vehicles or a class of vehicle; or

(*b*) badges issued under and in accordance with Regulations revoked by Regulation 2 and borne by vehicles or a class of vehicle.

shall, on and after the coming into operation of these Regulations, apply and operate as if the reference in that provision to any such badge as is mentioned in (*a*) or (*b*) above were a reference to a disabled person's badge issued, or having effect as if issued, under and in accordance with these Regulations, borne by vehicles or, as the case may require, by the same class of vehicles, and displayed on a vehicle in the relevant position.

(2) For the purposes of paragraph (1) and any order referred to therein, a vehicle shall be regarded as displaying a disabled person's badge in the relevant position when—

(*a*) in the case of a vehicle fitted with a front windscreen, the badge is exhibited thereon with the front facing forwards on the near side of and immediately behind the windscreen; and

(*b*) in the case of a vehicle not fitted with a front windscreen, the badge is exhibited in a conspicuous position on the front or near side of the vehicle.

[Regulation 13 is printed as amended by the Road Traffic Regulation Act 1984, s 144(1), and Sched 10, para 2.]

*   *   *

The Drivers' Hours (Goods Vehicles) (Exemptions) Regulations 1978

(SI 1978 No 1364)

[The text of these regulations is printed as amended by the Drivers' Hours (Goods Vehicles) (Exemptions) (Amendment) Regulations 1982 (SI 1982 No 1554) (3 December 1982).

The amending regulations are referred to in the notes to the main regulations only by their year and number. The date referred to above is the date on which the regulations came into force.]

* * *

2. Interpretation

(1) In these Regulations, unless the context otherwise requires—

'the Act' means the Transport Act 1968;

'the Community rules' means those provisions of Council Regulation (EEC) No 543/69 of 25th March 1969 on the harmonisation of certain social legislation relating to road transport (as last amended by Council Regulations (EEC) Nos 2827/77 and 2829/77, both of 12th December 1977) which regulate the driving and rest periods of drivers of goods and passenger vehicles and which apply in unmodified form to journeys or work in connection with international transport operations, but apply until 31st December 1980 in modified form, and thereafter in unmodified form, to journeys or work in connection with national transport operations in Great Britain;

'Community regulated journeys or work' means journeys or work to which the Community rules apply, whether in modified or unmodified form;

'domestic journeys or work' means journeys or work to which the Community rules do not apply but to which the provisions of Part VI of the Act do apply;

'the Harmonisation Regulations' means the Drivers' Hours (Harmonisation with Community Rules) Regulations 1978 *[SI 1978 No 1157]*;

'section 96' means section 96 of the Act;

and any other expression which is also used in Part VI of the Act has the same meaning as in that Part of that Act.

(2) The references in these Regulations to the Community rules as applying in modified form are references to those rules as temporarily modified by the Community Drivers' Hours Rules (Temporary Modifications) Regulations 1978 *[SI 1978 No 7]* and the references in these Regulations to the Community rules as applying in unmodified form are references to those rules as they have effect without that modification.

(3) Any reference in an entry in Column 1 of Part I of the Schedule to these Regulations to an emergency is a reference to such a case of emergency as is specified in Column 2 of that Part in relation to that entry, and any reference in an entry in Col-

umn 1 of Part II of the Schedule to these Regulations to a special need is a reference to such a special need as is specified in Column 2 of that Part in relation to that entry.

(4) Subject to paragraph (5) below, any reference in these Regulations to an enactment or instrument is a reference to that enactment or instrument as amended by any subsequent enactment or instrument.

(5) In interpreting a provision of these Regulations which grants an exemption from the requirements of any of subsections (1) to (6) of section 96, or imposes a condition in relation to such exemption, in a case (and only in a case) where apart from the exemption the subsection in question would apply to a driver in a form affected by the provisions of the Harmonisation Regulations, any reference in that provision to the subsection in question shall be construed as a reference to that subsection as amended by the Harmonisation Regulations and—

(a) the expression 'working day' in that provision shall be construed in accordance with the amendment to the definition of that expression made by Regulation 4 (3) of the Harmonisation Regulations, and

(b) the expression 'working week' in that provision shall be construed in accordance with the revised definition of that expression given in Regulation 4 (8), or Regulation 5 (6) of the Harmonisation Regulations (as the case may be), if, and only if, that revised definition would have been used in applying the requirements of the particular subsection of section 96 to that driver, had there been no such exemption.

[The Community Drivers' Hours Rules (Temporary Modifications) Regulations 1978 (SI 1978 No 7) have now lapsed.]

3. Exemptions from requirements as to drivers' hours

(1) For the purpose of enabling drivers of goods vehicles to deal with the cases of emergency and to meet the special needs specified in Parts I and II of the Schedule to these Regulations such drivers are hereby exempted from the requirements of the relevant subsections of section 96 to the extent specified in column 1 of the said Parts I and II in relation to them, subject, however, to the conditions specified or referred to therein in relation to them.

(2) For the purposes of paragraph (1) above 'the relevant subsections of section 96' means—

(a) in relation to a driver who spends time on duty to deal with an emergency—
   (i) where that time is spent by him on domestic journeys or work, subsections (1) to (6),
   (ii) where that time is spent by him on Community regulated journeys or work, subsections (2), (3) and (5),

(b) in relation to a driver who spends time on duty to meet a special need—
   (i) where that time is spent by him on domestic journeys or work, subsections (3) to (6),
   (ii) where that time is spent by him on Community regulated journeys or work, subsections (3) and (5).

(3) Where in a working day or a working week a driver spends time on duty to meet a special need and that time is spent on both domestic journeys or work and Community regulated journeys or work, then, in applying the provisions of these Regulations, account shall be taken of both the domestic and the Community regulated journeys or work in determining whether the time spent by the driver in the

working day or working week in question has been spent wholly or mainly in meeting the special need.

(4) Nothing in these Regulations shall exempt any driver from the relevant requirements of the Community rules in any case where they apply.

SCHEDULE

PART I

CASES OF EMERGENCY

Column 1 Drivers exempted, requirements exempted from and conditions of exemption	Column 2 Emergencies

A driver who spends time on duty to deal with an emergency—
 	
(1) is exempted from the requirements of section 96 (1), (2) and (3) in respect of any working day during which he spends time on such duty, subject to the condition that he does not during that day spend time on duty (otherwise than for dealing with an emergency) for a period of, or periods amounting in the aggregate to, more than 11 hours:
 	
Provided that where a driver spends time on duty to deal with an emergency which interrupts what would otherwise have been an interval for rest between two successive working days, this condition shall not preclude him from subsequently spending not more than 11 hours on duty (of which not more than 10 hours shall be spent in driving vehicles to which Part VI of the Act applies) for other purposes, if he has had, since he was last on duty for such other purposes, two or more intervals for rest which amount in the aggregate to a period of not less than 10 hours;
 	
(2) is exempted from the requirement of section 96 (4) in respect of the interval for rest between any working day during which he spends time on such duty and any succeeding working day, subject to the condition that he has between those days an interval for rest of not less than 10 hours, and in such a case subsections (1) to (3) and (8) of section 96 and sub-paragraph (1) above, shall in respect of each of the said working days mentioned above, apply in relation to the driver as if, for
	1. Events which—
	(a) cause or are likely to cause such—
	    (i) danger to the life or health of one or more individuals or animals, or
	    (ii) a serious interruption in the maintenance of public services for the supply of water, gas, electricity or drainage or of telecommunication or postal services, or
	    [(iii) a serious interruption in the use of roads railways or airports, or]
	(b) are likely to cause such serious damage to property,
	
	as to necessitate that taking of immediate action to prevent the occurrence or continuance of such danger or interruption or the occurrence of such damage.

Column 1	Column 2
Drivers exempted, requirements exempted from and conditions of exemption	Emergencies

the purposes of the expression 'working day' in each of those subsections, and in that sub-paragraph, he had had an interval for rest between the said days of not less than 11 hours;
 	
(3) is exempted from the requirement of section 96(5) in respect of any working week during which he spends time on such duty subject to the condition that he does not during that week spend time on duty (otherwise than for dealing with an emergency) for periods amounting in the aggregate to more than 66 hours;
 	
(4) is exempted from the requirement of section 96(6) in respect of any working week during which he spends time on such duty—
 	
  (a) subject to the conditions specified in Part III of this Schedule, and
 	
  (b) in a case where he spends time on such duty during the last 24 hours of that working week, subject also to the condition that he does not during that period of 24 hours after spending time on duty for dealing with an emergency, spend time on duty for any other purpose.	

[Part I of this Schedule is printed as amended by SI 1982 No 1554.]

PART II

CASES OF SPECIAL NEED

Column 1	Column 2
Drivers exempted, requirements exempted from and conditions of exemption	Special Needs

Post Office
 	
1.—(1) A driver of a goods vehicle which is used for the purposes of the Post Office is exempted from the requirements of—
 	
(*a*) section 96 (3) in respect of any working day to which this paragraph applies during which the time spent by him on duty is spent wholly or mainly in meeting a special need, subject to the condition that that working day does not exceed 14 hours; and
 	
(*b*) section 96 (5) and (6) in respect of any working week to which this paragraph applies during which the time spent by him on duty is spent wholly or mainly in meeting such a need, subject, in the case of the exemption from the requirements of—
 	
   (i) section 96 (5), to the condition that he is not on duty in that week for periods amounting in the aggregate to more than 66 hours, and
 	
   (ii) section 96 (6), to the conditions specified in Part III of this Schedule.
 	
(2) The working weeks to which this paragraph applies are any which fall wholly or partly in the month of December in any year, and the working days to which this paragraph applies are any which fall wholly or partly within any such working week.
	1. Work done wholly or mainly in connection with the handling of mail.

Column 1	Column 2
Drivers exempted, requirements exempted from and conditions of exemption	Special Needs

Carriage of food and drink

2.—(1) A driver is exempted from the requirements of—

(*a*) section 96 (3) in respect of any working day to which this paragraph applies during which the time spent by him on duty is spent wholly or mainly in meeting a special need, subject to the condition that that working day does not exceed 14 hours; and

(*b*) section 96 (5) and (6) in respect of any working week to which this paragraph applies during which the time spent by him on duty is spent wholly or mainly in meeting such a need, subject, in the case of the exemption from the requirements of—

   (i) section 96 (5), to the condition that he is not on duty in that week for periods amounting in the aggregate to more than 66 hours, and

   (ii) section 96 (6), to the conditions specified in Part III of this Schedule.

(2) The working weeks to which this paragraph applies are—

(*a*) the working week in which Good Friday falls;

(*b*) the working week which immediately precedes that in which the first Monday in May bank holiday falls;

(*c*) the working week which immediately precedes that in which the spring bank holiday Monday falls;

(*d*) the six working weeks which immediately precede the working week in which the summer bank holiday Monday falls; and

2. Work done wholly or mainly in connection with the carriage of food or drink other than—

(*a*) bread;

(*b*) milk;

(*c*) fodder or feeding stuffs for animals; or

(*d*) articles or substances used only as drugs.

Column 1	Column 2
Drivers exempted, requirements exempted from and conditions of exemption	Special Needs
(e) the working week in which 1st January falls and the two immediately preceding working weeks; and the working days to which this paragraph applies are any which fall wholly or partly within any such working week. In this paragraph the expression 'bank holiday' means a bank holiday under the Banking and Financial Dealings Act 1971 either generally or in the particular locality where the journey or part of the journey takes place. *Carriage of bread* 3.—(1) A driver is exempted from the requirements of— (a) section 96 (3) in respect of any working day to which this sub-paragraph applies during which the time spent by him on duty is spent wholly or mainly in meeting a special need, subject to the condition that that working day does not exceed 14 hours; (b) section 96 (5) in respect of any working week such as is mentioned in paragraph 2 (2) above during which the time spent by him on duty is spent wholly or mainly in meeting such a need, subject to the condition that he is not on duty in that week for periods amounting in the aggregate to more than 66 hours; and (c) section 96 (6) in respect of any working week during which the time spent by him on duty is spent wholly or mainly in meeting such a need, subject to the conditions specified in Part III of this Schedule.	3. Work done wholly or mainly in connection with the carriage of bread.

Column 1	Column 2
Drivers exempted, requirements exempted from and conditions of exemption	Special Needs

(2) The working days to which sub-paragraph (1) (*a*) above applies are—

(*a*) subject to sub-paragraph (3) below, any which fall wholly or partly on a Friday or on a Saturday; or

(*b*) any which fall wholly or partly within any working week such as is mentioned in paragraph 2 (2) above; or

(*c*) without prejudice to sub-paragraph (*b*) above, any two each of which falls wholly or partly within a period of 7 days immediately preceding a bank holiday.

In this sub-paragraph the expression 'bank holiday' has the same meaning as in paragraph 2 above.

(3) In a case where, by virtue of sub-paragraphs (1) and (2) (*a*) above, a driver is exempted from the requirements mentioned in the said sub-paragraph (1) in respect of a working day which falls wholly or partly on a Friday, the said sub-paragraph (2) (*a*) shall apply in his case as if the reference to a Saturday were omitted.

Carriage of milk

4. A driver is exempted from the requirements of—

(*a*) section 96 (3) in respect of any working day to which this sub-paragraph applies during which the time spent by him on duty is spent wholly or mainly in meeting a special need, subject to the condition that that working day does not exceed 14 hours; and

(*b*) section 96 (5) and (6) in respect of any working week during which the time spent by him on

4. Work done wholly or mainly in connection with the carriage of milk.

Column 1	Column 2
Drivers exempted, requirements exempted from and conditions of exemption	Special Needs
duty is spent wholly or mainly in meeting such a need, subject, in the case of the exemption from the requirements of—	

(i) section 96 (5), to the condition that he is not on duty in that week for periods amounting in the aggregate to more than 66 hours, and

(ii) section 96 (6), to the condition that he has in the 14 day period which comprises that working week and the next following working week a continuous period of not less than 48 hours for which he is off duty.

Carriage of liquid egg

5.—(1) A driver is exempted from the requirements of—

(a) section 96 (3) in respect of any working day to which this sub-paragraph applies during which the time spent by him on duty is spent wholly or mainly in meeting a special need, subject to the condition that that working day does not exceed 14 hours; and

(b) section 96 (5) and (6) in respect of any working week during which the time spent by him on duty is spent wholly or mainly in meeting such a need, subject, in the case of the exemption from the requirements of—

(i) section 96 (5), to the condition that he is not on duty in that week for periods amounting in the aggregate to more than 66 hours, and

(ii) section 96 (6), to the conditions specified in Part III of this Schedule.

5. Work done wholly or mainly in connection with the carriage of liquid egg in bulk.

Column 1	Column 2
Drivers exempted, requirements exempted from and conditions of exemption	Special Needs
(2) The working days to which sub-paragraph (1) (*a*) above applies are any which fall wholly or partly within any working week such as is mentioned in paragraph 2 (2) above.	
Carriage of animals	
6.—(1) A driver is exempted from the requirements of—	6. Work done wholly or mainly in connection with the carriage of animals.
(*a*) section 96 (3) in respect of any working day during which the time spent by him on duty is spent wholly or mainly in meeting a special need, subject to the condition that that working day does not exceed 14 hours;	
(*b*) section 96 (4) in respect of the interval for rest between that day and any succeeding working day, subject to the condition that he has between those days an interval for rest of not less than 10 hours; and	
(*c*) section 96 (5) and (6) in respect of any working week during which the time spent by him on duty is spent wholly or mainly in meeting such a need, subject, in the case of the exemption from the requirements of—	
(i) section 96 (5), to the condition that he is not on duty in that week for periods amounting in the aggregate to more than 66 hours, and	
(ii) section 96 (6), to the conditions specified in Part III of this Schedule.	
(2) In any case where a driver is exempted by virtue of paragraph (1) (*b*) above from the requirement of section 96 (4), subsections (1) to (3) and (8) of section 96 and the said sub-paragraph (1) (*b*) shall, in respect of	

Column 1	Column 2
Drivers exempted, requirements exempted from and conditions of exemption	Special Needs
each of the said working days mentioned in the said paragraph (1) (*b*), apply in relation to him as if, for the purposes of the expression 'working day' in each of those subsections, and in that sub-paragraph, he had had an interval for rest between the said days of not less than 11 hours.	
Carriage of animal waste not intended for human consumption	
7.—(1) A driver is exempted from the requirements of—	7. Work done wholly or mainly in connection with the carriage of animal waste not intended for human consumption.
(*a*) section 96 (3) in respect of any working day during which the time spent by him on duty is spent wholly or mainly in meeting a special need, subject to the condition that that working day does not exceed 14 hours;	
(*b*) section 96 (4) in respect of the interval for rest between that day and any succeeding working day, subject to the condition that he has between those days an interval for rest of not less than 10 hours; and	
(*c*) section 96 (5) in respect of any working week during which the time spent by him on duty is spent wholly or mainly in meeting such a need, subject to the condition that he is not on duty in that week for periods amounting in the aggregate to more than 66 hours.	
(2) In any case where a driver is exempted by virtue of paragraph (1) (*b*) above from the requirement of section 96 (4), subsections (1) to (3) and (8) of section 96 and the said sub-paragraph (1) (*b*) shall, in respect of each of the said working days mentioned in the said paragraph (1) (*b*), apply in relation to him as if, for the	

Column 1	Column 2
Drivers exempted, requirements exempted from and conditions of exemption	Special Needs

purposes of the expression 'working day' in each of those subsections, and in that sub-paragraph, he had had an interval for rest between the said days of not less than 11 hours.

Carriage of fish and agricultural produce, of things used for the repair or replacement of agricultural machinery, of certain materials used in agriculture and of felled trees.

8. A driver is exempted from the requirements of—

    (*a*) section 96 (3) in respect of any working day during which the time spent by him on duty is spent wholly or mainly in meeting a special need, subject to the condition that that working day does not exceed 14 hours; and

    (*b*) section 96 (5) and (6) in respect of any working week during which the time spent by him on duty is spent wholly or mainly in meeting such a need, subject, in the case of the exemption from the requirements of—

        (i) section 96 (5), to the condition that he is not on duty in that week for periods amounting in the aggregate to more than 66 hours, and

        (ii) section 96 (6), to the conditions specified in Part III of this Schedule.

8. Work done wholly or mainly in connection with—

    (*a*) the carriage of fish from the place where it has been landed direct to another place, where the carriage takes place immediately after the fish has been landed; or

    (*b*) the carriage of anything produced in the course of agriculture from the place where it is produced (being a place at which the business of agriculture is carried on) direct to another place, where the journey on which the produce is carried commenced during the harvest period for that produce.

    For the purposes of this paragraph a journey shall not be treated otherwise than as direct by reason only of any temporary interruption made for the purpose of transferring the produce from one means of transport to another; or

    (*c*) the carriage of anything used for or in connection with the repair or replacement of agricultural machinery (including fuel and lubricants for such machinery) at a time when it is being used in connection with the harvesting of such produce as aforesaid; or

Column 1	Column 2
Drivers exempted, requirements exempted from and conditions of exemption	Special Needs
	(d) the carriage of agricultural lime, seed or fertilizers, or of fodder or feeding stuffs for animals; or
	(e) the carriage of trees from any place where they have recently been felled.
	In this paragraph 'agriculture' has the same meaning as in Part VI of the Act, except that it does not include dairy farming or livestock breeding and keeping, and 'agricultural' shall be construed accordingly.
Blood transfusion service	
9. A driver is exempted from the requirement of section 96 (3) in respect of any working day during which the time spent by him on duty is spent wholly or mainly in meeting a special need, subject to the conditions that—	9. Work done wholly or mainly in connection with the collection and delivery of blood for the purposes of transfusion.
(a) that working day does not exceed 14 hours;	
(b) he is able to obtain rest and refreshment during that day for a period which is, or for periods which in the aggregate are, not less than the time by which the working day exceeds 10 hours; and	
(c) he has not taken advantage of the exemption conferred by this paragraph on more than one previous working day which forms part of the working week of which that day forms part.	

Column 1	Column 2
Drivers exempted, requirements exempted from and conditions of exemption	Special Needs

Distribution of newspapers, magazines and periodicals

10.—(1) A driver is exempted from the requirements of—	10. Work done wholly or mainly in connection with the distribution of newspapers, magazines or periodicals to wholesalers or to persons or premises for the purposes of their sale by retail by those persons or at those premises.

(*a*) section 96 (3) in respect of any working day during which the time spent by him on duty is spent wholly or mainly in meeting a special need, subject to the condition that that working day does not exceed 14 hours; and

(*b*) section 96 (4) in respect of the interval for rest between that day and any succeeding working day, subject to the condition that he has between those days an interval for rest of not less than 10 hours.

(2) In any case where a driver is exempted by virtue of sub-paragraph (1) (*b*) above from the requirement of section 96 (4), subsections (1) to (3) and (8) of section 96 and the said sub-paragraph (1) (*b*), shall, in respect of each of the said working days mentioned in the said paragraph (1) (*b*), apply in relation to him as if, for the purposes of the expression 'working day' in each of those subsections, and in that sub-paragraph, he had had an interval for rest between the said days of not less than 11 hours.

Carriage of materials used in building or civil engineering work

11. A driver is exempted from the requirements of—	11. Work done wholly or mainly in connection with the carriage of materials or components used in building or civil engineering work to or from sites where such work is being prepared or carried out.

(*a*) section 96 (3) in respect of any working day during which the time spent by him on duty is spent wholly or mainly in meeting a special need, subject to the condition that that working day does not exceed 14 hours; and

Column 1	Column 2
Drivers exempted, requirements exempted from and conditions of exemption	Special Needs

(*b*) section 96 (5) and (6) in respect of any working week during which the time spent by him on duty is spent wholly or mainly in meeting such a need, subject in the case of the exemption from the requirements of—

  (i) section 96 (5), to the condition that he is not on duty in that week for periods amounting in the aggregate to more than 66 hours, and

  (ii) section 96 (6), to the conditions specified in Part III of this Schedule.

Furniture removal and carriage of shop-fittings

12. A driver is exempted from the requirement of section 96 (3) in respect of any working day during which the time spent by him on duty is spent wholly or mainly in meeting a special need, subject to the condition that that working day does not exceed 14 hours.

12. Work done wholly or mainly in connection with furniture removal (that is to say, the carriage of household furniture and effects from one private residence to another or to or from a place where such furniture and effects are to be or have been put in store) or with the carriage of shopfittings to or from shops.

Carriage of explosives, radioactive substances and ships' stores.

13. A driver is exempted from the requirement of section 96 (3) in respect of any working day during which the time spent by him on duty is spent wholly or mainly in meeting a special need, subject to the condition that that working day does not exceed 14 hours.

13. Work done wholly or mainly in connection with—

  (*a*) the carriage of explosives (within the meaning of the Explosives Act 1875); or

  (*b*) the carriage of radioactive substances (within the meaning of the Radioactive Substances Act 1948); or

  (*c*) the delivery of stores to ships.

Column 1	Column 2
Drivers exempted, requirements exempted from and conditions of exemption	Special Needs

Carriage of exceptional loads when accompanied by the police

14. A driver is exempted from the requirements of—

    (*a*) section 96 (3) in respect of any working day during which the time spent by him on duty is spent wholly or mainly in meeting a special need, subject to the conditions that—

        (i) that working day does not exceed 14 hours, and

        (ii) he is off duty during that day for a period which is, or for periods which in the aggregate are, not less than the time by which that working day exceeds 11 hours; and

    (*b*) section 96 (5) and (6) in respect of any working week during which the time spent by him on duty is spent wholly or mainly in meeting such a need, subject, in the case of the exemption from the requirements of—

        (i) section 96 (5), to the condition that he is not on duty in that week for periods amounting in the aggregate to more than 66 hours, and

        (ii) section 96 (6), to the conditions specified in Part III of this Schedule.

14. Work done wholly or mainly in connection with the carriage of a load where, owing to its dimensions or weight, the vehicle by which it is carried is accompanied for the whole or the greater part of its journey by one or more motor vehicles each driven by a constable in uniform.

Carriage of goods by sea ferry

15. A driver is exempted from the requirement of section 96 (3) in respect of any working day during which the time spent by him on duty is spent wholly or mainly in meeting a special need, subject to the conditions that—

15. Work done wholly or mainly in connection with the carriage of goods where the journey on which they are carried—

    (*a*) involves their being ferried across the sea from one place

Column 1	Column 2
Drivers exempted, requirements exempted from and conditions of exemption	Special Needs
(a) that working day does n exceed 14 hours; and	within Great Britain to another such place, without being removed from the vehicle in which they are carried, and
(b) he is off duty during that day f a period which is, or for perio which in the aggregate are, n less than the time by which th working day exceeds 11 hours.	(b) is one during the whole of which the vehicle is driven or accompanied by the same driver.

PART III

CONDITIONS APPLICABLE TO EXEMPTIONS FROM SECTION 96 (6)

Where any entry in column 1 of this Schedule (other than entry No 4 in Part II) provides for an exemption from the requirement of section 96 (6) in relation to any such working week of a driver as is mentioned in that entry to enable that driver to spend time on duty to meet an emergency or a special need subject to the conditions specified in this Part of this Schedule, the conditions so referred to are the following—

(i) that the driver has, in respect of each working week in the course of which he has not had such a period off duty as is required by section 96 (6), a period of not less than 24 hours for which he is off duty,

(ii) that any such period is taken within a period of 28 days starting from the beginning of the working week in respect of which he is required to have that period and is taken by him in addition to any other period for which the driver is required by these conditions or by section 96 (6) to be off duty in the case of any other working week.

The Drivers' Hours (Harmonisation with Community Rules) Regulations 1978

(SI 1978 No 1157)

[The following summary of the general effect of these regulations, the European Communities Act 1972 and other instruments referred to in these regulations on the law relating to the hours of work for drivers of passenger and goods vehicles is taken from the explanatory note which was published with these regulations and shows which set of rules (ie Community or domestic) applies, or does not apply, to the particular kinds of journey or work in connection with passenger or goods vehicles. Notes appended to individual regulations on their effect are derived from the same source.]

A. PASSENGER VEHICLES

(1) *International journeys and work*

The Community rules (unmodified) apply. The domestic rules do not apply (Regulation 2). If a person who undertakes international journeys or work also undertakes domestic journeys or work, account has to be taken of the time spent on the international journeys or work in applying the limits in the domestic rules to the domestic journeys or work (Regulation 3).

(2) *National journeys and work*

The Community rules apply in modified form until 31st December 1980 and thereafter in unmodified form. The domestic rules do not apply (Regulation 2). If a person who undertakes national journeys or work also undertakes domestic journeys or work, account has to be taken of the time spent on the national journeys or work in applying the limits in the domestic rules to the domestic journeys or work (Regulation 3).

(3) *Domestic journeys or work*

Where a person only undertakes domestic journeys or work, the domestic rules alone apply.

B. GOODS VEHICLES

(1) *International journeys and work*

The Community rules (unmodified) apply. The domestic rules do not apply (Regulation 2). If in any period of seven days at the beginning of which a person has undertaken international journeys or work—

(a) that person also undertakes national journeys or work, the domestic rules will not, during that period, apply to the national journeys or work (Regulations 2 and 4 (1)),

(b) that person also undertakes domestic journeys or work, the domestic rules will during that period apply to those journeys or work without the limits on duty (Regulation 5) but, insofar as the domestic rules do apply, the time spent on the international journeys or work (and the national journeys or work, if relevant), must be taken into account in applying the limits imposed by the domestic rules (Regulation 3).

(2) *National journeys or work*

The Community rules apply in modified form until 31st December 1980 and thereafter in unmodified form. Except in a case where the person undertaking the national journeys or work has at some time during the previous 7 days undertaken international journeys or work (for this case see (1) above)—

(a) the duty limits in the domestic rules apply in an amended form to the national journeys or work (Regulation 4 (2)–(5)),

(b) if the person also undertakes domestic journeys or work, the domestic rules apply in an amended form to the domestic journeys or work (Regulation 4 (3)–(7)) and any time spent by that person on the national journeys or work has to be taken into account in applying the limits in the domestic rules to the domestic journeys or work (Regulation 3).

(3) *Domestic journeys or work*

Where a person only undertakes domestic journeys or work, the domestic rules alone apply.

C. PASSENGER AND GOODS VEHICLES

Where a person on any working day or in any working week drives or carries out work in connection with both passenger and goods vehicles, he is not to be treated for the purposes of the domestic rules as a goods vehicle driver unless at least half the time he spends with the passenger and goods vehicles is spent with the goods vehicles (Regulation 4 (9) and (10) and Regulation 5 (7)).

D. NOTES

In this Summary—

'international journeys or work', 'national journeys or work' and 'domestic journeys or work' have the meanings given in Regulation 1 (3);

'the Community rules' has the meaning given ino Regulation 1 (3) and the references to the Community rules as being modified or unmodified should be construed in accordance with Regulation 1 (4);

'the domestic rules' means the provisions of section 96 (1) to (9) of the Transport Act 1968 (these provisions applying in substantially altered form to passenger vehicles by virtue of the Drivers' Hours (Passenger and Goods Vehicles) (Modifications) Order *[SI 1971 No 818]*.]

1. Citation, commencement, revocation and interpretation

(1), (2) *[Omitted.]*

(3) In these Regulations—

'the Act' means the Transport Act 1968, as amended by paragraph 9 of Schedule 4 to the European Communities Act 1972 and by section 2 of the Road Traffic (Drivers' Ages and Hours of Work) Act 1976;

'the Community rules' means those provisions of Council Regulation (EEC) No 543/69 of 25th March 1969 on the harmonisation of certain social legislation relating to road transport (as last amended by Council Regulations (EEC) Nos 2827/77 and 2829/77, both of 12th December 1977) which regulate the driving and rest periods of drivers of goods and passenger vehicles and which apply in unmodified form to journeys or work in connection with international transport operations, but apply until 31st December 1980 in modified form, and thereafter in unmodified form, to journeys or work in connection with national transport operations in Great Britain;

'Community regulated journeys or work' means journeys or work to which the Community rules apply, whether in modified or unmodified form;

'domestic journeys or work' means journeys or work to which the Community rules do not apply but to which the provisions of Part VI of the Act do apply;

'goods vehicle' and 'passenger vehicle' mean, respectively, any goods vehicle and any passenger vehicle to which Part VI of the Act applies;

'international journeys or work' means those Community regulated journeys or work which are undertaken in connection with international transport operations and to which the Community rules apply in unmodified form;

'national journeys or work' means those Community regulated journeys or work which are undertaken in connection with national transport operations in Great Britain and to which, so long as the temporary modifications referred to in paragraph (4) below continue, the Community rules apply in modified form, and thereafter in unmodified form.

(4) The references in these Regulations to the Community rules as applying in modified form are references to those rules as temporarily modified by the Community Drivers' Hours Rules (Temporary Modifications) Regulations 1978 *[SI 1978 No 7]*, and the references in these Regulations to the Community rules as applying in unmodified form are references to those rules as they have effect without that modification.

(5) Subject to the provisions of these Regulations, any expression which is used in these Regulations and is defined in Part VI of the Act has the same meaning in these Regulations as in that Part.

(6) The references in these Regulations to sections 96 and 103 of the Act are references—

  (a) so far as relating to passenger vehicles, to those sections as modified by Part II of the Drivers' Hours (Passenger and Goods Vehicles) (Modifications) Order 1971 *[SI 1971 No 818]*, and

  (b) so far as relating to goods vehicles, to those sections as modified by the Drivers' Hours (Goods Vehicles) (Modifications) Order 1970 *[SI 1970 No 257]* and by Part III of the said Order of 1971.

(7) [The Interpretation Act 1978] shall apply for the interpretation of these Regulations as it applies for the interpretation of an Act of Parliament, and as if for the purpose of [section 17] of that Act these Regulations were an Act of Parliament and the Regulations revoked by paragraph (2) above were Acts of Parliament thereby repealed.

[Regulation 1 is printed as amended by the Interpretation Act 1978, s 17 (2).
The Community Drivers' Hours Rules (Temporary Modifications) Regulations 1978 (SI 1978 No 7) have lapsed.]

2. Section 96 of the Act not to apply in cases where the Community rules apply

Subject to Regulations 3, 4 and 5 below, the provisions of subsections (1) to (9) of section 96 of the Act (permitted driving time and periods of duty of drivers of passenger and goods vehicles) shall not apply in relation to the Community regulated journeys or work of the driver of a passenger vehicle or of a goods vehicle.

['Regulation 2 provides, in general, for the removal from Community regulated journeys and work of the drivers of passenger and goods vehicles of the section 96 limits on permitted driving times and periods of duty.']

3. Adaptation of sections 96 and 103 of the Act to take account of the operation of the Community rules in relation to the driving of passenger and goods vehicles

(1) Where a driver of a passenger or goods vehicle spends time in driving or on work partly on Community regulated journeys or work and partly on domestic journeys or work, then in applying, as respects the domestic journeys or work, the limits in subsections (1) to (9) of section 96 of the Act on periods of driving or duty or length of working day account shall be taken of the time spent by that driver in driving on the Community regulated journeys or in carrying out the Community regulated work and that time shall not be regarded for the purposes of any of those subsections as constituting or forming part of an interval for rest or an interval for rest and refreshment.

(2) The definition of 'the applicable Community rules' (inserted in section 103 (1) of the Act by section 2 (1) (*a*) of the Road Traffic (Drivers' Ages and Hours of Work) Act 1976) shall apply in relation to such of those rules as are embraced by the definition of 'the Community rules' in Regulation 1 (3) above.

['Regulation 3 deals with the case where the driver of a passenger or goods vehicle spends part of his time on Community regulated journeys or work and part on domestic journeys or work to which section 96 applies and provides that in applying the section 96 limits to the latter journeys and work account must be taken of the time spent by the driver on the Community regulated journeys and work.']

4. Additional provisions with respect to goods vehicle drivers undertaking national journeys or work but no international journeys or work

(1) This Regulation applies to a goods vehicle driver who undertakes national journeys or work (whether with or without domestic journeys or work) but it does not apply to him in any seven consecutive days' period at the beginning of which he undertakes international journeys or work.

(2) The provisions of Regulation 2 above shall not have the effect of causing the following provisions of section 96 of the Act to cease to apply in relation to the national journeys or work of a driver to whom this Regulation applies:—

    (i) subsection (2) (interval for rest between periods of duty),
    (ii) subsection (3) (the working day of a driver),
    (iii) subsection (5) (the working week of a driver), and
    (iv) subsections (7), (8) and (9) (modifications of requirements in certain cases) so far as they are applicable for the purposes of subsection (2), (3) or (5).

(3) For the purpose of the application of—

    (i) subsections (2), (3), (7) and (8) of section 96 of the Act in relation to the national journeys or work of a driver to whom this Regulation applies, and
    (ii) subsections (1) to (9) of that section in relation to the domestic journeys or work of such a driver,

the definition of 'working day' in section 103 (1) of the Act shall be amended by substituting for the words 'or (where permitted by virtue of section 96 (4) (*b*) of this Act) of not less than nine and a half hours' the words 'or, where permitted by Article 11 (1), (3) or (4) of Council Regulation (EEC) No 543/69 (daily rest) or by section 96 (4) of this Act as amended by Regulation 4 (6) of the Drivers' Hours (Harmonisation with Community Rules) Regulations 1978, of not less than ten, nine or, as the case may be, eight hours'.

(4) For the purpose of the application of subsection (2) of section 96 of the Act (interval for rest between periods of duty) in relation to the national and domestic journeys or work of a driver to whom this Regulation applies, in a case where the vehicle in connection with which the journeys or work are undertaken is not a vehicle referred to in Article 6 of Council Regulation (EEC) No 543/69 (heavy vehicles and vehicles with more than one trailer), that subsection shall be amended to read as follows:—

'(2) Subject to the provisions of this section, if on any working day a driver has been on duty for a period of, or for periods amounting in the aggregate to, five and a half hours and—

(*a*) during that period, or during or between any of those periods, the driver has not had—
(i) one interval of not less than half an hour, or
(ii) two intervals of not less than 20 minutes each, or
(iii) three intervals of not less than 15 minutes each,
in which he was able to obtain rest and refreshment; and

(*b*) the end of that period, or of the last of those periods, does not mark the end of that working day,

he shall at the end of that period, or of the last of those periods, have such an interval as aforesaid of not less than half an hour, but that interval may be reduced to—

(A) 20 minutes where during the period, or during or between any of the periods, mentioned above the driver has had one interval of at least 20 minutes in which he was able to obtain rest and refreshment, or

(B) 15 minutes where during that period, or during or between any of those periods, he has had two such intervals of at least 15 minutes each.'

(5) For the purpose of the application of subsection (3) of section 96 of the Act (the working day of a driver) in relation to the national and domestic journeys or work of a driver to whom this Regulation applies that subsection shall be amended to read as follows:—

'(3) Subject to the provisions of this section, the working day of a driver—

(*a*) except where paragraph (*b*) or (*c*) of this subsection applies, shall not exceed eleven hours;

(*b*) if during that day he is off duty for a period which is, or periods which taken together are, not less than the time by which his working day exceeds eleven hours, shall not exceed twelve and a half hours;

(*c*) where the vehicle of which he is driver is one manned by two drivers—
(i) shall, in a case where the vehicle has no bunk enabling crew members who are not performing any activity to lie down comfortably, not exceed 17 hours if during that working day that driver is for a period of, or for periods amounting in the aggregate to, at least 6 hours not required to perform any activity in connection with the operation of the vehicle, and

(ii) shall, in a case where the vehicle has such a bunk as aforesaid, not exceed 22 hours if during that working day that driver is for a period of, or for periods amounting in the aggregate to, at least 11 hours not required to perform any activity in connection with the operation of the vehicle.'

(6) For the purpose of the application of subsection (4) of section 96 of the Act (interval for rest) in relation to the domestic journeys or work of a driver to whom this Regulation applies that subsection shall be amended by substituting for paragraphs (a) and (b) thereof the following:—

'(a) subject to paragraphs (b) and (c) of this subsection, shall not be of less than eleven hours;

(b) may be reduced to nine hours not more than twice in any working week when such rest is taken at the place where the driver or the vehicle is based, or to eight hours not more than twice in any working week when such rest is taken elsewhere than at that place; and

(c) where the vehicle is manned by two drivers—
   (i) may, if the vehicle has no bunk enabling crew members who are not performing any activity to lie down comfortably, be reduced to ten hours during the 27 hour period preceding any time when the driver is on duty, or
   (ii) may, if the vehicle has such a bunk as aforesaid, be reduced to eight hours during the 30 hour period preceding any time when the driver is on duty.'

(7) For the purpose of the application of subsection (6) of section 96 of the Act (weekly off-duty periods) in relation to the domestic journeys or work of a driver to whom this Regulation applies that subsection shall be amended by substituting for the words 'being a period either falling wholly in that week' onwards the words 'being a period which is either immediately preceded or followed by such an interval for rest as is mentioned in subsection (4) above (as that subsection is amended by Regulation 4 (6) of the Drivers' Hours (Harmonisation with Community Rules) Regulations 1978).'

(8) As from 1st January 1979 the following provisions of section 103 of the Act, so far (and only so far) as they are relevant for the interpretation of—
   (i) subsections (1) to (9) of section 96 of the Act in their application to the domestic journeys or work of a driver to whom this Regulation applies who spends time in driving or on work partly on national journeys or work and partly on domestic journeys or work,
   (ii) subsections (2), (3), (5), (7) and (8) of the said section 96 in their application to the national journeys or work of such a driver, and
   (iii) paragraph (10) below,
shall be amended as follows, that is to say—

(a) in subsection (1) of the said section 103 the following shall be substituted for the definition of 'working week', namely—
' "working week" means any period of seven consecutive days';
and

(b) subsection (5) shall be omitted.

(9) Where a person drives both goods and passenger vehicles he shall not be regarded, in relation to the relevant period, as a goods vehicle driver for the purpose of this Regulation unless of the time which he spends in that period in driving, or on

work in connection with, the goods and passenger vehicles (whether on national or domestic journeys or work) at least half is spent in driving, or on work in connection with, the goods vehicles.

(10) In paragraph (9) above 'the relevant period' means—

(a) where the case concerns the application of subsection (1), (2) or (3) of section 96 of the Act with respect to a working day of the driver, that working day,

(b) where the case concerns the application of subsection (4) of the said section 96 with respect to an interval of rest following a working day of the driver, that working day, and

(c) where the case concerns the application of subsection (5), (6), (7) or (8) of the said section 96 with respect to a working week of the driver, that working week.

['Regulation 4 makes special provision for goods vehicle drivers who undertake Community regulated journeys or work on national transport operations but who do not carry out international transport operations. The effect of Regulation 4 is to secure that Regulation 2 does not cause subsection (2) (interval for rest between periods of duty), subsection (3) (restriction on the working day of a driver), subsection (5) (restriction on the working week of a driver) or subsections (7) to (9) (modifications of requirements in certain cases) of section 96 to cease to apply to those Community regulated journeys and work of such a driver. The regulation amends in relation both to the Community regulated journeys and work and to the domestic journeys and work of such a goods vehicle driver section 96 (2) (interval for rest between periods of duty) in certain cases only, and section 96 (3) (length of working day) of the 1968 Act, so as to take account of the operation of the provisions of Article 11 of Council Regulation (EEC) No 543/69 (daily rest period). It also amends in relation to the domestic journeys and work of such a goods vehicle driver section 96 (4) (daily rest period), section 96 (6) (weekly off-duty period) and the definition of "working day" in section 103 (1) of the 1968 Act, so as to take account of the provisions of the same Article of the EEC Regulation. In addition Regulation 4 amends, as from 1st January 1979 in relation to the domestic journeys and work of such a goods vehicle driver who spends time on Community regulated journeys or work, the definition of "working week" in section 103 (1) of the 1968 Act so as to reflect the fact that, as from that date, the Sunday to Saturday week (provided for in the 1968 Act) will be replaced by the any 7 consecutive days week ("the rolling week") in the Community rules as they apply to the national transport operations of a goods vehicle driver.']

5. Additional provisions with respect to goods vehicle drivers undertaking international journeys or work

(1) Where a goods vehicle driver undertakes international journeys or work and also domestic journeys or work (whether with or without national journeys or work), this Regulation applies to him during any period of seven consecutive days at the beginning of which the international journeys or work are undertaken.

(2) In relation to the domestic journeys or work of a driver to whom this Regulation applies sections 96 and 103 of the Act shall have effect during the period mentioned in paragraph (1) above subject to the adaptations mentioned in paragraphs (3) to (6) below.

(3) The definition of 'working day' in section 103 (1) and subsections (2) (interval for rest between periods of duty), (4) (interval for daily rest) and (6) (weekly off-duty periods) of section 96 shall be amended in the same way as is provided in Regulation 4 (3), (4), (6) ansd (7) above in relation to the domestic journeys or work of a driver to whom that Regulation applies.

(4) In subsection (2) (amended as mentioned in paragraph (3) above) of section 96 for the words 'on duty' the word 'driving' shall be substituted.

(5) Subsections (3) (the working day of a driver) and (5) (the working week of a driver) of section 96 shall not apply.

(6) In subsection (1) of section 103 the following shall be substituted for the definition of 'working week', namely—

' "working week" means any period of seven consecutive days;', and subsection (5) shall be omitted.

(7) Where in the period referred to in paragraph (1) above a person drives both goods and passenger vehicles, he shall not be regarded for the purposes of this Regulation as a goods vehicle driver unless of the time which he spends in that period in driving, or on work in connection with, the goods and passenger vehicles (both on the Community regulated and on the domestic journeys or work) at least half is spent in driving, or on work in connection with, the goods vehicles.

['Regulation 5 provides for the case of the goods vehicle driver whose Community regulated journeys or work consist of or include such journeys or work on international transport operations and who at any time within 7 days after the international journeys or work also undertakes domestic journeys or work outside the scope of the Community rules altogether. It amends sections 96 and 103 of the 1968 Act in relation to the latter journeys and work but makes no provision for applying any of the limits in section 96 of the 1968 Act to the Community regulated journeys or work of the driver. In the case of the domestic journeys or work of this driver the amendments to subsections (4) (daily rest period) and (6) (weekly off-duty period) of section 96, and to the definition of working day in section 103 (1), of the 1968 Act provided for in Regulation 4 are applied but, in addition, section 96 is further modified by the exclusion of the limits on duty for the working day and the working week of such a driver, subsection (2) of section 96 (intervals for rest between periods of duty) is amended so as to apply the limit to driving (instead of duty), and the definition of "working week" in section 103 is amended so as to apply the "rolling week" concept. These amendments preserve in relation to the international driver the substance of the modifications of Part VI of the 1968 Act provided for in the Drivers' Hours (Passenger and Goods Vehicles) (International Rules) Regulations 1973 [repealed by these regulations].']

The Drivers' Hours (Keeping of Records) Regulations 1976

(SI 1976 No 1447)

[The text of these regulations is printed as amended by:
  the Drivers' Hours (Keeping of Records) (Amendment) Regulations 1978 (SI 1978 No 1878) (1 February 1979); and
  the Drivers' Hours (Keeping of Records) Amendment) (No 2) Regulations 1978 (SI 1978 No 1938) (1 February 1979).
The amending regulations are referred to in the notes to the main regulations only by their years and numbers. The dates referred to above are the dates on which the regulations came into force.]

PART I

GENERAL

* * *

3. Interpretation

(1) In these Regulations, unless the context otherwise requires—

'the Act' means the Transport Act 1968;

'British goods vehicle' means a goods vehicle which, if a motor vehicle, is registered in the United Kingdom or, if a trailer, is drawn by a motor vehicle which is so registered;

'British passenger vehicle' means a passenger vehicle which is a public service vehicle registered in the United Kingdom:

['the Community rules' means those provisions of Council Regulation (EEC) No 543/69 of 25th March 1969 (as amended by Council Regulations (EEC) Nos 514/72 and 515/72, both of 28th February 1972, and by Council Regulations (EEC) Nos 2827/77 and 2829/77, both of 12th December 1977) which are directly applicable Community provisions relating to the driving of road vehicles;]

'driver's record book' means a book for recording matters relevant to the enforcement of the requirements of the Community rules or, as the case may be, Part VI of the Act, being a book which comprises—

    (i) a front sheet;
    (ii) instructions for the use of the book;
    (iii) daily sheets;
    (iv) an example of a completed daily sheet;
    (v) weekly reports,

and conforms to the model set out in Schedule 1 to these Regulations (this being also the model prescribed by the Community rules);

and any expression which is also used in Part V or Part VI of the Act has the same meaning as in the said Part V or Part VI respectively.

(2) Any reference in these Regulations, in relation to a driver's record book, to the front sheet, the instructions for use, a daily sheet or a weekly report is a reference to that part of the record book which is so styled in the model set out in Schedule 1 to these Regulations.

(3) Any reference in these Regulations to any enactment or instrument shall be construed as a reference to that enactment or instrument as amended by any subsequent enactment or instrument.

(4) [The Interpretation Act 1978] shall apply for the interpretation of these Regulations as it applies for the interpretation of an Act of Parliament, and as if for the purposes of [section 17] of that Act these Regulations were an Act of Parliament and the Regulations revoked by Regulation 2 of these Regulations were an Act of Parliament thereby repealed.

[Regulation 3 is printed as amended by the Interpretation Act 1978, s 17 (2), and SI 1978 No 1878.]

PART II

Keeping of Records by Drivers of Goods Vehicles
where Community Rules do not apply

4. Application of Part II

(1) This Part of these Regulations applies to drivers of goods vehicles and to employers of employee-drivers of such vehicles, but, except as provided in Part III of these Regulations, this Part does not apply in relation to a journey made or to work done by that driver in a case where the journey or, as the case may be, the work is a journey or work to which the Community rules apply.

(2) In this Part of these Regulations, except where the context otherwise requires, any reference to a vehicle is a reference to a goods vehicle.

5. Keeping of record books by drivers of goods vehicles

(1) Subject to the provisions of these Regulations—

(*a*) the driver of a goods vehicle shall enter, and the employer of an employee-driver of a goods vehicle shall cause any such driver to enter, in a driver's record book, in accordance with the instructions for use contained in that book, the information prescribed in the record book as information which is required to be furnished by a crew member, and

(*b*) the owner-driver of a goods vehicle and the employer of an employee-driver of such a vehicle shall make, in accordance with the said instructions, such entries in the record book as are required by the record book to be made therein by the undertaking,

and, subject as aforesaid, the driver and any such employer as aforesaid shall in all respects in relation to such record book comply, and the employer of any such employee-driver shall cause the driver to comply, with all the relevant instructions contained in the record book and relating to the issue, use, preservation and return of the record book.

(2) This Regulation and Regulation 6 below apply to a driver who in any working week drives goods and passenger vehicles as they apply to a driver who only drives

goods vehicle, and the information required to be furnished in the driver's record book by the driver of both goods and passenger vehicles shall be the required information in relation to his employments in connection with both goods and passenger vehicles, but if a driver of both goods and passenger vehicles has a different employer in relation to his employment in connection with goods vehicles from his employer in relation to his employment in connection with passenger vehicles, references in the foregoing paragraph of this Regulation and in Regulation 6 below to his employer shall be construed as references to his employer in relation to his employment in connection with goods vehicles.

6. Issue of record books in cases involving more than one employer

(1) If on the date of the coming into operation of these Regulations or at any time thereafter an employee-driver has more than one employer in relation to whom he is an employee-driver of a vehicle, the employer who is to issue a new driver's record book to him shall be the employer for whom the employee-driver first acts in the course of his employment on or after the said date or time.

(2) Where during the currency of a driver's record book an employee-driver ceases to be employed by an employer who has issued that book to him he shall return that book, including all duplicate and unused daily sheets and weekly reports, to that employer and, if he is at that time employed by some other person or persons in relation to whom he is an employee-driver of a vehicle, that other person, or if there is more than one such other person, that one of them for whom he first acts in the course of his employment after ceasing to be so employed as aforesaid, shall issue a new driver's record book to him in accordance with the requirements of these Regulations.

7. Form of drivers' record books—Supplemental provisions

(1) A driver's record book shall be numbered by perforation or stamping with the serial number of the book and shall have the standard A6 format (105 × 148 mm) or a larger format.

(2) A different serial number shall be given to each driver's record book used by an owner-driver or issued by an employer to his employee-drivers.

(3) Where a driver's record book contains more than fifteen daily sheets, it shall contain a duplicate of each of the daily sheets which are contained therein together with one sheet of carbon paper or other means whereby an entry in a daily sheet may be simultaneously reproduced on the duplicate of that sheet.

(4) Nothing in paragraph (3) of this Regulation shall preclude the use of a driver's record book which is furnished with duplicates of the daily sheets and the sheet of carbon paper as mentioned in that paragraph in a case where the record book contains fifteen or fewer daily sheets.

8. Manner of keeping drivers' record book

(1) Subject to the following provisions of these Regulations, the requirements contained in the following paragraphs of this Regulation shall be complied with as respects the making of entries in a driver's record book, the detachment and delivery of daily sheets and the return of record books.

(2) An owner-driver or an employer of an employee-driver shall, before the book is used, enter or secure that there is entered—

(a) on the front sheet of the record book the serial number of the operator's licence granted under Part V of the Act by virtue of which each goods vehicle used by the driver during the currency of the record book is an authorised vehicle for the purposes of the said Part V,

(b) on each of the daily sheets in the record book the serial number of the operator's licence granted as aforesaid by virtue of which each goods vehicle used by the driver in the course of the day in question is an authorised vehicle for the purposes of the said Part V, and

(c) on the front sheet of the record book the serial number of the book required by Regulation 7(1) of these Regulations and the number of daily sheets in the book.

(3) A driver shall, when making an entry in a daily sheet contained in a record book furnished with duplicates of the daily sheets, and when signing such a sheet, ensure by the use of carbon paper or otherwise that the entry or signature is simultaneously reproduced on the duplicate of that sheet.

(4) Where a daily sheet contained in a driver's record book furnished with duplicates of the daily sheets therein has been completed, the driver shall detach, and the employer of an employee-driver shall cause the driver to detach, the duplicate of that sheet from the book and—

(a) in a case where the daily sheet was completed by an employee-driver, he shall, within a period of seven days from the date of its being completed, deliver the duplicate sheet to the employer who issued or should have issued the book to him, and that employer shall cause the driver so to deliver the duplicate sheet, and, within a period of seven days from the date on which the employer receives the duplicate sheet, he shall examine and sign it; and

(b) in a case where the daily sheet was completed by an owner-driver, he shall, within a period of seven days from the date of its being completed, deliver the duplicate sheet to the address which is required to be entered on the front sheet of the record book:

Provided that a person shall not be treated as having failed to comply with any of the requirements of this paragraph with respect to the period within which a duplicate sheet shall be delivered or, as the case may be, examined or signed in any case where he can show that it was not reasonably practicable to comply with that requirement and that the requirement was otherwise complied with as soon as it was reasonably practicable to do so.

(5) Where an employee-driver uses a driver's record book which is not furnished with duplicates of the daily sheets in it, the employer to whom that record book is returned by the driver when it has been completed shall, within a period of seven days from the date of its return, examine and sign each of the daily sheets which have been used, unless he has previously examined and signed such sheet when the book was produced to him for inspection under Regulation 9 (6) of these Regulations.

(6) For the purposes of the instructions for use contained in a driver's record book, the book shall be regarded as completed—

(a) in the case of a book containing 15 or fewer daily sheets and no duplicates of the daily sheets, when all the daily sheets have been used or at the end of 28 days from the date on which the first sheet in the book was used, whichever is the earlier,

(b) in the case of any other book, when all the daily sheets have been used.

(7) No driver shall enter in any driver's record book any information which is required to be furnished by these Regulations if—

(i) in the case of an employee-driver, the book was not supplied to him by his employer, unless a driver's record book so supplied is not available to him, or

(ii) the is in possession of another such book in which he has entered information which is required to be so furnished and which is not completed.

9. Supply of information and production of drivers' record books by employers and employee-drivers

(1) Where an employee-driver has or has had during any period more than one employer in relation to whom he is an employee-driver—

(a) each employer, who is not an employer who is required by these Regulations to issue a driver's record book to that employee-driver, shall require that driver to produce his current driver's record book and shall enter on the front sheet contained therein the name and address of his undertaking and a statement that the holder of the record book is also a driver in his employment, and

(b) each employer of that employee-driver shall, whenever he is requested to do so by any of the other employers of that employee-driver, supply to that other employer such information as is specified in paragraph (4) of this Regulation and is in his possession.

(2) Where an employee-driver changes his employment, the employer by whom the employee-driver has ceased to be so employed shall on being so requested by the employee-driver, or his new employer, supply the employee-driver or the new employer with such information as is specified in paragraph (4) of this Regulation and is in his possession.

(3) Any information required to be supplied by the foregoing provisions of this Regulation shall, if so required by the person entitled to require it to be supplied, be supplied in writing.

(4) The information concerning an employee-driver which is to be supplied in accordance with the foregoing provisions of this Regulation is the following information relating to the whole or any part of the current working week of that driver, namely—

(a) any period during which that employee-driver has been off duty for a period of not less than twenty four hours in respect of that week as required by section 96 (6) of the Act or as so required by that provision as having effect in relation to that employee-driver by virtue of any exemption having effect under regulations made under section 96 (10) of the Act, and

(b) the number of hours for the purpose of the weekly limit under section 96 (5) of the Act for which that employee-driver has been on duty during that week.

(5) Any employee-driver shall produce his current driver's record book for inspection by the employer who issued it to him, or by any other person in relation to whom he is at any time during the period of the currency of that book an employee-driver, whenever required to do so by that employer or that other person.

(6) Any employee-driver shall return his current driver's record book to the employer who issued it to him at the end of any week beginning at midnight between Saturday and Sunday, if required to do so by that employer.

10. Preservation of driver's record books

(1) An owner-driver shall preserve his driver's record book intact when it has been completed or he has ceased to use it, and the employer of an employee-driver to whom

any driver's record book relating to that employee-driver has been returned shall preserve that book intact, for the period specified in paragraph (3) of this Regulation.

(2) Any owner-driver who has detached daily sheets from his driver's record book as required by Regulation 8 (4) of these Regulations and any employer of an employee-driver to whom any daily sheets have been delivered by his employee-driver as required by that provision shall also preserve those sheets for the period specified in paragraph (3) of this Regulation.

(3) The period for which drivers' record books and daily sheets must be preserved as required by this Regulation shall be one year reckoned, in the case of an owner-driver, from the day on which that book was completed or ceased to be used by him, or in the case of an employee-driver, from the day on which that book was returned to his employer.

(4) Where in accordance with the instructions for use in a driver's record book an employee-driver keeps a copy of a weekly report he shall preserve it intact for so long as the record book to which it relates remains in his possession, and where a copy of a weekly report is handed in by an employee-driver to his employer for signature by the employer, the employer shall preserve the copy intact until the expiration of one year from the end of the week concerned.

11. Registers of drivers' record books

(1) Subject to the following provisions of this Regulation, every owner-driver of a vehicle shall maintain a register in the form set out in Schedule 2 to these Regulations of all drivers' record books used by him and every employer of an employee-driver of a vehicle shall maintain such a register or more than one such register as provided for by paragraph (2) of this Regulation of all drivers' record books known by him to have been issued to or to be used by any of his employee-drivers, and every such owner-driver and employer as aforesaid shall make in that register or registers all such entries relating to the information to be recorded therein as is required by the form set out in the said Schedule 2 to be entered in that register or registers:

Provided that where a record book is not returned there shall be entered in the register, instead of the date of the return of the record book, the reason why the record book was not returned and the date when such entry was made.

(2) Where for the purpose of any trade, business or other activity carried on by him an employer of employee-drivers operates from more than one place vehicles which are driven by his employee-drivers, that employer may maintain for each such place a separate register of drivers' record books, each such register being a register complying with the requirements of paragraph (1) of this Regulation (subject to paragraph (4) of this Regulation) but relating only to the drivers' record books known by him to have been issued to or to be used by any of his employee-drivers in relation to the driving of vehicles operated from that place.

(3) An owner-driver and the employer of any employee-driver by whom any such register as aforesaid is required to be maintained shall preserve that register for a period of 12 months from whichever is the last to occur of the following dates, that is to say—

(a) the date on which he ceased to use a record book or on which there was returned to him the last of the books issued by him to any employee-driver, the use or issue of which is recorded in that register, or

(b) if any record book the issue of which by him is recorded in that register has not been returned to him as required by these Regulations, the date when the reason why the record book was not returned was entered in that register.

(4) Notwithstanding anything in the foregoing provisions of these Regulations, registers may be maintained in a form which differs from that set out in Schedule 2 to these Regulations (whether in size, layout, sequence, numbering, content or otherwise) so long as the register contains the same wording as in the form in the said Schedule and such register is so framed as to ensure that all the information required by the form in the said Schedule is required to be entered in the actual register and in such manner as to be readily identifiable by any person entitled under any enactment to inspect any such register.

12. Exemptions

(1) Where a driver does not during any period of twenty-four hours commencing at midnight drive any goods vehicle other than a vehicle the use of which is exempted from any requirement to have an operator's licence or, in the case of a vehicle in the public service of the Crown, would be so exempted by virtue of section 60 (2) of the Act, were it not such a vehicle, that driver and, if he is an employee-driver, his employer, shall be exempted for that period from the specified requirements.

(2) Where in any period of twenty-four hours beginning at midnight a driver does not drive a vehicle to which this Part of these Regulations applies for more than four hours and does not drive any such vehicle outside a radius of twenty-five miles from the operating centre of the vehicle, then he and, if he is an employee-driver, his employer shall be exempted for that period (hereinafter referred to as 'the exempted period') from the specified requirements:

Provided that where the exempted period is followed by a period of twenty-four hours in respect of any part of which a driver is not exempted from all the specified requirements the driver shall be required to enter in his driver's record book the date and time when his last working day ended if such day ended during the exempted period.

For the purposes of computing the said four hours no account shall be taken of any time spent in driving a vehicle elsewhere than on a road if the vehicle is being so driven in the course of operations of agriculture, forestry or quarrying or in the course of carrying out work in the construction, reconstruction, alteration or extension or maintenance of, or of a part of, a building, or of any other fixed works of construction or civil engineering (including works for the construction, improvement or maintenance of a road) and, for the purposes of this paragraph, where the vehicle is being driven on, or on a part of, a road in the course of carrying out of any work for the improvement or maintenance of, or of that part of, that road, it shall be treated as being driven elsewhere than on a road.

(3) In this Regulation the expression 'the specified requirements' means all the requirements of this Part of these Regulations as respects the entering of a current record in a driver's record book and, in the case of drivers, the having possession of such a book in accordance with the instructions for use contained in the book.

PART III

Provisions Supplementary to Community Rules
in Cases where those Rules apply

13. Application of Part III

This Part of these Regulations applies to drivers of British goods vehicles and (to the extent specified below) to drivers of British passenger vehicles and to the employers of such drivers, in cases where journeys which are made or work which is done by such drivers are journeys or work to which the Community rules apply, so as to impose in relation to those cases requirements which are additional to the requirements of the Community rules [with respect to the individual control books for drivers and crew members.]

[Regulation 13 is printed as amended by SI 1978 No 1878.]

14. Obligation of employers of employee-drivers

In a case where this Part of these Regulations applies the employer of an employee-driver of a British goods vehicle or British passenger vehicle shall cause such driver—

(a) to enter in a driver's record book a current record which shall give the information required by the Community rules as information which is required to be furnished by that driver, and otherwise to comply with all the requirements of those Rules with respect to the keeping of record books and matters related thereto; and

(b) to comply with such of the additional requirements contained in the following provisions of this Part of these Regulations as apply in relation to any such driver.

15. Application of certain Regulations in Part II—goods vehicles and passenger vehicles

In a case where this Part of these Regulations applies and the vehicles involved are either British goods vehicles or British passenger vehicles the provisions of Regulations 6 and 11 of these Regulations shall apply, and for the purposes of such application the references in those Regulations to a vehicle shall include references to goods vehicles and passenger vehicles.

16. Application of certain additional Regulations in Part II—goods vehicles only

In a case where this Part of these Regulations applies and the vehicles involved are British goods vehicles the provisions of Regulations 7(2), (3) and (4), 8, 9 and 10(2), (3) and (4) of these Regulations shall also apply but with the substitution—

(a) in paragraph (2) (c) of Regulation 8 for 'Regulation 7(1) of these Regulations' of 'the Community Rules';

(b) in paragraph (7) of Regulation 8 for 'these Regulations' of 'the Community Rules'; and

[(c) in Regulation 9, for paragraph (4), of the following paragraph—

(4) The information concerning an employee-driver which is to be supplied in accordance with the foregoing provisions of this Regulation is the following information relating to the period of 14 days immediately preceding the date on which the request for information is made or, in a case where there has been a change of employment the date on which that change occurred

(a) any weekly rest period taken by him during that period.

(b) the number of hours of driving undertaken by him on each day during that period, and

(c) the number of hours during which he has been on duty on each day during that period.]

[Regulation 16 is printed as amended by SI 1978 No 1878.]

[PART IV

PROVISIONS APPLICABLE IN CASES WHERE THE COMMUNITY RULES WITH
REGARD TO DRIVERS' HOURS APPLY BUT WHERE THE SPECIFIC REQUIREMENTS
OF THOSE RULES AS TO RECORD BOOKS DO NOT APPLY]

[The heading to Part IV was added when regs 17 to 20 were added by SI 1978 No 1878.]

[17. Application of Part IV

This Part of these Regulations applies to drivers, and to the employers of drivers,
who

(*a*) are drivers of British goods vehicles which are used for internal goods transport
operations carried out within a radius of 50 kilometres from the place where the
vehicle is based (including municipalities the centre of which is situated within
that radius), and

(*b*) spend not more than 4 hours in driving in the course of any day,

in cases where the journeys which are made or the work which is done by such drivers
are journeys or work to which the Community rules apply but where, by virtue of
Regulation 2(*c*) of the Community Road Transport Rules (Exemptions) Regulations
1978 *[SI 1978 No 1158]*, the drivers are exempted from the requirements of those rules
as respects individual control books, so as to impose in relation to those cases simplified requirements with respect to the keeping of records.]

[Part IV (regs 17 to 20) was added by SI 1978 No 1878.]

[18. Interpretation of Part IV

(1) In this Part of these Regulations

'day' means any period of 24 hours commencing at midnight;

'relevant day', in relation to a driver, means a day in the course of which he
spends not more than 4 hours in driving for the purpose of the transport operations mentioned in Regulation 17 (*a*) above:

'simplified record book' means a book for recording matters relevant to the
enforcement of the requirements of the Community rules, being a book which
comprises—

(i) a front sheet,
(ii) instructions for the use of the book,
(iii) weekly record sheets divided up into boxes for entrny of information
relating to each day in the week,

and conforms to the model set out in Schedule 3 to these Regulations.

(2) In determining for the purpose of this Part of these Regulations whether or not
a driver spends more than 4 hours in driving in the course of a day no account shall be
taken of any time spent in driving a vehicle elsewhere than on a road.]

[Part IV (regs 17 to 20) was added by SI 1978 No 1878.]

[19. Simplified record books

(1) Subject to the provisions of Regulation 20 below, in a case where this Part of
these Regulations applies—

(*a*) a driver shall keep, and the employer of a driver who is an employee-driver
shall cause that driver to keep, a simplified record book, and

(*b*) in relation to each relevant day of such driver the driver shall enter, and, where he is an employee-driver, his employer shall cause him to enter, in his simplified record book, in the appropriate boxes on the record sheet for the week in which the day in question falls, in accordance with the instructions for use contained in the book, the information prescribed in the record book as information which is required to be furnished by a driver;

and, subject as aforesaid, the driver and any such employer as aforesaid shall in all respects in relation to a simplified record book comply, and the employer of any such employee-driver shall cause the driver to comply, with all the relevant instructions contained in the record book and relating to the issue, use, preservation and return of the record book.

(2) No entry shall be made on a weekly record sheet in a simplified record book except in relation to a relevant day of the driver to whom the book relates.

(3) A simplified record book shall contain a duplicate of each weekly record sheet together with one sheet of carbon paper or other means whereby an entry on a weekly record sheet may be simultaneously reproduced on the duplicate of that sheet.

(4) Regulations 6, 7 (1) and (2), 8 (1), (2) (*a*) and (*c*), (3), (4), (6) (*b*) and (7), 9 (1), (2), (3), (4) (as amended by Regulation 16 of these Regulations), (5) and (6), 10 (1), (2) and (3) and 11 of these Regulations shall apply in relation to simplified record books as they apply in relation to drivers' record books, and for the purpose of this application—

(*a*) the references in those Regulations to the daily sheets shall be construed as references to the weekly record sheets,

(*b*) the words 'furnished with duplicates of the daily sheets' in Regulation 8 (3) and the words 'furnished with duplicates of the daily sheets therein' in Regulation 8 (4) shall be omitted, and

(*c*) in Regulation 6 the reference to the date of the coming into operation of these Regulations shall be construed as a reference to the coming into operation of this Part of these Regulations.]

[Part IV (regs 17 to 20) was added by SI 1978 No 1878.]

[20. Use of drivers' record books instead of simplified record books

(1) If in a case where this Part of these Regulations applies the driver keeps a driver's record book, he shall not keep, nor shall his employer cause him to keep, a simplified record book, but he shall make, in relation to each relevant day of his, the appropriate entries on a daily sheet in his driver's record book.

(2) For the purpose of paragraph (1) above the appropriate entries on a daily sheet in a driver's record book in relation to a relevant day of a driver are—

(*a*) the entries required by the instructions in that book to be made in boxes 1, 2, 3, 8, 9 and 12 on the sheet.

(*b*) in box 13 on the sheet an estimate of his driving time, and

(*c*) in box 16 on the sheet, in addition to the signature, the time of coming on duty and the time of going off duty.

(3) Where in any week a driver keeps, in accordance with this Regulation, a driver's record book instead of a simplified record book and every day on which he drives during the course of that week is a relevant day, it shall not be necessary for him to complete the weekly report in the driver's record book in respect of that week.]

[Part IV (regs 17 to 20) was added by SI 1978 No 1878.]

[PART V

PROVISIONS MODIFYING COMMUNITY RULES IN CASES
WHERE THOSE RULES APPLY]

[21. Application of Part V

This Part of these Regulations applies to the drivers of British passenger vehicles and to the employers of such drivers in cases where the journeys which are made or the work which is done are made or done in the course of national transport operations and are journeys or work to which the Community rules apply, so as to modify the requirements of those rules.]

[Part V (regs 21, 22) was added by SI 1978 No 1938.]

[22. Modified requirements as respects weekly reports—passenger vehicles

(1) In a case where this Part of these Regulations applies it shall not be necessary for the driver to make entries, or for the employer of such driver to cause him to make entries, in the boxes marked 'H' and 'I' in the weekly reports in his drivers' record book (these boxes being respectively the boxes for entry of the time spent on activities of the driver's employment, other than driving, and of the aggregate of the time spent on those activities and on driving).

(2) Paragraph 22 in the instructions for the use of the driver's record book (as set out in Schedule 1 to these Regulations) shall be suitably modified in the case of record books issued to drivers for use in the circumstances mentioned in paragraph (1) above, so as to indicate the effect of that paragraph.]

[Part V (regs 21, 22) was added by SI 1978 No 1938.]

[Schedule 1 is set out on pp 281–6.]

SCHEDULE 1

MODEL FOR DRIVER'S RECORD BOOK

(Note: The model set out below is that prescribed by Council Regulation (EEC) No 543/69 of 25th March 1969 as amended by Council Regulation (EEC) No 514/72 of 28th February 1972 and described by those Regulations as an 'individual control book'. The book must be of standard A6 format (105mm × 148mm) or a larger format).

[Documents (b) to (e) are reproduced with the permission of the Controller of Her Majesty's Stationery Office.]

MODEL INDIVIDUAL CONTROL BOOK

(a) Front Sheet

I   INDIVIDUAL CONTROL BOOK
         FOR CREW MEMBERS IN ROAD TRANSPORT

II Country ....

III Date book first used: .... 19...........

IV Date book last used: .... 19...........

V Surname, first name(s), date of birth and address of holder of book:
....
....

VI Name, address, telephone number and stamp (if any) of the undertaking:
....
....
....
....
....

VII Operator's Licence No (goods vehicles only).

Book No...
            (to be stamped or perforated)

(b) *Instructions*

INSTRUCTIONS
FOR THE USE OF THE INDIVIDUAL CONTROL BOOK

1.   This individual control book is issued in conformity with (specify relevant laws and regulations) ....

To the Undertaking

2.   After completing items V, VI and VII on the front sheet, issue a book to each crew member employed by you, in conformity with the laws and regulations referred to in paragraph 1 above.

3.   Keep a register showing the names of the persons to whom books have been issued, the serial number of each book issued, and the dates of issue. Require the holder to sign in the margin of the register.

4.   Give the holder the necessary instructions for correct use of the book.

5.   Examine the daily sheets and the weekly report every week or, if prevented from doing so, as soon thereafter as possible. Sign the weekly report.

6.   Withdraw the used books, observing the time-limit specified in paragraph 9 below, and hold them at the disposal of the authorized inspecting officers for not less than one year. Enter the date of the last daily sheet in the register referred to in paragraph 3 above.

To Crew Members

7.   This control book is personal. Carry it with you when on duty and produce it to any authorized inspecting officer on request. Hand it over to your employer when you leave the undertaking.

8.   Produce this control book to your employer every week or, if prevented from doing so, as soon thereafter as possible, so that he can check your entries and sign the weekly report.

9.   When the book is completed, keep it for two weeks so that you can produce it at any time to an authorized inspecting officer, and then hand it as soon as possible to your employer. Keep a copy of the weekly reports.

Front sheet

10. Make sure that your surname, first name(s), date of birth and address are filled in correctly (item V).

11. Enter the date on which you first use the book (item III).

12. After use, enter the date when you last used the book (item IV).

Daily sheet

13. Fill in a daily sheet for every day on which you have been employed as a crew member.

14. Enter in box 2 the registration number of any vehicle used during the day.

15.   The symbols used have the following meaning:

[symbol]   total period of uninterrupted rest before going on duty

[symbol]   daily rest period

[symbol]   breaks

[symbol]   driving periods

[symbol]   periods of attendance at work

16.   Enter your period of daily rest (symbol [symbol]), breaks (symbol [symbol]) and the
time during which you were engaged in activities represented by symbols 6 [symbol] and 7 [symbol]
by drawing a horizontal line across the hours concerned opposite the appropriate
symbol, and connect the horizontal lines by vertical lines. There will thus be
a continuous line over the full length of each strip (see example in the book).

17.   Entries must be made at the beginning and end of each period to which they relate.

18.   In box 16 ("Remarks") enter the name of the second driver, if any. This box may
also be used to explain any breach of the requirements or to correct particulars
given elsewhere (see paragraph 24). The employer or an inspecting officer may also
insert his remarks in this box.

19.   Opposite box 12, [symbol] enter the number of hours of uninterrupted rest (daily
rest) taken immediately before coming on duty. If this period begins in one day and
ends in the following day the figure will be the total achieved by adding together the
rest period taken at the end of the previous day and the rest period taken at the
beginning of the day to which the sheet relates.

20.   Before departure, enter opposite "Beginning of duty" in box 11 the number of
kilometres/miles shown on the recorder; at the end of duty, enter opposite "End
of duty" in box 11 the new number of kilometres/miles shown on the recorder and
note the total distance covered.

21.   Sign the daily sheet.

Weekly report

22.   This report should be made out at the end of every period of one week in which
one or more daily sheets have been made out. For days on which you were on duty
without being a crew member, ie for which there was no need to make out a daily
sheet, enter the figure "0" opposite box G and the duration of duty periods opposite
box H; if you did not engage in a particular activity, enter the figure "0" opposite
boxes G and H and add an explanation, such as "on leave", "day off".

23.   Enter opposite boxes F and G the figures shown opposite boxes 12 and 13 of the
relevant daily sheets.

General note

24.   No erasures, corrections or additions may be made in the book. Any mistakes,
even of form only, must be corrected under "Remarks" (box 16).

25.   No sheets may be destroyed.

26.   All entries must be made in ink or with a ball-point pen.

(c)   *Daily Sheet*

1. DAILY SHEET No.

2. Registration No. of vehicle(s)
   Operators Licence Nos.

3. Day of week and date

	1	2	3	4	5	6	7	8	9	10	11	12
4												
5												
6												
7												
	13	14	15	16	17	18	19	20	21	22	23	24
4												
5												
6												
7												

8. Place of coming on duty:

9. Place of going off duty:

10. Transport of goods.
    Permissible maximum weight of the combination of vehicles – Lorry with trailer or articulated vehicles (where applicable) :

10a. Passenger transport.
     System of daily rest selected:

11. Distance recorder: End of duty .... km/miles

                            Beginning of duty: .... km/miles

Total distance covered .... km/miles

Number of hours

12.

13.

14.

15. Total

     13 + 14

     If applicable.

16. Remarks and signature:

Book No.

(d) *Example of Completed Daily Sheet*

1. DAILY SHEET No. II		
2. Registration No. of vehicle(s) ABC 123 L Operators Licence Nos. D. 123456		3. Day of week and date Tuesday 7 September 1972

Book No. 21

4 5 6 7   4 5 6 7 (duty graph marked across 1–24 hour scale)

8. Place of coming on duty: Bristol

9. Place of going off duty: Nottingham

10. Transport of goods.
Permissible maximum weight of the combination of vehicles – Lorry with trailer or articulated vehicles 19 tons (where applicable)

10a. Passenger transport.
System of daily rest selected:

11. Distance recorder:	End of duty	21230	km/miles
	Beginning of duty	21090	km/miles
Total distance covered		140	km/miles

16. Remarks and signature: J. Smith

		Number of hours
12.	(symbol)	12
13.	(symbol)	6¼
14.	(symbol)	3
15. Total 13 + 14 If applicable		9¼

Note 1. In practice, boxes 10 and 10a will both be completed on the same daily sheet only where a crew member has carried out a passenger transport operation and a goods transport operation on the same day. In box 10a (completed only by crew members of passenger vehicles) the entry should be either "10 h" or "11 h", according to the system of daily rest periods applying to the crew member.

Note 2. Opposite box 12, if 12 hours is entered as the total period of uninterrupted rest taken prior to going on duty, this means that the driver went off duty at 7pm on the previous day, because adding the 5 hours from 7 pm to midnight on the previous day to the 7 hours entered in box 4 gives a total of 12 hours.

(e) *Weekly Report*

A. Surname and first name(s) of crew member

....

B. WEEKLY REPORT

C. From .... to .... 19.....inclusive

D. Days of the weekly period								J. Weekly total:
E. Daily sheet no.								
F. *								

Hours of occupational activities	G.								
	H.								
	I G+H								

K. Remarks: ....
....
....

L. Date of preceding weekly rest period: ....

M. Signature of crew member: ....

N. Signature of employer: ....

Book No ....

SCHEDULE 2

FORM OF REGISTER OF DRIVERS' RECORD BOOKS

Transport Act 1968/Council Regulation (EEC) No 543/69: Register of Record Books

REGISTER NO ....

PAGE NO ....

Name of Employer or Owner-Driver ....

Operator's Licence Number (Goods Vehicles) ....

Place at which Books Issued ....

1. Record Book Serial No	2. Issued to: (Driver's full name and address)	3. Date of Issue	4. Signature of employer issuing book	5. Name and address of any other known employer of driver	6. Date of return of book	7. Date of last daily sheet in book	8. Driver's signature

[SCHEDULE 3

Model for Simplified Record Book

(a) Front Sheet

SIMPLIFIED RECORD BOOK

FOR DRIVERS IN ROAD TRANSPORT

1.   Date book first used ....

2.   Date book last used ....

3.   Surname, first name(s), date of birth and address of holder of book

        ....

        ....

4.   Name, address, telephone number and stamp (if any) of undertaking

        ....

        ....

        ....

5.   Operator's Licence No ....

6.   Book No ....

7.   Number of weekly record sheets in book ....

(b) Instructions

Instructions for the use of the simplified record book

To the Undertaking

1. After completing items 4, 5, 6 and 7 on the front sheet, and consecutively numbering each weekly record sheet at box 1, issue a simplified record book to those drivers employed by you to whom Part IV of The Drivers' Hours (Keeping of Records) Regulations 1976 (SI 1976 No 1447) applies (Note: Part IV was added by The Drivers' Hours (Keeping of Records) (Amendment) Regulations 1978 (SI 1978 No 1878)). The simplified record book is NOT to be issued in any other circumstances. Nor is it to be issued to, or retained by, a driver who uses the full EEC type drivers' record book (because he chooses to do so or because he does other driving which requires him to do so).

2. Keep a register showing the names of the persons to whom books have been issued, the serial number of each book issued, and the dates of issue. Require the holder to sign in the margin of the register.

3. Give the holder the necessary instructions for correct use of the book.

4. Examine and sign each weekly record sheet at the end of the week to which it relates or, if prevented from doing so, as soon thereafter as possible.

5. Withdraw the used books, observing the time-limit specified in paragraph 8 below, and hold them at the disposal of the authorised inspecting officers for not less than one year. Enter the period covered by the last weekly record sheet in the register referred to in paragraph 2 above.

To Drivers

6. This record book is personal. Carry it with you when on duty and produce it to any authorised inspecting officer on request. Hand it over to your employer when you leave the undertaking.

7. Produce this record book to your employer at the end of every week or, if prevented from doing so, as soon thereafter as possible, so that he can check and countersign your entries.

8. When the book is completed, keep it for two weeks so that you can produce it at any time to an authorised inspecting officer, and then hand it as soon as possible to your employer.

Front Sheet

9. Make sure that your surname, first name(s), date of birth, and address are filled in correctly (item 3).

10. Enter the date on which you first use the book (item 1).

11. After use, enter the date when you last used the book (item 2).

Weekly Record Sheet

12. Enter details of work carried out on every day on which you do work as a driver.

13. Enter in box 4, for the day in question, the registration number of any vehicle used during that day.

14. Complete box 2 at the beginning of each week in which you do work as a driver.

15. Complete boxes 3, 5 and 6, for the day in question, at the beginning of each day on which you do work as a driver.

16. Complete boxes 7, 8 and 9 at the end of the day's work.

General

17. No sheets may be destroyed or mutilated.

18. All entries must be made in ink or with a ball-point pen.

(c) *Weekly Record Sheet for Local Goods Transport Operations*

1. Weekly Sheet No

2. Period covered by Sheet
   Week Commencing (Date)................................
   To Week Ending (Date)................................

Day 3.	Registration No of Vehicle(s) 4.	Place where Vehicle(s) Based 5.	Time of Going on Duty 6.	Time of Going Off Duty 7.	Estimated Time spent Driving 8.	Signature of Driver 9.

BOOK NO

10. Certification by employer.
    (Where applicable)

I have examined the entries in this sheet.
Signature........................Date................
Position held................................]

[*Schedule 3 was added by SI 1978 No 1878.*]

The Local Authorities' Traffic Orders (Exemptions for Disabled Persons) (England and Wales) Regulations 1971

(SI 1971 No 1493)

[The text of these regulations is printed as amended by:

the Local Authorities' Traffic Orders (Exemptions for Disabled Persons) (England and Wales) (Amendment) Regulations 1975 (SI 1975 No 267) (1 June 1975); and

the Local Authorities' Traffic Orders (Exemptions for Disabled Persons) (England and Wales) (Amendment) (No 2) Regulations 1975 (SI 1975 No 1562) (1 November 1975).

The amending regulations are referred to in the notes to the main regulations only by their years and numbers. The dates referred to above are the dates on which the regulations came into force.]

1. Commencement, citation and interpretation

(1) *[Omitted.]*

[(2) In these Regulations the following expressions have the meanings hereby respectively assigned to them:—

'the Act of [1984]' means the [Road Traffic Regulation Act 1984];

'the Act of 1970' means the Chronically Sick and Disabled Persons Act 1970;

'bus lane' means a road, or a part of the width of a road, the use of which by vehicles is restricted by or under any enactment, either in both directions or in one direction only and either at all times or at particular times only, to any or more of the following categories of vehicles—

    (i) public service vehicles (as defined in [the Public Passenger Vehicles Act 1981]) or particular classes of such vehicles,

    (ii) vehicles (not being motor cars) which are similar in construction to public service vehicles and are being used for the carriage of passengers, or particular classes of such vehicles,

    (iii) taxis,

    (iv) cycles,

and 'bus lane restriction', in relation to a bus lane, means the restriction by virtue of which the particular road, or the particular part of the width of a road, is a bus lane;

'disabled person' means a disabled person of a description prescribed by [Regulation 5 of the Disabled Persons (Badges for Motor Vehicles) Regulations 1982 *[SI 1982 No 1740]*];

'disabled person's badge' has the same meaning as in [Regulation 3 (1) of the Disabled Persons (Badges for Motor Vehicles) Regulations 1982];

'disabled person's vehicle' means a motor vehicle which—

(*a*) is driven by a disabled person, or

291

(*b*) is used by an institution (as defined in the said Regulations of [1982]) for carrying disabled persons as passengers, or

(*c*) is otherwise used for carrying disabled persons as passengers and is either—

  (i) a vehicle which is constructed or adapted for the carriage of not more than 12 passengers (exclusive of the driver) and is not a public service vehicle (as defined in [section 1 of the Public Passenger Vehicles Act 1981]), or

  (ii) a dual purpose vehicle as defined in [Regulation 3 (1) of the Motor Vehicles (Construction and Use) Regulations 1978 *[SI 1978 No 1017]*]

and is, in each case, a vehicle which, immediately before or after any period of waiting allowed by virtue of a provision of a kind required by Regulation 3 of these Regulations to be included in an order under the Act of [1984], has been or is to be driven by a disabled person or, as the case may be, has been or is to be used for carrying disabled persons as passengers;

'London local authority' means the Greater London Council, the Council of a London Borough, or the Common Council of the City of London;

'road', in relation to an order under [section 6 or 9 of the Act of 1984], includes a street as defined in [section 6 (6) of that Act].]

(3) Any reference in these Regulations to an order under any particular section of the Act of [1984] includes a reference to an order varying an order made, or having effect as if made, under that section.

(4) Any reference in these Regulations to any enactment shall be construed as a reference to that enactment as amended by or under any subsequent enactment.

(5) [The Interpretation Act 1978] shall apply for the interpretation of these Regulations as it applies for the interpretation of an Act of Parliament.

[Regulation 1 is printed as amended by SI 1975 No 267; the Interpretation Act 1978, ss 17(2), 23; the Motor Vehicles (Construction and Use) Regulations 1978 (SI 1978 No 1017), reg 3 (10); the Public Passenger Vehicles Act 1981, s 83 (1); and the Road Traffic Regulation Act 1984, s 144(1), and Sched 10, para 2.

The descriptions of a 'disabled person' prescribed by the Disabled Persons (Badges for Motor Vehicles) Regulations 1982 (SI 1982 No 1740), reg 5, are: a person who—

(*a*) receives a mobility allowance pursuant to section 37A of the Social Security Act 1975;

(*b*) uses a motor vehicle supplied by the Department of Health and Social Security, the Scottish Home and Health Department or the Welsh Office or is in receipt of a grant pursuant to section 5(2)(*a*) of the National Health Service Act 1977 or section 46 of the National Health Service (Scotland) Act 1978;

(*c*) is registered as blind under section 29 of the National Assistance Act 1948, or, in Scotland, is a blind person within the meaning of section 64(1) of that Act; or

(*d*) has a permanent and substantial disability which causes inability to walk or very considerable difficulty in walking.

The Disabled Persons (Badges for Motor Vehicles) Regulations 1982, reg 3(1), defines a disabled person's badge as—

a badge in the form prescribed by Regulation 4 issued by a local authority for display on a motor vehicle driven by a disabled person, or used for the carriage of a disabled person or of several disabled persons, and includes a duplicate badge issued pursuant to Regulation 8.

The Disabled Persons (Badges for Motor Vehicles) Regulations 1982, reg 3 (1), defines an 'institution' as 'an institution concerned with the care of the disabled'. Regulation 6 of those regulations provides: 'An institution is eligible to apply for the issue to it of a disabled person's badge for any motor vehicle or, as the case may be, for each motor vehicle, used by or on behalf of the institution to carry disabled persons'.

2. Application of Regulations

These Regulations apply—

(a) to orders made by a local authority (other than a London local authority) under any of the following provisions of the [Act of 1984], that is to say, [sections 1, 9, 35, 45 and 46], after the date of the coming into operation of these Regulations; and

(b) to orders made by the Greater London Council under any of the following provisions of the [Act of 1984], that is to say, [sections 6, 9, 45 and 46], after the date of the coming, into operation of these Regulations except that they do not apply to an order made after the said date by the said Council under any of the said sections in so far as the order applies in the City of London, the City of Westminster or the Royal Borough of Kensington and Chelsea, or any part of the London Borough of Camden [south of, and including, Euston Road].

[Regulation 2 is printed as amended by SI 1975 No 267 and the Road Traffic Regulation Act 1984, s 144(1), and Sched 10, para 2.
The main regulations came into operation on 1 December 1971; see reg 1 (1).
The power to make orders under the Road Traffic Regulation Act 1984 relates to traffic regulation orders outside Greater London (s 1), traffic regulation orders in Greater London (s 6), experimental traffic orders (s 9), provisions as to the use of local authority parking places (s 35), provision of parking places on the highway and charges therefor (s 45), and regulation of parking places on the highway (s 46).]

3. Exemptions in Orders for vehicles displaying disabled persons' badges

(1) Where an order under [section 1, 6 or 9 of the Act of 1984]—

(a) includes a provision; or

(b) applies a provision of an existing order under any such section, which provision prohibits the waiting of vehicles, or of any class of vehicles, in a road or part of a road and the provision is one which in relation to any particular vehicle prohibits that vehicle from waiting in that road or that part of a road either—

   (i) beyond a specified period of waiting by that vehicle permitted by that provision, or

   (ii) if less than a specified period has elapsed since a previous period of waiting by that vehicle in that road or that part of a road, as the case may be,

then in the case mentioned in (a) above, the order shall also include a provision for exempting from any such prohibition contained therein any disabled person's vehicle which displays in the relevant position a disabled person's badge issued by any local authority, and in the case mentioned as (b) above, the order shall also include a provision for exempting from any prohibition as applied and as originally enacted and subsequently extended (where this is the case) any disabled person's vehicle which displays in the relevant position a disabled person's badge issued by any local authority.

[(1A) Where an order under [section 1, 6 or 9 of the Act of 1984]—

(*a*) includes a provision, or

(*b*) applies a provision of an existing order under any such section, and the provision is one which—

    (i) prohibits the waiting of vehicles, or any class of vehicles, in a road or part of a road, except for the purpose of loading or unloading, and

    (ii) in relation to a particular vehicle would have the effect of prohibiting that vehicle from waiting in that road or that part of a road at all times in any day or during one or more specified periods in any day, and

    (iii) is not a provision applying to a bus lane at a time when the bus lane restriction is in operation, and

    (iv) is not a provision to which paragraph (1) of this Regulation refers,

then the order shall include the exemption provision described in paragraph (1B) of this Regulation.]

[(1B) The exemption provision referred to in paragraph (1A) above is a provision for exempting from the prohibition included in or applied by the order—

(*a*) in a case where the period of the prohibition is of 2 hours' duration or less, for the whole of that period, and

(*b*) in a case where the period of the prohibition is of more than 2 hours' duration, for a period of 2 hours (not being a period separated by an interval of less than 1 hour from a previous period of waiting by the same vehicle in the same road or part of a road on the same day)

any disabled person's vehicle in relation to which the following requirements are satisfied, namely, that—

    (i) in all cases a disabled person's badge is displayed in the relevant position on the vehicle, and

    (ii) in the case mentioned in (*b*) above, a parking disc, issued by a local authority, complying with the requirements of the British Standard Specification for Parking Discs (BS 4631: 1970), coloured orange, and capable of showing the quarter hour period during which a period of waiting begins, is displayed in a relevant position on the vehicle, and the driver, or other person in charge of the vehicle, marks on the parking disc the time at which the period of waiting has begun.]

[(1C) In paragraphs (1) and (1A) above the reference to an order [section 1 of the Act of 1984] shall include a reference to an order under [section 45] of that Act which, by virtue of [section 53 (1) (*a*)] of that Act, includes a provision for a purpose specified in paragraph (*c*) of [section 2 (2) of that Act.]

(2) Where an order under [section 6 or 45 of the Act of 1984]—

(*a*) includes a provision; or

(*b*) applies a provision of an existing order under either such section, which provision prohibits the waiting of vehicles, or of any class of vehicles, in a street-parking place or part of such a parking place and the provision is one which in relation to any particular vehicle prohibits that vehicle from waiting in that parking place or that part of a parking place either—

    (i) beyond a specified period of waiting by that vehicle permitted by that provision, or

    (ii) if less than a specified period has elapsed since a previous period of waiting by that vehicle in that parking place or that part of a parking place, as the case may be, then in the case mentioned in (*a*) above, the order shall also include a provision for exempting from any such prohibition contained therein any disabled person's vehicle which displays in the relevant position a disabled person's badge issued by any local authority, and in the case mentioned at (*b*) above, the order shall also include a provision for exempting from any prohibition as applied and as originally enacted and subsequently extended (where this is the case) any disabled person's vehicle which displays in the relevant position a disabled person's badge issued by any local authority.

(3) Where an order under [section 45 or 46 of the Act of 1984]—

(*a*) includes a provision; or

(*b*) applies a provision of an existing order under either such section, which provision prescribes—
   (i) a charge for a vehicle, or a vehicle of any class, left in a parking place,
   (ii) a time limit in relation to the leaving of, or waiting by, vehicles, or vehicles of any class, in a parking place, or
   (iii) a period which must elapse before a vehicle which has been taken away from a parking place may again be left therein.

then in the case mentioned in (*a*) above, the order shall also include a provision for exempting from any such matter prescribed therein any disabled person's vehicle which displays in the relevant position a disabled person's badge issued by any local authority, and in the case mentioned at (*b*) above, the order shall also include a provision for exempting from any matter prescribed and as applied and as originally enacted and subsequently extended (where this is the case) any disabled person's vehicle which displays in the relevant position a disabled person's badge issued by any local authority.

(4) Any provision for exemption required by this Regulation to be contained in any order referred to therein may be limited to the same class of vehicle as that to which the provision, from which exemption is required to be given by this Regulation, applies.

(5) For the purposes of this Regulation and any order referred to therein, a vehicle shall be regarded as displaying a disabled person's badge in the relevant position when—

(*a*) in the case of a vehicle fitted with a front windscreen, the badge is exhibited thereon with the obverse side facing forwards on the near side of and immediately behind the windscreen; and

(*b*) in the case of a vehicle not fitted with a front windscreen, the badge is exhibited in a conspicuous position on the vehicle.

[Regulation 3 is printed as amended by SI 1975 No 267, SI 1975 No 1562 and the Road Traffic Regulation Act 1984, s 144(1), and Sched 10, para 2.]

*   *   *

The Motor Cycles (Protective Helmets) Regulations 1980

(SI 1980 No 1279)

[The text of these regulations is printed as amended by:
the Motor Cycles (Protective Helmets) (Amendment) Regulations 1981 (SI 1981 No 374)
(1 April 1981).
The amending regulations are referred to in the notes to the main regulations only by their year
and number. The date referred to above is the date on which the regulations came into force.]

* * *

4.—(1) Save as provided in paragraph (2) below, every person driving or riding (otherwise than in a side-car) on a motor bicycle when on a road shall wear protective headgear.

(2) Nothing in paragraph (1) above shall apply to any person driving or riding on a motor bicycle if—

(*a*) it is a mowing machine;

(*b*) it is for the time being propelled by a person on foot; or

(*c*) he is a follower of the Sikh religion while he is wearing a turban.

(3) In this Regulation:—

'motor bicycle' means a two wheeled motor cycle, whether having a side-car attached thereto or not, and for the purposes of this definition any wheels of a motor cycle shall, if the distance between the centres of the areas of contact between such wheels and the road surface is less than 460 millimetres, be counted as one wheel; and

'protective headgear' means headgear which—

(*a*) is either—

(i) a helmet bearing a marking applied by its manufacturer indicating compliance with the specifications contained in one of the British Standards mentioned in Schedule 2 (whether or not as modified by any amendment), or

(ii) a helmet of a type manufactured for use by persons on motor cycles which by virtue of its shape, material and construction could reasonably be expected to afford to persons on motor bicycles a degree of protection from injury in the event of an accident similar to or greater than that provided by a helmet of a type prescribed by Regulation 5; and

(*b*) if worn with a chin cup attached to or held in position by a strap or other fastening provided on the helmet, is provided with an additional strap or other fastening (to be fastened under the wearer's jaw) for securing the helmet firmly to the head of the wearer; and

  (c) is securely fastened to the head of the wearer by means of the straps or other fastening provided on the headgear for that purpose.

5.—(1) The types of helmet hereby prescribed as types of helmet recommended as affording protection to persons on or in motor cycles from injury in the event of an accident are—

  (a) until 1st January 1982 helmets which as respects their shape, construction and other qualities—

    (i) conform—

      (a) in the case of a helmet manufactured before 1st March 1975, with any one of the British Standards mentioned in items 1, 2, 3 and 4 in Schedule 2,

      (b) in the case of a helmet manufactured on or after 1st March 1975, but before 2nd February 1977 with any one of the British Standards mentioned in items 2, 3, 4 and 5 in Schedule 2,

      (c) in the case of a helmet manufactured on or after 2nd February 1977 but before 1st July 1977 with any of the British Standards mentioned in items 3, 5 and 6 in Schedule 2,

      (d) in the case of a helmet manufactured on or after 1st July 1977 but before 1st October 1980 with any one of the British Standards mentioned in items 5, 6, 7 and 8 in Schedule 2

      [(e) in the case of a helmet manufactured on or after 1st October 1980 but before 1st April 1981 with one of the British Standards mentioned in items 7, 8, 9 and 10 in Schedule 2,]

      [(f) in the case of a helmet manufactured on or after 1st April 1981 with one of the British Standards mentioned in items 9 and 10 in Schedule 2, and]

    (ii) in the case of any helmet, is marked with the number of the British Standard with which it conforms and the certification mark of the British Standards Institution (whether or not it is required to be so marked by the British Standard in point);

  (b) on or after 1st January 1982 helmets which as respects their shape, construction and other qualities—

    (i) conform with one of the British Standards mentioned in [items 5, 6, 7, 8, 9 and 10 in Schedule 2], and

    (ii) are marked with the number of the British Standard with which they conform and the certification mark of the British Standards Institution (whether or not they are required to be so marked by the British Standard in point).

  (2) A reference in paragraph (1) above to a helmet which, as respects its shape, construction and other qualities, conforms with one of the British Standards mentioned in an item in Schedule 2 is a reference to a helmet which so conforms with one of those British Standards subject to such (if any) of the amendments to the relevant Standard mentioned in the relevant item as had effect at the time of the manufacture of the helmet.

 [Regulation 5 is printed as amended by SI 1981 No 374.]

  6. Nothing in Regulation 5 (1) shall be taken to authorise any person to apply any number or mark referred to therein in contravention of the Trade Descriptions Act 1968.

* * *

SCHEDULE 2

BRITISH STANDARDS

1. British Standard 2001: 1956 as amended by the following Amendment Slips:—

Number	Date of Publication
1	11th January 1957
2	23rd November 1959
3	27th February 1962
4	11th June 1964
5	13th March 1968
6	18th February 1972

2. British Standard 1869: 1960 as amended by the following Amendment Slips:—

Number	Date of Publication
1	29th May 1963
4	3rd December 1965
5	13th March 1968
6	10th August 1971
7	3rd January 1972
8	15th May 1973
9	1st February 1974
10	2nd September 1974
11	1st March 1975

3. British Standard 2495: 1960 as amended by the following Amendment Slips:—

Number	Date of Publication
1	29th May 1963
2	22nd February 1965
3	7th December 1965
4	22nd July 1966
5	10th August 1971
6	3rd January 1972
7	1st February 1974
8	1st March 1975

4. British Standard 2001: 1972 as amended by the following Amendment Slips:—

Number	Date of Publication
1	12th December 1972
2	26th January 1973
3	1st February 1974
4	2nd September 1974
5	1st March 1975

5. British Standard 5361: 1976

6. British Standard 2495: 1977

7. British Standard 5361: 1976 as amended by the following Amendment Slips:—

Number	Date of Publication
1	30th September 1977
2	31st August 1978
3	31st August 1979
4	29th February 1980

8. British Standard 2495: 1977 as amended by the following Amendment Slips:—

Number	Date of Publication
1	30th September 1977
2	31st August 1978
3	31st August 1979
4	29th February 1980

[9. British Standard 5361: 1976 as amended by the following Amendment Slips:—

Number	Date of Publication
1	30th September 1977
2	31st August 1978
3	31st August 1979
4	29th February 1980
5	27th February 1981]

[10. British Standard 2495: 1977 as amended by the following Amendment Slips:—

Number	Date of Publication
1	30th September 1977
2	31st August 1978
3	31st August 1979
4	29th February 1980
5	27th February 1981]

[Schedule 2 is printed as amended by SI 1981 No 374.]

The Motor Vehicles (Construction and Use) Regulations 1978

(SI 1978 No 1017)

[The text of these regulations is printed as amended by:

the Motor Vehicles (Construction and Use) (Amendment) Regulations 1978 (SI 1978 No 1233) (29 September 1978);

the Motor Vehicles (Construction and Use) (Amendment) (No 3) Regulations 1978 (SI 1978 No 1235) (1 October 1978);

the Motor Vehicles (Construction and Use) (Amendment) (No 5) Regulations 1978 (SI 1978 No 1317) (1 October 1978);

the Motor Vehicles (Construction and Use) (Amendment) Regulations 1979 (SI 1979 No 138) (13 March 1979);

the Motor Vehicles (Construction and Use) (Amendment) (No 2) Regulations 1979 (SI 1979 No 843) (16 August 1979);

the Motor Vehicles (Construction and Use) (Amendment) (No 3) Regulations 1979 (SI 1979 No 1062) (20 September 1979);

the Motor Vehicles (Construction and Use) (Amendment) (No 2) Regulations 1980 (SI 1980 No 139) (7 March 1980);

the Motor Vehicles (Construction and Use) (Amendment) Regulations 1980 (SI 1980 No 140) (5 March 1980);

the Motor Vehicles (Construction and Use) (Amendment) (No 3) Regulations 1980 (SI 1980 No 287) (8 April 1980);

the Motor Vehicles (Construction and Use) (Amendment) (No 4) Regulations 1980 (SI 1980 No 610) (30 May 1980);

the Motor Vehicles (Construction and Use) (Amendment) (No 5) Regulations 1980 (SI 1980 No 880) (28 July 1980);

the Motor Vehicles (Construction and Use) (Amendment) (No 6) Regulations 1980 (SI 1980 No 1166) (8 September 1980);

the Motor Vehicles (Construction and Use) (Amendment) (No 7) Regulations 1980 (SI 1980 No 1789) (24 December 1980);

the Motor Vehicles (Construction and Use) (Amendment) Regulations 1981 (SI 1981 No 261) (1 April 1981);

the Motor Vehicles (Construction and Use) (Amendment) (No 2) Regulations 1981 (SI 1981 No 697) (3 June 1981);

the Motor Vehicles (Construction and Use) (Amendment) (No 3) Regulations 1981 (SI 1981 No 915) (1 August 1981);

the Motor Vehicles (Construction and Use) (Amendment) (No 4) Regulations 1981 (SI 1981 No 1189) (except so far as noted otherwise against reg 75 post, 10 September 1981);

the Motor Vehicles (Construction and Use) (Amendment) (No 5) Regulations 1981 (SI 1981 No 1580) (7 December 1981);

the Motor Vehicles (Construction and Use) (Amendment) (No 6) Regulations 1981 (SI 1981 No 1663) (except so far as noted otherwise against regs 144A, 144B and 144C post, 29 December 1981);

the Motor Vehicles (Construction and Use) (Amendment) (No 7) Regulations 1981 (SI 1981 No 1688) (24 December 1981);

the Motor Vehicles (Construction and Use) (Amendment) Regulations 1982 (SI 1982 No 1057) (2 September 1982);

the Motor Vehicles (Construction and Use) (Amendment) (No 2) Regulations 1982 (SI 1982 No 1132) (7 September 1982);

the Motor Vehicles (Construction and Use) (Amendment) (No 3) Regulations 1982 (SI 1982 No 1223) (30 September 1982);

the Motor Vehicles (Construction and Use) (Amendment) (No 4) Regulations 1982 (SI 1982 No 1272) (1 October 1982);

the Motor Vehicles (Construction and Use) (Amendment) (No 5) Regulations 1982 (SI 1982 No 1422) (5 November 1982);

the Motor Vehicles (Construction and Use) (Amendment) (No 6) Regulations 1982 (SI 1982 No 1480) (19 November 1982);

the Motor Vehicles (Construction and Use) (Amendment) (No 7) Regulations 1982 (SI 1982 No 1576) (1 May 1983);

the Motor Vehicles (Construction and Use) (Amendment) Regulations 1983 (SI 1983 No 112) (14 March 1983);

the Motor Vehicles (Construction and Use) (Amendment) (No 2) Regulations 1983 (SI 1983 No 471) (1 May 1983);

the Motor Vehicles (Construction and Use) (Amendment) (No 3) Regulations 1983 (SI 1983 No 932) (1 November 1983);

the Motor Vehicles (Construction and Use) (Amendment) Regulations 1984 (SI 1984 No 195) (1 April 1984);

the Motor Vehicles (Construction and Use) (Amendment) (No 2) Regulations 1984 (SI 1984 No 331) (23 March 1984);

the Motor Vehicles (Construction and Use) (Amendment) (No 3) Regulations 1984 (SI 1984 No 386) (19 April 1984);

the Motor Vehicles (Construction and Use) (Amendment) (No 4) Regulations 1984 (SI 1984 No 679) (15 June 1984);

the Motor Vehicles (Construction and Use) (Amendment) (No 5) Regulations 1984 (SI 1984 No 813) (1 August 1984);

the Motor Vehicles (Construction and Use) (Amendment) (No 6) Regulations 1984 (SI 1984 No 1543) (1 November 1984); and

the Motor Vehicles (Construction and Use) (Amendment) (No 7) Regulations 1984 (SI 1984 No 1809) (1 March 1985).

The amending regulations are referred to in the notes to the main regulations only by their years and numbers. The dates referred to above are the dates on which the regulations came into force.

The main regulations have also been amended by the Motor Vehicles (Construction and Use) (Amendment) (No 4) Regulation 1978 (SI 1978 No 1263) (revoked by SI 1982 No 1480) but these do not affect the text of any regulation printed.]

ARRANGEMENT OF REGULATIONS

PART I

PRELIMINARY

Regulation

PART II

REGULATIONS GOVERNING THE CONSTRUCTION WEIGHT AND EQUIPMENT OF MOTOR VEHICLES AND TRAILERS

A *General*

B *Gas Containers*

*　　*　　*

C *Locomotives*

D *Motor Tractors*

PART III

REGULATIONS GOVERNING THE USE ON
ROADS OF MOTOR VEHICLES AND TRAILERS

PART IV

TESTING AND INSPECTION OF BRAKES, SILENCERS, STEERING GEAR, TYRES, LIGHTING EQUIPMENT AND REFLECTORS

PART V

PARTICULAR REGULATIONS RELATING TO VEHICLES FOR WHICH PLATING CERTIFICATES HAVE BEEN ISSUED

SCHEDULES

carrying wide or long loads or vehicles carrying loads or having fixed
appliances or apparatus which project

. . . .

9A.   Maximum sound levels (A weighting) in decibels (dB (A))

. . . .

11.   Ministry plate
12.   Distinguishing plates for motor cycles
12A.   Distinguishing plates for motor cycles first used on or after 1st Janu-
        ary 1982

*   *   *

PART I

PRELIMINARY

*   *   *

3. Interpretation

(1) In these Regulations, unless the context otherwise requires, the following
expressions have the meanings hereby assigned to them respectively, that is to say,—

'the 1960 Act' means the Road Traffic Act 1960;

'the [1984] Act' means the [Road Traffic Regulation Act 1984];

'the 1972 Act' means the Road Traffic Act 1972;

'the Designation of Approval Marks Regulations' means the Motor Vehicles
(Designation of Approval Marks) Regulations [1979 *[SI 1979 No 1088]*];

'the Lighting Regulations' means the Road Vehicles Lighting Regulations [1984
[SI 1984 No 812]];

'the Plating and Testing Regulations' means the Goods Vehicles (Plating and
Testing) Regulations [1982 *[SI 1982 No 1478]*];

'the Type Approval Regulations' means the Motor Vehicles (Type Approval)
Regulations [1980 *[SI 1980 No 1182]*];

'the Type Approval (Great Britain) Regulations' means the Motor Vehicles
(Type Approval) (Great Britain) Regulations [1984 *[SI 1984 No 981]*];

['agricultural motor vehicle' means a motor vehicle which is constructed or
adapted for use off roads for the purpose of agriculture, horticulture or forestry and which is primarily used for one or more of those purposes, but does
not include a dual-purpose vehicle;]

['agricultural trailer' means a trailer which is constructed or adapted for the
purpose of agriculture, horticulture or forestry and which is only used for one
or more of those purposes, but does not include an agricultural trailed
appliance;]

['agricultural trailed appliance' means a trailer—

(*a*) which is an implement constructed or adapted—

    (i) for use off roads for the purpose of agriculture, horticulture or for-
estry and which is only used for one or more of those purposes, and

    (ii) so that, save in the case of an appliance manufactured before 1st
December 1985, or a towed roller, its maximum gross weight is not
more than twice its unladen weight; but

(*b*) which is not—

    (i) a vehicle which is used primarily as living accommodation by one or more persons, and which is not also used for the carriage of goods or burden which are not needed by such one or more persons for the purpose of their residence in the vehicle; or

(ii) an agricultural implement rigidly but not permanently mounted on any vehicle whether or not any of the weight of the implement is supported by one or more of its own wheels except in a case where
—part of the weight of the implement is supported by one or more of its own wheels, and
—the longitudinal axis of the greater part of the implement is capable of articulating in the horizontal plane in relation to the longitudinal axis of the rear portion of the vehicle on which it is mounted;]

['agricultural trailed appliance conveyor' means an agricultural trailer which—

(a) has an unladen weight which does not exceed 510 kilograms;

(b) is clearly and indelibly marked with its unladen weight;

(c) has a pneumatic tyre fitted to each one of its wheels;

(d) is designed and constructed for the purpose of conveying one agricultural trailed appliance or one agricultural implement';]

['articulated bus' means a passenger vehicle so constructed that—

(a) it can be divided into two parts, both of which are vehicles and one of which is a motor vehicle, but cannot be so divided without the use of facilities normally available only at a workshop; and

(b) passengers carried by it can at all times pass from either part to the other;]

'articulated vehicle' means a heavy motor car or motor car with a trailer so attached to the drawing vehicle that part of the trailer is superimposed upon the drawing vehicle, and when the trailer is uniformly loaded not less than 20 per cent of the weight of its load is [borne by the drawing vehicle, but does not include an articulated bus];

'braking efficiency', in relation to the application of brakes to a motor vehicle at any time, means the maximum braking force capable of being developed by the application of those brakes, expressed as a percentage of the weight of the vehicle including any persons (not being fare paying or other travelling passengers) or load carried in the vehicle at that time;

'close-coupled', in relation to a trailer, means that the wheels on the same side of the trailer are so fitted that at all times while it is in motion they remain parallel to the longitudinal axis of the trailer, and that the distance between the centres of their respective areas of contact with the road surface does not exceed 1 metre;

['closely spaced' means—

(i) in the case of two axles, they are spaced at a distance apart of not more than 2.5 metres and not less than 1.02 metres; and

(ii) in the case of three axles, the outermost axles are spaced at a distance apart of 3.25 metres or less and no one of those three axles has a plated weight of more than 7500 kilograms;]

'composite trailer' means a combination of a converter dolly and a semi-trailer;

'converter dolly' means a trailer which is—

(a) equipped with two or more wheels,

(*b*) designed to enable a semi-trailer to move without any part of its weight being directly superimposed on the drawing vehicle, and

(*c*) not itself a part either of the semi-trailer or of the drawing vehicle;

'deck' means a floor or platform upon which seats are provided for the accommodation of passengers;

'direction indicator' means a device fitted to a motor vehicle or trailer for the purpose of intimating the intention of the driver to change the direction of the vehicle to the right or to the left;

'double-decked vehicle' means a vehicle having two decks one of which is wholly or partly above the other and each deck of which is provided with a gangway serving seats on that deck only;

'dual-purpose vehicle' means a vehicle constructed or adapted for the carriage both of passengers and of goods or burden of any description, being a vehicle of which the unladen weight does not exceed 2040 kilograms, and which either—

(i) is so constructed or adapted that the driving power of the engine is, or by the appropriate use of the controls of the vehicle can be, transmitted to all the wheels of the vehicle; or

(ii) satisfies the following conditions as to construction, namely:—

(*a*) the vehicle must be permanently fitted with a rigid roof, with or without a sliding panel;

(*b*) the area of the vehicle to the rear of the driver's seat must—

(i) be permanently fitted with at least one row of transverse seats (fixed or folding) for two or more passengers and those seats must be properly sprung or cushioned and provided with upholstered back-rests, attached either to the seats or to a side or the floor of the vehicle; and

(ii) be lit on each side and at the rear by a window or windows of glass or other transparent material having an area or aggregate area of not less than 1850 square centimetres on each side and not less than 770 square centimetres at the rear;

(*c*) the distance between the rearmost part of the steering wheel and the back-rests of the row of transverse seats satisfying the requirements specified in head (i) of the foregoing sub-paragraph (*b*) (or, if there is more than one such row of seats, the distance between the rearmost part of the steering wheel and the back-rests of the rearmost such row) must, when the seats are ready for use, be not less than one-third of the distance between the rearmost part of the steering wheel and the rearmost part of the floor of the vehicle;

'engineering plant' means—

(*a*) movable plant or equipment being a motor vehicle or trailer specially designed and constructed for the special purposes of engineering operations, and which cannot, owing to the requirements of those purposes, comply in all respects with the requirements of these Regulations and which is not constructed primarily to carry a load other than a load being either excavated materials raised from the ground by apparatus on the motor vehicle or trailer or materials which the vehicle or trailer is specially designed to treat while carried thereon; or

(*b*) a mobile crane which does not comply in all respects with the requirements of these Regulations;

'exhaust brake' means a device with which a vehicle is fitted as a means of using cylinder pressure or exhaust back pressure so as to provide for the vehicle a retarding force greater than would ordinarily result for a vehicle not so fitted;

'gangway' means the space provided for obtaining access from any entrance to the passengers' seats or from any such seat to an exit other than an emergency exit but does not include a staircase or any space in front of a seat which is required only for the use of passengers occupying that seat or that row of seats;

['gas' means any fuel that is wholly gaseous at 17·5°C. under a pressure of 1·013 bar absolute;]

['gas-fired appliance' means a device carried on a motor vehicle or trailer when in use on a road, which consumes gas and which is neither—

(a) a device owned or operated by or with the authority of the British Gas Corporation for the purpose of detecting gas, nor

(b) an engine for the propulsion of a motor vehicle, nor

(c) a lamp which consumes acetylene gas;]

'goods vehicle' means a motor vehicle constructed or adapted for use for the carriage of goods, or a trailer so constructed or adapted;

['gritting trailer' means a trailer which is in use on a road for the purpose of spreading grit or other matter so as to avoid or reduce the effect of ice or snow on the road;]

'half-decked vehicle' means any vehicle not being a single-decked vehicle or a double-decked vehicle;

['HP DIN' means the maximum useful power of an engine ascertained in accordance with Part 6 of the standard published in the Federal Republic of Germany by the Deutsches Institut für Normung with the number DIN 70020 and dated November 1976;]

'hours of darkness' means the time between half-an-hour after sunset and half-an-hour before sunrise;

'indivisible load' means a load which cannot without undue expense or risk of damage be divided into two or more loads for the purpose of conveyance on a road;

'industrial tractor' means a tractor, not being [an agricultural motor vehicle], which—

(a) has an unladen weight not exceeding 7370 kilograms,

(b) is designed and used primarily for work off roads, or for work on roads in connection only with road construction or maintenance (including any such tractor when fitted with an implement or implements designed primarily for use in connection with such work, whether or not any such implement is of itself designed to carry a load), and

(c) is so constructed as to be incapable of exceeding a speed of 20 miles per hour on the level under its own power;

['large passenger carrying vehicle' means a motor vehicle which is constructed or adapted to carry more than 8 seated passengers in addition to the driver;]

['liquefied petroleum gas' means—

(a) butane gas in any phase which meets the requirements contained in the specification of commercial butane and propane issued by the British

Standards Institution under the number BS 4250: 1975 and published on 29th August 1975, or

(b) propane gas in any phase which meets the requirements contained in the said specification, or

(c) any mixture of such butane gas and such propane gas;]

'locomotive' means a heavy locomotive or a light locomotive;

['Ministry plate' means a plate issued, or having effect as if issued, by the Secretary of State for a goods vehicle following the issue or amendment of a plating certificate and in the form in, and containing the particulars required by, Schedule 11, the said particulars being those shown in the plating certificate for the vehicle;]

'multi-pull means of operation', in relation to a braking system, means a device which causes the muscular energy of the driver to apply the brakes of that system progressively as a result of successive applications of that device by the driver;

'overall length' means the length of a vehicle measured between vertical planes at right angles to the longitudinal axis of the vehicle and passing through the extreme projecting points thereof exclusive of—

(a) any driving mirror;

(b) any starting handle;

(c) any hood when down;

(d) any expanding or extensible contrivance forming part of a turntable fire escape fixed to a vehicle;

(e) any telescopic fog lamp when extended;

(f) any snow-plough fixed in front of a vehicle;

(g) any post office letter box the length of which measured parallel to the longitudinal axis of the vehicle does nnot exceed 305 millimetres; and

(h) any container specially designed to hold and keep secure a seal issued for the purposes of customs clearance,

and, except for the purposes of Regulation 139, exclusive of any [front position lamp or side marker lamp with which the vehicle is fitted in accordance with the Lighting Regulations].

In ascertaining the extreme projecting points of a vehicle account shall be taken of any device or any receptacle on or attached to the vehicle which increases the carrying capacity of the vehicle unless—

(i) it is a tailboard which is let down while the vehicle is stationary in order to facilitate its loading or unloading,

(ii) it is a tailboard which is let down in order to facilitate the carriage of, but which is not essential for the support of, loads which are in themselves so long as to extend at least as far as the tailboard when in the upright position,

(iii) it is a receptacle which is constructed or adapted for the purpose of being lifted on or off vehicles with goods or burden contained therein and is from time to time actually used for that purpose in the ordinary course [of business, or];

[(iv) it is a plate, whether rigid or movable, fitted to a trailer constructed for the purpose of carrying other vehicles and designed to bridge the gap between that trailer and a motor vehicle constructed for that purpose and to which the trailer is attached so that, while the trailer is attached to the motor vehicle, vehicles which are to be carried by the motor vehicle may be moved from the trailer to the motor vehicle before a journey begins, and vehicles which have been carried on the motor vehicle may be moved from it to the trailer after a journey ends;]

'overall width' means the width of a vehicle measured between vertical planes parallel to the longitudinal axis of the vehicle and passing through the extreme projecting points thereof exclusive of—

(a) any driving mirror;

(b) any direction indicator;

(c) any snow-plough fixed in front of the vehicle;

(d) so much of the distortion of any tyre as is caused by the weight of the vehicle;

(e) in the case of vehicles registered before 2nd January 1939 so much of a swivelling window designed to allow the driver to give hand signals as projects when opened not more than 105 millimetres beyond the side of the vehicle; and

(f) any container specially designed to hold and keep secure a seal issued for the purposes of customs clearance,

and, except for the purposes of Regulation 139, exclusive of any [front position lamp or side marker lamp with which the vehicle is fitted in accordance with the Lighting Regulations].

In ascertaining the extreme projecting points of a vehicle account shall be taken of any device or any receptacle on or attached to the vehicle which increases the carrying capacity of the vehicle unless—

(i) it is a sideboard which is let down while the vehicle is stationary in order to facilitate its loading or unloading, or

(ii) it is a receptacle which is constructed or adapted for the purpose of being lifted on or off vehicles with goods or burden contained therein and is from time to time actually used for that purpose in the ordinary course of business;

'overhang' means the distance measured horizontally and parallel to the longitudinal axis of a vehicle between two vertical planes at right angles to that axis passing through the following two points, namely:—

(a) the rearmost point of the vehicle exclusive of—

(i) any hood when down;

(ii) any post office letter box the length of which measured parallel to the longitudinal axis of the vehicle does not exceed 305 millimetres;

(iii) any expanding or extensible contrivance forming part of a turntable fire escape fixed to a vehicle;

(iv) in the case of a motor car constructed solely for the carriage of passengers and their effects and adapted to carry not more than seven passengers exclusive of the driver, any luggage carrier fitted to the vehicle; and

(v) in the case of a public service vehicle constructed to draw a trailer, any part of the vehicle designed primarily for use as a means of attaching the trailer and any fitting designed for use in connection with such part, being a part and fitting the total length of which measured parallel to the longitudinal axis of the vehicle does not exceed 305 millimetres; and

(b)   (i) in the case of a motor vehicle having not more than three axles of which only one is not a steering axle, through the centre point of that axle;

        (ii) in the case of a motor vehicle having three axles of which the front axle is the only steering axle and of a motor vehicle having four axles of which the two foremost are the only steering axles, through a point 110 millimetres behind the centre of a straight line joining the centre points of the two rearmost axles; and

        (iii) in any other case through a point situated on the longitudinal axis of the vehicle and such that a line drawn from it at right angles to that axis will pass through the centre of the minimum turning circle of the vehicle;

'passenger vehicle' means a vehicle constructed solely for the carriage of passengers and their effects;

'pedestrian controlled vehicle' means a motor vehicle which is controlled by a pedestrian and not constructed or adapted for use or used for the carriage of a driver or passenger;

'pneumatic tyre' means a tyre which complies in all respects with the following requirements:—

(a) it shall be provided with, or together with the wheel upon which it is mounted shall form, a continuous closed chamber inflated to a pressure substantially exceeding atmospheric pressure when the tyre is in the condition in which it is normally used, but is not subjected to any load;

(b) it shall be capable of being inflated and deflated without removal from the wheel or vehicle;

(c) it shall be such that, when it is deflated and is subjected to a normal load, the sides of the tyre collapse;

['public service vehicle' has the meaning assigned to that expression in section 1 (1) (a) of the Public Passenger Vehicles Act 1981.]

['the Recording Equipment Regulation' has the same meaning as in section 82 of the 1972 Act;]

['public works vehicle' means a mechanically propelled vehicle which is specially designed for use on a road by or on behalf of any statutory undertaking (as defined in section 262 (13) of the Local Government Act 1972), highway authority, local authority, [water authority,] the Post Office, British Telecommunications or any police force for the purpose of works which such undertaking, authority or other body has a duty or a power to carry out, but excluding the carriage of persons other than crew or of goods other than goods needed for the works in respect of which the vehicle is being used;]

'recut pneumatic tyre' means any pneumatic tyre in which an existing tread pattern has been cut or burnt deeper or a new tread pattern has been cut or burnt except where the pattern is cut entirely in additional material added to the tyre for the purpose;

'registered', in relation to the date on which a vehicle was registered, means—

(a) in the case of a vehicle which was registered at any time under the Roads Act 1920, the date on which it was first so registered, and

(b) in the case of any other vehicle, the date on which it was first registered under the Vehicles (Excise) Act 1949, the Vehicles (Excise) Act 1962, or the Vehicles (Excise) Act 1971;

['relevant plate' means—

    (i) in relation to a vehicle which is fitted with a Ministry plate, that plate;

    (ii) in relation to a temporarily imported motor vehicle or a temporarily imported trailer, as defined in Regulation 86 (6), the plate referred to in that definition;

    (iii) in relation to any other vehicle, the plate with which it is equipped in accordance with Regulation 42;]

['relevant train weight' means—

    (i) in relation to a motor vehicle fitted with a Ministry plate, the weight shown in column (2) of that plate;

    (ii) in relation to a temporarily imported motor vehicle, as defined in Regulation 86 (6), the maximum train weight shown on the plate referred to in that definition;

    (iii) in relation to any other motor vehicle, the maximum train weight shown on the plate with which it is fitted in accordance with Regulation 42;]

'rigid vehicle' means a motor vehicle which is not constructed or adapted to form part of an articulated vehicle;

'safety glass' means glass so constructed or treated that if fractured it does not fly into fragments likely to cause severe cuts;

'semi-trailer' means a trailer which is constructed or adapted to form part of an articulated vehicle;

'single-decked vehicle' means a vehicle upon which no part of a deck or gangway is vertically above another deck or gangway;

'split braking system', in relation to a motor vehicle, means a braking system so designed and constructed that—

    (a) it comprises two independent sections of mechanism capable of developing braking force such that, excluding the means of operation, a failure of any part (other than a fixed member or a brake shoe anchor pin) of one of the said sections shall not cause a decrease in the braking force capable of being developed by the other section;

    (b) the said two sections are operated by a means of operation which is common to both sections;

    (c) the braking efficiency of either of the said two sections can be readily checked;

'stored energy', in relation to a braking system of a vehicle, means energy (other than the muscular energy of the driver or the mechanical energy of a spring) stored in a reservoir for the purpose of applying the brakes under the control of the driver, either directly or as a supplement to his muscular energy;

'straddle carrier' means a motor vehicle constructed to straddle and lift its load for the purpose of transportation;

'statutory power of removal' means a power conferred by or under any enactment to remove or move a vehicle from any road or from any part of a road;

'towing implement' means any device on wheels designed for the purpose of enabling a motor vehicle to draw another vehicle by the attachment of that device to that other vehicle in such a manner that part of that other vehicle is secured to and either rests on or is suspended from the device and some but not all of the wheels on which that other vehicle normally runs are raised off the ground;

'track laying', in relation to a vehicle, means that the vehicle is so designed and constructed that the weight thereof is transmitted to the road surface either by means of continuous tracks or by a combination of wheels and continuous tracks in such circumstances that the weight transmitted to the road surface by the tracks is not less than half the weight of the vehicle;

['train weight', in relation to a motor vehicle which may draw a trailer, means the maximum laden weight for the motor vehicle together with any trailer which may be drawn by it;]

'two-tone horn' means an instrument or apparatus which, when operated, automatically, produces a sound which alternates at regular intervals between two fixed notes;

'vehicle in the service of a visiting force or of a headquarters' has the same meaning as in Article 8 (6) of the Visiting Forces and International Headquarters (Application of Law) Order 1965 *[SI 1965 No 1536]*

'wheel' in the case of a motor vehicle or trailer means a wheel the tyre or rim of which when the vehicle is in motion on a road is in contact with the ground;

'wheeled' in relation to a vehicle means that the whole weight of the vehicle is transmitted to the road surface by means of wheels;

'wide tyre' means a pneumatic tyre as respects which its area of contact with the road surface is not less than 300 millimetres in width when measured at right angles to the longitudinal axis of the vehicle;

'works trailer' means a trailer designed for use in private premises and used on a road only in delivering goods from or to such premises to or from a vehicle on a road in the immediate neighbourhood, or in passing from one part of any such premises to another or to other private premises in the immediate neighbourhood or in connection with road works while at or in the immediate neighbourhood of the site of such works;

'works truck' means a motor vehicle (other than a straddle carrier) designed for use in private premises and used on a road only in delivering goods from or to such premises to or from a vehicle on a road in the immediate neighbourhooddd, or in passing from one part of any such premises to another or to other private premises in the immediate neighbourhood or in connection with road works while at or in the immediate neighbourhood of the site of such works.

(2) For the purpose of these Regulations, in determining when a motor vehicle is first used, the date of such first use shall be taken to be such date as is the earliest of the undermentioned relevant dates applicable to that vehicle:—

(*a*) in the case of a vehicle registered under the Roads Act 1920, the Vehicles (Excise) Act 1949, the Vehicles (Excise) Act 1962 or the Vehicles (Excise) Act 1971, the relevant date is the date on which it was first so registered; and

(*b*) in each of the following cases—

(i) in the case of a vehicle which is being or has been used under a trade licence as defined in section 16 of the Vehicles (Excise) Act 1971 (otherwise than for the purposes of demonstration or testing or of being delivered from premises of the manufacturer by whom it was made, or of a distributor of vehicles or dealer in vehicles, to premises of a distributor of vehicles, dealer in vehicles or purchaser thereof, or to premises of a person obtaining possession thereof under a hiring agreement or hire purchase agreement);

(ii) in the case of a vehicle belonging, or which has belonged, to the Crown which is or was used or appropriated for use for naval, military or air force purposes;

(iii) in the case of a vehicle belonging, or which has belonged, to a visiting force or a headquarters or defence organisation to which in each case the Visiting Forces and International Headquarters (Application of Law) Order 1965 applies;

(iv) in the case of a vehicle being a vehicle which has been used on roads outside Great Britain and which has been imported into Great Britain; and

(v) in the case of a vehicle being a vehicle which has been used otherwise than on roads after being sold or supplied by retail and before being registered;

the relevant date is the date of manufacture of the vehicle.

In sub-sub-paragraph (v) of this paragraph 'sold or supplied by retail' means sold or supplied otherwise than to a person acquiring solely for the purpose of resale or re-supply for a valuable consideration.

[(2A) For the purposes of these Regulations the date of manufacture of a vehicle to which the Motor Vehicles (Type Approval for Goods Vehicles) (Great Britain) Regulations 1982 *[SI 1982 No 1271]* apply shall, as regards any provisions of these Regulations, be the date of manufacture described in Regulation 2 (4) (*a*) of the said Regulations of 1982.]

(3) Except where otherwise provided in these Regulations a tyre shall not be deemed to be of soft or elastic material unless the said material is either—

(*a*) continuous round the circumference of the wheel; or

(*b*) fitted in sections so that so far as reasonably practicable no space is left between the ends thereof,

and is of such thickness and design as to minimise, so far as reasonably possible, vibration when the vehicle is in motion and so constructed as to be free from any defect which might in any way cause damage to the surface of a road.

(4) For the purpose of these Regulations a brake drum shall be deemed to form part of the wheel and not of the braking system.

(5) For the purpose of these Regulations other than Regulation 108 any two wheels of a motor vehicle or trailer shall be regarded as one wheel if the distance between the centres of the areas of contact between such wheels and the road surface is less than 460 millimetres.

(6) For the purpose of these Regulations other than Regulation 108, in counting the number of axles of and in determining the sum of the weights transmitted to the road surface by any one axle of a vehicle, where the centres of the areas of contact between all the wheels and the road surface can be included between any two vertical planes at right angles to the longitudinal axis of the vehicle less than 1.02 metres apart, those wheels shall be treated as constituting one axle.

(6A) For the purpose of Regulations 73, 86 (1) and (2), 87, 89 (3) and 137, and for the purpose of Regulation 101 except as provided in paragraph (1) (*e*) thereof, but not for the purpose of any other Regulations, a composite trailer shall be treated as one trailer (not being a semi-trailer or a converter dolly) only.

[(6AA) For the purposes of [Regulation 46D, Schedule 7, and the definitions in paragraph (1) of this Regulation of the expressions 'close-coupled' and 'closely spaced'], the distance between any two axles shall be obtained by measuring the shortest distance between the line joining the centres of the areas of contact with the road surface of the wheels of one axle and the line joining the centres of the areas of contact with the road surface of the wheels of the other axle.]

[(6B) The provisions of these Regulations relating to trailers shall not apply to any part of an articulated bus.]

(7) Any reference in these Regulations to any enactment shall be construed as a reference to that enactment as amended by any subsequent enactment.

(8) Any reference in these Regulations to any Community Directive shall be construed as a reference to that Directive as amended by the Act of Accession *[Cmnd 4862 II, Annex I, pp 120/128]*

(9) Any reference in these Regulations to a numbered Regulation or Schedule is a reference to the Regulation or Schedule bearing that number in these Regulations except where otherwise expressly provided.

(10) [The Interpretation Act 1978] shall apply for the interpretation of these Regulations as it applies for the interpretation of an Act of Parliament, and as if for the purpose of [section 17] of that Act these Regulations were an Act of Parliament and the Regulations revoked by Regulation 2 were Acts of Parliament thereby repealed.

(11) In so far as any consent, notice, direction or dispensation given, Ministry plate issued or any other thing done under a provision of the Regulations revoked by these Regulations could have been given, issued or done under a corresponding provision of these Regulations it shall not be invalidated by the revocation effected by Regulation 2 but shall have effect as if given, issued or done under that corresponding provision.

[The definitions in reg 3 (1) are printed as amended by the Interpretation Act 1978, ss 17 (2), 23, SI 1979 No 843, SI 1980 No 1166, SI 1981 No 261, SI 1981 No 1189, SI 1981 No 1580, SI 1981 No 1663, SI 1982 No 1057, SI 1982 No 1272, SI 1982 No 1480, SI 1982 No 1576, SI 1983 No 471, the Road Traffic Regulation Act 1984, s 144 (1), Sched 10, para 2, SI 1984 No 813, and SI 1984 No 1809.

Paragraph (2A) was added by SI 1982 No 1272.

Paragraph (6AA) was added by SI 1982 No 1576 and is printed as amended by SI 1983 No 471.

Paragraph (6B) was added by SI 1981 No 261.

Paragraph (10) is printed as amended by the Interpretation Act 1978, s 17 (2).

The Road Traffic Act 1960 has in effect been replaced by the Road Traffic Act 1972 and the Public Passenger Vehicles Act 1981. References to the Act of 1960 should be construed, as the context allows, as references to those Acts; see the Road Traffic Act 1972, s 205 (2), and Sched 10, para 3, and the Public Passenger Vehicles Act 1981, s 83; cf the Interpretation Act 1978, s 17.

In the definition of 'HP DIN', the document to which reference is made is obtainable from the British Standards Institution.

'Statutory undertaking' (sic) is defined by the Local Government Act 1972, s 262 (13), as meaning: 'any railway, light railway, tramway, road transport, water transport, canal, inland navigation, ferry, dock, harbour, pier or lighthouse undertaking, any telephone undertaking, any market undertaking or any undertaking for the supply of electricity, gas, hydraulic power . . .or district heating'. This definition is set out as amended by the Water Act 1973, s 40 (3), and Sched 9.]

4. Application and exemptions—General

(1) Except where the context otherwise requires these Regulations shall apply to wheeled vehicles only.

(2) Regulations 11, 12, 23, 24, 29, 49, 52 and 56 shall not apply to road rollers.

(3) Regulations 9 to 12 inclusive, 14 to 21 inclusive, 23 to 26 inclusive, 30 to 80 inclusive and 98 shall not apply to vehicles proceeding to a port for export.

(4) Regulations 12, 54, 63, 65, 66 and 69 shall not apply to any pedestrian controlled vehicle.

(5) Regulations 11, 12, 20, 52, 56, 60, 65, 77, 78, 80 and 82 to 94 inclusive shall apply only to motor vehicles and trailers used on highways.

[(5A) Regulations 85, 86 (1) to (3) and (6), 88, 89, 90, 91 and 94 do not apply to any agricultural motor vehicle, agricultural trailer, or agricultural trailed appliance.]

(6) Every motor vehicle registered before the expiration of one year from the making of any Regulation hereof (. . . other than a regulation contained in Part V of these Regulations) by which the requirements as regards the construction or weight of any class of vehicles are varied shall be exempt from the requirements of that Regulation for a period of five years from the making thereof provided that it complies with the requirements of the Regulations to which it would have been subject [immediately prior to the making of that Regulation [save that the provisions of this paragraph do not apply as regards a vehicle to which paragraph (2) of Regulation 46 or Regulation 89A apply].].

(7) Part II of these Regulations, except Regulations 9, 47, 48, 49, 53, 57, 62, 70, 73 and 74, shall not apply to any motor vehicle or trailer at any time brought temporarily into Great Britain by a person resident abroad, provided that such motor vehicle or trailer respectively complies in every respect with the requirements relating to motor vehicles or trailers contained in:—

(a) Article 21 and paragraph (1) of Article 22 of the Convention on Road Traffic concluded at Geneva on 19th September 1949 [Cmnd 7997], and Part I, Part II (so far as it relates to direction indicators and stop lights) and Part III of Annex 6 to that Convention; or

(b) paragraphs I, III and VIII of Article 3 of the International Convention relative to Motor Traffic concluded at Paris on 24th April 1926 [Treaty Series No 11 (1930)].

[(8) Part II of these Regulations, except Regulations 9, 47, 48, 49, 53, 57, 62 and 70, shall not apply to any motor vehicle manufactured in Great Britain which—

(a) complies with the requirements referred to in paragraph (7) above and contained in the Conventions of 1949 or, as the case may be, 1926 referred to in that paragraph as if the vehicle had been brought temporarily into Great Britain, and either

(b) is exempt from car tax by virtue of [section 7 (1) to (3) of the Car Tax Act 1983], or

(c) has been zero rated under [Regulation 49 or 50 of the Value Added Tax (General) Regulations 1980 [SI 1980 No 1536].]

(9) Regulations 9 to 12 inclusive, 14 to 20 inclusive, 22 to 32 inclusive, 36, 37, 39 to 94 inclusive, and 139 shall not apply to any vehicle in the service of a visiting force or of a headquarters.

(10) Part II of these Regulations and Regulations 80 to 114 inclusive and Regulation 142 shall not apply to—

(a) a motor vehicle which has been submitted for an examination under section 43 of the 1972 Act while it is being used on a road in connection with the carrying out of that examination and is being so used by a person who is empowered under the said section 43 to carry out that examination, or by a person acting under the direction of a person so empowered; or (*b*) a motor vehicle or trailer which has been submitted for an examination either under regulations under section 45 of the 1972 Act or under section 45 (3) or (4) of that Act while it is being used on a road in connection with the carrying out of that examination and is being so used by a person who is empowered under the said regulations to carry out that examination, or by a person acting under the direction of a person so empowered.

(11) Regulations 18, 20, 29 (4), 66, 69 and 118 (2) shall not apply to any motor car or motor cycle in respect of which a certificate has been issued by the Officer in Charge of the National Collections of Road Transport, the Science Museum, London, SW7, that it was designed before 1st January 1905 and constructed before 31st December 1905, and paragraphs (1) to (3), (5) to (7), (9) to (11) and (13) to (15) of Regulation 64 shall not apply to any such motor car if it complies with the provisions of paragraph (8) of the said Regulation 64 as though it were a vehicle first registered under the Motor Car Act 1903 before 1st January 1915 and paragraphs (1), (2), (5) and (6) of Regulation 67 shall not apply to any such motor cycle if it complies with the provisions of paragraph (4) of the said Regulation 67 as though it were a motor cycle first registered under the Motor Car Act 1903 or the Roads Act 1920 before 1st January 1927.

(12) The provisions of these Regulations applicable to trailers contained in Part II (except paragraph (2) of Regulation 8) and Regulations 81 and 126 shall not apply—

(*a*) to any towing implement which is being drawn by a motor vehicle while it is not attached to any vehicle except the one drawing it if the following conditions are satisfied, that is to say,—

    (i) the towing implement is not being so drawn during the hours of darkness, and

    (ii) the vehicle by which it is being so drawn is not driven at a speed exceeding 20 miles per hour; or

(*b*) to any vehicle which is being drawn by a motor vehicle in the exercise of a statutory power of removal.

(13) Any reference in these Regulations to a vehicle which is being drawn by a motor vehicle in the exercise of a statutory power of removal or to a broken down vehicle shall include a reference to any towing implement which is being used for the drawing of any such vehicle.

[Regulation 4 is printed as amended by the Interpretation Act 1978, ss 17 (2), 23, SI 1980 No 880, SI 1981 No 261, SI 1981 No 915, and SI 1984 No 1809.

The Car Tax Act 1983, s 7 (1) to (3), relates to relief from car tax for vehicles exported and remission of car tax for vehicles acquired for export.]

Application and exemptions—Type approval

5.—(1) This Regulation applies to a motor vehicle or trailer in respect of which—

(*a*) a type approval certificate has been issued by the [Secretary of State for Transport] under Regulation 5 of the Type Approval Regulations (which provides for the issue of such a certificate in respect of a vehicle which is proved as a type vehicle where it conforms to certain requirements as to design, construction, equipment and marking) or by the competent authority of any member State other than the United Kingdom under a provision of the law of that State which corresponds to the said Regulation 5; or

(*b*) a certificate of conformity has been issued by the manufacturer of the vehicle under Regulation 6 of those Regulations (which provides for the issue of such a certificate in respect of a vehicle where it is manufactured so as to conform with type vehicle in respect of such of the said requirements as apply in relation to that vehicle) or under a provision of the law of any member State other than the United Kingdom which corresponds to the said Regulation 6.

(2) Where in the case of any motor vehicle or trailer to which this Regulation applies the type approval certificate or, as the case may be, the certificate of conformity in question has been issued by reason of the vehicle's conforming to the requirements of a Community Directive specified in column 2 of the Table set out below *[pp 320–3]* (the Directives there specified being the Community Directives which are referred to in Part I of Schedule 2 to the Type Approval Regulations, and which contain requirements with respect to the design, construction, equipment and marking of vehicles or their components) then that one or more (as the case may be) of these Regulations which are specified opposite to that Dire;ctive in column 5 of the said table shall not apply to that vehicle if it is first used on or after the date specified opposite to that Directive in column 3 of the said table, and—

(a) in a case where a date is specified opposite to that Directive in column 4(b) of the said table but no date is specified opposite to that Directive in column 4(a) of the said table, the vehicle is first used before the date so specified in column 4(b) of the said table, or

(b) in a case where a date is specified opposite to that Directive in column 4(b) of the said table and a date is also specified opposite to that Directive in column 4(a) of the said table the vehicle is either manufactured before the date so specified in column 4(a) of the said table or first used before the date so specified in column 4(b) of the said table.

(3) In paragraph (1) above 'member State' has the same meaning as in the Type Approval Regulations.

[Regulation 5 is printed as amended by SI 1978 No 1233; the Minister of Transport Order 1979 (SI 1979 No 571); SI 1979 No 1062; SI 1980 No 139; SI 1980 No 880; the Transfer of Functions (Transport) Order 1981 (SI 1981 No 238); SI 1981 No 1189; SI 1981 No 1580; SI 1982 No 1223; SI 1982 No 1422; and SI 1982 No 1576.]

5A.—(1) This Regulation applies to a motor vehicle in respect of which a certificate of conformity or a Minister's approval certificate has been issued under section 47 of the 1972 Act (approval of design, construction etc. of vehicles).

[(2) Where in the case of a motor vehicle to which this Regulation applies:—

(a) the certificate has been issued because the vehicle, or the relevant part of the vehicle, conforms to a type approval requirement specified in either—

   (i) column 2 of Table A below *[p 324]* by reference to an item number and description of subject matter shown in [Schedule 1 to the Motor Vehicles (Type Approval) (Great Britain) Regulations 1984 *[SI 1984 No 981]*]; or

   (ii) column 2 of Table B below *[p 324]* by reference to an item number and description of subject matter shown in Schedule 1 to the Motor Vehicles (Type Approval for Goods Vehicles) (Great Britain) Regulations 1982.

(b) the vehicle is first used on or after the date specified opposite to that item number and description in column 3 of the said Table A or, as the case may be, the said Table B, and

(c) in a case where a date is specified opposite to that number and description in column 4 of the said Table A or, as the case may be, the said Table B, the vehicle is first used before that date.

then that one or more (as the case may be) of these Regulations which are specified opposite to that item number and description in column 5 of the said Table A or, as the case may be, the said Table B, shall not apply to that vehicle.]

Table *[ie table in reg 5]*

1 Item Number	2 Community Directive				3 Date on or after which the vehicle is first used	4		5 Regulations from which the vehicle is exempted
	(a) Reference Number	(b) Date	(c) Official Journal Reference	(d) Subject Matter		(a) Date before which the vehicle is manufactured	(b) Date before which the vehicle is first used	
1	70/157/EEC	6th February 1970	OJ L42, 23.2.1970, p 16 (SE 1970 (1), p 111).	The permissible sound level and the exhaust system of motor vehicles.	1st July 1973			31
1A	as amended by 73/350/EEC	7th November 1973	OJ L321, 22.11.73, p 33.	The permissible sound level and the exhaust system of motor vehicles.	1st March 1974			31
1B	and as amended by 77/212/EEC	8th March 1977	OJ L66, 12.3.1977, p 33.	The permissible sound level and the exhaust system of motor vehicles.	1st April 1977			31, [31A in so far as it relates to vehicles specified in paragraph (1) (a) thereof, and 31E]
[1C	and as amended by 81/334/EEC	13th April 1981	OJ L131, p 6.	The permissible sound level and exhaust system of motor vehicles	1st January 1982			31, 31A in so far as it relates to vehicles specified in paragraph (1) (a) thereof, and 31E]
2	70/220/EEC	20th March 1970	OJ L76, 6.4.1970, p 1 (SE 1970 (1), p 171).	Measures to be taken against air pollution by gases from spark ignition engines of motor vehicles.	10th November 1973	[1st October 1976]	1st April 1977	36

2A	as amended by 74/290/EEC	28th May 1974	OJ L159, 15.6.1974, p 61.	Measures to be taken against air pollution by gases from spark ignition engines of motor vehicles.	1st January 1975	[1st October 1980]	[1st April 1981]	36
2B	and as amended by 77/102/EEC	30th November 1976	OJ L32, 3.2.1977, p 32.	Measures to be taken against air pollution by gases from spark ignition engines of motor vehicles.	1st April 1977	[1st October 1981]	[1st April 1982]	36
[2C]	and as amended by 78/665/EEC	14th July 1978	OJ L223, 14.8.1978 p 48.	Measures to be taken against air pollution by gases from spark ignition engines of motor vehicles.	1st January 1979			36]
3	70/221/EEC	20th March 1970	OJ L76, 6.4.1970, p 23 (SE 1970 (1), p 192).	Liquid fuel tanks and rear protective devices for motor vehicles and their trailers.	1st July 1973			19 [and 46B]
[3A]	As amended by 79/490/EEC	18th April 1979	OJ L128 p 22.	Liquid fuel tanks and rear under-run protection	1st October 1981			19 and 46B]
4	70/387/EEC	27th July 1970	OJ L176, 10.8.1970, p 5 (SE 1970 (11), p 564).	The doors of motor vehicles and their trailers.	1st July 1973			15
5	70/388/EEC	27th July 1970	OJ L176, 10.8.1970, p 12 (SE 1970 (11), p 571).	Audible warning devices for motor vehicles.	1st July 1973			[29]
6	71/127/EEC	1st March 1971	OJ L68, 22.3.1971, p 1 (SE 1971 (1), p 136).	The rear-view mirrors of motor vehicles.	1st July 1973			23 (3) and 24 (5) (c).
[6A]	as amended by 79/795/EEC	20th July 1979	OJ L239 22.9.79 p 1.	The rear view mirrors of motor vehicles	1st February 1980			23 (3) and 24 (3), (5) (c) and (7) and 24A.

| 1 | 2 Community Directive | | | | 3 | 4 | | 5 |
Item Number	(a) Reference Number	(b) Date	(c) Official Journal Reference	(d) Subject Matter	Date on or after which the vehicle is first used	(a) Date before which the vehicle is manufactured	(b) Date before which the vehicle is first used	Regulations from which the vehicle is exempted
7	71/320/EEC	26th July 1971	OJ L202, 6.9.1971, p 37 (SE 1971 (III), p 746).	The braking devices of certain categories of motor vehicles and their trailers.	1st July 1973			13, 14, 51, 55, 59, 64, 71 and 75.
7A	as amended by 74/132/EEC	11th February 1974	OJ L74, 19.3.1974, p 7.	The braking devices of certain categories of motor vehicles and their trailers.	1st October 1974			13, 14, 51, 55, 59, 64, 71 and 75.
7B	and as amended by 75/524/EEC	25th July 1975	OJ L236, 8.9.1975, p 3.	The braking devices of certain categories of motor vehicles and their trailers.	1st January 1976			13, 14, 51, 55, 59, 64, 71 and 75.
[7C	and as amended by 79/489/EEC	18th April 1979	OJ L128, 26.5.79, p 12.	The braking devices of certain categories of motor vehicles and their trailers	18th April 1979			13, 14, 14A, 51, 55, 59, 64, 71 and 75.]
8	72/245/EEC	20th June 1972	OJ L152, 6.7.1972, p 15 (SE 1972 (II), p 637).	The suppression of radio interference produced by spark ignition engines fitted to motor vehicles.	1st April 1974			32
9	72/306/EEC	2nd August 1972	OJ L190, 20.8.1972, p 1 (SE 1972 (III), p 889).	The emission of pollutants from diesel engines for use in vehicles.	2nd February 1974			37
10	74/297/EEC	4th June 1974	OJ L165, 20.6.1974, p 16.	The interior fittings of motor vehicles (the behaviour of the steering mechanism in the event of an impact).	4th December 1975			16

11 ⋯	75/443/EEC	26th June 1975	OJ L196, 26.7.1975, p 1.	Reverse and speedometer equipment of motor vehicles.	1st January 1977	18
[13	75/541/EEC	28th June 1977	OJ L220, 29.8.77, p 95.	Safety belts and restraint systems of motor vehicles.	1st February 1979	17 (8) (c)]
[14	78/549/EEC	12th June 1978	OJ L168 26.6.78, p 45.	Wheel guards of motor vehicles	12th January 1979	66]
[15	78/1015/EEC	23rd November 1978	OJ L349 13.12.78, p 21.	The permissible sound level and exhaust system of motor-cycles.	1st October 1980	31B]
[16	74/151/EEC	4th March 1974	OJ L84, 28.3.74, p 25.	Parts and characteristics of wheeled agricultural or forestry tractors.	1st September 1975	31C]

[TABLE A] *[ie table to reg 5A]*

1. No	2. Item number in Schedule 1 to the Type Approval (Great Britain) Regulations, and subject matter		3. Date on or after which the vehicle is first used	4. Date before which the vehicle is first used	5. Regulations from which the vehicle is exempted
1.	[Item No 1 or No 1A]	Door latches and hinges	1st August 1978		15
2.	Item No 2	Radio-interference suppression	1st August 1978		32
[2A.	Item No 2A	Radio interference suppression	1st October 1979		32]
3.	Item No 3	Protective steering	1st August 1978		16
4.	Item No 4	Exhaust emissions (spark ignition engines)	1st August 1978	[1st April 1981]	36
[4A.	Item No 4A	Exhaust emissions (spark ignition engines)	1st August 1978	1st April 1982	36]
[4B.	Item No 4B	Exhaust emissions (spark ignition engines)	10th January 1979		36]
5.	Item No 5	Exhaust emissions (compression ignition engines)	1st August 1978		37
[5A.	Item No 5A	Exhaust emissions (compression ignition engines)	14th December 1981		37]
[6.	Item No 13C	Brakes	1st October 1979		13, 14 and 64]
[7.	Item No 13D	Brakes	1st June 1980		13, 14 and 64]
[8.	Item No 13A	Brakes	1st October 1978		13, 14, 14A and 64]
[9.	Item No 13B	Brakes	1st October 1979		13, 14, 14A and 64]

[TABLE B *[ie table to reg 5A]*

1. No	2. Item number in Schedule 1 to the Motor Vehicles (Type Approval for Goods Vehicles) (Great Britain) Regulations and subject matter	3. Date on or after which vehicle is first used	4. Date before which the vehicle is first used	5. Regulations from which the vehicle is exempted
1.	Item No 2—Exhaust emissions	1st October 1982		36
2.	Items No 3 and 3A—Exhaust emissions	1st October 1982		37
3.	Items No 5 and 5A—Radio interference suppression	1st October 1982		32
4.	Items No 6, 6A, 6B, 6C and 6D—Brakes	1st October 1982		13, 14, 14A, 59 and 64]

[Regulation 5A is printed as amended by the Interpretation Act 1978, ss 17 (2), 23; SI 1980 No 880; SI 1981 No 1189; SI 1982 No 1223; and SI 1982 No 1272.]

[5AA.—(1) This Regulation applies to an agricultural motor vehicle in respect of which a type approval certificate, a certificate of conformity or a Minister's approval certificate has been issued by virtue of the Agricultural or Forestry Tractors and Tractor Components (Type Approval) Regulations 1979 *[SI 1979 No 221, as amended by SI 1981 No 669 and SI 1983 No 709]* or by the competent authority of any Member State other than the United Kingdom under a provision of the law of that State which corresponds to those Regulations.

(2) Where in the case of an agricultural motor vehicle to which this Regulation applies the certificate mentioned in paragraph (1) above has been issued by reason of the vehicle's conforming to the requirements of a Community Directive specified in an item in column 2 of the Table below then the Regulation specified in that item in column 3 of that Table does not apply to that vehicle.

TABLE *[ie table to reg 5AA]*

1	2			3
Item No	Community Directive (in each case as amended by 82/890/EEC (OJ L378 (31.12.82) p 45))			Regulations from which vehicle is exempt
	(a) Reference No.	(b) Official Journal Reference	(c) Subject matters	
1	74/151/EEC	OJ L84 (28.3.74) p 25	Tanks for liquid fuel	19
2	74/151/EEC	OJ L84 (28.3.74) p 25	Audible warning devices	29
3	74/346/EEC	OJ L191 (15.7.74) p 1	Rear view mirrors	24
4	74/347/EEC (as amended by 79/1073/EEC)	OJ L191 (15.7.74) p 5 OJ L331 (27.12.79) p 20	Field of vision	22
5	74/347/EEC (as amended by 79/1073/EEC)	OJ L191 (15.7.74) p 5 OJ L331 (27.12.79) p 20	Windscreen wipers	27
6	75/322/EEC	OJ L147 (9.6.75) p 28	Suppression of radio interference from spark ignition engines	32
7	76/432/EEC	OJ L122 (8.5.76) p 1	Braking devices	79C
8	77/537/EEC	OJ L220 (28.8.77) p 38	Emission of pollutants from diesel engines	37]

[Regulation 5AA was inserted by SI 1984 No 1809.]

[5B.—(1) The provisions of the 1978 Regulations which are specified in column (2) of the Table below shall not apply in respect of a vehicle which is legibly and indelibly marked in a conspicuous and readily accessible position with a marking designated as an approval mark by Regulation 4 of the 1979 Regulations and shown at the item of Schedule 2 to the 1979 Regulations specified in column (3) of that Table or, in a case where two items of Schedule 2 to the 1979 Regulations are specified in the said column (3), with one of those markings.

(2) In this Regulation 'the 1978 Regulations' means these Regulations and 'the 1979 Regulations' means the Motor Vehicles (Designation of Approval Marks) Regulations 1979 *[SI 1979 No 1088, as amended].*]

[TABLE *[ie table to reg 5B.]*

(1)	(2)	(3)
Item No	1978 Regulations	Items in Schedule 2 to the 1979 Regulations
1	13	13, 13A, 13B, 13C
2	14	13, 13A, 13B, 13C
3	14A	13, 13A, 13B, 13C
4	51	13, 13B
5	55	13, 13B
6	59	13, 13A, 13B, 13C
7	64	13, 13A, 13B, 13C
8	67	13, 13B
9	75	13, 13B
10	101	13, 13A, 13B, 13C]

[Regulation 5B was added by SI 1980 No 880 and is printed as amended by SI 1982 No 1480.]

[6. (*a*) The provisions of the Regulations specified in column 2 of Table 1 below shall not apply to an agricultural motor vehicle provided that it is not driven at a speed in excess of 20 miles per hour;

(*b*) the provisions of the Regulations specified in column 2 of Table 2 below shall not apply to an agricultural motor vehicle notwithstanding that it is driven at a speed in excess of 20 miles per hour provided that it is not driven at a speed in excess of 40 miles per hour;

(*c*) the provisions of the Regulations specified in column 2 of Table 3 below shall not apply to an agricultural motor vehicle manufactured on or after 1st December 1985 and first used on or after 1st June 1986 if it is driven at a speed in excess of 20 miles per hour.]

TABLE 1 *[ie table to reg 6.]*

1 Item	2 Regulation	
1	12	(Springs)
2	18	(Speedometer)
3	24A	(Mirrors)
4	29(1)	(Audible warning instrument)
5	48 to 69	(Requirements relating to locomotives, motor tractors, motor cars, heavy motor cars and motor cycles)

TABLE 2 *[ie table to reg 6.]*

1 Item	2 Regulation	
1	48, 53, 57, 62	(Overall width)
2	54, 58, 63	(Overhang)
3	79C	(Brakes)
4	79D	(Tyres)

TABLE 3 *[ie table to reg 6.]*

1 Item	2 Regulation	
1	14A(2)(*cc*)	(Brakes)
2	24(2)(*b*)	(Mirrors)
3	26(6)(*a*)	(Safety glass)
4	28(2)	(Windscreen washers)
5	31C(1)	(Noise)
6	31D(2)(*c*)	(Noise)
7	37(2)	(Emissions)
8	37(3)(*a*)	(Emissions)]

[Regulation 6 is printed as substituted by SI 1984 No 1809.]

7. Provision as respects Trade Descriptions Act 1968

Where by a provision of any Regulation hereof any vehicle or any of its parts or equipment is required to be marked with a specification number or the registered certification trade mark of the British Standards Institution or with an approval mark, nothing in that provision shall be taken to authorise any person to apply any such number or mark to the vehicle, part or equipment in contravention of the Trade Descriptions Act 1968.

PART II

REGULATIONS GOVERNING THE CONSTRUCTION, WEIGHT AND EQUIPMENT OF MOTOR VEHICLES AND TRAILERS

A *General*

8. Construction

(1) Every motor cycle and invalid carriage shall be so constructed that it is a wheeled vehicle.

(2) Save as aforesaid every motor vehicle and trailer shall be so constructed that it is either a wheeled vehicle or a track laying vehicle.

[9. Overall length

(1) Save as provided in paragraphs (2) to (5) below, the overall length of a vehicle of a type specified in an item in column (2) of the Table below shall not exceed the maximum length specified in that item in column (3) of that Table.

(2) The provisions of paragraph (1) above do not apply to—

(*a*) an articulated vehicle constructed and normally used for the conveyance of indivisible loads of exceptional length if each wheel of the vehicle—

TABLE *[ie table to reg 9 (1)]*

(1)	(2)	(3)
Item No	Type of Vehicle	Maximum length (in metres)
1	An articulated vehicle	15.5
2	An articulated bus	18
3	A semi-trailer manufactured on or after 1st May 1983	12.2
4	A large passenger-carrying vehicle, not being an articulated bus, which is so constructed as to be capable of turning in either direction in a circle which, when traced at ground level by a vertical line passing through any part of the vehicle included in the overall length and the overall width of the vehicle, does not exceed in diameter 24 metres	12
5	A motor vehicle not of a type mentioned in item 1, 2 or 4	11
6	[A trailer which is neither a semi-trailer nor an agricultural trailed appliance]	7
[7	An agricultural trailed appliance manufactured on or after 1st December 1985	15]

    (i) is fitted with a pneumatic tyre, or

    (ii) is not fitted with a pneumatic tyre but the vehicle is not driven at a speed exceeding 12 miles per hour;

(b) a trailer constructed and normally used for the conveyance of indivisible loads of exceptional length;

(c) [agricultural trailed appliance manufactured before 1st December 1985];

(d) any broken-down vehicle which is being drawn by a motor vehicle in consequence of the breakdown; or

(e) a trolley vehicle in the course of construction or delivery.

(3) The provisions of paragraph (1) above have effect as if for the reference to 7 metres there were substituted a reference to 12 metres in the case of a trailer which—

    (i) has not less than 4 wheels and where the distance between the centres of the respective areas of contact with the road of the foremost and rearmost wheels on the same side of the trailer is not less than three-fifths of its overall length, and

    (ii) is drawn by a motor vehicle having an unladen weight of 2030 kilograms or more.

(4) The provisions of paragraph (1) above do not apply to a semi-trailer if it—

(a) forms part of an articulated vehicle of a type specified in paragraph (2) (a) above, or

(b) is constructed and normally used for the purpose of carrying at least two other wheeled vehicles.

(5) The provisions of paragraph (1) above do not apply to a trailer being drying or mixing plant designed for the production of asphalt or of bituminous or tar macadam and used mainly for the construction, repair or maintenance of roads or a road planing machine so used if the overall length of the trailer together with that of the motor vehicles by which it is drawn does not exceed 18.3 metres.

(6) For the purposes of this Regulation—

(a) [save as provided in sub-paragraph (c) below, the overall length] of a trailer excludes any part of the trailer designed primarily for use as a means of attaching it to another vehicle and any fitting designed for use in connection with any such part; and

(*b*) the overall length of a semi-trailer excludes the thickness of any front or rear wall or any other part [forward of any front wall or rearward of any rear wall] which does not increase the vehicle's load-carrying space[; and]]

[(*c*) the overall length of an agricultural trailed appliance includes any drawbar or other thing with which it is equipped for the purpose of being towed.]

[Regulation 9 is printed as substituted by SI 1982 No 1576 and subsequently amended by SI 1983 No 471, and SI 1984 No 1809. (Formerly, reg 9 had been amended by SI 1980 No 287, and SI 1981 No 261.)]

[9A. Turning circle

(1) Subject to the provisions of paragraph (2) below every vehicle (other than a vehicle adapted to carry not more than 16 passengers and having an overall length which does not exceed 7 metres) being used as a public service vehicle shall be so constructed as to be capable of turning in either direction inside a circle of 24 metres diameter without any of its outermost points projecting outside the circle.

(2) Every large passenger carrying vehicle (other than an articulated bus and a vehicle adapted to carry not more than 16 passengers and having an overall length which does not exceed 7 metres) manufactured on or after 1st October 1981 and first used on or after 1st April 1982 and every articulated bus first used on or after 1st April 1982 shall be constructed so as to comply with the provision relating to manoeuverability specified in paragraph 5.10 in Regulation 36 annexed to the Agreement concerning the adoption of Uniform Conditions of Approval and reciprocal recognition thereof for Motor Vehicle Equipment and Parts concluded at Geneva on 20th March 1958 *[Cmnd 2535]* as amended *[Cmnd 3562]* to which the United Kingdom is a party *[the instrument of accession was deposited with the Secretary-General of the United Nations on 15 January 1963]* as regards vehicles within the scope of that Regulation whether or not such large passenger vehicles or articulated buses are within such scope.]

[Regulation 9A was inserted by SI 1981 No 261.]

[9B. Provisions as to sections of articulated buses and direction-holding of articulated buses

(1) This Regulation applies to every articulated bus first used on or after 1st April 1982.

(2) The connecting section of the two parts of every articulated bus to which this Regulation applies shall be constructed so as to comply with the provisions relating to such a section specified in paragraph 5.9 in Regulation 36 annexed to the Agreement mentioned in Regulation [9A (2)] as regards vehicles within the scope of that Regulation.

(3) Every articulated bus to which this Regulation applies shall be constructed so that when the vehicle is moving in a straight line the longitudinal median planes of its two parts coincide and form a continuous plane without any deflection.]

[Regulation 9B was inserted by SI 1981 No 261 and is printed as amended by SI 1982 No 1057.]

10. Overall height of public service vehicles

[(1) The overall height of a large passenger carrying vehicle (other than an articulated bus) manufactured on or after 1st October 1981 and first used on or after 1st

April 1982 and the overall height of an articulated bus first used on or after 1st April 1982 shall not exceed 4·57 metres.

(2) The overall height of a public service vehicle not being a vehicle to which paragraph (1) above applies shall not exceed 4·57 metres.

(3) In this Regulation 'overall height' means the vertical distance between the ground and the point on the vehicle which is farthest from the ground, and for the purpose of determining the overall height—

> (a) the condition of the tyres of the vehicle shall be such as to comply with the requirements specified in paragraph (1) (b) of Regulation 107;
>
> (b) the vehicle shall be at its unladen weight (as provided in section 194 of the 1972 Act);
>
> (c) the surface of the ground under the vehicle shall be reasonably flat.]

[Regulation 10 is printed as substituted by SI 1981 No 261.]

* * *

[14A. Brakes

(1) Except as provided in paragraphs (2) and (3) below, the braking system of every motor vehicle of a category specified in an item in column 2 of the Table in Schedule 4A and the braking system of every trailer of a category specified in an item in column 3 of the said Table, and which is manufactured on or after 1st October 1982 and first used on or after 1st April 1983 shall comply with the construction, fitting and performance requirements specified in the same item in column 4 of the said Table:

Provided that it shall not be unlawful for any motor vehicle of a category specified in an item in column 2 or any trailer specified in an item in column 3 of the said Table and which is manufactured before 1st October 1982 or first used before 1st April 1983 to comply with the said requirements instead of with any other requirements relating to the construction of the braking system of such vehicles as are specified in these Regulations.

(2) The requirements specified in paragraph (1) above shall not apply to:—

> [(a) an agricultural trailer or agricultural trailed appliance that is not, in either case, drawn at a speed exceeding 20 miles per hour;]
>
> (b) a locomotive;
>
> (c) a motor tractor;
>
> [(cc) [an agricultural motor vehicle] which is not a motor tractor;]
>
> (d) a vehicle which is incapable by reason of its construction of exceeding a speed of 25 kilometres per hour on the level under its own power;
>
> (e) a works trailer;
>
> (f) a works truck; or
>
> (g) a public works vehicle;
>
> (h) a trailer designed and constructed, or adapted, to be drawn exclusively by a vehicle to which sub-paragraph (b), (c), (d), (f) or (g) of this paragraph applies.

(3) The requirements specified in column 4 of the Table in Schedule 4A shall apply—

> (a) in item 1, 2, 3, 4, 5 and 6 so that the requirement specified in paragraph 1.2.1 of Annex IV to the Council Directive shall apply—

    (i) before 1st October 1983 without regard to the amendment to that para-
graph contained in Commission Directive 79/489/EEC of 18th April
1979 *[OJ L 128 26.5.79, p 2]*, and

    (ii) on and after 1st October 1983 with regard to the said amendment;

(b) in items 2 and 3 with the proviso that the testing requirements specified in
paragraphs 1.5.1 and 1.5.2 of Annex II to the Council Directive shall apply in
relation to every vehicle in category M3, other than a double-decked vehicle
first used before 1st October 1983;

(c) in items 2 and 3 with the proviso that the requirements specified in paragraph
1.1.4.2 of Annex II to the Council Directive shall not apply in relation to a
vehicle which is in category M2 or category M3;

(d) in items 1, 2, 3, 4, 5 and 6, in the case of vehicles constructed or adapted for use
by physically handicapped drivers, the requirement in paragraph 2.1.2.1 of
Annex 1 to the Council Directive that the driver must be able to achieve the
braking action mentioned in that paragraph from his driving seat without
removing his hands from the steering control shall not apply provided that the
driver is able to achieve that action while one of his hands remains on the steering control;

[(e) in items 1, 2, 3, 4, 5, 6, 7, 8, 9 and 10 with the proviso that the requirements
specified in paragraph 1.1.4.2 of Annex II to the Council Directive shall not
apply in relation to a vehicle of a type of which either:—

    (i) compliance at the date of its manufacture with the requirements speci-
fied in Annex 13 to Regulation 13 (incorporating the 03 series of amendments which entered into force on 4th January 1979 and the 04 series of
amendments which entered into force on 11th August 1981) annexed to
the Agreement concerning the adoption of uniform conditions of approval for Motor Vehicle Equipment and Parts and reciprocal recognition
thereof concluded at Geneva on 20th March 1958 *[Cmnd 2535]* as
amended *[Cmnd 3562]* to which the United Kingdom is a party *[the instrument of accession dated 14 January 1963 was deposited with the Secretary-General
of the United Nations on 15 January 1963]* is evidenced by a document issued
by the Secretary of State pursuant to a test in respect of which the fee
numbered 1360C, 1361Z or 1362W prescribed in [Schedule 1 to the
Motor Vehicles (Type Approval and Approval Marks) (Fees) Regulations 1984 *[SI 1984 No 1404]* has been paid, or

    (ii) compliance at a later date with those requirements if any fitment has
been approved as a result of a notifiable alteration, within the meaning
in Regulation 41 of the Plating and Testing Regulations, having been
made: and]

(f) to a vehicle manufactured by British Leyland Limited and known as the Atlan-
tean Bus if such vehicle is manufactured on or after 1st October 1983 and first
used on or after 1st October 1984.

(4) In this Regulation—

(a) 'the Council Directive' means Council Directive 71/320/EEC of 26th July 1971
(which relates to the braking devices of certain categories of motor vehicles and
their trailers) *[OJ L 202, 6.9.71, p 37]* as amended by Commission Directive 75/
524/EEC of 25th July 1975 *[OJ L 236, 8.9.75, p 3]* and Commission Directive
79/489/EEC of 18th April 1979 *[OJ L 128, 26.5.79, p 12]* (the amendments to
Council Directive 71/320/EEC introduced by Commission Directive 74/132/
EEC of 11th February 1974 *[OJ L 74, 19.3.74, p 7]* not being relevant); and

(*b*) a reference to a vehicle in category M2 or category M3 is a reference to a vehicle categorised by that number and letter in Article 1 of the Council Directive.]

[Regulation 14A was added by SI 1981 No 1189 and is printed as amended by the Interpretation Act 1978, ss 17 (2), 23; SI 1982 No 1480; SI 1983 No 112; and SI 1984 No 1809.]

* * *

[17. Seat belts and anchorage points

(1) Except as provided by paragraph (2), this Regulation applies to—

(*a*) every motor car manufactured on or after 1st July 1964 and registered on or after 1st January 1965; and

(*b*) every three-wheeled motor cycle, the unladen weight of which exceeds 255 kilograms and which was manufactured on or after 1st March 1970 and first used on or after 1st September 1970.

(2) This Regulation does not apply to—

(*a*) a goods vehicle (other than a dual-purpose vehicle), being a motor car which—
   (i) was manufactured before 1st September 1966, or
  (ii) was registered before 1st April 1967, or
  (iii) is a vehicle manufactured on or after 1st October 1979 and first used on or after 1st April 1980 and has a maximum gross weight in Great Britain (determined in accordance with the provisions of Schedule 2) exceeding 3500 kilograms, or
  (iv) is a vehicle manufactured before 1st October 1981 or first used before 1st April 1982, which is of a model first manufactured before 1st October 1979 and has an unladen weight exceeding 1525 kilograms;

(*b*) a passenger vehicle or dual-purpose vehicle being in either case a vehicle constructed or adapted to carry more than twelve passengers exclusive of the driver;

(*c*) [an] [agricultural motor vehicle] or an industrial tractor which is not in either case a motor tractor;

(*d*) a motor tractor;

(*e*) a works truck;

(*f*) an electrically-propelled goods vehicle;

(*g*) a pedestrian-controlled vehicle;

(*h*) a vehicle which has been used on roads outside Great Britain and has been imported into Great Britain, whilst it is being driven after its importation into Great Britain on a journey from the place where it has arrived in Great Britain to a place of residence of the owner or driver of the vehicle, and on the journey from any such place to a place where, by previous arrangement, the vehicle will be provided with such anchorage points and seat belts as will comply with the requirements of this Regulation; or

(*i*) a vehicle which is incapable by reason of its construction of exceeding a speed of 16 miles per hour on the level under its own power.

(3) (*a*) This paragraph applies to every vehicle to which this Regulation applies being—
   (i) a vehicle constructed or adapted to have more than eight passenger seats exclusive of the driver's seat,

> (ii) a motor ambulance,
> (iii) a motor caravan,
> (iv) a vehicle in respect of which, or of a model of which, there is in force on 1st October 1979 a type approval certificate or a Minister's approval certificate issued pursuant to the Type Approval (Great Britain) Regulations, and which is manufactured before 1st October 1981 or first used before 1st April 1982, or
> (v)   any other vehicle to which this Regulation applies, not being a vehicle to which the Type Approval (Great Britain) Regulations apply, and which is manufactured before 1st October 1981 or first used before 1st April 1982.

(b) Every vehicle to which this paragraph applies shall be equipped with anchorage points which are designed to hold securely in position on the vehicle seat belts for the driver's seat and the specified passenger's seat (if any).

(c) The anchorage points required under sub-paragraph (b) above shall either—
> (i) at the date on which the vehicle is manufactured, comply—
>> (A) in the case of a vehicle to which either the Council Directive or the ECE Regulation applies, with the Council Directive requirements or with the ECE Regulation requirements, or
>> (B) in the case of a vehicle to which neither the Council Directive nor the ECE Regulation applies, with standards identical to the Council Directive requirements or the ECE Regulation requirements; or
> (ii) be fitted to a vehicle which was manufactured before 1st October 1981 or first used before 1st April 1982 and which is legibly and permanently marked—
>> (A) if it does not have integral seat belt anchorages and is a motor car manufactured on or after 1st September 1966 and registered on or after 1st April 1967 or a three-wheeled motor cycle manufactured on or after 1st April 1972 and first used on or after 1st October 1972, with the specification number of a British Standard for seat belt anchorage points, namely either BS AU 48: 1965 or BS AU 48a; or
>> (B) if it has integral seat belt anchorages provided on or after 1st January 1969 and is a motor car manufactured on or after 1st September 1966 and registered on or after 1st April 1967 or if it has integral seat belt anchorages provided on or after 1st July 1971 and is a three-wheeled motor cycle manufactured on or after 1st January 1971 and first used on or after 1st July 1971, with the specification number of a British Standard for seats with Integral Seat Belt Anchorages, namely either BS AU 140: 1967 or BS AU 140a.

(d) In any case where a vehicle (other than a motor cycle which was first used before 1st October 1972) is required to be marked in accordance with the provisions of sub-paragraph (c) (ii) (B) above, the seat, being a seat with integral seat belt anchorages, shall be legibly and permanently marked with the specification number of a British Standard for seats with Integral Seat Belt Anchorages followed by the suffix '1', namely, either BS AU 140/1: 1967 or BS AU 140a/1.

(4) Every vehicle to which this Regulation applies, not being a vehicle specified in paragraph (3) above, shall be equippped with anchorage points—

(a) which are designed to hold securely in position on the vehicle seat belts for every forward-facing seat constructed or adapted to accommodate one adult, and

(b) which, at the date on which the vehicle is manufactured, comply—
- (i) in the case of a vehicle to which either the Council Directive or the ECE Regulation applies, with the Council Directive requirements or with the ECE Regulation requirements, or
- (ii) in the case of a vehicle to which neither the Council Directive nor the ECE Regulation applies, with standards identical to the Council Directive requirements or the ECE Regulation requirements.

(5) Save as provided in paragraph (6)—

(a) every vehicle to which the Regulation applies which is a vehicle manufactured before 1st October 1980 or first used before 1st April 1981 shall be provided with—
- (i) a body-restraining seat belt, designed for use by an adult, for the driver's seat, and
- (ii) a body-restraining seat belt for the specified passenger's seat (if any); and

(b) every other vehicle to which this Regulation applies shall be provided with seat belts for the driver's seat and for the specified passenger's seat (if any) which belts—
- (i) restrain the upper and lower parts of the torso,
- (ii) include a lap belt,
- (iii) are anchored at no less than three points, and
- (iv) are designed for use by an adult.

(6) The requirements specified in paragraph (5) shall not apply—

(a) to a vehicle—
- (i) while it is being used under a trade licence within the meaning of the Vehicles (Excise) Act 1971, or
- (ii) not being a vehicle to which the Type Approval (Great Britain) Regulations apply, while it is being driven from premises of the manufacturer by whom it was made, or of a distributor of vehicles or dealer in vehicles—
    - (a) to premises of a distributor of or dealer in vehicles or of the purchaser of the vehicle, or
    - (b) to premises of a person obtaining possession of the vehicle under a hiring agreement or hire-purchase agreement; or

(b) in relation to the driver's seat or the specified passenger's seat (if any) of a vehicle which has been specially designed and constructed, or specially adapted, for the use of a person suffering from some physical defect or disability, in a case where a disabled person's seat belt for an adult person is provided for use for that seat.

(7) Every seat belt, other than a disabled person's seat belt, provided in pursuance of this Regulation shall be properly secured to all the anchorage points provided for it in pursuance of paragraphs (3) or (4).

(8) Subject to paragraph (9), where a seat belt other than—
- (i) a restraining device for a young person,

(ii) a seat belt comprising a lap belt and shoulder straps, or

(iii) a disabled person's seat belt

is provided in pursuance of this Regulation for a motor car or a motor cycle in either case manufactured on or after 1st October 1972 and first used on or after 1st April 1973, the following additional conditions shall apply as respects that seat—

(a) the belt shall be so arranged that a person can, when sitting in the seat for which the belt is provided and with the belt previously adjusted to fit him, remove the belt from the device required by sub-paragraph (c) of this paragraph and by using one hand, or by taking the belt with one hand and transferring it from one hand to the other, put the belt on;

(b) the fastenings by means of which the belt is secured on the wearer shall be so designed that they can be engaged with a single movement of one hand in one direction and released with such a movement in one direction;

(c) an efficient device, unlikely to become dislodged in normal use, for retaining the belt in position when stowed away shall be provided and the centre of the device shall be located not more than 75 millimetres behind a point which is in the same horizontal plane and is positioned on the rear side of the door aperture provided for access to the front seat:

For the purpose of determining the position of the said point the door and any rubber, felt or other soft trimming or sealing material around the door aperture shall be disregarded;

(d) the said device shall be at a sufficient height from the floor of the vehicle to ensure that, so far as is practicable, any part of the belt that would come in contact with the clothing of a person wearing the belt in normal circumstances does not lie on the floor when the belt is in the stowed position;

(e) it shall be possible to stow away the belt for retention on the device mentioned in sub-paragraph (c) of this paragraph without employing any manual device for adjusting the belt to fit [the wearer];

(f) the belt, after being put on by the wearer, shall either adjust automatically to fit him or be such that the said manual device shall be convenient to use and capable of being operated with one hand so as to [tighten the belt; and]

[(g) in the case of a vehicle manufactured on or after 1st October 1980 and first used on or after 1st April 1981—

(i) if it is a vehicle to which Council Directive 77/541/EEC of 28th June 1977 [OJ L220, 29.8.77, p 95] applies, the belt shall comply with the installation requirements specified in paragraphs 3.2.2 to 3.3.4 of Annex I to that Directive; or

(ii) if it is a vehicle to which that Directive does not apply the belt shall comply with standards identical to those installation requirements:

Provided that the requirements or standards, as the case may be, specified in this sub-paragraph shall not apply so as to require a seat belt to which paragraph (9) refers to comply with the requirement specified in the second paragraph (which relates to the locking or releasing of a seat belt by a single movement of either hand by the wearer) of paragraph 3.3.2 of the said Annex.]

(9) [The requirements specified in paragraph (8) (a) to (f) shall not apply to]—

(a) a seat belt fitted to a seat which is treated as a specified passenger's seat by virtue of the provision of sub-paragraph (ii) in the definition of 'specified passenger's seat' in paragraph (12), or

(b) a seat belt fitted to the specified passenger's seat of a goods vehicle which has an unladen weight of more than 915 kilograms and has more than one forward-facing seat for a passenger alongside the driver's seat, any such seats for passengers being joined together in a single structure.

(10) Every seat belt, other than a disabled person's seat belt or restraining device for a young person, provided for any person in any vehicle to which this Regulation applies, whether or not such seat belt is required to be provided, shall—

(a) in the case of a vehicle manufactured before 1st October 1980 or first used before 1st April 1981 be legibly and permanently marked—
   (i) in the case of a belt which was first fitted to the vehicle before 1st February 1979, with a British Standards mark; or
   (ii) in the case of a belt which was first fitted to the vehicle on or after 1st February 1979, with either a British Standards mark or with a designated approval mark; or

[(b) in the case of any other vehicle to which this Regulation applies, be legibly and permanently marked with a designated approval mark:

Provided that the requirement specified in sub-paragraph (b) above shall apply so that any belt in a vehicle to which Council Directive 77/541/EEC of 28th June 1977 does not apply, whether or not the belt is part of a restraint system as defined in paragraph 1.11 of Annex I to that Directive, shall be marked with a designated approval mark which does not include the letter 'Z' referred to in paragraph 10 (2) of Schedule 5 to the Motor Vehicles (Designation of Approval Marks) Regulations 1979 [SI 1979 No 1088 as amended by SI 1980 No 582].]

(11) Every seat belt, being a restraining device for a young person but not being a disabled person's seat belt, fitted to any vehicle to which this Regulation applies shall be legibly and permanently marked [with either a British Standards mark or a marking designated as an approval mark by Regulation 4 of the Motor Vehicles (Designation of Approval Marks) Regulations 1979 [SI 1979 No 1088 as amended by SI 1980 Nos 582 and 2027 and SI 1981 No 126] and shown in column (2) at item 44 in Schedule 2 to those Regulations.]

(12) (a) In this Regulation—

the expressions 'motor ambulance' and 'motor caravan' have the same meanings as are respectively assigned to them in Regulation 3(2) of the Type Approval (Great Britain) Regulations;

'body-restraining seat belt' means a seat belt designed to provide restraint for both the upper and lower parts of the trunk of the wearer in the event of an accident to the vehicle;

'British Standards mark' means a mark consisting of
   (i) the specification number of a British Standard for Seat Belt Assemblies for Motor Vehicles, namely either—
      (a) BS 3254: 1960 or
      (b) BS AU 160a in the case of a restraining device for an adult or BS AU 157a in the case of a restraining device for a young person, and
   (ii) the registered certification trade mark of the British Standards Institution;

'the Council Directive' means Council Directive 76/115/EEC of 18th December 1975 [OJ L24, 30.1.76, p 6];

'the Council Directive requirements' means the design and construction requirements specified in Annex I, paragraphs 4 and 5.5, and in Annex III to the Council Directive;

['designated approval mark' means the marking designated as an approval mark by Regulation 4 of the Motor Vehicles (Designation of Approval Marks) Regulations 1979 *[SI 1979 No 1088 as amended by SI 1980 No 582]* and shown in column (2) at item 16 of Schedule 2 to those Regulations or the marking designated as an approval mark by Regulation 5 of those Regulations and shown in column (2) at item 23 of Schedule 4 to those Regulations;]

'disabled person's seat belt' means a seat belt which has been specially designed and constructed, and not merely adapted, for use by an adult or young person suffering from some physical defect or disability and which is used solely by such a person;

'the ECE Regulation' means the Regulation numbered 14 of 30th January 1970 (as amended on 16th March 1971 and issued with revised text on 19th August 1976) annexed to the Agreement concerning the adoption of uniform conditions of approval for Motor Vehicle Equipment and Parts and reciprocal recognition thereof concluded at Geneva on 20th March 1958 *[Cmnd 2535]* as amended *[Cmnd 3562]*, to which the United Kingdom is a party;

'the ECE Regulation requirements' means the design, construction and equipment requirements in paragraphs 5, 6 and 7 of and in Annex 3 to the ECE Regulation;

'forward-facing seat' means a seat which is attached to a vehicle so that it faces towards the front of the vehicle in such a manner that a line passing through the centre of both the front and the back of the seat is at an angle of 30° or less to the longitudinal axis of the vehicle;

'lap belt' means a seat belt which passes across the front of the wearer's pelvic region;

'seat' includes any part designed for the accommodation of one adult of a continuous seat designed for the accommodation of more than one adult;

'seat belt' means a belt intended to be worn by a person in a vehicle and designed to prevent or lessen injury to its wearer in the event of an accident to the vehicle and includes, in the case of a restraining device for a young person, any special chair to which the belt is attached;

'seat with integral seat belt anchorages' means a seat which is fitted with all the anchorage points required for use in connection with the seat belt provided for that seat;

'specified passenger's seat' means—
  (i) in the case of a vehicle which has one forward-facing front seat alongside the driver's seat, such seat, and in the case of a vehicle which has more than one such seat, the one furthest from the driver's seat; or
  (ii) if the vehicle normally has no seat which is the specified passenger's seat under the last preceding sub-paragraph, the forward-facing front seat for a passenger which is foremost in the vehicle and furthest from the driver's seat, unless there is a fixed partition separating such seat from the space in front of it alongside the driver's seat;

'three-wheeled motor cycle' does not include a two-wheeled motor cycle with a side car attached to it.

(*b*) In this Regulation, unless the contrary intention appears, a reference to a paragraph followed by a number is a reference to the paragraph bearing that number in this Regulation.]

[Regulation 17 is printed as substituted by SI 1979 No 1062 (which substituted the above text for

reg 17 and for reg 17A as inserted by SI 1978 No 1233). Regulation 17 has subsequently been amended by SI 1980 No 610; SI 1981 No 697; and SI 1984 No 1809.]

[18. Speedometer

(1) Save as provided in paragraphs (2) and (3) below, to every motor vehicle first used on or after 1st October 1937 there shall be fitted an instrument so constructed and in such a position as at all times readily to indicate to the driver of the vehicle the speed thereof within a margin of accuracy of plus or minus 10 per cent, if and when he is driving at a speed exceeding 10 miles per hour.

[(1A) The indication mentioned in paragraph (1) above shall—

(*a*) in the case of a vehicle manufactured before 1st October 1983 or first used before 1st April 1984, be either in miles per hour or kilometres per hour;

(*b*) in the case of any other vehicle, be in both miles per hour and kilometres per hour so, however, that either of these indications may be temporarily replaced by the other by the operation of a switch.]

[(2) The provisions of paragraph (1) above do not apply to:—

(*a*) an invalid carriage first used before 1st April 1984;

(*b*) a motor cycle the cylinder capacity of the engine of which does not exceed 100 cubic centimetres first used before 1st April 1984;

(*c*) a works truck first used before 1st April 1984;

(*d*) a vehicle which it is at all times unlawful to drive at a speed exceeding 25 miles per hour;

(*e*) a vehicle which is incapable by reason of its construction of exceeding a speed of 25 miles per hour on the level under its own power;

(*f*) a vehicle marked in a conspicuous and readily accessible position with the marking designated as an approval mark by Regulation 4 of the Motor Vehicles (Designation of Approval Marks) Regulations 1979 *[SI 1979 No 1088]* and shown at item 39 in Schedule 2 to those Regulations.]

[(3) The provisions of paragraph (1) above do not apply to a vehicle which is equipped with recording equipment which is marked with a marking designated as an approval mark by Regulation 5 of the Motor Vehicles (Designation of Approval Marks) Regulations 1979 and shown at item 3 in Schedule 4 to those Regulations (whether or not the vehicle is required to be equipped with that equipment) and which, as regards the visual indications given by that equipment of the speed of the vehicle, complies with the requirements relating to the said indications and installation specified in the Recording Equipment Regulation.]

[Regulation 18 is printed as substituted by SI 1980 No 1789 and amended by SI 1982 No 1057.]

*　　*　　*

Mirrors

23.—(1) Save as provided in paragraph (2) of this Regulation—

(*a*) the following motor vehicles, that is to say, every passenger vehicle adapted to carry more than seven passengers exclusive of the driver and every goods vehicle, including every dual-purpose vehicle, but excluding locomotives and motor tractors, shall be equipped with at least two mirrors one of which shall be fitted externally on the off-side of the vehicle and the other either internally

mirrors shall be so constructed and fitted to the motor vehicle as to assist the driver, if he so desires, to become aware of traffic to the rear and on both sides rearwards; and

(b) every [agricultural motor vehicle] shall be equipped with a mirror fitted externally on the off-side of [the agricultural motor vehicle] and so constructed and fitted to [the agricultural motor vehicle] as to assist the driver, if he so desires, to become aware of traffic on that side rearwards, unless he can easily obtain a clear view of traffic to the rear (including traffic to the rear of any trailer being drawn) without having any mirror fitted to [the agricultural motor vehicle]; and

(c) subject to the provisions of the foregoing sub-paragraphs every motor vehicle shall be equipped either internally or externally with a mirror so constructed and fitted to the motor vehicle as to assist the driver, if he so desires, to become aware of traffic to the rear of the vehicle.

(2) Paragraph (1) of this Regulatmion shall not apply to—

(a) a two-wheeled motor cycle with or without a sidecar attached;

(b) [an agricultural motor vehicle with an unladen weight exceeding 7370 kilograms];

(c) a motor vehicle when drawing a trailer if a person is carried on the trailer in a position which affords an uninterrupted view to the rear and such a person is provided with efficient means of communicating to the driver the effect of signals given by the drivers of other vehicles to the rear thereof;

(d) a works truck if the driver can easily obtain a clear view of traffic to the rear;

(e) a pedestrian controlled vehicle;

(f) a vehicle to which Regulation 24 applies unless that vehicle is an excepted vehicle as defined in paragraph (8) of that Regulation; or

[(g) a vehicle to which Regulation 24A applies.]

(3) In the case of a motor vehicle first used on or after 1st April 1969 the edges of any mirror fitted internally to the vehicle to assist any person, if he so desires, to become aware of traffic to the rear of the vehicle shall be surrounded by some material such as will render those edges and that material unlikely to cause severe cuts in the event of the mirror or that material being struck by any occupant of the vehicle.

[Regulation 23 is printed as amended by SI 1982 No 1223, and SI 1984 No 1809.]

24.—(1) [This Regulation applies to such of the following vehicles as are not vehicles to which Regulation 24A applies]—

(a) every two-wheeled motor cycle manufactured on or after 1st April 1978 and first used on or after 1st October 1978,

(b) every Ford Transit motor car manufactured on or after 10th January 1978 and first used on or after 10th July 1978, and

(c) every motor vehicle (other than a two-wheeled motor cycle or a Ford Transit motor car) manufactured on or after 1st December 1977 and first used on or after 1st June 1978.

(2) Every vehicle to which this Regulation applies, which is

(a) a motor tractor,

[(b) an agricultural motor vehicle,]

(c) a locomotive,

(d) a works truck, or

(*e*) a vehicle which has a maximum design speed not exceeding 16 miles per hour and which does not fall within paragraph (3) below,

and which is not an excepted vehicle, shall be equipped with at least one exterior rear-view mirror fitted on the off-side of the vehicle.

[(3) Every vehicle to which this Regulation applies and which is not an excepted vehicle or a vehicle referred to in paragraph (2) (*a*), (*b*), (*c*) or (*d*) above shall be equipped—

(*a*) with at least one exterior rear-view mirror fitted on the off-side of the vehicle;

(*b*) save as provided in paragraph (4) below, with an interior rear-view mirror; and

(*c*) in a case where an interior rear-view mirror does not provide an adequate view of the road to the rear of the vehicle, with at least one exterior rear-view mirror fitted on the near-side of the vehicle.]

[(4) The requirement specified in paragraph (3) (*b*) above for an interior rear-view mirror shall not apply in any case where a vehicle is fitted with an exterior rear-view mirror on the off-side of the vehicle and on the near-side of the vehicle and an interior rear-view mirror would give the driver no view of the road to the rear of the vehicle.]

(5) Subject to paragraph (6) below, the following requirements shall apply to rear-view mirrors with which all vehicles to which this Regulation applies are equipped—

[(*a*) each rear-view mirror shall be legibly and indelibly marked in a conspicuous and readily accessible position with

    (i) in the case of a rear-view mirror attached to a two-wheeled motor cycle with or without a side car attached, the marking designated as an approval mark by Regulation 5 of the Motor Vehicles (Designation of Approval Marks) Regulation 1979 *[SI 1979 No 1088 as amended]* and shown at item 2, 2A or 29 in Schedule 4 to those Regulations; and

    (ii) in the case of a rear-view mirror attached to any motor vehicle other than a two-wheeled motor cycle with or without a side car attached, the marking so designated and shown at the said item 2 or 2A;]

(*b*) each rear-view mirror shall be fixed to the vehicle in such a way that it remains steady under normal driving conditions;

(*c*) each exterior rear-view mirror on a vehicle fitted with windows and a windscreen shall be visible to the driver, when in his driving position, through a side window or through the portion of the windscreen which is swept by the windscreen wiper;

(*d*) where the bottom edge of exterior rear-view mirror is less than 2 metres above the road surface when the vehicle is laden, that mirror shall not project more than 20 centimetres beyond the overall width of the vehicle or, in a case where the vehicle is drawing a trailer which has an overall width greater than that of the drawing vehicle, not more than 20 centimetres beyond the overall width of the trailer;

(*e*) each interior rear-view mirror shall be capable of being adjusted by the driver when in his driving position;

(*f*) except where the mirror is a spring back mirror, each exterior rear-view mirror on the driver's side of the vehicle shall be capable of being adjusted by the driver when in his driving position, but this requirement shall not prevent such a mirror from being locked into position from the outside of the vehicle.

[(6) Paragraph (5) (*a*) above does not apply to a rear-view mirror fitted to a large passenger carrying vehicle if that mirror complies with the relevant requirements with respect to construction and testing set out in either Annex I to Council Directive 71/127/EEC *[OJ L 68, 22.3.71, p 1 (SE 1971(I), p 136)]* other than the requirements specified in paragraphs 2.3.4 and 2.6 of that Annex, or Annex I to Commission Directive 79/795/EEC *[OJ L 239, 22.9.79]* other than the requirements specified in paragraphs 2.3.3 and 2.6 of that Annex.]

(7) The following additional requirement shall apply to rear-view mirrors with which vehicles are required to be equipped in accordance with paragraph (2) or (3) above, that is to say, each exterior rear-view mirror fitted to a vehicle which has a technically permissible maximum weight (as mentioned in Annex I to Council Directive 71/127/EEC) exceeding 3·5 metric tonnes shall be a Class II mirror (as described in that Annex) and each exterior rear-view mirror fitted to any other vehicle shall be either a Class II or a Class III mirror (as described in that Annex).

(8) In this Regulation—

'agricultural or forestry tractor' has the same meaning as in the Agricultural and Forestry Tractors (Type Approval) Regulations 1975 *[SI 1975 No 1475]*;

'excepted vehicle' means—
> (i) a two-wheeled motor cycle with or without a side car attached,
> (ii) a motor vehicle when drawing a trailer if a person is carried on the trailer in a position which affords an uninterrupted view to the rear and such a person is provided with efficient means of communicating to the driver the effect of signals given by the drivers of other vehicles to the rear thereof,
> (iii) a works truck if the driver can easily obtain a clear view of traffic to the rear,
> (iv) a pedestrian controlled vehicle, or
> (v) a vehicle which is merely a chassis when being driven from the place where it has been manufactured to the place where it is to receive a vehicle body;

'Ford Transit motor car' means a motor car manufactured by the Ford Motor Company Limited and known as the Ford Transit;

'rear-view mirror' means a mirror to assist the driver of a vehicle to become aware of traffic to the rear of the vehicle or rearwards on the sides of the vehicle or, where the mirror is an exterior mirror fitted on one side of the vehicle, rearwards on that side, or in a case where the vehicle is drawing a trailer, a mirror to assist the driver of the drawing vehicle to become aware of traffic to the rear of the trailer or rearwards on the sides of the drawing vehicle and the trailer, or where the mirror is an exterior mirror fitted on one side of the drawing vehicle, rearwards on that side of the drawing vehicle and the trailer;

'spring back mirror' means a rear-view mirror which, if knocked out of its alignment, can be returned to its former position without any need for its adjustment.

[Regulation 24 is printed as amended by SI 1982 No 1223, and SI 1984 No 1809.]

[24A.—(1) This Regulation applies to every vehicle which is—

(a) a motor vehicle referred to in Article 8 of the Council Directive being either—
> (i) a large passenger carrying vehicle, or
> (ii) a goods vehicle with a maximum gross weight exceeding 3500 kilograms; and

(*b*) manufactured on or after 1st October 1982 and first used on or after 1st April 1983.

(2) Save as provided in paragraph (3) below, every vehicle to which this Regulation applies shall be fitted with rear-view mirrors in accordance with the provisions specified in either—

(*a*) Regulation 24 as regards vehicles to which that Regulation applies, or

(*b*) paragraphs 3.1 to 3.4.6 of Annex I to the Council Directive.

(3) Every goods vehicle to which this Regulation applies and which is manufactured on or after 1st October 1984 and first used on or after 1st April 1985 shall be fitted with rear-view mirrors in accordance with the provisions of paragraphs 3.1 to 3.4.6 of Annex I to the Council Directive.

(4) In this Regulation—

'the Council Directive' means Council Directive 71/127/EEC of 1st March 1971 as amended by Commission Directive 79/795/EEC of 20th July 1979;

'maximum gross weight' means—

(*a*) in the case of a vehicle equipped with a Ministry plate in accordance with Regulation 148 or 149, the design gross weight shown in column (3) of that plate or, if no such weight is shown, the gross weight shown in column (2) of that plate;

(*b*) in the case of a vehicle not equipped with such a Ministry plate, but equipped with a plate in accordance with paragraph (2)(*a*), (*b*) or (*c*) or paragraph (2A) of Regulation 42, the maximum gross weight ascertained by reference to the particulars mentioned in the said paragraph (2)(*a*), (*b*) or (*c*) or (2A) as the case may be; and

'rear-view mirror' means a mirror defined as a 'rear-view mirror' in paragraph 1.1 of Annex I to the Council Directive and which is marked with a marking designated as an approval mark by Regulation 5 of the Motor Vehicles (Designation of Approval Marks) Regulations 1979 and shown at item 2 or 2A in Schedule 4 to those Regulations.]

[Regulation 24A was inserted by SI 1982 No 1223.]

* * *

27. Windscreen wipers

(1) Every vehicle which is fitted with a windscreen shall be fitted with one or more efficient automatic windscreen wipers, unless the driver can obtain an adequate view to the front of the vehicle without looking through the windscreen, for example by opening the windscreen or looking over it.

(2) The windscreen wipers required by the last preceding paragraph shall be capable of clearing the windscreen so that the driver has an adequate view of the road in front of the near and off sides of the vehicle in addition to an adequate view to the front of thet vehicle.

28. Windscreen washers

(1) Subject to the following paragraph, every motor vehicle, which is required to be fitted with one or more efficient automatic windscreen wipers by virtue of Regulation 27 shall be fitted with a windscreen washer capable of clearing, in conjunction

with those windscreen wipers, the area of the windscreen swept by those windscreen wipers of mud or other similar deposit.

(2) This Regulation shall not apply to [agricultural motor vehicles], vehicles which are incapable by reason of their construction of exceeding 20 miles per hour on the level under their own power or vehicles being used for the time being as stage carriages or on any journey incidental to such use.

[Regulation 28 is printed as amended by SI 1984 No 1809.]

[29. Audible warning instrument

(1) Every motor vehicle, other than a works truck and a pedestrian controlled vehicle, shall be fitted with a horn, and in the case of a motor vehicle first used on or after 1st August 1973 the sound emitted by any horn shall be continuous and uniform and not strident.

(2) Except as provided in paragraphs (3), (4) and (5) below, no motor vehicle shall be fitted with a bell, gong, siren or two-tone horn.

(3) The provisions of paragraph (2) above shall not apply so as to make it unlawful for the following vehicles to be fitted with a bell, gong, siren or two-tone horn:—

(*a*) motor vehicles used for fire brigade, ambulance or police purposes;

(*b*) motor vehicles owned by a body formed primarily for the purposes of fire salvage and used for those or similar purposes;

(*c*) motor vehicles owned by the Forestry Commission or by local authorities and used from time to time for the purposes of fighting fires;

(*d*) motor vehicles owned by the Secretary of State for Defence and used for the purposes of the disposal of bombs or explosives;

(*e*) motor vehicles used for the purposes of the Blood Transfusion Service provided under the National Health Service Act 1977 or under the National Health Service (Scotland) Act 1947;

(*f*) motor vehicles used by Her Majesty's Coastguard or the Coastguard Auxiliary Service to aid persons in danger or vessels in distress on or near the coast;

(*g*) motor vehicles owned by the National Coal Board and used for the purposes of rescue operations at mines;

(*h*) motor vehicles owned by the Secretary of State for Defence and used by the Royal Air Force Mountain Rescue Service for the purposes of rescue operations in connection with crashed aircraft or any other emergencies; and

(*i*) motor vehicles owned by the Royal National Lifeboat Institution and used for the purposes of launching lifeboats.

(4) The provisions of paragraphs (1) and (2) above shall not apply so as to make it unlawful for a motor vehicle to be fitted with an instrument or apparatus (not being a two-tone horn) designed to emit a sound for the purpose of informing members of the public that goods are on the vehicle for sale.

(5) Subject to paragraph (6) below, the provisions of paragraph (2) above shall not apply so as to make it unlawful for a vehicle to be fitted with a bell, gong or siren—

(*a*) if the purpose thereof is to prevent theft or attempted theft of the vehicle or its contents; or

(*b*) in the case of a large passenger-carrying vehicle, if the purpose thereof is to summon help for the driver, the conductor or an inspector while the vehicle is being used as a public service vehicle.

(6) Every bell, gong or siren fitted to a vehicle, other than a large passenger-carrying vehicle being used as a public service vehicle, by virtue of paragraph (5) above shall be fitted with a device designed to stop the bell, gong or siren emitting a noise for a continous period of more than 5 minutes, and every device fitted to a motor vehicle, other than a large passenger-carrying vehicle being used as a public service vehicle, first used on or after 1st October 1982 so as to cause a horn mentioned in paragraph (1) above to sound for the purpose of preventing theft or attempted theft of the vehicle or its contents shall be fitted with a device designed to stop the horn emitting a noise for a continuous period of more than 5 minutes.

(7) In this Regulation—

(a) 'horn' means an instrument, not being a bell, gong or siren capable of giving audible and sufficient warning of the approach or position of the vehicle to which it is fitted; and

(b) references to a bell, gong or siren include references to any instrument or apparatus capable of emitting a sound similar to that emitted by a bell, gong or siren.]

[Regulation 29 is printed as substituted by SI 1981 No 1580.]

30. Silencer

Every vehicle propelled by an internal combustion engine shall be fitted with a silencer, expansion chamber or other contrivance suitable and sufficient for reducing as far as may be reasonable the noise caused by the escape of the exhaust gases from the engine.

*   *   *

Noise

[31A.—(1) Except as provided in Regulation 31D (1) and (3), this Regulation applies to every motor vehicle, other than a motor vehicle to which Regulation 31E applies, being—

(a) a vehicle within the scope of Article 1 of the Council Directive, namely any motor vehicle intended for use on the road, with or without bodywork, having at least four wheels and a maximum design speed exceeding 25 kilometres per hour, with the exception of vehicles which run on rails, [agricultural motor vehicles] and machinery and public works vehicles—

    (i) in the case of a vehicle to which paragraph I.1.1; I.1.2; I.1.3; I.1.5; I.1.6; and I.1.7 of the Annex to the Council Directive applies, if manufactured on or after 1st April 1983 and first used on or after 1st October 1983,

    (ii) in the case of a vehicle to which paragraph I.1.4 of the Annex to the Council Directive applies—

        (a) being a vehicle manufactured by British Leyland Limited and known as the Atlantean Bus, if manufactured on or after 1st October 1983 and first used on or after 1st October 1984;

        (b) being any other vehicle, if manufactured on or after 1st April 1983 and first used on or after 1st October 1983;

(b) a vehicle not being within the scope of Article 1 of the Council Directive but which is manufactured on or after 1st April 1983 and first used on or after 1st October 1983 and which is:—

    (i) a vehicle which has a maximum design speed of 25 kilometres per hour or less but which would, if it had a maximum design speed exceeding 25 kilometres per hour, be within the scope of Article 1 of the Council Directive, or

(ii) a vehicle which is a mechanically propelled vehicle with three wheels (not being a motor cycle with a side-car attached),

(iii) a vehicle, not being a vehicle within the scope of sub-paragraph (i) and (ii), above, which is:—

(a) engineering plant,

(b) a locomotive, other than [an agricultural motor vehicle],

(c) a motor tractor other than an industrial tractor or [an agricultural motor vehicle],

(d) a public works vehicle, or

(e) a works truck.

[(2) Every vehicle mentioned in paragraph (1) (a) above shall be so constructed that if the conditions of measurement specified in an item in column (2) of the Table below exist, and the method of measurement specified in that item in column (3) of that Table is used and, in a case to which item 2 applies, the results are interpreted as specified in that item, its sound level, when measured by an instrument specified in that item in column (4) of that Table, does not exceed the limits specified in that item in column (5) of that Table, and the device designed to reduce the exhaust noise meets the requirements specified in that item in column (6) (a) of that Table if fibrous absorbent material is not used and in column (6) (b) of that Table if fibrous absorbent material is used.]

[for the table referred to in para (2), see p 346]

[(3) Every vehicle mentioned in paragraph (1) (b) above shall be so constructed that if the conditions of measurement specified in an item in column (2) of the Table below exist, and the method of measurement specified in that item in column (3) of that Table is used and, in a case to which item 2 applies, the results are interpreted as specified in that item, its sound level, when measured by an instrument specified in that item in column (4) of that Table, does not exceed the limits specified in that item in column (5) (a) of that Table in the case of a vehicle mentioned in sub-paragraph (i) or (ii) of the said paragraph (1) (b) and in column (5) (b) of that Table in the case of a vehicle mentioned in sub-paragraph (iii) of the said paragraph (1) (b).]

[for the table referred to in para (3), see p 347]

(4) In this regulation—

'the Council Directive' means Council Directive 70/157/EEC of 6th February 1970 on the approximation of the laws of Member States relating to the permissible sound level and the exhaust system of motor vehicles *[OJ L 42 23.2.70, p 16 (SE 1970 (I), p 111)]*, as amended by Commission Directive 73/350/EEC of 7th November 1973 *[OJ L 321 27.11.73, p 33]* and by Council Directive 77/212/EEC of 8th March 1977 *[OJ L 66 12.3.77, p 33]* [but excluding any amendments made by Commission Directive 81/334/EEC of 13th April 1981 *[OJ L 131, 18.5.81, p 6]*];

['the Commission Directive' means Council Directive 70/157/EEC as amended by Commission Directive 73/350/EEC, Council Directive 77/212/EEC and Commission Directive 81/334/EEC.]

'public works vehicle' means any mechanically propelled vehicle which is constructed for use on a road by any statutory undertaker (as defined in section 262 (13) of the Local Government Act 1972), highway authority, local authority, or the Post Office or the police for the purpose of works which such undertaking, authority or other body has a duty or a power to carry out.]

[TABLE *[following immediately after text of reg 31A(2)]*]

(1)	(2)	(3)	(4)	(5)	(6) Requirements of exhaust device	
					(a) If fibrous absorbent material is not used	(b) If fibrous absorbent material is used
Item No	Conditions of Measurement	Method of Measurement and Interpretation of Results	Instrument of Measurement	Limits of sound level		
1.	Conditions specified in paragraph I.3 of the Annex to the Council Directive.	Method specified in paragraph I.4.1 of the Annex to the Council Directive.	Instrument specified in paragraph I.2 of the Annex to the Council Directive.	Limits specified in paragraph I.1 of the Annex to the Council Directive.	Requirements specified in paragraph II.1 of the Annex to the Council Directive (except in so far as that paragraph refers to paragraphs II.2, II.4, II.5 and II.6).	Requirements specified in column 6(a) of this item plus those specified in paragraphs II.4 to II.4.1.4 and II.6 of the Council Directive.
2.	Conditions specified in paragraph 5.2.2.3 of Annex 1 to the Commission Directive.	Method specified in paragraph 5.2.2.4 of Annex 1 to the Commission Directive; Interpretation of results as specified in paragraph 5.2.2.5 of that Annex.	Instrument specified in paragraph 5.2.2.2 of Annex 1 to the Commission Directive.	Limits specified in paragraph 5.2.2.1 of Annex 1 to the Commission Directive.	Requirements specified in paragraph 5.1 of Annex 1 to the Commission Directive, and the marking requirements in paragraph 3 of that Annex.	Requirements specified in column 6(a) of this item plus those specified in paragraph 5.3.1 of Annex 1 to the Commission Directive.]

[TABLE *[following immediately after text of reg 31A(3)]*]

(1)	(2)	(3)	(4)	(5) Limits of Sound Level	
				(a)	(b)
Item No	Conditions of Measurement	Method of Measurement and Interpretation of Results	Instrument of Measurement	Vehicle referred in paragraph (1) (b) (i) or (ii) of this Regulation	Vehicle referred to in paragraph (1) (b) (iii) of this Regulation
1.	Conditions specified in paragraph I.3 of the Annex to the Council Directive.	Method specified in paragraph I.4.1 of the Annex to the Council Directive.	Instrument specified in paragraph I.2 of the Annex to the Council Directive.	Limits specified in paragraph I.1 of the Annex to the Council Directive.	89dB(A)
2.	Conditions specified in paragraph 5.2.2.3 of Annex 1 to the Commission Directive.	Method specified in paragraph 5.2.2.4 of Annex 1 to the Commission Directive; Interpretation of results as specified in paragraph 5.2.2.5 of that Annex.	Instrument specified in paragraph 5.2.2.2 of Annex 1 to the Commission Directive.	Limits specified in paragraph 5.2.2.1 of Annex 1 to the Commission Directive.	89dB(A)]

[Regulation 31A was inserted by SI 1980 No 1116 and is printed as amended by SI 1982 No 1422, and SI 1984 No 1809.

For the Local Government Act 1972, s 262 (13), see the note to reg 3.]

[31B.—(1) Except as provided in Regulation 31D (1), this Regulation applies to every vehicle manufactured on or after 1st October 1982 and first used on or after 1st April 1983 being—

(*a*) a motorcycle,

(*b*) a moped, or

(*c*) any other mechanically propelled vehicle with two wheels.

(2) Every motorcycle to which this Regulation applies shall be so constructed that when the conditions of measurement specified in paragraph 2.1.3 of Annex 1 to the Council Directive exist and the method of measurement specified in paragraphs 2.1.4 and 2.1.5.2 to 2.1.5.4 of that Annex is applied the sound level specified in paragraph 2.1.1 of that Annex is not exceeded when measured by an instrument specified in paragraph 2.1.2 of that Annex, and that the device designed to reduce the exhaust noise meets the requirements specified in paragraph 3.1 of that Annex [(except in so far as that paragraph relates to paragraph 3.2)] and, if fibrous absorbent material is used, the requirements specified in paragraphs 3.4.1 to 3.4.3 of that Annex.

(3) Every moped to which this Regulation applies shall be so constructed that its sound level satisfies requirements identical to those specified, in relation to motorcycles, in paragraph (2) above save that the maximum permissible sound level in dB (A) when all the conditions and methods of testing there specified, in relation to motorcycles, are employed shall not exceed 73.

(4) Every other vehicle to which this Regulation applies shall be so constructed that its sound level satisfies requirements identical to those specified, in relation to motorcycles, in paragraph (2) above save that the maximum permissible sound level in dB (A) when all the conditions and methods of testing specified in that paragraph, in relation to motorcycles, are employed shall not exceed in the case of a vehicle with an engine the capacity of which is specified in an item in column 2 of the Table below the level specified in that item in column 3 of that Table.

[Table *[ie table in reg 31B]*

1	2	3
Item No	Engine capacity of vehicle in cubic centimetres	Maximum permissible sound level in dB (A)
1.	80 or less	78
2.	More than 80 but not more than 125	80
3.	More than 125 but not more than 350	83
4.	More than 350 but not more than 500	85
5.	More than 500	86]

(5) In this Regulation—

'moped' has the meaning assigned to that expression in Regulation 46 (4);

'motorcycle' has the meaning assigned to that expression in Article 1 of the

Council Directive, namely, any two-wheeled vehicle, with or without a side-car, fitted with an engine, intended for use on the road and having a maximum design speed of more than 50 kilometres per hour;

'the Council Directive' means Council Directive 78/1015/EEC of 23rd November 1978 on the approximation of laws of Member States on the permissible sound level and exhaust system of motorcycles *[OJ L 349 13.12.78, p 21].*]

[Regulation 31B was inserted by SI 1980 No 1166 and is printed as amended by SI 1982 No 1422.]

[31C.—(1) Except as provided in Regulation 31D (1), this Regulation applies to every vehicle manufactured on or after 1st October 1982 and first used on or after 1st April 1983 being [an agricultural motor vehicle] or an industrial tractor.

(2) Every vehicle to which this Regulation applies shall be so constructed that when the conditions of measurement specified in paragraph I.3 of Annex VI of Council Directive 74/151/EEC *[OJ L 84 28.3.74, p 25]* exist and the method of measurement specified in paragraph I.4.1 of that Annex is applied, its sound level when measured by an instrument specified in paragraph I.2 of that Annex does not exceed—

(*a*) in the case of a vehicle with HP DIN of less than 90, 89dB (A), and

(*b*) in the case of a vehicle with HP DIN of 90 or more, 92dB (A),

and that the device designed to reduce the exhaust noise meets the requirements specified in paragraph II.1 of that Annex [(except in so far as that paragraph relates to paragraph II.2)] and, if fibrous absorbent material is used, the requirements specified in paragraphs II.4.1 to II.4.3 of that Annex.]

[Regulation 31C was inserted by SI 1980 No 1166 and is printed as amended by SI 1982 No 1422, and SI 1984 No 1809.]

[31D.—(1) Regulations 31, 31A, 31B, 31C, and 31E shall not apply to—

(*a*) a motor vehicle proceeding to a place where, by previous arrangement—
  (i) noise emitted by it is about to be measured for the purpose of ascertaining whether or not that vehicle complies with Regulation 31 or, as the case may be 31A, 31B, 31C or 31E, or
  (ii) the vehicle is about to be mechanically adjusted, modified or equipped for the purpose of securing that it so complies, or

(*b*) a motor vehicle returning from such a place immediately after the noise had been so measured.

(2) Regulation 31 shall apply to—

(*a*) a vehicle propelled by a compression ignition engine and which is of a type in respect of which a type approval certificate has been issued under the [Motor Vehicles (Type Approval) (Great Britain) Regulations 1984 *[SI 1984 No 981]*];

(*b*) a motorcycle (as defined in Regulation 31B (5)) which—
  (i) is first used on or after 1st October 1980;
  (ii) has an engine capacity not exceeding 50 cubic centimetres, and
  (iii) complies with the requirements specified (in relation to a vehicle to which Regulation 31B applies) in Regulation 31B (2); or

(*c*) [an agricultural motor vehicle] manufactured on or after 7th February 1975 and which complies with the requirements specified (in relation to the vehicle to which Regulation 31C applies) in Regulation 31C (2).

[(3) Regulations 31 and 31A do not apply to a vehicle specially constructed, and not merely adapted, for the purposes of fighting fires or salvage from fires on or in the vicinity of airports, having an engine power exceeding 300 HP DIN; and Regulations 31, 31A and 31C do not apply to road rollers.]]

[Regulation 31D was inserted by SI 1980 No 1166 and is printed as amended by the Interpretation Act 1978, ss 17(2), 23; SI 1982 No 1422; and SI 1984 No 1809.]

[31E.—(1) Except as provided in Regulation 31D (1), this Regulation applies to every vehicle which—

    (*a*) has a compression ignition engine;

    (*b*) is so constructed or adapted that the driving power of the engine is, or by the appropriate use of the controls of the vehicle can be, transmitted to all the wheels of the vehicle;

    (*c*) falls within category I.1.1, I.1.2, I.1.3 specified in Article 1 of Council Directive 77/212/EEC of 8th March 1977; and

    (*d*) is manufactured on or after 1st April 1983 and first used on or after 1st October 1983.

(2) Every vehicle to which this Regulation applies shall be so constructed that if the conditions of measurement specified in paragraph (2) of the Table below exist and the method of measurement specified in that item in column (3) of that Table is used and, in a case to which item 2 applies, the results are interpreted as specified in that item, its sound level when measured by an instrument specified in that item in column (4) of that Table does not exceed the limit specified in that item in column (5) of that Table and the device designed to reduce the exhaust noise meets the requirements specified in that item in column (5) (*a*) of that Table if fibrous absorbent material is not used and column (5) (*b*) of that Table if fibrous absorbent material is used.

[Regulation 31E was inserted by SI 1980 No 1166 and is printed as substituted by SI 1982 No 1422.]

*   *   *

41. *[Revoked.]*

42. Certain vehicles to be equipped with plates, etc

(1) [Paragraphs (2) and (2A) of this Regulation apply] to:—

[(*a*) every heavy motor car and motor car first used on or after 1st January 1968 not being—

    (i) a dual-purpose vehicle;

    (ii) [an agricultural motor vehicle];

    (iii) a works truck; or

    (iv) a pedestrian controlled vehicle; or

    (v) save as provided in sub-paragraph (*aa*) below, a passenger vehicle; and]

[(*aa*) every large passenger carrying vehicle (whether or not it is an articulated bus) manufactured on or after 1st October 1981 and first used on or after 1st April 1982; and]

  (*b*) every locomotive and motor tractor first used on or after 1st April 1973 not being—

    (i) [an agricultural motor vehicle];

    (ii) [an agricultural motor vehicle];

    (iii) an industrial tractor;

[Table *[following immediately after text of reg 31E(2)]*]

(1)	(2)	(3)	(4)	(5)	(6)	
					Requirements of exhaust device	
					(a)	(b)
Item No	Conditions of Measurement	Method of Measurement and Interpretation of Results	Instrument of Measurement	Limit of Sound level	If fibrous absorbent material is not used	If fibrous absorbent material is used
1.	Conditions specified in paragraph I.3 of the Annex to the Council Directive.	Method specified in paragraph I.4.1 of the Annex to the Council Directive.	Instrument specified in paragraph I.2 of the Annex to the Council Directive.	82dB(A)	Requirements specified in paragraph II.1 of the Annex to the Council Directive (except in so far as that paragraph refers to paragraphs II.2, II.4, II.5 and II.6).	Requirements specified in column (6)(a) of this item plus the requirements specified in paragraphs II.4 to II.4.1.4 and II.6 of the Annex to the Council Directive.
2.	Conditions specified in paragraph 5.2.2.3 of Annex 1 to the Commission Directive.	Method specified in paragraph 5.2.2.4 of Annex 1 to the Commission Directive; Interpretation of results as specified in paragraph 5.2.2.5 of that Annex.	Instrument specified in paragraph 5.2.2.2 of Annex 1 to the Commission Directive.	82dB(A)	Requirements specified in paragraph 5.1 of Annex 1 to the Commission Directive, and the marking requirements in paragraph 3 of that Annex.	Requirements specified in column (6)(a) of this item plus those specified in paragraph 5.3.1 of Annex 1 to the Commission Directive.]

    (iv) a works truck;

    (v) engineering plant;

    (vi) a pedestrian controlled vehicle; or

    (vii) a vehicle manufactured before 1st October 1972; and

(c) every trailer manufactured on or after 1st January 1968 which exceeds 1020 kilograms in weight unladen and is other than—

    (i) a trailer not constructed or adapted to carry any load, other than plant or special appliance or apparatus which is a permanent or essentially permanent fixture, and not exceeding 2290 kilograms in total weight;

    (ii) a living van not exceeding 2040 kilograms in weight unladen and fitted with pneumatic tyres;

    (iii) a works trailer;

    (iv) a trailer mentioned in Regulation 75 (4); or

    (v) a trailer which was manufactured and used outside Great Britain before it was first used in Great Britain; and

(d) every trailer which is a converter dolly manufactured on or after 1st January 1979 not being a trailer to which sub-paragraph (c) above applies.

[(2) Every motor vehicle and trailer to which this paragraph applies and which is first used before [1st October 1982] shall be equipped with either—

(a) a plate which is securely affixed to the vehicle in a conspicuous and readily accessible position, and which contains in the case of a heavy motor car, motor car, locomotive or motor tractor the particulars required by Part I of Schedule 2 and in the case of a trailer the particulars required by Part II of that Schedule, the said particulars being completed in accordance with Part III of that Schedule and the plate otherwise complying with the provisions contained in that Part, or

(b) a plate which is securely affixed to the vehicle in a conspicuous and readily accessible position, and which complies with the requirements specified in the Annex to Council Directive 76/114/EEC of 18th December 1975 [OJ L 24, 30.1.76, p 1] (which relates to statutory plates and inscriptions for motor vehicles and their trailers), as read with the following paragraphs of this Regulation and which contains—

    (i) in lieu of the requirements specified in paragraphs 2.1.4 and 2.1.6 of the said Annex the particulars specified in paragraph (3) of this Regulation,

    (ii) in lieu of the requirements specified in paragraph 2.1.5 of the said Annex the particulars specified in paragraph (4) of this Regulation, and

    (iii) in accordance with the provisions of the second part of paragraph 2.1.8 of the said Annex the particulars specified in paragraph (5) of this Regulation, or

(c) a plate which is securely affixed to the vehicle in a conspicuous and readily accessible position, and which complies with the requirements specified in the Annex to Council Directive 76/114/EEC of 18th December 1975 as amended by Commission Directive 78/507/EEC of 19th May 1978 [OJ L 155, 13.6.78, p 31], as, read with the following paragraphs of this Regulation and which contains—

    (i) in lieu of the requirements specified in paragraphs 2.1.4 and 2.1.6 of the said Annex as so amended the particulars specified in paragraph (3) of this Regulation,

    (ii) in lieu of the requirements specified in paragraph 2.1.5 of the said Annex as so amended the particulars specified in paragraph (4) of this Regulation, and

(iii) in accordance with the provisions of the second part of paragraph 2.1.8 of the said Annex as so amended the particulars specified in paragraph (5) of this Regulation.]

[(2A) Every motor vehicle and trailer to which this paragraph applies and which is first used on or after [1st October 1982] shall be equipped with either—

(a) a plate which complies with the requirements specified in paragraph (2) (a) of this Regulation, or

(b) a plate which complies with the requirements specified in paragraph (2) (c) of this Regulation.]

(3) The particulars referred to in [paragraphs (2) (b) (i) and (2) (c) (i) of this Regulation] are as follows—

(a) in the case of a motor vehicle—
   (i) the maximum gross weight in Great Britain referred to in item 10 in Part I of Schedule 2, and
   (ii) the maximum weight in Great Britain for each axle referred to in item 9 in Part I of Schedule 2;

(b) in the case of a trailer—
   (i) the maximum gross weight in Great Britain referred to in item 8 in Part II of Schedule 2, and
   (ii) the maximum weight in Great Britain for each axle referred to in item 7 in Part II of Schedule 2.

[(4) The particulars referred to in paragraph (2) (b) (ii) and (2) (c) (ii) of this Regulation are as follows—

(a) in the case of a motor vehicle which is constructed to form part of an articulated vehicle the maximum train weight referred to in item 8 in Part I of Schedule 2 if that weight is less than the maximum laden weight of the articulated vehicle, of which the motor vehicle is constructed to form part, referred to in Regulation 88 or Regulation 91, or the said maximum laden weight if that weight is less than the said maximum train weight;

(b) in the case of a motor vehicle which is not constructed to form part of an articulated vehicle the maximum train weight referred to in item 8 in Part I of Schedule 2 if that weight is less than the maximum laden weight of the motor vehicle and trailer referred to in Regulation 87, or the said maximum laden weight if that weight is less than the said maximum train weight.]

(5) The particulars referred to in [paragraphs (2) (b) (iii) and (2) (c) (iii) of this Regulation] are as follows:—

(a) in the case of a motor vehicle of which the maximum gross weight referred to in item 7 in Part I of Schedule 2 is more than the maximum gross weight in Great Britain referred to in item 10 in Part I of Schedule 2, the said maximum gross weight in a column to the right of the said maximum gross weight in Great Britain;

(b) in the case of a trailer of which the maximum gross weight referred to in item 6 in Part II of Schedule 2 is more than the maximum gross weight in Great Britain referred to in item 8 in Part II of Schedule 2, the said maximum gross weight in a column to the right of the said maximum gross weight in Great Britain;

(c) in the case of a semi-trailer the maximum gross weight referred to in item 6 in Part II of Schedule 2, in the right-hand column of the plate;

(*d*) in the case of a motor vehicle which is constructed to form part of an articulated vehicle, where the maximum laden weight of the articulated vehicle referred to in Regulation 88 or Regulation 91 is less than the maximum train weight referred to in item 8 in Part I of Schedule 2, the said maximum train weight in a column to the right of the said maximum laden weight;

(*e*) in the case of a motor vehicle which is not constructed to form part of an articulated vehicle, where the maximum laden weight of the motor vehicle and trailer referred to in Regulation 87 is less than the maximum train weight referred to in item 8 in Part I of Schedule 2, the said maximum train weight in a column to the right of the said maximum laden weight;

(*f*) in the case of a motor vehicle of which the maximum axle weight for each axle referred to in item 6 in Part I of Schedule 2 is more than the maximum weight in Great Britain for each axle referred to in item 9 in Part I of Schedule 2, the said maximum axle weight for each axle in a column to the right of the said maximum weight in Great Britain for each axle;

(*g*) in the case of a trailer of which the maximum weight for each axle referred to in item 4 in Part II of Schedule 2 is more than the maximum weight in Great Britain for each axle referred to in item 7 in Part II of Schedule 2, the said maximum weight for each axle in a column to the right of the said maximum weight in Great Britain for each axle;

(*h*) in the case of a semi-trailer the maximum load imposed on the drawing vehicle referred to in item 5 in Part II of Schedule 2, in the right-hand column of the plate.

(6) Part III of Schedule 2 shall apply for determining the relevant weights to be shown on a plate in accordance with paragraphs (3), (4) and (5) of this Regulation.

[Regulation 42 is printed as amended by SI 1978 No 1235; SI 1981 No 261; SI 1981 No 1580; SI 1982 No 1480; and SI 1984 No 1809.

In effecting an amendment to para (1)(a), SI 1984 No 1809, reg 38, Schedule (item 16), referred to 'reg 42 (1) (a) (iii)'; but the effect of the amendment (the substitution of 'an agricultural motor vehicle' for 'a land tractor') makes it apparent that the amendment should be made to reg 42 (1) (a) (ii), and effect has been given to the amendment accordingly.]

[42A.—(1) Save as provided in paragraph (3) below, every agricultural trailed appliance manufactured on or after 1st December 1985 shall be equipped with a plate affixed to the vehicle in a conspicuous and readily accessible position and which is clearly and indelibly marked with the particulars specified in paragraph (2) below.

(2) Those particulars are—

(*a*) the name of the manufacturer of the appliance;

(*b*) the year in which the appliance was manufactured;

(*c*) the maximum gross weight (calculated in accordance with Part II of Schedule 2 to these Regulations);

(*d*) the unladen weight (calculated in accordance with section 194 of the Road Traffic Act 1972); and

(*e*) the maximum load which would be imposed by the appliance on the drawing vehicle.

(3) In the case of a towed roller consisting of several separate rolls used in combination, a single plate shall satisfy the requirement specified in paragraph (2) above.]

[Regulation 42A was inserted by SI 1984 No 1809.]

43.—(1) Subject to paragraph (2) below, this Regulation applies to every motor vehicle manufactured on or after 1st October 1979 and first used on or after 1st April 1980 which is a passenger vehicle or a dual-purpose vehicle other than a vehicle which is a dual-purpose vehicle by reason only that it satisfies the requirements specified in paragraph (i) in the definition of 'dual-purpose vehicle' in Regulation 3 (1); and which—

(a) is adapted to carry not more than 8 passengers exclusive of the driver and either has 4 or more wheels or, if having only 3 wheels, has a maximum gross weight of more than 1000 kilograms, or

(b) has 3 wheels, a maximum gross weight not exceeding 1000 kilograms, and either a design speed exceeding 40 kilometres per hour or an engine with a capacity exceeding 50 cubic centimetres, and is not a motor cycle with a side-car attached.

(2) This Regulation does not apply to any vehicle specified in [Regulation 3 (2) . . .] of the Type Approval (Great Britain) Regulations.

[(3) Every motor vehicle to which this Regulation applies shall be equipped with a plate which is in a conspicuous and readily accessible position, is affixed to a vehicle part which is not normally subject to replacement and which—

(a) either—
  (i) shows clearly and indelibly the vehicle identification number in accordance with the requirements specified in paragraphs 3.4.4. and 3.1.2 in the Annex to Council Directive 76/114/EEC of 18th December 1975 *[OJ L 24 30.1.76, p 1]*, disregarding any amendments thereto, and the name of the manufacturner of the vehicle, or
  (ii) complies with the requirements specified in the Annex to Council Directive 76/114/EEC of 18th December 1975 as amended by Commission Directive 78/507/EEC of 19th May 1978 *[OJ L 155 13.6.78, p 31]*: and

(b) shows clearly and indelibly either—
  (i) the approval reference number of the type approval certificate which relates to the vehicle model or the model variant of the vehicle model, as the case may be, issued in accordance with the provisions of Regulation 9 (1) of, and Part I of Schedule 3 to, the Type Approval (Great Britain) Regulations, or
  (ii) the approval reference number of the Minister's approval certificate which relates to the vehicle, issued in accordance with the provisions of Regulation 9 (2) of, and Part I (A) of Schedule 4 to, the said Regulations:

Provided that the information required under sub-paragraph (b) above may be shown clearly and indelibly on an additional plate which is fitted in a conspicuous and readily accessible position and which is affixed to a vehicle part which is not normally subject to replacement.]

(4) The vehicle identification number of every motor vehicle to which this Regulation applies shall be marked on the chassis, frame or other similar structure, on the right-hand side of the vehicle, in a clearly visible and accessible position, and by a method such as hammering or stamping, in such a way that it cannot be obliterated or deteriorate.

(5) In this Regulation 'maximum gross weight' means the weight which a vehicle

is designed or adapted not to exceed when in normal use and travelling on a road laden.

[Regulation 43 is printed as amended by the Interpretation Act 1978, ss 17 (2), 23, and SI 1979 No 843.]

* * *

46. Distinguishing plates for motor cycles

[(1) Every motor cycle first used on or after 1st August 1977 and before 1st January 1982 and which is not—

(i) a motor cycle propelled by an internal combustion engine with a cylinder capacity exceeding 150 cubic centimetres; or

(ii) a mowing machine; or

(iii) a pedestrian controlled vehicle

shall be equipped with a plate which is securely affixed to the cycle in a conspicuous and readily accessible position and which either—

(*a*) states whether the motor cycle is a standard motor cycle or a moped;

(*b*) is in the form and of the size specified in Schedule 12;

(*c*) contains the further particulars specified for a motor cycle plate in that Schedule; and

(*d*) complies with the other requirements specified for a plate in that Schedule

or complies with the provisions specified in paragraph (2) below as regards the vehicles to which that paragraph relates.]

[(2) Every, motor cycle first used on or after 1st January 1982 and which is not—

(i) a motor cycle propelled by an internal combustion engine with a cylinder capacity exceeding 125 cubic centimetres;

(ii) a mowing machine; or

(iii) a pedestrian controlled vehicle

shall be equipped with a plate which is securely affixed to the cycle in a conspicuous position and which—

(*a*) states whether the motor cycle is a standard motor cycle or a moped;

(*b*) is in the form and of the size specified in Schedule 12A;

(*c*) contains the further particulars specified for a motor cycle plate in that Schedule; and

(*d*) complies with the other requirements specified for such a plate in that Schedule.]

(3) If a motor cycle to which this Regulation applies is altered so that it ceases to be a moped and becomes a standard motor cycle, an appropriate amendment shall be made to the plate required by [paragraph (1) or (2) above] or the motor cycle shall be equipped with the appropriate new plate.

(4) [The following expressions, where used in this Regulation or in Schedule 12 or Schedule 12A, have the meanings respectively assigned to them namely:—

['maximum engine power' means the maximum net power the motor cycle engine will develop, in kilowatts, when measured in accordance with the test conditions specified in the International Standard numbered ISO 4106 developed by the technical committee of the International Organisation for Standardisation, and approved by member bodies, including the United Kingdom, and published under the reference ISO 4106 1978—09—01;]

'moped' means a motor cycle which has a maximum design speed which does not exceed 30 miles per hour, a kerbside weight which does not exceed 250 kilograms, and, if propelled by an internal combustion engine, an engine with a cylinder capacity which does not exceed 50 cubic centimetres;

'kerbside weight', in relation to a motor cycle, means the weight of the cycle when it carries—

(a) no person thereon; and

(b) a full supply of fuel in its tank, an adequate supply of other liquids incidental to its propulsion and no load other than the loose tools and equipment with which it is normally equipped:

'maximum design speed', in relation to a motor cycle, means the maximum speed which the motor cycle is designed to achieve under its own power on a level road; and

['power to weight ratio' in relation to a motor cycle means the ratio of the maximum engine power to the kerbside weight of the vehicle measured, as regards the maximum engine power, in kilowatts and, as regards the kerbside weight, in 1000 kilograms;]

'standard motor cycle' means a motor cycle which is not a moped.

(5) For the purposes of this Regulation and Schedule 12 a motor cycle shall be regarded as having a maximum design speed which does not exceed 30 miles per hour if it cannot exceed that speed by more than 5 miles per hour when tested under the following conditions—

(a) the surface on which it is tested shall be dry asphalt or concrete;

(b) the rider shall be a person not exceeding 75 kilograms in weight;

(c) no passenger or load shall be carried;

(d) the test route shall be so located that acceleration to, and deceleration from, maximum speed can take place elsewhere than on the test route itself;

(e) the test route shall not have a gradient exceeding 5 per cent;

(f) the motor cycle shall be ridden in opposite directions along the test route and the speed recorded for the purpose of the test shall (in order to minimise the effect of wind resistance and gradient) be the average of speeds shown for each direction;

(g) when being driven along the test route, the motor cycle shall be driven in such manner and in such gear as to achieve the maximum speed of which it is capable; and

(h) if the motor cycle is fitted with a device which can, without the use of specialist tools or equipment, be readily modified or removed so as to increase its maximum speed, the test shall be carried out with the device in the modified condition or, as the case may be, without the device.

[Regulation 46 is printed as amended by 1981 No 915 (and correction slip thereto).]

[46A. Marking of weights on unbraked trailers

(1) On and after 1st October 1982 every unbraked trailer [other than one mentioned in Regulation 75 (4)] shall have its maximum gross weight (stated in kilograms) marked in a conspicuous and readily accessible position on the outside of the vehicle on its left or near side.

(2) In this Regulation—

'maximum gross weight', in relation to a trailer, means the weight which it is designed or adapted not to exceed when in use and travelling on a road laden; and

'unbraked trailer' means any trailer other than one which, whether or not Regulation 75 applies to it, is equipped with a braking system in accordance with that Regulation.]

[Regulation 46A was added by SI 1981 No 1189 and is printed as amended by SI 1983 No 113.]

[46B. Rear under-run protection

(1) Except as provided in paragraph (2) below, this Regulation applies to every goods vehicle being either—

(*a*) a motor vehicle with a maximum gross weight (determined as provided in Part I of Schedule 2 to these Regulations) which exceeds 3500 kilograms and which is manufactured on or after 1st October 1983 and first used on or after 1st April 1984; or

(*b*) a trailer with an unladen weight which exceeds 1020 kilograms and which is manufactured on or after 1st May 1983.

(2) This Regulation does not apply to—

(*a*) a motor vehicle which is incapable by reason of its construction of exceeding a speed of 15 miles per hour on the level under its own power;

(*b*) a motor car or a heavy motor car constructed or adapted to form part of an articulated vehicle;

(*c*) an agricultural trailer;

(*d*) engineering plant;

(*e*) a fire engine;

(*f*) [an agricultural motor vehicle];

(*g*) a vehicle fitted at the rear with apparatus [specially designed] for spreading material on a road;

(*h*) a vehicle so constructed that it can be unloaded by part of the vehicle being tipped rearwards;

(*i*) a vehicle owned by the Secretary of State for Defence and used for naval, military or air force purposes;

[(*j*) a vehicle to which no bodywork has been fitted and which is being driven or towed—

    (i) for the purpose of a quality or safety check by its manufacturer or a dealer in, or distributor of, such vehicles;

    (ii) to a place where, by previous arrangement, bodywork is to be fitted or work preparatory to the fitting of bodywork is to be carried out, or;

    (iii) by previous arrangement to premises of a dealer in, or distributor of, such vehicles;]

(*k*) a vehicle which is being driven or towed to a place where by previous arrangement a device is to be fitted so that it complies with this Regulation;

(*l*) a vehicle specially designed and constructed, and not merely adapted, to carry other vehicles loaded on it from the rear;

(*m*) a trailer specially designed and constructed, and not merely adapted, to carry round timber, beams or girders, being items of exceptional length;

[(*n*) a vehicle fitted with a tail lift so constructed that the lift platform forms part of the floor of the vehicle and this part has a length of at least 1 metre measured parallel to the longitudinal axis of the vehicle; or]

[(o) a trailer having a base or centre in a country outside Great Britain from which it normally starts its journeys, provided that a period of not more than 12 months has elapsed since the vehicle was last brought into Great Britain;]

[(p) a vehicle specially designed, and not merely adapted, for the carriage and mixing of liquid concrete[;]]

[(q) a vehicle designed and used solely for the delivery of coal by means of a special conveyor which is carried on the vehicle and when in use is fitted to the rear of the vehicle so as to render its being equipped with a rear under-run protective device impracticable; or]

[(r) [an agricultural trailed appliance].]

(3) Save as provided in paragraphs (4) and (5) below, every vehicle to which this Regulation applies shall be equipped with a rear under-run protective device.

(4) A vehicle to which this Regulation applies and which is fitted with a tail lift, bodywork or other part which renders its being equipped with a rear under-run protective device impracticable shall instead be equipped with [one or more devices which do not protrude beyond the overall width of the vehicle (excluding any part of the device or devices) and which comply with the following requirements]:—

(a) not more than 50 centimetres shall lie between one device and the device next to it;

(b) not more than 30 centimetres shall lie between the outermost end of a device nearest to the outermost part of the vehicle to which it is fitted and a vertical plane passing through the outer end of the rear axle of the vehicle on the same side of the vehicle or, in a case where the vehicle is fitted with more than one rear axle, through the outer end of the widest rear axle on the same side of [the vehicle, and paragraph II.5.4.2 in the Annex to the Council Directive shall not have effect in a case where this requirement is met];

(c) all the devices together shall have the characteristics specified in paragraphs II.5.4.1 to II.5.4.5.5.2 in the Annex to the Council Directive [save—

   (i) as provided in sub-paragraphs (a) and (b) above,

   (ii) that for the reference in paragraph II.5.4.1 in that Annex to 30 centimetres there is substituted a reference to 35 centimetres, and

   (iii) the distance of 40 centimetres specified in paragraph II.5.4.5 in that Annex may be measured exclusive of the said tail-lift, bodywork or other part.]

(5) The provisions of paragraph (3) above have effect so that:—

(a) in the case of a vehicle which is fitted with a demountable body, the characteristics specified in paragraph II.5.4.2 in the Annex to the Council Directive have effect as if the reference to 10 centimetres were a reference to 30 centimetres and as if in paragraph II.5.4.5.1 the reference to 30 centimetres were a reference to 35 centimetres; and

(b) in the case of a trailer with a single axle or two close-coupled axles, the height of 55 centimetres referred to in paragraph II.5.4.1 in that Annex is measured when the coupling of the trailer to the vehicle by which it is drawn is at the height recommended by the manufacturer of the trailer.

(6) In this Regulation:—

'rear under-run protective device' means a device within the description given in paragraph II.5.4 in the Annex to the Council Directive;

'the Council Directive' means Council Directive 70/221/EEC of 20th March 1970 *[OJ L76, 6.4.70, p 23]* as amended by Commission Directive 79/490/EEC of 18th April 1979 *[OJ L128, 26.5.79, p 22]*;

'outermost part', in relation to a vehicle, does not include a door, hinged side or other adjustable part of the vehicle when opened or extended or a driving mirror or direction indicator.]

[Regulation 46B was inserted by SI 1982 No 1576 and is printed as amended by SI 1983 No 471; SI 1984 No 195; SI 1984 No 813; and SI 1984 No 1809.]

[46C. Sideguards

(1) Save as provided in paragraph (2) below, on and after 1st May 1983 every semi-trailer [which has a relevant plate showing a gross weight exceeding 26000 kilograms] shall be securely fitted with a sideguard to give protection on any side of the vehicle where the distance between its foremost axle and the centre of its king pin, or in the case of a vehicle which has more than one king pin, the rearmost one, exceeds 4.5 metres.

(2) The requirements specified in paragraph (1) above do not apply—

(*a*) in a case where the relevant train weight of an articulated vehicle of which the semi-trailer forms a part does not exceed 32520 kilograms, or

(*b*) to a semi-trailer to which Regulation 46D applies or which is a vehicle mentioned in paragraph (2) of that Regulation [or]

[(*c*) until the 1st January 1984, to a semi-trailer forming part of an articulated vehicle the total laden weight of which does not exceed 32520 kilograms.]

(3) A sideguard with which a vehicle is by this Regulation required to be fitted shall comply with the specifications listed, in relation to vehicles to which Regulation 46D applies, in paragraph (5) (*a*) to (*k*) of that Regulation save as provided in paragraph (6) of that Regulation.]

[Regulation 46C was inserted by SI 1982 No 1576 and is printed as amended by SI 1983 No 471.]

[46D.—(1) Save as provided in paragraph (2) below, this Regulation applies to every goods vehicle being either—

(*a*) a motor vehicle with a maximum gross weight (determined as provided in Part I of Schedule 2 to these Regulations) which exceeds 3500 kilograms and which is manufactured on or after 1st October 1983 and first used on or after 1st April 1984; or

(*b*) a trailer with an unladen weight which exceeds 1020 kilograms and which is manufactured on or after 1st May 1983.

(2) This Regulation does not apply to—

(*a*) a motor vehicle which is incapable by reason of its construction of exceeding a speed of 15 miles per hour on the level under its own power;

(*b*) an agricultural trailer;

(*c*) engineering plant;

(*d*) a fire engine;

(*e*) [an agricultural motor vehicle];

(*f*) a vehicle so constructed that it can be unloaded by part of the vehicle being tipped sideways or rearwards;

(*g*) a vehicle owned by the Secretary of State for Defence and used for naval, military or air force purposes;

[(*h*) a vehicle to which no bodywork has been fitted and which is being driven or towed—

    (i) for the purpose of a quality or safety check by its manufacturer or a dealer in, or distributor of, such vehicles;

    (ii) to a place where, by previous arrangement, bodywork is to be fitted or work preparatory to the fitting of bodywork is to be carried out; or

    (iii) by previous arrangement to premises of a dealer in, or distributor of, such vehicles;]

(*i*) a vehicle which is being driven or towed to a place where by previous arrangement a sideguard is to be fitted so that it complies with this Regulation;

(*j*) a vehicle designed solely for use and used solely in connection with street cleansing, the collection or disposal of refuse or the collection or disposal of the contents of gullies or cesspools;

(*k*) a trailer specially designed and constructed, and not merely adapted, to carry round timber, beams or girders, being items of exceptional length;

(*l*) a motor car or a heavy motor car constructed or adapted to form part of an articulated vehicle;

[(*m*) a [[vehicle]] specially designed and constructed, and not merely adapted, to carry other vehicles loaded on it from the front or the rear;]

[(*n*) a trailer with a load platform—

    (i) no part of any edge of which is more than 60 millimetres inboard from the plane described in paragraph (5) (*c*) (i); and

    (ii) the upper surface of which is not more than 750 millimetres from the ground over whichever distance specified in paragraph (5) (*d*) to (*g*) would be applicable to the trailer if this exemption did not apply to it; . . .]

[(*o*) a trailer having a base or centre in a country outside Great Britain from which it normally starts its journeys, provided that a period of not more than 12 months has elapsed since the vehicle was last brought into Great Britain;]

[(*p*) [an agricultural trailed appliance].]

(3) Every vehicle to which this Regulation applies shall be securely fitted with a sideguard to give protection on any side of the vehicle where—

(*a*) in the case of a semi-trailer, the distance between the transverse vertical planes through the centre of its foremost axle and through the centre of its king pin or, in the case of a vehicle having more than one king pin, the rearmost one, exceeds 4.5 metres;

(*b*) in the case of any other vehicle, the distance between the centres of any two consecutive axles exceeds 3 metres.

(4) Save as provided in [paragraphs (6) and (7)] below, a sideguard with which a vehicle is by this Regulation required to be fitted shall comply with all the specifications listed in paragraph (5) below.

(5) The specifications mentioned in paragraph (4) above are as follows:—

[(*a*) the outermost surface of every sideguard shall be smooth, essentially rigid and either flat or horizontally corrugated, save that:—

(i) any part of the surface may overlap another provided that the overlapping edges face rearwards or downwards,

(ii) a gap not exceeding 25 millimetres measured longitudinally may exist between any two adjacent parts of the surface provided that the foremost edge of the rearward part does not protrude outboard of the rearmost edge of the forward part, and

(iii) domed heads of bolts or rivets may protrude beyond the surface to a distance not exceeding 10 millimetres;]

(*b*) no part of the lowest edge of a sideguard shall be more than 550 millimetres above the ground when the vehicle to which it is fitted is on level ground[, and in the case of a semi-trailer when its load platform is horizontal];

(*c*) in a case specified in an item in column 2 of the Table below the highest edge of a sideguard shall be as specified in that item in column 3 of that Table;

(*d*) the distance between the rearmost edge of a sideguard and the vertical plane passing through the foremost part of the tyre fitted to the wheel of that vehicle nearest to it shall not exceed 300 millimetres;

(*e*) the distance between the foremost edge of a sideguard fitted to a semi-trailer not fitted with landing legs and a transverse vertical plane passing through the centre of the vehicle's king pin or, if the vehicle has more than one king pin, the rearmost one, shall not exceed 3 metres;

(*f*) the foremost edge of a sideguard fitted to a semi-trailer fitted with landing legs shall not be more than—

(i) 250 millimetres from a transverse plane passing through the centre of the leg nearest to that edge in a case where that edge is not more than 3 metres from a transverse vertical plane passing through the centre of the vehicle's king pin or, if the vehicle has more than one king pin, the rearmost one; and

(ii) in any other case 3 metres from a transverse vertical plane passing through the centre of the vehicle's king pin or, if the vehicle has more than one king pin, the rearmost one;

(*g*) the distance between the foremost edge of a sideguard fitted to a vehicle other than a semi-trailer and a vertical plane passing through the rearmost part of the tyre fitted to the wheel of that vehicle nearest to the sideguard shall not exceed 300 millimetres if the vehicle is a motor vehicle and 500 millimetres if the vehicle is a trailer;

(*h*) the external edges of a sideguard shall be rounded at a radius of at least 2.5 millimetres;

(*i*) no sideguard shall be more than 30 millimetres inboard from a vertical plane passing through the external face of the tyre (excluding any distortion caused by the weight of the vehicle) fitted to the outermost wheel at the rear of the vehicle on the same side of the vehicle;

(*j*) no sideguard shall project beyond the plane from which, in the absence of a sideguard, the vehicle's overall width (as defined in Regulation 3) would fall to be measured;

(*k*) every sideguard shall cover an area extending to at least 100 millimetres downwards from its highest edge, 100 millimetres upwards from its lowest edge and 100 millimetres rearwards and inwards from its foremost edge, and no sideguard shall have a vertical gap measuring more than 300 millimetres nor any vertical surface measuring less than 100 millimetres; and (*l*) be capable of withstanding a force of 2 kilonewtons applied perpendicularly to any part of its surface by the centre of a ram the face of which is circular and not more than 220 millimetres in diameter, and during such application—

  (i) no part of the sideguard shall be deflected by more than 150 millimetres, and

  (ii) no part of the sideguard which is less than 250 millimetres from its rearmost part shall be deflected by more than 30 millimetres.

[In this paragraph 'tangential plane', in relation to a sideguard, means the vertical plane tangential to the external face of the outermost part of the tyre (excluding any distortion caused by the weight of the vehicle) fitted to the outermost wheel at the rear and on the same side of the vehicle.]

[(6) The provisions of paragraph (4) apply—

(*a*) in the case of an extendible trailer when it is, by virtue of the extending mechanism, extended to a length greater than its minimum, so as not to require, in respect of any additional distance solely attributable to the extension, compliance with the specifications mentioned in paragraph (5) (*d*) to (*g*);

(*b*) in the case of a vehicle designed and constructed, and not merely adapted, to be fitted with a demountable body or to carry a container (as defined in Regulation 80A (4)), when it is not fitted with a demountable body or carrying such a container as if it were fitted with such a body or carrying such a container; and

(*c*) only so far as is practicable in the case of—

  (i) a vehicle designed solely for the carriage of a fluid substance in a closed tank which is permanently fitted to the vehicle and provided with valves and hose or pipe connections for loading or unloading; and

  (ii) a vehicle which requires additional stability during loading or unloading or while being used for operations for which it is designed or adapted and is fitted on one or both sides with an extendible device to provide such stability.]

[(7) In the case of a motor vehicle to which this Regulation applies and which is of a type which was required to be approved under the Motor Vehicles (Type Approval for Goods Vehicles) (Great Britain) Regulations 1982 *[SI 1982 No 1271]* before 1st October 1983—

(*a*) if the bodywork of the vehicle covers the whole of the area specified as regards a sideguard in paragraph (5) (*b*), (*c*), (*d*) and (*g*) above the other provisions of that paragraph do not apply to that vehicle; and

(*b*) if the bodywork of the vehicle covers only part of that area the part of that area which is not so covered shall be fitted with a sideguard which complies with the provisions of paragraph (5) above save that there shall not be a gap between—

  (i) the rearmost edge of the sideguard or the rearmost part of the bodywork (whichever is furthest to the rear) and the vertical plane mentioned in (*d*) of more than 300 millimetres;

  (ii) the foremost edge of the sideguard or the foremost part of the bodywork (whichever is furthest to the front) and the vertical plane mentioned in (*g*) of more than 300 millimetres;

  (iii) any vertical or sloping edge of any part of the bodywork in question and the edge of the sideguard immediately forwards or rearwards thereof of more than 25 millimetres measured horizontally.]]

[Regulation 46D was inserted by SI 1982 No 1576 and is printed as amended by SI 1983 No 471; SI 1984 No 195; SI 1984 No 813; and SI 1984 No 1809.]

TABLE (SH7A)

[TABLE *[ie table to reg 46D]*

1 Item No	2 Case	3 Requirement about highest edge of sideguard

1	Where the floor of the vehicle to which the sideguard is fitted—
	  (i) extends laterally outside the tangential plane,
	  (ii) is not more than 1.85 metres from the ground,
	  (iii) extends laterally over the whole of the length as specified in sub-paragraphs (*d*) to (*g*) below of the sideguard with which the vehicle is required by this Regulation to be fitted, and
	  (iv) is wholly covered at its edge by a side-rave the lower edge of which is not more than 150 millimetres below the under-side of the floor.
		Not more than 350 millimetres below the lower edge of the side-rave.

2	Where the floor of the vehicle to which the sideguard is fitted—
	  (i) extends laterally as specified in sub-paragraph (i) in item 1 above, and
	  (ii) does not comply with one or more of the provisions specified in sub-paragraphs (ii), (iii) and (iv) in item 1 above,
	and any part of the structure of the vehicle is cut within 1.85 metres of the ground by the tangential plane.
		Not more than 350 millimetres below the structure of the vehicle where it is cut by the tangential plane.

3	Where—
	  (i) no part of the structure of the vehicle is cut within 1.85 metres of the ground by the tangential plane, and
	  (ii) the upper surface of the load carrying structure of the vehicle is less than 1.5 metres from the ground.
		Not less than the height of the upper surface of the load-carrying structure of the vehicle.

4	A vehicle specially designed and not merely adapted, for the carriage and mixing of liquid concrete.	Not less than 1 metre from the ground.
5	Any other case.	Not less than 1.5 metres from the ground. ;]

[46E. Containment and suppression of spray

(1) The requirements specified in paragraph (2) below apply in respect of every goods vehicle, except a vehicle of a class specified in paragraph (5) below, which is—

(a) a motor vehicle, manufactured on or after 1st October 1985, and first used on or after 1st April 1986 having a maximum gross weight (determined as provided in Part I of Schedule 2 to these Regulations) exceeding 12 tonnes,

(b) a trailer, manufactured on or after 1st May 1985, having a maximum gross weight (determined as provided in Part II of Schedule 2 to these Regulations) exceeding 3·5 tonnes, or

(c) a trailer, whenever manufactured, having a maximum gross weight (determined as provided in Part II of Schedule 2 to these Regulations) exceeding 16 tonnes and with 2 or more axles.

(2) The requirements referred to in paragraph (1) above are that—

(a) in the case of a trailer manufactured before 1st January 1975, on and after 1st October 1987,

(b) in the case of a trailer manufactured on or after 1st January 1975 but before 1st May 1985, on and after 1st October 1986,

(c) in the case of a trailer manufactured on or after 1st May 1985, on or after that date, and

(d) in the case of every other vehicle to which this Regulation applies, on and after 1st April 1986,

the vehicle shall be fitted, in relation to the wheels on each of its axles, with such containment devices as satisfy the technical requirements and other provisions about containment devices specified in the British Standards Specification:

Provided that—

in the case of a containment device fitted before 1st January 1985, the said requirements shall be deemed to be complied with if that containment device substantially conforms to those requirements.

(3) In this Regulation 'the British Standards Specification' means the British Standard Specification for Spray Reducing Devices for Heavy Goods Vehicles published under the reference BS AU 200: Part 1: 1984 and BS AU 200: Part 2: 1984 and references to a 'containment device', a 'suppression device' and an 'air/water separator' are references to the devices respectively so described in the British Standards Specification.

(4) Nothing in this Regulation derogates from any requirement specified in Regulations 61, 66 or 79.

(5) The classes of vehicle exempted from the requirements specified in paragraph (2) above are—

(a) a motor vehicle so constructed that the driving power of its engine is, or can by use of its controls be, transmitted to all the wheels on at least one front axle and on at least one rear axle;

(b) a motor vehicle where the shortest distance between the ground and the lowest part of that portion of the vehicle which lies within the area formed by the overall length of the vehicle and the middle 80 per cent of the shortest distance between the inner edges of any two wheels on opposite sides of the vehicle (excluding any bulging of the tyres near the ground) ascertained when the vehicle is—

    (i) fitted with suitable tyres inflated to a pressure recommended by the manufacturer, and

    (ii) standing on reasonably flat ground,

is not less than 400 millimetres;

(c) a works truck;

(d) a works trailer;

(e) a broken-down vehicle;

(f) a motor vehicle which is incapable by reason of its construction of exceeding a speed of 30 miles per hour on the level under its own power;

(g) a vehicle of a kind specified in sub-paragraphs (b), (c), (d), (f), (g), (h), (j), (k), (o), or (p) of Regulation 46D(2);

(h) a vehicle specially designed, and not merely adapted, for the carriage and mixing of liquid concrete;

(i) a vehicle which is being driven or towed to a place where by previous arrangement a device is to be fitted so that it complies with the requirements specified in paragraphs (1), (2) and (3) above;

(j) [an agricultural motor vehicle and an agricultural trailed appliance conveyor].]

[*Regulation 46E was inserted by SI 1984 No 1543 and is printed as amended by SI 1984 No 1809.*]

B *Gas Containers*

*   *   *

C *Locomotives*

48. Overall width

The overall width of a locomotive shall not exceed 2.75 metres.

*   *   *

Brakes

50. Every locomotive first used before 1st June 1955 shall be equipped with an efficient braking system, the brakes of which act upon all the wheels of the vehicle other than the steering wheels, and so designed and constructed that the application of the brakes will bring the vehicle to rest within a reasonable distance:

Provided that this Regulation shall not apply to a locomotive first used on or before 2nd January 1933 if the locomotive is propelled by steam and the engine thereof is capable of being reversed.

51.—[(1) This regulation applies to every locomotive first used on or after 1st June 1955.]

[(2) Every locomotive to which this paragraph applies shall be equipped with an efficient braking system or efficient braking systems in either case having two means of operation, so designed and constructed that notwithstanding the failure of any part thereof (other than a fixed member or a brake shoe anchor pin) through or by means of which the force necessary to apply the brakes is transmitted, there shall still be available for application by the driver brakes which—

(*a*) are sufficient under the most adverse conditions to bring the vehicle to rest within a reasonable distance, and

(*b*) apply to not less than half the number of the wheels of the vehicle:

Provided that this paragraph shall not apply in the case of a road roller if the vehicle is equipped with one braking system with one means of operation.]

[(2A) *[Revoked.]*]

(3) The application of one means of operation shall not affect or operate the pedal or hand lever of the other means of operation.

(4) No braking system shall be rendered ineffective by the non-rotation of the engine.

(5) All the brakes which are operated by one of the means of operation shall be capable of being applied by direct mechanical action without the intervention of any hydraulic, electric or pneumatic device.

(6) Where any brake shoe is capable of being applied by more than one means of operation, all the wheels of a locomotive to which [this paragraph applies] shall be fitted with brakes all of which are operated by one of the means of operation:
Provided that—

(*a*) where a vehicle has more than six wheels, at least four of which are steering wheels, it shall be a sufficient compliance with this paragraph if brakes are fitted to all the wheels, other than two steering wheels which are situated on opposite sides of the vehicle, and if all such brakes are operated by one of the means of operation;

(*b*) where a vehicle has more than four wheels and the drive is transmitted to all wheels other than the steering wheels without the interposition of a differential driving gear or similar mechanism between the axles carrying the driving wheels, it shall be deemed to be a sufficient compliance with this paragraph if one means of operation operates the brakes on two driving wheels situated on opposite sides of the vehicle and the other means of operation operates brakes on all the other wheels required to be fitted with brakes by this paragraph; and

(*c*) where means of operation are provided in addition to those prescribed by this Regulation such additional means of operation may be disregarded for the purposes of this paragraph.

(7) One at least of the means of operation shall be capable of causing brakes to be applied directly, and not through the transmission gear, to not less than half the number of the wheels of the vehicle:
Provided that where a locomotive to which [this paragraph applies] has more than four wheels and the drive is transmitted to all wheels other than the steering wheels without the interposition of a differential driving gear or similar mechanism between the axles carrying the driving wheels, it shall be deemed to be a sufficient compliance with this paragraph if the brakes applied by one means of operation act directly on two driving wheels on opposite sides of the vehicle and the brakes applied by the other means of operation act directly on all other driving wheels.

(8) For the purpose of this Regulation—

(*a*) not more than one front wheel shall be included in half the number of the wheels of the vehicle for the purposes aforesaid except that this provision shall not apply to a locomotive with more than three wheels, whether or not any brake shoe is capable of being applied by more than one means of operation, if as respects the fitting of its wheels with brakes and the operation of these brakes the provisions of paragraph (6) of this Regulation relating to such matters are complied with; and

(*b*) every moving shaft to which any part of a braking system or any means of operation therof is connected or by which it is supported shall be deemed to be part of that system.

[Regulation 51 is printed as amended by SI 1979 No 138, and SI 1984 No 1809.]

* * *

D *Motor Tractors*

53. Overall width

The overall width of a motor tractor shall not exceed 2.5 metres.

54. Overhang

The overhang of a motor tractor shall not exceed 1.83 metres.

55. Brakes

(1) [Every motor tractor, not being . . . an industrial tractor], shall be equipped] with an efficient braking system or efficient braking systems, in either case having two means of operation, so designed and constructed that, notwithstanding the failure of any part (other than a fixed member or a brake shoe anchor pin) through or by means of which the force necessary to apply the brakes is transmitted, there shall still be available for application by the driver to not less than half the number of the wheels of the vehicle brakes sufficient under the most adverse conditions to bring the vehicle to rest within a reasonable distance:

Provided that this paragraph shall not apply in the case of a road roller . . . , not propelled by steam, if the vehicle is equipped with one braking system with one means of operation.

[(1A) Every . . . industrial tractor] shall be equipped with an efficient braking system or efficient braking systems so designed and constructed that notwithstanding the failure of any part thereof there shall still be available for application by the driver a brake sufficient under the most adverse conditions to bring the vehicle to rest within a reasonable distance.]

(2) The application of one means of operation shall not affect or operate the pedal or hand lever of the other means of operation.

(3) In the case of vehicles first used on or after 1st April 1938 no braking system shall be rendered ineffective by the non-rotation of the engine:

Provided that this paragraph shall not apply in the case of any vehicle referred to in sub-paragraph (*b*) of paragraph (7) of this Regulation.

(4) In the case of a motor tractor first used on or after 1st April 1938 all the brakes which are operated by one of the means of operation shall be capable of being applied by direct mechanical action without the intervention of any hydraulic, electric or pneumatic device.

(5) [[Except in the case of . . . or an industrial tractor], where any brake shoe] is capable of being applied by more than one means of operation, all the wheels of the motor tractor shall be fitted with brakes all of which are operated by one of the means of operation:

Provided that where means of operation are provided in addition to those prescribed by this Regulation such additional means of operation may be disregarded for the purposes of this paragraph.

(6) In the case of a motor tractor first used after 14th January 1931, [other than . . . an industrial tractor], one at least of the means of operation shall be capable of causing brakes to be applied directly, and not through the transmission gear, to not less than half the number of the wheels of the vehicle:

Provided that where a motor tractor has more than four wheels and the drive is transmitted to all wheels other than the steering wheels without the interposition of a differential driving gear or similar mechanism between the axles carrying the driving wheels, it shall be deemed to be a sufficient compliance with this paragraph if the brakes applied by one means of operation act directly on two driving wheels on opposite sides of the vehicle and the brakes applied by the other means of operation act directly on all other driving wheels.

(7) For the purpose of this Regulation—

(a) in the case of a motor tractor first used on or after 1st October 1938—

    (i) not more than one front wheel shall be included in half the number of the wheels of the vehicle for the purposes aforesaid except that this provision shall not apply to a motor tractor with more than three wheels, whether or not any brake shoe is capable of being applied by more than one means of operation, if as respects the fitting of its wheels with brakes and the operation of those brakes the provisions of paragraph (5) of this Regulation relating to such matters are complied with, and

    (ii) every moving shaft to which any part of a braking system or any means of operation thereof is connected or by which it is supported shall be deemed to be part of that system; and

(b) in the case of a motor tractor propelled by steam the engine shall be deemed to be an efficient braking system with one means of operation if the engine is capable of being reversed and, in the case of a motor tractor first used on or after 1st October 1943, is incapable of being disconnected from any of the driving wheels of the vehicle except by the sustained effort of the driver.

[Regulation 55 is printed as amended by SI 1979 No 138, SI 1981 No 1580, and SI 1984 No 1809.]

*   *   *

E *Heavy Motor Cars*

57. Overall width

The overall width of a heavy motor car shall not exceed 2.5 metres.

58. Overhang

The overhang of a heavy motor car shall not exceed 60 per cent of the distance between the plane perpendicular to the longitudinal axis of the vehicle which passes through the centre or centres of the front wheel or wheels and the foremost vertical plane from which the overhang is to be measured as defined in Regulation 3:
Provided that—

(a) in the case of a vehicle designed for use and mainly used for the purpose of heating a road or other like surface in the process of construction, repair or maintenance, no part of the heating plant shall be taken into account when calculating the overhang; and

(*b*) this Regulation shall not apply in the case of—
    (i) a heavy motor car first used before 15th August 1928,
    (ii) a heavy motor car designed for use and used solely in connection with street cleansing, the collection or disposal of refuse or the collection or disposal of the contxents of gullies or cesspools,
    (iii) a works truck, . . .
    (iv) a heavy motor car designed so that it can dispose of its load by tipping to the rear, if the overhang does not exceed 1.15 metres [, or]
  [(v) an articulated bus.]

[Regulation 58 is printed as amended by SI 1981 No 261.]

59. Brakes

(1) Save as provided in paragraph (2) of this Regulation, every heavy motor car shall be equipped either with an efficient braking system having two means of operation or with two efficient braking systems each having a separate means of operation:

Provided that for the purpose of this paragraph no account shall be taken in the case of a heavy motor car first used on or after 1st January 1968 of a multi-pull means of operation, unless that means, at the first application, operates an hydraulic, electric or pneumatic device which causes brakes to be applied sufficient to have a total braking efficiency of not less than the total braking efficiency required by paragraph (5) (*b*) of this Regulation in relation to brakes as applied by a second independent means of operation.

[(2) Nothing in—

(*a*) any part of this Regulation shall apply to a heavy motor car to which Regulation 14A applies;

(*b*) paragraph (1) or (3) of this Regulation shall apply to a heavy motor car equipped with one efficient braking system with one means of operation and which is a split braking system.]

(3) Save as provided in paragraph (2) of this Regulation, the braking system or braking systems of every heavy motor car first used after 15th August 1928 shall be so designed and constructed that, notwithstanding the failure of any part (other than a fixed member or a brake shoe anchor pin) through or by means of which the force necessary to apply the brakes is transmitted, there shall still be available for application by the driver to not less than half the number of the wheels of the vehicle brakes sufficient under the most adverse conditions to bring the vehicle to rest within a reasonable distance.

(4) The braking system or braking systems of every heavy motor car to which Schedule 4 applies and first used before 1st January 1968 shall comply with the requirements of that Schedule relating to the efficiency of the brakes of such heavy motor cars.

(5) The braking system or braking systems of every heavy motor car first used on or after 1st January 1968, which is not a works truck or a pedestrian controlled vehicle, shall—

(*a*) have brakes acting on all the wheels of the vehicle which as applied by one means of operation have a total braking efficiency of not less than 50 per cent;

(*b*) except in the case mentioned in the following sub-paragraph (*c*), have brakes which as applied by a second independent means of operation have a total braking efficiency of not less than 25 per cent;

(c) in the case of a heavy motor car equipped with a split braking system in accordance with paragraph (2) of this Regulaton, have brakes which in the event of a failure of any part (other than a fixed member or a brake shoe anchor pin) of one of the independent sections comprised in the split braking system are such that there remain brakes applied by the other section sufficient to have a total braking efficiency of not less than 25 per cent.

(6) The braking system or braking systems of every heavy motor car first used after 15th August 1928 and before 1st January 1968 and which is a goods vehicle other than a pedestrian controlled vehicle or a works truck and is a rigid vehicle with two axles shall—

(a) have brakes which as applied by one means of operation have a total braking efficiency of not less than 45 per cent;

(b) except in the case mentioned in the following sub-paragraph (c), have brakes which as applied by a second independent means of operation have a total braking efficiency of not less than 20 per cent;

(c) in the case of a heavy motor car equipped with a split braking system in accordance with paragraph (2) of this Regulation, have brakes which in the event of a failure of any part (other than a fixed member or a brake shoe anchor pin) of one of the independent sections comprised in the split braking system are such that there remain brakes applied by the other section sufficient to have a total braking efficiency of not less than 20 per cent.

(7) The braking system or braking systems of every heavy motor car first used after 15th August 1928 and before 1st January 1968 and which is a goods vehicle other than a pedestrian controlled vehicle or a works truck and is a rigid vehicle with more than two axles or is constructed or adapted to form part of an articulated vehicle shall—

(a) have brakes which as applied by one means of operation have a total braking efficiency of not less than 40 per cent;

(b) except in the case mentioned in the following sub-paragraph (c), have brakes which as applied by a second independent means of operation have a total braking efficiency of not less than 15 per cent;

(c) in the case of a heavy motor car equipped with a split braking system in accordance with paragraph (2) of this Regulation, have brakes which in the event of a failure of any part (other than a fixed member or a brake shoe anchor pin) of one of the independent sections comprised in the split braking system are such that there remain brakes applied by the other section sufficient to have a total braking efficiency of not less than 15 per cent.

(8) The braking system or braking systems of every heavy motor car first used on or before 15th August 1928, not being a heavy motor car to which Schedule 4 applies, shall be sufficient under the most adverse conditions to bring the vehicle to rest within a reasonable distance.

(9) Paragraphs (1) and (3) of this Regulation shall not apply in the case of a works truck if it is equipped with one braking system having one means of operation.

(10) The application of one means of operation shall not affect or operate the pedal or hand lever of the other means of operation.

(11) In the case of vehicles first used on or after 1st April 1938 no braking system shall be rendered ineffective by the non-rotation of the engine:

Provided that this paragraph shall not apply in the case of any vehicle referred to in paragraph (16)(*b*) of this Regulation.

(12) All the brakes of a heavy motor car which are operated by one means of operation shall be capable of being applied by direct mechanical action without the intervention of any hydraulic, electric or pneumatic device:

Provided that this paragraph shall not apply to a heavy motor car which satisfies the requirements of Regulation 13 (2) of these Regulations.

(13) In the case of a heavy motor car first used before 1st January 1968, where any brake shoe is capable of being applied by more than one means of operation all the wheels of the heavy motor car shall be fitted with brakes all of which are operated by one of the means of operation:

Provided that—

(*a*) where a heavy motor car has more than six wheels, at least four of which are steering wheels, it shall be a sufficient compliance with this paragraph if brakes are fitted to all the wheels, other than two steering wheels which are situated on opposite sides of the vehicle, and all such brakes are operated by one of the means of operation;

(*b*) where a heavy motor car has more than four wheels and the drive is transmitted to all wheels other than the steering wheels without the interposition of a differential driving gear or similar mechanism between the axles carrying the driving wheels, it shall be deemed to be a sufficient compliance with this paragraph if one means of operation operates the brakes on two driving wheels situated on opposite sides of the vehicle and the other means of operation operates brakes on all the other wheels required to be fitted with brakes by this paragraph; and

(*c*) where means of operation are provided in addition to those prescribed by this Regulation such additional means of operation may be disregarded for the purposes of this paragraph.

(14) [Except in the case of a works truck with an unladen weight not exceeding 7,370 kilograms, one at least of the means of operation] shall be capable of causing brakes to be applied directly, and not through the transmission gear, to not less than half the number of the wheels of the vehicle:

Provided that—

(*a*) in the case of a heavy motor car having brakes acting on all the wheels of the vehicle and capable of being applied by one means of operation, any shaft leading from any differential driving gear of an axle to a driving wheel shall be deemed not to form part of the transmission gear;

(*b*) where in the case of any other heavy motor car it has more than four wheels and the drive is transmitted to all wheels other than the steering wheels without the interposition of a differential driving gear or similar mechanism between the axles carrying the driving wheels, it shall be deemed to be a sufficient compliance with this paragraph if the brakes applied by one means of operation act directly on two driving wheels on opposite sides of the vehicle and the brakes applied by the other means of operation act directly on all other driving wheels.

(15) Paragraphs (10) to (14) inclusive of this Regulation shall not apply to a heavy motor car first used on or before 15th August 1928.

(16) For the purposes of this Regulation—

(*a*) in the case of any motor vehicle—

(i) not more than one front wheel shall be included in half the number of the wheels of the vehicle for the purposes aforesaid except that this provision shall not apply either to a heavy motor car with more than three wheels, whether or not any brake shoe is capable of being applied by more than one means of operation, if as respects the fitting of its wheels with brakes and the operation of those brakes the provisions of paragraph (13) of this Regulation relating to such matters are complied with, or to a works truck, and

(ii) every moving shaft to which any part of a braking system or any means of operation thereof is connected or by which it is supported shall be deemed to be part of that system; and

(b) in the case of a heavy motor car propelled by steam and not used as a public service vehicle the engine shall be deemed to be an efficient braking system with one means of operation if the engine is capable of being reversed and, in the case of a heavy motor car first used on or after 1st January 1927, is incapable of being disconnected from any of the driving wheels of the vehicle except by the sustained effort of the driver.

[Regulation 59 is printed as amended by SI 1981 No 1189 and SI 1981 No 1580.]

*   *   *

61. Wings

A heavy motor car shall be equipped with wings or other similar fittings to catch, so far as practicable, mud or water thrown up by the rotation of the wheels, unless adequate protection is afforded by the body of the vehicle:
Provided that this Regulation shall not apply—

(a) in relation to the rear wheels of any heavy motor car for the time being forming part of an articulated vehicle if the trailer forming the remaining part of the articulated vehicle is used only for or, when empty, in connection with the carriage of round timber;

(b) in the case of a vehicle in an unfinished condition proceeding to a works for completion; or

(c) in the case of a works truck.

F *Motor Cars*

62. Overall width

The overall width of a motor car shall not exceed 2.5 metres.

63. Overhang

The overhang of a motor car shall not exceed 60 per cent of the distance between the plane perpendicular to the longitudinal axis of the vehicle which passes through the centre or centres of the front wheel or wheels and the foremost vertical plane from which the overhang is to be measured as defined in Regulation 3:
Provided that—

(a) in the case of a motor car first used before 1st January 1966 the overhang may be increased by not more than 76 millimetres, if the distance between the foremost and rearmost axles does not exceed 2.29 metres; and

(b) this Regulation shall not apply in the case of—
(i) a motor car first used on or before 2nd January 1933,

(ii) a motor car designed for use and used solely in connection with street cleansing, the collection or disposal of refuse or the collection or disposal of the contents of gullies or cesspools or as an ambulance, or

(iii) a works truck.

64. Brakes

(1) Save as provided in paragraph (2) of this Regulation, every motor car shall be equipped either with an efficient braking system having two means of operation or with two efficient braking systems each having a separate means of operation:

Provided that for the purpose of this paragraph no account shall be taken in the case of a motor car first used on or after 1st January 1968 of a multi-pull means of operation, unless that means, at the first application, operates an hydraulic, electric or pneumatic device which causes brakes to be applied sufficient to have a total braking efficiency of not less than the total braking efficiency required by paragraph (5)(b) of this Regulation in relation to brakes as applied by a second independent means of operation.

[(2) Nothing in—

(a) any part of this Regulation shall apply to a motor car to which Regulation 14A applies;

(b) paragraph (1) or (3) of this Regulation shall apply to a motor car equipped with one efficient braking system with one means of operation and which is a split braking system.]

(3) Save as provided in paragraph (2) of this Regulation, the braking system or braking systems of every motor car shall be so designed and constructed that notwithstanding the failure of any part (other than a fixed member or a brake shoe anchor pin) through or by means of which the force necessary to apply the brakes is transmitted there shall still be available for application by the driver to not less than half the number of the wheels of the vehicle brakes sufficient under the most adverse conditions to bring the vehicle to rest within a reasonable distance:

Provided that in the event of such failure as aforesaid it shall not be necessary for brakes to be available for application by the driver—

(a) in the case of a motor car first used before 1st October 1938, to more than two wheels;

(b) in the case of a vehicle having less than four wheels, to more than one wheel.

(4) The braking system or braking systems of every motor car to which Schedule 4 applies and first used before 1st January 1968 shall comply with the requirements of that Schedule relating to the efficiency of the brakes of such motor cars.

(5) The braking system or braking systems of every motor car first used on or after 1st January 1968 which is not a works truck or a pedestrian controlled vehicle shall—

(a) have brakes acting on all the wheels of the vehicle which as applied by one means of operation have a total braking efficiency of not less than 50 per cent;

(b) except in the case mentioned in the following sub-paragraph (c), have brakes which as applied by a second independent means of operation have a total braking efficiency of not less than 25 per cent;

(c) in the case of a motor car equipped with a split braking system in accordance with paragraph (2) of this Regulation, have brakes which in the event of a failure of any part (other than a fixed member or a brake shoe anchor pin) of one of the independent sections comprised in the split braking system are such that there remain brakes applied by the other section sufficient to have a total braking efficiency of not less than 20 per cent.

(6) The braking system, or braking systems of every motor car first used after 1st January 1915 and before 1st January 1968 and which is a goods vehicle exceeding 1525 kilograms in unladen weight other than a dual-purpose vehicle, a pedestrian controlled vehicle or a works truck and is a rigid vehicle with two axles shall—

(a) have brakes which as applied by one means of operation have a total braking efficiency of not less than 45 per cent;

(b) except in the case mentioned in the following sub-paragraph (c), have brakes which as applied by a second independent means of operation have a total braking efficiency of not less than 20 per cent;

(c) in the case of a motor car equipped with a split braking system in accordance with paragraph (2) of this Regulation, have brakes which in the event of a failure of any part (other than a fixed member or a brake shoe anchor pin) of one of the independent sections comprised in the split braking system are such that there remain brakes applied by the other section sufficient to have a total braking efficiency of not less than 20 per cent.

(7) The braking system or braking systems of every motor car first used after 1st January 1915 and before 1st January 1968 and which is a goods vehicle exceeding 1525 kilograms in unladen weight other than a dual-purpose vehicle, a pedestrian controlled vehicle or a works truck and is a rigid vehicle with more than two axles or is constructed or adapted to form part of an articulated vehicle shall—

(a) have brakes which as applied by one means of operation have a total braking efficiency of not less than 40 per cent;

(b) except in the case mentioned in the following sub-paragraph (c), have brakes which as applied by a second independent means of operation have a total braking efficiency of not less than 15 per cent;

(c) in the case of a motor car equipped with a split braking system in accordance with paragraph (2) of this Regulation, have brakes which in the event of a failure of any part (other than a fixed member or a brake shoe anchor pin) of one of the independent sections comprised in the split braking system are such that there remain brakes applied by the other section sufficient to have a total braking efficiency of not less than 15 per cent.

(8) Paragraphs (1) and (3) of this Regulation shall not apply in the case of a motor car first registered under the Motor Car Act 1903 before 1st January 1915 but—

(a) such a motor car shall be equipped with an efficient braking system;

(b) that system shall be so designed and constructed that brakes shall be available for application by the driver, in the case of a vehicle with not less than four wheels, to two wheels of the vehicle, and in the case of a vehicle with less than four wheels, to one wheel of the vehicle; and

(c) if such a motor car is not one to which Schedule 4 applies, the brakes required by the foregoing sub-paragraph to be available for application shall be brakes sufficient under the most adverse conditions to bring the vehicle to rest within a reasonable distance.

(9) The foregoing paragraphs of this Regulation shall not apply in the case of a works truck if it is equipped with one braking system with one means of operation.

(10) The application of one means of operation shall not affect or operate the pedal or hand lever of the other means of operation.

(11) In the case of vehicles first used on or after 1st April 1938, no braking system shall be rendered ineffective by the non-rotation of the engine:

Provided that this paragraph shall not apply in the case of any vehicle referred to in paragraph (15)(*b*) of this Regulation.

(12) All the brakes of a motor car which are operated by one of the means of operation shall be capable of being applied by direct mechanical action without the intervention of any hydraulic, electric or pneumatic device:

Provided that this paragraph shall not apply to a motor car which satisfies the requirements of Regulation 13 (2).

(13) In the case of a motor car first used before 1st January 1968 with more than three wheels where any brake shoe is capable of being applied by more than one means of operation all the wheels shall be fitted with brakes all of which are operated by one of the means of operation:

Provided that—

(*a*) where a motor car has more than six wheels, at least four of which are steering wheels, it shall be a sufficient compliance with this paragraph if brakes are fitted to all the wheels, other than two steering wheels which are situated on opposite sides of the vehicle, and all such brakes are operated by one of the means of operation;

(*b*) where a motor car has more than four wheels and the drive is transmitted to all wheels other than the steering wheels without the interposition of a differential driving gear or similar mechanism between the axles carrying the driving wheels, it shall be deemed to be a sufficient compliance with this paragraph if one means of operation operates the brakes on two driving wheels situated on opposite sides of the vehicle and the other means of operation operates brakes on all the other wheels required to be fitted with brakes by this paragraph;

(*c*) where means of operation are provided in addition to those prescribed by this Regulation such additional means of operation may be disregarded for the purposes of this paragraph;

(*d*) this paragraph shall not apply to a pedestrian controlled vehicle not exceeding 410 kilograms in weight unladen; and

(*e*) in the case of a motor car the unladen weight of which does not exceed 2040 kilograms or which is constructed solely for the carriage of passengers and their effects and adapted to carry not more than seven passengers exclusive of the driver, it shall be deemed to be a sufficient compliance with this paragraph if one means of operation operates brakes fitted to all but two of the wheels and, as respects each of those two wheels, operates a brake on the shaft leading thereto and no gearing is interposed between the brake and the wheel.

(14) [Except in the case of a works truck one at least of the means of operation] shall be capable of causing brakes to be applied directly and not through the transmission gear to not less than half the number of the wheels of the vehicle:

Provided that—

(*a*) in the case of a motor car having brakes acting on all the wheels of the vehicle and capable of being applied by one means of operation, any shaft leading from any differential driving gear of an axle to a driving wheel shall be deemed not to form part of the transmission gear;

(*b*) in the case of a motor car having more than four wheels and first used before

1st October 1938, it shall be deemed to be sufficient compliance with this paragraph if one of the means of operation applies brakes directly and not through the transmission gear to not less than two of the wheels of the vehicle; and

(c) where a motor car has more than four wheels and the drive is transmitted to all wheels other than the steering wheels without the interposition of a differential driving gear or similar mechanism between the axles carrying the driving wheels, it shall be deemed to be a sufficient compliance with this paragraph if the brakes applied by one means of operation act directly on two driving wheels on opposite sides of the vehicle and the brakes applied by the other means of operation act directly on all other driving wheels.

(15) For the purpose of this Regulation—

(a) in the case of a motor car first used on or after 1st October 1938—

    (i) not more than one front wheel shall be included in half the number of the wheels of the vehicle for the purposes aforesaid:

        Provided that this provision shall not apply—

        (1) to a motor car the unladen weight of which does not exceed 1020 kilograms,

        (2) to a motor car which is a passenger vehicle constructed or adapted to carry not more than seven passengers exclusive of the driver,

        (3) to a works truck, or

        (4) to a motor car with more than three wheels, whether or not any brake shoe is capable of being applied by more than one means of operation, if as respects the fitting of its wheels with brakes and the operation of those brakes the provisions of paragraph (13) of this Regulation relating to such matters are complied with, and

    (ii) every moving shaft to which any part of a braking system or any means of operation thereof is connected or by which it is supported shall be deemed to be part of that system; and

(b) in the case of a motor car propelled by steam and not used as a public service vehicle, the engine shall be deemed to be an efficient braking system with one means of operation if the engine is capable of being reversed and is incapable of being disconnected from any of the driving wheels of the vehicle except by the sustained effort of the driver.

[Regulation 64 is printed as amended by SI 1981 No 1189 and SI 1981 No 1580.]

*   *   *

66. Wings

A motor car shall be equipped with wings or other similar fittings to catch, so far as practicable, mud or water thrown up by the rotation of the wheels unless adequate protection is afforded by the body of the vehicle:

Provided that this Regulation shall not apply—

(a) in relation to the rear wheels of any motor car for the time being forming part of an articulated vehicle if the trailer forming the remaining part of the articulated vehicle is used only for or, when empty, in connection with the carriage of round timber;

(b) in the case of a vehicle in an unfinished condition proceeding to a works for completion; or

(c) in the case of a works truck.

G *Motor Cycles*

67. Brakes

(1) Save as provided in paragraph (4) of this Regulation, every motor cycle shall be equipped either with an efficient braking system having two means of operation or with two efficient braking systems each having a separate means of operation.

(2) Save as provided in paragraph (4) of this Regulation, the braking system or braking systems with which a motor cycle is required to be equipped shall be so designed and constructed that notwithstanding the failure of any part (other than a fixed member or a brake shoe anchor pin) through or by means of which the force necessary to apply the brakes is transmitted there shall still be available for application by the driver to at least one wheel of the vehicle brakes sufficient under the most adverse conditions to bring the vehicle to rest within a reasonable distance.

(3) The braking system or braking systems of every motor cycle to which Schedule 4 applies shall comply with the requirements of that Schedule relating to the efficiency of the brakes of such motor cycles.

(4) Paragraphs (1) and (2) of this Regulation shall not apply in the case of a motor cycle first registered under the Motor Car Act 1903 or the Roads Act 1920 before 1st January 1927 but—

(*a*) such a motor cycle shall be equipped with an efficient braking system, and

(*b*) that system shall be so designed and constructed that brakes shall be available for application by the driver to at least one wheel of the vehicle.

(5) The foregoing paragraphs of this Regulation shall not apply in the case of a works truck if it is equipped with one braking system having one means of operation.

(6) In the case of a motor cycle required to have two means of operating brakes, the application of one means of operation shall not affect or operate the pedal or hand lever of the other means of operation.

*   *   *

69. Wings

Every motor cycle other than a works truck shall be equipped with wings or other similar fittings to catch, so far as practicable, mud or water thrown up by the rotation of the wheels.

H *Invalid Carriages*

70. Overall Width

The overall width of an invalid carriage shall not exceed 2.2 metres.

71. Brakes

Every invalid carriage shall be equipped with an efficient braking system, the brakes of which act on at least two wheels of the vehicle, so designed and constructed that the application of the brakes shall bring the vehicle to rest within a reasonable distance.

72. Wings

Every invalid carriage shall be equipped with wings or other similar fittings to catch, so far as practicable, mud or water thrown up by the rotation of the wheels.

I *Trailers*

73. *[Revoked.]*

74. Overall width

(1) Save as provided in paragraph (3) of this Regulation, the overall width of a trailer shall not exceed 2.3 metres:

Provided that the said width may be—

(a) 2.5 metres in the case of a trailer in relation to which the conditions mentioned in paragraph (2) of this Regulation are complied with [or an agricultural trailed appliance];

(b) exceeded by not more than 380 millimetres in the case of a trailer which is in use by a travelling showman in connection with his business and was in such use before 15th January 1931; and

(c) exceeded by not more than 150 millimetres in the case of a trailer manufactured before 1st January 1933 which has been converted from use with solid tyres to use with pneumatic tyres if the width of no part of the vehicle exceeds 2.3 metres except in so far as such increase is rendered necessary by the conversion.

(2) The conditions referred to in paragraph (1) of this Regulation are that:—

(a) every wheel of the trailer is fitted with a pneumatic tyre;

(b) the trailer is drawn by a locomotive, a motor tractor or a heavy motor car or, where the trailer forms part of an articulated vehicle the other part of which is a motor car, the motor car exceeds 2030 kilograms in weight unladen;

(c) every wheel of the vehicle (not being a locomotive) by which the trailer is drawn is fitted with a pneumatic tyre; and

(d) the outermost part of the trailer comprised in its overall width and on either side of the trailer does not extend more than 305 millimetres outwards beyond the outermost part comprised in the overall width of the vehicle by which it is being drawn on the same side, when the longitudinal axis of that vehicle and the longitudinal axis of the trailer lie in parallel vertical planes.

[(3) The provisions of paragraph (1) above do not apply to—

(a) a trailer which is a trolley vehicle in the course of construction or delivery; or

(b) a broken down vehicle which is being drawn by a motor vehicle in consequence of the breakdown.]

[Regulation 74 is printed as amended by SI 1984 No 1809.]

[74A. Minimum ground clearance

(1) Every trailer which is—

(a) a goods vehicle; and

(b) manufactured on or after 1st April 1984

shall have a minimum ground clearance of not less than 160 millimetres if the trailer has an axle interspace of more than 6 metres but less than 11.5 metres, and a minimum ground clearance of not less than 190 millimetres if the trailer has an axle interspace of 11.5 metres or more.

(2) In this Regulation—

'axle interspace' means—

> (i) in the case of a semi-trailer, the distance between the point of support of the semi-trailer at its forward end and, if it has only one axle, the centre of that axle or, if it has more than one axle, the point half way between the centre of the rearmost axle at the rear and the centre of the foremost axle at the rear, and
>
> (ii) in the case of any other trailer, the distance between the centre of its front axle or, if it has more than one axle at the front, the point half way between the centre of the foremost axle at the front and the centre of the rearmost axle at the front, and the centre of its rear axle or, if it has more than one axle at the rear, the point half way between the centre of the foremost axle at the rear and the centre of the rearmost axle at the rear;

'ground clearance' means the shortest distance between the lowest part of that portion of the trailer (excluding any part of a suspension, steering or braking system attached to any axle, any wheel and any air skirt) which lies within the area formed by the overall width of the trailer and the middle 70 per cent of the axle interspace and the ground ascertained when the trailer—

> (a) is fitted with suitable tyres which are inflated to a pressure recommended by the manufacturer, and
>
> (b) is as near as may be horizontal and standing on ground which is reasonably flat.]

[Regulation 74A was inserted by SI 1983 No 471.]

Brakes

75.—(1) [Save as provided in paragraphs (3) and (4) of this Regulation [and without derogating from paragraph (4A) of this Regulation], every trailer, other than an agricultural trailer, manufactured before 1st January 1968 and every agricultural trailer whenever manufactured which, in either case, has a maximum gross weight exceeding 750 kilograms] shall be equipped with an efficient braking system the brakes of which are capable of being applied when it is being drawn—

> (a) to at least two wheels in the case of a trailer having not more than four wheels;
>
> (b) to at least four wheels in the case of a trailer having more than four wheels; and
>
> (c) in the case of trailers manufactured after 1st April 1938, to at least half the number of wheels of the trailer,

and so constructed that—

> (i) the brakes can be applied either by the driver of the drawing vehicle or by some other person on such vehicle or the trailer,
>
> (ii) in the case of a trailer forming part of an articulated vehicle and being permanently attached to the drawing vehicle, the brakes are capable of being set so as effectively to prevent two at least of the wheels from revolving when the trailer is not being drawn, and
>
> (iii) in the case of any other trailer, the brakes are capable of being set so as effectively to prevent two at least of the wheels from revolving when the trailer, whether it is attached to the drawing vehicle or not, is not being drawn:

Provided that the provisions of item (i) of this paragraph shall not apply in the case a trailer if the brakes of the trailer automatically come into operation on the overrun of the trailer.

[In this paragraph—

'maximum gross weight' has the meaning given by Regulation 46A (2); and 'permanently attached' means that the trailer can only be detached from the drawing vehicle by an operation involving the use of facilities which are normally found only in a workshop.]

(2) Save as provided in paragraphs (3) and (4) of this Regulation, every trailer manufactured on or after 1st January 1968, except an agricultural trailer, [and which has a maximum gross weight exceeding 750 kilograms] shall be equipped with an efficient braking system so designed and constructed that—

(a) when the trailer is being drawn, the brakes of that braking system are capable of being applied to all the wheels of the trailer by the driver of the drawing vehicle using the means of operation applying those of the brakes of the drawing vehicle which were designed and constructed to have the highest braking efficiency of any of the brakes of any braking system with which the drawing vehicle is equipped;

(b) when the trailer is being drawn, in the event of a failure of any part (other than a fixed member or a brake shoe anchor pin) of the braking system with which the drawing vehicle is equipped (excluding the means of operation of a split braking system) or of any part (other than as aforesaid) of the braking system with which the trailer is equipped, brakes shall still be capable of being applied to at least two wheels of the trailer or, in the case of a two-wheeled trailer, to one wheel in the manner indicated in the last preceding sub-paragraph or by the driver using any other means of operation of a braking system with which the drawing vehicle is by these Regulations required to be equipped;

(c) when the trailer is stationary—
   (i) the brakes of that system can also be applied to at least two wheels of the trailer and released by a person standing on the ground by a means of operation fitted to the trailer;
   (ii) the braking force of that system can, when applied in the manner indicated in sub-paragraph (a) or (c) (i) of this paragraph, at all times be maintained in operation by direct mechanical action without the intervention of any hydraulic, electric or pneumatic device; and
   (iii) such braking force, when so applied and so maintained in operation by direct mechanical action, is capable of holding the trailer stationary on a gradient of at least 1 in 6.25 without the assistance of stored energy:

Provided that the provisions of sub-paragraphs (a) and (b) of this paragraph shall not apply in the case of a trailer if the brakes of the trailer automatically come into operation on the overrun of the trailer.

[(3) where—
   (i) a motor vehicle to which Regulation 5 applies by virtue of its conforming to the requirements of Council Directive 71/320/EEC of 26th July 1971 or, where appropriate, to the requirements of that Directive as amended by the amending Directives specified in Regulation 5 is drawing a trailer to which that Regulation does not sapply, or
   (ii) a motor vehicle to which Regulation 5A applies, being a vehicle in respect of which a certificate of conformity or Minister's approval certificate has been issued under section 47 of the 1972 Act indicating that the requirements (other than requirements of marking) specified in EEC Regulation 13 (as defined in Regulation 101 (7)) have been satisfied, is drawing a trailer, or
   (iii) a motor vehicle to which Regulation 5B applies is drawing a trailer to which that Regulation does not apply, [or]

[(iv) motor vehicle to which Regulation 14A applies is drawing a trailer to which that Regulation does not apply,]
paragraph (2) (b) of this Regulation shall apply to the trailer as if the words 'or of any part (other than as aforesaid) of the braking system with which the trailer is equipped' were omitted.]

(4) Paragraphs (1), (2) and (3) of this Regulation shall not apply to—

[(a) any agricultural trailed appliance or agricultural trailed appliance conveyor drawn by a motor vehicle;]

(b) any trailer designed for use and used for street cleansing which does not carry any load other than its necessary gear and equipment;

[(bb) before 1st October 1986 any gritting trailer, or on or after 1st October 1986 a gritting trailer the maximum gross weight of which does not exceed 2000 kilograms;]

[(bbb) before 1st October 1986, any trailer which has an unladen weight not exceeding 102 kilograms and which was manufactured before 1st October 1982;]

(c) any broken down vehicle which is being drawn by a motor vehicle in consequence of the breakdown;

(d) any agricultural trailer manufactured before 1st July 1947 when drawn by a motor tractor or a land tractor which is not a motor tractor if—
  (i) its laden weight does not exceed 4070 kilograms,
  (ii) it is the only trailer so drawn, and
  (iii) it is not drawn at a speed exceeding 10 miles per hour; . . .

(e) [any trailer manufactured before 19th November 1982 used only] for the carriage of plant and materials for producing gas for the propulsion of the drawing vehicle if the drawing vehicle is either a goods vehicle weighing not less than 2030 kilograms in weight unladen [or a large passenger-carrying vehicle;]

[(f) any trailer to which Regulation 14A applies[; or]]

[(g) any trailer being drawn by a motor cycle by virtue of Regulation 130 (e).]

[(4A) The brakes of every agricultural trailer manufactured on or after 1st December 1985 shall be capable of achieving a braking efficiency of not less than 25 per cent.
In this paragraph 'braking efficiency' means the maximum braking force capable of being developed by the application of brakes expressed as a percentage of the total of the maximum axle weights of the trailer shown on the plate which is affixed to it in accordance with Regulation 42 or, if there is no such plate affixed to it, the total of the maximum axle weights which the trailer was designed to have.]

(5) In the case of trailers manufactured on or after 1st April 1938 [not being agricultural trailers], the braking system shall be so constructed that it is not rendered ineffective by the non-rotation of the engine of the drawing vehicle.

[Regulation 75 is printed as amended by SI 1980 No 880; SI 1981 No 1189; SI 1981 No 1663, SI 1983 No 112; SI 1984 No 386; and SI 1984 No 1809.

The amendments effected by SI 1981 No 1189 came into force, as respects the amendments incorporated into the text relating to paras (1) and (2), on 1 October 1981. (The amendments effected by that instrument to paras (3) and (4) took effect on the same date as the other provisions of that instrument, namely 10 September 1981. SI 1981 No 1189 also effected, from the earlier date, an amendment to para (1) which was superseded by an amendment (also effected by SI 1981 No 1189) which took effect on 1 October 1981.)]

76.—[(1) Where—

    (i) a trailer to which Regulation 5 applies by virtue of its conforming to the requirements of Council Directive 71/320/EEC of 26th July 1971 or, where appropriate, to the requirements of that Directive as amended by the amending Directives specified in Regulation 5, is drawn by a motor vehicle to which that Regulation does not apply, or

    (ii) a trailer to which Regulation 5B applies is drawn by a motor vehicle to which that Regulation does not apply [or]

    [(iii) a trailer to which Regulation 14A applies is drawn by a motor vehicle to which that Regulation does not apply,]

then the braking system of the drawing vehicle shall be so constructed that in the event of a failure of any part (other than a fixed member or a brake shoe anchor pin) of the service braking system with which the drawing vehicle is equipped (excluding the means of operation of a split braking system) brakes shall still be capable of being applied to at least two wheels of the trailer or, in the case of a two-wheeled trailer, to one wheel by the driver using the secondary braking system of the drawing vehicle.]

(2) In this Regulation 'service braking system' means the braking system which was designed and constructed to have the highest braking efficiency of any braking system with which the drawing vehicle is equipped and 'secondary braking system' means a braking system applied by a second independent means of operation or by one of the independent sections comprised in a split braking system

[Regulation 76 is printed as amended by SI 1980 No 880 and SI 1981 No 1189.]

*   *   *

79. Wings

The rear wheels of every trailer or, in the case of a two-wheeled trailer both its wheels, shall be equipped with wings or other similar fittings to catch, so far as practicable, mud or water thrown up by the rotation of the wheels, unless adequate protection is afforded by the body of the trailer:

Provided that this Regulation shall not apply to—

    (*a*) trailers in an unfinished condition proceeding to a works for completion;

    (*b*) [agricultural trailed appliances];

    (*c*) [agricultural trailed appliance conveyors];

    (*d*) living vans;

    (*e*) watercarts;

    (*f*) trailers used only for or, when empty, in connection with the carriage of round timber;

    (*g*) trailer pumps used for fire brigade purposes;

    (*h*) trailers drawn by a vehicle the maximum speed of which is restricted by virtue of the provisions of Schedule 5 to the 1967 Act to 12 miles per hour or less; or

    (*i*) any broken down vehicle which is being drawn in consequence of the breakdown.

[Regulation 79 is printed as amended by SI 1984 No 1809.]

[J *Agricultural Motor Vehicles*]

[Note: the above heading was inserted by SI 1984 No 1809.]

[79A. Overall width

The overall width of an agricultural motor vehicle shall not exceed 2.5 metres.]

[Regulation 79A was inserted by SI 1984 No 1809.]

[79B. Overhang

In the case of an agricultural motor vehicle the distance measured horizontally and parallel to the longitudinal axis of the rear portion of the vehicle between two vertical planes at right angles to that axis passing through the rearmost point of the vehicle and the through the centre of the rear or rearmost axle shall not exceed 3 metres.]

[Regulation 79B was inserted by SI 1984 No 1809.]

[79C. Brakes

(1) This Regulation applies to an agricultural motor vehicle, and references in this Regulation to a vehicle are references to an agricultural motor vehicle.

(2) Every braking system fitted to a vehicle manufactured on or after 1st December 1985 and first used on or after 1st June 1986 shall have a total braking efficiency of not less than 25 per cent.

(3) Every vehicle which was first used before 9th February 1980 shall be equipped with an efficient braking system or efficient braking systems, in either case having two means of operation, so designed and constructed that, notwithstanding the failure of any part (other than a fixed member or a brake shoe anchor pin) through or by means of which the force necessary to apply the brakes is transmitted, there shall still be available for application by the driver to not less than half the number of the wheels of the vehicle brakes sufficient under the most adverse conditions to bring the vehicle to rest within a reasonable distance:
Provided that this paragraph does not apply in the case of a road roller, or a vehicle not propelled by steam which is equipped with one braking system with one means of operation.

(4) Every vehicle first used on or after 9th February 1980 shall be equipped with an efficient braking system or efficient braking systems so designed and constructed that notwithstanding the failure of any part thereof there shall still be available for application by the driver a brake sufficient under the most adverse conditions to bring the vehicle to rest within a reasonable distance.

(5) The application of one means of operation shall not affect or operate the pedal or hand lever of the other means of operation.

(6) In the case of vehicles first used on or after 1st April 1938 no braking system shall be rendered ineffective by the non-rotation of the engine:
Provided that this paragraph does not apply in the case of any vehicle referred to in paragraph (7)(*b*) below.

(7) For the purpose of this Regulation—

(*a*) in the case of a vehicle first used on or after 1st October 1938—
    (i) not more than one front wheel shall be included in half the number of the wheels of the vehicle, and
    (ii) every moving shaft to which any part of a braking system or any means of operation thereof is connected or by which it is supported shall be deemed to be part of that system;

(*b*) in the case of a vehicle propelled by steam the engine shall be deemed to be an efficient braking system with one means of operation if the engine is capable of being reversed and, in the case of a vehicle first used on or after 1st October 1943, is incapable of being disconnected from any of the driving wheels of the vehicle except by the sustained effort of the driver; and

(c) 'braking efficiency' means the maximum braking force capable of being developed by the application of brakes expressed as a percentage of the total maximum axle weights which the vehicle is designed to have.]

[Regulation 79C was inserted by SI 1984 No 1809.]

*   *   *

PART III

REGULATIONS GOVERNING THE USE ON ROADS OF MOTOR VEHICLES AND TRAILERS

80. Markings on locomotives, tractors and heavy motor cars

The owner of a locomotive, motor tractor or heavy motor car [not being in any case an agricultural motor vehicle] shall cause the unladen weight of the vehicle to be painted or otherwise plainly marked upon some conspicuous place on the left or near side of the vehicle:

Provided that this Regulation shall not apply to a heavy motor car not registered under the Roads Act 1920, the Vehicles (Excise) Act 1949, the Vehicles (Excise) Act 1962 or the Vehicles (Excise) Act 1971 [nor to a vehicle the unladen weight of which is shown on its Ministry plate].

[Regulation 80 is printed as amended by SI 1982 No 1272.]

[80A. Indications of overall travelling height

(1) This Regulation applies to—

(a) every motor vehicle which is constructed or adapted so as to be capable of hoisting and carrying a skip;

(b) every motor vehicle which is—
   (i) carrying a container, or
   (ii) drawing a trailer or semi-trailer carrying a container; and

(c) every motor vehicle which is—
   (i) engineering plant, or
   (ii) carrying engineering equipment, or
   (iii) drawing a trailer or semi-trailer carrying engineering equipment.

(2) On and after 6th March 1979, no person shall use or cause or permit to be used on a road a vehicle to which this Regulation applies if the overall travelling height exceeds 12 feet unless there is carried in the vehicle in the manner specified in paragraph (3) of this Regulation a notice clearly indicating, in feet and inches and in figures not less than 40 millimetres tall, the overall travelling height.

(3) The notice referred to in paragraph (2) of this Regulation shall be attached to the vehicle in such manner that it can be read by the driver when in the driving position.

(4) In this Regulation:—

'container' means an article of equipment, not being a motor vehicle or trailer, having a volume of at least 8 cubic metres, constructed wholly or mostly of metal and intended for repeated use for the carriage of goods or burden;

'engineering equipment' means engineering plant and any other plant or equipment designed and constructed for the purposes of engineering operations;

'overall travelling height' means not less than and not above one inch more than—

      (i) in the case of a motor vehicle which is not drawing a trailer or a semi-trailer, the distance between the ground and the point on the motor vehicle, or any load which is being carried by or any equipment which is fitted to the said vehicle, which is farthest from the ground, and

     (ii) in the case of a motor vehicle which is drawing a trailer or a semi-trailer, the distance between the ground and the point on the motor vehicle or any trailer or semi-trailer which it is drawing, or any load which is being carried on or any equipment which is fitted to any part of the said combination of vehicles, which is farthest from the ground.

and for the purpose of determining the overall travelling height—

(a) the condition of the tyres of the motor vehicle and of any trailer or semi-trailer which it is drawing shall be such as to comply with the requirements specified in paragraph (1) (b) of Regulation 107.

(b) the surface under the motor vehicle and any trailer or semi-trailer which it is drawing and any load which is being carried on and any equipment which is fitted to any part of the said combination of vehicles and which projects beyond any part of the said combination of vehicles shall be reasonably flat, and

(c) any equipment which is fitted to the motor vehicle or any trailer or semi-trailer which it is drawing shall be stowed in the position in which it is to proceed on the road;

'skip' means an article of equipment designed and constructed to be carried on a road vehicle and to be placed on a road or other land for the storage of materials, or for the removal and disposal of rubble, waste, household or other rubbish or earth.]

[Regulation 80A was added by SI 1978 No 1317.]

81. *[Revoked.]*

[Note: an amendment to reg 81 (4) (e) purports to be made by SI 1984 No 1809, reg 38, Schedule (item 27); this amendment would seem to have no effect by reason of the prior revocation of reg 81 (see SI 1984 No 813, reg 6).]

82. Laden weight of locomotive

(1) Save as provided in paragraph (2) of this Regulation, the laden weight of a locomotive shall not exceed 20830 kilograms.

(2) The laden weight of a locomotive which is equipped with suitable and sufficient springs between each wheel and the frame of the vehicle and every wheel of which is fitted with a pneumatic tyre or a tyre of soft or elastic material shall not exceed—

(a) in the case of a vehicle with less than six wheels, 22360 kilograms;

(b) in the case of a vehicle with six wheels, 26420 kilograms; or

(c) in the case of a vehicle with more than six wheels, 30490 kilograms.

(3) The total weight transmitted to the road surface by any two wheels of a loco-motive in line transversely shall not exceed 11180 kilograms:

Provided that this paragraph shall not apply to a road roller or to a vehicle with not more than four wheels first used before 1st June 1955.

83. Weight of trailers drawn by a locomotive

The maximum total weight of all trailers, whether wheeled or track laying and whether laden or unladen, drawn by a locomotive whether wheeled or track laying shall not exceed 40650 kilograms.

84. Laden weight of heavy motor car or motor car, being a public service vehicle

(1) [Save as provided in paragraphs (1A) and (2) of this Regulation], in the case of a heavy motor car or motor car which is a public service vehicle the total weight transmitted to the road surface by any two wheels in line transversely shall not exceed 9150 kilograms and the sum of the weight so transmitted by all the wheels shall not exceed 14230 kilograms.

[(1A) This Regulation does not apply to a vehicle to which Regulation 89A applies.]

(2) In the case of a heavy motor car or motor car having brakes which as applied by one means of operation have a total braking efficiency of not less than 50 per cent and which as applied by a second independent means of operation or as applied on a failure in the case of a split braking system have a total braking efficiency of not less than 25 per cent the following provisions shall apply—

(a) the total weight transmitted to the road surface by any two wheels in line trans-versely may amount to but shall not exceed 10170 kilograms, if each such wheel is fitted with either two pneumatic tyres having the centres of their areas of contact with the road surface not less than 300 millimetres apart measured at right angles to the longitudinal axis of the vehicle or with a wide tyre; and

(b) the sum of the weights transmitted to the road surface by all the wheels of the vehicle may amount to but not exceed, where the distance between the front and rear axles is at least 3.25 metres but less than 3.65 metres, 15250 kilo-grams, and where the distance between the front and the rear axles is at least 3.65 metres, 16260 kilograms.

For the purposes of this sub-paragraph (b) the distances between any two axles shall be obtained in the same manner as is provided in paragraph 1 of Schedule 6.

(3) For the purpose of this Regulation the weight transmitted to the road surface by a vehicle shall be taken to be the weight so transmitted by the vehicle when it is complete and fully equipped for service with a full supply of water, oil and fuel and loaded with weights of 63.5 kilograms per person placed in the correct relative pos-itions for [each person, whether passenger or crew, for whom a seat is provided and any conductor intended to be carried on a vehicle otherwise than in a crew seat] and, in the case of a public service vehicle registered after 31st December 1954 in which by or under any enactment more than eight standing passengers may be carried, with additional weights of 63.5 kilograms per person for each standing passenger in excess of eight reasonably distributed in the space in which any such passengers may be so carried.

[Regulation 84 is printed as amended by SI 1981 No 261, and SI 1982 No 1057.]

85. Laden weight of heavy motor car or motor car, not being a public service vehicle

(1) [Save as provided in paragraphs (1A) and (2) of this Regulation], in the case of a heavy motor car or motor car which is not a public service vehicle, the weight transmitted to the road surface by any one wheel where no other wheel is in the same line transversely shall not exceed 4580 kilograms, the total weight so transmitted by any two wheels in line transversely shall not exceed 9150 kilograms and the sum of the weights so transmitted by all the wheels shall not exceed—

(a) in the case of a vehicle with not more than four wheels, 14230 kilograms;

(b) in the case of a vehicle with more than four wheels but not more than six wheels, 20330 kilograms; and

(c) in the case of a vehicle with more than six wheels, 24390 kilograms,

so, however, that in relation to a vehicle first used on or after 1st June 1973, not being a vehicle to which Regulation 89 applies and in so far as it is a vehicle to which either of sub-paragraphs (b) and (c) of this paragraph applies, for the weight limits of 20330 kilograms and 24390 kilograms specified in those sub-paragraphs there shall be substituted respectively weight limits of 16260 kilograms and 18290 kilograms.

[(1A) This Regulation does not apply to a vehicle to which Regulation 89A applies.]

(2) In the case of a prior 1968 vehicle, a post 1968 vehicle or a temporarily imported vehicle the following provisions shall apply—

(i) the weight transmitted to the road surface by any one wheel where no other wheel is in the same line transversely may amount to but shall not exceed 5090 kilograms, and the total weight so transmitted by any two wheels in line transversely may amount to but shall not exceed 10170 kilograms if each such wheel is fitted with either two pneumatic tyres having the centres of their areas of contact with the road surface not less than 300 millimetres apart measured at right angles to the longitudinal axis of the vehicle or with a wide tyre; and

(ii) if it is fitted with a number of axles specified in column 1 of paragraph 2 of Schedule 6 as respects which the measurements apply as so specified, the sum of the weights transmitted to the road surface by all the wheels of the vehicle may amount to but shall not exceed the weight specified in relation to that vehicle in column 2 of the said paragraph:

Provided that the provisions of sub-paragraph (ii) of this paragraph shall not apply to a motor vehicle when drawing a trailer other than a trailer to which Regulation 86 (3) applies.

(3) In this Regulation—

'a prior 1968 vehicle' means a heavy motor car or motor car (other than a public service vehicle)—

(a) first used before 1st January 1968;

(b) equipped with a plate complying with the requirements of Regulation 42, whether that Regulation applies to that vehicle or not; and

(c) having brakes which as applied by one means of operation have a total braking efficiency of not less than 50 per cent and which as applied by a second independent means of operation or as applied on a failure in the case of a split braking system have a total braking efficiency of not less than 25 per cent;

'a post 1968 vehicle' means a heavy motor car or motor car (other than a public service vehicle) first used on or after 1st January 1968;

'a temporarily imported vehicle' means a heavy motor car or motor car (other than a public service vehicle) brought temporarily into Great Britain by a person resident abroad which—

(a) is not registered under the Vehicles (Excise) Act 1971;

(b) complies with the requirements mentioned in Regulation 4 (7);

(c) carries a plate securely affixed to it in a conspicuous and readily accessible position issued by the competent authority in the country where it is registered indicating the permissible maximum weight for the vehicle in that country; and

(d) has brakes which as applied by one means of operation have a total braking efficiency of not less than 50 per cent and which as applied by a second independent means of operation or as applied on a failure in the case of a split braking system have a total braking efficiency of not less than 25 per cent.

[Regulation 85 is printed as amended by SI 1981 No 261.]

86. Laden weight of trailer

(1) Save as provided in paragraph (3) of this Regulation, the total weight transmitted to the road surface by any two wheels of a trailer in line transversely shall not exceed 9150 kilograms.

(2) Save as provided in paragraph (3) of this Regulation, the total laden weight of a trailer with less than six wheels and not forming part of an articulated vehicle shall not exceed 14230 kilograms.

(3) In the case of—

(a) a trailer equipped with a plate complying with the requirements of Regulation 42, whether that Regulation applies to that trailer or not; or

(b) a temporarily imported trailer;

which in either case is drawn by a prior 1968 vehicle, a post 1968 vehicle or a temporarily imported motor vehicle the following provisions shall apply—

(i) the weight transmitted to the road surface by any two wheels of the trailer in line transversely may amount to but shall not exceed 10170 kilograms if each wheel is fitted with either two pneumatic tyres having the centres of their areas of contact with the road surface not less than 300 millimetres apart measured at right angles to the longitudinal axis of the vehicle or with a wide tyre, and

(ii) if it is fitted with a number of axles specified in column 1 of paragraph 2 of Schedule 6 as respects which the measurements apply as so specified, the sum of the weights transmitted to the road surface by all the wheels of the trailer may amount to but shall not exceed the weight specified in relation to that trailer in column 2 of the said paragraph.

(4) Save as provided in paragraph (5) of this Regulation, the total laden weight of a trailer—

(a) manufactured before 27th February 1977 and having no other brakes than a parking brake and brakes which automatically come into operation on the overrun of the trailer shall not exceed 3560 kilograms,

(b) manufactured on or after 27th February 1977 and fitted with brakes which automatically come into operation on the overrun of the trailer, whether or not it is fitted with any other brake, shall not exceed 3500 kilograms.

(5) The requirement specified in sub-paragraph (b) of paragraph (4) of this Regulation shall not apply to an agricultural trailer which—

(a) is being drawn by [an agricultural motor vehicle],

(b) is fitted with brakes which automatically come into operation on the overrun of the trailer, and

(c) complies with the requirements specified in paragraph (1) of Regulation 75 including the requirement that the brakes can be applied either by the driver of the drawing vehicle or by some other person on such vehicle or the trailer.

(6) In this Regulation—

'a prior 1968 vehicle' means a motor tractor, heavy motor car or motor car—

(a) first used before 1st January 1968;

(b) equipped with a plate complying with the requirements of Regulation 42, whether that Regulation applies to the vehicle or not; and

(c) which while drawing a trailer mentioned in paragraph (3) of this Regulation has brakes which (whether assisted by the brakes on the trailer or not) as applied by one means of operation have a total braking efficiency of not less than 50 per cent and as applied by a second independent means of operation or as applied on a failure in the case of a split braking system have a total braking efficiency of not less than 25 per cent;

'a post 1968 vehicle' means a motor tractor, heavy motor car or motor car—

(a) first used on or after 1st January 1968;

(b) which, in the case of a motor tractor, is equipped with a plate as specified in Regulation 42 and which complies with the requirements relating to a braking system specified in paragraph (5) of Regulation 59 notwithstanding that the provisions of Regulations 42 and 59 (5) do not apply to such tractor; and

(c) which, while drawing a trailer mentioned in paragraph (3) of this Regulation has brakes which (whether assisted by the brakes on the trailer or not) as applied by one means of operation have a total braking efficiency of not less than 50 per cent, and as applied by a second independent means of operation or as applied on a failure in the case of a split braking system have a total braking efficiency of not less than 25 per cent;

'a temporarily imported motor vehicle' means a motor tractor, heavy motor car or motor car brought temporarily into Great Britain by a person resident abroad which—

(a) is not registered under the Vehicles (Excise) Act 1971;

(b) complies with the requirements mentioned in Regulation 4 (7);

(c) carries a plate securely affixed to it in a conspicuous and readily accessible position issued by the competent authority in the country where it is registered indicating the permissible maximum weight for the vehicle in that country; and

(d) while drawing a trailer mentioned in paragraph (3) of this Regulation has brakes which (whether assisted by the brakes of the trailer or not) as applied by one means of operation have a total braking efficiency of not less than 50 per cent and as applied by a second independent means of operation or as applied on a failure in the case of a split braking system have a total braking efficiency of not less than 25 per cent;

'a temporarily imported trailer' means a trailer whenever manufactured brought temporarily into Great Britain by a person resident abroad which—

(*a*) complies with the requirements mentioned in Regulation 4 (7); and

(*b*) carries a plate securely affixed to it in a conspicuous and readily accessible position issued by the competent authority in a country outside Great Britain indicating the permissible maximum weight for the trailer in that country.

[Regulation 86 is printed as amended by SI 1984 No 1809.]

[87. Laden weight of vehicle and trailer

[Except as provided in Regulation 96A (2), the] total laden weight of a trailer, not being a semi-trailer, together with that of the motor vehicle by which it is drawn shall not, in a case specified in an item in column (2) of the Table below, exceed the weight specified in that item in column (3) of that Table.]

[TABLE *[ie table in reg 87]*

(1) Item No	(2) Vehicle Combination	(3) Maximum weight (in kilograms)
1	[A wheeled trailer drawn by a wheeled motor tractor, a wheeled heavy motor car or a wheeled motor car, and which—]	
	(*a*) is fitted with power-assisted brakes which can be operated by the driver of the drawing vehicle and are not rendered ineffective by the non-rotation of its engine; and	
	(*b*) is drawn by a vehicle which is equipped with a warning device so placed as to be readily visible to the driver when in the driving seat in order to indicate an impending deficiency or failure in the vacuum or pressure system	32520
2	A wheeled trailer drawn by a wheeled motor tractor, a wheeled heavy motor car or wheeled motor car not being a combination of vehicles mentioned in item 1	24390
3	A track laying trailer drawn by a motor tractor, heavy motor car or motor car, whether wheeled or track laying, and a wheeled trailer, drawn by a track laying vehicle being a motor tractor, heavy motor car or motor car, not being a combination of vehicles mentioned in item 1 or 2	22360.]

[Regulation 87 is printed as substituted by SI 1982 No 1576 and as amended by SI 1983 No 471, and SI 1984 No 1809.]

88. Laden weight of articulated vehicle

(1) Save as provided in paragraph (2) of this Regulation, the total laden weight of an articulated vehicle shall not exceed—

(*a*) if the trailer has less than four wheels, 20330 kilograms, and

(*b*) if the trailer has four wheels or more, 24390 kilograms.

(2) In the case of an articulated vehicle formed by—

(*a*) a trailer equipped with a plate complying with the requirements of Regulation 42, whether that Regulation applies to the trailer or not, or a temporarily imported trailer; and

(*b*) a prior 1968 vehicle, a post 1968 vehicle or a temporarily imported motor vehicle,

where the articulated vehicle is fitted with a number of axles specified in column 1 of paragraph 3 of Schedule 6 as respects which the measurements apply as so specified, the sum of the weights transmitted to the road surface by all the wheels of the articulated vehicle may amount to but shall not exceed the weight specified in relation to that vehicle in column 2 of the said paragraph.

(3) For the purpose of this Regulation, 'a temporarily imported trailer' has the same meaning as in Regulation 86 (6) and 'a prior 1968 vehicle', 'a post 1968 vehicle' and 'a temporarily imported motor vehicle' have the same meanings as in the definitions of those terms in that Regulation subject, however, to any reference to a motor tractor in those definitions being omitted.

89. Laden weight of certain vehicles not part of articulated vehicles

(1) [Save as provided in paragraph (2) below, this Regulation applies to]—

(*a*) a heavy motor car or motor car—
  (i) equipped with a plate complying with the requirements of Regulation 42,
  (ii) having brakes which as applied by one means of operation have a total braking efficiency of not less than 50 per cent and which as applied by a second independent means of operation or as applied on a failure in the case of a split braking system have a total braking efficiency of not less than 25 per cent, and
  (iii) not forming part of an articulated vehicle;

(*b*) [a temporarily imported motor vehicle] as defined in Regulation 85 (3)—
  (i) if the plate which it carries indicates a permissible maximum weight for each axle thereof, and
  (ii) not forming part of an articulated vehicle;

(*c*) a trailer—
  (i) equipped with a plate complying with the requirements of Regulation 42,
  (ii) drawn by a motor tractor, heavy motor car or motor car which in each case whilst drawing the trailer has brakes which (whether assisted by the brakes on the trailer or not) as applied by one means of operation have a total braking efficiency of not less than 50 per cent and as applied by a second independent means of operation or as applied on a failure in the case of a split braking system have a total braking efficiency of not less than 25 per cent, and
  (iii) not forming part of an articulated vehicle;

(*d*) a temporarily imported trailer as defined in Regulation 86 (6)—

    (i)   if the plate which it carries indicates a permissible maximum weight for each axle thereof;

    (ii) drawn by a motor tractor, heavy motor car or motor car which in each case whilst drawing the trailer has brakes which comply with the provision of sub-paragraph (c)(ii) above, and

    (iii) not forming part of an articulated vehicle; and

(e) a composite trailer which—

    (i)   consists of a converter dolly equipped with a plate which complies with the requirements of Regulation 42 and a semi-trailer which is equipped with such a plate, and

    (ii) is drawn by a motor tractor, a heavy motor car, or a motor car which in each case whilst drawing the composite trailer has brakes which comply with the provisions specified in sub-paragraph (c)(ii) above:

(2) Nothing in Regulation 85 and Regulation 86 (other than paragraph (4) of that Regulation) shall apply to a vehicle [to which this Regulation applies, and nothing in this Regulation shall apply to a vehicle to which Regulation 89A applies.]

(3) In the case of a vehicle to which this Regulation applies, the sum of the weights transmitted to the road surface by all the wheels of the vehicle may, subject to the provisions of Regulation 86 (4), amount to but shall not exceed such weight as is specified in Part I of Schedule 7 and is relevant to the class of vehicle in column 1 of that part in which it falls:

Provided that nothing in this paragraph shall apply so as to require a vehicle first used before 1st June 1973 to be used on a road at a weight below that at which it could have been used under Regulation 85 (1)(b) and (c).

[Regulation 89 is printed as amended by SI 1981 No 261, and SI 1982 No 1576.]

[89A. Laden weight of large passenger carrying vehicles

(1) This Regulation applies to—

(a) every large passenger carrying vehicle being an articulated bus, and

(b) every large passenger carrying vehicle not being an articulated bus, manufactured on or after 1st October 1981 and first used on or after 1st April 1982.

(2) In the case of a vehicle to which this Regulation applies, the sum of the weights transmitted to the road surface by all the wheels of the vehicle may amount to but shall not exceed such weight as is specified in Part I of Schedule 7 and is relevant to the class of vehicle in column 1 of the Part in which it falls.

(3) In the case of a vehicle to which this Regulation applies the total weight transmitted to the road surface by any two wheels in line transversely shall not exceed—

(a) 10,170 kilograms if each such wheel is fitted with two pneumatic tyres having the centre of their areas of contact with the road surface not less than 300 millimetres apart measured at right angles to the longitudinal axis of the vehicle or a wide tyre; or

(b) 9,150 kilograms in any other case.

(4) For the purposes of this Regulation the weight transmitted to the road surface shall be calculated with reference to the vehicle when it is complete and fully equipped for service with—

(a) a full supply of water, oil and fuel; and

(b) weights of 63.5 kilograms for each person—

    (i) being a person (including [crew]) for whom a seat is provided in the position in which they may be seated, and

(ii) [being a person (including crew) who may by or under any enactment be carried standing, reasonably distributed in the space in which any such person may be so carried, save that in the case of a public service vehicle (not being an articulated bus) only the number of such persons exceeding 8 (excluding crew) shall be taken into account.]

[Regulation 89A was added by SI 1981 No 261 and is printed as amended by SI 1982 No 1057.]

90. Laden weight of certain motor vehicles forming part of articulated vehicles

(1) This Regulation applies to—

(*a*) a heavy motor car or motor car complying with the provisions of sub-paragraphs (i) and (ii) of paragraph (1)(*a*) of Regulation 89 and forming part of an articulated vehicle; and

(*b*) a temporarily imported vehicle as defined in Regulation 85 (3) complying with the provisions of sub-paragraph (i) of paragraph (1)(*b*) of Regulation 89 and forming part of an articulated vehicle.

[(2) Save as provided in paragraph (3) below, the weight transmitted to the surface of the road by all the wheels of a vehicle to which this Regulation applies and which has—

(*a*) the number of axles specified in an item in column (2) in Part II of Schedule 7,

(*b*) in a case where an intermediate axle weight is specified in that item in column (3) of that Part, an intermediate axle weight of the amount there specified, and

(*c*) axle spacings as specified in that item in column (4) of that Part

may amount to but shall not exceed the weight specified in that item in column (5) of that Part:

Provided that in the case of a vehicle of a kind specified in item 3 in the said Part the vehicle has a relevant train weight of more than 32520 kilograms.]

[(3) This Regulation does not apply so as to require a vehicle first used before 1st June 1973 to be used on a road at a weight below that at which it could have been used under Regulation 85 (1)(*b*) and (*c*), and nothing in Regulation 85 applies to a vehicle to which this Regulation applies.]

[(4) In this Regulation and in Part II of Schedule 7—

'intermediate axle weight' means the highest weight shown for any axle in column 2 of a Ministry plate and carried on the vehicle or, if no such plate is carried on the vehicle, the highest maximum weight in Great Britain shown for any axle in the plate complying with the requirement of Regulation 42 or the highest weight shown for any axle in the plate mentioned in Regulation 89 (1)(*b*)(i) with which the vehicle is equipped, any such axle not being the foremost or rearmost.]

[Regulation 90 is printed as amended by SI 1982 No 1576.]

91. Laden weight of certain articulated vehicles

(1) This Regulation applies to an articulated vehicle formed by—

(*a*) a heavy motor car or motor car to which Regulation 90 (1)(*a*) applies or a temporarily imported vehicle to which Regulation 90 (1)(*b*) applies; and

(*b*) a trailer which—
(i) is equipped with a plate complying with the requirements of Regulation 42, or
(ii) is a temporarily imported trailer as defined in Regulation 86 (6),

the said heavy motor car or motor car in each case whilst drawing the trailer having brakes which (whether assisted by the brakes on the trailer or not) as applied by one means of operation have a total braking efficiency of not less than 50 per cent and as applied by a second independent means of operation or as applied on a failure in the case of a split braking system have a total braking efficiency of not less than 25 per cent.

(2) Nothing in Regulation 88 shall apply to an articulated vehicle to which this Regulation applies.

[(3) In the case of an articulated vehicle to which this regulation applies, if the relevant axle spacing is a distance [specified in an item in Part III of Schedule 7], where the drawing vehicle has 2 axles, in column (2)(*a*), and where the drawing vehicle has at least 3 axles, in column (2)(*b*), the total weight transmitted to the surface of the road by all the wheels of the vehicle shall not exceed—

(*a*) the maximum weight specified in that item in column (3) of the said Part III; and

(*b*) as regards an articulated vehicle of a type specified in an item in column (2) in Part IIIA of Schedule 7, the maximum weight specified in that item in column (3) of that Part;

and in the case of an articulated vehicle to which this Regulation applies which has a relevant axle spacing specified in column (2) of the said Part III at item 13 to 18 the overall length of the articulated vehicle shall not be less than the length specified in that item in column (4) of the said Part III.]

[(4) In this Regulation and in Part III of Schedule 7 'relevant axle spacing' means the distance between the rearmost axle of the semi-trailer and the rearmost axle of the drawing vehicle.]

[Regulation 91 is printed as amended by SI 1982 No 1576 and SI 1983 No 471.]

92. Total weights for certain closely spaced axles, etc

[(1) This Regulation applies to—

(*a*) a motor car or a heavy motor car (in either case whether or not forming part of an articulated vehicle) to which Regulation 89 (1)(*a*)(i) and (ii) or (*b*)(i) applies;

(*b*) a trailer (whether or not forming part of an articulated vehicle) to which Regulation 89 (1)(*c*)(i) and (ii) or (*d*)(i) and (ii) applies; and

(*c*) an agricultural motor vehicle, an agricultural trailer, and an agricultural trailed appliance.]

[(2) Save as provided in paragraph (3) below, where two closely spaced axles of a vehicle to which this Regulation applies are spaced at a distance specified in an item in column (2) in Part IV of Schedule 7 the total weight transmitted to the surface of the road by all the wheels of those axles shall not exceed—

(*a*) in a case where the plated weight of neither of the axles exceeds one half of the weight shown in that item in column (3) of that Part, the weight specified in that item in the said column (3);

(*b*) in a case where the plated weight of one of the axles exceeds one half of the weight shown in that item in column (3) of that Part but does not exceed 10170 kilograms the weight specified in that item in column (4) of that Part;

(*c*) in a case other than one mentioned in sub-paragraph (*a*) or (*b*) above, the weights shown in that item in column (5) of that Part.]

[(3) The provisions of paragraph (2) above shall not apply so as to require a vehicle first used before 1st June 1973 fitted with closely spaced axles to be used on a road at a weight as respects the wheels of those axles below that at which it could have been used under Regulation 94.]

[(4) Where any two adjoining axles of three closely spaced axles of a vehicle to which this regulation applies are spaced at such a distance apart as is specified in an item in column (2) of Part V of Schedule 7, the total weight transmitted to the surface of the road by all the wheels of each of those axles shall not exceed the weight shown in that item in column (3) in that Part:

Provided that nothing in this paragraph shall apply to prevent a vehicle being used on a road—

(i) if the vehicle was first used before 1st June 1973, at a weight as respects those closely spaced axles below that at which it could have been used under Regulation 94; or

(ii) with axle weights shown on the plating certificate issued for the vehicle current on 30th April 1983.]

(5) Where the plated weight of any one of three adjacent axles of a vehicle to which this Regulation applies, being a trailer forming part of an articulated vehicle, exceeds [7500 kilograms], the total weight transmitted to the road surface by all the wheels of those axles may amount to but shall not exceed such weight as is specified in Part VI of Schedule 7 and is relevant to those axles by virtue of the provision made in that Part:

Provided that nothing in this paragraph shall apply so as to require a vehicle first used before 1st June 1973 to be used on a road at a weight as respects the wheels of any of those axles below that at which it could have been used under Regulation 94.

(6) In this Regulation—

. . .

'plated weight', in relation to an axle, means the weight for that axle shown in column 2 of a Ministry plate . . . and carried on the vehicle or, if no such plate is carried on the vehicle, the maximum weight in Great Britain shown for that axle in the plate complying with the requirements of Regulation 42 or the weight shown for that axle in the foreign plate with which the vehicle is equipped;

'foreign plate' means the plate mentioned in Regulation 89 (1)(b)(i) or 89 (1)(d)(i).

(7) Nothing in sub-paragraphs (b) and (c) of Regulation 94 shall apply to a vehicle to which this Regulation applies.

[Regulation 92 is printed as amended by SI 1982 No 1576, and SI 1984 No 1809.]

[93. Wheel and axle weights for certain vehicles

(1) This Regulation applies to the same vehicles to which Regulation 92 applies, and sub-paragraphs (b) and (c) of Regulation 94 do not apply to a vehicle to which this Regulation applies.

(2) In the case of a vehicle to which this Regulation applies the weight transmitted to the road by one or more wheels of the vehicle as mentioned in an item in column (2) of the Table below shall not exceed the maximum weight specified in that item in column (3) of that Table.]

[TABLE *[ie table to reg 93 (2)]*

(1) Item No	(2) Wheel criteria	(3) Maximum weight (in kilograms)
1	More than two wheels in line transversely—	
	(*a*) in the case of a vehicle manufactured before 1st May 1983 and the wheels are on— (i) one of two closely spaced axles, or (ii) any one of three adjacent axles are mentioned in Regulation 92 (5), and	
	(*b*) in any case of a vehicle manufactured on or after 1st May 1983.	10170
2	More than two wheels in line transversely in the case of a vehicle manufactured before 1st May 1983 where the wheels are otherwise than as mentioned in (*a*) of item 1.	11180
3	Two wheels in line transversely on the sole driving axle of a motor vehicle where the relevant train weight shown on the plate of that vehicle exceeds 32520 kilograms if each such wheel is fitted with—	
	(*a*) a wide tyre, or	
	(*b*) two pneumatic tyres having the centres of their areas of contact with the road surface not less than 300 millimetres apart measured at right angles to the longitudinal axis of the vehicle.	10500
4	Two wheels in line transversely in a case other than that mentioned in item 3 above if each wheel is fitted with—	
	(*a*) a wide tyre, or	
	(*b*) two pneumatic tyres having the centres of their areas of contact with the road surface not less than 300 millimetres apart measured at right angles to the longitudinal axis of the vehicle	10170
5	Two wheels in line transversely otherwise than as mentioned in item 4	9150
6	One wheel if—	
	(*a*) no other wheel is in the same line transversely; and	
	(*b*) the wheel is fitted with either— (i) a wide tyre, or (ii) two pneumatic tyres having the centres of their areas of contact with the road surface not less than 300 millimetres apart measured at right angles to the longitudinal axis of the vehicle	5090

[TABLE *[ie table to reg 93 (2) continued]*

(1) Item No	(2) Wheel criteria	(3) Maximum weight (in kilograms)
7	One wheel if— (*a*) no other wheel is in the same line transversely; and (*b*) the wheel is not fitted with tyres as mentioned in item 6 above	4580]

[Regulation 93 was substituted by SI 1982 No 1576.]

94. Distribution of weight

Save as provided in Regulations 92 and 93, in the case of a heavy motor car, motor car or trailer, whether laden or unladen, the weight transmitted by more than two wheels to any strip of the road surface upon which the vehicle rests contained between any two parallel lines drawn on that surface at right angles to the longitudinal axis of the vehicle—

(*a*) less than 1.02 metres apart shall not exceed 11180 kilograms;

(*b*) less than 1.22 metres apart but 1.02 metres or more apart shall not exceed 16260 kilograms; and

(*c*) less than 2.13 metres apart but 1.22 metres or more apart shall not exceed 18300 kilograms.

[94A. Weight restriction for agricultural trailed appliances

No person shall use, or cause or permit to be used, on a road an agricultural trailed appliance which is equipped with a plate in accordance with Regulation 42A and which exceeds the maximum gross weight referred to in paragraph (2)(*c*) of that Regulation.]

[Regulation 94A was inserted by SI 1984 No 1809.]

95. Additional weight restrictions

(1) In this Regulation 'plate', in relation to a vehicle, means the plate with which it is required to be equipped by Regulation 42.

[(2) Paragraph 4 of this Regulation applies to—

(*a*) a goods vehicle being a heavy motor car or motor car to which Regulation 42 applies and for which no Ministry plate has been issued, and

(*b*) a locomotive or motor tractor to which Regulation 42 applies.]

(3) . . .

(4) As respects a motor vehicle to which this paragraph applies, whether or not drawing or being drawn by another vehicle, the following provisions of this paragraph shall apply—

(*a*) neither the maximum gross weight shown in its plate nor the maximum gross weight in Great Britain shown in its plate shall be exceeded;

(*b*) neither the maximum axle weight for each axle shown in its plate nor the maximum axle weight in Great Britain for each axle shown in its plate shall be exceeded:

Provided that this sub-paragraph shall not apply in the case of any axle being one of two or more axles to which the following sub-paragraph applies;

(c) where any two or more axles are fitted with a compensating arrangement in accordance with Regulation 11, neither the sum of the maximum axle weights for those axles so fitted shown in its plate nor the sum of the maximum weights in Great Britain for those axles so fitted shown in its plate shall be exceeded;

(d) the maximum train weight (if any) shown in its plate shall not be exceeded.

(5) Paragraph (6) of this Regulation applies to a goods vehicle, being a trailer to which Regulation 42 applies, and for which no plating certificate has been issued.

(6) As respects a trailer to which this paragraph applies, the following provisions of this paragraph shall apply—

(a) neither the maximum gross weight shown in its plate nor the maximum gross weight in Great Britain shown in its plate shall be exceeded;

(b) neither the maximum axle weight for each axle shown in its plate nor the maximum axle weight in Great Britain for each axle shown in its plate shall be exceeded:
    Provided that this sub-paragraph shall not apply in the case of any axle being one of two or more axles to which the following sub-paragraph applies;

(c) where any two or more axles are fitted with a compensating arrangement in accordance with Regulation 11, neither the sum of the maximum axle weights for those axles so fitted shown in its plate nor the sum of the maximum axle weights in Great Britain for those axles so fitted shown in its plate shall be exceeded.

(7) Nothing in Regulations 82 and 85 to 94 shall be taken to permit any such weight as is mentioned in the preceding provisions of this Regulation to be exceeded and nothing in this Regulation shall be taken to permit any weight mentioned in any of the said Regulationss 85 to 94 which is applicable to the vehicle in question to be exceeded.

[Regulation 95 is printed as amended by SI 1982 No 1272.]

[95A. Height of certain vehicles

(1) Save as provided in paragraph (3) below, no person shall use or cause or permit to be used on a road any semi-trailer having a relevant plate showing a gross weight exceeding 26000 kilograms if—

(a) any part of the structure of the vehicle is more than 4.2 metres from the ground when the vehicle is on level ground; and

(b) the total laden weight of the semi-trailer and the vehicle by which it is drawn exceeds 32520 kilograms.

(2) For the purpose of this Regulation the structure of a vehicle includes any detachable structure attached to the vehicle for the purpose of containing any load, but does not include any load which is not a detachable structure or any sheeting or other readily flexible means of covering or securing a load.

(3) This Regulation does not apply to any vehicle while it is being loaded or unloaded.]

[Regulation 95A was inserted by SI 1982 No 1576.]

96. *[Revoked.]*

[96A. Weight limits for agricultural motor vehicles and agricultural trailers

(1)

(a) The sum of the weights transmitted to the road surface by all the wheels of an agricultural motor vehicle or a balanced agricultural trailer may amount to but shall not exceed such weight as is specified in Part I of Schedule 7 and is relevant to the class of vehicle in Column 1 of that Part in which it falls, provided that in the case of an agricultural motor vehicle this shall not exceed 24390 kilograms, and in the case of a balanced agricultural trailer this shall not exceed 18290 kilograms.

For the purposes of this paragraph, in the case of an agricultural motor vehicle, the 'maximum axle weight' shall mean the maximum permissible axle weight as specified by the manufacturer.

(b) In the case of an unbalanced agricultural trailer the sum of the weights transmitted to the road surface by all the wheels of the trailer together with the weight imposed by the trailer on the drawing vehicle shall not exceed 18290 kilograms.

(c) In the case of an agricultural trailed appliance the sum of the weights transmitted to the road surface by all the wheels of the appliance together with the weight imposed by the appliance on the drawing vehicle shall not exceed 14230 kilograms.

(2) The total weight transmitted to the surface of a road by all the wheels of an agricultural motor vehicle and any trailer or trailers which it is drawing shall not exceed—

(a) in the case of an agricultural motor vehicle drawing an unbalanced agricultural trailer where the distance between the rearmost axle of the trailer and the rearmost axle of the drawing vehicle does not exceed 2.9 metres, 20000 kilograms;

(b) in any other case, 24390 kilograms.

(3) In this Regulation—

(a) 'balanced agricultural trailer' means an agricultural trailer the whole of the weight of which is borne by its own wheels, and

(b) 'unbalanced agricultural trailer' means an agricultural trailer not more than 35 per cent of the weight of which is borne by the drawing vehicle and the rest of the weight of which is borne by its own wheels.]

[Regulation 96A was inserted by SI 1984 No 1809.]

97. Maintenance and use of vehicle so as not to be a danger, etc

(1) A motor vehicle, every trailer drawn thereby and all parts and accessories of such vehicle and trailer shall at all times be in such condition, and the number of passengers carried by such vehicle or trailer, the manner in which any passengers are carried in or on such vehicle or trailer, and the weight, distribution, packing and adjustment of the load of such vehicle or trailer shall at all times be such that no danger is caused or is likely to be caused to any person in or on the vehicle or trailer or on a road:

Provided that in the case of a public service vehicle the provisions of this Regulation with regard to the number of passengers carried shall be deemed to be complied with if the number does not exceed that for the time being permitted by regulations made or having effect as if made under [section 26 of the Public Passenger Vehicles Act 1981] with regard to the carrying capacity of public service vehicles.

(2) The load carried by a motor vehicle or trailer shall at all times be so secured, if necessary by physical restraint other than its own weight, and be in such a position, that neither danger nor nuisance is likely to be caused to any person or property by reason of the load or any part thereof falling or being blown from the vehicle or by reason of any other movement of the load or any part thereof in relation to the vehicle.

(3) No motor vehicle or trailer shall be used for any purpose for which it is so unsuitable as to cause or be likely to cause danger or nuisance to any person in or on the vehicle or trailer or on a road.

[Regulation 97 is printed as amended by the Interpretation Act 1978, s 17 (2) (a).]

98. Maintenance of speedometer

[(1) Every instrument for indicating speed fitted to

(a) a motor vehicle in compliance with the requirements of Regulation 18 (1), or

(b) a motor vehicle to which, by virtue of Regulation 5, Regulation 18 (1) does not apply, or

(c) a motor vehicle marked with the marking specified in Regulation 18 (2) (g), shall be kept free from any obstruction which might prevent its being easily read and shall at all material times be maintained in good working order[, or]

[(d) a motor vehicle to which Regulation 18 (3) relates and which is not, under the Recording Equipment Regulation, required to be equipped with the recording equipment mentioned in that paragraph.]

(2) In this Regulation 'all material times' means all times when the motor vehicle is in use on a road except—

(a) when the vehicle is being used on a journey during which, as a result of a defect, the instrument ceased to be in good working order, or

(b) when, as a result of a defect, the instrument has ceased to be in good working [order and steps have been taken to have the vehicle equipped with all reasonable expedition, by means of repairs or replacement, with an instrument which is in good working order.]

[Regulation 98 is printed as substituted by SI 1980 No 1789 and as amended by SI 1982 No 1057.]

99. Maintenance of power to weight ratio

(1) No person shall use or cause or permit to be used any ancillary equipment on a motor vehicle to which Regulation 44 applies while the vehicle is in motion on a road at a speed in excess of 5 miles per hour, unless the power of the engine remaining available to drive the vehicle is at least 4.4 kilowatts for every 1000 kilograms of the relevant weight.

(2) For the purpose of this Regulation 'ancillary equipment' means machinery or apparatus forming part of the vehicle or mounted thereon, used for purposes not connected with the driving of the vehicle and 'relevant weight' has the meaning given in Regulation 44.

100. Maintenance of glass

All glass or other transparent material fitted to motor vehicles shall be maintained in such condition that it does not obscure the vision of the driver while the vehicle is being driven on a road.

Maintenance of brakes

101.—(1) [Every part of every braking system and of the means of operation thereof fitted to a motor vehicle or a trailer, not being—

    (i) a motor vehicle or a trailer to which Regulation 5 applies by virtue of the vehicle's conforming to the requirements of Council Directive 71/320/EEC of 26th July 1971 (which relates to the braking devices of certain categories of motor vehicles and their trailers) or, where appropriate, to the requirements of that Directive as amended by the amending Directives specified in Regulation 5, or

    (ii) a motor vehicle to which Regulation 5A applies; or

    (iii) a motor vehicle or a trailer to which Regulation 14A applies shall

at all times while the motor vehicle or trailer is used on a road—]

    (a) be maintained in good and efficient working order and be properly adjusted;

    (b) in the case of motor vehicles to which Schedule 4 applies and first used before 1st January 1968 be so maintained that the brakes forming part of the system comply with the requirements as to the efficiency of brakes which are applicable to such a vehicle by virtue of the provisions contained in Regulations 59 (4), 64 (4) and 67 (3);

    (c) [in the case of motor vehicles to which paragraph (5) of either Regulation 59 or Regulation 64 or paragraph (3) of Regulation 67 applies], where such a vehicle is not being used while drawing a trailer, be so maintained that the brakes forming part of the system comply with the requirements as to the efficiency of brakes which are applicable to such a vehicle by virtue of the provisions contained in [any of such paragraphs];

    (d) in the case of motor vehicles to which paragraph (6) or (7) of either Regulation 59 or Regulation 64 applies, where such a vehicle is not being used while drawing a trailer, be so maintained that the brakes forming part of the system comply with the requirements as to the efficiency of brakes which are applicable to such a vehicle by virtue of the provisions contained in any of such paragraphs;

    [(e) in the case of a motor vehicle to which Regulation 13 (2) applies, be so maintained that the system complies with the requirements as to its braking force specified in Regulation 13 (2)(b)(ii); and]

    [(f) in the case of a trailer to which Regulation 75 (2) applies, be so maintained that the system complies with the requirements as to its braking force specified in Regulation 75 (2)(c)(iii), and for the purposes of this sub-paragraph a reference to a trailer to which Regulation 75 (2) applies shall, in the case of a composite trailer, be deemed to be a reference to the semi-trailer which forms part of the composite trailer.]

    [(g) in the case of an agricultural motor vehicle to which Regulation 79C (2) applies, be so maintained as to be capable of achieving a braking efficiency equivalent to that specified in that Regulation;]

    [(h) in the case of an agricultural trailer to which Regulation 75 (4A) applies, be so maintained as to be capable of achieving a braking efficiency equivalent to that specified in that Regulation;]

    [(i) in the case of an agricultural motor vehicle to which Regulation 5AA applies because it conforms to the requirements of the Council Directive mentioned in item 7 of the Table in paragraph (2) of that Regulation, be so maintained as to comply with the performance standards and characteristics which are specified in that Directive in relation to the vehicle.]

(2) [Where a motor vehicle to which Regulation 59 (5), 64 (5) or 67 (3) applies] is being used while drawing a trailer manufactured on or after 1st January 1968 (other than a trailer not required by these Regulations to be equipped with a braking system), whether or not that motor vehicle and trailer together form an articulated vehicle, then every part of every braking system with which that motor vehicle is equipped and every part of every braking system with which the trailer is equipped shall be so maintained that, when the brakes of any braking system of that motor vehicle [(being a system to which Regulation 59 (5), 64 (5) or 67 (3) applies)] are applied by their means of operation and the brakes of any braking system of that trailer applied by that same means of operation are applied, those brakes together produce the same total braking efficiencies as would be required of the brakes of such a motor vehicle when applied by that means of operation if that motor vehicle were not drawing a trailer.

(3) [Where a motor vehicle to which Regulation 59 (5), 64 (5) or 67 (3) applies], being a goods vehicle, is being used while drawing a trailer manufactured before 1st January 1968 (other than a trailer not required by these Regulations to be equipped with a braking system), whether or not that motor vehicle and trailer together form an articulated vehicle, then every part of every braking system with which that motor vehicle is equipped and every part of every braking system with which the trailer is equipped shall be so maintained that, when the brakes of any braking system of the motor vehicle [(being a system to which Regulation 59 (5), 64 (5) or 67 (3) applies)] are applied by their means of operation they produce (whether assisted by the brakes on the trailer or not) the same total braking efficiencies as would be required of the brakes of such a motor vehicle when applied by that means of operation if that motor vehicle were not drawing a trailer and if it were treated as being a motor vehicle first used before 1st January 1968 [and in the case of a vehicle to which Regulation 59 (5) or 64 (5) applies, as having to comply with regulation 59 (7) or, as the case may be, Regulation 64 (7)] notwithstanding that the said paragraph does not apply to that motor vehicle.

(4) Where a motor vehicle to which paragraph (6) or (7) of either Regulation 59 or Regulation 64 applies is being used while drawing a trailer (whenever manufactured) other than a trailer not required by these Regulations to be equipped with a braking system, whether or not that motor vehicle and trailer together form an articulated vehicle, then every part of every braking system with which that motor vehicle is equipped and every part of every braking system with which the trailer is equipped shall be so maintained that, when the brakes of any braking system with which the motor vehicle is equipped are applied by their means of operation, they produce (whether assisted by the brakes on the trailer or not) the same total braking efficiencies as would be required of the brakes of such a motor vehicle when applied by that means of operation if that motor vehicle were not drawing a trailer, and if, in the case of a motor vehicle to which the said paragraph (6) applies, it were treated as being a motor vehicle having to comply with paragraph (7) of either Regulation 59 or Regulation 64.

(5) Where a motor vehicle to which paragraph (2) of Regulation 13 applies is attached to a trailer manufactured on or after 1st January 1968 (other than a trailer not required by these Regulations to be equipped with a braking system), whether or not that motor vehicle and trailer together form an articulated vehicle, and the combination of those vehicles is stationary, then every part of every braking system with which that motor vehicle is equipped and every part of every braking system with which the trailer is equipped shall be so maintained that the brakes of those systems as applied by the means of operation specified in the said paragraph (2) can together

produce a braking force sufficient to hold the combination of vehicles stationary on a gradient of at least 1 in 6.25 without the assistance of stored energy.

(6) For the purposes of this Regulation the date of the manufacture of a trailer shall in the case of a composite trailer be deemed to be the date of the manufacture of the semi-trailer which forms part of the composite trailer.

[(7) [Revoked.]]

[Regulation 101 is printed as amended by SI 1980 No 880; SI 1981 No 1189; SI 1981 No 1580; SI 1982 No 1480; and SI 1984 No 1809.]

[**101A.**—(1) This Regulation applies to every motor vehicle or trailer mentioned in sub-paragraph (i), (ii) or (iii) of Regulation 101 (1) and to every motor vehicle or trailer to which, by virtue of item 10 in the Table in Regulation 5B, Regulation 101 does not apply.

(2) The braking system of every motor vehicle or trailer to which this Regulation applies shall at all times when the vehicle is in use on a road be maintained [in good and efficient working order and be properly adjusted and] so that—

(a) if it is a vehicle to which Regulation 14A applies, the requirements as to construction and fitting and, save as provided in paragraphs (3) to (6) below, the requirements as to performance, referred to in Regulation 14A (1) are complied with;

(b) if it is a vehicle to which, by virtue of Regulation 5, Regulation 14A does not apply, the requirements as to construction and fitting and, save as provided in paragraphs (3) to (6) below, the requirements as to performance, specified in the Directives mentioned in item 7, 7A, 7B or 7C in the Table in Regulation 5 are complied with;

(c) if it is a vehicle to which, by virtue of Regulation 5A, Regulation 14A does not apply, the requirements as to design and construction and equipment specified in items 13A, 13B, 13C or 13D in Schedule 1 to the [Motor Vehicles (Type Approval) (Great Britain) Regulations 1984 [SI 1984 No 981]] and, save as provided in paragraphs (3) to (6) below, the requirements as to performance specified in the instrument or other document mentioned, respectively, in relation to those items in column 3 of the said Schedule, are complied with;

[(cc) if it is a vehicle to which, by virtue of regulation 5A, Regulation 14A does not apply, the requirements as to design and construction and equipment specified in items 6, 6A, 6B, 6C or 6D in Schedule 1 to the Motor Vehicles (Type Approval for Goods Vehicles) (Great Britain) Regulations 1982 and, save as provided in paragraphs (3) to (6) below, the requirements as to performance specified in the instrument or other document mentioned, respectively, in relation to those items in column 3 of the said Schedule, are complied with;]

(d) if it is a vehicle to which, by virtue of Regulation 5B, Regulation 14A does not apply, the requirements as to design and construction with which the vehicle must comply in order to qualify for the marking designated as an approval mark in [item 13, 13A, 13B or 13C] in Schedule 2 to the Motor Vehicles (Designation of Approval Marks) Regulations 1979 and, save as provided in paragraphs (3) to (6) below, the requirements as to performance specified in the Regulations mentioned respectively in relation to those items in column 3 of the said Schedule, are complied with.

(3) (a) The service braking system of every motor vehicle to which this Regulation

applies shall at all times when the vehicle is in use on a road and not drawing a trailer have a total braking efficiency of not less than 50 per cent; and

(b) where a motor vehicle to which this Regulation applies is in use on a road and drawing a trailer the service braking system of the combination of the motor vehicle and the trailer shall at all times have a total braking efficiency of not less than 45 per cent.

(4) The secondary braking system of every motor vehicle to which this Regulation applies shall at all times when the vehicle is in use on a road have a total braking efficiency of not less than 25 per cent.

(5) The parking braking system of every motor vehicle or trailer to which this Regulation applies shall at all times when the vehicle is in use on a road be capable of holding the vehicle stationary on a gradient of at least 16 per cent.

(6) The parking braking system of every motor vehicle to which this Regulation applies shall at all times when the vehicle is in use on a road and drawing one or more trailers with a permissible maximum weight specified in Schedule 6 or 7, be capable of holding the combination of vehicles stationary on a gradient of at least 12 per cent without the use of stored energy and without the assistance of any brake fitted to the trailer.

(7) In this Regulation—

'service braking system' means the braking system of a vehicle which is designed and constructed to have the highest braking efficiency of any braking system with which the vehicle is equipped;

'secondary braking system' means a braking system of a vehicle applied by a secondary means of operation independent of the service braking system or by one of the sections comprised in a split braking system; and

'parking brake' means the brake with which a vehicle is required to be fitted in order to comply with the requirement specified in Regulation 13 (1) or (2), or with the requirement by virtue of which, in accordance with Regulation 13 (3)(c), it is exempt from the requirement specified in Regulation 13 (1) or (2).]

[Regulation 101A was added by SI 1981 No 1189 and is printed as amended by SI 1982 No 1272 and SI 1982 No 1480.]

102. Maintenance of steering gear

All steering gear fitted to a motor vehicle shall at all times while the vehicle is used on a road be maintained in good and efficient working order and be properly adjusted.

[102A. Maintenance of seat belts and anchorage points

(1) This Regulation applies to every seat belt with which a motor vehicle is required to be provided in accordance with Regulation 17 and to the anchorages, fastenings, adjusting device and retracting mechanism (if any) of every such seat belt.

(2) For the purposes of this Regulation the anchorages and anchorage points of a seat belt shall, in the case of a seat with integral seat belt anchorages, include the system by which the seat assembly itself is secured to the vehicle structure.

(3) The anchorage points provided for seat belts shall be used only as anchorages for the seat belts for which they are intended to be used or capable of being used.

(4) Save as provided in paragraph (5) below—

(a) all load-bearing members of the vehicle structure or panelling within 30 centimetres of each anchorage point shall be maintained in a sound condition and free from serious corrosion, distortion or fracture;

(b) the adjusting device and (if fitted) the retracting mechanism of the seat belt shall be so maintained that the belt may be readily adjusted to the body of the wearer, either automatically or manually, according to the design of the device and (if fitted) the retracting mechanism;

(c) the seat belt and its anchorages, fastenings and adjusting device shall be maintained free from any obvious defect which would be likely to affect adversely the performance by the seat belt of the function of restraining the body of the wearer in the event of an accident to the vehicle;

(d) the buckle or other fastening of the seat belt shall—
    (i) be so maintained that the belt can be readily fastened or unfastened,
    (ii) be kept free from any temporary or permanent obstruction, and
    (iii) except in the case of a disabled person's seat belt, be readily accessible to a person sitting in the seat for which the seat belt is provided;

(e) the webbing or other material which forms the seat belt shall be maintained free from cuts or other visible faults (as, for example, extensive fraying) which would be likely to affect adversely the performance of the belt when under stress;

(f) the ends of every seat belt, other than a disabled person's seat belt, shall be securely fastened to the anchorage points provided for them; and

(g) the ends of every disabled person's seat belt shall, when the seat belt is being used for the purpose for which it was designed and constructed, be securely fastened either to some part of the structure of the vehicle or to the seat which is being occupied by the person wearing the belt so that the body of the person wearing the belt would be restrained in the event of an accident to the vehicle.

(5) No requirement specified in paragraph (4) above applies if—

(a) the vehicle is being used on a journey after the start of which the requirement ceased to be complied with; or

(b) the vehicle is being used after the requirement ceased to be complied with and steps have been taken for such compliance to be restored with all reasonable expedition.

(6) Expressions which are used in this Regulation and are defined in Regulation 17 have the same meaning in this Regulation as they have in Regulation 17.]

[Regulation 102A is printed as substituted by SI 1982 No 1132. (Formerly reg 102A had been amended by SI 1978 No 1233 and SI 1979 No 1062.)]

103. Maintenance of windscreen wipers

Every windscreen wiper required by these Regulations to be fitted to a motor vehicle shall at all times while the vehicle is used on a road be maintained in good and efficient working order and be properly adjusted.

104. Maintenance of petrol tank

Every motor vehicle shall at all times be so maintained that—

(a) any tank, in which petroleum spirit as defined in section 23 of the Petroleum (Consolidation) Act 1928 used either for the propulsion of the vehicle or for the driving of any ancillary engine or equipment forming part of the vehicle is contained, is reasonably secure against its being damaged, and

(b) the leakage of any liquid or vapour from the said tank is adequately prevented so, however, that nothing in this paragraph shall be taken to preclude the tank being fitted with a device which by the intake of air or the emission of vapour relieves changes in pressure in the tank.

105, 106. *[Revoked.]*

[105A. Maintenance of rear under-run protective device

(1) Every rear under-run protective device fitted to:—

(a) a vehicle in compliance with the requirements of Regulation 46B, or

(b) a vehicle to which, by virtue of Regulation 5, Regulation 46B does not apply

and every device fitted to a vehicle in accordance with paragraph (4) or (5) of Regulation 46B shall at all times when the vehicle is on a road be maintained free from any obvious defect which would be likely to affect adversely the performance of the device in the function of giving resistance in the event of an impact from the rear.

(2) In this Regulation 'rear under-run protective device' has the same meaning as in Regulation 46B.]

[Regulation 105A was inserted by SI 1982 No 1576.]

[105B. Maintenance of sideguards

Every sideguard fitted to a vehicle in compliance with the requirements of Regulation 46C or Regulation 46D shall at all times when the vehicle is on a road be maintained free from any obvious defect which would be likely to affect adversely the effectiveness of the device.]

[Regulation 105B was inserted by SI 1982 No 1576.]

[105C. Maintenance of devices for containment and suppression of spray

Every part of every containment device with which a vehicle is required to be fitted by the provisions of Regulation 46E shall at all times when the vehicle is on a road be maintained free from any obvious defect which would be likely to affect adversely the effectiveness of the device.]

[Regulation 105C was inserted by SI 1984 No 1543.]

Condition and maintenance of tyres

107.—(1) Save as provided in paragraphs (2) and (3) of this Regulation, no person shall use or cause or permit to be used on a road any motor vehicle or trailer a wheel of which is fitted with a pneumatic tyre, if—

(a) the tyre is unsuitable having regard to the use to which the motor vehicle or trailer is being put or to the types of tyres fitted to its other wheels;

(b) the tyre is not so inflated as to make it fit for the use to which the motor vehicle or trailer is being put;

(c) the tyre . . . has a cut in excess of 25 millimetres or 10 per cent of the section width of the tyre, which ever is the greater, measured in any direction on the outside of the tyre and deep enough to reach the [ply or cord];

(d) the tyre has any [lump, bulge or tear] caused by separation or partial failure of its structure;

(*e*) the tyre has any portion of the ply or cord . . . exposed; or

[(*f*) the base of any groove which showed in the original tread pattern of the tyre is not clearly visible;]

[(*g*) either (i) the grooves of the tread pattern of the tyre do not have a depth of at least 1 millimetre throughout a continuous band measuring at least three-quarters of the breadth of the tread and round the entire outer circumference of the tyre;

or (ii) in a case where the original tread pattern of the tyre did not extend beyond three-quarters of the breadth of the tread the base of any groove which showed in the original tread pattern does not have a depth of at least 1 millimetre.]

(2) Paragraph (1) of this Regulation shall not prohibit the use on a road of a motor vehicle or trailer by reason only of the fact that a wheel of the vehicle or trailer is fitted with a tyre which is deflated or not fully inflated and which has any of the defects described in sub-paragraph (*c*), (*d*) or (*e*) of paragraph (1) of this Regulation, if the tyre and the wheel to which it is fitted are so constructed as to make the tyre in that condition fit for the use to which the motor vehicle or trailer is being put and the outer sides of the wall of the tyre are so marked as to enable the tyre to be identified as having been constructed to comply with the requirements of this paragraph.

[(3)(*a*) Nothing in paragraph (1) above applies to—

[(i) an agricultural motor vehicle that is not driven at a speed in excess of 20 miles per hour,

(ii) an agricultural trailer,

(iii) an agricultural trailed appliance,

(iv) an agricultural trailed appliance conveyor,]

(v) *[revoked]*

(vi) a broken down vehicle or a vehicle proceeding to a place where it is to be broken up, being drawn, in either case, by a motor vehicle at a speed not exceeding 20 miles per hour;

(*b*) Nothing in paragraph 1(*f*) and (*g*) above applies to—

(i) a motor cycle having three wheels the unladen weight of which does not exceed 102 kilogrammes and which is incapable of exceeding 12 miles per hour on the level under its own power, or

(ii) a pedestrian controlled works truck;

(*c*) Nothing in paragraph (1) (*g*) above applies to a motorcycle with an engine capacity which does not exceed 50 cubic centimetres.]

[(4) No person shall use or cause or permit to be used on a road any motor vehicle or trailer a wheel of which is fitted with a recut pneumatic tyre if—

(*a*) its ply or cord has been cut or exposed by the recutting process, or

(*b*) it has been wholly or partially recut, in a pattern other than the manufacturer's recut tread pattern.]

(5) Without prejudice to paragraphs (1) and (4) of this Regulation, all the tyres of a motor vehicle or trailer shall at all times while the vehicle or trailer is used on a road be maintained in such condition as to be fit for the use to which the vehicle or trailer is being put, and as to be free from any defect which might in any way cause damage to the surface of the road or danger to persons on or in the vehicle or to other persons using the road.

(6) [(*a*)] For the purposes of this Regulation—

['breadth of tread' means the breadth of that part of the tyre which can contact the road under normal conditions of use measured at 90 degrees to the peripheral line of the tread;]

['original tread pattern' means—
— in the case of a re-treaded tyre, the tread pattern of the tyre immediately after the tyre was re-treaded,
— in the case of a wholly recut tyre, the manufacturer's recut tread pattern,
— in the case of a partially recut tyre, on that part of the tyre which has been recut, the manufacturer's recut tread pattern, and on the other part, the tread pattern of the tyre when new, and
— in the case of any other tyre, the tread pattern of the tyre when the tyre was new;]

'tie-bar' means any part of a tyre moulded in the tread of the tyre for the purpose of bracing two or more features of such tread pattern; . . .

['tread pattern' means the combination of plain surfaces and grooves extending across the breadth of the tread and round the entire outer circumference of the tyre but excludes:—
(a) any tie bars or tread wear indicators,
(b) any features which are designed to wear out substantially before the rest of the pattern under normal conditions of use; and
(c) any other minor features; and]

'tread wear indicator' means any bar, not being a tie-bar, projecting from the base of the tread pattern of a tyre and moulded between two or more features of the tread pattern of a tyre for the purpose of indicating the extent of the wear of such tread pattern[;]

[(b) The references in paragraph (1)(g)(i) above to grooves are references
— in so far as a tyre has been recut, to the grooves of the manufacturer's recut tread pattern; and
— in so far as a tyre has not been recut, to the grooves which showed when the tyre was new.]

[Regulation 107 is printed as amended by SI 1982 No 932, and SI 1984 No 1809.]

108.—(1) No person shall use or cause or permit to be used on a road a vehicle if pneumatic tyres of different types of structure are fitted to the same axle of the vehicle.

(2) Save as provided in paragraph (3) of this Regulation, no person shall use or cause or permit to be used on a road a motor vehicle having only two axles each of which is equipped with one or two single wheels if—

(a) a diagonal-ply tyre or a bias-belted tyre is fitted on the rear axle of the vehicle and a radial-ply tyre is fitted on the front axle of the vehicle; or

(b) a diagonal-ply tyre is fitted on the rear axle of the vehicle and a bias-belted tyre is fitted on the front axle of the vehicle.

(3) Paragraph (2) of this Regulation shall not apply to a vehicle to an axle of which there are fitted wide tyres not being wide tyres which were specially constructed for use on engineering plant [or to a vehicle which is incapable by reason of its construction of exceeding a speed of 30 miles per hour on the level under its own power].

(4) No person shall use or cause or permit to be used on a road a motor vehicle if—

(a) pneumatic tyres of one type of structure are fitted on a steerable axle of the vehicle and tyres of a different type of structure are fitted on another steerable axle of the vehicle; or (*b*) pneumatic tyres of one type of structure are fitted on a driven axle of the vehicle not being a steerable axle and tyres of a different type of structure are fitted on another driven axle of the vehicle not being a steerable axle.

(5) For the purposes of this Regulation—

'axle' includes—

      (i) two or more stub axles which are fitted on opposite sides of the longitudinal axis of the vehicle so as to form—

          (*a*) a pair in the case of two stub axles, and

          (*b*) pairs in the case of more than two stub axles, and

      (ii) a single stub axle which is not one of a pair;

'a bias-belted tyre' means a pneumatic tyre, the structure of which is such that the ply cords extend to the bead so as to be laid at alternate angles of substantially less than 90° to the peripheral line of the tread, and are constrained by a circumferential belt comprising two or more layers of substantially inextensible cord material laid at alternate angles smaller than those of the ply cord structure;

'a diagonal-ply tyre' means a pneumatic tyre, the structure of which is such that the ply cords extend to the bead so as to be laid at alternate angles of substantially less than 90° to the peripheral line of the tread, but not being a bias-belted tyre;

'a driven axle' means an axle through which power is transmitted from the engine of the vehicle of which the axle forms part to the wheels on that axle;

'a radial-ply tyre' means a pneumatic tyre, the structure of which is such that the ply cords extend to the bead so as to be laid at an angle of substantially 90° to the peripheral line of the tread, the ply cord structure being stabilised by a substantially inextensible circumferential belt;

'stub axle' means an axle on which only one wheel is mounted; and

'type of structure', in relation to a tyre, means a type of structure of a tyre of a kind defined in the foregoing provisions of this paragraph.

[Regulation 108 is printed as amended by SI 1983 No 932.]

Maintenance and use of vehicles so as not to emit smoke, etc

109. No person shall use or cause or permit to be used on a road any motor vehicle from which any smoke, visible vapour, grit, sparks, ashes, cinders, or oily substance is emitted if the emission thereof causes or is likely to cause damage to any property or injury to any person who is actually at the time or who reasonably may be expected on the road, or is likely to cause danger to any such person as aforesaid.

[**110.** No person shall use or cause or permit to be used on a road—

(*a*) a motor vehicle to which paragraph (1) or (4) of Regulation 37 applies, or

[(*b*) an agricultural motor vehicle of a type specified in Regulation 5AA in respect of which a type approval certificate has been issued in relation to Item 8 in the Table to that Regulation, or]

(*c*) a motor vehicle to which Regulation 5 applies by virtue of the vehicle's conforming to the requirements of Council Directive 72/306/EEC of 2nd August 1972 *[OJ L 190, 20.8.72, p 1 (SE 1972 (III) p 889)]*

if the fuel injection equipment, the engine speed governor or any other parts of the engine by which it is propelled have in any way been altered or adjusted so as to increase by such alteration or adjustment the emission of smoke from that vehicle.]

[Regulation 110 is printed as substituted by SI 1979 No 843 and as subsequently amended by SI 1984 No 1809.]

111. Where a motor vehicle, being a vehicle propelled by a compression ignition engine, is fitted with a device to facilitate the starting of the engine by causing it to be supplied with excess fuel—

(*a*) the device shall be maintained in such a condition that it does not cause the engine to be supplied with excess fuel while the vehicle is in motion on a road; and

(*b*) no person shall use the device, or cause or permit it to be used, so as to cause it to supply the engine with excess fuel while the vehicle is in motion on a road:

Provided that paragraph (*b*) of this Regulation shall not apply as respects a device such as is mentioned in sub-paragraph (ii) of the proviso to Regulation 34 (2).

112. The engine of every motor vehicle to which Regulation 35 applies shall at all times while the vehicle is used on a road be so maintained that the means by which (in compliance with that Regulation) vapours or gases in the engine crank case or in other parts of the engine are prevented from escaping into the atmosphere are in good and efficient working order.

113. Contents of lavatories, etc

No person shall cause or permit the contents of any closet, urinal, lavatory basin or sink carried by a motor vehicle or trailer or of any tank into which such closet, urinal, lavatory basin or sink drains to be discharged or to leak on to a road.

Excessive noise

114. No person shall use or cause or permit to be used on a road any motor vehicle or trailer which causes any excessive noise:

Provided that it shall be a good defence to proceedings taken in respect of a contravention of this Regulation—

(i) to prove that the noise or continuance of the noise in respect of which the proceedings are taken was due to some temporary or accidental cause and could not have been prevented by the exercise of due diligence and care on the part of the owner or driver of the motor vehicle, or

(ii) in the case of proceedings against the driver or person in charge of the motor vehicle who is not the owner thereof, to prove that the noise arose through a defect in design or construction of the motor vehicle or trailer or through the negligence or fault of some other person whose duty it was to keep the motor vehicle or trailer in proper condition or in a proper state of repair or adjustment or properly to pack or adjust the load of such motor vehicle or trailer as the case may be and could not have been prevented by the exercise of reasonable diligence and care on the part of such driver or other person in charge of the motor vehicle.

115. No motor vehicle shall be used on a road in such manner as to cause any excessive noise which could have been avoided by the exercise of reasonable care on the part of the driver.

116. Limitation of noise by measurement

(1) Except as provided in paragraph (4) below, this Regulation applies to any vehicle which is a motor vehicle first used on or after 1st January 1931 or which is a trailer.

(2) Subject to the following provisions of this Regulation, no person shall use or cause or permit to be used on a road any vehicle to which this Regulation applies if—

(a) at a time when the noise emitted by that vehicle is measured under the conditions set out in Schedule 10 by an apparatus of the kind prescribed by paragraph (5) below, there is indicated by that apparatus in relation to the said noise so measured a sound level (A weighting) in decibels which exceeds the maximum sound level permitted in relation to that vehicle by paragraph (3) below, and

(b) the sound level of such noise as is described in paragraph 4 of Schedule 10 when measured in accordance with the provisions of that paragraph is found to be at least 10 decibels (A weighting) below the sound level indicated as herein before provided by the said apparatus in relation to the noise emitted by the vehicle.

[(3) The maximum sound level permitted for the purpose of paragraph (2) above shall be—

(a) in the case of a motor vehicle first used before 1st November 1970, the sound level (A weighting) in decibels shown in an item in column 3 of Schedule 9A in relation to the class of vehicle shown in that item in column 2 of Schedule 9A;

(b) in the case of a motor vehicle first used on or after 1st November 1970 but not being a vehicle to which sub-paragraph (c) below applies, the sound level (A weighting) in decibels shown in an item in column 4 of Schedule 9A in relation to the class of vehicle shown in that item in column 2 of Schedule 9A;

(c) in the case of a vehicle to which Regulation 31A, 31B, 31C or 31E applies the sound level (A weighting) in decibels shown in an item in column 5 of Schedule 9A in relation to the class of vehicle shown in that item in column 2 of Schedule 9A.]

(4) This Regulation shall not apply—

[(a) a motor vehicle proceeding to a place where, by previous arrangement—

    (i) noise emitted by it is about to be measured for the purpose of ascertaining whether or not that vehicle complies with Regulation 31 or, as the case may be 31A, 31B, 31C or 31E; or

    (ii) the vehicle is about to be mechanically adjusted, modified or equipped for the purpose of securing that it so complies; or]

[(b) a motor vehicle returning from such a place immediately after the noise had been so measured; or]

(c) to a vehicle at a time when it is stationary otherwise than through enforced stoppage owing to the necessities of traffic and at the same time Regulation 117, by virtue of the proviso thereto, does not apply in relation to that vehicle, or

(d) to a motor vehicle first used before 1st November 1970 at a time when an exhaust brake with which that vehicle is fitted is in operation, or

[(e) a vehicle to which Regulation 31D (3) applies.]

(5) The apparatus prescribed for the purposes of paragraph (2) above shall be a noise meter of the same kind as that prescribed for the purposes of paragraph (1) of Regulation 31, and paragraph (3) of that Regulation shall have effect in relation to this Regulation as if any references therein to paragraph (1) of Regulation 31 were references to paragraph (2) of this Regulation.

(6) It shall be a good defence to proceedings taken in respect of the use of a vehicle

which does not comply with this Regulation to prove the matters which would, by virtue of either proviso (i) or proviso (ii) to Regulation 114, constitute a good defence to proceedings taken in respect of the use of a motor vehicle which does not comply with that Regulation.

(7) The definition of sound level (A weighting) in decibels specified in Regulation 31 (5) shall apply for the purposes of this Regulation and Schedules 9 and 10.

(8) In this Regulation and Schedule 10, any reference to noise emitted by a vehicle shall be construed as including a reference to noise howsoever arising which is attributable to any load, burden or goods carried on or by the vehicle or to anything (other than an audible warning instrument fitted in accordance with Regulation 29 (1) or an instrument or apparatus fitted in accordance with Regulation 29 (6)) fitted to it, or attributable to the manner in which the vehicle is loaded or fitted.

(9) Where any motor vehicle to which this Regulation applies is drawing a trailer, this Regulation and Schedules 9 and 10 shall have effect in relation to that motor vehicle as if any reference to it were a reference both to the motor vehicle and to the trailer drawn thereby.

(10) *[Revoked.]*

[Regulation 116 is printed as amended by SI 1980 No 1166.]

Other limitations as to noise

[116A. No person shall use or cause or permit to be used on a road any vehicle propelled by an internal combustion engine—

(*a*) so that the exhaust gases from the engine escape into the atmosphere without first passing through the silencer, expansion chamber or other contrivance with which the vehicle is required by Regulation 30 to be fitted;

(*b*) with any such silencer, expansion chamber or other contrivance altered or replaced in such a way that the alteration or replacement increases the noise made by the escape of the exhaust gases so that the vehicle does not comply with Regulation 116B; or

(*c*) with any such silencer, expansion chamber or other contrivance which is not in good and efficient working order.]

[Regulation 116A was inserted by SI 1982 No 1422.]

[116B.—(1) No person shall use or cause or permit to be used on a road any motor vehicle—

(*a*) to which Regulation 31, 31A, 31B, 31C or 31E applies or

(*b*) to which any of those Regulations would apply save for the provisions of Regulation 5

unless it is fitted with such parts as are required to enable it to comply—

(i) if the vehicle is one mentioned in sub-paragraph (*a*) above, with requirements specified in the regulation mentioned in that sub-paragraph which applies to the vehicle; or

(ii) if the vehicle is one mentioned in sub-paragraph (*b*) above, with the requirements specified in the community directive mentioned in the Table in Regulation 5 with reference to which the vehicle is exempt from the Regulation in question.

(2) Nothing in paragraph (1) above derogates from any requirement specified in regulation 116.]

[Regulation 116B was inserted by SI 1982 No 1422.]

[116C.—(1) No person shall use, or cause or permit to be used, on a road any motorcycle or moped first used on or after 1st January 1985 if the silencer which forms part of its exhaust system is not either—

(a) that with which the vehicle was fitted when it was first used; or

(b) clearly and indelibly marked with either—

  (i) the relevant British Standard marking indicating that it has been tested in accordance with test 2, or

  (ii) a reference to its make and type specified by the manufacturer of the vehicle.

(2) No person shall use, or cause or permit to be used, on a road any motorcycle or moped which is fitted with an exhaust system any part of which is marked with the words 'NOT FOR ROAD USE' or words to the like effect.

(3) In this Regulation—

'British Standard marking' means a marking specified in paragraph 6.1 of the British Standard Specification for replacement motorcycle and moped exhaust systems, which came into effect on 30th September 1983 issued by the British Standard Institution under reference number BS AU 193: 1983, and 'test 2' means the test so described in that Specification and therein specified;

'exhaust system' means a complete set of components through which the exhaust gases escape from the engine unit of a motorcycle or moped including those which are necessary to limit the noise caused by the escape of those gases; and

'moped' and 'motorcycle' have the same meanings as in Regulation 31B.

(4) Nothing in this Regulation derogates from any requirement specified in Regulation 116, 116A, or 116B.]

[Regulation 116C was inserted by SI 1984 No 679.]

117. Stopping of engine when stationary

The driver of every motor vehicle shall, when the vehicle is stationary otherwise than through enforced stoppage owing to the necessities of traffic, stop the action of any machinery attached to or forming part of such vehicle so far as may be necessary for the prevention of noise:

Provided that this Regulation shall not apply—

(a) so as to prevent the examination or working of the machinery attached to or forming part of a motor vehicle where any such examination or working is rendered necessary by any failure or derangement of the said machinery or where the machinery attached to or forming part of the vehicle is required to be worked for some ancillary purpose; or

(b) in the case of a motor vehicle which is propelled by gas produced in plant carried on the vehicle or on a trailer drawn by the vehicle.

118. Use of audible warning instruments

(1) Subject to the provisions of this Regulation, no person shall—

(a) in the case of a vehicle which is stationary on a road, at any time, other than at times of danger due to another moving vehicle on or near the road, or

(b) in the case of a vehicle which is in motion on a restricted road, between 23.30 hours and 07.00 hours in the following morning,

sound or cause or permit to be sounded any instrument or apparatus fitted to or otherwise carried on the vehicle, being an instrument or apparatus capable of giving audible and sufficient warning of its approach or position.

(2) Subject to the provisions of this Regulation and without prejudice to the provisions of the foregoing paragraph, no person shall sound or cause or permit to be sounded a gong, bell, siren, any instrument or apparatus capable of making a sound similar to that emitted by a gong, bell or siren, or a two-tone horn, fitted to or otherwise carried on a vehicle (whether it is stationary or not).

[(3) Nothing in paragraph (1) or (2) above shall prevent—

  (a) the sounding of an instrument or apparatus fitted to, or otherwise carried on a vehicle at a time when the vehicle is being used for one of the relevant purposes specified in Regulation 29 (3) and it is necessary or desirable to do so either to indicate to other road users the urgency of the purposes for which the vehicle is being used, or to warn other road users of the presence of the vehicle on the road;

  (b) the sounding of a horn (not being a two-tone horn), bell, gong or siren—

    (i) to raise alarm as to the theft or attempted theft of the vehicle or its contents; or

    (ii) in the case of a large passenger vehicle, to summon help for the driver, the conductor or an inspector while the vehicle is being used as a public service vehicle.]

[(4) Subject to the provisions of section 62 of the Control of Pollution Act 1974 and notwithstanding the provisions of paragraphs (1) and (2) above, a person may sound or cause or permit to be sounded an instrument or apparatus other than a two-tone horn fitted to or otherwise carried on a vehicle, being an instrument or apparatus designed to emit a sound for the purpose of informing members of the public that the vehicle is conveying goods for sale, if—

  (a) when the apparatus or instrument is sounded, it is sounded only for that purpose; and

  (b) the apparatus or instrument is sounded otherwise than between 1900 hours and 1200 hours on the following day.]

[(5) Every device mentioned in Regulation 29 (6) shall at all times be maintained in good and efficient working order.]

[(6) Expressions which are used in this Regulation and in Regulation 29 have the same meaning in this Regulation as they have in Regulation 29 and the expression 'restricted road' in paragraph (1) above means a road which is a restricted road for the purpose of [section 81 of the Road Traffic Regulation Act 1984.]

[Regulation 118 is printed as amended by SI 1981 No 1580, and the Road Traffic Act 1984, s 144 (1), Sched 10, para 2.

The Control of Pollution Act 1974, s 62, regulates the use of loudspeakers in streets.]

Duties relating to driving and stopping

119. No person while actually driving a motor vehicle on a road shall be in such a position that he cannot have proper control of that vehicle or that he cannot retain a full view of the road and traffic ahead and no person shall cause or permit any other person while actually driving a motor vehicle on a road to be in such a position as aforesaid.

120. No person shall cause or permit a motor vehicle to travel backwards for a greater distance or time than may be requisite for the safety or reasonable convenience of the occupants of that vehicle or of other traffic on the road:

Provided that this Regulation shall not apply in the case of a road roller or other road plant while actually engaged in the construction, maintenance or repair of roads.

121. The driver of every vehicle propelled by steam (other than a motor car) shall, unless two persons are carried on it for the purpose of driving or attending to the vehicle, stop the vehicle whenever it is necessary to attend to the furnace.

122. No person in charge of a motor vehicle or trailer shall cause or permit the motor vehicle or trailer to stand on a road so as to cause any unnecessary obstruction thereof.

123.—(1) Save as provided in paragraph (2) of this Regulation, no person shall, except with the permission of a police officer in uniform, cause or permit any motor vehicle to stand on any road during the hours of darkness otherwise than with the left or near side of the vehicle as close as may be to the edge of the carriageway.

(2) This Regulation shall not apply to—

(*a*) any motor vehicle when it is being used for fire brigade, ambulance or police purposes or for defence purposes (including civil defence purposes) if compliance with this Regulation would hinder or be likely to hinder the use of the vehicle for the purpose for which it is being used on that occasion;

(*b*) any motor vehicle standing on a part of a road specially set aside for the parking of vehicles or as a stand for hackney carriages or as a stand for public service vehicles or as a place at which such vehicles may stop for a longer time than is necessary for the taking up and setting down of passengers where compliance with this Regulation would conflict with the provisions of any order, regulations or byelaws governing the use of such part of a road for that purpose;

(*c*) any motor vehicle waiting to set down or pick up passengers in accordance with regulations made or directions given by a chief officer of police in regard to such setting down or picking up;

(*d*) any motor vehicle on any road in which vehicles are allowed to proceed in one direction only; or

(*e*) any motor vehicle whilst it is being used in connection with
   (i) any building operation or demolition,
   (ii) the repair of any other vehicle,
   (iii) the removal of any obstruction to traffic,
   (iv) the maintenance, repair or reconstruction of any road, or
   (v) the laying, erection, alteration or repair in or near to any road of any sewer, of any main, pipe or apparatus for the supply of gas, water or electricity, of any telegraph or telephone wires, cables, posts or supports or of the apparatus of any electric transport undertaking if, in any such case, compliance with this Regulation would hinder or be likely to hinder the use of the vehicle for the purpose for which it is being used on that occasion.

124.—(1) No person shall cause or permit to be on a road any motor vehicle which is not attended by a person duly licensed to drive it unless the engine is stopped and the relevant parking brake is effectively set.

Provided that the requirements of this Regulation as to the stopping of the engine shall not apply in the case of—

(a) a fire brigade vehicle the engine of which is being used for any fire brigade purpose;

(b) a vehicle which is propelled by gas produced in plant carried on the vehicle or on a trailer drawn by the vehicle;

(c) a vehicle when it is being used for police or ambulance purposes; or

(d) a vehicle engaged in operations which require its engine to be used—

  (i) to drive special machinery or apparatus forming part of the vehicle or mounted thereon, such machinery or apparatus being that used for purposes other than in connection with the driving of the vehicle, or

  (ii) to maintain the electrical power in the batteries of the vehicle at a level required for the driving of such machinery or apparatus,

so, however, that paragraph (d) of this proviso shall not have effect in the case of a vehicle which is stationary on a road in such a position or in such condition or in such circumstances (including the gradient of the road) as to be likely to cause danger to any person or property.

(2) In this Regulation, 'relevant parking brake' means—

(a) in the case of a motor vehicle to which Regulation 5 applies, being a vehicle to which that Regulation applies by virtue of the vehicle's conforming to the requirements of Council Directive 710/320/EEC of 26th July 1971 *[OJ L 202, 6.9.71, p 37 (SE 1971 (III), p 746)]*, or, where appropriate, to the requirements of that Directive as amended by the amending Directives specified in Regulation 5, the parking brake provided in accordance with those requirements; and

(b) in the case of any other motor vehicle, the parking brake provided in accordance with Regulation 13.

125. Opening of doors

No person shall open or cause or permit to be opened any door of a motor vehicle or trailer on a road so as to cause injury or danger to any person.

Application of brakes of trailers

126.—(1) Where a trailer is drawn by a motor vehicle whether wheeled or track laying the driver (or in the case of a locomotive one of the persons employed in driving or tending the locomotive) shall be in a position readily to operate any brakes required to be fitted to the trailer as well as the brakes of the motor vehicle unless a person other than the driver is in a position and competent efficiently to apply the brakes of the trailer:

Provided that this Regulation shall not apply in the case of trailers which, in compliance with these Regulations, are fitted with brakes which automatically come into operation on the overrun of the trailer or where a motor vehicle is drawing a broken down vehicle, whether or not in consequence of a breakdown, in such a manner that the broken down vehicle cannot be steered by its own steering gear.

(2) In this Regulation, the reference to the brakes required to be fitted to a trailer means—

(a) in the case of a trailer to which Regulation 5 applies, being a trailer to which that Regulation applies by virtue of the trailer's conforming to the requirements of Council Directive 71/320/EEC of 26th July 1971 *[OJ L 202, 6.9.71, p 37 (SE 1971 (III), p 746)]*, or, where appropriate, to the requirements of that

Directive as amended by the amending Directives specified in Regulation 5, the brakes fitted in accordance with those requirements; and

[(*aa*) in the case of a trailer to which Regulation 5B applies, the brakes fitted in accordance with ECE Regulation 13 (as defined in Regulation 101 (7)); and]

(*b*) in the case of any other trailer, the brakes fitted in accordance with the requirements of these Regulations.

[Regulation 126 is printed as amended by SI 1980 No 880.]

127. No person in charge of a motor vehicle, whether wheeled or track laying, or trailer drawn thereby shall cause or permit such trailer to stand when detached from the drawing vehicle unless one at least of the wheels of the trailer is prevented from revolving by the setting of [the brake or the use of a chain, chock or other efficient device].

[Regulation 127 is printed as amended by SI 1981 No 1189.]

128. Restriction on distance between motor vehicles and trailers and marking of trailer connections

(1) Where a motor vehicle is drawing a trailer solely by means of a rope or chain or, in a case where more than one trailer is being drawn, where a trailer is attached to another trailer solely by such means, the length of the rope or chain shall be such that the distance between the nearest points of the trailer and the vehicle to which it is so attached cannot exceed 4.5 metres.

(2) Where a motor vehicle is drawing a trailer or trailers and the distance between the nearest points of the trailer or, as the case may be, of any trailer so drawn and the vehicle to which it is attached exceeds 1.5 metres steps shall be taken to render the means whereby that trailer is attached to that vehicle clearly visible to other persons using the road within a reasonable distance from either side of either vehicle.

(3) For the purposes of this Regulation, in determining the nearest points of two vehicles any part of either vehicle designed primarily for use as a means of attaching the one vehicle to the other and any fitting designed for use in connection with any such part shall be disregarded.

[128A. Use of plates, etc, between motor vehicle and trailer

(1) Save as provided in paragraph (2) below, no person shall use or cause or permit to be used any motor vehicle constructed for the purpose of carrying other vehicles or any trailer constructed for that purpose so that while such vehicle or trailer is on a road any part of the weight of any vehicle which is being carried rests on a plate of a kind mentioned in paragraph (iv) in the definition in Regulation 3 (1) of 'overall length'.

(2) The provisions of paragraph (1) above do not apply—

(*a*) while the motor vehicle or trailer constructed for the purpose of carrying other vehicles is being loaded or unloaded; or

(*b*) if the plate is folded or withdrawn so that it cannot be used for the purpose mentioned in paragraph (1) above.]

[Regulation 128A was inserted by SI 1983 No 471.]

Restrictions on the use of vehicles to draw trailers and of trailers drawn

129. Every sidecar fitted to a motor cycle shall be so attached that the wheel thereof is not wholly outside perpendicular planes at right angles to the longitudinal axis of the motor cycle passing through the extreme projecting points in the front and in the rear of the motor cycle.

[**130.**—(1) Save as provided in paragraph (2) below, no person shall use, or cause or permit to be used, on a road—

(*a*) a motor cycle drawing behind it more than one trailer;

(*b*) a motor cycle drawing behind it any trailer carrying a passenger;

(*c*) a motor cycle drawing behind it a trailer with an unladen weight exceeding 254 kilograms or an overall width exceeding 1.5 metres;

(*d*) a motor cycle with not more than two wheels, without a sidecar, and with an engine capacity which does not exceed 125 cubic centimetres drawing behind it any trailer; or

(*e*) a motor cycle with not more than 2 wheels, without a sidecar and with an engine capacity exceeding 125 cubic centimetres drawing behind it any trailer unless—

(i) the trailer has an overall width not exceeding 1 metre,

(ii) the distance between the rear axle of the motor cycle and the rearmost part of the trailer does not exceed 2.5 metres,

(iii) the motor cycle is clearly and indelibly marked in a conspicuous and readily accessible position with its kerbside weight,

(iv) the trailer is clearly and indelibly marked in a conspicuous and readily accessible position with its unladen weight, and

(v) the laden weight of the trailer does not exceed 150 kilograms or two thirds of the kerbside weight of the motor cycle, whichever is the [least].

(2) The provisions of paragraph (1)(*b*) above do not apply if the trailer is a broken-down motorcycle and one passenger is riding it, and the provisions of paragraph (1)(*d*) and (*e*)(iii) to (v) above do not apply in respect of a brokendown motorcycle.

(3) In this Regulation 'kerbside weight' has the same meaning as in Regulation 46 (4).]

[Regulation 130 was substituted by SI 1984 No 386 and is printed as amended by SI 1984 No 679.]

131. *[Revoked.]*

132. No straddle carrier or invalid carriage shall draw a trailer.

133. No trailer shall be used for the conveyance of passengers for hire or reward:
Provided that this Regulation shall not apply to a trailer, being either a broken down motor vehicle or a trailer carrying a broken down motor vehicle, while being drawn in consequence of a breakdown of the said motor vehicle if the following conditions are fulfilled—

(*a*) the trailer is not drawn at a speed in excess of 30 miles per hour; and

(*b*) where the trailer is, or is carrying, a broken down motor vehicle constructed or adapted to carry more than 7 passengers exclusive of the driver or any other broken down motor vehicle carrying more than 8 persons, it is attached to the drawing vehicle by means of a rigid draw bar.

134. No trailer which is a living van and either has less than 4 wheels or is a four-wheeled trailer having two close-coupled wheels on each side shall be used for the carriage of any passenger:

Provided that this Regulation shall not apply to a trailer while it is being tested by the manufacturer by whom it was made, or by the repairer by whom it is being or has been repaired, or by a distributor of trailers or a dealer in trailers.

[135.—(1) [No trailer shall in any circumstances be drawn by an articulated bus, and no trailer shall be drawn by a public service vehicle which is not an articulated bus except—]

    (*a*) in a case where one public service vehicle is drawing another public service vehicle to meet the circumstances of an emergency if neither vehicle is carrying any passenger; or

    (*b*) in a case where the drawing of the trailer and the means by which the trailer is attached to the drawing vehicle have been approved in writing by a certifying officer.

(2) In this Regulation 'certifying officer' has the same meaning as is assigned to that expression in [section 7 (1) of the Public Passenger Vehicles Act 1981.]

[Regulation 135 was substituted by SI 1980 No 287 and is printed as amended by the Interpretation Act 1978, s 17 (2)(a), and SI 1981 No 261.]

136.—[(1) Where a motor vehicle is drawing only one trailer the overall length shall not exceed 18 metres:

Provided that—

    (*a*) this paragraph shall not apply where the trailer being drawn is either—

        (i) a trailer constructed and normally used for the conveyance of indivisible loads of exceptional length, or

        (ii) a broken down vehicle being drawn by a motor vehicle in consequence of the breakdown; and

    (*b*) this paragraph has effect in relation to a combination of vehicles consisting of a motor vehicle which is a showman's vehicle and a trailer which is a living van as if for the reference to 18 metres there were substituted a reference to 22 metres.]

[(1A) In paragraph (1) above—

    ['living van' means a vehicle which is used primarily as living accommodation by one or more persons, and which is not also used for the carriage of goods or burden which are not needed by such one or more persons for the purpose of their residence in the vehicle;] and

    'showman's vehicle' has the meaning given by paragraph 7 of Schedule 3 to the Vehicles (Excise) Act 1971.]

(2) Where a motor vehicle is drawing two or more trailers or only one trailer constructed and normally used for the conveyance of indivisible loads of exceptional length, the overall length of the motor vehicle shall not exceed 9.2 metres and, unless the conditions specified in paragraphs 1 and 2 of Schedule 8 have been complied with, the overall length of the combination of vehicles shall not exceed 25.9 metres.

(3) Where a motor vehicle is drawing two trailers only one such trailer may exceed 7 metres in overall length, and, where a motor vehicle is drawing three trailers, no trailer in the combination of vehicles shall exceed 7 metres in overall length.

(4) For the purposes of this Regulation the reference to the combination of vehicles

shall be construed in the same manner as provided in sub-paragraph (*g*) of Regulation 139 for the purposes of Regulation 140 and the overall length of such a combination shall be measured in the manner provided in sub-paragraph (*h*) of Regulation 139.

[Regulation 136 is printed as amended by SI 1981 No 1580, and SI 1984 No 331.]

[136A. Restrictions with respect to unbraked trailers

(1) The laden weight of an unbraked trailer in use on a road shall not exceed its maximum gross weight.

(2) Save as provided in paragraph (3) below, no unbraked trailer shall be drawn on a road by a vehicle if the kerbside weight of the drawing vehicle is less than twice the unladen weight of the trailer together with the weight of any load which the trailer is carrying.

(3) The provision specified in paragraph (2) above shall not apply—

(*a*) to an agricultural trailer;

[(*aa*) a trailer mentioned in Regulation 75(4); or]

(*b*) before 1st October 1986 to any trailer being—
    (i) a gritting trailer, or
    (ii) a trailer not exceeding 102 kilograms in weight unladen.

(4) In this Regulation—

'kerbside weight' has the meaning given by Regulation 3 (1) of the Lighting Regulations; and

'maximum gross weight' and 'unbraked trailer' have the meanings respectively given by Regulation 46A (2).]

[Regulation 136A was added by SI 1981 No 1189 and is printed as amended by SI 1983 No 112.]

[136B. Restriction on width in relation to agricultural vehicles

No person shall use, or cause or permit to be used, on a road an agricultural motor vehicle drawing a trailer in such a manner that the longitudinal axes of the motor vehicle and the trailer are parallel but in different vertical planes if the overall width of the two vehicles, measured as if the motor vehicle and the trailer were one vehicle, exceeds 2.5 metres.]

[Regulation 136B was inserted by SI 1984 No 1809.]

[137.—(1) No person shall use, or cause or permit to be used, on a road any vehicle of a type specified in an item in column 2 of the Table below if it is drawing more trailers than the number specified in that item in column 3 of that Table.

(2) For the purpose of this Regulation—

(*a*) 'trailer' does not include a vehicle used solely for carrying water for the purpose of the drawing vehicle;

(*b*) an articulated vehicle when being drawn by another motor vehicle because the articulated vehicle has broken down shall, if the articulated vehicle is unladen, be treated in relation to the drawing vehicle as a single trailer;

(*c*) a towed roller used for the purposes of agriculture, horticulture or forestry and

TABLE *[ie table to reg 137]*

1 Item No	2 Type of drawing vehicle	3 Maximum number of trailers
1.	Locomotive	3
2.	Motor tractor	1, if laden.
3.	Motor tractor	2, if both unladen.
4.	Motor car	2 if one is a towing implement and the other is secured to and either rests on or is suspended from the towing implement; 1 in any other case.
5.	Heavy motor car	2 if one is a towing implement and the other is secured to and either rests on or is suspended from the towing implement; 1 in any other case.
6.	Agricultural motor vehicle	2 unladen agricultural trailers; or 1 agricultural trailer, whether laden or unladen, and 1 agricultural trailed appliance; or 2 agricultural trailed appliances.

consisting of several separate rolls shall be treated as one agricultural trailed appliance.]

[Regulation 137 is printed as substituted by SI 1984 No 1809.]

[137A. Restrictions on the use of agricultural motor vehicles, agricultural trailers, and agricultural trailed appliances

(1) No person shall use, or cause or permit to be used, on a road an agricultural motor vehicle drawing one or more trailers unless the ratio of weight as between the drawing vehicle and the trailer, or the trailers, is not greater than 1 to 4:

Provided that this requirement does not apply in a case where the brakes fitted to each trailer in compliance with Regulation 75 are operated directly by the service braking system fitted to the motor vehicle.

(2) No person shall use, or cause or permit to be used, on a road, any motor vehicle towing one or more agricultural trailers unless—

(a) each trailer is either a balanced agricultural trailer (as defined in Regulation 96A(3)) or an unbalanced agricultural trailer (as there defined); and

(b) each trailer, if its gross weight exceeds 14230 kilograms, is fitted with brakes as mentioned in the proviso to paragraph (1) above.

(3) No person shall use, or cause or permit to be used, on a road, an agricultural trailer manufactured on or after 1st December 1985 which is drawn by a motor vehicle manufactured on or after 1st December 1985 and first used on or after 1st June 1986 unless—

(a) the brakes fitted to the trailer in accordance with Regulation 75 (4A) can be applied progressively by the driver of the drawing vehicle, from his normal driving position and while keeping proper control of that vehicle, using a means of operation mounted on the drawing vehicle; or

(b) the brakes fitted to the trailer automatically come into operation on the over-run of the trailer.]

[Regulation 137A was inserted by SI 1984 No 1809.]

138. Attendants on trailers and certain other vehicles

(1) The requirements of section 34 of the 1972 Act with regard to the employment of drivers and attendants shall not apply in the following cases, that is to say:—

(a) in the case of any articulated vehicle;

[(b) where an agricultural motor vehicle is towing an agricultural trailer, an agricultural trailed appliance or an agricultural trailed appliance conveyor;]

(c) where a trailer with not more than two wheels is drawn by a motor car or a motor cycle or where a four-wheeled trailer having two close-coupled wheels on each side is drawn by a motor car;

(d) where a motor tractor is drawing—
   (i) any closed trailer specially constructed and used for the conveyance of meat between docks and railway stations or between wholesale markets and docks or railway stations,
   (ii) any machine or implement used for the purpose of the maintenance, repair or cleansing of roads, or
   (iii) any trailer designed for use and used solely in connection with street cleansing, the collection or disposal of refuse or the collection or disposal of the contents of gullies or cesspools;

(e) where a works truck is drawing any works trailer and the weight unladen of each vehicle does not exceed 1525 kilograms;

(f) *[Revoked.]*

(g) where a motor vehicle is drawing a trailer which has no brakes other than a parking brake and brakes which automatically come into operation on the overrun of the trailer;

(h) in the case of any road roller;

(i) where a motor vehicle belonging to the Secretary of State for Defence and being used for naval, military or air force purposes is drawing a trailer fitted with brakes which can be applied by the driver of the drawing vehicle;

(j) where a motor vehicle is drawing a broken down vehicle, whether or not in consequence of a breakdown, in such a manner that the broken down vehicle cannot be steered by its own steering gear;

(k) where a vehicle is being drawn by a motor vehicle in the exercise of a statutory power of removal in such manner that the vehicle being so drawn cannot be steered by its own steering gear;

(l) where a towing implement is being drawn by a motor vehicle while it is not attached to any vehicle except the one drawing it; or

(m) where a motor vehicle is drawing a trailer or trailers and every such trailer is fitted with power assisted or power operated brakes which can be operated by the driver of the drawing vehicle and are not rendered ineffective by the non-rotation of the engine of the drawing vehicle—
   (i) where one such trailer is drawn; or
   (ii) where two or more such trailers are drawn, if one attendant is carried either on the drawing vehicle or a trailer for the purpose of attending to the trailers.

(2) The requirements of the said section 34 with regard to the employment of persons to drive or attend a locomotive whilst being driven on a highway shall not apply in the case of a locomotive propelled by the combustion of liquid fuel or by electrical power, whether or not the locomotive is drawing a trailer or trailers.

(3) The provisions of this Regulation shall not be treated as prejudicing the operation of any provision of Regulation 140 in so far as it provides, in relation to the use of a vehicle on a road, for compliance with the conditions specified in paragraph 2 of Schedule 8 (which relates to the employment of persons in attending to vehicles and their load).

[Regulation 138 is printed as amended by SI 1981 No 1663, and SI 1984 No 1809.]

[138A. Maintenance of ground clearance of trailers

(1) Save as provided in paragraph (2) below, every trailer to which Regulation 74A relates shall at all times when the trailer is in use on a road be maintained so that its minimum ground clearance is not less than that specified in paragraph (1) of Regulation 74A.

(2) The requirement specified in paragraph (1) above shall not apply

(*a*) in the case of a trailer which is fitted with a suspension system with which, by the operation of a control, the trailer may be lowered or raised—

    (i) while that system is being operated to enable the trailer to pass under a bridge or other obstruction over a road, and

    (ii) to the extent that such system is operated so that no part of the trailer (excluding any wheel) touches the ground or is likely to do so; or

(*b*) in the case of a trailer while it is being loaded or unloaded.]

[Regulation 138A was inserted by SI 1983 No 471.]

Restrictions on use of vehicles carrying wide or long loads or having fixed appliances or apparatus

139. For the purposes of this Regulation, Regulation 140, and Schedule 8—

(*a*) the expression 'lateral projection', in relation to a load carried by a vehicle, means that part of the load which extends beyond a side of the vehicle;

(*b*) the width of any lateral projection shall be measured between vertical planes parallel to the longitudinal axis of the vehicle and passing through the extreme projecting point of the vehicle on that side on which the projection lies and that part of the projection furthest from that point;

(*c*) references to a special appliance or apparatus, in relation to a vehicle, are references to any crane or other special appliance or apparatus fitted to the vehicle which is a permanent or essentially permanent fixture;

(*d*) the expressions 'forward projection' and 'rearward projection'—

    (i) in relation to a load carried in such a manner that its weight rests on only one vehicle, mean respectively that part of the load which extends beyond the foremost point of the vehicle and that part which extends beyond the rearmost point of the vehicle.

    (ii) in relation to a load carried in such a manner that part of its weight rests on more than one vehicle, mean respectively that part of the load which extends beyond the foremost point of the foremost vehicle by which the load is carried except where the context otherwise requires and that part of the load which extends beyond the rearmost point of the rearmost vehicle by which the load is carried, and

(iii) in relation to any special appliance or apparatus, mean respectively that part of the appliance or apparatus which, if it were deemed to be a load carried by the vehicle, would be a part of a load extending beyond the foremost point of the vehicle and that part which would be a part of a load extending beyond the rearmost point of the vehicle,

and references in Regulation 140 and in Schedule 8 to a forward projection or to a rearward projection in relation to a vehicle shall be construed accordingly;

(e) the length of any forward projection or of any rearward projection shall be measured between vertical planes at right angles to the longitudinal axis of the vehicle and passing—

    (i) in the case of a forward projection, through the foremost point of the vehicle and that part of the projection furthest from that point, and

    (ii) in the case of a rearward projection, through the rearmost point of the vehicle and that part of the projection furthest from that point.

      In this and the foregoing sub-paragraph the expression 'vehicle' shall not include any special appliance or apparatus or any part thereof which is a forward projection or a rearward projection within the meaning of this Regulation;

(f) references to the distance between vehicles, in relation to vehicles carrying a load, are references to the distance between the nearest points of any two adjacent vehicles by which the load is carried, measured when the longitudinal axis of each vehicle lies in the same vertical plane.

      For the purposes of this sub-paragraph, in determining the nearest point of two vehicles any part of either vehicle designed primarily for use as a means of attaching the one vehicle to the other and any fitting designed for use in connection with any such part shall be disregarded;

(g) references to a combination of vehicles, in relation to a motor vehicle which is drawing one or more trailers, are references to the motor vehicle and the trailer or trailers drawn thereby, including any other motor vehicle which is used for the purpose of assisting in the propulsion of the trailer or the trailers on the road;

(h) the overall length of a combination of vehicles shall be taken as the distance between the foremost point of the drawing vehicle comprised in the combination and the rearmost point of the rearmost vehicle comprised therein, measured when the longitudinal axis of each vehicle comprised in the combination lies in the same vertical plane;

(i) the extreme projecting point of a vehicle shall be taken as excluding any part of, or part of the equipment of, a vehicle which by virtue of sub-paragraphs (a) to (f) of the definition of the overall width of a vehicle contained in Regulation 3 (1) falls to be excluded in determining that overall width;

(j) the foremost or, as the case may be, the rearmost points of a vehicle shall be taken as excluding any part of, or part of the equipment of, a vehicle which by virtue of sub-paragraphs (a) to (h) of the definition of the overall length of a vehicle contained in Regulation 3 (1) falls to be excluded in determining that overall length[; and]

[(k) an agricultural implement rigidly, but not permanently, mounted on an agricultural motor vehicle, agricultural trailer or agicultural trailed appliance whether or not part of its weight is supported by one or more of its own wheels, shall not be treated as a load, or special appliance, on that vehicle.]

[Regulation 139 is printed as amended by SI 1984 No 1809.]

140.—(1) No load shall be carried on a vehicle where the overall width of the vehicle together with the width of any lateral projection or projections of its load exceeds 4.3 metres.

(2) Subject to the following provisions of this Regulation, no load shall be carried on a vehicle—

(*a*) where the load has a lateral projection exceeding 305 millimetres in width; or

(*b*) where the overall width of the vehicle together with the width of any lateral projection or projections of its load exceeds 2.9 metres:
  Provided that this paragraph shall not apply—
  (i) to the carriage of an indivisible load if—
    (*a*) it is not reasonably practicable to comply with the requirements of the said paragraph, and
    (*b*) the conditions specified in paragraph 1 of Schedule 8 have been complied with, and
    (*c*) where the overall width of the vehicle together with the width of any lateral projection or projections of its load exceeds 3.5 metres, the conditions specified in paragraph 2 of Schedule 8 have been complied with; or
  (ii) to the carriage of loose agricultural produce not baled or crated.

(3) Where a load is carried in such a manner that its weight rests—

(*a*) on one vehicle being a heavy motor car or a trailer the overall length of the heavy motor car or, as the case may be, of the trailer together with the length of any forward and of any rearward projection of the load shall not exceed 27.4 metres; or

(*b*) on more than one vehicle being—
  (i) a motor vehicle drawing one trailer whether forming part of an articulated vehicle or not, or
  (ii) any other combination of vehicles,

then, in the case at (i) above, the overall length of the trailer together with the length of any forward projection of the load extending beyond the foremost point of the trailer and of any rearward projection of the load shall not exceed 27.4 metres and, in the case at (ii) above, the overall length of the vehicles together with the distance between vehicles and the length of any forward and of any rearward projection of the load shall not exceed 27.4 metres.

(4) Subject to the following provisions of this Regulation—

(*a*) no load shall be carried on a vehicle where the overall length of the vehicle together with the length of any forward projection and of any rearward projection of the load exceeds 18.3 metres, and as respects a motor vehicle which is drawing a trailer or trailers, no load shall be carried in such a manner that its weight rests on more than one of the vehicles being—
  (i) the motor vehicle and one trailer whether forming part of an articulated vehicle or not, or
  (ii) any another combination of vehicles,

if, in the case at (i) above, the overall length of the trailer together with the length of any forward projection of the load extending beyond the foremost point of the trailer and of any rearward projection of the load exceeds 18.3 metres and, in the case at (ii) above the overall length of the vehicles together with the distance between vehicles and the length of any forward and of any rearward projection of the load exceeds 18.3 metres; and

(b) without prejudice to the foregoing sub-paragraph, no load shall be carried on a trailer drawn by a motor vehicle or in such a manner that part of its weight rests on more than one trailer so drawn where the overall length of the combination of vehicles together with the length of any forward projection of the load extending beyond the foremost point of the drawing vehicle comprised in the combination and the length of any rearward projection of the load extending beyond the rearmost point of the rearmost vehicle comprised therein exceeds 25.9 metres,

unless the conditions specified in paragraphs 1 and 2 of Schedule 8 have been complied with.

(5) Subject to the following provisions of this Regulation, no vehicle having a special appliance or apparatus which—

(a) has a forward projection exceeding 1.83 metres in length but not exceeding 3.05 metres in length, shall be used on a road unless the conditions specified in paragraphs 2 and 3 of Schedule 8 have been complied with;

(b) has a rearward projection exceeding 1.07 metres in length but not exceeding 1.83 metres in length, shall be used on a road unless the condition specified in paragraph 4 of Schedule 8 has been complied with;

(c) has a rearward projection exceeding 1.83 metres in length but not exceeding 3.05 metres in length, shall be used on a road unless the condition specified in paragraph 3 of Schedule 8 has been complied with;

(d) has a forward or rearward projection exceeding 3.05 metres in length, shall be used on a road unless the conditions specified in paragraphs 1, 2 and 3 of Schedule 8 have been complied with.

(6) Subject to the following provisions of this Regulation, no load shall be carried on a vehicle—

(a) where the load has a forward projection exceeding 1.83 metres in length but not exceeding 3.05 metres in length, unless the conditions specified in paragraphs 2 and 3 of Schedule 8 have been complied with;

(b) where the load has a rearward projection exceeding 1.07 metres in length but not exceeding 1.83 metres in length, unless the condition specified in paragraph 4 of Schedule 8 has been complied with;

(c) where the load has a rearward projection exceeding 1.83 metres in length but not exceeding 3.05 metres in length, unless the condition specified in paragraph 3 of Schedule 8 has been complied with;

(d) where the load has a forward or a rearward projection exceeding 3.05 metres in length, unless the conditions specified in paragraphs 1, 2 and 3 of Schedule 8 have been complied with;

(e) where the load is carried on an articulated vehicle not exceeding 15 metres in overall length and which is not constructed and normally used for the conveyance of indivisible loads of exceptional length and where the overall length of the articulated vehicle together with any forward or rearward projections of the load exceeds 16.8 metres, unless the condition specified in paragraph 1 of Schedule 8 has been complied with:

Provided that—

(a) this paragraph shall not apply—

(i) to the carriage of a load which consists, whether wholly or partly, of a boat used for racing and propelled solely by oars if any provision of this paragraph would otherwise apply by reason only of the boat being so carried that it has a forward projection or, as the case may be, a rearward projection, or

    (ii) to the carriage of a load by a straddle carrier; and

(*b*) notwithstanding that sub-paragraphs (*c*) and (*d*) of this paragraph provide for the condition specified in paragraph 3 of Schedule 8 to be complied with as respects a load which has a rearward projection specified in either of such sub-paragraphs, that condition in relation to the exhibition of the end projection surface on that rearward projection need not be complied with in the case of such a load which carries a rear marking in accordance with [the Lighting Regulations].

(7) Subject to the following provisions of this Regulation, where the load or part of the load carried by a vehicle consists, whether wholly or partly, of a boat used for racing and propelled solely by oars, the boat shall not be so carried that it has a forward projection or a rearward projection—

(*a*) exceeding 1.07 metres in length unless the condition specified in paragraph 4 of Schedule 8 has been complied with; or

(*b*) exceeding 3.05 metres in length unless the conditions specified in paragraphs 1 and 4 of Schedule 8 have been complied with.

(8) Subject to the following provisions of this Regulation, no load shall be carried on a straddle carrier where the load has a rearward projection exceeding 1.07 metres in length unless the condition specified in paragraph 4 of Schedule 8 has been complied with:

Provided that this paragraph shall not apply in the case of a vehicle used in passing from one part of any private premises to any other part thereof or to other private premises in the immediate neighbourhood.

(9) Subject to the following provisions of this Regulation, no load shall be carried on a straddle carrier—

(*a*) where the load has a forward projection exceeding 1.83 metres in length;

(*b*) where the load has a rearward projection exceeding 3.05 metres in length;

(*c*) where the overall length of the vehicle together with the length of any forward projection and of any rearward projection of its load exceeds 12.2 metres:

Provided that this paragraph shall not apply in the case of a vehicle used in passing from one part of any private premises to any other part thereof or to other private premises in the immediate neighbourhood if—

    (i) the vehicle is not driven at a speed exceeding 12 miles per hour, and

    (ii) where the overall length of the vehicle together with the length of any forward projection and of any rearward projection of its load exceeds 12.2 metres the conditions specified in paragraphs 1 and 2 of Schedule 8 have been complied with.

(10) In a case where a vehicle has a special appliance or apparatus or is carrying a load or a boat used for racing as mentioned in paragraph (7) of this Regulation and the appliance or apparatus, the load or the said boat has, in relation to the vehicle, a forward projection or a rearward projection, and another vehicle is attached to that end of the vehicle from which the appliance or apparatus or, as the case may be, the load or the said boat projects and is attached to that vehicle in such manner that—

(*a*) in the case where there is a forward projection, the foremost point of that other vehicle extends beyond the foremost part of the projection or, in the case where there is a rearward projection, the rearmost point of that other vehicle extends beyond the rearmost part of the projection; or

(*b*) in the case where there is a forward projection, the foremost part of the projection extends beyond the foremost point of that other vehicle or, in the case where there is a rearward projection, the rearmost part of the projection extends beyond the rearmost point of that other vehicle,

then—

(i) in either of the cases mentioned in sub-paragraph (*a*) of this paragraph, the provisions of paragraphs (5), (6) and (7) of this Regulation, in so far as they provide for compliance with paragraphs 3 or 4 of Schedule 8, shall not apply as respects any such projection, and

(ii) in either of the cases mentioned in sub-paragraph (*b*)) of this paragraph, the provisions of the said paragraphs (5), (6) and (7), in so far as they provide for compliance with the said paragraph 3 or 4, shall apply as if each of the references in the said paragraphs (5), (6) and (7) to a forward projection and to a rearward projection were treated respectively as a reference to so much of a forward projection as extends beyond the foremost point of that other vehicle and to so much of a rearward projection as extends beyond the rearmost point of that other vehicle measured, in either case, when the longitudinal axis of each vehicle lies in the same vertical plane between vertical planes at right angles to the said longitudinal axis and passing, in the case of a forward projection, through the foremost point of the said other vehicle and that part of the projection furthest from that point or, in the case of a rearward projection, through the rearmost point of the said other vehicle and that part of the projection furthest from that point.

(11) This Regulation shall not apply to any motor vehicle or trailer being used—

(*a*) for fire brigade, ambulance or police purposes or for defence purposes (including civil defence purposes); or

(*b*) in connection with the removal of any obstruction to traffic,

if, in any such case, compliance with any provision of this Regulation would hinder or be likely to hinder the use of the vehicle for the purpose for which it is being used on that occasion.

[(12) No person shall use, or cause or permit to be used, on a road an agricultural implement rigidly, but not permanently, mounted on an agricultural motor vehicle, agricultural trailer, or agricultural trailed appliance whether or not part of its weight is supported by one or more of its own wheels, if—

(*a*) the overall width of the vehicle together with the lateral projection of the implement exceeds 2.5 metres;

(*b*) the implement projects more than 1 metre forwards or rearwards of the vehicle, so, however, that this restriction shall not apply in a case where:—

(i) part of the weight of the implement is supported by one or more of its own wheels, and

(ii) the longitudinal axis of the greater part of the implement is capable of articulating in the horizontal plane in relation to the longitudinal axis of the rear portion of the vehicle.]

[Regulation 140 is printed as amended by SI 1984 No 813, and SI 1984 No 1809.]

141. Passengers on motor cycles

If any person in addition to the driver is carried astride any two-wheeled motor cycle (whether a sidecar is attached thereto or not) suitable supports or rests for the feet shall be available on such cycle for that person.

[141A. Use of sidecars

(1) This Regulation applies to every two-wheeled motor cycle first registered on or after 1st April 1981 not being a motor cycle brought temporarily into Great Britain by a person resident abroad.

(2) No person shall use, or cause or permit to be used on a road on or after 1st August 1981 any two-wheeled motor cycle to which this Regulation applies if there is a sidecar attached to the right (or off-side) of the motor cycle.]

[Regulation 141A was added by SI 1980 No 140.]

142. Mascots

No mascot shall be carried by a motor vehicle first used on or after 1st October 1937 in any position where it is likely to strike any person with whom the vehicle may collide unless the mascot is not liable to cause injury to such person by reason of any projection thereon.

143. Television sets

(1) No person shall use or install for use in a motor vehicle a television receiving apparatus if the screen thereof is partly or wholly, and whether directly or in any reflection, visible to the driver whilst in the driving seat or if the controls thereof, other than the sound volume control and the main switch are within reach of the driver whilst in the driving seat.

(2) No person shall use a television receiving apparatus in a motor vehicle under circumstances and in a position such that it might cause distraction to the driver of any other vehicle on the road.

144. Implements suspended from lifting appliances

Where a vehicle is fitted with any apparatus or appliance designed for lifting and part of the apparatus or appliance consists of an implement to facilitate lifting which is suspended from the apparatus or appliance, the implement shall at all times while the vehicle is in motion on a road and when the implement is not attached to any load supported by the appliance or apparatus be so secured either to the appliance or apparatus or to some part of the vehicle that no danger is caused or is likely to be caused to any person on the vehicle or on the road.

[144A. Use of gas propulsion systems

(1) No person shall use or cause or permit to be used on a road any gas propulsion system of a vehicle unless the whole of such system is in a safe condition.

(2) No person shall use or cause or permit to be used in any gas supply system for the propulsion of a vehicle when the vehicle is on a road any fuel except liquefied petroleum gas.

(3) No person shall use or cause or permit to be used on a road any vehicle which is propelled by gas unless the gas container in which such fuel is stored is on the motor vehicle, and not on any trailer, and in the case of an articulated vehicle on the portion of the vehicle to which the engine is fitted.]

[Regulation 144A was added by SI 1981 No 1663, with effect from 19 February 1982.]

[144B. Use of gas-fired appliances—general

(1) No person shall use or cause or permit to be used in or on a vehicle on a road any gas-fired appliance unless the whole of such appliance and the gas system attached thereto is in an efficient and safe condition.

(2) No person shall use or cause or permit to be used in any gas-fired appliance in or on a vehicle on a road any fuel except liquefied petroleum gas.

(3) No person shall use or cause or permit to be used in or on a vehicle on a road any gas-fired appliance unless the vehicle is so ventilated that—

(*a*) an ample supply of air is available for the operation of the appliance,

(*b*) the use of the appliance does not adversely affect the health or comfort of any person using the vehicle, and

(*c*) any unburnt gas is safely disposed of to the outside of the vehicle.

(4) No person shall use or cause or permit to be used on a road—

(*a*) a vehicle in or on which there is one gas-fired appliance unless the gas supply for such appliance is shut off at the point where it leaves the container or containers at all times when the appliance is not in use,

(*b*) a vehicle in or on which there is more than one gas-fired appliance each of which has the same supply of gas unless the gas supply for such appliances is shut off at the point where it leaves the container or containers at all times when none of such appliances is in use, or

(*c*) a vehicle in or on which there is more than one gas-fired appliance each of which does not have the same supply of gas unless each gas supply for such appliances is shut off at the point where it leaves the container or containers at all times when none of such appliances which it supplies is in use.]

[Regulation 144B was added by SI 1981 No 1663, with effect from 19 February 1982.]

[144C. Use of gas-fired appliances when a vehicle is in motion

(1) All the provisions specified in this Regulation apply to every motor vehicle and trailer other than a vehicle constructed or adapted for the conveyance of goods under controlled temperatures, and the provisions specified in paragraph (3) (*d*) below (but no other provisions specified in this Regulation) apply to a vehicle constructed or adapted for the conveyance of goods under controlled temperatures.

(2) No person shall use or cause or permit to be used in any vehicle to which this Regulation applies, while the vehicle is in motion on a road, any gas-fired appliance except—

(*a*) a gas-fired appliance which is fitted to engineering plant while the plant is being used for the purposes of the engineering operations for which it was designed, or

(*b*) a gas-fired appliance which is permanently attached to a large passenger carrying vehicle, provided that any appliance for heating or cooling the interior of the vehicle for the comfort of the driver and any passengers does not expose a naked flame on the outside of the appliance, or

(*c*) in any other vehicle, a refrigerating appliance or an appliance which does not expose a naked flame on the outside of the appliance and which is permanently attached to the vehicle and designed for the purpose of heating any part of the interior of the vehicle for the comfort of the driver and any passengers.

(3) No person shall use or cause or permit to be used in any vehicle to which this Regulation applies, while the vehicle is in motion on a road, any gas-fired appliance unless—

(a) in the case of an appliance to which sub-paragraph (2) (a) above refers, the appliance complies with the requirements specified in paragraphs 12 and 13 of Schedule 3A and the gas system to which it is attached complies with the requirements specified in paragraphs 2 to 9 and 15 of Schedule 3A;

(b) in the case of an appliance to which sub-paragraph (2) (b) above refers, the appliance complies with the requirements specified in paragraphs 12, 13 and 14 of Schedule 3A and the gas system to which it is attached complies with the requirements specified in paragraphs 2 to 9, 11 and 15 of Schedule 3A;

(c) in the case of an appliance to which sub-paragraph (2) (c) above refers, the appliance complies—

    (i) in the case of any such appliance fitted to a motor vehicle, with the requirements specified in paragraphs 12, 13 and 14 of Schedule 3A, and

    (ii) in any other case, with the requirements specified in paragraphs 12 and 13 of Schedule 3A

and the gas system to which the appliance is attached complies with the requirements specified in paragraphs 2 to 9 and 15 of Schedule 3A; and

(d) in all cases, the appliance is fitted with a valve which stops the supply of gas to the appliance if the appliance fails to perform its function and causes gas to be emitted.]

[Regulation 144C was added by SI 1981 No 1663, with effect from 19 February 1982.]

PART IV

Testing and Inspection of Brakes, Silencers, Steering Gear, Tyres, Lighting Equipment and Reflectors

145. Testing of brakes, etc

(1) Any police constable in uniform and any person for the time being appointed by the Secretary of State as a certifying officer or public service vehicle examiner under Part III of the 1960 Act or as an examiner appointed under Part IV of that Act or under section 56 (1) of the 1972 Act or appointed by the Commissioner of Police of the Metropolis to examine and inspect public carriages for the purposes of the Metropolitan Public Carriage Act 1869, or appointed by the police authority for a police area to act, under the directions of the Chief Officer of Police, for the purposes of section 53 of the 1972 Act, who shall produce his authority if required, is hereby empowered to test and inspect the brakes, silencers, steering gear, [and tyres] of any motor vehicle or trailer on any premises where that motor vehicle or trailer is, subject however to the consent of the owner of the premises.

(2) The power conferred by this Regulation to test and inspect the brakes, silencers, steering gear, [and tyres] of a vehicle on any premises where the vehicle is shall not be exercised unless either the owner of the vehicle consents or notice of the date and time at which it is proposed to carry out the test and inspection has been given to him in accordance with the provisions of paragraph (3) of this Regulation.

(3) The said notice shall be given to the owner of the vehicle personally or left at his address not less than 48 hours before the time of the proposed test and inspection or shall be sent to him not less than 72 hours before that time by recorded delivery service at his address.

(4) The provisions of paragraph (2) of this Regulation shall not apply in the case of a test and inspection made within 48 hours of an accident to which section 25 of the 1972 Act applies and in which the vehicle has been involved.

(5) For the purposes of this Regulation, the owner of the vehicle shall be deemed to be—

(a) in the case of a vehicle which is for the time being registered under the Vehicles (Excise) Act 1971 and is not being used under a trade licence under that Act the person appearing as the owner of the vehicle in the register kept by the Secretary of State under that Act;

(b) in the case of a vehicle used under a trade licence, the holder of the licence; and

(c) in the case of a vehicle exempt from excise duty by virtue of the Motor Vehicles (International Circulation) Order 1975 *[SI 1975 No 1208]*, the person resident outside the United Kingdom who has brought the vehicle into Great Britain,

and in cases (a) and (b) the address of the owner as shown on the said register or, as the case may be, on the licence may be treated as his address.

[Regulation 145 is printed as amended by SI 1984 No 813.

Part III of the Road Traffic Act 1960 is now the Public Passenger Vehicles Act 1981. Examiners were appointed under s 183 (1) of the Act of 1960 (ie under Part IV of that Act); see now the Road Traffic Act 1972, s 56 (1).]

PART V
Particular Regulations Relating to Vehicles for which Plating Certificates have been Issued

146. Interpretation

In this Part of these Regulations, unless the context otherwise requires, the following expressions have the meanings hereby assigned to them respectively, that is to say—

'axle weight', in relation to each axle of a motor vehicle or trailer, means the sum of the weights transmitted to the road surface by all the wheels of that axle;

'design gross weight', in relation to a vehicle, means the gross weight of the vehicle at or below which in the opinion of the [Secretary of State for Transport] or of a person authorised in that behalf by the [Secretary of State for Transport] the vehicle could safely be driven on roads;

'design', in relation to the gross weight, each axle weight or the train weight of a motor vehicle or trailer, means any such weight at or below which in the opinion of the [Secretary of State for Transport] or a person authorised in that behalf by the [Secretary of State for Transport] the vehicle could safely be driven on roads;

'gross weight', in relation to a motor vehicle, means the sum of the weights transmitted to the road surface by all the wheels of the vehicle;

'gross weight', in relation to a trailer, means the sum of the weights transmitted to the road surface by all the wheels of the trailer and includes any weight of the trailer imposed on the drawing vehicle;

. . . . .

'Ministry test date disc' means a plate issued by the [Secretary of State for Transport] for a goods vehicle, being a trailer, following the issue of a goods vehicle test certificate for that trailer under the Plating and Testing Regulations and containing the following particulars namely:—

(a) the identification mark allotted to that trailer and shown in that certificate;

(b) the date until which that certificate is valid;

(c) the number of the vehicle testing station shown in the said certificate;

. . . . .

[Regulation 146 is printed as amended by the Minister of Transport Order 1979 (SI 1979 No 571), the Transfer of Functions (Transport) Order 1981 (SI 1981 No 238), SI 1982 No 1272, and SI 1982 No 1576.]

147. Application of Part V

This Part of these Regulations applies to goods vehicles, being goods vehicles of a class to which the Plating and Testing Regulations apply, for which a plating certificate has been issued.

Ministry plates for goods vehicles

[148.—(1) Every goods vehicle to which this part of these Regulations applies shall, from the date specified in paragraph (2) below, be equipped with a Ministry plate securely affixed, so as to be legible at all times, in a conspicuous and readily accessible position, and in the cab of the vehicle if it has one.

(2) The date mentioned in paragraph (1) above is—

(a) in the case of a vehicle to which the Motor Vehicles (Type Approval for Goods Vehicles) (Great Britain) Regulations 1982 apply, 14 days after the plate was issued;

(b) in the case of any other vehicle, the relevant date as defined in section 46 (1) of the 1972 Act.]

[Regulation 148 was substituted by SI 1982 No 1272.]

149. Every goods vehicle to which this Part of these Regulations applies, being a trailer for which a goods vehicle test certificate is issued under the Plating and Testing Regulations, shall as from each date such a certificate is issued . . . , carry in the relevant position and in legible condition a Ministry test date disc issued for that trailer following the issue of that test certificate until the date of expiry of that test certificate or the date of issue of a further test certificate for that trailer, whichever date is the earlier, and shall not display that disc after that one of such dates as is the earlier.

In this Regulation 'relevant position' means a conspicuous and readily accessible position, being such that the disc is clearly visible by daylight from the nearside of the road.

[Regulation 149 is printed as amended by SI 1982 No 1272.]

150. Weight restrictions

(1) As respects a goods vehicle to which this Part of these Regulations applies, whether laden or unladen and whether or not drawing or being drawn by another vehicle, the following provisions of this Regulation shall apply as from the relevant date mentioned in Regulation 148 . . . namely,—

(a) the gross weight shown in column (2) of the plating certificate for that vehicle shall not be exceeded;

(b) the axle weight for each axle shown in column (2) of the plating certificate for that vehicle shall not be exceeded:

Provided that this sub-paragraph shall not apply in the case of any axle being one of two or more axles to which the following sub-paragraph applies;

(c) where any two or more axles are fitted with a compensating arrangement in accordance with Regulation 11, the sum of the axle weights for all the axles so fitted shall not exceed the sum of such weights for those axles as are shown in column (2) of the said plating certificate.

(2) As respects a goods vehicle to which this Part of these Regulations applies, being a motor vehicle, the train weight (if any) shown in column (2) of the plating certificate for that vehicle shall not be exceeded.

(3) Nothing in any plate mentioned in Regulation 42 with which a goods vehicle to which this Part of these Regulations applies is equipped or in Regulations 85 to 94 shall be taken to permit any such weight as is mentioned in the preceding provisions of this Regulation to be exceeded and nothing in paragraph (1) or (2) of this Regulation shall be taken to permit any weight mentioned in any of the said Regulations 85 to 94 which is applicable to the vehicle in question to be exceeded.

[Regulation 150 is printed as amended by SI 1982 No 1272.]

151. Additional markings

(1) Without prejudice to the provision of Regulation 148, any weight which by virtue of Regulation 150 may not be exceeded in the case of a goods vehicle to which this Part of these Regulations applies may be marked on the near side of the vehicle, the off side of the vehicle or on both sides of the vehicle.

(2) Where at any time by virtue of any provisions contained in Regulation 85, 86, 89 or 90 a goods vehicle to which this Part of these Regulations applies may not be used in excess of a weight, being a weight equal to the sum of the weights transmitted to the road surface by all the wheels of the vehicle and less than the gross weight which may not be exceeded by that vehicle by virtue of Regulation 150, the first mentioned weight may be marked on the near side of the vehicle, the off side of the vehicle or on both sides of the vehicle.

(3) Where at any time by virtue of any provision contained in Regulation 87, 88 or 91 a goods vehicle to which this Part of these Regulations applies is drawing, or being drawn by, another vehicle and those vehicles may not be used together in excess of a laden weight applicable to those vehicles by virtue of any such provision, that weight may be marked on the near side of that goods vehicle, the off side of that vehicle or on both sides of the vehicle.

[152. Alteration of braking requirements

(1) This Regulation applies to a goods vehicle being a motor vehicle to which this Part of these Regulations applies and to which Regulation 59 (5), (6) or (7) or Regulation 64 (5), (6) or (7) applies.

(2) In relation to a vehicle to which this Regulation applies, the requirements specified in Regulation 59 (5), (6) or (7) or, as the case may be, in Regulation 64 (5), (6) or (7) shall, as from the date on which a plating certificate has been issued . . . , have effect as though to each of the said paragraphs of whichever of those Regulations is applicable there were attached a proviso that the requirements as to braking efficiencies specified in the paragraphs shall not be treated as being complied with unless those efficiencies are capable of being produced when the sum of the weights transmitted to the road surface by all the wheels of the vehicle is either—

(*a*) equal to the design gross weight shown in the plating certificate in force as respects the vehicle, or

(*b*) if no such weight is shown in such certificate, equal to the gross weight shown in column (2) of that certificate.

(3) Notwithstanding the provisions of paragraph (2) above, as from the date on which a plating certificate has been issued . . . , no person shall use or cause or permit to be used on a road a vehicle to which this Regulation applies if it does not comply with the requirements specified in Regulation 59 (5), (6) or (7) or, Regulation 64 (5), (6) or (7) without regard to the proviso mentioned in paragraph (2) above and in Regulation 101 (1)(*c*) and (*d*).]

[Regulation 152 is printed as substituted by SI 1981 No 1189 and as amended by SI 1982 No 1272.]

153. Additional provisions as to braking requirements

(1) This Regulation applies to a goods vehicle being a motor vehicle to which this part of these Regulations applies and to which Regulation 101A applies.

[(2) In relation to a vehicle to which this Regulation applies and which is of a type specified in an item in column 2 of the Table below, the requirements as to braking efficiencies imposed by the Regulation specified in that item in column 3 of that Table shall, as from the date on which a plating certificate is issued have effect as though there were attached to them a condition that they shall not be complied with unless the braking efficiences in point are capable of being produced when the sum of the weights transmitted to the road by all the wheels of the vehicle is as specified in that item—

(*a*) in column 4(*a*) of that Table if the weight there specified is shown in the plating certificate for the vehicle,

(*b*) in column 4(*b*) of that Table if the weight mentioned in column 4(*a*) of the Table is not shown in that certificate.

(3) Notwithstanding the provisions of paragraph (2) above, as from the date on which a plating certificate has been issued no person shall use or cause or permit to be used on a road a vehicle to which this Regulation applies if it does not comply with the requirement specified in Regulation 101A without regard to the proviso mentioned in paragraph (2) above.]

[Regulation 153 is printed as substituted by SI 1981 No 1189 and as amended by SI 1982 No 1272, SI 1982 No 1480, and SI 1983 No 112.

The reference in para (3) to 'the proviso' related to the use of the words 'a proviso' in para (2) (as originally enacted); the corresponding words in para (2) (as substituted) are 'a condition'.]

154. Tyres

Each axle of every goods vehicle to which this Part of these Regulations applies shall as from the date a plating certificate is issued for the vehicle . . . , be equipped with tyres which, as respects strength, are designed and maintained adequately to support the axle weight shown in column (2) of that certificate for that axle.

[Regulation 154 is printed as amended by SI 1982 No 1272.]

[TABLE *[ie table in reg 153 (2)]*]

1	2	3	4	
			Sum of weights transmitted to the road by all the wheels of the vehicle	
Item No	Type of Vehicle	Regulation imposing requirements as to braking efficiencies	(a) Where design weights are specified in plating certificate	(b) Where design weights are not specified in plating certificate
1	Motor vehicle whether or not equipped to draw a trailer	101A (3)(a) 101A (4) 101A (5)	The design gross weight of the vehicle as specified in column (3) of the plating certificate	The gross weight not to be exceeded in Great Britain as specified in column (2) of the plating certificate
2	Motor vehicle equipped to draw a trailer	[101A (3)(b)] 101A (6)	The design gross and train weights of the motor vehicle as specified in column (3) of the plating certificate	The gross and train weights not to be exceeded in Great Britain as specified in column (2) of the plating certificate
3	Trailer	101A (5)	The design gross weight of the vehicle as specified in column (3) of the plating certificate	The gross weight not to be exceeded in Great Britain as specified in column (2) of the plating certificate]

SCHEDULE 1

Regulations Revoked by Regulation 2

*　　　*　　　*

SCHEDULE 2

Plates for Certain Vehicles

*　　　*　　　*

SCHEDULE 3

Gas Containers

[SCHEDULE 3A

Gas Systems

Definitions

1. In this Schedule—

'check valve' means a device which permits the flow of gas in one direction and prevents the flow of gas in the opposite direction;

'design pressure' means the pressure which a part of a gas system has been designed and constructed safely to withstand;

'double-check valve' means a device which consists of two check valves in series and which permits the flow of gas in one direction and prevents the flow of gas in the opposite direction;

'excess flow valve' means a device which automatically and instantaneously reduces to a minimum the flow of gas through the valve when the flow rate exceeds a set value;

'fixed gas container' means a gas container which is attached to a vehicle permanently and in such a manner that the container can be filled without being moved;

'gas container' means any container, not being a container for the carriage of gas as goods, which is fitted to or carried on a motor vehicle or trailer and is intended for the storage of gas for either—

(*a*) the propulsion of the motor vehicle, or

(*b*) the operation of a gas-fired appliance;

'high pressure' means a pressure exceeding 1.0325 bar absolute;

'high pressure pipeline' means a pipeline intended to contain gas at high pressure;

'pipeline' means any pipe or passage connecting any two parts of a gas propulsion system of a vehicle or of a gas-fired appliance supply system on a vehicle or any two points on the same part of any such system;

'portable gas container' means a gas container which may be attached to a vehicle but which can readily be removed;

'pressure relief valve' means a device which opens automatically when the pressure in the part of the gas system to which it is fitted exceeds a set value, reaches its maximum flow capacity when the set value is exceeded by 10 per cent and closes automatically when the pressure falls below a set value; and

'reducing valve' means a device which automatically reduces the pressure of the gas passing through it, and includes regulator devices.

Gas containers

2.—(1) Every gas container shall—

(*a*) be capable of withstanding the pressure of the gas which may be stored in the container at the highest temperature which the gas is likely to reach,

(*b*) if fitted inside the vehicle be so arranged as to prevent so far as is practicable the possibility of gas entering the engine, passenger or living compartments due to leaks or venting from the container or valves, connections and gauges immediately adjacent to it, and the space containing these components shall be so ventilated and drained as to prevent the accumulation of gas,

(*c*) be securely attached to the vehicle in such a manner as not to be liable to displacement or damage due to vibration, or other cause, and

(*d*) be so placed and so insulated or shielded as not to suffer any adverse effect from the heat of the exhaust system of any engine or any other source of heat.

(2) Every portable gas container shall be either—

(*a*) hermetically sealed, or

(*b*) fitted with a valve or cock to enable the flow of gas from the container to be stopped.

(3) Every fixed gas container shall

(*a*) be fitted with—

  (i) at least one pressure relief valve, and

  (ii) at least one manually operated valve which may be extended by an internal dip tube inside the gas container so as to indicate when the container has been filled to the level corresponding to the filling ratio specified in the British Standards Institution Specification for Filling Ratios and Developed Pressures for Liquefiable and Permanent Gases (as defined, respectively, in paragraphs 3.2 and 3.5 of the said Specification) published in May 1976 under the number BS 5355, and

(*b*) be conspicuously and permanently marked with its design pressure.

(4) If any fixed gas container is required to be fitted in a particular attitude or location, or if any device referred to in subparagraph (3) above requires the container to be fitted in such a manner, then every such gas container shall be conspicuously and permanently marked to indicate that requirement.

(5) If the operation of any pressure relief valve or other device referred to in subparagraph (3) above may cause gas to be released from the gas container, an outlet shall be provided to lead such gas to the outside of the vehicle so as not to suffer any adverse effect from the heat of the exhaust system of any engine or any other source of heat, and that outlet from the pressure relief valve shall not be fitted with any other valve or cock.

Filling systems for fixed gas containers

3.—(1) Every connection for filling a fixed gas container shall be on the outside of the vehicle.

(2) There shall be fitted to every fixed gas container either—

 a) a manually operated shut-off valve and an excess flow valve, or

(*b*) a manually operated shut-off valve and a single check valve, or

 (*c*) a double-check valve,

and all parts of these valves in contact with gas shall be made entirely of suitable metal except that they may contain non-metal washers and seals provided that such washers and seals are supported and constrained by metal components.

(3) In every case where a pipe is attached to a gas container for the purpose of filling the gas container there shall be fitted to the end of the pipe furthest from the gas container a check valve or a double-check valve.

(4) There shall be fitted over every gas filling point on a vehicle a cap which shall—

(a) prevent any leakage of gas from the gas filling point,

(b) be secured to the vehicle by a chain or some other suitable means,

(c) be made of suitable material, and

(d) be fastened to the gas filling point by either a screw thread or other suitable means.

Pipelines

4.—(1) Every pipeline shall be fixed in such a manner and position that—

(a) it will not be adversely affected by the heat of the exhaust system of any engine or any other source of heat,

(b) it is protected from vibration and strain in excess of that which it can reasonably be expected to withstand, and

(c) in the case of a high pressure pipeline it is so far as is practicable accessible for inspection.

(2) Save as provided in sub-paragraph (4) below, every high pressure pipeline shall be—

(a) a rigid line of steel, copper or copper alloy of high pressure hydraulic grade, suitable for service on road vehicles and designed for a minimum service pressure rating of not less than 75 bar absolute, and

(b) effectively protected against, or shielded from, or treated so as to be resistant to, external corrosion throughout its length unless it is made from material which is corrosion resistant under the conditions which it is likely to encounter in service.

(3) No unsupported length of any high pressure pipeline shall exceed 600 millimetres.

(4) Flexible hose may be used in a high pressure pipeline if—

(a) it is reinforced either by stainless steel wire braid or by textile braid,

(b) its length does not exceed 500 millimetres, and

(c) save in the case of a pipeline attached to a gas container for the purpose of filling that container the flexibility which it provides is necessary for the construction or operation of the gas system of which it forms a part.

(5) If a high pressure pipeline or part of such a pipeline is so constructed or located that it may, in the course of its normal use (excluding the supply of fuel from a gas container), contain liquid which is prevented from flowing, a relief valve shall be incorporated in that pipeline.

Unions and joints

5.—(1) Every union and joint on a pipeline or gas container shall be so constructed and fitted that it will—

(a) not be liable to work loose or leak when in use, and

(b) be readily accessible for inspection and maintenance.

(2) Every union on a high pressure pipeline or on a gas container shall be made of suitable metal but such a union may contain non-metal washers and seals provided that such washers and seals are supported and constrained by metal components.

Reducing valves

6. Every reducing valve shall be made of suitable materials and be so fitted as to be readily accessible for inspection and maintenance.

Pressure relief valves

7.—(1) Every pressure relief valve which is fitted to any part of a gas system (including a gas container) shall—

(a) be made entirely of suitable metal and so constructed and fitted as to ensure that the cooling effect of the gas during discharge shall not prevent its effective operation,

(b) be capable, under the most extreme temperatures likely to be met (including exposure to fire), of a discharge rate which prevents the pressure of the contents of the gas system from exceeding its design pressure,

(c) have a maximum discharge pressure not greater than the design pressure of the gas container,

(d) be so designed and constructed as to prevent unauthorised interference with the relief pressure setting during service, and

(e) have outlets which are—

(i) so sited that so far as is reasonably practicable in the event of an accident the valve and its outlets are protected from damage and the free discharge from such outlets is not impaired, and

(ii) so designed and constructed as to prevent the collection of moisture and other foreign matter which could adversely affect their performance.

(2) The pressure at which a pressure relief valve is designed to start lifting shall be clearly and permanently marked on every such valve.

(3) Every pressure relief valve which is fitted to a gas container shall communicate with the vapour space in the gas container and not with any liquefied gas.

Valves and cocks

8.—(1) A valve or cock shall be fitted to every supply pipeline as near as practicable to every fixed gas container and such valve or cock shall by manual operation enable the supply of gas from the gas container to the gas system to be stopped, and save as provided in sub-paragraph (2) below, shall—

(a) if fitted on the outside of the vehicle, be readily visible and accessible from the outside of the vehicle, or

(b) if fitted inside the vehicle be readily accessible for operation and be so arranged as to prevent so far as is practicable the possibility of gas entering the engine, passenger or living compartments due to leaks, and the space containing the valve or cock shall be so ventilated and drained as to prevent the accumulation of gas in that space.

(2) Where a fixed gas container supplies no gas system other than a gas propulsion system and the gas container is so located that it is not practicable to make the valve

or cock referred to in sub-paragraph (1) above readily accessible there shall be fitted an electrically-operated valve which shall either be incorporated in the valve or cock referred to in sub-paragraph (1) above or be fitted immediately downstream from it and shall—

(a) be constructed so as to open when the electric power is applied and to close when the electric power is cut off.

(b) be so fitted as to shut off the supply of gas from the gas container to the gas system when the engine is not running, and

(c) if fitted inside the vehicle be so arranged as to prevent as far as is practicable the possibility of gas entering the engine, passenger or living compartments due to leaks, and the space containing the valve shall be so ventilated and drained as to prevent the accumulation of gas in that space.

(3) A notice clearly indicating the position, purpose and method of operating every valve or cock referred to in sub-paragraphs (1) and (2) above shall be fixed—

(a) in all cases, in a conspicuous position on the outside of the vehicle, and

(b) in every case where the valve or cock is located inside the vehicle in a conspicuous position adjacent to the gas container.

(4) In the case of a high pressure pipeline for the conveyance of gas from the gas container an excess flow valve shall be fitted as near as practicable to the gas container and such valve shall operate in the event of a fracture of the pipeline or other similar failure.

(5) All parts of every valve or cock referred to in this paragraph which are in contact with gas shall be made of suitable metal, save that they may contain non-metal washers and seals provided that such washers and seals are supported and constrained by metal components.

Gauges

9. Every gauge connected to a gas container or to a pipeline shall be so constructed as to be unlikely to deteriorate under the action of the gas used or to be used and shall be so constructed and fitted that—

(a) no gas can escape into any part of the vehicle as a result of any failure of the gauge, and

(b) in the event of any failure of the gauge the supply of gas to the gauge can be readily stopped:

Provided that the requirement specified in sub-paragraph (b) above shall not apply in respect of a gauge fitted as an integral part of a gas container.

Propulsion systems

10.—(1) Every gas propulsion system shall be so designed and constructed that—

(a) the supply of gas to the engine is automatically stopped by the operation of a valve when the engine is not running at all or is not running on the supply of gas, and

(b) where a reducing valve is relied on to comply with sub-paragraph (a) above, the supply of gas to the engine is automatically stopped by the operation of an additional valve when the engine is switched off.

(2) Where the engine of a vehicle is constructed or adapted to run on one or more fuels as alternatives to gas, the safety and efficiency of the engine and any fuel system shall not be impaired by the presence of any other fuel system.

Special requirements for large passenger carrying vehicles

11. In the case of a large passenger carrying vehicle there shall be fitted as near as practicable to the gas container—

(a) a valve which shall stop the flow of gase into the gas supply pipeline in the event of the angle of tilt of the vehicle exceeding that referred to in Regulation 6 of the Public Service Vehicles (Conditions of Fitness, Equipment, Use and Certification) Regulations 1981 *[SI 1981 No 257]*, and

(b) a valve which shall stop the flow of gas into the gas supply pipeline in the event of the deceleration of the vehicle exceeding 5g.

[The angle of tilt referred to in the Public Service Vehicles (Conditions of Fitness, Condition, Use and Certification) Regulations 1981, reg 6, is 28 degrees from the horizontal in the case of a double-decked vehicle or 35 degrees from the horizontal in the case of a single-decked vehicle or a half-decked vehicle.]

Gas-fired appliances

12. Every part of a gas-fired appliance shall be—

(a) so designed and constructed that leakage of gas is unlikely to occur; and

(b) constructed of materials which are compatible with each other and with the gas used.

13. Every gas-fired appliance shall be—

(a) so located as to be easily inspected and maintained,

(b) so located and either insulated or shielded that its use shall not cause or be likely to cause danger due to the presence of any flammable material,

(c) so constructed and located as not to impose undue stress on any pipe or fitting, and

(d) so fastened or located as not to work loose or move in relation to the vehicle.

14. With the exception of catalytic heating appliances, every appliance of the kind described in Regulation 144C (2) (b) or (c) which is fitted to a motor vehicle shall be fitted with a flue which shall be—

(a) connected to an outlet which is on the outside of the vehicle,

(b) constructed and located so as to prevent any expelled matter from entering the vehicle, and

(c) located so that it will not cause any adverse effect to, or suffer any adverse effect from, the exhausts outlet of any engine or any other source of heat.

General requirements

15. Every part of a gas propulsion system or a gas-fired appliance system, excluding the appliance itself, shall be—

(a) so far as is practicable so located or protected as not to be exposed to accidental damage,

(b) soundly and properly constructed of materials which are compatible with one another and with the gas used or to be used and which are capable of withstanding the loads and stresses likely to be met in operation, and

(c) so designed and constructed that leakage of gas is unlikely to occur.]

[Schedule 3A was added by SI 1981 No 1663.]

SCHEDULE 4

REQUIREMENTS WITH RESPECT TO THE EFFICIENCY OF THE BRAKES OF CERTAIN MOTOR VEHICLES

1. This Schedule applies to a motor vehicle which is a heavy motor car, a motor car or a motor cycle and is not—

(a) a goods vehicle the unladen weight of which exceeds 1525 kilograms;

[(b) a large passenger carrying vehicle;]

(c) an articulated vehicle or a vehicle constructed or adapted for the purpose of forming part of an articulated vehicle;

[(d) a works truck;]

[(e) a pedestrian controlled vehicle; or]

[(f) a vehicle to which Regulation 14A applies;]

and references to a motor vehicle in the following provisions of this Schedule shall be construed accordingly.

In this paragraph 'goods vehicle' does not include a dual-purpose vehicle.

[Paragraph 1 is printed as amended by SI 1981 No 1189.]

2. For the purposes of this Schedule a two-wheeled motor cycle shall not, by reason that a sidecar is attached thereto, be treated as three-wheeled.

3. In the case of a motor vehicle having at least four wheels and required to have two means of operating brakes—

(a) if each means of operation applies brakes to at least four wheels, the brakes as applied by one of the means shall have a total braking efficiency of not less than 50 per cent and the brakes as applied by the other means shall have a total braking efficiency of not less than 25 per cent;

(b) if only one of the means of operation applies brakes to at least four wheels, the brakes as applied by that means shall have a total braking efficiency of not less than 50 per cent and the brakes as applied by the other means shall have a total braking efficiency of not less than 25 per cent; and

(c) if neither means of operation applies brakes to at least four wheels, the brakes as applied by one of the means shall have a total braking efficiency of not less than 30 per cent and the brakes as applied by the other means shall have a total braking efficiency of not less than 25 per cent.

4. In the case of a three-wheeled motor vehicle required to have two means of operating brakes—

(a) if each means of operation applies brakes to all three wheels, the brakes as applied by one of the means shall have a total braking efficiency of not less than 40 per cent and the brakes as applied by the other means shall have a total braking efficiency of not less than 25 per cent;

(b) if only one of the means of operation applies brakes to all three wheels, the brakes as applied by that means shall have a total braking efficiency of not less than 40 per cent and the brakes as applied by the other means shall have a total braking efficiency of not less than 25 per cent; and

(c) if neither means of operation applies brakes to all three wheels, the brakes as applied by one of the means shall have a total braking efficiency of not less than 30 per cent and the brakes as applied by the other means shall have a total braking efficiency of not less than 25 per cent.

5. In the case of a motor vehicle, being a two-wheeled motor cycle, required to have more than one means of operating brakes, the brakes as applied by one of the means shall have a total braking efficiency of not less than 30 per cent and the brakes as applied by the other means shall have a total braking efficiency of not less than 25 per cent.

6. In the case of a motor vehicle not required to have two means of operating brakes—

(a) if the vehicle has at least four wheels and one or more means of operation applying brakes to at least four wheels, the brakes as applied by that means or one of those means shall have a total braking efficiency of not less than 50 per cent;

(b) if the vehicle has at least four wheels and no means of operation applying brakes to at least four wheels, the brakes as applied by the means or one of the means of operation shall have a total braking efficiency of not less than 30 per cent;

(c) if the vehicle is three-wheeled and has one or more means of operation applying brakes to all three wheels, the brakes as applied by that means or one of those means shall have a total braking efficiency of not less than 40 per cent;

(d) if the vehicle is three-wheeled and has no means of operation applying brakes to all three wheels, the brakes as applied by the means or one of the means of operation shall have a total braking efficiency of not less than 30 per cent; and

(e) if the vehicle is two-wheeled, the brakes as applied by the means or one of the means of operation shall have a total braking efficiency of not less than 30 per cent.

[SCHEDULE 4A

REQUIREMENTS WITH RESPECT TO THE CONSTRUCTION, FITTING AND PERFORMANCE OF THE BRAKES OF CERTAIN MOTOR VEHICLES AND TRAILERS

In this Schedule—

'maximum gross weight' means—

(a) in the case of a vehicle equipped with a Ministry plate in accordance with Regulation 148 or 149, the design gross weight shown in column (3) of that plate or, if no such weight is shown, the gross weight shown in column (2) of that plate;

(b) in the case of a vehicle not equipped with such a Ministry plate, but which is equipped with a plate in accordance with paragraph (2)(a), (b) or (c) or paragraph (2A) of Regulation 42, the weights ascertained by reference to the particulars mentioned in the said paragraph 2(a), (b) or (c) or (2A) as the case may be;

(c) in any other case the weight the vehicle is designed or adapted not to exceed when travelling on a road laden; and

'the Council Directive' has the meaning assigned to that expression in Regulation 14A (4).]

TABLE *[ie table to Sched 4A]*

1	2	3	4
Item No.	Category of Motor Vehicle	Category of trailer	Construction Fitting and performance Requirements
1.	A passenger vehicle or a dual-purpose vehicle which is constructed or adapted to carry [more than 2 passengers but] not more than 8 passengers (exclusive of the driver) and which either— (*a*) has 4 or more wheels or, if having only 3 wheels, has a maximum gross weight exceeding 1,000 kilograms, or (*b*) has only 3 wheels, a maximum gross weight of 1,000 kilograms or less, and either a design speed exceeding 40 kilometres per hour or an engine capacity exceeding 50 cubic centimetres, and is not a motor cycle with a side-car attached.		The requirements set out in relation to category M1 vehicles in Annexes I, II and VII to the Council Directive and, if relevant, in Annexes III, IV, V and VI to the Council Directive.
2.	A passenger vehicle or a dual-purpose vehicle which is constructed or adapted to carry more than 8 passengers (exclusive of the driver) and which has a maximum gross weight of 5,000 kilograms or less.		The requirements set out in relation to category M2 vehicles in Annexes I, II and VII to the Council Directive and, if relevant, in Annexes III, IV, V and VI to the Council Directive.
3.	A passenger vehicle or a dual-purpose vehicle which is constructed or adapted to carry more than 8 passengers (exclusive of the driver) and which has a maximum gross weight exceeding 5,000 kilograms.		The requirements set out in relation to category M3 vehicles in Annexes I, II and VII to the Council Directive and, if relevant, in Annexes III, IV, V and VI to the Council Directive.
4.	A dual-purpose vehicle which is not of a class to which item 1, 2 or 3 above applies or a goods vehicle which has a maximum gross weight of 3,500 kilograms or less and is not a motorcycle with a side-car attached.		The requirements set out in relation to category N1 vehicles in Annexes I, II and VII to the Council Directive and, if relevant, in Annexes III, IV, V and VI to the Council Directive.
5.	A goods vehicle which has a maximum gross weight [exceeding 3,500 kilograms] but which does not exceed 12,000 kilograms.		The requirements set out in relation to category N2 vehicles in Annexes I, II and VII to the Council Directive and, if relevant, in Annexes III, IV, V and VI to the Council Directive.

1	2	3	4
Item No.	Category of Motor Vehicle	Category of trailer	Construction Fitting and performance Requirements
6.	A goods vehicle which has a maximum gross weight which exceeds 12,000 kilograms.		The requirements set out in relation to category N3 vehicles in Annexes I, II and VII to the Council Directive and, if relevant, in Annexes III, IV, V and VI to the Council Directive.
7.		A trailer which has a maximum gross weight of 750 kilograms or less.	The requirements set out in relation to category 01 vehicles in Annexes I, II and VII to the Council Directive and, if relevant, in Annexes III, IV, V, VI and VIII to the Council Directive.
8.		A trailer which has a maximum gross weight which exceeds 750 kilograms but which does not exceed 3,500 kilograms.	The requirements set out in relation to category 02 vehicles in Annexes I, II and VII to the Council Directive and, if relevant, in Annexes III, IV, V, VI and VIII to the Council Directive.
9.		A trailer which has a maximum gross weight which exceeds 3,500 kilograms but which does not exceed 10,000 kilograms.	The requirements set out in relation to category 03 vehicles in Annexes I, II and VII to the Council Directive and relevant, in Annexes III, IV, V, VI and VIII to the Council Directive.
10.		A trailer which has a maximum gross weight which exceeds 10,000 kilograms.	The requirements set out in relation to category 04 vehicles in Annexes I, II and VII to the Council Directive and, if relevant, in Annexes III, IV, V, VI, and VIII to the Council Directive.

[Schedule 4A was added by SI 1981 No 1189 and is printed as amended by SI 1982 No 1480.]

SCHEDULE 5

[Revoked.]

*   *   *

SCHEDULE 6

Permissible Maximum Weights

1. For the purposes of this Schedule the distance between any two axles shall be obtained by measuring the shortest distance between the line joining the centres of the points of contact with the road surface of the wheels of one axle and the line joining the centres of the points of contact with the road surface of the wheels of the other axle.

Column 1

Column 2
Kilograms

2. Heavy motor cars, motor cars and trailers in each case not forming part of an articulated vehicle:—
(*a*) in the case of a vehicle with two axles—
    (i) where the distance between the axles is at least 3·25 metres but less than 3·65 metres 15250
    (ii) where the distance between the axles is at least 3·65 metres. 16260
(*b*) in the case of a vehicle with three axles, where the distance between the foremost and rearmost axles is at least 5·48 metres..... 22360
(*c*) in the case of a vehicle with more than three axles—
    (i) where the distance between the foremost and rearmost axles is at least 7·01 metres but less than 7·92 metres........... 26420
    (ii) where the distance between the foremost and rearmost axles is at least 7·92 metres 28450

3. Articulated vehicles:—
(*a*) in the case of an articulated vehicle with three axles—
    (i) where the distance between the foremost and rearmost axles is less than 5·48 metres.. 20330
    (ii) where the distance between the foremost and rearmost axles is at least 5·48 metrese... 24390
(*b*) in the case of an articulated vehicle with four axles—
    (i) where the distance between the foremost and rearmost axles is less than 7·01 metres.. 24390
    (ii) where the distance between the foremost and rearmost axles is at least 7·01 metres but less than 7·92 metres........... 26420
    (iii) where the distance between the foremost and rearmost axles is at least 7·92 metres but less than 9·75 metres........... 28450
    (iv) where the distance between the foremost and rearmost axles is at least 9·75 metres but less than 11·58 metres 30490
    (v) where the distance between the foremost and rearmost axles is at least 11·58 metres 32520
(*c*) in the case of an articulated vehicle with more than four axles—
    (i) where the distance between the foremost and rearmost axles is less than 7·01 metres.. 24390
    (ii) where the distance between the foremost and rearmost axles is at least 7·01 metres but less than 7·92 metres........... 26420
    (iii) where the distance between the foremost and rearmost axles is at least 7·92 metres but less than 8·99 metres........... 28450
    (iv) where the distance between the foremost and rearmost axles is at least 8·99 metres but less than 9·75 metres........... 30490
    (v) where the distance between the foremost and rearmost axles is at least 9·75 metres 32520

SCHEDULE 7

Permissible Maximum Weights, etc

For the purposes of this Schedule—
  (1) . . .
  (2) where by virtue of any provision made in Part I, II or III of this Schedule two or more maximum weights specified in any such Part are applicable to any vehicle,

the highest of such maximum weights shall be treated as being the weight which the vehicle must not exceed, and where by virtue of any provision made in Part IV, V or VI of this Schedule two or more maximum weights are applicable to the axles of a vehicle, the highest of such maximum weights shall be treated as being the weight which those axles must not exceed.

PART I

Maximum permissible weights for heavy motor cars and motor cars and trailers in each case not forming part of an articulated vehicle

For the purposes of this Part of this Schedule—

'closely spaced' has the same meaning as in Regulation 92;

'maximum axle weight' means the highest weight shown for any axle in column 2 of a Ministry plate as defined in Regulation 146 and carried on the vehicle or, if no such plate is carried on the vehicle, the highest maximum weight in Great Britain shown for any axle in the plate complying with the requirements of Regulation 42 or the highest weight shown for any axle in the foreign plate with which the vehicle is equipped;

'foreign plate' means the plate mentioned in Regulation 89 (1) (*b*) (i) or 89 (1) (*d*) (i).

Column 1 Class of vehicle	Column 2 *Kilograms*
(*a*) Two axled vehicles—	
(i) where the distance between the axles is less than 2·65 metres and part (ii) of this item does not apply	14230
(ii) where the distance between the axles is less than 2·65 metres and—	
(*a*) the vehicle is a trailer,	
(*b*) the vehicle has two closely spaced axles,	
(*c*) the distance between the foremost axle of the trailer and the rear axle of the motor vehicle by which it is drawn is at least 4·2 metres, and	
(*d*) both the trailer and the motor vehicle by which it is drawn are vehicles to which Regulation 89 applies........	16260
[(iii) except in a case mentioned in item (iv) below, where the distance between the axles is at least 2.65 metres	16260]
[(iv) where the distance between the axles is at least 3 metres and the vehicle is a trailer...	18000]
(*b*) Three axled vehicles—	
Their weight shall not exceed 16260 kilograms except in a case below, where the weight opposite that case shall apply—	
(i) where the distance between the foremost and rearmost axle is at least 3 metres...	18290
(ii) where the distance between the foremost and rearmost axle is at least 3·2 metres and the maximum axle weight is not more than 8130 kilograms	20330
(iii) where the distance between the foremost and rearmost axle is at least 3·9 metres and the maximum axle weight is more than 8130 kilograms...	20330

	Column 1 Class of vehicle	Column 2 *Kilograms*
(iv)	where the distance between the foremost and rearmost axle is at least 3·9 metres and the maximum axle weight is not more than 8640 kilograms	22360
(v)	where the distance between the foremost and rearmost axle is at least 4·6 metres and the maximum axle weight is more than 8640 kilograms	22360
(vi)	where the distance between the foremost and rearmost axle is at least 4·9 metres and the maximum axle weight is not more than 9400 kilograms	24390
(vii)	where the distance between the foremost and rearmost axle is at least 5·1 metres and the maximum axle weight is more than 9400 kilograms	24390

(*c*) Vehicles with four or more axles—

Their weight shall not exceed 18290 kilograms except in a case below, where the weight opposite that case shall apply—

(i)	where the distance between the foremost and rearmost axle is at least 3·7 metres and the maximum axle weight is not more than 8640 kilograms	20330
(ii)	where the distance between the foremost and rearmost axle is at least 4·6 metres and the maximum axle weight is not more than 8640 kilograms	22360
(iii)	where the distance between the foremost and rearmost axle is at least 4·7 metres and the maximum axle weight is not more than 8640 kilograms	24390
(iv)	where the distance between the foremost and rearmost axle is at least 5 metres and the maximum axle weight is not more than 9150 kilograms	24390
(v)	where the distance between the foremost and rearmost axle is at least 5·6 metres and the maximum axle weight is not more than 9150 kilograms	26420
(vi)	where the distance between the foremost and rearmost axle is at least 6 metres and the maximum axle weight is not more than 9660 kilograms	26420
(vii)	where the distance between the foremost and rearmost axle is at least 5·9 metres and the maximum axle weight is not more than 9150 kilograms	28450
(viii)	where the distance between the foremost and rearmost axle is at least 6·3 metres and the maximum axle weight is not more than 9660 kilograms	28450
(ix)	where the distance between the foremost and rearmost axle is at least 6·3 metres and the maximum axle weight is not more than 9400 kilograms	390490
(x)	where the distance between the foremost and rearmost axle is at least 6·5 metres and the maximum axle weight is not more than 9660 kilograms	30490

PART II

Maximum permissible weights for heavy motor cars and motor cars in each case forming part of an articulated vehicle

*   *   *

[PART III (see Regulation 91)
Maximum weight of articulated vehicles

(1) Item No	(2) Relevant axle spacing (in metres)		(3) Maximum weight (in kilograms)	(4) Minimum overall length (in metres)
	(a) Where motor vehicle has 2 axles	(b) Where motor vehicle has at least 3 axles		
1	[at least 2.0]	[at least 2.0]	20330	—
2	at least 2.2	at least 2.2	22360	—
3	at least 2.6	at least 2.6	23370	—
4	at least 2.9	at least 2.9	24390	—
5	at least 3.2	at least 3.2	25410	—
6	at least 3.5	at least 3.5	26420	—
7	at least 3.8	at least 3.8	27740	—
8	at least 4.1	at least 4.1	28450	—
9	at least 4.4	at least 4.4	29470	—
10	at least 4.7	at least 4.7	30490	—
11	at least 5.0	at least 5.0	32500	—
12	at least 5.3	at least 5.3	32520	—
13	at least 5.5	at least 5.4	33000	10.0
14	at least 5.8	at least 5.6	34000	10.3
15	at least 6.2	at least 5.8	35000	10.5
16	at least 6.5	at least 6.0	36000	11.0
17	at least 6.7	at least 6.2	37000	11.5
18	at least 6.9	at least 6.3	38000	12.0]

[PART IIIA (see Regulation 91)

(1) Item No	(2) Type of articulated vehicle	(3) Maximum weight (in kilograms)
1	Motor vehicle and semi-trailer having a total of 3 axles	24390
2	Motor vehicle and semi-trailer having a total of 4 axles or motor vehicle first used before 1st April 1973 and semi-trailer having a total of 5 or more axles	32520
3	Motor vehicle first used on or after 1st April 1973 and semi-trailer having a total of 5 or more axles	38000]

[PART IV (see Regulation 92(2))
Maximum weights for two closely spaced axles

(1)	(2)	(3)	(4)	(5)
Item No	Distance between axles (in metres)	Maximum weight when plated weight of neither axle exceeds one half of the specified weight (in kilograms)	Maximum weight in cases not within column (3) when plated weight of neither axle exceeds 10170 kilograms (in kilograms)	Maximum weight in cases not within column (3) or (4) (in kilograms)
1	at least 1.02	16260	12200	10500
2	at least 1.05	17280	15260	10500
3	at least 1.20	18300	16270	15260
4	at least 1.35	18800	17280	16500
5	at least 1.50	19320	18300	18000
6	at least 1.80	20000	19000	19000
7	at least 1.85	20340	19320	19320]

[PART V (see Regulation 92(4))
Maximum weights for three closely spaced axles

(1)	(2)	(3)
Item No	Smallest distance between any adjoining axles of three closely spaced axles (in metres)	Maximum weight for any one of three closely spaced axles (in kilograms)
1	at least 0.70	6000
2	at least 0.80	6200
3	at least 0.90	6400
4	at least 1.00	6600
5	at least 1.10	6900
6	at least 1.20	7100
7	at least 1.35	7500]

PART VI

Maximum weight for three adjacent axles

For the purposes of this Part of this Schedule—

'intermediate axle weight' means the weight shown for the axle, being the middle axle of three adjacent axles, in column 2 of a Ministry plate as defined in Regulation 146 and carried on the vehicle or, if no such plate is carried on the vehicle, the maximum weight in Great Britain shown for that axle in the plate complying with the requirements of Regulation 42 or the weight shown for that axle in the foreign plate with which the vehicle is equipped;

'foreign plate' means the plate mentioned in Regulation 89 (1) (*b*) (i) or 89 (1) (*d*) (i).

The total weight transmitted to the road surface by the wheels of three adjacent axles shall not exceed 18290 kilograms except in a case below, where the weight opposite that case shall apply—

Kilograms

(i)   where the distance between the foremost and rearmost axle
is at least 3 metres and the intermediate axle weight is not
more than 8390 kilograms   20330

(ii) where the distance between the foremost and rearmost axle
is at least 3.8 metres and the intermediate axle weight is not
more than 8640 kilograms

(iii) where the distance between the formost and rearmost axle
is at least 4.6 metres and the intermediate axle weight is not
more than 9150 kilograms   24390

[Schedule 7 is printed as amended by SI 1982 No 1576, and SI 1983 No 471.]

SCHEDULE 8

CONDITIONS TO BE COMPLIED WITH IN RELATION TO THE USE OF VEHICLES CARRYING
WIDE OR LONG LOADS OR VEHICLES CARRYING LOADS OR HAVING FIXED APPLIANCES OR
APPARATUS WHICH PROJECT

PART 1

1. The conditions referred to in paragraph (2) of Regulation 136 and in paragraphs
(2), (4), (5), (6), (7) and (9) of Regulation 140 as the conditions specified in paragraph 1 of this Schedule are as follows:—

(*a*) save in so far as the chief officer of police of any police area in which it is proposed that the vehicle or vehicles in question will be used dispenses, as respects
the use of the vehicle or vehicles in that area, with any of the requirements contained in this and in the following sub-paragraph as to length of notice or particulars to be given, the owner of the vehicle or vehicles shall, before using the
vehicle, or, as the case may be, the vehicles on a road, give at least two clear
days' notice of the intended use (excluding Sundays, any bank holiday, Christ-
mas Day or Good Friday) to the chief officer of police of any such area as aforesaid.

In this sub-paragraph—

(i)   'chief officer of police' and 'police area', in relation to England and
Wales, have respectively the same meanings as in the Police Act 1964,
and in relation to Scotland, have respectively the same meanings as in
the Police (Scotland) Act 1967, and

(ii) the expression 'bank holiday', in relation to notice of the intended use of
a vehicle on a road, means a day which is a bank holiday by or under the
Banking and Financial Dealings Act 1971, either generally or in the
locality in which the road is situated;

(*b*) the notice referred to in the foregoing sub-paragraph shall contain particulars
of the time, date and route of the journey and—

(i)   in a case where this paragraph applies by virtue of paragraph (2) of
Regulation 140 particulars of the overall length and overall width of the
vehicle by which the load is to be carried and of the width of any lateral
projection or projections of its load,

(ii) in a case where this paragraph applies by virtue of paragraph (4) (*a*) of
Regulation 140 particulars of the overall length and overall width of
each vehicle by which the load is to be carried and of the length of any
forward projection and of any rearward projection of the load and,

where the load is to be carried by more than one vehicle, of the distance between vehicles,

(iii) in a case where this paragraph applies by virtue of Regulation 136 or paragraph (4) (*b*) of Regulation 140, particulars of the overall length of the combination of vehicles to be used and, in the second-mentioned case, particulars of the length of any forward projection and of any rearward projection of the load, being the projection or projections thereof as mentioned in the said paragraph (4) (*b*), and

(iv) in a case where this paragraph applies by virtue of paragraphs (5), (6), (7) or (9) of Regulation 140, particulars of the overall length of the vehicle to be used and of the length of any forward projection and of any rearward projection of its special appliance or apparatus or, as the case may be, of its load; and

(*c*) subject to any variations in the time, date or route of the journey which the owner of the vehicle or vehicles may be directed to make by any such chief officer of police as aforesaid, and subject to any delay which may be occasioned by reason of a direction given by a police constable, in the interests of road safety or to avoid undue traffic congestion, to the driver of a vehicle to halt it in a place on or adjacent to the road on which the vehicle is travelling, the vehicle or, as the case may be, the vehicles shall be used only in circumstances which accord with the particulars given in compliance with the foregoing subparagraph as to the time, date and route of the journey and only if any dimension or measurement relating to the vehicle or the vehicles (including that relating to a combination of vehicles), to a special appliance or apparatus or to a load, being a dimension or measurement of which particulars have been given as aforesaid, is not exceeded.

For the purposes of this sub-paragraph and of item (iv) of the foregoing subparagraph; the reference to a load shall, in a case where this paragraph applies by virtue of paragraph (7) of Regulation 140, be treated as a reference to a boat used for racing as mentioned in the said paragraph (7).

2. The conditions referred to in paragraph (2) of Regulation 136 and in paragraphs (2), (4), (5), (6) and (9) of Regulation 140 as the conditions specified in paragraph 2 of this Schedule are that at least one person in addition to the person or persons employed in driving the motor vehicle in question shall be employed in attending to that vehicle and its load and any other vehicle or vehicles drawn by that vehicle and the load or loads carried on the vehicle or vehicles so drawn and to give warning to the driver of the said motor vehicle and to any other person of any danger likely to be caused to any such other person by reason of the presence of the said vehicle or vehicles on the road:

Provided that, where three or more motor vehicles as respects which the conditions in this paragraph are applicable are travelling together in convoy, it shall be sufficient compliance with this paragraph if only the foremost and rearmost vehicles in the convoy are attended in the manner prescribed in this paragraph.

For the purpose of this paragraph—

(*a*) in a case where a motor vehicle is drawing a trailer or trailers any person employed in pursuance of section 34 of the 1972 Act in attending that vehicle or any such trailer shall be treated as being an attendant required by this paragraph so long as he is also employed to discharge the duties mentioned in this paragraph, and

(*b*) in a case where a motor vehicle is drawing a trailer or trailers and another motor vehicle is used for the purpose of assisting in their propulsion on the road, the person or persons employed in driving that other motor vehicle shall not be treated as a person or persons employed in attending to the first-mentioned vehicle or any vehicle or vehicles drawn thereby.

3. The conditions referred to in paragraphs (5) and (6) of Regulation 140 as the conditions specified in paragraph 3 of this Schedule are as follows:—

(a) there shall be exhibited on every relevant projection such a number of plane unbroken surfaces as are required by the following provisions of this paragraph, the said surfaces to be of the size, shape and colour specified in those provisions and to be situated in accordance therewith.

In this sub-paragraph the expression 'relevant projection' means any such forward or rearward projection as is mentioned in sub-paragraph (a), (c), or (d) of the said paragraph (5) or of the said paragraph (6);

(b) subject to the provisions of sub-paragraph (e) of this paragraph, three surfaces shall be exhibited of which one (hereafter referred to as 'the end projection surface') shall be of the shape and colour shown in the diagram first set out in Part II of this Schedule and shall conform with the dimensions there shown in relation to the size and colouring of that surface, and the other two, and any surface additional to those two required by the said sub-paragraph (e), (each hereafter referred to as a 'side projection surface') shall be of the shape and colour shown in the diagram secondly set out in the said Part II and shall conform with the dimensions there shown in relation to the size and colouring of that surface;

(c) the end projection surface shall be exhibited so that it may be seen, in the case of a forward projection, from the front thereof or, in the case of a rearward projection, from the rear thereof and shall be situated so that—
   (i) it lies, as near as practicable, in a vertical plane at right angles to the longitudinal axis of the vehicle and passing through a point not more than 0.6 metres from the extreme end of the projection,
  (ii) the vertical distance between the carriageway of the road and the nearest point on the surface does not exceed 2.5 metres,
 (iii) the surface and any object or device by means of which it is exhibited impedes, as little as possible, the view of the driver to the front or, as the case may be, to the rear of the vehicle, and
 (iv) every part of the surface is clearly visible to other persons using the road within a reasonable distance from that end of the projection from which the surface may be seen as provided by the foregoing provisions of this sub-paragraph;

(d) the two side projection surfaces shall be exhibited so that one may be seen from one side of the projection and the other may be seen from the other side thereof and each surface shall be situated so that—
   (i) it lies, as near as practicable, in a vertical plane parallel to the longitudinal axis of the vehicle,
  (ii) no part of it extends beyond the end of the projection,
 (iii) the horizontal distance between it and the end projection surface or a rear marking carried in accordance with [the Lighting Regulations] does not exceed 0.9 metres,
 (iv) the vertical distance between the carriageway of the road and any point on at least one side of the surface does not exceed 2.5 metres, and
  (v) every part of the surface is clearly visible to other persons using the road within a reasonable distance from that side of the projection from which

the surface may be seen as provided by the foregoing provisions of this sub-paragraph;

(e) in the case of a forward projection exceeding 4.5 metres in length or a rearward projection exceeding 5.1 metres in length such a number of side projection surfaces additional to the two side projection surfaces required by sub-paragraph (b) of this paragraph shall be exhibited on each side of the projection as to ensure that the horizontal distance between the foremost or, as the case may be, the rearmost point of the vehicle and that part of any side projection surface exhibited on the same side nearest that point, or between the nearest points of adjacent side projection surfaces exhibited on the same side, does not exceed in the case of such surfaces exhibited on a forward projection, 2.4 metres or, in the case of such surfaces exhibited on a rearward projection, 3.6 metres.

For the purposes of this sub-paragraph the expression 'the vehicle' shall not include any special appliance or apparatus or any part thereof which is a forward projection or a rearward projection within the meaning of Regulation 139;

(f) the provisions of items (i), (iv) and (v) of sub-paragraph (d) of this paragraph shall apply in relation to the additional side projection surfaces exhibited in accordance with the foregoing sub-paragraph as they apply in relation to the side projection surfaces referred to in the said sub-paragraph (d); and

(g) every surface exhibited in compliance with the foregoing provisions of this paragraph shall be kept clean and unobscured and during the hours of darkness shall be illuminated by means of lamps sufficient to render the surface readily distinguishable from a reasonable distance and so shielded that only light reflected from the surface is visible to other persons using the road:

Provided that the conditions in sub-paragraph (b) so far as it relates to side projection surfaces and the condition in sub-paragraph (d) shall not apply by reason only that a vehicle has a special appliance or apparatus, or is carrying a load, which has a rearward projection exceeding 1.8 metres in length but not exceeding 3 metres in length.

[Paragraph 3 is printed as amended by SI 1984 No 813.]

4. The condition referred to in paragraphs (5), (6), (7) and (8) of Regulation 140 as the condition specified in paragraph 4 of this Schedule is that steps shall have been taken to render the relevant projection clearly visible to other persons using the road within a reasonable distance, in the case of a forward projection, from the front thereof or, in the case of a rearward projection, from the rear thereof and, in either case, from either side thereof.

In this paragraph the expression 'relevant projection' means any such forward or rearward projection as is mentioned in sub-paragraph (b) of the said paragraph (5) or of the said paragraph (6) or in the said paragraph (7) or the said paragraph (8).

PART II

Projection Markers

DIAGRAM OF END PROJECTION SURFACE

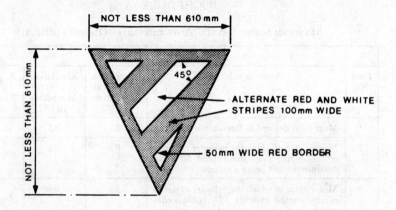

NOT LESS THAN 610mm

NOT LESS THAN 610mm

45°

ALTERNATE RED AND WHITE
STRIPES 100mm WIDE

50mm WIDE RED BORDER

DIAGRAM OF SIDE PROJECTION SURFACE

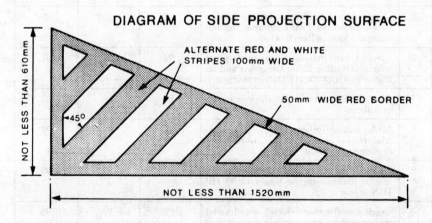

NOT LESS THAN 610mm

ALTERNATE RED AND WHITE
STRIPES 100mm WIDE

50mm WIDE RED BORDER

45°

NOT LESS THAN 1520mm

[The above diagrams are reproduced with the permission of the Controller of Her Majesty's stationery office.]

SCHEDULE 9

Maximum Sound Levels

*　　*　　*

[SCHEDULE 9A

Maximum Sound Levels (A weighting) in Decibels (dB (A))

1	2	3	4	5
Item No	Class of vehicle	Regulation 116 (3)(a) Maximum dB (A)	Regulation 116 (3) (b) Maximum dB (A)	Regulation 116 (3)(c) Maximum dB (A)
1.	Moped (as defined in Regulation 46 (4))	83	83	79
2.	Motor cycle of which the cylinder capacity of the engine does not exceed 50 cubic centimetres, not being a moped	83	83	81
3.	Motor cycle of which the cylinder capacity of the engine exceeds 125 cubic centimetres	90	89	89
4.	Motor cycle not being a vehicle in item 1, 2 or 3 above	90	85	83
5.	Goods vehicle having a maximum gross weight exceeding 3500 kilograms, but not being a vehicle in item 6 below	92	92	89
6.	Goods vehicle having a maximum gross weight exceeding 12000 kilograms and an engine power of 200 HP DIN or more	92	94	91
7.	Goods vehicle not being a vehicle in item 5 or 6 above	88	88	85
8.	Motor tractor (other than . . . an industrial tractor), locomotive . . . , works truck or engineering plant	92	92	92
9.	[Agricultural motor vehicle] or industrial tractor with an engine power of 90 HP DIN or less	92	92	92
10.	[Agricultural motor vehicle] or industrial tractor with an engine power greater than 90 HP DIN	92	92	95
11.	Passenger vehicle constructed for the carriage of more than 8 passengers (exclusive of the driver), or to which Regulation 31E applies but not being a vehicle in item 12 below	92	92	85
12.	Passenger vehicle constructed for the carriage of more than 8 passengers (exclusive of the driver), and having an engine power equal to or exceeding 200 HP DIN	92	94	88

1	2	3	4	5
Item No	Class of vehicle	Regulation 116 (3)(a) Maximum dB (A)	Regulation 116 (3) (b) Maximum dB (A)	Regulation 116 (3)(c) Maximum dB (A)
13.	Passenger vehicle not being a vehicle in item 11 or 12 above	87	87	83
14.	Vehicle not being a vehicle in any item above	92	92	92]

[Schedule 9A was inserted by SI 1980 No 1166 and is printed as amended by SI 1984 No 1809.]

SCHEDULE 10

MEASUREMENT OF NOISE

*   *   *

SCHEDULE 11

MINISTRY PLATE

PLATE	DEPARTMENT OF TRANSPORT Road Traffic Act 1972, Sections 40 and 45 Examination of Goods Vehicles			Serial No
				MAKE
REGISTRATION / IDENTIFICATION MARK (where applicable)	CHASSIS / SERIAL No (where marked on vehicle)	YEAR OF ORIGINAL REGISTRATION (where applicable)	YEAR OF MANUFACTURE	MODEL (where applicable)
(1) DESCRIPTION OF WEIGHTS APPLICABLE TO VEHICLE	(2) WEIGHTS NOT TO BE EXCEEDED IN GREAT BRITAIN KILOGRAMS	(3) DESIGN WEIGHTS (if higher than shown in col (2)) KILOGRAMS		Space for Authenticating Stamp
AXLE WEIGHT (Axles numbered from front to rear) AXLE 1				
AXLE 2				
AXLE 3				DATE OF ISSUE OF PLATING CERTIFICATE.
AXLE 4				
GROSS WEIGHT (see warning opposite)				WARNING 1. A reduced gross weight may apply in certain cases to a vehicle towing or being towed by another. 2. A reduced train weight may apply depending on the type of trailer drawn. 3. All weights shown are subject to fitting of correct tyres.
TRAIN WEIGHT (see warning opposite)				

SCHEDULE 11—Notes

Notes: A Ministry Plate may contain the words 'MINISTRY OF TRANSPORT' or 'DEPARTMENT OF THE ENVIRONMENT' instead of the words 'DEPARTMENT OF TRANSPORT', and may contain the words 'Road Safety Act 1967, Sections 8 and 9' instead of the words 'Road Traffic Act 1972, Sections 40 and 45'. It may also contain additional columns in Columns (2) and (3) showing the weights in tons.

[(2) Entries in respect of train weight are required in the cases of—
    (a) a motor vehicle constructed or adapted to form part of an articulated vehicle, and
    (b) a rigid vehicle which is constructed or adapted to draw a trailer and is manufactured on or after 1st October 1982 and first used on or after 1st April 1983.]

[(2A) A ministry plate shall contain the words 'Road Traffic Act 1972, Sections 40 and 47' instead of the words 'Road Traffic Act 1972, Sections 40 and 45' in a case where the Motor Vehicles (Type Approval for Goods Vehicles) (Great Britain) Regulations 1982 apply.]

[(2B) A Ministry plate shall show the unladen weight and function of the vehicle in a case where the Motor Vehicles (Type Approval for Goods Vehicles) (Great Britain) Regulations 1982 apply.]

[*Schedule 11 and notes are printed as amended by SI 1982 No 1272.*]

SCHEDULE 12

DISTINGUISHING PLATES FOR MOTOR CYCLES

1. The plate shall be firmly attached to a part of the motor cycle which is not normally subject to replacement during the life of the motor cycle.

2. The plate shall be in the form shown in the diagram in this paragraph, shall have dimensions not less than those shown in that diagram and shall show the information provided for in that diagram and detailed in the Notes below.

Diagram of Plate

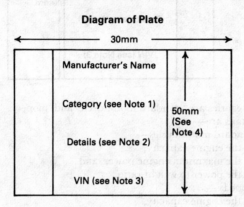

Notes: 1. The categories are 'standard motor cycle' and 'moped';
2. The details are—
(a) for standard motor cycles and mopeds—
the engine capacity; and
(b) for mopeds only—
(i) the kerbside weight, and
(ii) the maximum design speed.
3. The vehicle identification number (VIN) shall be marked in the form used by the manufacturer to identify any one individual vehicle.

3. The information on the plate shall be shown in characters not less than 4 millimetres in height and in the positions on the plate indicated in the diagram above.

4. No information, other than that provided for in the diagram above, shall be marked within the rectangle which is shown by the heavy lines in that diagram.

[SCHEDULE 12A

DISTINGUISHING PLATES FOR MOTOR CYCLES FIRST USED ON OR AFTER 1ST JANUARY 1982

1. The plate shall be firmly attached to a part of the motor cycle which is not normally subject to replacement during the life of the motor cycle.

2. The plate shall be in the form shown in the diagram in this paragraph, shall have dimensions not less than those shown in that diagram and shall show the information provided for in that diagram and detailed in the Notes below.

Diagram of Plate

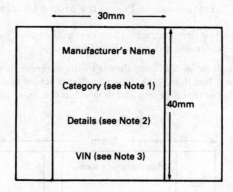

Notes: 1. The categories are 'standard motor cycle' and 'moped'.
　　　　2. The details are—
　　　(a) for standard motor cycles—
　　　　　　(i) the engine capacity,
　　　　　　(ii) the maximum engine power, and
　　　　　　(iii) the power to weight ratio;
　　　(b) for mopeds—
　　　　　　(i) the engine capacity,
　　　　　　(ii) the kerbside weight, and
　　　　　　(iii) the maximum design speed.
　　　　3. The vehicle identification number (VIN) shall be marked in the form used
　　　　　by the manufacturer to identify any one individual vehicle.

The Motor Vehicles (Driving Licences) Regulations 1981

(SI 1981 No 952)

[The text of these regulations is printed as amended by:
   the Motor Vehicles (Driving Licences) (Amendment) (No 2) Regulations 1982 (SI 1982 No 230) (29 March 1982).
   the Motor Vehicles (Driving Licences) (Amendment) (No 4) Regulations 1982 (SI 1982 No 937) (1 October 1982 and 1 February 1983); and
   the Motor Vehicles (Driving Licences) (Amendment) Regulations 1984 (SI 1984 No 274) (5 April 1984).
The amending regulations are referred to in the notes to the main regulations only by their year and number. The date referred to above is the date on which the regulations came into force.

   The main regulations have also been amended by the Motor Vehicles (Driving Licences) (Amendment) Regulations 1982 (SI 1982 No 99), the Motor Vehicles (Driving Licences) (Amendment) (No 3) Regulations 1982 (SI 1982 No 423), the Motor Vehicles (Driving Licences) (Amendment) Regulations 1983 (SI 1983 No 1662), and the Motor Vehicles (Driving Licences) (Amendment) (No 2) Regulations 1984 (SI 1984 No 737), but these do not affect the text of any regulation printed.]

PART I

PRELIMINARY

*   *   *

3. Interpretation

(1) In these Regulations, unless the context otherwise requires, the following expressions have the meanings hereby respectively assigned to them, that is to say:—

'Act of 1960' means the Road Traffic Act 1960;

'Act of 1972' means the Road Traffic Act 1972;

'clerk to the traffic commissioners' means the clerk to the traffic commissioners for any traffic area constituted for the purposes of [the Public Passenger Vehicles Act 1981];

'controlled by a pedestrian' in relation to a vehicle means that the vehicle either—
   (a) is constructed or adapted for use under such control; or
   (b) is constructed or adapted for use either under such control or under the control of a person carried on it but is not for the time being in use under, or proceeding under, the control of a person carried on it;

'disability' includes disease;

'full licence' means a licence other than a provisional licence;

'group' in relation to a class of motor vehicles means a group of motor vehicles of the classes specified in the second column of Schedule 3, and a group identified by a letter means the group corresponding to the letter in the first column of that Schedule;

463

'kerbside weight' has the same meaning as in Regulation 46 (4) of the Motor Vehicles (Construction and Use) Regulations 1978 *[SI 1978 No 1017]*;

'licence' means a licence to drive a motor vehicle granted under Part III of the Act of 1972;

'licensing authority' means the Secretary of State;

'maximum design speed' has the same meaning as in Regulation 46 (4) of the Motor Vehicles (Construction and Use) Regulations 1978;

'moped' means—

    (i) in the case only of motor cycles which are first used on or after 1st August 1977, a motor cycle (not being a motor vehicle of group K) which has a maximum design speed which does not exceed 30 mph, a kerbside weight which does not exceed 250 kg, and, if propelled by an internal combustion engine, an engine the cylinder capacity of which does not exceed 50 cc, or

   (ii) in the case only of motor cycles which are first used before 1st August 1977, a motor cycle which has an engine with a cylinder capacity not exceeding 50 cc and is equipped with pedals by means of which the cycle is capable of being propelled;

'part of a test' means Part I or Part II, as the case may require, of the test for motor bicycles prescribed by Regulation 18;

'provisional licence' means a licence granted by virtue of section 88 (2) of the Act of 1972;

'test' means a test of competence to drive conducted under section 85 of the Act of 1972 [and includes a reference to part of a test];

'vehicle propelled by electrical power' means a vehicle of which the motive power is solely derived from any electrical storage battery carried on the vehicle and not connected to any source of power when the vehicle is in motion;

'vehicle with automatic transmission' means a vehicle in which the driver is not provided with any means whereby he may, independently of the use of the accelerator or the brakes, vary gradually the proportion of the power being produced by the engine which is transmitted to the road wheels of the vehicle.

(2) In determining for the purpose of these Regulations when a motor cycle is first used, the date of such first use shall be taken to be such date as is the earliest of the undermentioned relevant dates applicable to that cycle—

(*a*) in the case of a motor cycle registered under the Roads Act 1920, the Vehicles (Excise) Act 1949, the Vehicles (Excise) Act 1962 or the Vehicles (Excise) Act 1971, the relevant date is the date on which it was first so registered; and

(*b*) in each of the following cases:—

    (i) in the case of a motor cycle which is being or has been used under a trade licence as defined in section 16 of the Vehicles (Excise) Act 1971 (otherwise than for the purposes of demonstration or testing or of being delivered from premises of the manufacturer by whom it was made, or of a distributor of vehicles or dealer in vehicles to premises of a distributor of vehicles, dealer in vehicles or purchaser thereof, or to premises of a person obtaining possession thereof under a hiring agreement or hire purchase agreement);

   (ii) in the case of a motor cycle which belongs or has belonged to the Crown and which is or was used or appropriated for use for naval, military or air force purposes;

 (iii) in the case of a motor cycle which belongs or has belonged to a visiting force or a headquarters or defence organisation to which in each case the Visiting Forces and International Headquarters (Application of Law) Order 1965 *[SI 1965 No 1536]* applies;

 (iv) in the case of a motor cycle which has been used on roads outside Great Britain and has been imported into Great Britain; and

 (v) in the case of a motor cycle which has been used otherwise than on roads after being sold or supplied by retail and before being registered,

the relevant date is the date of manufacture of the cycle.

In this paragraph 'sold or supplied by retail' means sold or supplied otherwise than to a person acquiring solely for the purpose of re-sale or re-supply for a valuable consideration.

(3) The provisions of Regulation 46 (5) of the Motor Vehicles (Construction and Use) Regulations 1978 shall apply for determining, for the purposes of the definition of 'moped' in paragraph (1) above, whether the maximum design speed of a motor cycle does not exceed 30 mph.

(4), (5) *[Omitted.]*

[Regulation 3 is printed as amended by the Interpretation Act 1978, s 17 (2) (a), and SI 1982 No 230.]

PART II

LICENCES

4. Minimum ages for holding or obtaining licences

(1) Subsection (1) of section 96 of the Act of 1972 (which specifies the minimum age for holding or obtaining a licence to drive certain classes of motor vehicles) shall have effect as if in the Table in that subsection—

 (*a*) in item 2, the age of 17 were substituted for the age of 16 in relation to all motor cycles other than—

  (i) mopeds,

  (ii) motor cycles which are mowing machines, or

  (iii) motor cycles which are vehicles controlled by a pedestrian;

 (*b*) in item 3, the age of 16 were substituted for the age of 17 in the case of a person to whom an award of a mobility allowance has been made in pursuance of section 37A of the Social Security Act 1975 *[section 37A was inserted by section 22 (1) of the Social Security Pensions Act 1975]* provided that where the award was made before he attained the age of 16 it is in force when he attains that age;

 (*c*) in item 4, in relation to an agricultural tractor which—

  (i) is so constructed that the whole of its weight is transmitted to the road surface by means of wheels;

  (ii) has an overall width not exceeding 8 feet;

  (iii) is chargeable with duty under section 1 of the Vehicles (Excise) Act 1971 by reference to paragraph 1 of Schedule to that Act as being an agricultural machine or, by virtue of the provisions of section 7 (1) of that Act, is not chargeable with duty thereunder; and

  (iv) is driven without a trailer attached to it, other than a trailer which has an overall width not exceeding 8 feet and which is either a two-wheeled or close-coupled four-wheeled trailer,

the age of 16 were substituted for the age of 17, but in the case of a person who has not passed the test of competence prescribed under section 85 (2) of the Act of 1972 to drive such a tractor, only while taking, proceeding to or returning from, such a test;

(d) in item 6, the age of 17 were substituted for the age of 21 in relation to a road roller falling within that item if the roller—
   (i) is propelled otherwise than by steam;
   (ii) has an unladen weight not exceeding $11\frac{1}{2}$ tons; and
   (iii) is not constructed or adapted for the conveyance of a load other than the following articles, that is to say, water, fuel, accumulators and other equipment used for the purpose of propulsion, loose tools, loose equipment and objects such as are mentioned in paragraph (3) below,

and if no wheel of the roller is fitted with a pneumatic, soft or elastic tyre;

(e) in item 6, the age of 18 were substituted for the age of 21 in the case of a person who fulfils the conditions—
   (i) that he is employed by a registered employer, and
   (ii) that he is a registered employee of such an employer,

in relation to any vehicle (other than a road roller) which is a heavy goods vehicle (hgv) of a class to which his training agreement applies and is owned by his employer or by a registered hgv driver training establishment;

(f) in item 6, the age of 18 were substituted for the age of 21 in relation to a large passenger vehicle where—
   (i) the driver of the vehicle is not engaged in the carriage of passengers and either holds a licence to drive a public service vehicle granted under [section 22 of the Public Passenger Vehicles Act 1981], is undergoing a test of his ability to drive a public service vehicle in pursuance of Regulations for the time being in force under that section, or is acting under the suspervision of a person who holds such a licence; or
   (ii) the driver holds such a licence and is engaged in the carriage of passengers—
      (a) on a regular service over a route which does not exceed 50 kilometres; or
      (b) on a national transport operation when the vehicle used is constructed and equipped to carry not more than 15 persons including the driver,

and in either case the operator of the vehicle holds a PSV operator's licence, granted under Part I of the Transport Act 1980, not being a licence which is of no effect by reason of its suspension;

(g) in items 5 and 6, the age of 17 were substituted for the ages of 18 and 21 respectively in the case of members of the armed forces of the Crown in relation to any vehicle when being used in the course of urgent work of national importance in accordance with an order of the Defence Council in pursuance of the Defence (Armed Forces) Regulations 1939 which were continued permanently in force, in the form set out in Part C of Schedule 2 to the Emergency Laws (Repeal) Act 1959, by section 2 of the Emergency Powers Act 1964.

[(h) in items 5 and 6, the age of 17 were substituted for the ages of 18 and 21 respectively in the case of a member of the armed forces of the Crown when receiving instruction in the driving of heavy goods vehicles of any class in preparation for a test of competence prescribed under section 119 of the Act of 1972 to drive vehicles of that class, or when taking, proceeding to, or returning from any such test.]

(2) For the purposes of paragraph (1)(c) above any implement fitted to a tractor shall be deemed to form part of the tractor notwithstanding that it is not a permanent or essentially permanent fixture, and in that paragraph—

    (i) 'overall width', in relation to a vehicle, means the width of the vehicle measured between vertical planes parallel to the longitudinal axis of the vehicle and passing through the extreme projecting points thereof exclusive of any driving mirror and so much of the distortion of any tyre as is caused by the weight of the vehicle; and

    (ii) 'close-coupled', in relation to a trailer, means that the wheels on the same side of the trailer are so fitted that at all times while it is in motion they remain parallel to the longitudinal axis of the trailer, and that the distance between the centres of their respective areas of contact with the road surface edoes not exceed 33 inches.

(3) For the purposes of paragraph 1(d) above the unladen weight of a vehicle shall be treated as including the weight of any object for the time being attached to the vehicle, being an object specially designed to be so attached for the purpose of temporarily increasing the vehicle's gross weight.

(4) In paragraph 1(e) above and in this paragraph—

'heavy goods vehicle' has the same meaning as in section 124 of the Act of 1972;

'registered' means registered for the time being by the Training Committee in accordance with the relevant provisions of the training scheme;

'the Training Committee' means the committee which has been established by the employers' associations and the trade unions in the road goods transport industry with a constitution approved by the Secretary of State and which is known as the National Joint Training Committee for Young HGV Drivers in the Road Goods Transport Industry;

'the training scheme means the scheme which has been established by the Training Committee with the approval of the Secretary of State for training young drivers of hgvs and which provides for—

    (a) the registration by the Training Committee of employers who are willing and able to provide hgv driver training for persons employed by them.

    (b) the registration by the Training Committee of persons operating establishments for providing hgv driver training,

    (c) a syllabus for hgv driver training, and

    (d) the registration by the Training Committee of individual employees who are undergoing, or are to undergo, hgv driver training in the service of a registered employer in accordance with a form of agreement approved by the Training Committee;

and 'training agreement', in relation to an individual who is undergoing, or is to undergo, such training as aforesaid, means his agreement therefor with his registered employer in pursuance of the training scheme.

(5) In paragraph (1)(f) above ' "large passenger vehicle" means a motor vehicle which is constructed solely to carry passengers and their effects and is adapted to carry more than nine persons inclusive of the driver' and expressions used which are also used in the Community Drivers' Ages and Hours of Work Regulations have the same meaning as in that instrument.

(6) In paragraph (5) above, 'the Community Drivers' Ages and Hours of Work Regulation' means Council Regulation (EEC) 543/69 on the harmonisation of certain social legislation relating to road transport *[OJ L 77/49 of 29.3.69]* as amended by

Council Regulations (EEC) Nos 514/72 *[OJ L 67/1 of 20.3.72]*, 515/72 *[OJ L 67/11 of 20.3.72]* and 2827/77 *[OJ L 334/1 of 24.1.77]* as read with Regulation 3 of the Community Road Transport Rules (Exemptions) Regulations 1978 *[SI 1978 No 1158]*.

(7) *[Omitted.]*

[Regulation 4 is printed as amended by the Interpretation Act 1978, s 17 (2) (a), and SI 1984 No 274.]

*   *   *

[7. Duration of provisional licences

For the purposes of subsection (1A) of section 89 of the Act of 1972 there is hereby prescribed—

> (i) a motor cycle of a class falling within group D,
> (ii) a period of two years, and
> (iii) the circumstances that the applicant for the licence is a person whose previous provisional licence authorising the driving of a motor cycle of a class included in group D was revoked under section 87 of the Act of 1972, or surrendered by him, because he was suffering from a relevant or prospective disability and who applies for a licence to continue in force for a period equal to the remainder of the period for which that previous licence would have authorised the driving of such a motor cycle at the time of surrender or revocation.]

[Regulation 7 was substituted (with effect from 1 October 1982) by SI 1982 No 937].

8. Conditions attached to provisional licences

(1) Subject to the provisions of paragraphs (2), (3) and (4) of this Regulation the holder of a provisional licence shall comply with the following conditions in relation to motor vehicles of a class which he is authorised to drive by virtue of the provisional licence, that is to say he shall not drive or ride such a motor vehicle—

> (a) otherwise than under the supervision of a qualified driver who is present with him in or on the vehicle;
>
> (b) unless a distinguishing mark in the form set out in Schedule 2 is displayed on the vehicle in such manner as to be clearly visible to other persons using the road from within a reasonable distance from the front and from the back of the vehicle;
>
> (c) while it is being used to draw a trailer; and
>
> (d) in the case of a motor bicycle not having attached thereto a side-car, while carrying on it a person who is not a qualified driver:

Provided that where the holder of a provisional licence has passed a test which authorises him to be granted a full licence to drive or ride a particular class of vehicles the above-mentioned conditions shall cease to apply in relation to the driving or riding (as the case may be) by him of motor vehicles of that class.

(2) The condition specified in paragraph (1)(a) of this Regulation shall not apply when the holder of the provisional licence—

> (a) is undergoing a test or a test of competence to drive heavy goods vehicles under Part IV of the Act of 1972; or
>
> (b) is driving a vehicle (not being a motor car) constructed to carry only one person and not adapted to carry more than one person; or
>
> (c) is driving a vehicle the unladen weight of which does not exceed 16 hundred-

weight, being a vehicle propelled by electrical power, constructed or adapted to carry only one person and constructed or adapted for the carriage of goods or burden of any description; or

(*d*) is driving a road roller the unladen weight of which does not exceed 3 tons, being a vehicle constructed or adapted for the carriage of goods or burden of any description; or

(*e*) is riding a motor bicycle, whether or not having attached thereto a side-car; or

(*f*) is driving a motor vehicle on a road in an exempted island.

(3) The condition specified in paragraph (1)(*c*) of this Regulation shall not apply when the holder of the provisional licence is driving an agricultural tractor, nor shall it prevent the holder of a provisional licence from driving an articulated vehicle.

(4) The condition specified in paragraph (1)(*d*) of this Regulation shall not apply when the holder of the provisional licence is riding a pedal cycle of the tandem type to which additional means of propulsion by mechanical power are attached.

(5) In this Regulation—

'exempted island' means any island outside the mainland of Great Britain from which motor vehicles, unless constructed for special purposes, can at no time be conveniently driven to a road in any other part of Great Britain by reason of the absence of any bridge, tunnel, ford or other way suitable for the passage of such motor vehicles but this expression 'exempted island' does not include any of the following islands, namely, the Isle of Wight, St. Mary's (Isles of Scilly), the islands of Arran, Barra, Bute, Great Cumbrae, Islay, the island which comprises Lewis and Harris, Mainland (Orkney), Mainland (Shetland), Mull, the island which comprises North Uist, Benbecula and South Uist, Skye and Tiree;

'leg disability' means a disability which consists solely of any one or more of the following:—
(*a*) the absence of a leg or legs,
(*b*) the deformity of a leg or legs,
(*c*) the loss of use of a leg or legs,

reference to a leg including reference to a foot or part of a leg or foot, and reference to loss of use, in relation to a leg or foot, including reference to a deficiency of movement or power in the leg or foot;

'qualified driver' means a person who holds—
(i) the case of the supervision of the driver of any vehicle including a motor car, a full licence authorising him to drive as a full licence holder the motor vehicle being driven by the holder of the provisional licence, or
(ii) in the case only of the supervision of the driver of a motor car by a person whose licence is limited, in pursuance of an application in that behalf by him or under section 87 (4) (ii) of the Act of 1972, solely on account of a leg disability to motor vehicles of a particular construction or design, a full licence authorising him so to drive motor cars of a class falling within the same group as the motor car being driven by the holder of the provisional licence.

*   *   *

[10. Full licences not carrying provisional entitlement

(1) Section 88 (4) of the Act of 1972 shall not apply in the case of a licence which—

(*a*) is limited to vehicles of a particular construction or design whether pursuant to an application in that behalf by the holder of the licence or pursuant to section 87 (4) (ii) of the Act of 1972; or

(*b*) authorises its holder to drive vehicles of a class included in group K only.

(2) Section 88 (4) of the Act of 1972 in its application to a full licence granted on or after 1st October 1982 which does not authorise the driving of a vehicle of a class included in group A, B, C or E shall have effect subject to the limitation that it shall not authorise the holder of such a licence to drive any motor cycle of a class included in group D subject to the same conditions as if he were authorised by a provisional licence to drive the last mentioned vehicles.]

[Regulation 10 was substituted by SI 1982 No 937.]

11. Signature of licences

Every person to whom a licence is granted shall forthwith sign it in ink with his usual signature.

12. Lost or defaced licences

(1) If the holder of a licence satisfies the licensing authority that the licence has been lost or defaced the licensing authority shall, on payment of the fee prescribed in Regulation 6, issue to him a duplicate licence and shall endorse thereon any particulars endorsed upon the original licence and the duplicate so issued shall have the same effect as the original.

(2) If at any time while a duplicate licence is in force the original licence is found, the person to whom the original licence was issued, if it is in his possession, shall return it to the licensing authority, or if it is not in his possession, but he becomes aware that it is found, shall take all reasonable steps to obtain possession of it and if successful shall return it as soon as may be to the licensing authority.

*   *   *

24. Statement of date of birth

The circumstances in which a person specified in section 161 (1) of the Act of 1972 shall, on being required by a police constable, state his date of birth are as follows:—

(1) where that person fails to produce forthwith for examination his licence on being required to do so by a police constable under the said section 161 (1); or

(2) where, on being so required, that person produces a licence—

(*a*) which the police constable in question has reason to suspect—
    (i) was not granted to that person, or
    (ii) was granted to that person in error, or
    (iii) contains an alteration in the particulars entered on the licence (other than as described in paragraph (*b*) below) made with intent to deceive; or

(*b*) in which the driver number has been altered, removed or defaced.

For the purposes of this paragraph 'driver number' means the number described as the driver number in the licence.

[24A. Learner motor cycles

For the purposes of section 88 (2) (*c*) of the Act of 1972 (provisional licence not to authorize the driving of certain motor cycles) the first use of a motor cycle shall be taken to have occurred on the date of first use as determined in accordance with paragraph (2) of Regulation 3.

[Regulation 24A was inserted (with effect from 1 February 1983) by SI 1982 No 937.]

*   *   *

[29. Effect of changes in classification of vehicles by reason of deletion of group M

(1) The deletion of group M in Schedule 3 to these Regulations by Regulation 9(*e*) of the Motor Vehicles (Driving Licences) (Amendment) (No 4) Regulations 1982 *[SI 1982 No 937]* shall not affect—

(*a*) any entitlement of a holder of a licence for vehicles of a class included in that group granted before the date of coming into operation of the said Regulation 9(*e*) to drive vehicles of that class, and vehicles of any other class included in that group, in pursuance of the licence, or

(*b*) any such licence ceasing to be in force whether before or after that date, any right that the person who held the licence would have had to grant of a further licence on or after that date authorising him to drive such vehicles.

(2) In licences (whether full or provisional) issued before the date of coming into operation of Regulation 9(*e*) of the Motor Vehicles (Driving Licences) (Amendment) (No 4) Regulations 1982 any reference to groups A or B shall be construed for all purposes on and after that date as a reference to the groups as prescribed in these Regulations on and after that date.]

[Regulation 29 was inserted by SI 1982 No 937 with effect from 1 October 1982.

The date on which reg 9 (e) of the Motor Vehicles (Driving Licences) (Amendment) (No 4) Regulations 1982 (SI 1982 No 937) came into operation was 1 February 1983; see reg 1 (2) of SI 1982 No 937.]

*   *   *

SCHEDULE 3

GROUPS OF MOTOR VEHICLES FOR DRIVING TEST PURPOSES

Group	Class of vehicle included in the group	Additional requirements	Additional groups covered
A	A vehicle without automatic transmission, of any class not included in any other group.	1, 2, 3, 4, 5, 6, 7, 8, 9 and 10	B, C, E, F, K, [L and N]
B	A vehicle with automatic transmission, of any class not included in any other group.	1, 2, 3, 4, 5, 6, 7, 8, 9 and 10	E, F, K and L
C	Motor tricycle weighing not more than 425 kg. unladen, but excluding any vehicle included in group E, J, K or L.	1, 2, 3, 4, 5, 6, 9 and 10 and if fitted with a means for reversing, 7 and 8	E, K and L
D	Motor bicycle (with or without sidecar) but excluding any vehicle included in group E [or K]	1, 2, 3, 4, 5, 6, 9 and 10	C [and E]
E	Moped	1, 2, 3, 4, 5, 6, 9 and 10	—
F	Agricultural tractor, but excluding any vehicle included in group H.	1, 2, 3, 4, 5, 6, 7, 9 and 10	K
G	Road roller	1, 2, 3, 4, 5, 6, 7, 9 and 10	—
H	Track-laying vehicle steered by its tracks	1, 2, 3, 4, 5, 6, 9, 10 and 12	—
J	Invalid carriage	1, 2, 3, 4, 5, 6, 9 and 10	—
K	Mowing machine or pedestrian controlled vehicle	1, 2, 3, 4, 5 and 6	—
L	Vehicle propelled by electrical power but excluding any vehicle included in group [D, E, J or K]	1, 2, 3, 4, 5, 6, 9 and 10 and, if fitted with a means of reversing, 7 and 8	K
M	[deleted]		—
N	Vehicle exempted from duty under section 7(1) of the Vehicles (Excise) Act 1971.	1, 2, 3, 4, 5 and 6	—

[Schedule 3 is printed as amended by reg 9 of SI 1982 No 937. Regulation 9 (a) effected the amendments noted against Group A and reg 9 (e) deleted the Group M entries; these amendments took effect on 1 February 1983. The amendments to Groups D and L were effected by reg 9 (b) to (d) and took effect on 1 October 1982.]

*　　　*　　　*

The Motor Vehicles (Tests) Regulations 1981

(SI 1981 No 1694)

*   *   *

[6. Exemptions

(1) *[Omitted.]*

[(1A) [Added by SI 1982 No 814; lapsed.]

(2) Pursuant to section 44 (6) the Secretary of State hereby exempts from section 44 (1) the use of a vehicle—

(*a*)   (i) for the purpose of submitting it by previous arrangement for, or bringing it away from, an examination, or

       (ii) in the course of an examination, for the purpose of taking it to, or bringing it away from, any place where a part of the examination is to be or, as the case may be, has been, carried out, or of carrying out any part of the examination, the person so using it being either—

          (A) an examiner, or a Ministry Inspector or an inspector appointed by a designated council, or

          (B) a person acting under the personal direction of an examiner, a Ministry Inspector or a designated Council, or

       (iii) where a test certificate is refused on an examination—

          (A) for the purpose of delivering it by previous arrangement at, or bringing it away from, a place where work is to be or has been done on it to remedy for a further examination the defects on the ground of which the test certificate was refused; or

          (B) for the purpose of delivering it, by towing it, to a place where the vehicle is to be broken up;

(*b*)–(*g*) *[Omitted.]*

*   *   *

The Motor Vehicles (Type Approval) (EEC Manufacturers) Regulations 1981

(SI 1981 No 493)

1. Citation, commencement and interpretation

(1) *[Omitted.]*

(2) In these Regulations expressions which are also used in Part II of the Road Traffic Act 1972 have the same meanings as in that Part.

2. Application of provisions relating to type approval certificates and certificates of conformity

(1) Subject to paragraph (2), the provisions—

(*a*) of sections 47 to 50 of the Road Traffic Act 1972 (approval of design, construction, etc., of vehicles and vehicle parts); and

(*b*) of regulations made thereunder before the coming into operation of these Regulations,

so far as relating to type approval certificates and certificates of conformity, shall apply in relation to vehicles and vehicle parts manufactured in a member State of the Economic Community (other than the United Kingdom) or in Northern Ireland as they apply in relation to vehicles and vehicle parts manufactured in Great Britain.

(2) Nothing in the said provisions as applied by paragraph (1) shall require the Secretary of State for Transport to issue a type approval certificate before the expiration of the period of 12 months beginning with the day on which these Regulations come into operation.

(3) In consequence of paragraph (1) above any reference in the said provisions to a vehicle or vehicle part (including a reference which is to be construed as including such a reference) shall be construed as including a reference to a vehicle or vehicle part manufactured in a member State of the Economic Community (other than the United Kingdom) or in Northern Ireland.

[These regulations came into operation on 27 April 1981; reg 1 (1).]

474

The Motor Vehicles (Type Approval) (Great Britain) Regulations 1984

(SI 1984 No 981)

*   *   *

2. Interpretation

(1) In these Regulations—

'the Construction and Use Regulations' means the Motor Vehicles (Construction and Use) Regulations 1978) *[SI 1978 No 1017, as amended]*;

'dual-purpose vehicle' means a vehicle constructed or adapted for the carriage both of passengers and of goods or burden of any description, being a vehicle of which the unladen weight does not exceed 2040 kilograms, and which satisfies the following conditions as to construction, namely:—

  (*a*) the vehicle must be permanently fitted with a rigid roof, with or without a sliding panel;

  (*b*) the area of the vehicle to the rear of the driver's seat must—

      (i) be permanently fitted with at least one row of transverse seats (fixed or folding) for two or more passengers and those seats must be properly sprung or cushioned and provided with upholstered back-rests, attached either to the seats or to a side or the floor of the vehicle; and

      (ii) be lit on each side and at the rear by a window or windows of glass or other transparent material having an area or aggregate area of not less than 1850 square centimetres on each side and not less than 770 square centimetres at the rear; and

  (*c*) the distance between the rearmost part of the steering wheel and the back-rests of the row of transverse seats satisfying the requirements specified in sub-paragraph (*b*)(i) above or, if there is more than one such row of seats, the distance between the rearmost part of the steering wheel and the back-rests of the rearmost such row must, when the seats are ready for use, be not less than one-third of the distance between the rearmost part of the steering wheel and the rearmost part of the floor of the vehicle;

'maximum gross weight' means, in relation to a vehicle, the weight which it is designed or adapted not to exceed when in normal use and travelling on a road laden;

'motor ambulance' means a motor vehicle which is specially designed and constructed (and not merely adapted) for carrying, as equipment permanently fixed to the vehicle, equipment used for medical, dental or other health purposes and is used primarily for the carriage of persons suffering from illness, injury or disability;

'motor caravan' means a motor vehicle which is constructed or adapted for the carriage of passengers and their effects and which contains, as permanently installed equipment, the facilities which are reasonably necessary for enabling the vehicle to provide mobile living accommodation for its users;

'the prescribed type approval requirements', in relation to a vehicle or a vehicle part subject to type approval requirements, means the type approval requirements prescribed therefor by these Regulations;

'the type approval requirements' means the requirements with respect to the design, construction, equipment or marking of vehicles or vehicle parts which—

(a) relate to the items numbered in column (1) and listed in column (2) of Schedule 1, and

(b) are contained in instruments or other documents, and consist of the requirements, specified against each such item in column (3) of Schedule 1, and

(2) *[Omitted.]*

(3) For the purposes of these Regulations—

(a) a motor vehicle is to be regarded as being manufactured on or after a particular date if it is first assembled on or after that date, even if it includes one or more parts which were manufactured before that date, and

(b) the provisions of Regulation 3 (2) of the Construction and Use Regulations shall apply for determining when a motor vehicle is first used.

(4) *[Omitted.]*

[In para (1), only selected definitions are included.]

3. Application

(1) Subject to paragraph (2) these Regulations apply to—

(a) every motor vehicle manufactured on or after 1st October 1977 and first used on or after 1st August 1978 which is constructed solely for the carriage of passengers and their effects or is a dual-purpose vehicle and in either case which—

    (i) is adapted to carry not more than eight passengers exclusive of the driver and either has four or more wheels or, if having only three wheels, has a maximum gross weight of more than 1000 kilograms, or

    (ii) has three wheels, a maximum gross weight not exceeding 1000 kilograms, and either a design speed exceeding 40 kilometres per hour or an engine with a capacity exceeding 50 cubic centimetres, and is not a motor cycle with a side-car attached, and

(b) parts of any such motor vehicles.

(2) These Regulations do not apply to, or to parts of—

(a) a motor ambulance;

(b) a motor caravan;

(c) a motor vehicle brought temporarily into Great Britain by a person resident abroad;

(d) a vehicle in the service of a visiting force or of a headquarters (as defined in Article 8(6) of the Visiting Forces and International Headquarters (Application of Law) Order 1965) *[SI 1965 No 1536]*;

(e) a motor vehicle which is imported by an individual into Great Britain and in relation to which the following conditions are satisfied—

    (i) the vehicle has been purchased outside Great Britain for the personal use of the individual importing it or of his dependants,

    (ii) the vehicle has been so used by that individual or his dependants on roads outside Great Britain before it is imported,

    (iii) the vehicle is intended solely for such personal use in Great Britain, and

    (iv) the individual importing the vehicle intends, at the time when [application is first made for a licence for the vehicle under the Vehicles (Excise) Act 1971], to remain in Great Britain for not less than twelve months from that time;

(f) a motor vehicle which is to be exported from Great Britain and which—

    (i) is exempt from car tax by virtue of paragraph 7 of Schedule 7 to the Finance Act 1972 *[para 7 was amended by the Finance (No 2) Act 1975, s 23(1) and the Finance Act 1981, s 17(4), and para 8 was amended by the Act of 1975, s 23(2)]*,

    (ii) is a vehicle in relation to which there has been a remission of car tax by virtue of paragraph 8 of that Schedule, or

    (iii) has been zero-rated under Regulation 49 or 50 of the Value Added Tax (General) Regulations 1980 *[SI 1980 No 1536]*;

(g) a motor vehicle which is of a new or improved type, or is fitted with equipment of a new or improved type, and which has been constructed to that type, or fitted with that equipment, for the purposes of tests or trials or for use as a prototype, and—

    (i) is not intended for general use on roads, and

    (ii) in the case of a vehicle first used on a road on or after 21st August 1984, remains in the ownership and the use of—

        (A) the manufacturer of the vehicle if the vehicle is of a new or improved type, or

        (B) the manufacturer of the equipment if the vehicle is fitted with equipment of a new or improved type or the manufacturer of the vehicle on which that equipment is used;

(h) a motor vehicle which is of a new or improved type provided that—

    (i) a final examination has been carried out in respect of a vehicle to which the vehicle is alleged to conform following a written application made either—

        (A) in the manner approved in accordance with Regulation 5, for a type approval certificate for the type, or

        (B) in the manner approved in accordance with Regulation 6, for a Minister's approval certificate,

    and as a result of the examination the Secretary of State is satisfied that the relevant type approval requirements specified in Schedule 1 are complied with;

    (ii) the Secretary of State has been notified of the vehicle identification number in a manner approved by him;

    (iii) the vehicle is being used for no purpose other than for, or in connection with, publicity, demonstration or evaluation of that type of vehicle; and

    (iv) until, following the examination mentioned in sub-paragraph (i) of this sub-paragraph, there has been issued a type approval certificate or, as the case may be, a Minister's approval certificate, the vehicle—

        (A) remains in the ownership of the person who made the application referred to in the said sub-paragraph (i), and

        (B) is not offered for sale or supply or sold or supplied by retail;

(i) a motor vehicle to which sections 45 to 51 and 62 have become applicable after a period of use on roads during which, by virtue of section 188(4) (which relates to vehicles in the public service of the Crown), those sections did not apply to that vehicle; or (*j*) a motor vehicle constructed or assembled by a person not ordinarily engaged in the trade or business of manufacturing motor vehicles of that description.

[Regulation 3 is printed as amended by the Motor Vehicles (Type Approval) (Great Britain) (Amendment) (No 2) Regulations 1984 (SI 1984 No 1761) with effect from 13 December 1984.

The Finance Act 1972, Sched 7, was repealed (before the enactment of these regulations) by the Car Tax Act 1983. It is not certain whether the Interpretation Act 1978, s 17(2)(a), applies in such circumstances; for the corresponding provisions of the 1983 Act, see s 7(1)–(3).]

*   *   *

The Motor Vehicles (Type Approval for Goods Vehicles) (Great Britain) Regulations 1982

(SI 1982 No 1271)

[The text of these regulations is printed as amended by:
  the Motor Vehicles (Type Approval for Goods Vehicles) (Great Britain) (Amendment) Regula-
  tions 1984 (SI 1984 No 697) (20 June 1984)
The amending regulations are referred to in the notes to the main regulations only by their year and
number. The date referred to above is the date on which the regulations came into force.]

1. *[Omitted.]*

2. Interpretation

(1) In these regulations—

'the Construction and Use Regulations' means the Motor Vehicles (Construction and Use) Regulations 1978 *[SI 1978 No 1017, as amended]*;

'the Great Britain Regulations' means the Motor Vehicles (Type Approval) (Great Britain) Regulations 1979 *[SI 1979 No 1092, as amended]*;

'the Plating and Testing Regulations' means the Goods Vehicles (Plating and Testing) Regulations 1971 *[SI 1971 No 352, as amended]*;

'appropriate information document'—
  (i) in relation to a vehicle subject to type approval requirements, means a document in the form set out in Part I of Schedule 2, and
  (ii) in relation to a vehicle part subject to type approval requirements, means a document in the form set out in Part II of Schedule 2;

'bi-purpose vehicle' means a vehicle constructed or adapted for the carriage of both goods and not more than 8 passengers, not being a vehicle to which the Great Britain Regulations apply nor a motor ambulance or a motor caravan;

'break-down vehicle' has the meaning given in Schedule 2 to the Plating and Testing Regulations;

'dual-purpose vehicle' has the meaning given in Regulation 3(1) of the Construction and Use Regulations;

'motor ambulance' and 'motor caravan' have the meanings given respectively in Regulation 2(1) of the Great Britain Regulations;

'prescribed alteration' means an alteration to a vehicle to which these Regulations apply which varies the number or nominal diameter of the tyres or the wheels and which is made before the vehicle is first used;

'prescribed fee', in relation to any matter provided for in these Regulations, means the fee prescribed for such matter in Regulations under section 50(1);

'prescribed type approval requirements', in relation to a vehicle or vehicle part subject to type approval requirements, means the type approval requirements prescribed therefor by these Regulations;

'public works vehicle' has the meaning given in Regulation 3(1) of the Construction and Use Regulations;

'slow vehicle' means a vehicle incapable by reason of its construction of a speed of more than 25 kilometres per hour on the level under its own power;

'type approval requirements' means, in relation to any vehicle to which these Regulations apply, the determination of—

(a) the weights mentioned in Regulation 5;

(b) the requirements with respect to the design, construction, equipment or marking of such vehicles or their parts which—

(i) relate to the items numbered in column (1) and listed in column (2) of Schedule 1, and

(ii) are contained in instruments or other documents, and consist of the requirements, specified against each such item in column (3) of Schedule 1; and

'vehicle subject to type approval requirements' and 'vehicle part subject to type approval requirements' have the meanings given in Regulation 4.

(2), (3) *[Omitted.]*

(4) For the purpose of these Regulations—

(a) a vehicle is to be regarded as being manufactured on or after a particular date if it is assembled to the stage where it includes all the parts of the vehicle which it needs to have to comply with any one or more of the prescribed type approval requirements; and

(b) the date on which a vehicle is to be regarded as being first used is the date on which it is first registered under the Vehicles (Excise) Act 1971.

(5) *[Omitted.]*

[The Goods Vehicles (Plating and Testing) Regulations 1971 (SI 1971 No 352), as amended, have been revoked and replaced by the Goods Vehicles (Plating and Testing) Regulations 1982 (SI 1982 No 1478). The term 'break-down vehicle' is not defined in Sched 2 to the 1982 regulations; the definition in reg 3(1) of those regulations is: 'a motor vehicle on which there is mounted apparatus designed for raising a disabled vehicle wholly or partly from the ground or for drawing a disabled vehicle when so raised, and which is not used for the conveyance of goods other than a disabled vehicle wholly raised by that apparatus and which carries no other load other than articles required for the operation of, or in connection with, that apparatus or otherwise for dealing with disabled vehicles'.

The Motor Vehicles (Type Approval) (Great Britain) Regulations 1979 (SI 1975 No 1092), as amended have been revoked and replaced by the Motor Vehicles (Type Approval) (Great Britain) Regulations 1984 (SI 1984 No 981).

Regulation 4 of these regulations (reg 4(7)): 'A vehicle to which, or to a part of which, any such requirement as is mentioned in paragraph (1) is for the time being applicable is referred to in these regulations as "a vehicle subject to type approval requirements" and a vehicle part to which any such requirement is so applicable is referred to in these regulations as "a vehicle part subject to type approval requirements" '.

Regulation 5 of these regulations is concerned with plated weights.]

3. Application of Regulations

(1) Subject to paragraph (2), these Regulations apply to—

(a) every motor vehicle manufactured on or after 1st October 1982 and first used on or after 1st April 1983 and which

(i) has three or more wheels, and

(ii) is either a goods vehicle, the [tractive] unit of an articulated vehicle or a bi-purpose vehicle; and

(b) parts of any such vehicles.

(2) These Regulations do not apply to, or to the parts of, any of the following vehicles, that is to say—

(a) a vehicle brought temporarily into Great Britain and which—
  (i) displays a registration mark mentioned in Regulation 5 of the Motor Vehicles (International Circulation) Regulations 1971 *[SI 1971 No 937]*, and
  (ii) complies in every respect with the requirements relating to motor vehicles contained in:—
    (A) Article 21 and paragraph (1) of Article 22 of the Convention on Road Traffic concluded at Geneva on 19th September 1949 *[Cmnd 7997]*, and Part I, Part II (so far as it relates to direction indicators and stop lights) and Part III of Annex 6 to that Convention; or
    (B) paragraphs I, III and VIII of Article 3 of the International Convention relative to Motor Traffic concluded at Paris on 24th April 1926 *[TS No 11 (1930)]*

(b) a vehicle which is to be exported from Great Britain and which either—
  (i) has not been used on a road in Great Britain for any purpose except that of proceeding from the place where it was manufactured to the place from which it is to be taken out of Great Britain, or
  (ii) satisfies the criteria of—
    (A) being exempt from car tax by virtue of [section 7(1) to (3) of the Car Tax Act 1983],
    (B) being a vehicle in relation to which there has been a remission of car tax by virtue of paragraph 8 of that Schedule, or
    (C) being zero-rated under [Regulation 49 or 50 of the Value Added Tax (General) Regulations 1980 *[SI 1980 No 1536]*],

(c) a vehicle in the service of a visiting force or of a headquarters (as defined in Article 8(6) of the Visiting Forces and International Headquarters (Application of Law) Order 1965 *[SI 1965 No 1536]*;

(d) a vehicle to which sections 45 to 51 and 65 have become applicable after a period of use on roads during which, by virtue of section 188(4) (which relates to vehicles in the public service of the Crown), those sections did not apply to that vehicle;

[(e) a motor vehicle which is of a new or improved type, or is fitted with equipment of a new or improved type, and which has been constructed to that type or fitted with that equipment, for the purposes of tests or trials or for use as a prototype, and—
  (i) is not intended for general use on roads, and
  (ii) in the case of a vehicle first used on a road on or after 20th June 1984, remains in the ownership and the use of—
    (A) if the vehicle is of a new or improved type the manufacturer of the vehicle, or
    (B) if the vehicle is fitted with equipment of a new or improved type the manufacturer of the equipment or the manufacturer of the vehicle on which that equipment is used;]

[(ee) a motor vehicle the unladen weight of which does not exceed 1525 kilograms which is of a new or improved type provided that—
  (i) a final examination has been carried out in respect of a vehicle to which the vehicle is alleged to conform following a written application made either—

      (A) in the manner approved in accordance with Regulation 7 for a type approval certificate for the type, or

      (B) in the manner approved in accordance with Regulation 8 for a Minister's approval certificate in respect of a vehicle of the type,

   and as a result of the examination the Secretary of State is satisfied that the relevant type approval requirements specified in Schedule 1 are complied with;

  (ii) the Secretary of State has been notified of the vehicle identification number in a manner approved by him;

  (iii) the vehicle is being used for no purpose other than for, or in connection with, publicity, demonstration or evaluation of that type of vehicle; and

  (iv) until, following the examination mentioned in sub-paragraph (i), there has been issued a type approval certificate or, as the case may be, a Minister's approval certificate, the vehicle—

      (A) remains in the ownership of the person who made the application referred to in sub-paragraph (i); and

      (B) is not offered for sale or supply, or sold or supplied, by retail;]

(f) a motor tractor, a light locomotive and a heavy locomotive;

(g) engineering plant, a land tractor, a pedestrian-controlled vehicle, a straddle carrier, a works truck and a vehicle which is track-laying (all as defined in Regulation 3(1) of the Construction and Use Regulations);

(h) a vehicle [the use of which on a road is authorised by] Article 15, 17 or 18 of the Motor Vehicles (Authorisation of Special Types) General Order 1979 *[SI 1979 No 1198]*;

(i) a tower wagon as defined in Schedule 4 to the Vehicles (Excise) Act 1971;

(j) a fire engine (including an air field crash tender);

(k) a road roller;

(l) a vehicle propelled by steam;

(m) a vehicle constructed for the purpose of preventing or reducing the effect of snow or ice on roads, either by spreading grit or other material, by scooping or sweeping, or by other means;

(n) a two-wheeled motor cycle, with or without a sidecar;

(o) an electrically-propelled vehicle;

(p) a break-down vehicle;

(q) a vehicle the weight of which unladen does not exceed 1525 kilograms constructed or assembled by a person not ordinarily engaged in the trade or business of manufacturing vehicles of that description;

(r) a vehicle the weight of which unladen does not exceed 1525 kilograms imported by an individual into Great Britain and in relation to which the following conditions are satisfied—

  (i) the vehicle has been purchased outside Great Britain for the personal use of the individual importing it or of his dependents,

  (ii) the vehicle has been so used by that individual or his dependents on roads outside Great Britain before it is imported,

  (iii) the vehicle is intended solely for such person use in Great Britain, and

  (iv) the individual importing the vehicle intends, at the time when the vehicle is imported, to remain in Great Britain for not less than twelve months from that time;

(s) a motor ambulance; or

(*t*) a motor caravan.

[Regulation 3 is printed as amended by the Interpretation Act 1978, ss 17(2), 23, and SI 1984 No 697.

The Car Tax Act 1983, s 7(1)–(3), relates to relief from car tax for vehicles exported and remission of car tax for vehicles acquired for export.

Articles 15, 17 and 18 of the Motor Vehicles (Authorisation of Special Types) General Order 1979 (SI 1979 No 1198) refer to vehicles for moving excavating material, vehicles fitted with moveable platforms and vehicles for carrying or drawing abnormal indivisible loads, respectively.

In Sched 4 to the Vehicles (Excise) Act 1971, the term 'tower wagon' is defined as meaning: 'a goods vehicle- (a) into which there is built, as part of the vehicle, any expanding or extensible contrivance designed for facilitating the erection, inspection, repair, or maintenance of overhead structures or equipment; and (b) which is neither constructed nor adapted for use nor used for the conveyance of any load, except such a contrivance and articles used in connection therewith'.]

The Motor Vehicles (Wearing of Seat Belts) Regulations 1982

(SI 1982 No 1203)

1, 2. *[Omitted.]*

3. (1) In these Regulations—

'the Construction and Use Regulations' means the Motor Vehicles (Construction and Use) Regulations 1978 *[SI 1978 No 1017 as amended]*;

'the Driving Licences Regulations' means the Motor Vehicles (Driving Licences) Regulations 1981 *[SI 1981 No 952 as amended]*

'disabled person's seat belt' has the same meaning as in Regulation 17(12) of the Construction and Use Regulations;

'disabled person's vehicle' means a vehicle which has been specially designed and constructed, or specially adapted, for the use of a person suffering from some physical defect or disability;

'private hire vehicle' means a motor vehicle constructed or adapted to seat fewer than 9 passengers, other than a taxi or a public service vehicle, which is provided for hire with the services of a driver for the purpose of carrying passengers and which displays a sign pursuant to either section 21 of the Vehicles (Excise) Act 1971 or section 48(2) of the Local Government (Miscellaneous Provisions) Act 1976 or any similar enactment;

'public service vehicle' has the same meaning as in section 1 of the Public Passenger Vehicles Act 1981;

'specified passenger's seat' has the same meaning as in Regulation 17(12) of the Construction and Use Regulations;

'taxi' has the same meaning as in section 64(3) of the Transport Act 1980;

'trade licence' has the same meaning as in section 38(1) of the Vehicles (Excise) Act 1971.

(2) In these Regulations a reference to any Act or subordinate legislation (as defined in section 21(1) of the Interpretation Act 1978) includes a reference to that Act or subordinate legislation as from time to time extended, amended, re-enacted or applied.

(3) In these Regulations, unless the context otherwise requires, any reference to a numbered Regulation is a reference to the Regulation bearing that number in these Regulations.

4. Save as provided in Regulation 5, every person shall wear a seat belt of a description specified in Regulation 7 if he is—

(1) driving a motor vehicle of a class specified in Regulation 6; or

(2) riding in a motor vehicle of that class in—

(*a*) the specified passenger's seat, or

(*b*) a forward facing seat alongside the driver's seat which is not the specified passenger's seat and the specified passenger's seat is not occupied by another person (whether or not that person is over the age of 14 years).

5. The requirement specified in Regulation 4 does not apply to a person who is—

(*a*) using a vehicle constructed or adapted for the delivery or collection of goods or mail to consumers or addresses, as the case may be, whilst engaged in making local rounds of deliveries or collections;

(*b*) driving the vehicle whilst performing a manoeuvre which includes reversing;

(*c*) a qualified driver (as defined in Regulation 8(5) of the Driving Licences Regulations) and is supervising the holder of a provisional licence (as defined in Regulation 3(1) of those Regulations) while that holder is performing a manoeuvre which includes reversing;

(*d*) the holder of a valid certificate in a form supplied by the Secretary of State, containing the information required by it, and signed by a registered medical practitioner to the effect that it is inadvisable on medical grounds for him to wear a seat belt;

(*e*) a constable protecting or escorting another person;

(*f*) not a constable but is protecting or escorting another person by virtue of powers the same as or similar to those of a constable for that purpose;

(*g*) in the service of a fire brigade and is donning operational clothing or equipment;

(*h*) the driver of—
    (i) a taxi which is being used for seeking hire, or answering a call for hire, or carrying a passenger for hire, or
    (ii) a private hire vehicle which is being used to carry a passenger for hire;

(*i*) a person by whom, as provided in the Driving Licences Regulations, a test of competence to drive is being conducted and his wearing of a seat belt would endanger himself or any other person;

(*j*) occupying a seat for which the seat belt either—
    (i) does not comply with the requirements of Regulation 102A of the Construction and Use Regulations, or
    (ii) has an inertia reel mechanism which is locked as a result of the vehicle being, or having been, on a steep incline; or

(*k*) riding in a vehicle, being used under a trade licence, for the purpose of investigating or remedying a mechanical fault in the vehicle.

6. The classes of vehicle mentioned in Regulation 4 are—

(*a*) a vehicle to which Regulation 17 of the Construction and Use Regulations applies; and

(*b*) a vehicle which is equipped with anchorage points and seat belts and to which that Regulation would apply if it were not for the circumstances that the vehicle—
    (i) is proceeding to a port for export;
    (ii) has been brought temporarily into Great Britain by a person resident abroad;
    (iii) is within the provisions of Regulation 4(8) of the Construction and Use Regulations (which relates to vehicles subject to certain tax exemptions by virtue of their impending export);

(iv) is in the service of a visiting force or headquarters (as defined in Article 8(6) of the Visiting Forces and International Headquarters (Application of Law) Order 1965 *[SI 1965 No 1536]*);

(v) is within the provisions of Regulation 4(10) of the Construction and Use Regulations (which relates to vehicles subject to certain exemptions relating to tests of satisfactory conditions);

(vi) is being used under a trade licence; or

(vii) is not a vehicle to which the [Motor Vehicles (Type Approval) (Great Britain) Regulations 1984 *[SI 1984 No 981]*] applies but which is being driven from premises of the manufacturer by whom it was made, or of a distributor of vehicles or dealer in vehicles

—to premises of a distributor of or dealer in vehicles of the purchaser of the vehicle, or

—to premises of a person obtaining possession of the vehicle under a hiring agreement or hire-purchase agreement.

[Regulation 6 is printed as amended by the Interpretation Act 1978, ss 17(2), 23.]

7. The descriptions of seat belt referred to in Regulation 4 are—

(*a*) as regards a driver's seat or a specified passenger's seat in respect of which a seat belt is required to be fitted by Regulation 17 of the Construction and Use Regulations—

(i) in the case of a disabled person's vehicle, a disabled person's seat belt;

(ii) in the case of any other vehicle to which that Regulation applies, a seat belt which complies with the requirements specified in paragraphs (5), (7), (8) and (10) of that Regulation;

(*b*) as regards a driver's seat or a specified passenger's seat in respect of which a seat belt is not required to be fitted by that Regulation, the seat belt fitted to the vehicle in respect of that seat;

(*c*) as regards a seat mentioned in Regulation 4(2)(*b*), the seat belt fitted to the vehicle in respect of that seat.

The Motor Vehicles (Wearing of Seat Belts by Children) Regulations 1982

(SI 1982 No 1342)

1. *[Omitted.]*

2. In these Regulations—
'adult seat belt' means:—
  (a) in the case where the seat belt is one mentioned in paragraph (5) of Regulation 17 of the Construction and Use Regulations, one which complies with the requirements specified in paragraphs (5), (7), (8) and (10) of that Regulation;
  (b) in a case where the seat belt is not one to which paragraph (5) of that Regulation applies, the belt fitted to the vehicle for use by a person occupying the seat in question;

'the Construction and Use Regulations' means the Motor Vehicles (Construction and Use) Regulations 1978 *[SI 1978 No 1017, as amended]*;

'restraining device for a young person' means a seat belt which is marked with a marking referred to in Regulation 17(11) of the Construction and Use Regulations; and

'seat belt' and 'specified passenger's seat' have the meanings respectively given to those expressions in Regulation 17(12) of the Construction and Use Regulations.

3. The provisions of section 33B(1) of the Road Traffic Act 1972 do not apply in respect of a child for whom there is a valid certificate in a form supplied by the Secretary of State, containing the information required by it, and signed by a registered medical practitioner to the effect that it is inadvisable on medical grounds for him to wear a seat belt.

4. The provisions of the said section 33B(1) apply only in respect of a vehicle which is of a class specified in Regulation 6 of the Motor Vehicles (Wearing of Seat Belts) Regulations 1982 *[SI 1982 No 1203]* (which relates to vehicles to which seat belts for certain seats are required to be fitted and to vehicles to which, but for the use being made of them, that requirement would apply).

5. The provisions of the said section 33B(1) do not apply to a person driving on a road a motor vehicle in respect of a child who occupies either—
  (a) a forward facing seat alongside the driver's seat if every other part of the vehicle which is designed to be used as a seat (including the specified passenger's seat and any seat which may be folded) is occupied by another person (whether a child or not); or
  (b) a seat for which no restraining device for a young person is provided, and
    (i) the seat belt provided for that seat is an adult seat belt which has an

487

inertia reel mechanism which is locked as a result of the vehicle being or having been, on a steep incline, or

(ii) the seat belt provided for that seat is an adult seat belt which does not comply with the requirements of Regulation 102A of the Construction and Use Regulations.

6. The descriptions of seat belt prescribed for the purpose of the said section 33B(1) are—

(*a*) for a child under 1 year of age, a restraining device for a young person appropriate to the weight of the child in accordance with the indication of weight shown on the marking referred to in Regulation 17(11) of the Construction and Use Regulations;

(*b*) for a child of 1 year of age or more who is not disabled, either any type of a restraining device for a young person or an adult seat belt;

(*c*) for a child of 1 year of age or more who is disabled, either—

(i) any type of a restraining device for a young person; or

(ii) an adult seat belt; or

(iii) a seat belt which has been specially designed and constructed, and not merely adapted, for use by a person suffering from some physical defect or disability.

The Motorways Traffic (England and Wales) Regulations 1982

(SI 1982 No 1163)

[The text of these regulations is printed as amended by the Motorways Traffic (England and Wales) (Amendment) Regulations 1983 (SI 1983 No 374) (16 April 1983); and the Motorways Traffic (England and Wales) (Amendment) Regulations 1984 (SI 1984 No 1479) (17 October 1984).

The amending regulations are referred to in the notes to the main regulations only by their years and numbers. The dates referred to above are the dates on which the regulations came into force.]

ARRANGEMENT OF REGULATIONS

1, 2. *[Omitted.]*

3. Interpretation

(1) In these Regulations, the following expressions have the meanings hereby respectively assigned to them:—

(*a*) 'the Act of [1984]' means the [Road Traffic Regulation Act 1984];

(*b*) ['carriageway' means that part of a motorway which—

    (i) is provided for the regular passage of vehicular motor traffic along the motorway; and

    (ii) where a hard shoulder is provided, has the approximate position of its left-hand or near-side edge marked with a traffic sign of the type shown in diagram 1012.1 in Schedule 2 to the Traffic Signs Regulations and General Directions 1981 *[SI 1981 No 859]*.]

(*c*) 'central reservation' means that part of a motorway which separates the carriageway to be used by vehicles travelling in one direction from the carriageway to be used by vehicles travelling in the opposite direction;

489

(*d*) 'excluded traffic' means traffic which is not traffic of Classes I or II;

(*e*) 'hard shoulder' means a part of the motorway which is adjacent to and situated on the left hand or near side of the carriageway when facing in the direction in which vehicles may be driven in accordance with Regulation 6, and which is designed to take the weight of a vehicle;

(*f*) 'motorway' means any road or part of a road to which these Regulations apply by virtue of Regulation 4;

(*g*) 'verge' means any part of a motorway which is not a carriageway, a hard shoulder, or a central reservation.

(2) A vehicle shall be treated for the purposes of any provision of these Regulations as being on any part of a motorway specified in that provision if any part of the vehicle (whether it is at rest or not) is on the part of the motorway so specified.

(3) Any provision of these Regulations containing any prohibition or restriction relating to the driving, moving or stopping of a vehicle, or to its remaining at rest, shall be construed as a provision that no person shall use a motorway by driving, moving or stopping the vehicle or by causing or permitting it to be driven or moved, or to stop or remain at rest, in contravention of that prohibition or restriction.

(4) In these Regulations references to numbered classes of traffic are references to the classes of traffic set out in Schedule 4 to the Highways Act 1980.

[Regulation 3 is printed as amended by the Road Traffic Regulation Act 1984, s 144 (1), and Sched 10, para 2, and SI 1984 No 1479.]

4. Application

These Regulations apply to every special road or part of a special road which can only be used by traffic of Classes I or II, but shall not apply to any part of any such road until such date as may be declared in accordance with the provisions of [section 1(4) of the Act of 1984] to be the date on which it is open for use as a special road.

[Regulation 4 is printed as amended by the Road Traffic Regulation Act 1984, s 144 (1), and Sched 10, para 2.]

5. Vehicles to be driven on the carriageway only

Subject to the following provisions of these Regulations, no vehicle shall be driven on any part of a motorway which is not a carriageway.

6. Direction of driving

(1) Where there is a traffic sign indicating that there is no entry to a carriageway at a particular place, no vehicle shall be driven or moved onto that carriageway at that place.

(2) Where there is a traffic sign indicating that there is no left or right turn into a carriageway at a particular place, no vehicle shall be so driven or moved as to cause it to turn to the left or (as the case may be) to the right into that carriageway at that place.

(3) Every vehicle on a length of carriageway which is contiguous to a central reservation, shall be driven in such a direction that the central reservation is at all times on the right hand or off side of the vehicle.

(4) Where traffic signs are so placed that there is a length of carriageway (being a length which is not contiguous to a central reservation) which can be entered at one

end only by vehicles driven in conformity with paragraph (1) of this Regulation, every vehicle on that length of carriageway shall be driven in such a direction only as to cause it to proceed away from that end of that length of carriageway towards the other end thereof.

(5) Without prejudice to the foregoing provisions of this Regulation, no vehicle which—

(a) is on a length of carriageway on which vehicles are required by any of the foregoing provisions of this Regulation to be driven in one direction only and is proceeding in or facing that direction, or

(b) is on any other length of carriageway and is proceeding in or facing one direction.

shall be driven or moved so as to cause it to turn and proceed in or face the opposite direction.

7. Restriction on stopping

(1) Subject to the following provisions of this Regulation, no vehicle shall stop or remain at rest on a carriageway.

(2) Whether it is necessary for a vehicle which is being driven on a carriageway to be stopped while it is on a motorway—

(a) by reason of a breakdown or mechanical defect or lack of fuel, oil or water, required for the vehicle; or

(b) by reason of any accident, illness or other emergency; or

(c) to permit any person carried in or on the vehicle to recover or move any object which has fallen onto a motorway; or

(d) to permit any person carried in or on the vehicle to give help which is required by any other person in any of the circumstances specified in the foregoing provisions of this paragraph,

the vehicle shall, as soon and in so far as is reasonably practicable, be driven or moved off the carriageway on to, and may stop and remain at rest on, any hard shoulder which is contiguous to that carriageway.

(3)(a) A vehicle which is at rest on a hard shoulder shall so far as is reasonably practicable be allowed to remain at rest on that hard shoulder in such a position only that no part of it or of the load carried thereby shall obstruct or be a cause of danger to vehicles using the carriageway.

(b) A vehicle shall not remain at rest on a hard shoulder for longer than is necessary in the circumstances or for the purposes specified in paragraph 2 of this Regulation.

(4) Nothing in the foregoing provisions of this Regulation shall preclude a vehicle from stopping or remaining at rest on a carriageway while it is prevented from proceeding along the carriageway by the presence of any other vehicle or any person or object.

8. Restriction on reversing

No vehicle on a motorway shall be driven or moved backwards except in so far as it is necessary to back the vehicle to enable it to proceed forwards or to be connected to any other vehicle.

9. Restriction on the use of hard shoulders

No vehicle shall be driven or stop or remain at rest on any hard shoulder except in accordance with paragraphs (2) and (3) of Regulation 7.

10. Vehicles not to use the central reservation or verge

No vehicle shall be driven or moved or stop or remain at rest on a central reservation or verge.

11. Vehicles not to be driven by learner drivers

No motor vehicle shall be driven on a motorway by a person who is authorised to drive that vehicle only by virtue of his being the holder of a provisional licence under section 88(2) of the Road Traffic Act 1972, unless, since the date of coming into force of the said provisional licence that person has passed a test prescribed under section 85 of the Road Traffic Act 1972 sufficient to entitle him under that Act to be granted a licence, other than a provisional licence, authorising him to drive that vehicle on a road.

12. Restriction on use of right hand or off side lane

[(1) This Regulation applies to—

(a) a goods vehicle which has an operating weight exceeding 7.5 tonnes;

(b) a motor vehicle constructed solely for the carriage of passengers and their effects the overall length of which exceeds 12 metres;

(c) a motor vehicle drawing a trailer, and

(d) a motor vehicle other than a motor vehicle constructed solely for the carriage of passengers and their effects which does not fall within sub-paragraphs (a), (b) or (c) and which is a heavy motor car, a motor tractor, a light locomotive or a heavy locomotive.

(2) Subject to the provisions of paragraph (3) below, no vehicle to which this Regulation applies shall be driven or moved or stop or remain at rest on the right hand or offside lane of a length of carriageway which has three or more traffic lanes at any place where all the lanes are open for use by traffic proceeding in the same direction.

(3) The prohibition contained in paragraph (2) above shall not apply to a vehicle while it is being driven on any right hand or offside lane such as is mentioned in that paragraph in so far as it is necessary for the vehicle to be driven to enable it to pass another vehicle which is carrying or drawing a load of exceptional width.

(4) In this Regulation—

'goods vehicle' and 'operating weight' have the same meanings as in [sections 138(3) and 138(2) respectively of the Act of 1984], and

'overall length' has the same meaning as in Regulation 3(1) of the Motor Vehicles (Construction and Use) Regulations 1978 *[SI 1978 No 1017]*.]

[Regulation 12 is printed as substituted by SI 1983 No 374, and as amended by the Road Traffic Regulation Act 1984, s 144 (1), and Sched 10, para 2.]

13. Restrictions affecting persons on foot on a motorway

No person shall at any time while on foot go or remain on any part of a motorway other than a hard shoulder except in so far as it is necessary for him to do so to reach a hard shoulder or to secure compliance with any of these Regulations or to recover or move any object which has fallen on to a motorway or to give help which is required by any other person in any of the circumstances specified in paragraph (2) of Regulation 7.

14. Restrictions affecting animals carried in vehicles

The person in charge of any animal which is carried by a vehicle using a motorway shall, so far as is practicable, secure that—

(a) the animal shall not be removed from or permitted to leave the vehicle while the vehicle is on a motorway, and

(b) if it escapes from, or it is necessary for it to be removed from, or permitted to leave, the vehicle—

(i) it shall not go or remain on any part of the motorway other than a hard shoulder, and

(ii) it shall whilst it is not on or in the vehicle be held on a lead or otherwise kept under proper control.

15. Use of motorway by excluded traffic

(1) Excluded traffic is hereby authorised to use a motorway on the occasions or in the emergencies and to the extent specified in the following provisions of this paragraph, that is to say—

(a) traffic of Classes III or IV may use a motorway for the maintenance, repair, cleaning or clearance of any part of a motorway or for the erection, laying, placing, maintenance, testing, alteration, repair or removal of any structure, works or apparatus in, on, under or over any part of a motorway;

(b) pedestrians may use a motorway—

(i) when it is necessary for them to do so as a result of an accident or emergency or of a vehicle being at rest on a motorway in any of the circumstances specified in paragraph (2) of Regulation 7, or

(ii) in any of the circumstances specified in sub-paragraphs (b), (d), (e) or (f) of paragraph (1) of Regulation 16.

(2) The Secretary of State may authorise the use of a motorway by any excluded traffic on occasion or in emergency or for the purpose of enabling such traffic to cross a motorway or to secure access to premises abutting on or adjacent to a motorway.

(3) Where by reason of any emergency the use of any road (not being a motorway) by any excluded traffic is rendered impossible or unsuitable the Chief Officer of Police of the police area in which a motorway or any part of a motorway is situated, or any officer of or above the rank of superintendent authorised in that behalf by that Chief Officer, may—

(a) authorise any excluded traffic to use that motorway or that part of a motorway as an alternative road for the period during which the use of the other road by such traffic continues to be impossible or unsuitable, and

(b) relax any prohibition or restriction imposed by these Regulations in so far as he considers it necessary to do so in connection with the use of that motorway or that part of a motorway by excluded traffic in pursuance of any such authorisation as aforesaid.

16. Exceptions and relaxations

(1) Nothing in the foregoing provisions of these Regulations shall preclude any person from using a motorway otherwise than in accordance with the provisions in any of the following circumstances, that is to say—

(a) where he does so in accordance with any direction or permission given by a constable in uniform or with the indication given by a traffic sign;

(b) where, in accordance with any permission given by a constable, he does so for the purpose of investigating any accident which has occurred on or near a motorway;

(c) where it is necessary for him to do so to avoid or prevent an accident or to obtain or give help required as the result of an accident or emergency, and he does so in such manner as to cause as little danger or inconvenience as possible to other traffic on a motorway;

(d) where he does so in the exercise of his duty as a constable or as a member of a fire brigade or of an ambulance service;

(e) where it is necessary for him to do so to carry out in an efficient manner—
   (i) the maintenance, repair, cleaning, clearance, alteration or improvement of any part of a motorway, or
   (ii) the removal of any vehicle from any part of a motorway, or
   (iii) the erection, laying, placing, maintenance, testing, alteration, repair or removal of any structure, works or apparatus in, on, under or over any part of a motorway; or

(f) where it is necessary for him to do so in connection with any inspection, survey, investigation or census which is carried out in accordance with any general or special authority granted by the Secretary of State.

(2) Without prejudice to the foregoing provisions of these Regulations, the Secretary of State may relax any prohibition or restriction imposed by these Regulations.

The Passenger and Goods Vehicles
(Recording Equipment) Regulations 1979

(SI 1979 No 1746)

[The text of these regulations is printed as amended by the Passenger and Goods Vehicles (Recording Equipment) (Amendment) Regulations 1984 (SI 1984 No 144) (13 March 1984).

The amending regulations are referred to in the notes to the main regulations only by their year and number. The date referred to above is the date on which the regulations came into force.]

1. Commencement, citation, revocation and interpretation

(1), (2) *[Omitted.]*

(3) In these Regulations—

'the Act of 1968' means the Transport Act 1968;

'the Community Recording Equipment Regulation' means Council Regulation (EEC) No 1463/70 of 20th July 1970 on the introduction of recording equipment in road transport, as amended by Council Regulations (EEC) Nos 1787/73 and 2828/77, and as read with the Community Road Transport Rules (Exemptions) Regulations 1978 *[SI 1978 No 1158]*.

2. Installation and use of recording equipment

[Substitutes ss 97–97B for s 97 of the Transport Act 1968 (above) and makes provision for their commencement.]

3. Consequential adaptations of enactments

[Amends the Transport Act 1968, ss 98, 99 and 103 (above), and the Road Traffic (Foreign Vehicles) Act 1972, Sched 1.]

[4. Installation or repair of recording equipment, checks and inspections

(1) The Secretary of State shall be the competent authority in Great Britain—

(*a*) for the approval of fitters and workshops for the installation or repair of recording equipment in accordance with Article 14 of the Community Recording Equipment Regulation; and

(*b*) for the nomination of bodies for the carrying out of checks and inspections of recording equipment in accordance with Chapter VI of Annex I to that Regulation.

(2) Any approval or nomination under this Regulation shall be in writing, shall specify its scope, shall provide for its withdrawal by the Secretary of State on notice given by him and, if the Secretary of State thinks fit, may contain conditions.

(3) Such conditions may in particular relate to—

(*a*) the fees to be charged for installing or repairing or, as the case may be, checking or inspecting recording equipment;

(*b*) the place where and equipment by means of which such activities are, or are to be, carried out;

(*c*) the procedure to be adopted in carrying out such activities;

(*d*) the records to be kept and the evidence to be furnished of the carrying out of such activities;

(*e*) the training of persons for carrying out such activities;

(*f*) the inspection by or on behalf of the Secretary of State of places where and equipment by means of which such activities are, or are to be, carried out; and

(*g*) the display, at the places where such activities are carried out, of signs indicating that such activities are carried out there by fitters or workshops approved or, as the case may be, bodies nominated, by the Secretary of State.

(4) The Secretary of State shall publish from time to time lists of—

(*a*) the fitters and workshops for the time being approved by him; and

(*b*) the bodies for the time being nominated by him;

and any list published under sub-paragraph (*a*) above shall specify the mark to be placed by each approved fitter or workshop on any seals which he or they affix to any recording equipment.

(5) In this Regulation 'recording equipment' means equipment for recording information as to the use of a vehicle.]

[Regulation 4 was substituted by SI 1984 No 144 (and a correction slip dated February 1984).]

5. Period of retention of records by crew members

(1) The period for which Article 17 of the Community Recording Equipment Regulation requires the crew members of a vehicle registered in Great Britain to be able to produce record sheets relating to national transport operations shall be two days.

(2) In this Regulation 'registered' means registered under section 19 of the Vehicles (Excise) Act 1971, or the corresponding provision of any earlier enactment.

The 'Pelican' Pedestrian Crossings Regulations and General Directions 1969

(SI 1969 No 888)

[The text of these regulations and directions is printed as amended by:
the 'Pelican' Pedestrian Crossings (Amendment) Regulations and General Directions 1979
(SI 1979 No 401) (1 June 1979).

The amending regulations and directions are referred to in the notes to the main regulations and directions only by their year and number. The date referred to above is the date on which the regulations and directions came into force.]

ARRANGEMENT

PART I
GENERAL

PART II
REGULATIONS

SCHEDULES

PART III

GENERAL DIRECTIONS

PART I

GENERAL

*   *   *

3. Interpretation

(1) In this Instrument unless the context otherwise requires the following expressions have the meanings hereby respectively assigned to them:—

'the appropriate Minister' means, in relation to a crossing established on a road in Scotland, Wales or Monmouthshire, the Secretary of State, and in relation to a crossing established on a road in England excluding Monmouthshire, the [Secretary of State for Transport];

'carriageway' does not include that part of any road which consists of a street refuge or central reservation, whether within the limits of a crossing or not;

'central reservation' means any provision, not consisting of a street refuge, made in a road for separating one part of the carriageway of that road from another part of that carriageway for the safety or guidance of vehicular traffic using that road;

'crossing' means a crossing for foot passengers established either—

(a) by a local authority in accordance with the provisions for the time being in force of a scheme submitted and approved under [section 23 of the Road Traffic Regulation Act 1984], or

(b) in the case of a trunk road, by the Secretary of State or the [Secretary of State for Transport] in the discharge of the duty imposed on him by [section 24 of the Road Traffic Regulation Act 1984];

'one-way street' means any road on which the driving of vehicles otherwise than in one direction is prohibited at all times;

' "Pelican" crossing' means a crossing—

(a) at which there are traffic signs of the size, colour and type prescribed by Regulation 3 (1) of and Schedule 1 to the Regulations contained in Part II of this Instrument, and

(b) the presence and limits of which are indicated in accordance with Regulation 3 (2) of and Schedule 2 to the Regulations contained in Part II of this Instrument;

'stop line' in relation to the driver of a motor vehicle approaching a 'Pelican' crossing means the white line indicating the approach to the crossing in accordance with paragraph 3 of Schedule 2 to the Regulations contained in Part II of this Instrument, which is parallel to the limits of the crossing and on the same side of the crossing as the driver;

'stud' means any mark or device on the carriageway, whether or not projecting above the surface thereof;

'vehicular traffic light signal', 'pedestrian light signal' and 'indicator for pedestrians' means respectively the traffic signals of those descriptions prescribed by Regulation 3 (1) of and Schedule 1 to the Regulations contained in Part II of this Instrument.

(2) Any reference in this Instrument to a light shown by a signal or indicator is a reference to a light of constant intensity unless the contrary intention appears.

(3) Any reference in this Instrument to any enactment or instrument shall be construed, unless the context otherwise requires, as a reference to that enactment or instrument as amended, re-enacted or replaced by any subsequent enactment or instrument.

(4) [The Interpretation Act 1978] shall apply for the interpretation of this Instrument as it applies for the interpretation of an Act of Parliament, and as if for the purposes of [section 17] of that Act this Instrument were an Act of Parliament and the Instrument revoked by paragraph 2 of this Part of this Instrument were an Act of Parliament thereby repealed.

[Paragraph 3 is printed as amended by the Secretary of State for the Environment Order 1970 (SI 1970 No 1681); the Interpretation Act 1978, s 17 (2); the Minister of Transport Order 1979 (SI 1979 No 571); the Transfer of Functions (Transport) Order 1981 (SI 1981 No 238); and the Road Traffic Regulation Act 1984, s 144 (1), and Sched 10, para 2.]

PART II

REGULATIONS

* * *

3. 'Pelican' crossings

(1) The provisions of Schedule 1 to these Regulations shall have effect as respects the size, colour and type of traffic signs which are to be placed at or near a crossing for the purpose of constituting it a 'Pelican' crossing.

(2) The provisions of Schedule 2 to these Regulations shall have effect for regulating the manner in which the presence and limits of a crossing are to be indicated for the purpose of constituting it a 'Pelican' crossing.

4. Variations in dimensions

(1) Any variation in a dimension (other than as to the height of a letter) specified in any of the diagrams in Parts II and III of Schedule 1 to these Regulations shall be treated as permitted by these Regulations if the variation—

(a) in the case of a dimension of less than 50 millimetres, does not exceed 10% of that dimension;

(b) in the case of a dimension of 50 millimetres or more but less than 300 millimetres, does not exceed 5% of that dimension; or

(c) in the case of a dimension of 300 millimetres or more, does not exceed $2\frac{1}{2}$% of that dimension.

(2) Any variation in a dimension as to the height of a letter specified in either of the diagrams in Part III of Schedule 1 to these Regulations shall be treated as permitted by these Regulations if the variation does not exceed 5% of that dimension.

(3) Any variation in a dimension of a white line or gap specified in Schedule 2 to these Regulations shall be treated as permitted by these Regulations if the variation—

(a) in the case of a dimension of 3 metres or more, does not exceed 15% of that dimension;

(b) in the case of a dimension of 300 millimetres or more but less than 3 metres, does not exceed 20% of that dimension; or

(c) in the case of a dimension of less than 300 millimetres, where the actual dimension exceeds the dimension so specified, does not exceed 20% of the dimension so specified, and where the actual dimension is less than the dimension so specified, does not exceed 10% of the dimension so specified.

(4) Any variation in the angle between a row of studs and the edge of a carriageway or longitudinal broken line specified in Schedule 2 shall be treated as permitted by these Regulations if the variation does not exceed 20 degrees.

5. Significance of traffic signs

Regulations 6 and 7 of these Regulations are made under section 54 of the Act of 1967 and shall have effect for the purpose of prescribing the warnings, information, requirements and prohibitions which are to be conveyed to traffic by signs of the size, colour and type prescribed by Regulation 3 (1) of and Schedule 1 to these Regulations.

[The Act of 1967 was repealed and replaced by the Road Traffic Act 1984. For the provision of the latter corresponding to s 54 of the Act of 1967, see s 64.]

6. Significance of the vehicular traffic light signals

(1) The vehicular traffic light signal at a 'Pelican' crossing shall convey the following information, requirements and prohibitions:—

(a) the green light shall convey the information that vehicular traffic may proceed across the crossing;

(b) the amber light shall convey the prohibition that vehicular traffic shall not proceed beyond the stop line, or, if the stop line is not for the time being visible, beyond the vehicular traffic light signal facing such traffic on the side of the carriageway on which vehicles approach the crossing, except in the case of any vehicle which when the amber light is first shown is so close to the said line or signal that it cannot safely be stopped before passing the line or signal;

(c) the red light shall convey the prohibition that vehicular traffic shall not proceed beyond the stop line, or, if the stop line is not for the time being visible, beyond the vehicular traffic light signal facing such traffic on the side of the carriageway on which vehicles approach the crossing; and

(d) the flashing amber light shall convey the information that vehicular traffic may proceed across the crossing but that every foot passenger, if the foot passenger is on the carriageway within the limits of that crossing before any part of a vehicle has entered those limits, has the right of precedence within those limits over that vehicle, and the requirement that the driver of a vehicle shall accord such precedence to any such foot passenger.

(2) Vehicular traffic passing the vehicular traffic light signal in accordance with the foregoing provisions of this Regulation shall proceed with due regard to the safety of other users of the road and subject to the direction of any police constable or traffic warden in uniform who may be engaged in the regulation of traffic.

7. Significance of the traffic signs for pedestrians

(1) The traffic signs for pedestrians at a 'Pelican' crossing shall convey to foot passengers the warnings and information mentioned in the following paragraphs of this Regulation.

(2) The pedestrian light signal shall convey to foot passengers the following warnings and information:—

(*a*) the red light shown by the pedestrian light signal shall convey to a foot passenger the warning that he should not in the interests of safety use the crossing;

(*b*) the green light shown by the pedestrian light signal shall convey to a foot passenger the information that he may use the crossing and drivers of vehicles may not cause their vehicles to enter the limits of the crossing; and

(*c*) the flashing green light shown by the pedestrian light signal shall convey—

    (i) to a foot passenger who is already on the crossing when the flashing green light is first shown the information that he may continue to use the crossing, that vehicular traffic may proceed across the crossing, and that if he is on the carriageway within the limits of the crossing, before any part of a vehicle has entered those limits he has the right of precedence within those limits over that vehicle, and

    (ii) to a foot passenger who is not already on the crossing when the flashing green light is first shown the warning that he should not in the interests of safety start to cross the carriageway.

(3) When the word 'WAIT' shown by the indicator for pedestrians is illuminated it shall convey to a foot passenger the same warning as that conveyed by the red light shown by the pedestrian light signal.

(4) Any audible signal emitted by any device for emitting audible signals provided in conjunction with the indicator for pedestrians shall convey to a foot passenger the information that he may use the crossing and drivers of vehicles may not cause their vehicle to enter the limits of the crossing.

8. Movement of traffic and precedence of pedestrians

Regulations 9, 10, 11 and 12 of these Regulations are made under section 23 of the Act of 1967 and shall have effect with respect to the movement of traffic (including foot passengers) and the precedence of the foot passengers over vehicles at and in the vicinity of a 'Pelican' crossing.

[The Act of 1967 has been repealed and replaced by the Road Traffic Regulation Act 1984. For the provision of the latter corresponding to s 23 of the Act of 1967, see s 25.]

9. Requirements with respect to the stopping of vehicles on the approach to a 'Pelican' crossing

(1) Subject to the provisions of paragraph (2) of this Regulation, the driver of a vehicle shall not cause the vehicle or any part thereof to stop on the carriageway between—

(*a*) a 'Pelican' crossing, the approach to which is indicated by a pattern of studs as provided in paragraph 3 of Schedule 2 to these Regulations, and

(*b*) the line of studs in that pattern situated furthest from the crossing, on the side of the road on which the pattern of studs is placed, or, if the road is a one-way street, on either side of the road.

(2) Nothing in paragraph (1) of this Regulation shall apply—

(*a*) so as to prevent a vehicle stopping on any length of road or any side thereof so long as may be necessary to enable the vehicle, if it cannot be used for such purpose without stopping on that length of road or side thereof, to be used in connection with any building operation or demolition, the removal of any obstruction to traffic, the maintenance, improvement or reconstruction of that length of road or side thereof, or the laying, erection, alteration or repair in or near to that length of road of any sewer or of any main, pipe or apparatus for the supply of gas, water or electricity, or of any telegraphic line as defined in the Telegraph Act 1878;

(*b*) so as to prevent a vehicle stopping on any length of road or any side thereof to enable the vehicle, if it cannot be used for such purpose without stopping on that length of road or side thereof to be used for fire brigade, ambulance or police purposes;

(*c*) to a pedal bicycle not having a side-car attached thereto, whether additional means of propulsion by mechanical power are attached to the bicycle or not; or

(*d*) to a vehicle stopping for the purpose of complying with a requirement or prohibition indicated by the vehicular traffic light signals at the crossing, or where the driver of the vehicle is obliged to stop in order to avoid an accident, or is prevented from proceeding by circumstances beyond his control.

[In the Telegraph Act 1878, the term 'telegraphic line' is defined in s 2 as: 'telegraphs, posts, and any work (within the meaning of the Telegraph Act 1863) and also any cables, apparatus, pneumatic or other tube, pipe, or thing whatsoever used for the purpose of transmitting telegraphic messages or maintaining telegraphic communications, and includes any portion of a telegraphic line as defined by this Act'. In the Telegraph Act 1863, the term 'work' is defined by s 3 as including telegraphs and posts.]

10. Prohibition against the proceeding of vehicles across a 'Pelican' crossing

When the vehicular traffic light signal is showing a red light, the driver of a vehicle shall not cause the vehicle or any part thereof to proceed beyond the stop line, or, if that line is not for the time being visible or there is no stop line, beyond the vehicular traffic light signal facing the driver on the side of the carriageway on which vehicles approach the crossing.

11. Precedence of pedestrians over vehicles on a 'Pelican' crossing

When the vehicular traffic light signal at a 'Pelican' crossing is showing a flashing amber light every foot passenger, if the foot passenger is on the carriageway within the limits of that crossing before any part of a vehicle has entered those limits, shall have precedence within those limits over that vehicle, and the driver of a vehicle shall accord such precedence to any such foot passenger.

12. Prohibitions against the waiting of vehicles and pedestrians on a 'Pelican' crossing

(1) The driver of a vehicle shall not cause the vehicle or any part thereof to stop within the limits of a 'Pelican' crossing unless either he is prevented from proceeding by circumstances beyond his control or it is necessary for him to stop in order to avoid an accident.

(2) No foot passenger shall remain on the carriageway within the limits of a 'Pelican' crossing longer than is necessary for the purpose of passing over the crossing with reasonable dispatch.

SCHEDULE 1

THE SIZE, COLOUR AND TYPE OF TRAFFIC SIGNS
AT A 'PELICAN' CROSSING

PART I

Traffic Signs

1. The traffic signs which are to be placed at or near a crossing for the purpose of constituting it a 'Pelican' crossing shall consist of a combination of—

(a) vehicular traffic light signals,

(b) pedestrian light signals, and

(c) indicators for pedestrians,
of the size, colour and type prescribed by the following provisions of this Schedule.

Vehicular traffic light signals

2. The vehicular traffic light signals shall be as follows:—

(a) three lights shall be used, one red, one amber, and one green;

(b) the lamps showing the aforesaid lights shall be arranged vertically, the lamp showing red light being the uppermost and that showing the green light the lowermost;

(c) each lamp shall be separately illuminated and the effective diameter of the lens thereof shall be not less than 200 millimetres nor more than 215 millimetres;

(d) the height of the centre of the lens in the lamp showing the amber light from the surface of the carriageway in the immediate vicinity shall be not less than 2.4 metres nor more than 4.0 metres;

Provided that if the vehicular traffic light signals are placed at or near a crossing in accordance with this paragraph any additional vehicular traffic light signals placed over the carriageway shall be of such a height that the centre of the lens in the lamp showing the amber light from the surface of the carriageway in the immediate vicinity is not less than 6.1 metres nor more than 9 metres;

(e) the centres of the lenses of adjacent lamps shall not be more than 360 millimetres apart;

(f) the lamp showing the amber light shall be capable of showing a steady light or a flashing light such that it flashes at a rate of not less than 70 nor more than 90 flashes per minute;

(g) the word 'STOP' in black lettering may be placed upon the lens of the lamp showing a red light and no other lettering shall be used upon the lenses.

Pedestrian light signals

3.—(1) The pedestrian light signals shall be of the size, colour and type shown either in Diagram 1 or in Diagram 2 in Part II of this Schedule *[not reproduced]*.

(2) The height of the lower edge of the container enclosing the light signals from the surface of the carriageway in the immediate vicinity shall be not less than 2·1 metres nor more than 2·6 metres.

(3) The said signals shall be so designed that—

(a) the red figure shown in the said Part II of this Schedule can be internally illuminated by a steady light;

(*b*) the green figure shown in the said Part II of this Schedule can be internally illuminated by a steady light or by a flashing light flashing at a rate of not less than 70 nor more than 90 flashes per minute; and

(*c*) when one signal is illuminated the other signal is not illuminated.

Indicator for pedestrians

4.—(1) The indicator for pedestrians shall be of the size, colour and type shown either in Diagram 1 or in Diagram 2 set out in Part III of this Schedule *[not reproduced]*.

(2) The indicator for pedestrians shall be so designed and constructed that the word 'WAIT' as shown in each of the said diagrams can be illuminated so that it appears in white letters on a blue ground and there is incorporated in the indicator a device (hereinafter referred to as 'a push button') which can be used by foot passengers with the effect hereinafter described.

(3) A device for emitting audible signals may be provided in conjunction with an indicator for pedestrians.

Sequence of signals

5.—(1) The vehicular traffic and pedestrian light signals and the indicators for pedestrians when they are placed at or near any crossing shall be so designed and constructed that—

(*a*) before the signals and indicators are operated by the pressing of a push button or as described in paragraph 6 of this Schedule the vehicular traffic light signal shows a green light, the pedestrian light signal shows a red light, the word 'WAIT' in the indicator for pedestrians is not illuminated and any device for emitting audible signals is silent;

(*b*) when a push button is pressed—

(i) after the expiration of the vehicle period but before the vehicular traffic light signals are showing an amber light, the signals and indicators, unless they are working as described in paragraph 6 (*b*) of this Schedule, are caused to show lights in the sequences specified in descending order in column 1 in the case of vehicular traffic light signals, in column 2 in the case of pedestrian light signals and in column 3 in the case of the indicators for pedestrians of [either the table in Part IV or the table in Part V of this Schedule];

(ii) when the vehicular traffic light signals are showing an amber light or a red light, there is no effect;

(iii) when the pedestrian light signals are showing a flashing green light, the word 'WAIT' in each of the indicators for pedestrians is illuminated immediately and the signals and indicators are caused to show lights in the sequence specified in sub-paragraph (i) of this paragraph at the end of the next vehicle period;

(iv) after the pedestrian light signals have ceased to show a flashing green light and before the end of the next vehicle period, the word 'WAIT' in each of the indicators for pedestrians is illuminated and the signals and indicators are caused to show lights in the sequence specified in sub-paragraph (i) of this paragraph at the end of the vehicle period;

(*c*) the periods, during which lights are shown by the signals and the indicators, commence and terminate in relation to each other as shown in the columns of [either the table in Part IV or the table in Part V of this Schedule] as if each horizontal line therein represented one moment in time, subsequent moments occurring in descending order, but the distances between the horizontal lines do not represent the lengths of the periods during which the lights shown by the signals and the indicator are, or are not, lit.

(2) Where a device for emitting audible signals is provided in conjunction with an indicator for pedestrians placed at or near any crossing it shall be so designed and constructed that—

(a) when a push-button is pressed—

  (i) after the expiration of the vehicle period but before the vehicular traffic light signals are showing an amber light, a regular pulsed sound is emitted throughout the period when the pedestrian light signals are showing a green light and the vehicular traffic light signals are at the same time showing a red light;

  (ii) when the vehicular light signals are showing an amber or red light, there is no effect;

  (iii) when the pedestrian light signals are showing a flashing green light or at the end of this period and before the end of the next vehicle period, a regular pulsed sound is emitted throughout the period when the pedestrian light signals next show a green light and the vehicular traffic light signals next show at the same time a red light;

(b) the period, during which the audible signal is given, commences and terminates in relation to the periods during which the light signals specified in sub-paragraph (i) of this paragraph are given as shown in the columns in [either the table in Part IV or the table in Part V of this Schedule] as if each horizontal line had the significance specified in that paragraph.

(3) In this paragraph 'vehicle period' means such period as may be fixed from time to time in relation to a 'Pelican' crossing, which commences when the vehicular traffic light signals cease to show a flashing amber light and during which the vehicular traffic light signals show a green light.

[Paragraph 5 of Sched 1 is printed as amended by SI 1979 No 401.]

Operation by remote control

6. The vehicular traffic light signals, pedestrian signals, indicators for pedestrians and any device for emitting audible signals, when they are placed at or near any crossing may also be so designed and constructed that they can by remote control be made to operate:—

(a) as if a push button had been pressed;

(b) so that the pressing of a push button has no effect, other than causing the word 'WAIT' in each of the indicators for the pedestrians to be illuminated, until normal operation is resumed.

STATUTORY INSTRUMENTS

SCHEDULE 1

PARTS II and III

*   *   *

PART IV

Sequence of vehicular traffic light signals 1.	Sequence of pedestrian signals		
	Pedestrian light signals 2.	Indicator for pedestrians 3.	Audible signal 4.
Green light	Red light	The word 'WAIT' is illuminated	None
Amber light			
Red light			
	Green light	The word 'WAIT' is not illuminated	Regular pulsed sound
Flashing amber light	Flashing green light	The word 'WAIT' is illuminated	None
	Red light		
Green light			

[PART V

Sequence of vehicular traffic light signals 1.	Sequence of pedestrian signals		
	Pedestrian light signals 2.	Indicator for pedestrians 3.	Audible signal 4.
Green light	Red light	The word 'WAIT' is illuminated	None
Amber light			
Red light			
	Green light	The word 'WAIT' is not illuminated	Regular pulsed sound
Flashing amber light	Flashing green light	The word 'WAIT' is illuminated	None]
Green light	Red light		

[Part V of Sched 1 was inserted by SI 1979 No 401.]

SCHEDULE 2

THE MANNER OF INDICATING THE PRESENCE AND LIMITS OF A 'PELICAN' CROSSING

Manner of indicating the limits of the crossing

1.—(1) Every crossing which is a 'Pelican' crossing and its limits shall be indicated by two lines of studs placed across the carriageway or between the edge of the carriageway and a street or central reservation in accordance with the following provisions of this paragraph.

(2) Each line formed by the outside edges of the studs shall be so separated from the other line so formed that the distance between any point on one of those lines and the nearest point on the other line shall be not less than 2·4 metres nor more than 5 metres or such greater distance (not being more than 10 metres) [as may be appropriate having regard to the layout of the carriageway and the extent to which it is used by pedestrians];

Provided that the foregoing provisions of this sub-paragraph shall be regarded as having been complied with in the case of any crossing which for the most part complies with those provisions notwithstanding that those provisions may not be so complied with as respects the distance from one or more points on one line to the nearest point on the other line, so long as the general indication of the lines is not thereby materially impaired.

(3) The studs of which each line is constituted shall be so placed that the distance from the centre of any one stud to the centre of the next stud in the line is not less than 500 millimetres nor more than 720 millimetres, and a distance of not more than 1·3 metres is left between the edge of the carriageway central reservation or street refuge at either end of the line and the centre of the stud nearest thereto:

Provided that the foregoing provisions of this sub-paragraph shall be regarded as having been complied with in the case of any line where most of the studs constituting it comply with those provisions notwithstanding that those provisions may not be complied with as respects one or more such studs, so long as the general indication of the line is not thereby materially impaired.

(4) Studs shall not be fitted with reflecting lenses and shall be—

(a) white, silver or light grey in colour;

(b) square or circular in plan, the sides of a square stud and the diameter of a circular stud not being less than 95 millimetres nor more than 110 millimetres in length; and

(c) so fixed that they do not project more than 15 millimetres above the carriageway at their highest points nor more than 6 millimetres at their edges.

[Paragraph 1 of Sched 2 is printed as amended by SI 1979 No 401.]

2. A crossing or its limits shall not be deemed to have ceased to be indicated in accordance with the provisions of the foregoing paragraph by reason only of the discoloration or temporary removal or displacement of one or more studs in any line so long as the general indication of the line is not thereby materially impaired.

Manner of indicating the vehicular approach to the crossing

3.—(1) Subject to the following provisions of this paragraph, the approach for vehicular traffic to a 'Pelican' crossing shall be indicated by a pattern of studs placed and white lines marked on the carriageway in accordance with the following provisions of this paragraph.

(2) On a road, not being a one-way street, and where the crossing is not a crossing which extends only between the edge of the carriageway and a street refuge or a central reservation, the pattern of studs and white lines shall be indicated on each side of the crossing and shall comply with the following requirements, the relevant dimensions being those shown without brackets:—

(a) There shall be a transverse stop line 200 millimetres (300 millimetres) wide from the edge of the carriageway to the centre of the carriageway on the side of the carriageway on which vehicles approach the crossing, parallel to the line of studs indicating the limits of the crossing on the side of the crossing nearer to the approaching vehicles, and not less than 1·7 metres nor more than 2·0 metres from such line of studs.

(b) There shall be a longitudinal broken line 100 millimetres wide along the centre of the carriageway extending from the end of the transverse stop line away from the crossing and consisting of three (five) strips 4·0 metres (6·0 metres) long and two (four) gaps 2·0 metres :(3·0 metres) long arranged alternately in such a manner that the first strip adjoins the transverse stop line.

(c) There shall be two rows of studs from the edge of the carriageway to the centre of the carriageway on the side of the carriageway on which vehicles approach the crossing, complying with the following requirements:—

    (i) The two rows shall be parallel to each other.

    (ii) The row of studs further from the crossing shall be not less than 14·0 metres (23·5 metres) nor more than 16·0 metres (26·5 metres) from the line of studs indicating the limits of the crossing on the side of the crossing nearer to the approaching vehicles except where such distances would be inappropriate having regard to the layout and conditions at the place where the crossing is situated.

    (iii) If the edge of the carriageway and the longitudinal broken line are parallel at the places where the two rows of studs meet them the two rows of studs shall be straight and at right angles to the edge of the carriageway and in any other case the two rows of studs shall be curved as appropriate so as to meet the edge of the carriageway or the longitudinal broken line at a right angle.

    (iv) Each row of studs shall have the same number of studs.

    (v) The two rows of studs shall be not less than 300 millimetres nor more than 410 millimetres apart, measured between the centres of the studs.

    (vi) There shall be not more than 1·3 metres between the edge of the carriageway and the centre of the nearest stud thereto in each row.

    (vii) There shall be not less than 500 millimetres nor more than 720 millimetres between the centre of any stud in a row and the centre of the next stud thereto in that row.

    (viii) There shall be not less than 500 millimetres nor more than 720 millimetres between the centre of the longitudinal broken line and the centre of the nearest stud thereto in each row.

(3) On a road, being a one-way street, or where a crossing extends only between the edge of the carriageway and a street refuge or a central reservation, the pattern of studs and white lines shall be indicated on the side of the crossing on which vehicles approach the crossing and shall comply with the following requirements, the relevant dimensions being those shown without brackets:—

(a) There shall be a transverse stop line 200 millimetres (300 millimetres) wide from one edge of the carriageway to the other, in the case of a crossing on a one-way street, or, in the case of a crossing which extends only between the edge of the carriageway and a street refuge or a central reservation, from the edge of the carriageway to the centre of the carriageway or to the edge of the central reservation, as the case may be, in each case parallel to the nearer line of studs indicating the limits of the crossing and not less than 1·7 metres nor more than 2·0 metres from such line of studs.

(b) There shall be a longitudinal broken line 100 millimetres wide along the centre of the carriageway extending from the centre of the transverse stop line in the case of a crossing on a one-way street, or, in the case of a crossing which extends only between the edge of the carriageway and a central refuge from the end of the transverse stop line away from the crossing and consisting of three (five) strips 4·0 metres (6·0 metres) long and two (four) gaps 2·0 metres (3·0 metres) long arranged alternately in such a manner that the first strip adjoins the transverse stop line.

(c) There shall be two rows of studs from one edge of the carriageway to the other, in the case of a crossing on a one-way street, or, in the case of a crossing which extends only between the edge of the carriageway and a street refuge or a central reservation, from that edge of the carriageway to the centre of the carriageway, or to the edge of the central reservation, as the case may be, in each case complying with the following requirements:—

(i) The two rows shall be parallel to each other.

(ii) The row of studs further from the crossing shall be not less than 14·0 metres (23·5 metres) nor more than 16.0 metres (26.5 metres) from the nearer line of studs indicating the limits of the crossing except where such distances would be inappropriate having regard to the layout and conditions at the place where the crossing is situate.

(iii) If the two edges of the carriageway and the longitudinal broken line, or the edge of the carriageway and the edge of the central reservation, are parallel at the places where the two rows meet them, the two rows of studs shall be straight and at right angles to the edge of the carriageway and in any other case the two rows of studs shall be curved as appropriate so as to meet the edge of the carriageway, or the edge of the central reservation, or the longitudinal broken line, as the case may be, at a right angle.

(iv) Each row of studs shall have the same number of studs.

(v) The two rows of studs shall be not less than 300 millimetres apart nor more than 410 millimetres apart, measured between the centres of the studs.

(vi) There shall be not more than 1·3 metres between the edge or centre of the carriageway, or the edge of the central reservation, as the case may be, and the centre of the nearest stud thereto in each row.

(vii) Except in the case of the two studs in each row which lie one on each side of the longitudinal centre line, there shall be not less than 500 millimetres nor more than 720 millimetres between the centre of any stud in a row and the centre of the next stud thereto in that row.

(viii) There shall be not less than 500 millimetres nor more than 720 millimetres between the centre of the longitudinal centre line and the centre of the nearest stud thereto in each row on each side thereof.

(4) In the case of a road on which a speed limit on the driving of motor vehicles is not in force by virtue of any enactment—

(a) of 30 miles per hour or less, where figures appear in the last two preceding subparagraphs in brackets alongside other figures in relation to the dimensions of the pattern of studs, the figures in brackets shall apply in substitution for the said other figures;

(b) of 40 miles per hour or less, where figures appear in the last two preceding subparagraphs in brackets alongside other figures in relation to the dimensions of the pattern of white lines, the figures in brackets shall apply in substitution for the said other figures.

(5) The transverse stop line may be omitted or its angle in relation to and its distance from the crossing varied and the longitudinal broken line may be omitted having regard to the layout and conditions at the place where the crossing is situate.

(6) The requirements of this paragraph shall be regarded as having been complied with in the case of any pattern of studs or white lines if most of the studs or the lengths of white lines comply with those requirements notwithstanding that one or more studs or some of the lengths of white line may not comply with those requirements so long as the general appearance of the pattern of studs or white lines is not thereby materially impaired.

(7) The approach to a crossing shall not be regarded as having ceased to be indicated by a pattern of studs or white lines in accordance with the foregoing provisions by reason only of the discoloration, temporary removal or displacement of one or more studs in the pattern of studs or a length of white line in the pattern of white lines so long as the general appearance of the pattern of studs or white lines is not thereby materially impaired.

(8) The provisions of sub-paragraph (4) of paragraph 1 of this Schedule shall apply to the studs mentioned in this paragraph as they apply to the studs mentioned in that sub-paragraph.

(9) Where the appropriate authority is satisfied in relation to a particular approach to a crossing that by reason of the existence at or near that crossing of a road junction which is on the same side of that crossing and on the same side of the road as that approach—

(a) the application of Regulation 9 of the Regulations contained in Part II of this Instrument in relation to that approach will not be appropriate unless the pattern of studs by which that approach is to be indicated is varied as hereinafter provided, or

(b) that the application of the said Regulation 9 in relation to that approach would be inappropriate even if the pattern of studs were varied as aforesaid,

then, in the case mentioned in (a) of this sub-paragraph, that approach shall be indicated in accordance with the foregoing provisions of this paragraph varied by the substitution for the distance of not less than 14·0 metres nor more than 16·0 metres specified in paragraph 3 (2) of this Schedule, or for the said distance of not less than 23·5 metres nor more than 26·5 metres, as the case may be, of such shorter distance (not being less than 9 metres) as the appropriate authority may think fit, and, in the case mentioned in (b) of this sub-paragraph, it shall not be necessary for that approach to be indicated in accordance with this paragraph.

Provided that for the purpose of the application of this sub-paragraph to a crossing which is on a road which is a one-way street the foregoing provisions of this sub-paragraph shall have effect as if the words 'and on the same side of the road' were omitted.

In this sub-paragraph the expression 'appropriate authority' means, in relation to an approach to a crossing which is on a trunk road in England, [the Secretary of State for Transport] and in relation to an approach to a crossing which is on a trunk road in Scotland, or Wales, the Secretary of State, and, in relation to an approach to any other crossing, the Council in whose scheme under [section 23 of the Road Traffic Regulation Act of 1984] the crossing is for the time being included.

[Paragraph 3 of Sched 2 is printed as amended by the Secretary of State for the Environment Order 1970 (SI 1970 No 1681); the Minister of Transport Order 1979 (SI 1979 No 571); the Transfer of Functions (Transport) Order 1981 (SI 1981 No 238); and the Road Traffic Regulation Act 1984, s 144 (1), and Sched 10, para 2.]

PART III

GENERAL DIRECTIONS

* * *

2. Number of traffic signals

(1) The vehicular traffic light signals, pedestrian light signals and indicators for pedestrians placed at or near a 'Pelican' crossing which extends from one edge of the carriageway to the opposite edge of the carriageway on a road which is not a one-way

street shall be placed so that there are [at least] two vehicular traffic light signals, one pedestrian light signal and one indicator for pedestrians on each side of the carriageway:

Provided that—

(a) where there is a street refuge or central reservation on the crossing, the said vehicular traffic light signals shall be so placed that there is one on each side of the carriageway and two on the refuge or reservation;

(b) one or more additional indicators for pedestrians shall be placed on the refuge or reservation; and

(c) if vehicular traffic light signals are placed at or near a crossing in accordance with this paragraph additional vehicular traffic light signals may be [placed over or at the side of the carriageway].

(2) The said light signals and indicators placed at or near a 'Pelican' crossing which extends only between the edge of the carriageway and a street refuge or a central reservation or a 'Pelican' crossing on a road which is a one-way street shall be placed so that [at least] one vehicular traffic light signal, one pedestrian light signal and one indicator for pedestrians are on each end of the crossing on the side of the carriageway on which vehicles approach the crossing:

Provided that—

(a) where there is a street refuge or central reservation on a 'Pelican' crossing on a road which is a one-way street an additional vehicular traffic light signal shall be placed on the refuge or central reservation;

(b) one or more additional indicators for pedestrians shall be placed on the refuge or reservation; and

(c) if vehicular traffic light signals are placed at or near a crossing in accordance with this paragraph additional vehicular traffic light signals may be [placed over or at the side of the carriageway].

[Direction 2 is printed as amended by SI 1979 No 401.]

3. Manner of placing traffic signals

Subject to the following provisions of these Directions the light signals and indicators placed at or near any 'Pelican' crossing in accordance with the foregoing provisions of these Directions shall be so arranged that—

(a) each vehicular traffic light signal shall face the stream of traffic it is intended to control,

(b) each pedestrian light signal at either end of the crossing shall be so placed as to be clearly visible to any person who is about to use the crossing at the other end of the crossing, and

(c) each indicator for pedestrians shall be so placed that the push button in the indicator is readily accessible to foot passengers who wish to press it.

4. *[Revoked.]*

5. Colouring of containers and posts

(1) The containers of the vehicular traffic light signals and of the pedestrian light signals shall be coloured black and may be mounted on a black backing board with a white border not less than 45 millimetres nor more than 55 millimetres in width.

(2) Where a vehicular traffic light signal, a pedestrian light signal or an indicator

for pedestrians is mounted on a post specially provided for the purposes, that part of the post which extends above ground level shall be coloured grey and may have one white band not less than 140 millimetres nor more than 160 millimetres in depth, the lower edge of the band being not less than 1·5 metres nor more than 1·7 metres above the level of the surface of the ground in the immediate vicinity.

[6. Approval of mechanisms and sequence adjustments

(1) Vehicular traffic light signals, pedestrian light signals and indicators for pedestrians may be placed at or near any 'Pelican' crossing only if the apparatus (including the content of all instructions stored in, or executable by, it) used to secure that the signals and indicators comply with the relevant provisions of the Regulations contained in Part II of this Instrument is of a type which has been approved in writing by or on behalf of the [Secretary of State for Transport].

(2) Without prejudice to the provisions of paragraph (1) above, where such signals and indicators as are mentioned in that paragraph are adjusted at any time, whether before or after they have been erected for the first time, so as to operate in accordance with the alternative sequences illustrated in Part V of Schedule 1, to the Regulations contained in Part II of this Instrument, those signals and indicators shall not be displayed in operation at or near a 'Pelican' crossing unless approval in writing to the making of that adjustment has first been given by or on behalf of the [Secretary of State for Transport.]

[Direction 6 is printed as substituted by SI 1979 No 401 and as amended by the Minister of Transport Order 1979 (SI 1979 No 571) and the Transfer of Functions (Transport) Order 1981 (SI 1981 No 238).]

7. Special cases

Nothing in these Directions shall be taken to limit the power of the appropriate Minister by any special Direction to dispense with, add to or modify any of the requirements of these Directions in relation to any particular case.

The Public Service Vehicles (Conduct of Drivers, Conductors and Passengers) Regulations 1936

(SR & O 1936 No 619)

[The text of these regulations is printed as amended by:
  the Public Service Vehicles (Conduct of Drivers, Conductors and Passengers) (Amendment) Regulations 1975 (SI 1975 No 461) (16 April 1975); and
  the Public Service Vehicles (Conduct of Drivers, Conductors and Passengers) (Amendment) Regulations 1980 (SI 1980 No 915) (31 July 1980)
The amending regulations are referred to in the notes to the regulations by their years and numbers. The dates referred to above are the dates on which the regulations came into force.]

PART I

*   *   *

2. In these Regulations unless the context otherwise requires the following expressions have the meanings hereby respectively assigned to them:—

'Vehicle' means public service vehicle;

'Driver' means a person licensed to drive a vehicle;

'Conductor' means a person [employed] to act as conductor of a vehicle or, in the case of a vehicle where there is no conductor, the driver;

'Authorised person' means any employee of the licensee (including the conductor) on duty upon or in connection with the vehicle;

'Stage Carriage', 'Express Carriage' and 'Contract Carriage' have the meanings assigned to them in the [Public Passenger Vehicles Act 1981].

['wireless telegraphy apparatus' has the meaning assigned to it by section 19 of the Wireless Telegraphy Act 1949.]

[Regulation 2 is printed as amended by the Road Traffic Act 1960, Sched XIX, para 3, SI 1975 No 461, SI 1980 No 915 and the Public Passenger Vehicles Act 1981, s 83 (1).

Section 19 of the Wireless Telegraphy Act 1949 provides:

(1) In this Act, except where the context otherwise requires, the expression 'wireless telegraphy' means the emitting or receiving, over paths which are not provided by any material substance constructed or arranged for that purpose, of electromagnetic energy of a frequency not exceeding three million megacycles a second, being energy which either—

(*a*) serves for the conveying of messages, sound or visual images (whether the messages, sound or images are actually received by any person or not), or for the actuation or control of machinery or apparatus; or

(*b*) is used in connection with the determination of position, bearing, or distance, or for the gaining of information as to the presence, absence, position or motion of any object or of any objects of any class.

and references to stations for wireless telegraphy and apparatus for wireless telegraphy or wireless telegraphy apparatus shall be construed as references to stations and apparatus for the emitting or receiving as aforesaid of such electromagnetic energy as aforesaid:

Provided that where—

(i) a station or apparatus for wireless telegraphy cannot lawfully be used without a wireless telegraphy licence or could not lawfully be used without such a licence but for regulations under section one of this Act; and

(ii) any such electro-magnetic energy as aforesaid which is received by that station or apparatus serves for the conveying of messages, sound or visual images; and

(iii) any apparatus is electrically coupled with that station or apparatus for the purpose of enabling any person to receive any of the said messages, sound or visual images,

the apparatus so coupled shall itself be deemed for the purposes of this Act to be apparatus for wireless telegraphy.]

3. The [Interpretation Act 1978] applies for the purpose of the interpretation of these Regulations as it applies for the interpretation of an Act of Parliament.

[Regulation 3 is printed as amended by the Interpretation Act 1978, s 17 (2).]

PART II
DRIVERS AND CONDUCTORS

4. A driver or a conductor, when acting as such,

(a) shall behave in a civil and orderly manner;

(b) shall not smoke in or on a vehicle during a journey or when it has passengers on board;

(c) shall take all reasonable precautions to ensure the safety of passengers in or on or entering or alighting from the vehicle;

(d) shall not wilfully deceive or refuse to inform any passenger or intending passenger as to the destination or route of the vehicle or as to the fare for any journey;

[(e) shall, if requested by any police constable or other person having reasonable cause, give particulars of his name, and the name and address of the person by whom he is employed and, in the case of a driver, of his licence;]

(f) shall not, at any reasonable time, obstruct or neglect to give all reasonable information and assistance to any person having authority to examine the vehicle.

[Regulation 4 is printed as amended by SI 1980 No 915.]

5. A driver, when acting as such, shall not when the vehicle is in motion speak to the conductor or any other person unless it is necessary to do so on grounds of safety.

[Provided that this Regulation shall not apply to any communication by the driver with an authorised person on operational matters or in an emergency by means of wireless telegraphy apparatus.]

[Regulation 5 is printed as amended by SI 1975 No 461.]

6. A conductor, when acting as such,

(a) shall not when the vehicle is in motion distract the driver's attention without reasonable cause or speak to him unless it is necessary to do so in order to give directions as to the stopping of the vehicle;

(*b*) shall take all reasonable precautions to ensure that every means provided for indicating the route fares and destination of the vehicle are clearly and correctly displayed;

(*c*) shall to the best of his ability take steps whenever necessary to enforce the provisions of these Regulations relating to the conduct of passengers.

7. A driver of a stage carriage or an express carriage, when acting as such,

(*a*) shall, when picking up or setting down passengers, stop the vehicle as close as may be to the left or near side of the road;

(*b*) shall not cause the vehicle to remain stationary on a road longer than is reasonably necessary to pick up or set down passengers except at a stand or place where such vehicles are permitted to stop for a longer time than is necessary for that purpose.

8. A conductor of a stage carriage or an express carriage, when acting as such, shall not, except for sufficient reason, by failing to signal to the driver to start, cause the vehicle to remain stationary on a road longer than is reasonably necessary to pick up or set down passengers except at a stand or place where the vehicle is permitted to stop for a longer time than is necessary for that purpose.

PART III
PASSENGERS

9. When a public service vehicle is carrying passengers or waiting to pick up passengers a passenger or intending passenger shall not

(i) use obscene or offensive language or conduct himself in a riotous or disorderly manner;

(ii) enter or alight from the vehicle otherwise than by the doors or openings provided for the purpose;

(iii) when entering or attempting to enter the vehicle wilfully and unreasonably impede passengers seeking to enter the vehicle or to alight therefrom;

(iv) enter or remain in or on the vehicle when requested not to do so by an authorised person on the ground that the vehicle is carrying its full complement of passengers or that the operator is debarred from picking up passengers at the place in question by reason of the conditions attached to his road service licence;

(v) travel in or on the upper deck of the vehicle unless he occupies a seat provided for that purpose, or in or on any part of the vehicle not provided for the conveyance of passengers;

(vi) wilfully do or cause to be done with respect to any part of the vehicle or its equipment anything which is calculated to obstruct or interfere with the working of the vehicle or to cause injury or discomfort to any person;

(vii) when the vehicle is in motion distract the driver's attention without reasonable cause or speak to him unless it is necessary to do so in order to give directions as to the stopping of the vehicle;

(viii) give any signal which might be interpreted by the driver as a signal from the conductor to start;

(ix) spit upon or from or wilfully damage, soil or defile any part of the vehicle;

(x) when in or on the vehicle distribute printed or similar matter of any description or distribute any article for the purpose of advertising;

(xi) wilfully remove, displace, deface or alter any number plate, notice board, fare table, route indicator, or destination board or any printed or other notice or advertisement in or on the vehicle;

(xii) when in or on the vehicle to the annoyance of other persons use or operate any noisy instrument or make or combine with any other person or persons to make any excessive noise by singing, shouting or otherwise;

(xiii) when in or on the vehicle throw any money to be scrambled for by any person on the road or footway; or throw out of the vehicle any bottle liquid or litter or any article or thing likely to annoy persons or to cause danger or injury to any person or property;

(xiv) throw any article from the vehicle or attach to or trail from the vehicle any streamer, balloon, flag or other article in such manner as to overhang the road;

(xv) wilfully obstruct or impede any authorised person;

(xvi) except in the case of a contract carriage, smoke or carry a lighted pipe, cigar or cigarette in or on any part of the vehicle in or on which a notice is exhibited that smoking is prohibited;

(xvii) except in the case of a contract carriage when in or on the vehicle beg, sell or offer for sale any article.

10. When a stage or express carriage is carrying passengers or is waiting to pick up passengers, a passenger or intending passenger shall not

(a) if his condition is such as to be offensive to passengers, or the condition of his dress or clothing is such that it may reasonably be expected to soil or injure the linings or cushions of the vehicle or the clothing of other passengers, enter or remain in or on the vehicle after an authorised person shall have requested him either not to enter or to leave the vehicle and in such latter case shall have tendered to him the amount of any fare previously paid;

(b) enter or travel in or on a vehicle with loaded firearms, or any dangerous or offensive article or, except with the consent of an authorised person, bring into or on to the vehicle any bulky or cumbersome article or place any such article elsewhere in or on the vehicle than as directed by an authorised person;

(c) bring any animal into or on to the vehicle without the consent of an authorised person or retain any animal in or on the vehicle after being requested by an authorised person to remove it or place any animal elsewhere in or on the vehicle than as directed by an authorised person.

[**11.** (a) No passenger on a stage or express carriage shall use or attempt to use in relation to the journey which he is taking or intending to take—

(i) any ticket which has been altered or defaced; or

(ii) any ticket which has been issued to another person if such ticket bears thereon an indication that it is not transferable; or

(iii) without reasonable excuse, any period or season ticket which has expired.

(b) Every passenger on a stage or express carriage shall—

(i) declare, if so requested by the driver or the conductor, the journey he has taken or intends to take:

(ii) where the vehicle is being operated by a driver without a conductor, immediately on boarding the vehicle, unless otherwise directed by an authorised person or by notice displayed on the vehicle, pay to the driver the fare for the journey he intends to take, or insert in any fare collection equipment provided on the vehicle coins of such denominations as may be required to pay that fare, and where the vehicle is not being so operated, if so requested by the conductor, pay the fare for the journey he intends to take or has taken, and in either case accept any ticket provided therefor:

Provided that this sub-paragraph shall not apply if the passenger is already the holder of a ticket in respect of the journey he intends to take or has taken and he complies with any directions on the ticket or by notice on the vehicle or given by an authorised person, as to the inspection, perforation, endorsement or cancellation of the ticket by such person;

(iii) produce his ticket, if any, when required to do so by an authorised person or, if he fails to produce his ticket, pay, by whichever of the means specified in sub-paragraph (ii) of this paragraph is appropriate, the fare for the journey he intends to take or has taken;

(iv) on completion of the journey for which he has paid the fare leave the vehicle if so requested by the driver or the conductor or pay, by whichever of the means specified in sub-paragraph (ii) of this paragraph is appropriate, the fare for any journey which he takes or intends to take on the vehicle by way of continuation of that journey, or, where so directed by an authorised person or by a notice on the vehicle, pay the fare for that further journey on leaving the vehicle;

(v) on demand by an authorised person surrender on completion of the journey any ticket issued to him in respect of the journey;

(vi) on demand by an authorised person surrender any period or season ticket held by him at the expiry of the period for which it was issued to him.

(c) No passenger shall without reasonable excuse leave or attempt to leave a stage or express carriage without having paid the fare for the journey he has taken.]

[Regulation 11 was substituted by SI 1975 No 461.]

12. (a) Any passenger contravening these Regulations may be removed from the vehicle by the driver or conductor or, on the request of the driver or conductor, by any police constable.

(b) A passenger in or on a vehicle who is reasonably suspected by the driver or conductor of contravening these Regulations shall give his name and address to a police constable or to the driver or conductor on demand.

The Road Vehicles (Registration and Licensing) Regulations 1971

(SI 1971 No 450)

[The text of these regulations is printed as amended by:
the Road Vehicles)(Registration and Licensing) (Amendment) Regulations 1972 (SI 1972 No 1865) (29 December 1972);
the Road Vehicles (Registration and Licensing) (Amendment) (No 2) Regulations 1975 (SI 1975 No 1342) (1 September 1975);
the Road Vehicles (Registration and Licensing) (Amendment) Regulations 1976 (SI 1976 No 1680) (9 November 1976);
the Road Vehicles (Registration and Licensing) (Amendment) Regulations 1983 (SI 1983 No 1248) (14 September 1983); and
the Road Vehicles (Registration and Licensing) (Amendment) Regulations 1984 (SI 1984 No 814) (1 August 1984).
The amending regulations are referred to in the notes by their years and numbers. The dates referred to above are the dates on which the regulations came into force.

The main regulations have also been amended by the Road Vehicles (Registration and Licensing) (Amendment) Regulations 1973 (SI 1973 No 870); the Road Vehicles (Registration and Licensing) (Amendment) Regulations 1975 (SI 1975 No 1089); the Road Vehicles (Registration and Licensing) (Amendment) (No 2) Regulations 1976 (SI 1976 No 2089); the Road Vehicles (Registration and Licensing) (Amendment) Regulations 1977 (SI 1977 No 230); the Road Vehicles (Registration and Licensing) (Amendment) Regulations 1978 (SI 1978 No 1536); but these do not affect the text of any regulation set out in this work.]

* * *

ARRANGEMENT OF REGULATIONS

PART I

PRELIMINARY

PART II

LICENSING AND REGISTRATION

PART III

EXHIBITION OF LICENCES AND REGISTRATION MARKS

*　　　　*　　　　*

PART V

TRADE LICENCES

*　　　　*　　　　*

PART I

PRELIMINARY

*　　　　*　　　　*

3. Interpretation

(1) In these Regulations, unless the context otherwise requires, the following expressions have the meanings hereby respectively assigned to them, that is to say:—

'the Act' means the Vehicles (Excise) Act 1971;

'agricultural machine' has the same meaning as in Schedule 3 to the Act;

'bicycle' means a mechanically propelled bicycle (including a motor scooter, a bicycle with an attachment for propelling it by mechanical power and a mechanically propelled bicycle used for drawing a trailer or sidecar) not exceeding 8 hundredweight in weight unladen;

['invalid carriage] means a mechanically propelled vehicle (including a cycle with an attachment for propelling it by mechanical power) which does not exceed [10] hundredweight in weight unladen and is adapted and used or kept on a road for an invalid or invalids;

'owner' in relation to a vehicle means the person by whom the vehicle is kept . . . and the expression 'ownership' shall be construed accordingly;

'pedestrian controlled vehicle' means a mechanically propelled vehicle with three or more wheels which does not exceed 8 hundredweight in weight unladen and which is neither constructed nor adapted for use nor used for the carriage of a driver or passenger;

'road' has the same meaning as in [section 196 of the Road Traffic Act 1972];

'trade licence' has the meaning assigned to it by section 16 of the Act;

'trade plates' has the meaning assigned thereto in Regulation 31 of these Regulations;

'tricycle' means a mechanically propelled tricycle (including a motor scooter and a tricycle with an attachment for propelling it by mechanical power) not exceeding 8 hundredweight in weight unladen and not being a pedestrian controlled vehicle;

'works truck' means a mechanically propelled vehicle designed for use in private premises and used on a road only in delivering goods from or to such premises to or from a vehicle on a road in the immediate neighbourhood, or in passing from one part of any such premises to another or to other private premises in the immediate neighbourhood or in connection with road works while at or in the immediate neighbourhood of the site of such works.

(2) Any reference in these Regulations to any enactment shall be construed as a reference to that enactment as amended by or under any subsequent enactment.

(3) The [Interpretation Act 1978] shall apply for the interpretation of these Regulations as it applies for the interpretation of an Act of Parliament, and as if for the purposes of [section 17] of that Act these Regulations were an Act of Parliament and the Regulations revoked by Regulation 2 of these Regulations were Acts of Parliament thereby repealed.

[Regulation 3 is printed as amended by the Road Traffic Act 1972, Sched 10, para 3, SI 1972 No 1865, SI 1975 No 1342, and the Interpretation Act 1978, s 17 (2).

Selected definitions only are reproduced in para (1).

Regulation 31 (1) states that 'The [Secretary of State for Transport] shall issue to every holder of a trade licence in respect of that licence two plates . . . appropriate to the class of vehicles on which they will be used showing the general registration mark assigned to the holder of the licence'. *The text of reg 31 (1) is set out as amended by the Minister of Transport Order 1979 (SI 1979 No 571) and the Transfer of Functions (Transport) Order 1981 (SI 1981 No 238).]*

[3A. Exclusion for electrically assisted pedal cycles

The provisions of Parts II and III of these Regulations do not apply to an electrically assisted pedal cycle for the time being prescribed for the purposes of [section 140 of the Road Traffic Regulation Act 1984] and section 193 of the Road Traffic Act 1972.]

[Regulation 3A was inserted by SI 1983 No 1248 and is printed as amended by the Road Traffic Regulation Act 1984, s 144 (1), and Sched 10, para 2.]

*   *   *

PART II

LICENSING AND REGISTRATION

*   *   *

12. Notification of change of ownership

(1) On a change of ownership of a mechanically propelled vehicle the previous owner of the vehicle shall deliver the registration book issued in respect of the vehicle and may deliver any current licence issued in respect of the vehicle to the new owner and shall notify in writing forthwith the change of ownership to the [Secretary of State for Transport] stating the registration mark of the vehicle, its make and class and the name and address of the new owner.

(2) Upon acquiring the vehicle the new owner shall—

(a) if he intends to use or keep the vehicle upon public roads otherwise than under a trade licence, forthwith insert his name and address in the appropriate part of the registration book and deliver it to the [Secretary of State for Transport];

(b) if he does not intend to use or keep the vehicle upon public roads, forthwith notify the [Secretary of State for Transport] in writing that he is the owner of the vehicle, and he shall state in such notification the registration mark of the vehicle, its make and class, the name and address of the previous owner and the fact that he does not intend to use or keep the vehicle on public roads;

(c) if he intends to use the vehicle upon public roads solely under a trade licence, at the expiration of three months from the date when he became the owner of the vehicle or, if a further change of ownership occurs, on the date of that change, whichever is the sooner, notify the [Secretary of State for Transport] in writing of his name and address and those of the previous owner.

[Regulation 12 is printed as amended by the Minister of Transport Order 1979 (SI 1979 No 571) and the Transfer of Functions (Transport) Order 1981 (SI 1981 No 238).]

13. Notification of change of address of owner

If the owner of a mechanically propelled vehicle changes his address he shall forthwith enter particulars of his new address in the space provided in the registration book issued in respect of the vehicle and send the book to the [Secretary of State for Transport].

[Regulation 13 is printed as amended by the Minister of Transport Order 1979 (SI 1979 No 571) and the Transfer of Functions (Transport) Order 1981 (SI 1981 No 238).]

*   *   *

PART III

EXHIBITION OF LICENCES AND REGISTRATION MARKS

16. Exhibition of licences

(1) Every licence issued under the Act and in force for a mechanically propelled vehicle, excepting a tramcar, shall be fixed to and exhibited on the vehicle in accordance with the provisions of this Regulation at all times while the vehicle is being used or kept on a public road:

Provided that when such a licence is delivered up with an application for a new licence to [any post office authorised for the time being to issue vehicle licences in accordance with arrangements for that purpose made between the Post Office and the [Secretary of State for Transport]], no licence shall be required to be fixed to and exhibited on the vehicle until the new licence is obtained, when that licence shall be deemed to be the licence in force for the vehicle for the purposes of this Regulation.

(2) Each such licence shall be fixed to the vehicle in a holder sufficient to protect the licence from any effects of the weather to which it would otherwise be exposed.

(3) The licence shall be exhibited on the vehicle:—

(a) in the case of an invalid vehicle, tricycle or bicycle, other than a case specified in sub-paragraph (b) or (c) of this paragraph, on the near side of the vehicle in front of the driving seat so that all the particulars thereon are clearly visible by daylight from the near side of the road;

(b) in the case of a bicycle drawing a side-car or to which a side-car is attached when the bicycle is being kept on a public road, on the near side of the handle-bars of the bicycle or on the near side of the side-car in front of the driving seat so that all the particulars thereon are clearly visible by daylight from the near side of the road;

(c) in the case of any vehicle fitted with a glass windscreen in front of the driver extending across the vehicle to its near side, on or adjacent to the near side . . . of the windscreen, so that all particulars thereon are clearly visible by daylight from the near side of the road;

(d) in the case of any other vehicle, if the vehicle is fitted with a driver's cab containing a near side window, on such window, or on the near side of the vehicle in front of the driver's seat or towards the front of the vehicle in the case of a pedestrian controlled vehicle and not less than 2 feet 6 inches and not more than 6 feet above the surface of the road, so that in each case all the particulars thereon are clearly visible by daylight from the near side of the road.

[Regulation 16 is printed as amended by SI 1972 No 1865, SI 1976 No 1680, the Minister of Transport Order 1979 (SI 1979 No 571) and the Transfer of Functions (Transport) Order 1981 (SI 1981 No 238).]

* * *

[**19.**—(1) Save as provided in paragraph (2) below, no person shall use or cause or permit to be used on a road during the hours of darkness any motor vehicle unless every letter and number of the registration mark displayed on the back of—

(a) the motor vehicle if it is not drawing a trailer, or

(b) the trailer if the motor vehicle is drawing one trailer, or

(c) the rearmost trailer if the motor vehicle is drawing more than one trailer,

is illuminated so as to be easily legible in the absence of fog from every part of the relevant area, the diagonal of the square governing that area being—

(i) 15 metres in the case of a bicycle, an invalid vehicle and a pedestrian controlled vehicle, and

(ii) 18 metres in the case of any other vehicle.

(2) The provisions of paragraph (1) above do not apply in respect of:—

(a) a works truck; or

(b) a vehicle which is not required to be fitted with a rear registration plate.]

[Regulation 19 is printed as substituted by SI 1984 No 814.]

* * *

22. Trailers

(1) Subject to paragraph (3) of this Regulation, where one or more trailers are attached to a mechanically propelled vehicle the owner of the vehicle shall ensure that there is displayed on the trailer or rearmost trailer (as the case may be) the registration mark of the mechanically propelled vehicle, and that such registration mark is fixed to and displayed on the trailer as if the trailer were a vehicle of the same class or description as the mechanically propelled vehicle.

(2) Where the registration mark of a mechanically propelled vehicle is fixed to and displayed on a trailer attached to it in accordance with the foregoing paragraph, the requirements of these Regulations as to the fixing to and display of a registration mark on the back of a mechanically propelled vehicle shall not apply to the vehicle drawing the trailer.

(3) Where the mechanically propelled vehicle is a restricted vehicle, the registration mark fixed to and displayed on the trailer in accordance with paragraph (1) of this Regulation may, instead of being that of the vehicle to which the trailer is attached, be that of any other restricted vehicle belonging to the owner of the vehicle to which the trailer is attached, and in such a case the duty in the said paragraph (1) as to fixing and display shall apply as if the other restricted vehicle were the vehicle to which the trailer was attached.

(4) In this Regulation 'restricted vehicle' means a vehicle mentioned in section 7 (1) of the Act or paragraph 2 (1) of Schedule 3 thereto.

* * *

PART V

TRADE LICENCES

* * *

30. Notification of change of address etc

If the holder of a trade licence changes the name of his business or his business address he shall notify this fact and the new name or address forthwith to the [Secretary of State for Transport] and shall at the same time send to the [Secretary of State for Transport] the licence for any necessary amendment.

[Regulation 30 is printed as amended by the Minister of Transport Order 1979 (SI 1979 No 571) and the Transfer of Functions (Transport) Order 1981 (SI 1981 No 238.]

* * *

32. Alteration of trade plates and similar offences

(1) No person shall alter, deface, mutilate or add anything to any trade plate or exhibit upon any mechanically propelled vehicle any trade plate which has been altered, defaced, mutilated or added to as aforesaid or upon which the figures or particulars have become illegible or the colour has become altered by fading or otherwise.

(2) No person shall exhibit on any mechanically propelled vehicle anything which could be mistaken for a trade plate.

33. Exhibition of trade plates and licences

No person shall use a vehicle on a public road by virtue of a trade licence except in accordance with the following provisions, that is to say—

(a) there shall be fixed to and displayed on the vehicle the trade plates issued by the [Secretary of State for Transport] in such a manner that, if the trade plates contained a registration mark assigned to the vehicle, the provisions of Regulations 18 and 19 of these Regulations would be complied with, notwithstanding the vehicle may not have been first registered on or after 1st October 1938 or it is a works truck or an agricultural machine; and

(b) where in accordance with the provisions of the preceding paragraph a trade plate is required to be fixed to the front of a vehicle, the trade plate so fixed shall be that containing means for fixing the licence thereto, and the trade licence shall be fixed to the vehicle by means of that plate and exhibited on that plate so as to be at all times clearly visible by daylight.

[Regulation 33 is printed as amended by the Minister of Transport Order 1979 (SI 1979 No 571) and the Transfer of Functions (Transport) Order 1981 (SI 1981 No 238).]

34. Restriction on use of trade plates and licences

No person, not being the holder of a trade licence, shall use on a public road a vehicle on which there is displayed a trade plate or a trade licence, so, however, that nothing in this Regulation shall apply so as to prevent a person with the consent of the holder of the trade licence from driving a vehicle when the vehicle is being used on a public road by virtue of a trade licence and by the holder thereof.

Purposes for which a vehicle may be used

35—(1) In this Regulation, 'business purpose', in relation to a motor trader, means—

(a) a purpose connected with his business as a manufacturer or repairer of or dealer in mechanically propelled vehicles, or

(b) a purpose connected with his business as a manufacturer or repairer of or dealer in trailers carried on in conjunction with his business as a motor trader.

(2) For the purposes of sub-paragraphs (a) to (k) of paragraph (4) of this Regulation, where a mechanically propelled vehicle is used on a public road by virtue of a trade licence and that vehicle is drawing a trailer, the vehicle and trailer shall be deemed to constitute a single vehicle.

(3) Save as provided in Regulation 36 of these Regulations, no person, being a motor trader and the holder of a trade licence, shall use any mechanically propelled vehicle on a public road by virtue of that licence unless it is a vehicle which is temporarily in his possession in the course of his business as a motor trader or a recovery vehicle kept by him for the purpose of dealing with disabled vehicles in the course of that business.

(4) Save as provided in the said Regulation 36 and without derogation from the provisions of the last preceding paragraph of this Regulation, no person, being a motor trader and the holder of a trade licence, shall use any mechanically propelled vehicle on a public road by virtue of that licence for a purpose other than a business purpose and other than one of the following purposes:—

(a) for its test or trial or the test or trial of its accessories or equipment in the ordinary course of construction or repair or after completion in either such case;

(b) for proceeding to or from a public weighbridge for ascertaining its unladen weight or to or from any place for its registration or inspection by a person acting on behalf of the [Secretary of State for Transport];

(c) for its test or trial for the benefit of a prospective purchaser, for proceeding at the instance of a prospective purchaser to any place for the purpose of such test or trial, or for returning after such test or trial;

(d) for its test or trial for the benefit of a person interested in promoting publicity in regard to it, for proceeding at the instance of such a person to any place for the purpose of such test or trial, or for returning after such test or trial;

(e) for delivering it to the place where the purchaser intends to keep it;

(f) for demonstrating its operation or the operation of its accessories or equipment when being handed over to the purchaser;

(g) for delivering it from one part of his premises to another part of his premises, or for delivering it from his premises to the premises of, or between parts of premises of, another manufacturer or repairer of or dealer in mechanically propelled vehicles or removing it from the premises of another manufacturer or repairer of or dealer in mechanically propelled vehicles direct to his own business;

(h) for proceeding to or returning from a workshop in which a body or a special type of equipment or accessory is to be or has been fitted to it or in which it is to be or has been painted or repaired;

(i) for proceeding from the premises of a manufacturer or repairer of or dealer in mechanically propelled vehicles to a place from which it is to be transported by train, ship or aircraft or for proceeding to the premises of such a manufacturer, repairer or dealer from a place to which it has been so transported;

(j) for proceeding to or returning from any garage, auction room or other place at which vehicles are usually stored or usually or periodically offered for sale and at which the vehicle is to be or has been stored or is to be or has been offered for sale as the case may be;

(k) for proceeding to or returning from a place where it is to be or has been tested, or for proceeding to a place where it is to be broken up or otherwise dismantled; or

(l) in the case of a recovery vehicle—
    (i) for proceeding to or returning from a place where assistance is to be, or has been, rendered to a disabled vehicle,
    (ii) for proceeding to or returning from a place where it is to be, or has been, held available for rendering assistance to a disabled vehicle, or
    (iii) for carrying a disabled vehicle, or for towing such a vehicle (whether with the assistance of a trailer or not), from the place where it has broken down or from such other place where it is subsequently for the time being situated to a place for repair or storage or breaking up.

[Regulation 35 is printed as amended by the Minister of Transport Order 1979 (SI 1979 No 571) and the Transfer of Functions (Transport) Order 1981 (SI 1981 No 238).]

36. No person, being a motor trader and who is a manufacturer of mechanically propelled vehicles and the holder of a trade licence, shall use any mechanically propelled vehicle, kept by him solely for the purposes of conducting research and development in the course of his business as such a manufacturer, on a public road by virtue of that licence except for such a purpose.

37. No person, being a vehicle tester and the holder of a trade licence, shall use any mechanically propelled vehicle on a public road by virtue of that licence for any purpose other than testing it or any trailer drawn thereby or any of the accessories or equipment on such vehicle or trailer in the course of his business as a vehicle tester.

Conveyance of goods or burden

38.—(1) No person, being a motor trader and the holder of a trade licence, shall use a mechanically propelled vehicle on a public road by virtue of that licence for the conveyance of goods or burden of any description other than—

(a) a load which is carried by a vehicle being used for a relevant purpose and is carried solely for the purpose of testing or demonstrating the vehicle or any of its accessories or equipment and which is returned to the place of loading without having been removed from the vehicle except for such last mentioned purpose or in the case of accident:

In this sub-paragraph 'relevant purpose' means a purpose mentioned in Regulation 35 (4) (*a*), (*c*), (*d*) and (*f*) of these Regulations; or

(*b*) in the case of a recovery vehicle, being used for a relevant purpose, any such load as is referred to in the definition of such a vehicle contained in section 16 (8) of the Act or a load consisting of a disabled vehicle:

In this sub-paragraph 'relevant purpose' means a purpose mentioned in Regulation 35 (4) (*l*) of these Regulations; or

(*c*) any load built in as part of the vehicle or permanently attached thereto: or

(*d*) a load consisting of parts, accessories or equipment designed to be fitted to the vehicle and of tools for so fitting them, the vehicle being used for a relevant purpose:

In this sub-paragraph 'relevant purpose' means a purpose mentioned in Regulation 35 (4) (*g*), (*h*) or (*i*) of these Regulations; or

(*e*) a load consisting of a trailer, the vehicle carrying the trailer being used for a relevant purpose:

In this sub-paragraph 'relevant purpose' means a purpose mentioned in Regulation 35 (4) (*e*), (*h*) or (*i*) of these Regulations.

(2) No person, being a motor trader and who is a manufacturer of mechanically propelled vehicles and the holder of a trade licence, shall use any mechanically propelled vehicle, kept by him solely for the purpose of conducting research and development in the course of his business as such a manufacturer, on a public road by virtue of that licence for the conveyance of goods or burden of any description other than—

(*a*) a load which is carried solely for the purpose of testing the vehicle or any of its accessories or equipment and which is returned to the place of loading without having been removed from the vehicle except for such purpose or in the case of accident; or

(*b*) any load built in as part of the vehicle or permanently attached thereto,

and nothing in the last preceding paragraph of this Regulation shall be taken as applying to a mechanically propelled vehicle the use of which is restricted by this paragraph.

(3) For the purposes of this Regulation and the next succeeding Regulation, where a vehicle is so constructed that a trailer may by partial superimposition be attached to the vehicle in such a manner as to cause a substantial part of the weight of the trailer to be borne by the vehicle, the vehicle and the trailer shall be deemed to constitute a single vehicle.

39. No person, being a vehicle tester and the holder of a trade licence, shall use a mechanically propelled vehicle on a public road by virtue of that licence for the conveyance of goods or burden of any description other than—

(*a*) a load which is carried solely for the purpose of testing or demonstrating the vehicle or any of its accessories or equipment and which is returned to the place of loading without having been removed from the vehicle except for such purpose or in the case of accident; or

(*b*) any load built in as part of the vehicle or permanently attached thereto.

40. Carriage of passengers

(1) No person, being the holder of a trade licence, shall use a mechanically propelled vehicle on a public road by virtue of that licence for carrying any person on the vehicle or on any trailer drawn thereby other than—

(a) the driver of the vehicle, being the holder of the licence, an employee of the holder, or any other person driving with the consent of the holder while (except in the case of a vehicle which is constructed to carry only one person) accompanied by the holder or an employee of his;

(b) any person required to be on the vehicle or trailer by or by virtue of the [Road Traffic Act 1972];

(c) any person carried for the purpose of fulfilling his statutory duties in connection with an inspection of the vehicle or trailer;

(d) any person in a disabled vehicle being towed;

(e) the holder of the trade licence or an employee of his, if in either case his presence is necessary for the purpose for which the vehicle is being used;

(f) an employee of the holder of the trade licence proceeding to a place for the purpose of driving vehicles on behalf of the holder of the trade licence in the course of his business as a motor trader;

(g) a prospective purchaser or his servant or agent or any person requested to accompany the said prospective purchaser, or in the case of a vehicle being used for the purpose mentioned in Regulation 35 (4) (f) of these Regulations, the purchaser or his servant or agent or any person requested to accompany the said purchaser; or

(h) a person mentioned in Regulation 35 (4) (d) of these Regulations.

(2) Where a person coming within sub-paragraph (g) or (h) of the preceding paragraph of this Regulation is carried he shall be accompanied (except in the case of a vehicle which is constructed to carry only one person) by the holder of the trade licence or an employee of his.

[Regulation 40 is printed as amended by the Road Traffic Act 1972, Sched 10, para 3.]

*   *   *

The Road Vehicles Lighting Regulations 1984

(SI 1984 No 812)

ARRANGEMENT OF REGULATIONS

PART I—Preliminary

PART II—Regulations Governing the Fitting of Lamps, Reflectors, Rear Markings and Devices

PART III—Regulations Governing the Maintenance and Use of Lamps, Reflectors, Rear Markings and Devices

PART IV—Testing and Inspection of Lighting Equipment and Reflectors

SCHEDULES

1. Obligatory lamps, reflectors, rear markings and devices
2. Part I   Front position lamps to which Regulation 16 applies
   Part II Front position lamps to which Regulation 17 applies
3. Part I   Dim-dip lighting devices to which Regulation 16 applies
   Part II Dim-dip lighting devices to which Regulation 17 applies
4. Part I   Dipped-beam headlamps to which Regulation 16 applies
   Part II Dipped-beam headlamps to which Regulation 17 applies
5. Part I   Main-beam headlamps to which Regulation 16 applies
   Part II Main-beam headlamps to which Regulation 17 applies
6. Front fog lamps to which Regulation 17 applies
7. Direction indicators to which either Regulation 16 or 17 applies
   Part I   General requirements
   Part II Arrangements of indicators
8. Part I   Hazard warning signal devices to which Regulation 16 applies
   Part II Hazard warning signal devices to which Regulation 17 applies
9. Part I   Side marker lamps to which Regulation 16 or 19 applies
   Part II Side marker lamps to which Regulation 17 applies
10. Part I   Rear position lamps to which Regulation 16 applies
    Part II Rear position lamps to which Regulation 17 applies
11. Part I   Rear fog lamps to which Regulation 16 applies
    Part II Rear fog lamps to which Regulation 17 applies
12. Part I   Stop lamps to which Regulation 16 applies
    Part II Stop lamps to which Regulation 17 applies
13. Reversing lamps to which Regulation 17 applies
14. Rear registration plate lamps to which Regulation 16 applies
15. Warning beacons to which Regulation 17 applies
16. Part I   Side reflex reflectors to which Regulation 16 applies
    Part II Side reflex reflectors to which Regulation 17 applies
17. Part I   Rear reflex reflectors to which Regulation 16 applies
    Part II Rear reflex reflectors to which Regulation 17 applies
18. Part I   Rear markings to which Regulation 16 applies
    Part II Rear markings to which Regulation 17 applies
19. Part I   Pedal reflex reflectors to which Regulation 16 applies
    Part II Pedal reflex reflectors to which Regulation 17 applies

. . . .

The Secretary of State for Transport in exercise of the powers
- (i) s 40(1), (2A) and (3) of the Road Traffic Act 1972 as regards vehicles, other than cycles not being motor vehicles;
- (ii) s 66(1) and (3) of that Act as regards cycles not being motor vehicles; and
- (iii) s 41(3) of that Act as regards the provisions referred to in Regulation 1(2) below

all of which powers are now vested in him, and of all other enabling powers, and after consultation with representative organisations in accordance with section 199(2) of that Act, hereby makes the following Regulations:—

PART I

1. Commencement, citation and exercise of powers

(1) These Regulations shall come into operation on 1st August 1984 and may be cited as the Road Vehicles Lighting Regulations 1984.

(2) The Secretary of State is satisfied that—

(a) it is requisite that the provisions mentioned in paragraph (3), which vary the requirements about the construction of the vehicles to which those provisions apply, shall apply to such of those vehicles as are registered under the Vehicles (Excise) Act 1971 before the expiration of 1 year from the making of these Regulations; and

(b) notwithstanding that those provisions will then apply to those vehicles, no undue hardship or inconvenience will be caused thereby.

(3) The provisions referred to in paragraph (2) are as follows:—

Number of Regulation or Schedule, if appropriate	Summary of requirement
Regulation 13(1)	The requirement for a stop lamp and a rear fog lamp to show a steady light is extended to all other lamps except a headlamp when used manually to signal the presence of the vehicle to which it is fitted, a direction indicator, a warning beacon, a special warning lamp, an illuminated sign on a police vehicle and an anti-lock brake indicator.
Regulation 15	The former restriction on the fitting of a lamp similar to a blue warning beacon is extended to a warning beacon of any colour and to a special warning lamp, whether such lamps are in working order or not.
Regulation 19	A requirement is introduced for side marker lamps to be fitted to a vehicle as mentioned in the Table in that Regulation during conditions of seriously reduced visibility in daytime as well as during the hours of darkness.
Schedule 1	The exemption from the need to fit stop lamps and direction indicators to a vehicle first used on or after 1st January 1936 equipped with front and rear position lamps which are not electrically operated is not preserved.
Schedule 2 Part I 2(b)(i)(B)(2)	Solo motor bicycles are no longer permitted to be fitted with a single obligatory front position lamp on the nearside of the vehicle.
Schedules 4, 5 and 6	Vehicles of a kind which were specified in Regulation 14(2) of the Road Vehicles Lighting Regulations 1971 [SI 1971 No 694] are no longer permitted to be fitted with headlamps or front fog lamps emitting light of any colour other than white or yellow.

Number of Regulation or Schedule, if appropriate	Summary of requirement
Schedules 4 and 5	The requirement for the aim of headlamps to be capable of adjustment is extended to optional head-lamps on all vehicles and to obligatory headlamps on vehicles of a kind which were specified in Regulation 14(2) of the Road Vehicles Lighting Regulations 1971.
Schedule 7 Part I 6	A requirement is introduced that— (a) a track-laying vehicle, (b) a motor cycle first used on or after 1st September 1965, or (c) any motor vehicle to which Regulation 70A of the Road Vehicles Lighting Regulations 1971 [SI 1971 No 694, as amended by SI 1977 No 1560] applied shall not be fitted with a direction indicator of a colour other than amber.
Schedule 7 Part I 11(a)	A new requirement is introduced for direction indicators to perform efficiently regardless of the speed of the vehicle.
Schedule 12 Part I 6	The option of amber for the colour of stop lamps for a track-laying vehicle is not preserved.
Schedule 17 Part I 7(b)	A requirement is introduced to prohibit the fitting of triangular-shaped reflectors to any vehicle other than a trailer.
—	Except as is specified in Regulation 7, the exemptions from the need to fit headlamps to a vehicle of a kind which was specified in Regulation 14(2)(f), (ff) or (g) of the Road Vehicles Lighting Regulations 1971 are not preserved.
—	The exemptions from the need to fit stop lamps and direction indicators to a vehicle of a kind which is mentioned in Regulation 4(8), (9) and (10) of the Construction and Use Regulations are not preserved.

2. Revocation

[Omitted.]

3. Interpretation

(1) Unless the context otherwise requires, any reference in these Regulations—

(a) to a numbered Regulation or Schedule is a reference to the Regulation or Schedule bearing that number in these Regulations,

(b) to a numbered paragraph is to the paragraph bearing that number in the Regulation or Schedule in which the reference occurs,

(c) to a numbered or lettered sub-paragraph is to the sub-paragraph bearing that number or letter in the paragraph in which the reference occurs.

(2) In these Regulations, unless the context otherwise requires—

'the Act' means the Road Traffic Act 1972;

'the Construction and Use Regulations' means the Motor Vehicles (Construction and Use) Regulations 1978 *[SI 1978 No 1017, as amended]*;

'the Designation of Approval Marks Regulations' means the Motor Vehicles (Designation of Approval Marks) Regulations 1979 *[SI 1979 No 1088, as amended]*;

'articulated bus', 'articulated vehicle', 'dual-purpose vehicle', 'engineering plant', 'industrial tractor', 'large passenger-carrying vehicle', 'overall length', 'overall width', 'passenger vehicle', 'pedestrian-controlled vehicle', 'vehicle in the service of a visiting force or of a headquarters', 'wheel', 'wheeled', 'works trailer' and 'works truck' have the meanings given respectively by Regulation 3(1) of the Construction and Use Regulations;

'agricultural vehicle' means a vehicle constructed or adapted for agriculture, grass cutting, forestry, land levelling, dredging or similar operations and primarily used for one or more of these purposes, and includes any trailer drawn by an agricultural vehicle;

'angles of visibility' means the horizontal and vertical angles throughout which the whole of the apparent surface of a lamp or reflector is visible, disregarding any part of the apparent surface which may be obscured by any part of the vehicle, provided that the lamp or reflector remains visible throughout the angles specified in the relevant Schedule below;

'apparent surface' means the orthogonal projection of a light-emitting surface in a plane perpendicular to the direction of observation;

'breakdown vehicle' means a vehicle used to attend an accident or breakdown or to draw a broken down vehicle;

'Chief Officer of Police' and 'police area', in relation to England and Wales, have the same meanings as in the Police Act 1964, and, in relation to Scotland, have the same meanings as in the Police (Scotland) Act 1967;

'circuit-closed tell-tale' means a light showing that a device has been switched on;

'combat vehicle' means a vehicle of a type described at item 1, 2 or 3 in column 1 of Schedule 1 to the Motor Vehicles (Authorisation of Special Types) General Order 1979 *[SI 1979 No 1198]*;

'daytime hours' means the time between half an hour before sunrise and half an hour after sunset;

'dim-dip lighting device' means a device which complies with the requirements specified in Part I of Schedule 3;

'dipped beam' means a beam of light emitted by a lamp which illuminates the road ahead of the vehicle without causing undue dazzle or discomfort to oncoming drivers or other road users;

'direction indicator' means a lamp on a vehicle used to indicate to other road users that the driver intends to change direction to the right or to the left;

'emergency vehicle' means—

(a) a motor vehicle used for fire brigade or police purposes;

(b) an ambulance, being a motor vehicle (other than an invalid carriage) which is constructed or adapted for the purposes of conveying sick, injured or disabled persons and which is used for such purposes;

(c) a motor vehicle owned by a body formed primarily for the purposes of fire salvage and used for those or similar purposes;

(d) a motor vehicle owned by the Forestry Commission or by a local authority and used from time to time for the purposes of fighting fires;

(e) a motor vehicle owned by the Secretary of State for Defence and used—
  (i) for the purposes of the disposal of bombs or explosives,
  (ii) by the Naval Emergency Monitoring Organisation for the purposes of a nuclear accident or an incident involving radio-activity,
  (iii) by the Royal Air Force Mountain Rescue Service for the purposes of rescue operations or any other emergencies, or
  (iv) by the Royal Air Force Armament Support Unit;

(f) a motor vehicle primarily used for the purposes of the Blood Transfusion Service provided under the National Health Service Act 1977 or under the National Health (Scotland) Act 1978;

(g) a motor vehicle used by Her Majesty's Coastguard or Coastguard Auxiliary Service for the purposes of giving aid to persons in danger or vessels in distress on or near the coast;

(h) a motor vehicle owned by the National Coal Board and used for the purposes of rescue operations at mines;

(i) a motor vehicle owned by the Royal National Lifeboat Institution and used for the purposes of launching lifeboats; and

(j) a motor vehicle primarily used for the purposes of conveying any human tissue for transplanting or similar purposes;

'extreme outer edge', in relation to a side of a vehicle, means the plane parallel with the median longitudinal plane of the vehicle, and coinciding with its lateral outer edge, disregarding the projection of—

(a) so much of the distortion of any tyre as is caused by the weight of the vehicle,

(b) any connections for tyre pressure gauges,

(c) any anti-skid devices which may be mounted on the wheels,

(d) rear-view mirrors,

(e) lamps and reflectors

(f) customs seals affixed to the vehicle, and devices for securing and protecting such seals, and

(g) special equipment;

'front fog lamp' means a lamp used to improve the illumination of the road in front of a motor vehicle in conditions of seriously reduced visibility;

'front position lamp' means a lamp used to indicate the presence and width of a vehicle when viewed from the front;

'hazard warning signal device' means a device which is capable of operating simultaneously all the direction indicators with which a vehicle, or a combination of vehicles, is fitted for the purpose of warning other persons of a temporary obstruction on the road;

'headlamp' means a lamp used to illuminate the road in front of a vehicle and which is not a front fog lamp;

'home forces' means the naval, military or air forces of Her Majesty raised in the United Kingdom;

'home forces' vehicle' means a vehicle owned by, or in the service of, the home forces and used for naval, military or air force purposes;

'horse-drawn', in relation to a vehicle, means that the vehicle is drawn by a horse or other animal;

'hours of darkness' means the time between half an hour after sunset and half an hour before sunrise;

'illuminated area', in relation to a lamp, means the area of the orthogonal projection of the light-emitting surface on a vertical plane (touching the surface of the lamp) at right angles to the longitudinal axis of the vehicle to which it is fitted, such projection being bounded by the edges of straight-edged screens situated in that plane and each allowing only 98 per cent of the total intensity of the light to be shown in the direction parallel to the longitudinal axis of the vehicle and, for the purposes of determining the lower, upper and lateral edges of a lamp, only screens having a horizontal or vertical edge shall be considered;

'installation and performance requirements', in relation to any lamp, reflector, rear marking or device, means the requirements specified in the Schedule hereto relating to that lamp, reflector, rear marking or device;

'kerbside weight' means—
  (a) in relation to a motor vehicle, the weight of the vehicle when it carries—
      (i) no person,
      (ii) a full supply of fuel in its tank, an adequate supply of other liquids incidental to its propulsion and no load other than the loose tools and equipment with which the vehicle is normally equipped, and
  (b) in relation to a trailer, the weight of the trailer when it carries no person and it is otherwise unladen;

'light-emitting surface', in relation to a lamp, means that part of the exterior surface of the lens through which light is emitted when the lamp is lit, and in relation to a reflex reflector means that part of the exterior surface of the reflex reflector through which light can be reflected;

'main beam' means a beam of light emitted by a lamp which illuminates the road over a long distance ahead of the vehicle;

'matched pair', in relation to lamps, means a pair of lamps in respect of which—
  (a) both lamps emit light of substantially the same colour and intensity; and
  (b) both lamps are of the same size and of such a shape that they are symmetrical to one another;

'maximum distance from the side of the vehicle' means the maximum distance from that side (the side being determined by reference to 'extreme outer edge') to the nearest edge of the illuminated area in the case of a lamp or the reflecting area in the case of a reflex reflector;

'maximum height above the ground' means the height above which no part of the illuminated area in the case of a lamp, or the reflecting area in the case of a reflex reflector, extends when the vehicle is at its kerbside weight and when each tyre with which the vehicle is fitted is inflated to the pressure recommended by the manufacturer of the vehicle;

'maximum speed' means, in relation to a motor vehicle, the maximum speed the vehicle can attain on the level under its own power;

'minimum height above the ground' means the height below which no part of the illuminated area in the case of a lamp, or the reflecting area in the case of a reflex reflector, extends when the vehicle is at its kerbside weight and when each tyre with which the vehicle is fitted is inflated to the pressure recommended by the manufacturer of the vehicle;

'motor bicycle combination' means a combination of a solo motor bicycle and a sidecar;

'movable platform' means a platform which is attached to, and may be moved by means of, an extensible boom;

'obligatory', in relation to a lamp, reflector, rear marking or device, means a lamp, reflector, rear marking or device with which a vehicle, its load or equipment is required by these Regulations to be fitted;

'operational tell-tale' means a warning device readily visible or audible to the driver and showing whether a device that has been switched on is operating correctly or not;

'optional', in relation to a lamp, reflector, rear marking or device, means a lamp, reflector, rear marking or device with which a vehicle, its load or equipment is not required by these Regulations to be fitted;

'pair', in relation to lamps, reflectors or rear markings, means a pair of lamps, reflectors or rear markings, one on each side of the vertical plane passing through the longitudinal axis of the vehicle, in respect of which—

　(a) each lamp, reflector or rear marking is at the same height above the ground, and

　(b) each lamp, reflector or rear marking is at the same distance from the said vertical plane,

these requirements being complied with so far as practicable in the case of an asymmetric vehicle;

'pedal cycle' means a vehicle which is not constructed or adapted to be propelled by mechanical power and which is equipped with pedals, including an electrically-assisted pedal cycle prescribed for the purposes of section 193 of the Act and [section 140 of the Road Traffic Regulation Act 1984];

'pedal reflex reflector' means a reflex reflector attached to or incorporated in the pedals of a pedal cycle or motor bicycle;

'rear fog lamp' means a lamp used to render a vehicle more readily visible from the rear in conditions of seriously reduced visibility;

'rear marking' means a marking of the size, colour and type indicated in Part I, Section B of Schedule 18;

'rear position lamp' means a lamp used to indicate the presence and width of a vehicle when viewed from the rear;

'rear reflex reflector' means a reflex reflector used to indicate the presence and width of a vehicle when viewed from the rear;

'rear registration plate lamp' means a lamp used to illuminate the rear registration plate;

'reflecting area' means, in relation to a reflex reflector fitted to a vehicle, the area of the orthogonal projection on a vertical plane—

　(a) at right angles to the longitudinal axis of the vehicle of that part of the reflector designed to reflect light in the case of a rear reflex reflector, and

　(b) parallel to the longitudinal axis of the vehicle of that part of the reflector designed to reflect light in the case of a side reflex reflector;

'reversing lamp' means a lamp used to illuminate the road to the rear of a vehicle for the purpose of reversing and to warn other road users that the vehicle is reversing or about to reverse;

'road clearance vehicle' means a mechanically propelled vehicle used for dealing with frost, ice or snow on roads;

'separation distance' between two lamps or two reflex reflectors means, except where otherwise specified, the distance between the orthogonal projections in a plane perpendicular to the longitudinal axis of the vehicle of the illuminated areas of the two lamps or the reflecting areas of the two reflectors;

'side marker lamp' means a lamp fitted to the side of a vehicle or its load and used to render the vehicle more visible to other road users;

'side reflex reflector' means a reflector fitted to the side of a vehicle or its load and used to render the vehicle more visible from the side;

'solo motor bicycle' means a motor bicycle without a sidecar;

'special equipment' means the movable platform of a vehicle fitted with such a platform, the apparatus for moving the platform and any jacks fitted to the vehicle for stabilising it while the movable platform is in use;

'special warning lamp' means a lamp, fitted to the front or rear of an emergency vehicle, capable of emitting a blue flashing light and not any other kind of light;

'stop lamp' means a lamp used to indicate to road users that the brakes of a vehicle or combination of vehicles are being applied;

'trailer' means a vehicle constructed or adapted to be drawn by another vehicle;

'vehicle' means a vehicle of any description and includes a machine or implement of any kind drawn or propelled along roads whether by hand, horse or mechanical power;

'visiting vehicle' has the meaning given by Regulation 3(1) of the Motor Vehicles (International Circulation) Regulations 1971 *[SI 1971 No 937]*;

'warning beacon' means a lamp that is capable of emitting a flashing or rotating beam of light throughout 360° in the horizontal plane;

'work lamp' means a lamp used to illuminate a working area or the scene of an accident, breakdown or roadworks in the vicinity of the vehicle to which it is fitted.

(3) Material designed primarily to reflect light is, when reflecting light, to be treated for the purposes of these Regulations as showing a light, and material capable of reflecting an image is not, when reflecting the image of a light, to be so treated.

(4) In these Regulations—

(*a*) except in the case of a dipped-beam headlamp, a main-beam headlamp and a front fog lamp, a reference to one lamp includes any combination of two or more lamps, whether identical or not, having the same function and emitting light of the same colour, if it comprises devices the projection of the aggregate illuminated areas of which in a vertical plane perpendicular to the median longitudinal plane of the vehicle occupies 60 per cent or more of the area of the smallest rectangle circumscribing the projections of those illuminated areas; and

(*b*) a reference to two lamps includes—

    (i) a single illuminated area which—

        (A) is placed symmetrically in relation to the median longitudinal plane of the vehicle,

        (B) extends on both sides to within 400 millimetres of the extreme outer edge of the vehicle,

        (C) is not less than 800 millimetres long, and

        (D) is illuminated by not less than two sources of light, and

    (ii) any number of illuminated areas which—

(A) are juxtaposed,

(B) if on the same transverse plane have illuminated areas which occupy not less than 60 per cent of the area of the smallest rectangle circumscribing the projections of their illuminated areas,

(C) are placed symmetrically in relation to the median longitudinal plane of the vehicle,

(D) extend on both sides to within 400 millimetres of the extreme outer edge of the vehicle,

(E) do not have a total length of less than 800 millimetres, and

(F) are illuminated by not less than two sources of light.

(5) The angles of visibility specified in the Schedules to these Regulations shall be treated as being satisfied if they are satisfied when every door, tailgate, boot lid, engine cover or cab is in the closed position, provided that at all times every front and rear position lamp, direction indicator and rear reflector, in each case being an obligatory lamp or reflector, remains visible to the front or rear as appropriate.

(6) For the purposes of these Regulations, in determining when a motor vehicle is first used, the date of such first use shall be taken to be the date which is prescribed as the date of first use by Regulation 3(2) of the Construction and Use Regulations for the purposes of those Regulations. In the case of a motor bicycle combination, the date of manufacture or first use of the sidecar shall be disregarded.

(7) Any reference in these Regulations to a vehicle having any number of wheels is a reference to a vehicle having that number of wheels the tyres or rims of which are in contact with the ground when the vehicle is in motion on a road and any two such wheels shall be treated as one wheel if the distance between the centres of the areas of contact between them and the ground is less than 460 millimetres.

(8) For the purposes of these Regulations, the unladen weight of a motor vehicle shall be calculated in accordance with section 194 of the Act.

(9) For the purposes of these Regulations, maximum gross weight shall be determined in accordance with the provisions of Part I of Schedule 2 to the Construction and Use Regulations in the case of a motor vehicle, and Part II of Schedule 2 to those Regulations in the case of a trailer.

[Regulation 3 is printed as amended by the Road Traffic Regulation Act 1984, s 144 (1), and Sched 10, para 2.

The meaning of 'Chief Officer of Police' and 'police area' is set out in Sched 8 to the Police Act 1964, as amended by the Statute Law (Repeals) Act 1971 and the Local Government Act 1972, Sched 30, as follows:

Police area	Police Authority	Chief Officer of Police
The City of London	The Common Council	The Commissioner of City of London Police
The metropolitan police district	The Secretary of State	The Commissioner of Police of the Metropolis
A county	The police committee	The chief constable
A combined area	The combined police authority	The chief constable

4. Exemptions—General

(1) Where a provision is applied by these Regulations to a motor vehicle first used on or after a specified date it does not apply to that vehicle if it was manufactured at least six months before that date.

(2) Where an exemption from, or relaxation to, a provision is applied by these Regulations to a motor vehicle first used before a specified date it shall also apply to a motor vehicle first used on or after that date if it was manufactured at least six months before that date.

(3) Nothing in these Regulations shall require any lamp or reflector to be fitted during daytime hours to—

(a) a vehicle not fitted with any front or rear position lamp,

(b) an incomplete vehicle proceeding to a works for completion,

(c) a pedal cycle,

(d) a pedestrian-controlled vehicle,

(e) a horse-drawn vehicle,

(f) a vehicle drawn or propelled by hand, or

(g) a combat vehicle.

(4) For the purposes of these Regulations, a lamp shall not be treated as being a lamp if it is—

(a) so painted over or masked that it is not capable of being immediately used or readily put to use; or

(b) an electric lamp which is not provided with any system of wiring by means of which that lamp is, or can readily be, connected with a source of electricity.

5. Exemptions—Temporarily imported vehicles and vehicles proceeding to a port for export

Part II of these Regulations does not apply to—

(a) any vehicle having a base or centre in a country outside Great Britain from which it normally starts its journeys, provided that a period of not more than 12 months has elapsed since the vehicle was last brought into Great Britain;

(b) a visiting vehicle;

(c) any combination of two or more vehicles, one of which is drawing the other or others, if the combination includes any vehicle of the type mentioned in paragraph 5(a) or (b); or

(d) a vehicle proceeding to a port for export

if in each case the vehicle or combination of vehicles complies in every respect with the requirements about lighting equipment and reflectors relating thereto contained in a Convention mentioned in Regulation 4(7) of the Construction and Use Regulations.

6. Exemptions—Vehicles towing or being towed

(1) No motor vehicle first used before 1st April 1986 and no pedal cycle or trailer manufactured before 1st October 1985 is required by Regulation 16 to be fitted with any rear position lamp, stop lamp, rear direction indicator, rear fog lamp or rear reflector whilst a trailer fitted with any such lamp or reflector is attached to its rear.

(2) No trailer manufactured before 1st October 1985 is required by Regulation 16 to be fitted with—

(a) any front position lamp whilst being drawn by a passenger vehicle or a dual-purpose vehicle;

(b) any stop lamp, rear fog lamp or rear direction indicator whilst being drawn by a motor vehicle which is not required by Regulation 16 to be fitted with any such lamp.

(3) No trailer is required by Regulation 16 to be fitted with any stop lamp or direction indicator whilst being drawn by a motor vehicle fitted with one or two stop lamps and two or more direction indicators if the dimensions of the trailer are such that when the longitudinal axes of the drawing vehicle and the trailer lie in the same vertical plane such stop lamps and at least one direction indicator on each side of the vehicle are visible to an observer in that vertical plane from a point 6 metres behind the rear of the trailer whether it is loaded or not.

(4) No rear marking is required to be fitted to any vehicle by Regulation 16 if another vehicle in a combination of which it forms part would obscure any such marking.

(5) In the case of any lamp, reflector or rear marking fitted to a vehicle forming part of a combination of vehicles, the angles of visibility specified in the Schedules to these Regulations shall be treated as being satisfied if they would have been satisfied but for the presence of other vehicles in the combination.

(6) No broken down vehicle whilst being drawn is required by these Regulations either to be fitted with any lamp, reflector or rear marking, except rear position lamps and rear reflectors, when on a road during the hours of darkness or, if fitted, to be maintained in accordance with Regulation 20.

7. Exemptions—Military vehicles

(1) Regulation 16 does not apply to a home forces' vehicle or to a vehicle in the service of a visiting force or of a headquarters whilst being used—

(a) in connection with training which is certified in writing for the purposes of this Regulation by a person duly authorised in that behalf to be training on a special occasion and of which not less than 48 hours' notice has been given by that person to the Chief Officer of Police of every police area in which the place selected for the training is wholly or partly situate; or

(b) on manoeuvres within such limits and during such period as may from time to time be specified by Order in Council under the Manoeuvres Act 1958.

(2) Where not less than 6 nor more than 12 vehicles being home forces' vehicles or vehicles of a visiting force or of a headquarters are proceeding together in a convoy on tactical or driving exercises which are authorised in writing by a person duly authorised in that behalf, and of which not less than 48 hours' notice in writing has been given by that person to the Chief Officer of Police of every police area through which it is intended that the convoy shall pass and the interval between any two vehicles in such a convoy does not exceed 20 metres—

(a) front position lamps shall be required only on the vehicle leading the convoy;

(b) rear position lamps shall be required only on the rearmost vehicle provided that every other vehicle in the convoy carries a bright light under the vehicle illuminating either a part of the vehicle or anything attached to the vehicle or the road surface beneath the vehicle, in such a manner that the presence of the vehicle can be detected from the rear.

(3) No lamp is required to be fitted to any home forces' vehicle or any vehicle in the service of a visiting force or of a headquarters if the vehicle is constructed or adapted for combat and is such that compliance with these provisions is impracticable and it is fitted with two red rear position lamps and two red rear reflex reflectors when on a road during the hours of darkness. Such lamps and reflectors need not meet any of the requirements specified in Schedules 10 and 17.

(4) Part II of these Regulations does not apply to a vehicle in the service of a visiting force or of a headquarters if the vehicle complies in every respect with the requirements as to lighting equipment and reflectors relating thereto contained in a Convention referred to in Regulation 5.

8. Exemptions—Invalid carriages

The provisions of Regulation 6 of the Use of Invalid Carriages on Highways Regulations 1970 *[SI 1970 No 1391]* apply for the purposes of these Regulations as they apply for the purposes of the said Regulations of 1970.

[Regulation 6 of the Use of Invalid Carriages on Highways Regulations 1970 (SI 1970 No 1391) provides as follows:

(1) Subject to paragraph (3) below, an invalid carriage when on the carriageway of any road shall during the hours of darkness carry—

(*a*) one lamp showing to the front a white light visible from a reasonable distance;

(*b*) one lamp showing to the rear a red light visible from a reasonable distance; and

(*c*) one unobscured and efficient red reflector facing to the rear.

(2) Every such lamp shall be kept properly trimmed, lighted and in a clean and efficient condition, and every such lamp and reflector shall be attached to the vehicle in such a position and manner, and shall comply with such conditions with respect thereto, as are specified in the Schedule to these Regulations.

(3) The foregoing provisions of this Regulation shall not apply in relation to a vehicle when it is on the carriageway of a road for the purpose only of crossing that carriageway in the quickest manner practicable in the circumstances.

(4) In this Regulation—

(*a*) 'road' means any highway and any other road to which the public has access not being (in either case) a footway within the meaning of section 20(2) of the said Act of 1970, and

(*b*) 'hours of darkness' means the time between half-an-hour after sunset and half-an-hour before sunrise.

The Act of 1970 to which para (4)(b) of reg 6 refers is the Chronically Sick and Disabled Persons Act 1970. Section 20(2) of that Act (as amended by the Highways Act 1980) defines 'footway' as 'a way which is a footway, footpath or bridleway within the meaning of the Highways Act 1980'.]

9. Exemptions—Vehicles drawn or propelled by hand

A vehicle drawn or propelled by hand which has an overall width, including any load, not exceeding 800 millimetres is required by these Regulations to be fitted with lamps and reflectors only when it is used on the carriageway of a road during the hours of darkness otherwise than—

(*a*) close to the near side or left hand edge of the carriageway, or

(*b*) to cross the road.

10. Provision as respects Trade Descriptions Act 1968

Where by any provision in these Regulations any vehicle or any of its parts or equipment is required to be marked with a specification number or a registered certification trade mark of the British Standards Institution or with any approval mark, nothing in that provision shall be taken to authorise any person to apply any such number or mark to the vehicle, part or equipment in contravention of the Trade Descriptions Act 1968.

PART II

[Regulations Governing the Fitting of Lamps, Reflectors, Rear Markings and Devices]

11. Colour of light shown by lamps and reflectors

(1) No person shall use, or cause or permit to be used, on a road a vehicle which is readily capable of showing a red light to the front, except red light from—

- (a) a red and white chequered domed lamp, or a red and white segmented mast-mounted flashing beacon, fitted to a fire service control vehicle and intended for use at the scene of an emergency;
- (b) reflex reflective material or a reflex reflector designed primarily to reflect light to one or both sides of the vehicle and attached to or incorporated in any wheel or tyre of—
    - (i) a pedal cycle and any sidecar attached to it;
    - (ii) a solo motor bicycle or motor bicycle combination; or
    - (iii) an invalid carriage; or
- (c) a traffic sign which is attached to a vehicle and prescribed as authorised for that purpose under [section 64 of the Road Traffic Regulation Act 1984].

(2) No person shall use, or cause or permit to be used, on a road a vehicle which is readily capable of showing any light to the rear, other than a red light, except—

- (a) amber light from a direction indicator;
- (b) white light from a reversing lamp;
- (c) white light from a work lamp;
- (d) light to illuminate the interior of a vehicle;
- (e) light from an illuminated rear registration plate;
- (f) light for the purposes of illuminating a taxi meter;
- (g) in the case of a large passenger-carrying vehicle, light for the purposes of illuminating a route indicator;
- (h) blue light and white light from a chequered domed lamp fitted to a police control vehicle and intended for use at the scene of an emergency;
- (i) white light from a red and white chequered domed lamp, or a red and white segmented mast-mounted flashing beacon, fitted to a fire service control vehicle and intended for use at the scene of an emergency;
- (j) blue light from a warning beacon or rear special warning lamp fitted to an emergency vehicle;
- (k) amber light from a warning beacon fitted to—
    - (i) a road clearance vehicle;
    - (ii) a vehicle constructed or adapted for the purpose of collecting refuse;
    - (iii) a breakdown vehicle;

   (iv) a vehicle having a maximum speed not exceeding 25 miles per hour;

   (v) a vehicle having an overall width exceeding 2.9 metres;

   (vi) a vehicle used for the purposes of testing, maintaining, improving, cleansing or watering roads or for any purpose incidental to any such use;

   (vii) a vehicle used for the purpose of inspecting, cleansing, maintaining, adjusting, renewing or installing any apparatus which is in, on, under or over a road, or for any purpose incidental to any such use;

   (viii) a vehicle used for or in connection with any purpose for which it is authorised to be used on roads by an Order under section 42 of the Act and any vehicle used to escort such a vehicle;

   (ix) a vehicle used by Her Majesty's Customs and Excise for the purpose of testing fuels;

(*l*) green light from a warning beacon fitted to a vehicle used by a medical practitioner registered by the General Medical Council (whether with full, provisional or limited registration);

(*m*) yellow light from a warning beacon fitted to a vehicle for use at airports;

(*n*) reflected light from amber pedal reflex reflectors;

(*o*) reflected light of any colour from reflex reflective material or a reflex reflector designed primarily to reflect light to one or both sides of the vehicle and attached to or incorporated in any wheel or tyre of—

   (i) a pedal cycle and any sidecar attached to it;

   (ii) a solo motor bicycle or motor bicycle combination; or

   (iii) an invalid carriage;

(*p*) reflected light from amber reflex reflective material on a road clearance vehicle;

(*q*) reflected light from yellow reflex reflective registration plates;

(*r*) reflected light from yellow reflex reflective material incorporated in a rear marking of a type specified in Part I Section B of Schedule 18 and fitted to—

   (i) a motor vehicle having a maximum gross weight exceeding 7500 kilograms;

   (ii) a motor vehicle first used before 1st August 1982 having an unladen weight exceeding 3000 kilograms;

   (iii) a trailer having a maximum gross weight exceeding 3500 kilograms;

   (iv) a trailer manufactured before 1st August 1982 having an unladen weight exceeding 1000 kilograms;

   (v) a trailer which forms part of a combination of vehicles one of which is of a type mentioned in a previous item of this sub-paragraph; or

   (vi) a load carried by any vehicle of a type mentioned in this sub-paragraph; or

(*s*) light of any colour from a traffic sign attached to a vehicle and authorised as mentioned in Regulation 11(1)(*c*).

[Regulation 11 is printed as amended by the Road Traffic Regulation Act 1984, s 144 (1), and Sched 10, para 2.]

12. Movement of lamps and reflectors

(1) Save as provided in paragraph (2), no person shall use, or cause or permit to be used, on a road any vehicle to which, or to any load or equipment of which, there is fitted a lamp, reflector or marking which is capable of being moved by swivelling, deflecting or otherwise while the vehicle is in motion.

(2) Paragraph (1) does not apply in respect of—

(a) a headlamp which can be dipped only by the movement of the headlamp or its reflector;

(b) a headlamp which is capable of adjustment so as to compensate for the effect of the load carried by the vehicle;

(c) a lamp or reflector which can be deflected to the side by the movement of, although not necessarily through the same angle as, the front wheel or wheels of the vehicle when turned for the purpose of steering the vehicle;

(d) a headlamp or front fog lamp which can be wholly or partially retracted or concealed;

(e) a direction indicator fitted to a motor vehicle first used before 1st April 1986;

(f) a work lamp;

(g) a warning beacon;

(h) an amber pedal reflex reflector; or

(i) reflex reflective material or a reflex reflector of any colour which is fitted so as to reflect light primarily to one or both sides of the vehicle and is attached to or incorporated in any wheel or tyre of—

　　(i) a pedal cycle and any sidecar attached to it;

　　(ii) a solo motor bicycle or motor bicycle combination; or

　　(iii) an invalid carriage.

13. Lamps to show a steady light

(1) Save as provided in paragraph (2), no person shall use, or cause or permit to be used, on a road any vehicle which is fitted with a lamp which emits a flashing light.

(2) Paragraph (1) does not apply in respect of—

(a) a direction indicator;

(b) a headlamp being flashed manually to signal the presence of the vehicle to which it is fitted;

(c) a warning beacon or special warning lamp;

(d) a lamp or illuminated sign fitted to a vehicle used for police purposes; or

(e) a green warning lamp used as an anti-lock brake indicator.

14. Filament lamps

No person shall use, or cause or permit to be used, on a road any motor vehicle first used on or after 1st April 1986 or any trailer manufactured on or after 1st October 1985, equipped with any lamp of a type that is required by any Schedule to these Regulations to be marked with an approval mark, unless every such lamp is fitted with a filament lamp referred to in the Designation of Approval Marks Regulations in—

(1) Regulation 4 and Schedule 2, items 2 or 2A, 8, 20, 37 or 37A; or

(2) Regulation 5 and Schedule 4, item 18.

15. Restrictions on fitting of warning beacons, special warning lamps and similar devices

(1) Save as provided in Regulation 11, no person shall use, or cause or permit to be used, on a road any vehicle which is fitted with—

(a) a warning beacon or a special warning lamp, or

(*b*) a device which resembles a warning beacon or a special warning lamp.

(2) The provisions of paragraph (1) apply in respect of a device, warning beacon or special warning lamp whether the same is in working order or not.

16. Obligatory lamps, reflectors, rear markings and devices

(1) Save as provided in the foregoing provisions of these Regulations and in paragraph (2), no person shall use, or cause or permit to be used, on a road any vehicle of a class specified in an item in column 2 of Schedule 1 unless it is equipped with lamps, reflectors, rear markings and devices which—

(*a*) are of a type specified in that item in column 3 of that Schedule, and

(*b*) comply with the relevant installation and performance requirements referred to in that item in column 4 of that Schedule.

(2) The requirements specified in paragraph (1) do not apply in respect of a lamp, reflector, rear marking or device of a type specified in an item in column 3 of Schedule 1 in the case of a vehicle specified in column 5 of that Schedule, nor to any lamp, reflector, rear marking or device to which Regulation 17 applies.

(3) The requirements specified in paragraph (1) apply without prejudice to any additional requirement specified in Regulation 18 or 19.

17. Optional lamps, reflectors, rear markings and devices

No person shall use, or cause or permit to be used, on a road any vehicle which is fitted with an optional lamp, reflector, rear marking or device specified in an item in column 2 of the Table below unless it complies with the provisions or, in the case of a direction indicator, the relevant provisions, contained in the Schedule, or part of the Schedule, referred to in that item in column 3 of that Table.

TABLE

1	2	3
Item No	Type of lamp, reflector, rear marking or device	Schedule, or Part of Schedule containing provisions with which compliance is required
1	Front position lamp	Schedule 2, Part II
2	Dim-dip lighting device	Schedule 3, Part II
3	Dipped-beam headlamp	Schedule 4, Part II
4	Main-beam headlamp	Schedule 5, Part II
5	Front fog lamp	Schedule 6
6	Director indicator	Schedule 7, Parts I and II
7	Hazard warning signal device	Schedule 8, Part II
8	Side marker lamp	Schedule 9, Part II
9	Rear position lamp	Schedule 10, Part II
10	Rear fog lamp	Schedule 11, Part II
11	Stop lamp	Schedule 12, Part II
12	Reversing lamp	Schedule 13
13	Warning beacon	Schedule 15
14	Side reflex reflector	Schedule 16, Part II
15	Rear reflex reflector	Schedule 17, Part II
16	Rear marking	Schedule 18, Part II
17	Pedal reflex reflector	Schedule 19, Part II

18. Projecting trailers and vehicles carrying overhanging or projecting loads or equipment

(1) No person shall use, or cause or permit to be used, on a road in the circumstances mentioned in paragraph (2)—

(a) any trailer which forms part of a combination of vehicles which projects laterally beyond any preceding vehicle in the combination; or

(b) any vehicle or combination of vehicles which carries a load or equipment

in either case under the conditions specified in an item in column 2 of the Table below, unless the vehicle or combination of vehicles complies with the requirements specified in that item in column 3 of that Table.

TABLE *[ie table to reg 18(1)]*

1	2	3
Item No	Conditions	Requirements
1	A trailer which is not fitted with front position lamps and which projects laterally on any side so that the distance from the outermost part of the projection to the outermost part of the illuminated area of the obligatory front position lamp on that side fitted to any preceding vehicle in the combination exceeds 400 millimetres.	A lamp showing white light to the front shall be fitted to the trailer so that the outermost part of the illuminated area is not more than 400 millimetres from the outermost projection of the trailer. The installation and performance requirements relating to front position lamps do not apply to any such lamp.
2	A trailer which is not fitted with front position lamps and which carries a load or equipment which projects laterally on any side of the trailer so that the distance from the outermost projection of the load or equipment to the outermost part of the illuminated area of the obligatory front position lamp on that side fitted to any preceding vehicle in the combination exceeds 400 millimetres.	A lamp showing white light to the front shall be fitted to the trailer or the load or equipment so that the outermost part of the illuminated area is not more than 400 millimetres from the outermost projection of the load or equipment. The installation and performance requirements relating to front position lamps do not apply to any such lamp.
3	A vehicle which carries a load or equipment which projects laterally on any side of the vehicle so that the distance from the outermost part of the load or equipment to the outermost part of the illuminated area of the obligatory front or rear position lamp on that side exceeds 400 millimetres.	Either— (a) the obligatory front or rear position lamp shall be transferred from the vehicle to the load or equipment; or (b) an additional front or rear position lamp shall be fitted to the vehicle, load or equipment. All the installation, performance and maintenance requirements relating to front or rear position lamps shall in either case be complied with except that for the purpose of determining the lateral position of such lamps any reference to the vehicle shall be taken to include the load or equipment except special equipment on a vehicle fitted with a movable platform or the jib of any crane.

1	2	3
Item No	Conditions	Requirements
4	A vehicle which carries a load or equipment which projects beyond the rear of the vehicle or, in the case of a combination of vehicles, beyond the rear of the rearmost vehicle in the combination, more than— (*a*) 2 metres in the case of an agricultural vehicle or a vehicle carrying a fire escape; or (*b*) 1 metre in the case of any other vehicle.	An additional rear lamp capable of showing red light to the rear visible from a reasonable distance shall be fitted to the vehicle or the load in such a position that the distance between the lamp and the rearmost projection of the load or equipment does not exceed 2 metres in the case mentioned in sub-paragraph (*a*) in column 2 of this item or 1 metre in any other case. The installation and performance requirements relating to rear position lamps do not apply to any such additional lamp.
5	A vehicle which carries a load or equipment which obscures any obligatory lamp, reflector or rear marking.	Either— (*a*) the obligatory lamp, reflector or rear marking shall be transferred to a position on the vehicle, load or equipment where it is not obscured; or (*b*) an additional lamp, reflector or rear marking shall be fitted to the vehicle, load or equipment. All the installation, performance and maintenance requirements relating to obligatory lamps, reflectors or rear markings shall in either case be complied with.

(2) The circumstances referred to in paragraph (1) are—

(*a*) as regards item 5 in the Table, in so far as it relates to obligatory stop lamps and direction indicators, all circumstances; and

(*b*) as regards items 1 to 4 in the Table and item 5 in the Table, except in so far as it relates to obligatory stop lamps and direction indicators, the circumstances of hours of darkness and of seriously reduced visibility.

19. Additional side marker lamps

(1) Save as provided in paragraph (2), no person shall use, or cause or permit to be used, on a road during the hours of darkness, or in seriously reduced visibility during daytime hours, any vehicle or combination of vehicles of a type specified in an item in column 2 of the Table below unless each side of the vehicle or combination of vehicles is fitted with the side marker lamps specified in that item in column 3 and those lamps are kept lit.

TABLE *[ie table to reg 19(1)]*

1	2	3
Item No	Vehicle or combination of vehicles	Side marker lamps
1	A vehicle or a combination of vehicles the overall length of which (including any load) exceeds 18.3 metres.	(*a*) One lamp no part of the light-emitting surface of which is more than 9.15 metres from the foremost part of the vehicle or vehicles (in either case inclusive of any load);

1	2	3
Item No	Vehicle or combination of vehicles	Side marker lamps
		(b) One lamp no part of the light-emitting surface of which is more than 3.05 metres from the rearmost part of the vehicle or vehicles (in either case inclusive of any load); and (c) Such other lamps as are required to ensure that not more than 3.05 metres separates any part of the light-emitting surface of one lamp and any part of the light-emitting surface of the next lamp.
2	A combination of vehicles the overall length of which (including any load) exceeds 12.2 metres but does not exceed 18.3 metres and carrying a load supported by any two of the vehicles but not including a load carried by an articulated vehicle.	(a) One lamp no part of the light-emitting surface of which is forward of, or more than 1530 millimetres rearward of, the rearmost part of the drawing vehicle; (a) If the supported load extends more than 9.15 metres rearward of the rearmost part of the drawing vehicle, one lamp no part of the light-emitting surface of which is forward of, or more than 1530 millimetres rearward of, the centre of the length of the load.

(2) The requirements specified in paragraph (1) do not apply to—

(a) a combination of vehicles where any vehicle being drawn in that combination has broken down; or

(b) a vehicle (not being one of a combination of vehicles)—

    (i) having a special applicance or apparatus of a kind specified in Regulation 140(5) of the Construction and Use Regulations; or

    (ii) carrying a load of a kind specified in Regulation 140(6), (7) or (8) of those Regulations

if the conditions specified in paragraph 3 (which provides for the special marking of projections from vehicles) of Schedule 8 to those Regulations are complied with in relation to the special applicance or load as if the said conditions had been expressed in the said Regulation 140 to apply in the case of every special applicance or apparatus or load of a kind specified in paragraph (5), (6), (7) or (8) of that Regulation.

(3) Every side marker lamp fitted in accordance with this Regulation shall comply with Schedule 9.

PART III

REGULATIONS GOVERNING THE MAINTENANCE AND USE OF LAMPS, REFLECTORS, REAR MARKINGS AND DEVICES

20. Maintenance of lamps, reflectors, rear markings and devices

(1) Save as provided in paragraph (4), no person shall use, or cause or permit to be used, on a road any vehicles unless every front position lamp, rear position lamp, headlamp, rear registration plate lamp, side marker lamp, rear fog lamp, reflex reflector and rear marking with which it is required by these Regulations to be fitted and

every stop lamp and direction indicator with which it is fitted is clean and in good working order.

(2) No person shall use, or cause or permit to be used, on a road any vehicle which is required by these Regulations to be fitted with a hazard warning signal device unless that device is in good working order.

(3) No person shall use, or cause or permit to be used, on a road any vehicle fitted with a dipped-beam headlamp, front fog lamp, rear fog lamp or reversing lamp, whether or not the lamp is required by these Regulations to be fitted to the vehicle, unless the lamp is maintained so that its aim will not cause undue dazzle or inconvenience to other persons using the road.

(4) The provisions of paragraph (1) do not apply in respect of—

(a) a rear fog lamp on a vehicle which is part of a combination of vehicles any part of which is not required by these Regulations to be fitted with a rear fog lamp;

(b) a rear fog lamp on a motor vehicle drawing a trailer;

(c) a defective lamp or reflector fitted to a vehicle in use on a road during daytime hours if such a lamp or reflector became defective during the journey which is in progress or if arrangements have been made to remedy the defect with all reasonable expedition; or

(d) a lamp, reflector or rear marking which, during daytime hours, is fitted to a combat vehicle.

21. Requirements about the use of front and rear position lamps, rear registration plate lamps and side marker lamps

(1) Save as provided in paragraphs (2) and (3), no person shall—

(a) use, or cause or permit to be used, on a road any vehicle during the hours of darkness or any vehicle which is in motion during daytime hours in seriously reduced visibility; or

(b) allow to remain at rest, or cause or permit to be allowed to remain at rest, on a road any vehicle during the hours of darkness

unless every front position lamp, rear position lamp, rear registration plate lamp and side marker lamp with which the vehicle is required by these Regulations to be fitted is kept lit and, in the case of—

(i) a motor bicycle combination which is only fitted with a front position lamp on the sidecar, or a trailer to the front of which no other vehicle is attached and which is not required to be fitted with front position lamps, a pair of front position lamps is fitted and kept lit; or

(ii) a solo motor bicycle which is not required to be fitted with a front position lamp, a front position lamp is fitted and kept lit.

(2) The provisions of paragraph (1) do not apply in respect of a vehicle of a class specified in paragraph (4) which is parked on a road on which a speed limit of 30 miles per hour or less is in force and the vehicle is parked—

(a) in a parking place for which provision is made under [section 6], or which is authorised under [section 32] or designated under [section 45, of the Road Traffic Regulation Act 1984], or which is set apart as a parking place under some other enactment or instrument and the vehicle is parked in a manner which does not contravene the provision of any enactment or instrument relating to the parking place; or

(b) in a lay-by—

(i) the limits of which are indicated by a traffic sign consisting of the road marking shown in diagram 1010 in Schedule 2 of the Traffic Signs Regulations and General Directions 1981 *[SI 1981 No 859]*; or

(ii) the surface of which is of a colour or texture which is different from that of the part of the carriageway of the road used primarily by through traffic; or

(iii) the limits of which are indicated by a continuous strip of surface of a different colour or texture from that of the surface of the remainder of the carriageway of the road; or

(*c*) elsewhere than in such a parking place or lay-by if—

  (i) the vehicle is parked on—

    (A) a road on which the driving of vehicles otherwise than in one direction is prohibited at all times and its left or near side is as close as may be and parallel to the left-hand edge of the carriageway or its right or off side is as close as may be and parallel to the right-hand edge of the carriageway, or

    (B) a road on which such a prohibition does not exist and its left or near side is as close as may be and parallel to the edge of the carriageway, and

  (ii) no part of the vehicle is less than 10 metres from the junction of any part of the carriageway of any road with the carriageway of the road on which it is parked whether that junction is on the same side of the road as that on which the vehicle is parked or not.

(3) The provisions of paragraph (1) do not apply in respect of—

(*a*) a solo motor bicycle or a pedal cycle being pushed along the left-hand edge of a carriageway;

(*b*) a pedal cycle waiting to proceed provided it is kept to the left-hand or near side edge of a carriageway; or

(*c*) a vehicle which is parked in an area outlined by lamps or traffic signs so as to prevent the presence of the vehicle, its load or equipment being a danger to persons using the road.

(4) The classes of vehicles referred to in paragraph (2) are—

(*a*) a motor vehicle being a goods vehicle the unladen weight of which does not exceed 1525 kilograms;

(*b*) a passenger vehicle other than a large passenger-carrying vehicle;

(*c*) an invalid carriage; and

(*d*) a motor cycle or a pedal cycle in either case with or without a sidecar.

Provided that this paragraph does not include—

  (i) a vehicle to which a trailer is attached; or

  (ii) a vehicle or a vehicle carrying a load which in either case is required to be fitted with lamps by Regulation 18.

[Regulation 21 is printed as amended by the Road Traffic Regulation Act 1984, s 144 (1), and Sched 10, para 2.]

22. Requirements about the use of headlamps and front fog lamps

(1) Save as provided in paragraph (2), no person shall use, or cause or permit to be used, on a road a vehicle which is fitted with obligatory dipped-beam headlamps unless every such lamp is kept lit—

(*a*) during the hours of darkness, except on a road which is a restricted road for the purposes of [section 81 of the Road Traffic Regulation Act 1984] by virtue of a system of street lighting when it is lit; and

(*b*) in seriously reduced visibility.

(2) The provisions of paragraph (1) do not apply—

(*a*) in the case of a motor vehicle fitted with one obligatory dipped-beam headlamp or a solo motor bicycle or motor bicycle combination fitted with a pair of obligatory dipped-beam headlamps, if a main-beam headlamp or a front fog lamp, is kept lit;

(*b*) in the case of a motor vehicle, other than a solo motor bicycle or motor bicycle combination, fitted with a pair of obligatory dipped-beam headlamps, if—

    (i) a pair of main-beam headlamps is kept lit; or

    (ii) a pair of front fog lamps which is so fitted that the outermost part of the illuminated area of each lamp in the pair is not more than 400 millimetres from the outer edge of the vehicle is kept lit;

(*c*) to a vehicle being drawn by another vehicle;

(*d*) to a vehicle while being used to propel a snow plough; or

(*e*) to a vehicle which is parked.

(3) No light provided by a dim-dip lighting device shall be deemed to satisfy the requirements of this Regulation.

[Regulation 22 is printed as amended by the Road Traffic Regulation Act 1984, s 144 (1), and Sched 10, para 2.]

23. Restrictions on the use of lamps other than those to which Regulation 21 refers

No person shall use, or cause or permit to be used, on a road any vehicle on which any lamp, hazard warning signal device or warning beacon of a type specified in an item in column 2 of the Table below is used in a manner specified in column 3 in that item.

TABLE

1	2	3
Item No	Type of lamp, hazard warning signal device or warning beacon	Manner of use prohibited
1	Headlamp	(*a*) Used so as to cause undue dazzle or discomfort to other persons using the road. (*b*) Used so as to be lit when a vehicle is parked.
2	Front fog lamp	(*a*) Used so as to cause undue dazzle or discomfort to other persons using the road. (*b*) Used so as to be lit at any time other than in conditions of seriously reduced visibility. (*c*) Used so as to be lit when a vehicle is parked.
3	Rear fog lamp	(*a*) Used so as to cause undue dazzle or discomfort to the driver of a following vehicle.

1	2	3
Item No	Type of lamp, hazard warning signal device or warning beacon	Manner of use prohibited
		(*b*) Used so as to be lit at any time other than in conditions of seriously reduced visibility. (*c*) Save in the case of an emergency vehicle, used so as to be lit when a vehicle is parked.
4	Reversing lamp	Used so as to be lit except for the purpose of reversing the vehicle.
5	Hazard warning signal device	Used other than for the purpose of— (i) warning persons using the road of a temporary obstruction when the vehicle is at rest; or (ii) in the case of a large passenger-carrying vehicle, for the purpose of summoning assistance for the driver or any person acting as a conductor or inspector on the vehicle.
6	Warning beacon emitting blue light and special warning lamp	Used so as to be lit except— (i) at the scene of an emergency; or (ii) when it is necessary or desirable either to indicate to persons using the road the urgency of the purpose for which the vehicle is being used, or to warn persons of the presence of the vehicle or a hazard on the road.
7	Warning beacon emitting amber light	Used so as to be lit except— (i) at the scene of an emergency; (ii) when it is necessary or desirable to warn persons of the presence of the vehicle; and (iii) in the case of a breakdown vehicle, while it is being used in connection with, and in the immediate vicinity of, an accident or breakdown, or while it is being used to draw a broken-down vehicle.
8	Warning beacon emitting green light	Used so as to be lit except whilst occupied by a medical practitioner registered by the General Medical Council (whether with full, provisional or limited registration) and used for the purposes of an emergency.
9	Warning beacon emitting yellow light	Used so as to be lit on a road.
10	Work lamp	(*a*) Used so as to cause undue dazzle or discomfort to the driver of any vehicle. (*b*) Used so as to be lit except for the purpose of illuminating a working area, accident, breakdown or works in the vicinity of the vehicle.
11	Any other lamp	Used so as to cause undue dazzle or discomfort to other persons using the road.

PART IV

TESTING AND INSPECTION OF LIGHTING EQUIPMENT AND REFLECTORS

24. Testing and inspection of lighting equipment and reflectors

The provisions of Regulation 145 of the Construction and Use Regulations apply in respect of lighting equipment and reflectors with which a vehicle is required by these Regulations to be fitted in the same way as they apply in respect of brakes, silencers, steering gear and tyres.

SCHEDULE 1

(see Regulation 16)

OBLIGATORY LAMPS, REFLECTORS, REAR MARKINGS AND DEVICES

1	2	3	4	5
Item No	Class of Vehicle	Type of lamp, reflector, rear marking or device	Schedule in which relevant installation and performance requirements are specified	Exceptions
1	Motor vehicle having three or more wheels not being a vehicle to which any other item in this Schedule applies	Front position lamp	Schedule 2: Part I	None.
		Dim-dip lighting device	Schedule 3: Part I	A vehicle having a maximum speed not exceeding 25 miles per hour;
				A vehicle first used before 1st April 1987;
				A home forces' vehicle
		Dipped-beam headlamp	Schedule 4: Part I	A vehicle having a maximum speed not exceeding 15 miles per hour;
				A vehicle first used before 1st April 1986 being an agricultural vehicle or a works truck;
				A vehicle first used before 1st January 1931.

Main-beam headlamp	Schedule 5: Part I	A vehicle having a maximum speed not exceeding 25 miles per hour;
		A vehicle first used before 1st April 1986 being an agricultural vehicle or a works truck;
		A vehicle first used before 1st January 1931.
Direction indicator	Schedule 7: Parts I and II	A vehicle having a maximum speed not exceeding 15 miles per hour;
		An agricultural vehicle having an unladen weight not exceeding 255 kilograms;
		A vehicle first used before 1st April 1986 being an agricultural vehicle, an industrial tractor or a works truck;
		A vehicle first used before 1st January 1936.
Hazard warning signal device	Schedule 8: Part I	A vehicle not required to be fitted with direction indicators;
		A vehicle first used before 1st April 1986.
Rear position lamp	Schedule 10: Part I	None.

1	2	3	4	5
Item No	Class of Vehicle	Type of lamp, reflector, rear marking or device	Schedule in which relevant installation and performance requirements are specified	Exceptions
		Rear fog lamp	Schedule 11: Part I	A vehicle having a maximum speed not exceeding 25 miles per hour; A vehicle first used before 1st April 1986 being an agricultural vehicle or a works truck; A vehicle first used before 1st April 1980; A vehicle having an overall width which does not exceed 1300 millimetres.
		Stop lamp	Schedule 12: Part I	A vehicle having a maximum speed not exceeding 25 miles per hour; A vehicle first used before 1st April 1986 being an agricultural vehicle or a works truck; A vehicle first used before 1st January 1936.
		Rear registration plate lamp	Schedule 14	A vehicle not required to be fitted with a rear registration plate.

Side reflex reflector	Schedule 16: Part I	A vehicle having a maximum speed not exceeding 25 miles per hour; A goods vehicle— (a) first used on or after 1st April 1986 the overall length of which does not exceed 6 metres; or (b) first used before 1st April 1986 the overall length of which does not exceed 8 metres; A passenger vehicle; An incomplete vehicle proceeding to a works for completion or to a place where it is to be stored or displayed for sale; A vehicle primarily constructed for moving excavated material and being used by virtue of an Order under Section 42 of the Act; A mobile crane or engineering plant.
Rear reflex reflector	Schedule 17: Part I	None
Rear marking	Schedule 18: Part I	A vehicle having a maximum speed not exceeding 25 miles per hour;

1	2	3	4	5
Item No	Class of Vehicle	Type of lamp, reflector, rear marking or device	Schedule in which relevant installation and performance requirements are specified	Exceptions
				A vehicle first used before 1st August 1982 the unladen weight of which does not exceed 3050 kilograms; A vehicle the maximum gross weight of which does not exceed 7500 kilograms; A passenger vehicle not being an articulated bus; A tractive unit for an articulated vehicle; An incomplete vehicle proceeding to a works for completion or to a place where it is to be stored or displayed for sale; A vehicle first used before 1st April 1986 being an agricultural vehicle, a works truck or engineering plant; A vehicle first used before 1st January 1940;

				Exceptions
2	Solo motor bicycle and motor bicycle combination	Front position lamp	Schedule 2: Part I	A home forces' vehicle; A vehicle constructed or adapted for— (a) fire fighting or fire salvage; (b) servicing or controlling aircraft; (c) heating and dispensing tar or other material for the construction or maintenance of roads; or (d) transporting two or more vehicles or vehicle bodies or two or more boats.
				A solo motor bicycle fitted with a headlamp.
		Dipped-beam headlamp	Schedule 4: Part I	A vehicle first used before 1st January 1931.
		Main-beam headlamp	Schedule 5: Part I	A vehicle having a maximum speed not exceeding 25 miles per hour; A vehicle first used before 1st January 1972 and having an engine with a capacity of less than 50 cubic centimetres; A vehicle first used before 1st January 1931.

1	2	3	4	5
Item No	Class of Vehicle	Type of lamp, reflector, rear marking or device	Schedule in which relevant installation and performance requirements are specified	Exceptions
		Direction indicator	Schedule 7: Parts I and II	A vehicle having a maximum speed not exceeding 25 miles per hour; A vehicle first used before 1st April 1986; A vehicle which can carry only one person or which, in the case of a motor bicycle combination, can carry only the rider and one passenger in the sidecar and which is constructed or adapted primarily for use off roads (whether by reason of its tyres, suspension, ground clearance or otherwise).
		Rear position lamp	Schedule 10: Part I	None.
		Stop lamp	Schedule 12: Part I	A vehicle having a maximum speed not exceeding 25 miles per hour; A vehicle first used before 1st April 1986 and having an engine capacity of less than 50 cubic centimetres;

		Rear registration plate lamp	Schedule 14	A vehicle first used before 1st January 1936. A vehicle not required to be fitted with a rear registration plate.
		Rear reflex reflector	Schedule 17: Part I	None.
3	Pedal cycle	Front position lamp	Schedule 2: Part I	None.
		Rear position lamp	Schedule 10: Part I	None.
		Rear reflex reflector	Schedule 17: Part I	None.
		Pedal reflex reflector	Schedule 19: Part I	A pedal cycle manufactured before 1st October 1985.
4	Pedestrian-controlled vehicle, horse-drawn vehicle and track-laying vehicle	Front position lamp	Schedule 2: Part I	None.
		Rear position lamp	Schedule 10: Part I	None.
		Rear reflex reflector	Schedule 17: Part I	None.
5	Vehicle drawn or propelled by hand	Front position lamp	Schedule 2: Part I	None.
		Rear position lamp	Schedule 10: Part I	A vehicle fitted with a rear reflex reflector.
		Rear reflex reflector	Schedule 17: Part I	A vehicle fitted with a rear position lamp.
6	Trailer drawn by a motor vehicle	Front position lamp	Schedule 2: Part I	A trailer with an overall width not exceeding 1600 millimetres;

1	2	3	4	5
Item No	Class of Vehicle	Type of lamp, reflector, rear marking or device	Schedule in which relevant installation and performance requirements are specified	Exceptions
				A trailer manufactured before 1st October 1985 the overall length of which, excluding any drawbar and any fitting for its attachment, does not exceed 2300 millimetres.
		Direction indicator	Schedule 7: Parts I and II	A trailer manufactured before 1st September 1965; An agricultural vehicle or a works trailer.
		Side marker lamp	Schedule 9: Part I	A trailer the overall length of which, excluding any drawbar and any fitting for its attachment, does not exceed 9.15 metres.
		Rear position lamp	Schedule 10: Part I	None.
		Rear fog lamp	Schedule 11: Part I	A trailer manufactured before 1st April 1980; A trailer the overall width of which does not exceed 1300 millimetres;

		An agricultural vehicle or a works trailer.
Stop lamp	Schedule 12: Part I	An agricultural vehicle or a works trailer.
Rear registration plate lamp	Schedule 14	A trailer not required to be fitted with a rear registration plate.
Side reflex reflector	Schedule 16: Part I	A trailer the overall length of which, excluding any draw-bar, does not exceed 5 metres;
		An incomplete trailer proceeding to a works for completion or to a place where it is to be stored or displayed for sale;
		Engineering plant;
		A trailer primarily constructed for moving excavated material and which is being used by virtue of an order under section 42 of the Act.
Rear reflex reflector	Schedule 17: Part I	None.
Rear marking	Schedule 18: Part I	A trailer manufactured before 1st August 1982 the unladen weight of which does not exceed 1020 kilograms;

1	2	3	4	5
Item No	Class of Vehicle	Type of lamp, reflector, rear marking or device	Schedule in which relevant installation and performance requirements are specified	Exceptions
				A trailer the maximum gross weight of which does not exceed 3500 kilograms; An incomplete trailer proceeding to a works for completion or to a place where it is to be stored or displayed for sale; An agricultural vehicle, a works trailer or engineering plant; A trailer drawn by a large passenger-carrying vehicle; A home forces' vehicle; A trailer constructed or adapted for— (a) fire fighting or fire salvage; (b) servicing or controlling aircraft; (c) heating and dispensing tar or other material for the construction or maintenance of roads;

		(d) carrying asphalt or macadam, in each case being mixing or drying plant; or (e) transporting two or more vehicles or vehicle bodies or two or more boats.	None. None.
		Schedule 10: Part I Schedule 17: Part I	
		Rear position lamp Rear reflex reflector	
7	Trailer drawn by a pedal cycle		

SCHEDULE 2

(See Regulations 16 and 17)

PART I

FRONT POSITION LAMPS TO WHICH REGULATION 16 APPLIES

1. Number—

(a) Any vehicle not covered by sub-paragraph (b), (c), (d), (e) or (f):   Two

(b) A pedal cycle with less than four wheels and without a sidecar: One

(c) A solo motor bicycle: One

(d) A motor bicycle combination with a headlamp on the motor bicycle: One, on the sidecar

(e) A vehicle drawn or propelled by hand which has an overall width including any load not exceeding 1250 millimetres: One

(f) An invalid carriage: One

2. Position:

(a) Longitudinal: No requirement

(b) Lateral—
  (i) Where two front position lamps are required to be fitted—
    (A) Maximum distance from the side of the vehicle—
      (1) A motor vehicle first used on or after 1st April 1986:   400 millimetres
      (2) A trailer manufactured on or after 1st October 1985:   150 millimetres
      (3) Any other vehicle manufactured on or after 1st October 1985:   400 millimetres
      (4) A motor vehicle first used before 1st April 1986 and any other vehicle manufactured before 1st October 1985:   510 millimetres
    (B) Minimum separation distance between front position lamps: No requirement
  (ii) Where one front position lamp is required to be fitted—
    (A) A sidecar forming part of a motor bicycle combination: On the centre-line of the sidecar or on the side of the sidecar furthest from the motor bicycle
    (B) Any other vehicle: On the centre-line or offside of the vehicle

(c) Vertical—
   (i) Maximum height above the ground—

(A) Any vehicle not covered by sub-paragraph (B), (C) or (D):	1500 millimetres or, if the structure of the vehicle makes this impracticable, 2100 millimetres
(B) A motor vehicle first used before 1st April 1986 and a trailer manufactured before 1st October 1985;	2300 millimetres
(C) A motor vehicle, first used on or after 1st April 1986, having a maximum speed not exceeding 25 miles per hour;	2100 millimetres
(D) A large passenger-carrying vehicle and a road clearance vehicle:	No requirement
(ii) Minimum height above the ground:	No requirement

3. Angles of visibility—

(a) A motor vehicle (not being a motor bicycle combination or an agricultural vehicle) first used on or after 1st April 1986 and a trailer manufactured on or after 1st October 1985—

(i) Horizontal—	
(A) Where one lamp is required to be fitted:	80° to the left and to the right
(B) Where two lamps are required to be fitted:	Either 80° outwards and 45° inwards or 45° outwards and 80° inwards
(ii) Vertical—	
(A) Any case not covered by sub-paragraph (B):	15° above and below the horizontal
(B) Where the highest part of the illuminated area of the lamp is less than 750 millimetres above the ground:	15° above and 5° below the horizontal
(b) Any other vehicle:	Visible to the front

4. Markings—

(a) A motor vehicle (other than a solo motor bicycle or a motor bicycle combination) first used on or after 1st January 1972 and a trailer manufactured on or after 1st October 1985:	An approval mark
(b) A solo motor bicycle and a motor bicycle combination in either case first used on or after 1st April 1986:	An approval mark
(c) Any other vehicle:	No requirement

5. Size of illuminated area:	No requirement
6. Colour:	White or, if incorporated in a headlamp which is capable of emitting only a yellow light, yellow

7. Wattage: No requirement

8. Intensity—
 (*a*) A front position lamp bearing any of the mark-   No requirement
      ings mentioned in paragraph 4:
 (*b*) Any other front position lamp: Visible from a reasonable
                                                             distance

9. Electrical connections: No requirement

10. Tell-tale: No requirement

11. Other requirements—
 (*a*) Except in the case of a vehicle covered by sub-paragraph (*b*), where two front
      position lamps are required to be fitted they shall form a pair.
 (*b*) In the case of a trailer manufactured before 1st October 1985 and a motor
      bicycle combination, where two front position lamps are required to be fitted
      they shall be fitted on each side of the longitudinal axis of the vehicle.

12. Definitions—

In this Schedule—

 'approval mark' means—
    (*a*) in relation to a solo motor bicycle or a motor bicycle combination, a
         marking designated as an approval mark by Regulation 4 of the Designa-
         tion of Approval Marks Regulations and shown at item 50A of Schedule 2
         to those Regulations, and
    (*b*) in relation to any other motor vehicle or any trailer, either—
         (i) a marking designated as an approval mark by Regulation 5 of the
             Designation of Approval Marks Regulations and shown at item 5
             of Schedule 4 to those Regulations, or
         (ii) a marking designated as an approval mark by Regulation 4 of the
             Designation of Approval Marks Regulations and shown at item 7
             of Schedule 2 to those Regulations.

PART II

FRONT POSITION LAMPS TO WHICH REGULATION 17 APPLIES

Any number may be fitted, and the only requirement prescribed by these Regulations
in respect of any which are fitted is that specified in paragraph 6 as regards front
position lamps to which Regulation 16 applies.

SCHEDULE 3

(See Regulations 16 and 17)

PART I

DIM-DIP LIGHTING DEVICES TO WHICH REGULATION 16 APPLIES

1. Every dim-dip lighting device shall whenever the obligatory front lamps of the
vehicle are switched on and either—

    (i) the engine of the vehicle is running, or

    (ii) the key or devices which control the starting or stopping of the engine are in the normal position for driving the vehicle

automatically supply sufficient current to cause to be emitted either—

    (A) lights as specified in paragraph 2 below, or

    (B) lights as specified in paragraph 3 below.

2. The lights referred to in paragraph 1(A) above are a light to the front from the dipped-beam filament of each of a pair of obligatory headlamps, each such light having, so far as is reasonably practicable, an intensity—

    (*a*) in the case of a halogen filament lamp, of 10 per cent of the normal intensity of the dipped beam, or

    (*b*) in the case of any other type of filament lamp, of 15 per cent of the normal intensity of the dipped beam.

3. The lights referred to in paragraph 1(B) above are a white light to the front from each lamp of any pair of front lamps each of which has an illuminated area of not less than 150 square centimetres and which are fitted in a position in which obligatory headlamps emitting a dipped beam may lawfully be fitted, each such light having an intensity of not less than 200 candelas, measured from directly in front of the centre of the lamp in a direction parallel to the longitudinal axis of the vehicle, and not more than 400 candelas in any direction.

PART II

Dim-Dip Lighting Devices to which Regulation 17 applies

The requirements prescribed by these Regulations in respect of a dim-dip lighting device which is fitted are all those specified in this Schedule as regards a dim-dip lighting device to which Regulation 16 applies.

SCHEDULE 4

(See Regulations 16 and 17)

PART I

Dipped-beam Headlamps to which Regulation 16 applies

1. Number—

    (*a*) Any vehicle not covered by sub-paragraph (*b*),   Two
         (*c*), (*d*) or (*e*):

    (*b*) A solo motor bicycle and a motor bicycle com-   One
         bination:

    (*c*) A motor vehicle with three wheels, other than a   One
         motor bicycle combination, first used before 1st
         January 1972:

(*d*) A motor vehicle with three wheels, other than a   One
motor bicycle combination, first used on or
after 1st January 1972 and which has an
unladen weight of not more than 400 kilogrammes and an overall width of not more
than 1300 millimetres:

(*e*) A large passenger-carrying vehicle first used   One
before 1st October 1969:

2. Position—

   (*a*) Longitudinal: No requirement

   (*b*) Lateral—
     (i) Where two dipped-beam headlamps are
        required to be fitted—
        (A) Maximum distance from the side of
           the vehicle—
           (1) Any vehicle not covered by sub-   400 millimetres
               paragraph (2) or (3):
           (2) A vehicle first used before 1st   No requirement
               January 1972:
           (3) An agricultural vehicle, engineering   No requirement
               plant and an industrial tractor:
        (B) Minimum   separation   distance   No requirement
           between a pair of dipped-beam
           headlamps:
     (ii) Where one dipped-beam headlamp is
        required to be fitted—
        (A) Any vehicle not covered by sub-   (i) On the centre-line of the
           paragraph (B):   motor vehicle (disregarding
                                         any sidecar forming part of
                                         a motor bicycle combi-
                                         nation), or
                                         (ii) At any distance from
                                         the side of the motor vehicle
                                         (disregarding any sidecar
                                         forming part of a motor
                                         bicycle combination) pro-
                                         vided that a duplicate lamp
                                         is fitted on the other side so
                                         that together they form a
                                         matched pair. In such a
                                         case, both lamps shall be
                                         regarded   as   obligatory
                                         lamps.
        (B) A large passenger-carrying vehicle   No requirement
           first used before 1st October 1969:

   (*c*) Vertical—
     (i) Maximum height above the ground—
        (A) Any vehicle not covered by sub-   1200 millimetres
           paragraph (B):

(B) A vehicle first used before 1st January 1952, an agricultural vehicle, a road clearance vehicle, an aerodrome fire tender, an aerodrome runway sweeper, an industrial tractor, engineering plant and a home forces' vehicle:	No requirement
(ii) Minimum height above the ground—	
(A) Any vehicle not covered by sub-paragraph (B):	500 millimetres
(B) A vehicle first used before 1st January 1956:	No requirement

3. Angles of visibility: No requirement

4. Markings—

(a) Any vehicle not covered by sub-paragraph (b), (c) or (d):	An approval mark or a British Standard mark
(b) A motor vehicle first used before 1st April 1986:	No requirement
(c) A three-wheeled motor vehicle, not being a motor bicycle combination, first used on or after 1st April 1986 and having a maximum speed not exceeding 50 miles per hour:	No requirement
(d) A solo motor bicycle and a motor bicycle combination:	No requirement

5. Size of illuminated area: No requirement

6. Colour: White or yellow

7. Wattage—

(a) A motor vehicle with four or more wheels first used on or after 1st April 1986:	No requirement
(b) A three-wheeled motor vehicle, not being a motor bicycle combination, first used on or after 1st April 1986—	
(i) having a maximum speed not exceeding 50 miles per hour:	24 watts minimum
(ii) having a maximum speed exceeding 50 miles per hour:	No requirement
(c) A motor vehicle with four or more wheels first used before 1st April 1986:	30 watts minimum
(d) A three-wheeled motor vehicle, not being a motor bicycle combination, first used before 1st April 1986:	24 watts minimum
(e) A solo motor bicycle and a motor bicycle combination—	
(i) having an engine not exceeding 250 cubic centimetres and a maximum speed not exceeding 25 miles per hour:	10 watts minimum

(ii) having an engine not exceeding 250   15 watts minimum
cubic centimetres and a maximum speed
exceeding 25 miles per hour:

(iii) having an engine exceeding 250 cubic   24 watts minimum
centimetres:

8. Intensity: No requirement

9. Electrical connections: No requirement

10. Tell-tale: No requirement

11. Other requirements—

(a) Every dipped-beam headlamp shall be so constructed that the direction of the beam of light emitted therefrom can be adjusted whilst the vehicle is stationary.

(b) Where two dipped-beam headlamps are required to be fitted, they shall form a matched pair and shall be capable of being switched on and off simultaneously and not otherwise.

12. Definitions—

In this Schedule—

'approval mark' means either—

(a) a marking designated as an approval mark by Regulation 5 of the Designation of Approval Marks Regulations and shown at item 12 or 13 or 14 or 16 or, in the case of a vehicle having a maximum speed not exceeding 25 miles per hour, 27 or 28 of Schedule 4 to those Regulations, or

(b) a marking designated as an approved mark by Regulation 4 of the Designation of Approval Marks Regulations and shown at item 1A or 1B or 1C or 1E or 5A or 5B or 5C or 5E or 8C or 8E or 8F or 8G or 8H or 8K or 8L or 20C or 20D or 20E or 20F or 20G or 20H or 20K or 20L or 31A or 31C or, in the case of a vehicle having a maximum speed not exceeding 25 miles per hour, 1H or 1I or 5H or 5I of Schedule 2 to those Regulations; and

'British Standard mark' means the specification for sealed beam headlamps published by the British Standards Institution under the reference BS AU 40: Part 4a: 1966 as amended by Amendment AMD 2188 published in December 1976, namely 'B.S. AU 40'.

PART II

DIPPED-BEAM HEADLAMPS TO WHICH REGULATION 17 APPLIES

Any number may be fitted, and the only requirements prescribed by these Regulations in respect of any which are fitted are those specified in paragraphs 2(c), 6 and 11(a) as regards dipped-beam headlamps to which Regulation 16 applies.

SCHEDULE 5

(See Regulations 16 and 17)

PART I

MAIN-BEAM HEADLAMPS TO WHICH REGULATION 16 APPLIES

1. Number—

(*a*)	Any vehicle not covered by sub-paragraph (*b*), (*c*) or (*d*):	Two
(*b*)	A solo motor bicycle and motor bicycle combination:	One
(*c*)	A motor vehicle with three wheels, other than a motor bicycle combination, first used before 1st January 1972:	One
(*d*)	A motor vehicle with three wheels, other than a motor bicycle combination, first used on or after 1st January 1972 and which has an unladen weight of not more than 400 kilogrammes and an overall width of not more than 1300 millimetres:	One

2. Position—

(*a*) Longitudinal — No requirement

(*b*) Lateral—

    (i) Where two main-beam headlamps are required to be fitted—

        (A) Maximum distance from the side of the vehicle: — The outer edges of the illuminated areas must in no case be closer to the side of the vehicle than the outer edges of the illuminated areas of the obligatory dipped-beam headlamps.

        (B) Maximum separation distance between a pair of main-beam headlamps: — No requirement

    (ii) Where one main-beam headlamp is required to be fitted: — (i) On the centre-line of the motor vehicle (disregarding any sidecar forming part of a motor bicycle combination), or
(ii) At any distance from the side of the vehicle (disregarding any sidecar forming part of a motor bicycle combination) provided that a duplicate lamp is fitted on the other side so that together they form a matched pair. In such a

	case, both lamps shall be treated as obligatory lamps.
(c) Vertical:	No requirement
3. Angles of visibility:	No requirement
4. Markings—	
(a) Any vehicle not covered by sub-paragraph (b), (c) or (d):	An approval mark or a British Standard mark
(b) A motor vehicle first used before 1st April 1986:	No requirement
(c) A three-wheeled motor vehicle, not being a motor bicycle combination, first used on or after 1st April 1986 and having a maximum speed not exceeding 50 miles per hour:	No requirement
(d) A solo motor bicycle and a motor bicycle combination:	No requirement
5. Size of illuminated area:	No requirement
6. Colour:	White or yellow
7. Wattage—	
(a) A motor vehicle, other than a solo motor bicycle or motor bicycle combination, first used on or after 1st April 1986:	No requirement
(b) A motor vehicle, other than a solo motor bicycle or a motor bicycle combination, first used before 1st April 1986:	30 watts minimum
(c) A solo motor bicycle and a motor bicycle combination—	
(i) having an engine not exceeding 250 cubic centimetres:	15 watts minimum
(ii) having an engine exceeding 250 cubic centimetres:	30 watts minimum
8. Intensity:	No requirement
9. Electrical connections:	Every main-beam headlamp shall be so constructed that the light emitted therefrom—
	(a) can be deflected at the will of the driver to become a dipped beam, or
	(b) can be extinguished by the operation of a device which at the same time either—

(i) causes the lamp to emit a dipped beam, or

(ii) causes another lamp to emit a dipped beam.

10. Tell-tale—

(*a*) Any vehicle not covered by sub-paragraph (*b*): A circuit-closed tell-tale shall be fitted

(*b*) A motor vehicle first used before 1st April 1986: No requirement

11. Other requirements—

(*a*) Every main-beam headlamp shall be so constructed that the direction of the beam of light emitted therefrom can be adjusted whilst the vehicle is stationary.

(*b*) Except in the case of a large passenger-carrying vehicle first used before 1st October 1969, where two main-beam headlamps are required to be fitted, they shall form a matched pair and shall be capable of being switched on and off simultaneously and not otherwise.

12. Definitions—

In this Schedule—

'approval mark' means—

(*a*) a marking designated as an approval mark by Regulation 5 of the Designation of Approval Marks Regulations and shown at item 12 or 13 or 17 of Schedule 4 to those Regulations; or

(*b*) a marking designated as an approval mark by Regulation 4 of the Designation of Approval Marks Regulations and shown at item 1A or 1B or 1F or 5A or 5B or 5F or 8C or 8D or 8E or 8F or 8M or 8N or 20C or 20D or 20E or 20F or 20M or 20N or 31A or 31D of Schedule 2 to those Regulations; and

'British Standard mark' means the specification for sealed beam headlamps published by the British Standards Institution under the reference BS AU 40: Part 4a: 1966 as amended by Amendment AMD 2188 published in December 1976, namely 'B.S. AU 40'.

PART II

Main-beam Headlamps to which Regulation 17 applies

Any number may be fitted, and the only requirements prescribed by these Regulations in respect of any which are fitted are those specified in paragraphs 6, 9 and 11(a) as regards main-beam headlamps to which Regulation 16 applies.

SCHEDULE 6

(See Regulation 17)

FRONT FOG LAMPS TO WHICH REGULATION 17 APPLIES

1. Number: No requirement

2. Position—

    (*a*) Longitudinal: No requirement

    (*b*) Lateral—

        (i) Where a pair of front fog lamps is used in conditions of seriously reduced visibility in place of the obligatory dipped beam headlamps—

            Maximum distance from side of vehicle: 400 millimetres

        (ii) In all other cases: No requirement

    (*c*) Vertical—

        (i) Maximum height above the ground—

            (A) Any vehicle not covered by sub-paragraph (B):   1200 millimetres

            (B) An agricultural vehicle, a road clearance vehicle, an aerodrome fire tender, an aerodrome runway sweeper, an industrial tractor, engineering plant and a home forces' vehicle: No requirement

        (ii) Minimum height above the ground: No requirement

3. Angles of visibility: No requirement

4. Markings—

    (*a*) A vehicle first used on or after 1st April 1986:   An approval mark

    (*b*) A vehicle first used before 1st April 1986:   No requirement

5. Size of illuminated area: No requirement

6. Colour: White or yellow

7. Wattage: No requirement

8. Intensity: No requirement

9. Electrical connections: No requirement

10. Tell-tale: No requirement

11. Definitions—

In this Schedule 'approval mark' means either—

    (*a*) a marking designated as an approval mark by Regulation 5 of the Designation of Approval Marks Regulations and shown at item 19 of Schedule 4 to those Regulations, or (*b*) a marking designated as an approval mark by Regulation 4 of the Designation of Approval Marks Regulations and shown at item 19 or 19A of Schedule 2 to those regulations.

SCHEDULE 7
(See Regulations 16 and 17)

DIRECTION INDICATORS TO WHICH EITHER REGULATION 16 OR 17 APPLIES

PART I
GENERAL REQUIREMENTS

1. Number—

The minimum and maximum number of direction indicators fitted on each side of a vehicle, whether required to be so fitted or not, is as follows—

(*a*) A motor vehicle with three or more wheels, not being a motor bicycle combination, first used on or after 1st April 1986:

A single front indicator (Category 1), one or two (but not more than two) rear indicators (Category 2) and at least one side repeater indicator (Category 5) or, in the case of a motor vehicle having a maximum speed not exceeding 25 miles per hour, a single front indicator (Category 1) and one or two (but not more than two) rear indicators (Category 2). Additional indicators may be fitted to the side (excluding the front and rear) of any motor vehicle.

(*b*) A trailer manufactured on or after 1st October 1985 drawn by a motor vehicle:

One or two (but not more than two) rear indicators (Category 2) or, in the case of a trailer towed by a solo motor bicycle or a motor bicycle combination, one or two (but not more than two) rear indicators (Category 12). Additional indicators may be fitted to the side (excluding the front and rear) of any trailer.

(*c*) A solo motor bicycle first used on or after 1st April 1986:

A single front indicator (Category 1 or 11) and a single rear indicator (Category 2 or 12). Additional indicators may be fitted to the side (excluding the front and rear) of any solo motor bicycle.

(*d*) A motor bicycle combination first used on or after 1st April 1986:

A single front indicator (Category 1 or 11) and a single rear indicator (Category 2 or 12). Additional indicators may be fitted to the side (excluding the front and rear) of any motor bicycle combination.

(*e*) A motor vehicle first used on or after 1st January 1936 and before 1st April 1986, a trailer manufactured on or after 1st January 1936 and before 1st October 1985, a pedal cycle with or without a sidecar or trailer, a horse-drawn vehicle and a vehicle drawn or propelled by hand:

Any arrangement of indicators so as to satisfy the requirements for angles of visibility in paragraph 3. However, not more than one front indicator and not more than two rear indicators may be fitted. Additional indicators may be fitted to the side (excluding the front and rear) of any vehicle.

(*f*) A motor vehicle first used before 1st January 1936 and any trailer manufactured before that date:

Any arrangement of indicators so as to make the intention of the driver clear to other road users.

2. Position—
  (*a*) Longitudinal—
    (i) A side repeater indicator which is required to be fitted in accordance with paragraph 1(a)(i):

Within 2600 millimetres of the front of the vehicle

    (ii) Any other indicator:

No requirement

  (*b*) Lateral—
    (i) Maximum distance from the side of the vehicle—
      (A) Any vehicle not covered by sub-paragraph (B):

400 millimetres. However, where the vertical distance between the illuminated areas of any rear indicator and any rear position lamp is less than 300 millimetres, the distance between the outer edge of the vehicle and the outer edge of the illuminated area of the said indicator shall not exceed by more than 50 millimetres the distance between the extreme outer edge of the vehicle and the outer edge of the illuminated area of the said rear position lamp.

(B) A motor vehicle first used before 1st April 1986, a trailer manufactured before 1st October 1985, a solo motor bicycle, a pedal cycle, a horse-drawn vehicle and a vehicle drawn or propelled by hand:	No requirement

(ii) Minimum separation distance between indicators on opposite sides of a vehicle—

(A) A motor vehicle, other than a solo motor bicycle or a motor bicycle combination, first used on or after 1st April 1986, a trailer manufactured on or after 1st October 1985, a horse-drawn vehicle, a pedestrian-controlled vehicle and a vehicle drawn or propelled by hand:	500 millimetres or, if the overall width of the vehicle is less than 1400 milli-metres, 400 millimetres
(B) A solo motor bicycle having an engine exceeding 50 cubic centi-metres and first used on or after 1st April 1986—	
(1) Front indicators:	300 millimetres
(2) Rear indicators:	240 millimetres
(3) Side repeater indicators:	No requirement
(C) A solo motor bicycle having an engine not exceeding 50 cubic centi-metres and first used on or after 1st April 1986 and a pedal cycle—	
(1) Front indicators:	240 millimetres
(2) Rear indicators:	180 millimetres
(3) Side repeater indicators:	No requirement
(D) A motor bicycle combination first used on or after 1st April 1986:	400 millimetres
(E) A motor vehicle first used before 1st April 1986 and a trailer manufac-tured before 1st October 1985:	No requirement

(iii) Minimum separation distance between a front indicator and any dipped-beam headlamp or front fog lamp—

(A) Every front indicator fitted to a motor vehicle, other than a solo motor bicycle or a motor bicycle combination, first used on or after 1st April 1986:	40 millimetres. However, this shall not apply if the luminous intensity in the reference axis of the indi-cator is at least 400 can-delas.
(B) Every front indicator fitted to a solo motor bicycle or a motor bicycle combination in either case first used on or after 1st April 1986:	100 millimetres
(C) Any front indicator fitted to any other vehicle:	No requirement

(c) Vertical—
    (i) Maximum height above the ground—

(A) Any vehicle not covered by sub-paragraph (B) or (C):	1500 millimetres or, if the structure of the vehicle makes this impracticable, 2300 millimetres. However, if two pairs of rear indicators are fitted, one pair may be mounted at any height.
(B) A motor vehicle first used before 1st April 1986 and a trailer manufactured before 1st October 1985:	No requirement
(C) A motor vehicle having a maximum speed not exceeding 25 miles per hour:	No requirement
(ii) Minimum height above the ground:	350 millimetres

3. Angles of visibility—

    (a) A motor vehicle first used on or after 1st April 1986 and a trailer manufactured on or after 1st October 1985—

        (i) Horizontal (see diagrams in Part II of this Schedule)—

(A) Every front or rear indicator fitted to a motor vehicle, other than a solo motor bicycle or a motor bicycle combination, having a maximum speed of not less than 25 miles per hour and every rear indicator fitted to a trailer:	80° outwards and 45° inwards
(B) Every front or rear indicator fitted to a solo motor bicycle or a motor bicycle combination:	80° outwards and 20° inwards
(C) Every front or rear indicator fitted to a motor vehicle, other than a solo motor bicycle or a motor bicycle combination, having a maximum speed not exceeding 25 miles per hour:	80° outwards and 3° inwards
(D) Every side repeater indicator fitted to a motor vehicle or a trailer:	Between rearward angles of 5° outboard and 60° outboard or, in the case of a motor vehicle having a maximum speed not exceeding 25 miles per hour where it is impracticable to comply with the 5° angle, this may be replaced by 10°.

        (ii) Vertical—

(A) Any vehicle not covered by sub-paragraph (B) or (C):	15° above and below the horizontal

(B) A motor vehicle having a maximum speed not exceeding 25 miles per hour where the highest part of the illuminated area of the lamp is less than 1900 millimetres above the ground:

15° above and 10° below the horizontal

(C) Where the highest part of the illuminated area of the lamp is less than 750 millimetres above the ground:

15° above and 5° below the horizontal

(b) A motor vehicle first used before 1st April 1986, a trailer manufactured before 1st October 1985, a pedal cycle, horse-drawn vehicle and a vehicle drawn or propelled by hand:

Such that at least one (but not necessarily the same) indicator on each side is plainly visible to the rear in the case of a trailer and both to the front and rear in the case of any other vehicle.

4. Markings—

(a) A motor vehicle, other than a solo motor bicycle or a motor bicycle combination, first used on or after 1st April 1986 and a trailer, other than a trailer drawn by a solo motor bicycle or a motor bicycle combination, manufactured on or after 1st October 1985: ·

An approval mark and, above such mark, the following numbers—

(a) in the case of a front indicator, '1';

(b) in the case of a rear indicator, '2';

(c) in the case of a side repeater indicator, '5'.

(b) A solo motor bicycle and a motor bicycle combination in either case first used on or after 1st April 1986, a trailer, manufactured on or after 1st October 1985, drawn by such a solo motor bicycle or a motor bicycle combination, a pedal cycle, a horse-drawn vehicle and a vehicle drawn or propelled by hand:

An approval mark and, above such mark, the following numbers—

(a) in the case of a front indicator, '1' or '11';

(b) in the case of a rear indicator, '2' or '12';

(c) in the case of a side repeater indicator, '5'.

(c) A motor vehicle first used before 1st April 1986 and a trailer manufactured before 1st October 1985:

No requirement

5. Size of illuminated area:

No requirement

6. Colour—

(a) Any vehicle not covered by sub-paragraph (b):

Amber

(b) Any indicator fitted to a motor vehicle first used before 1st September 1965 and any trailer drawn thereby—

(i) if it shows only the front:

White or amber

(ii) if it shows only the rear:

Red or amber

(iii) if it shows both to the front and to the rear:

Amber

7. Wattage—

    (*a*) Any front or rear indicator which emits a flash-   15 to 36 watts
        ing light and does not bear an approval mark:

    (*b*) Any other indicator: No requirement

8. Intensity—

    (*a*) An indicator bearing an approval mark: No requirement

    (*b*) An indicator not bearing an approval mark: Such that the light is plainly
                                           visible from a reasonable
                                         distance

9. Electrical connections—

    (*a*) All indicators on one side of a vehicle together with all indicators on that side of any trailer drawn by the vehicle, while so drawn, shall be operated by one switch.

    (*b*) All indicators on one side of a vehicle or combination of vehicles showing a flashing light shall flash in phase, except that in the case of a solo motor bicycle, a motor bicycle combination and a pedal cycle, the front and rear direction indicators on one side of the vehicle may flash alternately.

10. Tell-tale—

    (*a*) One or more indicators on each side of a vehicle to which indicators are fitted shall be so designed and fitted that the driver when in his seat can readily be aware when it is in operation; or

    (*b*) The vehicle shall be equipped with an operational tell-tale for front and rear indicators (including any rear indicator on the rearmost of any trailers drawn by the vehicle).

11. Other requirements—

    (*a*) Every indicator (other than a semaphore arm, that is an indicator in the form of an illuminated sign which when in operation temporarily alters the outline of the vehicle to the extent of at least 150 millimetres measured horizontally and is visible from both the front and rear of the vehicle) shall when in operation show a light which flashes constantly at the rate of not less than 60 nor more than 120 flashes per minute. However, in the event of a failure, other than a short-circuit, of an indicator, any other indicator on the same side of the vehicle or combination of vehicles may continue to flash, but the rate may be less than 60 or more than 120 flashes per minute. Every indicator shall when in operation perform efficiently regardless of the speed of the vehicle.

    (*b*) Where two front or rear direction indicators are fitted to a motor vehicle first used on or after 1st April 1986, and two rear direction indicators are fitted to a trailer manufactured on or after 1st October 1985, in each case they shall be fitted so as to form a pair. Where four rear direction indicators are fitted to a motor vehicle first used on or after 1st April 1986 and to a trailer manufactured on or after 1st October 1985, they shall be fitted so as to form two pairs.

12. Definitions—

In this Schedule 'approval mark' means either—

    (*a*) a marking designated as an approval mark by Regulation 5 of the Designation of Approval Marks Regulations and shown at item 9 of Schedule 4 to those Regulations; or

(b) a marking designated as an approval mark by Regulation 4 of the Designation of Approval Marks Regulations and shown at item 6 or, in the case of a solo motor bicycle or a motor bicycle combination, a pedal cycle, a horse-drawn vehicle, or a vehicle drawn or propelled by hand, at item 50 of Schedule 2 to those Regulations.

PART II

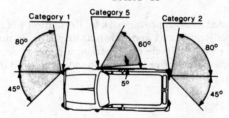

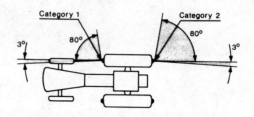

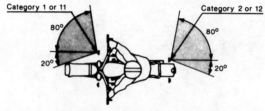

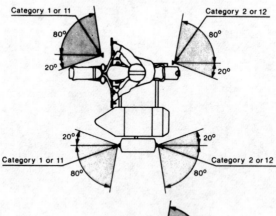

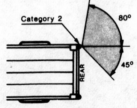

SCHEDULE 8

(See Regulations 16 and 17)

PART I

HAZARD WARNING SIGNAL DEVICES TO WHICH REGULATION 16 APPLIES

Every hazard warning signal device shall—

(a) be operated by one switch,

(b) cause all the direction indicators with which a vehicle or a combination of vehicles is equipped to flash in phase,

(c) be provided with a closed-circuit tell-tale in the form of a flashing light which may operate in conjunction with any direction indicator tell-tale, and

(d) be able to function even if the device which controls the starting and stopping of the engine is in a position which makes it impossible to start the engine.

PART II

HAZARD WARNING SIGNAL DEVICES TO WHICH REGULATION 17 APPLIES

The requirements prescribed by these Regulations in respect of a hazard warning signal device which is fitted are all those specified in this Schedule as regards a hazard warning signal device to which Regulation 16 applies.

SCHEDULE 9

(See Regulations 16, 17 and 19)

PART I

SIDE MARKER LAMPS TO WHICH REGULATION 16 OR 19 APPLIES

1. Number—

(a) Any trailer not covered by sub-paragraph (b):	One on each side
(b) Long vehicles and vehicle combinations to which Regulation 19 applies:	The numbers required by Regulation 19

2. Position—

(a) Longitudinal—	
(i) Any trailer not covered by sub-paragraph (ii):	Such that no part of the light-emitting surface is forward of, or more than 1530 millimetres to the rear of, the centre point of the overall length of the trailer.
(ii) Long vehicles and vehicle combinations, including any loads, to which Regulation 19 applies:	As specified in Regulation 19
(b) Lateral:	No requirement

(c) Vertical—
    (i) Maximum height above the ground: 2300 millimetres
    (ii) Minimum height above the ground: No requirement

3. Angles of visibility—

   (a) Horizontal: 70° to the left and to the right when viewed in a direction at right angles to the longitudinal axis of the vehicle

   (b) Vertical: No requirement

4. Markings: No requirement

5. Size of light-emitting surface: Not less than 490 square millimetres in the case of each of the surfaces through which the red light or the white light is emitted

6. Colour: White when viewed from the front and red when viewed from the rear

7. Wattage: 7 watts maximum

8. Intensity: Visible from a reasonable distance

9. Electrical connections: No requirement

10. Tell-tale: No requirement

PART II

SIDE MARKER LAMPS TO WHICH REGULATION 17 APPLIES

Any number may be fitted, and the only requirement prescribed by these Regulations in respect of any which are fitted is that specified in paragraph 6 as regards side marker lamps to which Regulation 16 or 19 applies.

SCHEDULE 10

(See Regulations 16 and 17)

PART I

REAR POSITION LAMPS TO WHICH REGULATION 16 APPLIES

1. Number—

   (a) Any vehicle not covered by sub-paragraph (b), Two
     (c), (d), (e), (f) or (g):

(b) A large passenger-carrying vehicle first used before 1st April 1955: — One

(c) A solo motor bicycle: — One

(d) A pedal cycle with less than four wheels and without a sidecar: — One

(e) A trailer drawn by a pedal cycle and a trailer, the overall width of which does not exceed 800 millimetres, drawn by a solo motor bicycle or by a motor bicycle combination: — One

(f) A vehicle drawn or propelled by hand: — One

(g) A motor vehicle having three or more wheels and a maximum speed not exceeding 25 miles per hour and a trailer drawn by any such vehicle if, in either case, the structure of the vehicle makes it impracticable to meet all of the relevant requirements of paragraphs 2 and 3 below with two lamps: — Four

2. Position:

(a) Longitudinal: — At or near the rear

(b) Lateral—

   (i) Where two lamps are required to be fitted—

     (A) Maximum distance from the side of the vehicle—

      (1) Any vehicle not covered by sub-paragraph (2): — 400 millimetres

      (2) A motor vehicle first used before 1st April 1986 and any other vehicle manufactured before 1st October 1985: — 800 millimetres

     (B) Minimum separation distance between pair of rear position lamps—

      (1) Any vehicle not covered by sub-paragraph (2): — 500 millimetres or, if the overall width of the vehicle is less than 1400 millimetres, 400 millimetres.

      (2) A motor vehicle first used before 1st April 1986 and any other vehicle manufactured before 1st October 1985: — No requirement

   (ii) Where one lamp is required to be fitted: — On the centre-line or off side of the vehicle

   (iii) Where four lamps are required to be fitted—

     (A) Maximum distance from the side of the vehicle—

      (1) One pair of lamps: — Such that they satisfy the relevant requirements in sub-paragraph 2(b)(i)(A)

(2) The other pair of lamps:	No requirement
(B) Minimum separation distance between rear position lamps—	
(1) One pair of lamps:	Such that they satisfy the relevant requirements in sub-paragraph 2(b)(i)(B)
(2) The other pair of lamps:	No requirement

(c) Vertical—
   (i) Maximum height above the ground where one or two rear position lamps are required to be fitted—

(A) Any vehicle not covered by sub-paragraph (B) or (C):	1500 millimetres or, if the structure of the vehicle makes this impracticable, 2100 millimetres
(B) A large passenger-carrying vehicle first used before 1st April 1986:	No requirement
(C) A motor vehicle first used before 1st April 1986 not being a large passenger-carrying vehicle, a trailer manufactured before 1st October 1985, an agricultural vehicle, a horse-drawn vehicle, an industrial tractor and engineering plant:	2100 millimetres

   (ii) Maximum height above the ground where four rear position lamps are required to be fitted—

(A) One pair of lamps:	Such that they satisfy the relevant requirements in paragraph 2(c)(i)
(B) The other pair of lamps:	No requirement

   (iii) Minimum height above the ground—

(A) A vehicle not covered by sub-paragraph (B):	350 millimetres
(B) A motor vehicle first used before 1st April 1986 and any other vehicle manufactured before 1st October 1985:	No requirement

3. Angles of visibility—

(a) A motor vehicle, other than a motor bicycle combination, first used on or after 1st April 1986 and a trailer manufactured on or after 1st October 1985—
   (i) Horizontal—

(A) Where two lamps are required to be fitted:	Either 45° inwards and 80° outwards or 80° inwards and 45° outwards
(B) Where one lamp is required to be fitted:	80° to the left and to the right
(C) Where four lamps are required to be fitted—	

(1) The outer pair of lamps:	0° inwards and 80° outwards
(2) The inner pair of lamps:	Either 45° inwards and 80° outwards or 80° inwards and 45° outwards

(ii) Vertical—

(A) Where one or two rear position lamps are required to be fitted—

(1) Any vehicle not covered by sub-paragraph (2) or (3):	15° above and below the horizontal
(2) Where the highest part of the illuminated area of the lamp is less than 1500 millimetres above the ground:	15° above and 10° below the horizontal
(3) Where the highest part of the illuminated area of the lamp is less than 750 millimetres above the ground:	15° above and 5° below the horizontal

(B) Where four rear position lamps are required to be fitted—

(1) One pair of lamps:	Such that they satisfy the relevant requirements in paragraph 3(a)(ii)(A)
(2) The other pair of lamps:	Visible to the rear
(b) A motor vehicle, other than a motor vehicle combination, first used before 1st April 1986 and any other vehicle manufactured before 1st October 1985:	Visible to the rear
(c) A vehicle drawn or propelled by hand, a pedal cycle, a horse-drawn vehicle and a motor bicycle combination:	Visible to the rear

4. Markings—

(a) A motor vehicle or a trailer not covered by sub-paragraph (b), (c) or (d):	An approval mark
(b) A motor vehicle first used before 1st January 1974 and a trailer, other than a trailer drawn by a pedal cycle, manufactured before that date:	No requirement
(c) A solo motor bicycle and a motor bicycle combination, in each case first used before 1st April 1986, and a trailer manufactured before 1st October 1985 and drawn by a solo motor bicycle or a motor bicycle combination:	No requirement
(d) A pedal cycle, a trailer drawn by a pedal cycle, a horse-drawn vehicle and a vehicle drawn or propelled by hand:	A British Standard mark

5. Size of illuminated area:	No requirement
6. Colour:	Red
7. Wattage:	No requirement

8. Intensity—

    (*a*) A rear position lamp bearing any of the mark-   No requirement
         ings mentioned in paragraph 4:

    (*b*) Any other rear position lamp: Visible from a reasonable
                                                distance

9. Electrical connections: No requirement

10. Tell-tale: No requirement

11. Other requirements—

Except in the case of a motor vehicle first used before 1st April 1986, any other vehicle manufactured before 1st October 1985 and a motor bicycle combination, where two rear position lamps are required to be fitted they shall form a matched pair and where four rear position lamps are required to be fitted they shall form two matched pairs and each pair shall be capable of being switched on and off simultaneously and not otherwise.

12. Definitions—

In this Schedule—

    'approval mark' means—

        (*a*) in relation to a solo motor bicycle, a motor bicycle combination and a trailer drawn by a solo motor bicycle or a motor bicycle combination, a marking designated as an approval mark by Regulation 4 of the Designation of Approval Marks Regulations and shown at item 50A of Schedule 2 to those Regulations, and

        (*b*) in relation to any other motor vehicle or any trailer, either—

            (i) a marking designated as an approval mark by Regulation 5 of the Designation of Approval Marks Regulations and shown at item 6 or, if combined with a stop lamp, at item 8 of Schedule 4 to those Regulations, or

           (ii) a marking designated as an approval mark by Regulation 4 of the Designation of Approval Marks Regulations and shown at item 7A or, if combined with a stop lamp, at item 7C of Schedule 2 to those Regulations; and

    'British Standard mark' means the specification for cycle rear lamps published by the British Standards Institution under the reference 3648:1963 as amended by Amendment PD 6137 published in May 1967, namely 'B.S. 3648'.

PART II

Rear Position Lamps to which Regulation 17 applies

Any number may be fitted, and the only requirement prescribed by these Regulations in respect of any which are fitted is that specified in paragraph 6 as regards rear position lamps to which Regulation 16 applies.

SCHEDULE 11

(See Regulations 16 and 17)

PART I

REAR FOG LAMPS TO WHICH REGULATION 16 APPLIES

1. Number:	One
2. Position—	
(*a*) Longitudinal:	At or near the rear of the vehicle
(*b*) Lateral—	
(i) Where one rear fog lamp is fitted:	On the centre-line or off side of the vehicle (disregarding any sidecar forming part of a motor bicycle combination)
(ii) Where two lamps are fitted:	No requirement
(*c*) Vertical—	
(i) Maximum height above the ground—	
(A) Any vehicle not covered by sub-paragraph (B):	1000 millimetres
(B) An agricultural vehicle, engineering plant and a motor tractor:	2100 millimetres
(ii) Minimum height above the ground:	250 millimetres
(*d*) Minimum separation distance between a rear fog lamp and a stop lamp—	
(i) In the case of a rear fog lamp which does not share a common lamp body with a stop lamp:	A distance of 100 millimetres between the light-emitting surfaces of the lamps when viewed in a direction parallel to the longitudinal axis of the vehicle
(ii) In the case of a rear fog lamp which shares a common lamp body with a stop lamp:	100 millimetres
3. Angles of visibility—	
(*a*) Horizontal:	25° inwards and outwards. However, where two rear fog lamps are fitted it shall suffice if throughout the sector so defined at least one lamp (but not necessarily the same lamp) is visible.
(*b*) Vertical:	5° above and below the horizontal
4. Markings:	An approval mark

5. Size of illuminated area:　　　　　　No requirement

6. Colour:　　　　　　　　　　　　　Red

7. Wattage:　　　　　　　　　　　　No requirement

8. Intensity:　　　　　　　　　　　No requirement

9. Electrical connections:　　　　　　No rear fog lamp shall be fitted to any vehicle so that it can be illuminated by the application of any braking system on the vehicle.

10. Tell-tale:　　　　　　　　　　　A circuit-closed tell-tale shall be fitted.

11. Other requirements—

Where two rear fog lamps are fitted to a motor vehicle first used on or after 1st April 1986 or to a trailer manufactured on or after 1st October 1985 they shall form a matched pair.

12. Definitions—

In this Schedule 'approval mark' means either—

(a) a marking designated as an approval mark by Regulation 5 of the Designation of Approval Marks Regulations and shown at item 20 of Schedule 4 to those Regulations, or

(b) a marking designated as an approval mark by Regulation 4 of the Designation of Approval Marks Regulations and shown at item 38 of Schedule 2 to those Regulations.

PART II

REAR FOG LAMPS TO WHICH REGULATION 17 APPLIES

1. In the case of a motor vehicle first used before 1st April 1980 and any other vehicle manufactured before 1st October 1979, any number may be fitted and the only requirements prescribed by these Regulations in respect of any which are fitted are those specified in paragraphs 2(d), 6 and 9 as regards rear fog lamps to which Regulation 16 applies.

2. In the case of a motor vehicle first used on or after 1st April 1980 and any other vehicle manufactured on or after 1st October 1979, not more than two may be fitted and the requirements prescribed by these Regulations in respect of any which are fitted are all those specified in this Schedule as regards rear fog lamps to which Regulation 16 applies except those specified in paragraph 1.

SCHEDULE 12

(See Regulations 16 and 17)

PART I

Stop Lamps to which Regulation 16 applies

1. Number—

(a) Any vehicle not covered by sub-paragraph (b) or (c):	Two
(b) A solo motor bicycle, a motor bicycle combination, an invalid carriage and a trailer drawn by a solo motor bicycle or a motor bicycle combination:	One
(c) Any other motor vehicle first used before 1st January 1971 and any other trailer manufactured before that date:	One

2. Position—

(a) Longitudinal:	At or towards the rear of the vehicle
(b) Lateral—	
(i) Maximum distance from the side of the vehicle—	
(A) Where two or more stop lamps are fitted:	At least one on each side of the longitudinal axis of the vehicle
(B) Where only one stop lamp is fitted:	On the centre-line or off side of the vehicle (disregarding any sidecar forming part of a motor bicycle combination)
(ii) Minimum separation distance between two obligatory stop lamps:	400 millimetres
(c) Vertical—	
(i) Maximum height above the ground—	
(A) Any vehicle not covered by sub-paragraph (B):	1500 millimetres or, if the structure of the vehicle makes this impracticable, 2100 millimetres
(B) A motor vehicle first used before 1st January 1971, a trailer manufactured before that date and a motor vehicle having a maximum speed not exceeding 25 miles per hour:	No requirement
(ii) Minimum height above the ground—	
(A) Any vehicle not covered by sub-paragraph (B):	350 millimetres
(B) A motor vehicle first used before 1st January 1971 and a trailer manufactured before that date:	No requirement

3. Angles of visibility—

    (*a*) A motor vehicle first used on or after 1st January 1971 and a trailer manufactured on or after that date—

        (i) Horizontal: 45° to the left and to the right

        (ii) Vertical—

            (A) Except in a case specified in sub-paragraph (B) or (C):   15° above and below the horizontal

            (B) Where the highest part of the illuminated area of the lamp is less than 1500 millimetres above the ground: 15° above and 10° below the horizontal

            (C) Where the highest part of the illuminated area of the lamp is less than 750 millimetres above the ground: 15° above and 5° below the horizontal

    (*b*) A motor vehicle first used before 1st January 1971 and a trailer manufactured before that date: Visible to the rear

4. Markings—

    (*a*) Any vehicle not covered by sub-paragraph (*b*) or (*c*):   An approval mark

    (*b*) A motor vehicle first used before 1st February 1974 and a trailer manufactured before that date: No requirement

    (*c*) A solo motor bicycle and a motor bicycle combination, in each case first used before 1st April 1986, and a trailer manufactured before 1st October 1985 drawn by a solo motor bicycle or a motor bicycle combination: No requirement

5. Size of illuminated area: No requirement

6. Colour: Red

7. Wattage—

    (*a*) A stop lamp fitted to a motor vehicle first used before 1st January 1971 or a trailer manufactured before that date and a stop lamp bearing an approval mark: No requirement

    (*b*) Any other stop lamp: 15 to 36 watts

8. Intensity: No requirement

9. Electrical connections—

    (*a*) Every stop lamp fitted to—

        (i) a solo motor bicycle or a motor bicycle combination first used on or after 1st April 1986 shall be operated both by the application of the front braking system and by the application of the rear braking system;

        (ii) any other motor vehicle, shall be operated by the application of a braking system.

(b) The braking systems mentioned in paragraph (a) are those which are designed to be used to bring the vehicle when in motion to a halt.

(c) Every stop lamp fitted to a trailer drawn by a motor vehicle shall be operated by the application of the braking system of that motor vehicle.

10. Tell-tale: No requirement

11. Other requirements—

Where two stop lamps are required to be fitted, they shall form a pair.

12. Definitions—

In this Schedule 'approval mark' means—

(a) in relation to a solo motor bicycle, a motor bicycle combination or a trailer drawn by a solo motor bicycle or a motor bicycle combination, a marking designated as an approval mark by Regulation 4 of the Designation of Approval Marks Regulations and shown at item 50A of Schedule 2 to those Regulations, and

(b) in relation to any other vehicle, either—

  (i) a marking designated as an approval mark by Regulation 5 of the Designation of Approval Marks Regulations and shown at item 7 or, if combined with a rear position lamp, at item 8 of Schedule 4 to those Regulations; or

  (ii) a marking designated as an approval mark by Regulation 4 of the Designation of Approval Marks Regulations and shown at item 7B or, if combined with a rear position lamp, at item 7C of Schedule 2 to those Regulations.

PART II

Stop Lamps to which Regulation 17 applies

Any number may be fitted, and the requirements prescribed by these Regulations in respect of any which are fitted are all those specified in this Schedule as regards stop lamps to which Regulation 16 applies except those specified in paragraphs 1 and 2(b)(ii).

SCHEDULE 13

(See Regulation 17)

Reversing Lamps to which Regulation 17 applies

1. Number: Not more than two

2. Position: No requirement

3. Angles of visibility: No requirement

4. Markings—

(a) A motor vehicle first used on or after 1st April   An approval mark
1986 and a trailer manufactured on or after 1st
October 1985:

(*b*) A motor vehicle first used before 1st April 1986 and a trailer manufactured before 1st October 1985:

No requirement

5. Size of illuminated area:

No requirement

6. Colour:

White

7. Wattage—

    (*a*) A reversing lamp bearing an approval mark:

No requirement

    (*b*) A reversing lamp not bearing an approval mark:

The total wattage of any one reversing lamp shall not exceed 24 watts.

8. Intensity:

No requirement

9. Electrical connections:

No requirement

10. Tell-tale—

    (*a*) A motor vehicle first used on or after 1st July 1954, provided that the electrical connections are such that the reversing lamp or lamps cannot be illuminated other than automatically by the selection of the reverse gear of the vehicle:

No requirement

    (*b*) Any other motor vehicle first used on or after 1st July 1954:

A circuit-closed tell-tale shall be fitted.

    (*c*) A motor vehicle first used before 1st July 1954:

No requirement

    (*d*) Any vehicle which is not a motor vehicle:

No requirement

11. Definitions—

In this Schedule 'approval mark' means either—

    (*a*) a marking designated as an approval mark by Regulation 5 of the Designation of Approval Marks Regulations and shown at item 21 of Schedule 4 to those Regulations, or

    (*b*) a marking designated as an approval mark by Regulation 4 of the Designation of Approval Marks Regulations and shown at item 23 or 23A of Schedule 2 to those Regulations.

SCHEDULE 14

(See Regulation 16)

REAR REGISTRATION PLATE LAMPS TO WHICH REGULATION 16 APPLIES

1. Number:

At least one

2. Position:

Such that the lamp or lamps are capable of adequately illuminating the rear registration plate

3. Angles of visibility: No requirement

4. Markings—

    (*a*) A motor vehicle first used on or after 1st April   An approval mark
         1986 and a trailer manufactured on or after 1st
         October 1985:

    (*b*) A motor vehicle first used before 1st April 1986   No requirement
         and a trailer manufactured before 1st October
         1985:

5. Size of illuminated area: No requirement

6. Colour: No requirement

7. Wattage: No requirement

8. Intensity: No requirement

9. Electrical connections: No requirement

10. Tell-tale: No requirement

11. Definitions—

In this Schedule 'approval mark' means—

    (*a*) in relation to a solo motor bicycle, a motor bicycle combination and a trailer
         drawn by a solo motor bicycle or a motor bicycle combination, a marking
         designated as an approval mark by Regulation 4 of the Designation of Appro-
         val Marks Regulations and shown at item 50A of Schedule 2 to those Regula-
         tions, and

    (*b*) in relation to any other motor vehicle and any other trailer, either—
        (i) a marking designated as an approval mark by Regulation 5 of the Desig-
            nation of Approval Marks Regulations and shown at item 10 of Schedule
            4 to those Regulations, or
        (ii) a marking designated as an approval mark by Regulation 4 of the Desig-
            nation of Approval Marks Regulations and shown at item 4 of Schedule
            2 to those Regulations.

SCHEDULE 15

(See Regulation 17)

Warning Beacons to which Regulation 17 applies

1. Number: No requirement

2. Position—

Every warning beacon shall be so mounted on the vehicle that the centre of the lamp
is at a height not less than 1200 millimetres above the ground.

3. Angles of visibility—

The light shown from at least one beacon (but not necessarily the same beacon) shall
be visible from any point at a reasonable distance from the vehicle.

4. Markings: No requirement

5. Size of illuminated area: No requirement

6. Colour: Blue, amber, green or yellow in accordance with Regulation 11

7. Wattage: No requirement

8. Intensity: No requirement

9. Electrical connections: No requirement

10. Tell-tale: No requirement

11. Other requirements—

The light shown by any one warning beacon shall be displayed not less than 60 nor more than 240 equal times per minute and the intervals between each display of light shall be constant.

SCHEDULE 16

(See Regulations 16 and 17)

PART I

SIDE REFLEX REFLECTORS TO WHICH REGULATION 16 APPLIES

1. Number—

(a) A motor vehicle first used on or after 1st April 1986 and a trailer manufactured on or after 1st October 1985: On each side: two and as many more as are sufficient to satisfy the requirements of paragraph 2(a)

(b) A motor vehicle first used before 1st April 1986 and a trailer manufactured before 1st October 1985: On each side: Two

2. Position—

(a) Longitudinal—

(i) A motor vehicle first used on or after 1st April 1986 and a trailer manufactured on or after 1st October 1985—

(A) Maximum distance from the front of the vehicle, including any drawbar, in respect of the foremost reflector on each side: 3 metres

(B) Maximum distance from the rear of the vehicle in respect of the rearmost reflector on each side: 1 metre

(C) Maximum separation distance between the reflecting areas of adjacent reflectors on the same side of the vehicle:	3 metres
(ii) A motor vehicle first used before 1st April 1986 and a trailer manufactured before 1st October 1985—	
(A) Maximum distance from the rear of the vehicle in respect of the rearmost reflector on each side:	1 metre
(B) The other reflector on each side of the vehicle:	Towards the centre of the vehicle
(b) Lateral:	No requirement
(c) Vertical—	
(i) Maximum height above the ground—	
(A) A motor vehicle first used on or after 1st April 1986 and a trailer manufactured on or after 1st October 1985:	900 millimetres or, if the structure of the vehicle makes this impracticable, 1500 millimetres
(B) A motor vehicle first used before 1st April 1986 and a trailer manufactured before 1st October 1985:	1500 millimetres
(ii) Minimum height above the ground:	350 millimetres
(d) Alignment:	Vertical and facing squarely to the side

3. Angles of visibility—

(a) A motor vehicle first used on or after 1st April 1986 and a trailer manufactured on or after 1st October 1985—	
(i) Horizontal:	45° to the left and to the right when viewed in a direction at right angles to the longitudinal axis of the vehicle
(ii) Vertical—	
(A) Except in a case specified in sub-paragraph (B):	15° above and below the horizontal
(B) Where the highest part of the reflecting area is less than 750 millimetres above the ground:	15° above and 5° below the horizontal
(b) A motor vehicle first used before 1st April 1986 and a trailer manufactured before 1st October 1985:	Plainly visible to the side

4. Markings: An approval mark

5. Size of reflecting area: No requirement

6. Colour—

    (a) Any vehicle not covered by sub-paragraph (b):   Amber

(*b*) A solo motor bicycle, a motor bicycle combination, a pedal cycle with or without a sidecar attached thereto or an invalid carriage:	No requirement
7. Other requirements:	No side reflex reflector shall be triangular.

8. Definitions—

    (*a*) In this Schedule 'approval mark' means either—

        (i) a marking designated as an approval mark by Regulation 4 of the Designation of Approval Marks Regulations and shown at item 3 of Schedule 2 to those Regulations and which includes the Roman numeral I, or

        (ii) a marking designated as an approval mark by Regulation 5 of the Designation of Approval Marks Regulations and shown at item 4 of Schedule 4 to those Regulations and which includes the Roman numeral I; and

    (*b*) In this Schedule references to 'maximum distance from the front of the vehicle' and 'maximum distance from the rear of the vehicle' are references to the maximum distance from that end of the vehicle (as determined by reference to the overall length of the vehicle exclusive of any special equipment) beyond which no part of the reflecting area of the side reflex reflector extends.

PART II

SIDE REFLEX REFLECTORS TO WHICH REGULATION 17 APPLIES

Any number may be fitted, and the only requirements prescribed by these Regulations in respect of any which are fitted are those specified in paragraphs 6 and 7 as regards side reflex reflectors to which Regulation 16 applies.

SCHEDULE 17

(See Regulations 16 and 17)

PART I

REAR REFLEX REFLECTORS TO WHICH REGULATION 16 APPLIES

1. Number—

(*a*) Any vehicle not covered by sub-paragraph (*b*) or (*c*):	Two
(*b*) A solo motor bicycle, a pedal cycle with less than four wheels and with or without a sidecar, a trailer drawn by a pedal cycle, a trailer the overall width of which does not exceed 800 millimetres drawn by a solo motor bicycle or a motor bicycle combination and a vehicle drawn or propelled by hand:	One
(*c*) A motor vehicle having three or more wheels and a maximum speed not exceeding 25 miles	Four

per hour and a trailer drawn by any such vehicle if, in either case, the structure of the vehicle makes it impracticable to meet all of the requirements of paragraphs 2 and 3 below with two reflectors:

2. Position—

(*a*)	Longitudinal:	At or near the rear
(*b*)	Lateral—	

   (i) Where two rear reflectors are required to be fitted—

      (A) Maximum distance from the side of the vehicle—

(1) Any vehicle not covered by sub-paragraph (2), (3) or (4):	400 millimetres
(2) A large passenger-carrying vehicle first used before 1st October 1954 and a horse-drawn vehicle manufactured before 1st October 1985:	No requirement
(3) A vehicle constructed or adapted for the carriage of round timber:	765 millimetres
(4) Any other motor vehicle first used before 1st April 1986 and any other vehicle manufactured before 1st October 1985:	610 millimetres

      (B) Minimum separation distance between a pair of rear reflectors—

(1) Any vehicle not covered by sub-paragraph (2):	600 millimetres or, if the overall width of the vehicle is less than 1300 millimetres, 400 millimetres
(2) A motor vehicle first used before 1st April 1986 and any other vehicle manufactured before 1st October 1985:	No requirement

(ii) Where one rear reflector is required to be fitted:	On the centre-line or off side of the vehicle

  (iii) Where four rear reflectors are required to be fitted—

      (A) Maximum distance from the side of the vehicle—

(1) One pair of reflectors:	Such that they satisfy the relevant requirements in sub-paragraph 2(*b*)(i)(A)
(2) The other pair of reflectors:	No requirement

      (B) Minimum separation distance between rear reflectors—

(1) One pair of reflectors:	Such that they satisfy the relevant requirements in sub-paragraph 2(*b*)(i)(B)
(2) The other pair of reflectors:	No requirement

(c) Vertical—
    (i) Maximum height above the ground where one or two rear reflectors are required to be fitted—

(A) Any vehicle not covered by sub-paragraph (B):	900 millimetres or, if the structure of the vehicle makes this impracticable, 1200 millimetres
(B) A motor vehicle first used before 1st April 1986 and any other vehicle manufactured before 1st October 1985:	1525 millimetres

    (ii) Maximum height above the ground where four rear reflectors are required to be fitted—

(A) One pair of reflectors:	Such that they satisfy the relevant requirements in paragraph 2(c)(i)
(B) The other pair of reflectors:	2100 millimetres

    (iii) Minimum height above the ground—

(A) Any vehicle not covered by sub-paragraph (B):	350 millimetres
(B) A motor vehicle first used before 1st April 1986 and any other vehicle manufactured before 1st October 1985:	No requirement

  (d) Alignment: Vertical and facing squarely to the rear

3. Angles of visibility—

  (a) A motor vehicle (not being a motor bicycle combination) first used on or after 1st April 1986 and a trailer manufactured on or after 1st October 1985—
    (i) Where one or two rear reflectors are required to be fitted—
      (A) Horizontal—

(1) Where two rear reflectors are required to be fitted:	30° inwards and outwards
(2) Where one rear reflector is required to be fitted:	30° to the left and to the right

      (B) Vertical—

(1) Except in a case specified in sub-paragraph (2)	15° above and below the horizontal
(2) Where the highest part of the reflecting area is less than 750 millimetres above the ground:	15° above and 5° below the horizontal

    (ii) Where four rear reflectors are required to be fitted—

(A) One pair of reflectors:	Such that they satisfy the relevant requirements in paragraph 3(a)(i)

(B) The other pair of reflectors: — Plainly visible to the rear

(b) A motor vehicle (not being a motor bicycle combination) first used before 1st April 1986 and a trailer manufactured before 1st October 1985: — Plainly visible to the rear

(c) A motor bicycle combination, a pedal cycle, a sidecar attached to a pedal cycle, a horse-drawn vehicle and a vehicle drawn or propelled by hand: — Plainly visible to the rear

4. Markings—

(a) A motor vehicle first used—
    (i) On or after 1st April 1986: — (A) An approval mark incorporating 'I' or 'IA', or (B) A British Standard mark which is specified in sub-paragraph (i) of the definition of 'British Standard mark' below followed by 'LI' or 'LIA'.

    (ii) On or after 1st July 1970 and before 1st April 1986: — (A) Any of the markings mentioned in sub-paragraph (a)(i) above, or (B) In the case of a vehicle manufactured in Italy, an Italian approved marking.

    (iii) Before 1st July 1970: — No requirement

(b) A trailer (other than a broken-down motor vehicle) manufactured—
    (i) On or after 1st October 1985: — (A) An approval mark incorporating 'III' or 'IIIA', or (B) A British Standard mark which is specified in sub-paragraph (i) of the definition of 'British Standard mark' below followed by 'LIII' or 'LIIIA'.

    (ii) On or after 1st July 1970 and before 1st October 1985: — (A) Any of the markings mentioned in sub-paragraph (b)(i) above, or (B) In the case of a vehicle manufactured in Italy, an Italian approved marking.

    (iii) Before 1st July 1970: — No requirement

(c) A pedal cycle manufactured—
    (i) On or after 1st July 1970: — (A) An approval mark incorporating 'I' or 'IA', or (B) A British Standard mark which is specified in sub-paragraph (i) of the definition of 'British Stan-

dard mark' below followed by 'LI' or 'LIA', or

(C) A British Standard mark which is specified in sub-paragraph (ii) of the definition of 'British Standard mark' below.

    (ii) Before 1st July 1970:   No requirement

(*d*) A horse-drawn vehicle and a vehicle drawn or propelled by hand in either case manufactured—

    (i) On or after 1st July 1970:   (A) An approval mark incorporating 'I' or 'IA', or

(B) A British Standard mark which is specified in sub-paragraph (i) of the definition of 'British Standard mark' followed by 'LI' or 'LIA'.

    (ii) Before 1st July 1970:   No requirement

5. Size of reflecting area: No requirement

6. Colour: Red

7. Other requirements—

(*a*) Except in the case of a motor vehicle used before 1st April 1986, any other vehicle manufactured before 1st October 1985 and a motor bicycle combination, where two rear reflectors are required to be fitted they shall form a pair. Where four rear reflectors are required to be fitted they shall form two pairs.

(*b*) No vehicle, other than a trailer or a broken-down motor vehicle being towed, may be fitted with triangular-shaped rear reflectors.

8. Definitions—

In this Schedule—

(*a*) 'approval mark' means either—

    (i) a marking designated as an approval mark by Regulation 4 of the Designation of Approval Marks Regulations and shown at item 3 or 3A or 3B of Schedule 2 to those Regulations, or

    (ii) a marking designated as an approval mark by Regulation 5 of the Designation of Approval Marks Regulations and shown at item 4 of Schedule 4 to those Regulations;

(*b*) 'British Standard mark' means either—

    (i) the specification for reflex reflectors for vehicles, including cycles, published by the British Standards Institution under the reference B.S. AU 40: Part 2: 1965, namely 'AU 40', or

    (ii) the specification for photometric and physical requirements of reflective devices published by the British Standards Institution under the reference BS 6102: Part 2: 1982, namely 'BS 6102/2'; and

(*c*) 'Italian approved marking' means—

a mark approved by the Italian Ministry of Transport, namely, one including two separate groups of symbols consisting of 'IGM' or 'DGM' and 'C.1' or 'C.2'.

PART II

REAR REFLEX REFLECTORS TO WHICH REGULATION 17 APPLIES

Any number may be fitted, and the only requirements prescribed by these Regulations in respect of any which are fitted are those specified in paragraphs 6 and 7(*b*) as regards rear reflex reflectors to which Regulation 16 applies.

SCHEDULE 18

(See Regulations 16 and 17)

PART I

REAR MARKINGS TO WHICH REGULATION 16 APPLIES

SECTION A

General requirements

1. Number—
   (*a*) A motor vehicle the overall length of which—

(i) does not exceed 13 metres:	A rear marking shown in diagram 1, 2 or 3 in Section B of this Schedule
(ii) exceeds 13 metres:	A rear marking shown in diagram 4 or 5 in Section B of this Schedule

   (*b*) A trailer if it forms part of a combination of vehicles the overall length of which—

(i) does not exceed 11 metres:	A rear marking shown in diagram 1, 2 or 3 in Section B of this Schedule
(ii) exceeds 11 metres but does not exceed 13 metres:	A rear marking shown in diagram 1, 2, 3, 4 or 5 in Section B of this Schedule
(iii) exceeds 13 metres:	A rear marking shown in diagram 4 or 5 in Section B of this Schedule

2. Position—

(*a*) Longitudinal:	At or near the rear of the vehicle
(*b*) Lateral—	
(i) A rear marking shown in diagram 2, 3 or 5 in Section B of this Schedule:	Each part shall be fitted as near as practicable to the outermost edge of the vehicle on the side thereof on which it is fitted so that no part of the marking projects beyond the outermost part of the vehicle on either side.

(ii) A rear marking shown in diagram 1 or 4 in Section B of this Schedule:	The marking shall be fitted so that the vertical centre-line of the marking lies on the vertical plane through the longitudinal axis of the vehicle and no part of the marking projects beyond the outermost part of the vehicle on either side.
(c) Vertical:	The lower edge of every rear marking shall be at a height of not more than 1700 milli-metres nor less than 400 millimetres above the ground whether the vehicle is laden or unladen.
(d) Alignment:	The lower edge of every rear marking shall be fitted hori-zontally. Every part of a rear marking shall lie within 20° of a transverse vertical plane at right angles to the longitudinal axis of the vehicle.
3. Angles of visibility:	Plainly visible to the rear, except while the vehicle is being loaded or unloaded.
4. Markings:	A British Standard mark
5. Size:	In accordance with Sections B and C of this Schedule
6. Colour:	Red fluorescent material in the stippled areas shown in any of the diagrams in Sec-tion B of this Schedule and yellow reflex reflecting material in any of the areas so shown, being areas not stippled and not constitut-ing a letter. All letters shall be coloured black.

7. Other requirements—

The two parts of every rear marking shown in diagrams 2, 3 or 5 in Section B of this Schedule shall form a pair.

8. Definitions—

In this Schedule 'British Standard mark' means the specification for rear marking plates for vehicles published by the British Standards Institution under the reference BS AU 152:1970, namely 'BS AU 152'.

SECTION B

Size, Colour and Type of Rear Markings

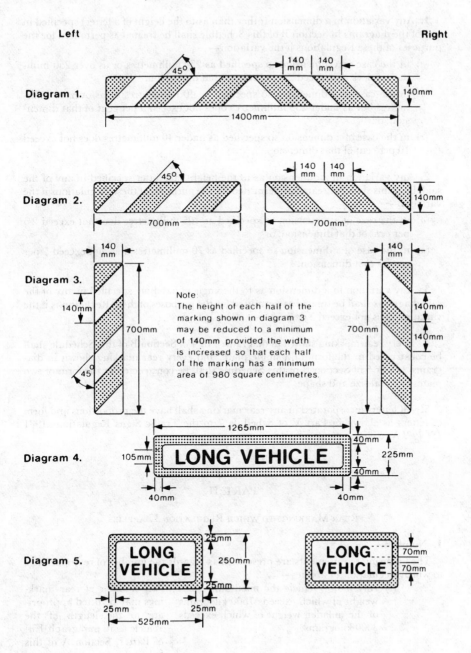

Left

Right

Diagram 1.

45°

140 mm | 140 mm

140mm

1400mm

Diagram 2.

45°

700mm

140 mm | 140 mm

140mm

700mm

Diagram 3.

140 mm

140mm

700mm

45°

Note:
The height of each half of the marking shown in diagram 3 may be reduced to a minimum of 140mm provided the width is increased so that each half of the marking has a minimum area of 980 square centimetres.

140 mm

140mm

140mm

700mm

Diagram 4.

1265mm

LONG VEHICLE

105mm

40mm

40mm

225mm

40mm

40mm

Diagram 5.

LONG VEHICLE

25mm

250mm

25mm

25mm | 25mm

525mm

LONG VEHICLE

70mm

70mm

SECTION C

ADDITIONAL PROVISIONS RELATING TO THE SIZE AND FORM OF REAR MARKINGS

1. Any variation in a dimension (other than as to the height of a letter) specified in any of the diagrams in Section B of this Schedule shall be treated as permitted for the purposes of these Regulations if the variation—

    (*a*) in the case of a dimension so specified as 250 millimetres or as over 250 millimetres does not exceed 2.5 per cent of that dimension;

    (*b*) in the case of a dimension so specified as 40 millimetres or as over 40 millimetres but as under 250 millimetres does not exceed 5 per cent of that dimension; or

    (*c*) in the case of a dimension so specified as under 40 millimetres does not exceed 10 per cent of that dimension.

2. Any variation in a dimension as to the height of a letter specified in any of the said diagrams shall be treated as permitted for the purposes of these Regulations if the variation—

    (*a*) in the case of a dimension so specified as 105 millimetres does not exceed 2·5 per cent of that dimension; or

    (*b*) in the case of a dimension so specified as 70 millimetres does not exceed 5 per cent of that dimension.

3. Any variation in a dimension as to the angle of hatching specified in any of the said diagrams shall be treated as permitted for the purposes of these Regulations if the variation does not exceed 5 degrees.

4. Every rear marking shown in diagrams 1 or 4 of Section B of this Schedule shall be constructed in the form of a single plate, and every rear marking shown in diagrams 2, 3 or 5 of Section B of this Schedule shall be constructed in the form of two plates of equal size and shape.

5. All letters incorporated in any rear marking shall have the proportions and form of letters as shown in Part V of Schedule 7 to the Traffic Signs Regulations 1981 *[SI 1981 No 859]*.

PART II

REAR MARKINGS TO WHICH REGULATION 17 APPLIES

1. Number—

The following requirements are prescribed as regards the number of rear markings to which Regulation 17 applies—

    (i) Any motor vehicle the maximum gross weight of which exceeds 7500 kilograms or the unladen weight of which exceeds 3000 kilograms: Any number of rear markings may be fitted appropriate to the length of the vehicle as in paragraph 1(*a*) of Part I, Section A of this Schedule.

(ii) Any trailer the maximum gross weight of which exceeds 3500 kilograms or the unladen weight of which exceeds 1000 kilograms:

Any number of rear markings may be fitted appropriate to the length of the combination of vehicles as in paragraph 1(*b*) of Section A of Part I of this Schedule.

(iii) Any trailer which is being drawn by a vehicle which is itself required or permitted to be fitted with a rear marking:

Any number of rear markings may be fitted appropriate to the length of the combination of vehicles as in paragraph 1(*b*) of Section A of Part I of this Schedule.

(iv) Any other vehicle:

No rear marking may be fitted.

2. Other provisions—

The requirements specified in relation to rear markings to which Regulation 16 applies in paragraphs 2 to 7 of Section A of Part I of this Schedule and in Sections B and C of that Part are prescribed as regards rear markings to which Regulation 17 applies.

SCHEDULE 19

(See Regulations 16 and 17)

PART I

PEDAL REFLEX REFLECTORS TO WHICH REGULATION 16 APPLIES

1. Number:

Two reflectors on each pedal

2. Position—
  (*a*) Longitudinal:

On the leading edge and the trailing edge of each pedal.

  (*b*) Lateral:

No requirement

  (*c*) Vertical:

No requirement

3. Angles of visibility:

Such that the reflector on the leading edge of each pedal is plainly visible to the front and the reflector on the trailing edge of each pedal is plainly visible to the rear.

4. Markings:

A British Standard mark

5. Size of reflecting area:

No requirement

6. Colour:

Amber

7. Definitions—

In this Schedule 'British Standard mark' means the specification for photometric and physical requirements of reflective devices published by the British Standards Institution under the reference BS 6102: Part 2: 1982, namely 'BS 6102/2'.

PART II

PEDAL REFLEX REFLECTORS TO WHICH REGULATION 17 APPLIES

Any number may be fitted, and the only requirement prescribed by these Regulations in respect of any which are fitted is that specified in paragraph 6 as regards pedal reflex reflectors to which Regulation 16 applies.

*   *   *

The 70 miles per hour, 60 miles per hour and 50 miles per hour (Temporary Speed Limit) Order 1977

[This order was varied by the 70 miles per hour, 60 miles per hour and 50 miles per hour (Temporary Speed Limit) (Variation) Order 1978 with effect from 23 August 1978. This order, which would otherwise have expired on 30 November 1978, was continued in force indefinitely by the 70 miles per hour (Temporary Speed Limit) (Continuation) Order 1978 (SI 1978 No 1548).]

*   *   *

2. Subject to Article 4 below, no person shall during the period of this Order drive a motor vehicle—

(*a*) at a speed exceeding 50 miles per hour on the lengths of dual carriageway road specified in Part I of Schedule 1 to this Order.

(*b*) at a speed exceeding 60 miles per hour on the lengths of dual carriageway road specified in Schedule 2 to this Order, or

(*c*) at a speed exceeding 70 miles per hour on any other length of dual carriageway road.

3. Subject to Article 4 below, no person shall during the period of this Order drive a motor vehicle—

(*a*) at a speed exceeding 50 miles per hour on the lengths of single carriageway road specified in Part II of Schedule 1 to this Order, or

(*b*) at a speed exceeding 60 miles per hour on any other length of single carriageway road.

4. Nothing in this Order shall prohibit a person from driving a motor vehicle on a length of road at a speed exceeding that which would apply to that length under Article 2 or 3 above in a case where a higher speed limit is, after the coming into operation of this Order, prescribed in relation to that length by means of an Order under [section 84 of the Road Traffic Regulation Act 1984].

[Article 4 is printed as amended by the Road Traffic Regulation Act 1984, s 144 (1), and Sched 10, para 2.]

SCHEDULE 1

PART I

Lengths of Dual Carriageway Road for which a 50 miles per hour speed limit is prescribed

Any dual carriageway sections of any of the lengths of road described in Part II of this Schedule.

PART II

Lengths of Single Carriageway Road for which a 50 miles per hour speed limit is prescribed

[In certain instances the lengths of road described below in this Part of this Schedule include short sections of dual carriageway road. These sections are covered by Part I of this Schedule.]

A *Trunk Roads*

*   *   *

B *Other Roads*

*   *   *

SCHEDULE 2
Lengths of Dual Carriageway Road for which a 60 miles per hour speed limit is prescribed

A *Trunk Roads*

*   *   *

B *Other Roads*

*   *   *

The Traffic Signs Regulations and General Directions 1981

(SI 1981 No 859)

ARRANGEMENT OF REGULATIONS

[The text of these regulations and general directions is printed as amended by:
the Traffic Signs (Amendment) Regulations 1982 (SI 1982 No 1879) (10 February 1983);
the Traffic Signs General (Amendment) Directions 1982 (SI 1982 No 1880) (10 February 1983); and
the Traffic Signs General (Amendment) Directions 1983 (SI 1983 No 1086) (25 August 1983);
the Traffic Signs (Amendment) Regulations 1983 (SI 1983 No 1088) (25 August 1983); and
the Traffic Signs (Amendment) Regulations and General Directions 1984 (SI 1984 No 966) (13 August 1984).

The amending regulations are referred to in the notes by their years and numbers. The dates referred to above are the dates on which the regulations and directions came into force.]

PART I

TRAFFIC SIGNS REGULATIONS

*   *   *

SECTION II

Miscellaneous General Provisions

SECTION III

Traffic Signs shown in Schedule 1

PART I
TRAFFIC SIGNS REGULATIONS
*   *   *

SECTION II

Miscellaneous General Provisions

6. Authorisations by the Secretary of State

Nothing in these Regulations shall be taken to limit the powers of the Secretary of State under section 54 of the Act to authorise the erection or retention of traffic signs of a character not prescribed by these Regulations.

7. Application of section 22 of the Road Traffic Act 1972 to signs and disqualification for offences

(1) Section 22 of the Road Traffic Act 1972 shall apply—

(a) to signs of the type shown in any of the diagrams 601.1, 602, 603, 606, 610, 616 and [649.2] and to the sign of the type shown in diagram 602 when used in combination with that shown in diagram 602.1, (*b*) to the red signal when shown by the light signals prescribed by Regulation 31, by Regulation 31 as varied by Regulation 32, or by Regulation 33,

(*c*) to the road marking shown in diagram 1013.1 insofar as that marking conveys the requirements specified in Regulation 23 (2),

(*d*) *[Revoked.]*

[(*e*) until 1st January 1985 to any sign of the type shown in diagram 649 in Schedule 1 to the 1975 Regulations or in diagram 649.1 in Schedule 1 to these Regulations, and]

(*f*) to any sign which in accordance with Regulation 3 (2) is treated as if prescribed by these Regulations, if it is a road marking of the type shown in the diagram numbered 1013 in Schedule 2 to the Regulations of 1964 insofar as that marking conveys the requirements specified in Regulation 23 (2) thereof.

(2) The signs specified hereby for the purposes of the paragraph appearing in column 5 of Part I of Schedule 4 to the said Act of 1972 in relation to section 22 thereof, are:—

(*a*) the sign shown in the diagram numbered 601.1,

(*b*) the sign shown in the diagram numbered [649.2],

(*c*) the red signal when shown by light signals prescribed by Regulation 31, by Regulation 31 as varied by Regulation 32, or by Regulation 33,

(*d*) the road marking shown in the diagram numbered 1013.1 insofar as that marking conveys the requirements specified in Regulation 23 (2),

(*e*) *[Revoked.]*

[(*f*) until 1st January 1985 any sign of the type shown in diagram 649 in Schedule 1 to the Regulations of 1975 or in diagram 649.1 in Schedule 1 to these Regulations, and]

(*g*) the road marking shown in the diagram numbered 1013 in Schedule 2 to the Regulations of 1964 insofar as it conveys the requirements specified in Regulation 23 (2) thereof which marking is in accordance with Regulation 3 (2) treated as if prescribed by these Regulations.

[Regulation 7 is printed as amended by SI 1984 No 966.]

8. Variations in dimensions

(1) Any variation in a dimension (other than a dimension as to the height of a letter or expressed as being the maximum or, as the case may be, minimum) specified in any of the diagrams in Schedule 1 or Schedules 3 to 6 shall be treated as permitted by these Regulations if the variation—

(*a*) in the case of a dimension so specified as 300 millimetres or as over 300 millimetres, does not exceed 5% of that dimension,

(*b*) in the case of a dimension so specified as 50 millimetres or as over 50 millimetres but as under 300 millimetres, does not exceed 7.5% of that dimension, or

(*c*) in the case of a dimension so specified as under 50 millimetres, does not exceed 10% of that dimension.

(2) Any variation in a dimension as to the height of a letter specified in any of the diagrams in Schedule 1 shall be treated as permitted by these Regulations if the variation—

(a) in the case of a dimension so specified as 100 millimetres or as over 100 milli- metres does not exceed 5% of that dimension, or

(b) in the case of a dimension so specified as under 100 millimetres, does not exceed 7.5% of that dimension.

(3) Without prejudice to the next following paragraph, any variation in a dimen- sion (other than a dimension expressed in diagrams 1003.4, 1013.1, 1027.1, 1040 to 1045 or 1055 as being the maximum, or as the case may be, minimum) specified in any of the diagrams in Schedule 2 shall be treated as permitted by these Regulations if the variation—

(a) in the case of a dimension so specified as 3 metres or as over 3 metres, does not exceed 15% of that dimension,

(b) in the case of a dimension so specified as 300 millimetres or as over 300 milli- metres but as under 3 metres, does not exceed 20% of that dimension, or

(c) in the case of a dimension so specified as under 300 millimetres, does not exceed 30% of the dimension so specified, and is not less than 20% of the dimension so specified.

(4) Any variation in a dimension as to the angle of hatching specified in any of the diagrams in Schedule 2 except diagrams 1043 to 1045 shall be treated as permitted by these Regulations if the variation does not exceed 5 degrees.

Section III

Traffic Signs shown in Schedule I

9. Signs to be of the sizes, colours and types shown in diagrams

Subject to the provisions of these Regulations, a traffic sign for conveying—

(a) to vehicular traffic on roads a warning of the description specified in or under a diagram in Part I of Schedule 1 shall be of the size, colour and type shown in the diagram relating to that warning;

(b) to vehicular traffic on roads a requirement, prohibition or restriction specified in or under a diagram in Part II of Schedule 1 (other than a requirement shown in diagram 601.1, 602, 602.1, [649.1 or 649.2]) shall be of the size, colour and type shown in the diagram relating to that requirement, prohibition or restriction;

(c) to traffic on a road other than a motorway information of a directional nature of the description specified in or under a diagram in Part III of Schedule 1 shall be of the size, colour and type shown in the diagram relating to that infor- mation;

(d) to traffic on roads information of the description specified in or under a dia- gram in Part IV of Schedule 1 shall be of the size, colour and type shown in the diagram relating to that information:
   Provided that until 1st January 1992 a traffic sign indicating a stopping place for stage or scheduled express carriages may, notwithstanding that it is not of the size, colour and type shown in any of the diagrams 845 to 852, be of a circular or rectangular shape of not less than 30 square centimetres on which the lettering shall be shown coloured black, dark brown, dark blue or dark red on a white or yellow background, or white or yellow on a red, blue, green, brown or black background if such sign so indicating is situated on or near any road immediately after the coming into operation of these Regulations;

(e) to traffic on a motorway information of a directional or other nature specified in or under a diagram in Part V of Schedule 1 shall be of the size, colour and type shown in the diagram relating to that information.

[Regulation 9 is printed as amended by SI 1984 No 966.
These regulations came into operation on 13 August 1981; see Part III.]

9A. Sign shown in diagram 610 and its significance

(1) Subject to the provisions of these Regulations, a traffic sign for conveying to vehicular traffic on roads the requirement specified in paragraph (2) or (3) shall be of the size, colour and type shown in diagram 610.

(2) Except as provided in paragraph (3) the requirement conveyed by the sign shown in diagram 610 shall be that vehicular traffic passing the sign must keep to the left of the sign where the arrow is pointed downwards to the left, or to the right of the sign where the arrow is pointed downwards to the right.

(3) On an occasion when a vehicle is being used for fire brigade, ambulance or police purposes and the observance of the requirement specified in paragraph (2) would be likely to hinder the use of that vehicle for the purpose for which it is being used on that occasion, then, instead of that requirement, the requirement conveyed by the traffic sign in question shall be that the vehicle shall not proceed beyond that sign in such a manner or at such a time—

    (i) as is likely to cause danger to the driver of any vehicle proceeding on or from another road or on or from another part of the same road; or

    (ii) as is likely to cause danger to non-vehicular traffic proceeding on or from another road or on or from another part of the same road.

10. *[Revoked.]*

[11.—(1) The requirements conveyed by a sign of the size, colour and type shown in a diagram of a type specified in an item in column 2 of the Table below are specified in that item in column 3 of that Table.

(2) In this Regulation—

    'abnormal transport unit' means—

      (a) a motor vehicle or a vehicle combination—

        (i) the overall length of which, inclusive of the load (if any) on the vehicle or the combination, exceeds 55 feet;

        (ii) the overall width of which, inclusive of the load (if any) on the vehicle or the combination, exceeds 9 feet 6 inches; or

        (iii) the maximum gross weight of which exceeds 38 tonnes; or

      (b) a motor vehicle, or a vehicle combination, which in either case is incapable of proceeding, or is unlikely to proceed, over an automatic half-barrier level crossing or an automatic open crossing (R) at a speed exceeding 5 miles per hour;

    'automatic half-barrier level crossing' means a level crossing where a road is crossed by a railway and where barriers are installed to descend automatically across part of the road when a train approaches;

    'automatic open crossing (R)' means a level crossing without automatic barriers where a road is crossed by a railway and where light signals are so installed as to be operated automatically by the trains approaching the crossing and the operation of the signals is monitored remotely from the crossing;

'driver', in relation to an abnormal transport unit, means where that unit is a single motor vehicle the driver of that vehicle and, where that unit is a vehicle combination, the driver of the only or the foremost motor vehicle forming part of that combination;

'major road' means the road at a road junction into which road there emerges vehicular traffic from a minor road;

'minor road' means a road at a road junction on which road there is placed the sign shown in diagram 601.1 or 602; and

'vehicle combination' means a combination of vehicles made up of one or more motor vehicles and one or more trailers all of which are linked together when travelling.]

[Regulation 11 is printed as substituted by SI 1984 No 966.]

TABLE *[ie table in reg 11(1)]*

1 Item No.	2 Type of diagram of sign	3 Requirements of sign
1.	601.1	(i) Every vehicle shall stop before crossing the transverse line shown in diagram 1002.1 or, if that line is not clearly visible, before entering the major road in respect of which the sign shown in diagram No. 601.1 has been provided; (ii) no vehicle shall proceed past the transverse line shown in diagram 1002.1 or, if that line is not clearly visible, enter the major road in respect of which the sign shown in diagram No. 601.1 has been provided, so as to be likely to cause danger to the driver of any other vehicle on the major road or to cause that driver to change the speed or course of his vehicle so as to avoid an accident.
2.	602	No vehicle shall cross the transverse line shown in diagram 1003 nearest to the major road at the side of which that line is drawn, or if that line is not clearly visible, enter that major road, so as to be likely to cause danger to the driver of any other vehicle or to cause that driver to change the speed or course of his vehicle so as to avoid an accident.
3.	602 when used with 602.1	No vehicle shall cross the transverse line shown in diagram 1003 nearest to the level

1 Item No.	2 Type of diagram of sign	3 Requirements of sign
		crossing at the side of which that line is drawn or, if that line is not clearly visible, enter that level crossing, so as to be likely to cause danger to the driver of any railway vehicle or to cause the driver to change the speed or course of his vehicle so as to avoid an accident.
4.	649.1 and 649.2	No abnormal transport unit or, in relation to sign 649.1, no motor vehicle or vehicle combination which would be an abnormal transport unit if in sub-paragraph (*a*)(iii) of the definition of that expression in paragraph (2) below the reference to 38 tonnes were a reference to 32.5 tonnes, shall proceed onto or over an automatic half-barrier level crossing or an automatic open crossing (R) unless— (*a*) the driver of the unit has used a telephone provided at or near the crossing for the purpose of obtaining from a person, authorised in that behalf by the railway authority, permission for the unit to proceed; (*b*) that permission has been obtained before the unit proceeds; and (*c*) the unit proceeds in accordance with any terms attached to that permission. Provided that sub-paragraphs (*b*) and (*c*) above shall not apply if— (i) on the use by the driver of the telephone placed at or near the crossing he receives an indication for not less than two minutes that the telephone at the other end of the telephone line is being called, but no duly authorised person answers it or he receives no indication at all due to a fault or malfunction of the telephone; and (ii) the driver then drives the unit on to the crossing with the reasonable expectation of crossing it within times specified in a railway notice at that telephone as being times between which trains do not normally travel over that crossing.

* * *

13. Dimensions

(1) Where as respects any diagram in Schedule 1 a dimension for the sign shown in the diagram is indicated in one or more sets of brackets against a dimension not indicated in brackets, any dimension indicated in a set of brackets may be treated as an alternative to the dimension not so indicated.

(2) Where a sign shown in any of the diagrams 606 to 614, 616 or 637 to 645 is placed temporarily on a road by a constable or a person acting under the instructions (whether general or specific) of the chief officer of police for the purposes of a temporary statutory provision any dimension specified for the sign in such a diagram may be reduced so long as any dimension shown in the diagram for measurement horizontally is not reduced to less than 200 millimetres.

(3) A sign shown in a diagram in Part III of Schedule 1 other than in diagrams 717, 726, 734.7 and 754 and a sign shown in a diagram in Part V of that Schedule other than in any of the diagrams 901.1, 910, 912 to 915, and 916.1 to 920 shall be of such dimensions having regard to the character of the road and the speed of the vehicular traffic generally using it as are necessary to accommodate any place name, route symbol, route number, arrow, any indication of distance, or any other indication which in accordance with these Regulations may be shown therein and it is appropriate to show for the purpose for which the sign is placed on a road.

[(4) In any diagram in Schedule 1 and, subject to Regulation 20(2), in Schedule 2, any alternative dimension adopted for a sign shall be so selected that that alternative is matched by the selection of the alternative for every other dimension for which an indication is given in the said diagrams and which corresponds in numerical ascending or descending order with that alternative so adopted.]

[Regulation 13 is printed as amended by SI 1982 No 1879.]

14. Proportions and form of letters and numerals

(1) Subject to the provisions of paragraphs (2) to (4) of this Regulation, and without prejudice to Regulation 12 (1) (*l*) (variant requirements to signs there specified), all letters incorporated in the signs shown in the diagrams in Schedule 1 other than in diagrams 742.1 to 742.4, 828.1 and 849 to 852 shall have the proportions and form shown in either Part I, Part II, Part V or Part VI of Schedule 7, all numerals incorporated in the signs shown in the diagrams in Schedule 1 shall have the proportions and form shown in Part III or Part VII of Schedule 7 and all other characters incorporated in the signs shown in the diagrams in Schedule 1 shall have the proportions and form shown in Part IV or Part VIII of Schedule 7.

(2) Letters and numerals used for the purposes of indicating a route number on the sign shown in diagram 757 and on any sign shown in a diagram in Part V of Schedule 1 shall have the proportions and form shown in Part IX of Schedule 7.

(3) Any arrow to be used in any of the signs shown in diagrams 703.3, 718.3 or 908.2 when those signs are erected over the carriageway on structures on which there is also mounted equipment for displaying the signs shown in diagram 6021 in Schedule 6 shall have the proportion and form of the arrow shown in the last diagram in Part IV of Schedule 7 and any such arrow to be used in any of the signs first abovementioned when those signs are erected over the carriageway on structures on which

no such equipment is also mounted shall have the proportion and form of the arrow shown in the penultimate diagram in the said Part IV.

(4) Subject to and within the limits of any dimension specified as maximum or minimum in diagrams 743.1 and 744.1 any letters, numerals or other characters incorporated in those diagrams may have proportions and form other than the proportions and form shown in any Part of Schedule 7.

15. Illumination of signs by steady lighting

(1) In this Regulation (except in paragraph (6) as respects the sign shown in diagram 828.1) and in Regulations 16 and 17 the references to lighting shall be construed as references to steady lighting.

(2) Subject to the provisions of paragraph (7), this paragraph applies to the signs shown in diagrams 606, 609 to 616, 617 (except when used with the sign shown in diagram 618), 619, 619.1, 621 to 622.2 [622.4 and 625] in constructing the following sub-paragraphs—

(a) when the signs shown in diagrams 606 and 612 to 614 are fixed to light signals prescribed by Regulation 31, or by Regulation 31 as varied by Regulation 32, they shall be illuminated by a means of internal lighting at all times except when the light signals to which they are fixed are being maintained or repaired;

(b) when the signs shown in diagrams 606, 609 to 611 [616 and 625] are mounted in a bollard fitted with a means of lighting them internally, they shall be illuminated throughout the hours of darkness by that means of internal lighting;

(c) without prejudice to the next following sub-paragraph, if a sign specified in sub-paragraph (a) above when not so fixed, or a sign specified in sub-paragraph (b) above when not so mounted, or any other sign to which this paragraph applies is erected on a road within 50 metres of any lamp lit by electricity which forms part of a system of street-lighting furnished by means of at least three such lamps placed not more than 183 metres apart, that sign shall be illuminated by a means of internal or external lighting either for so long as the said system is illuminated, or throughout the hours of darkness, unless it is erected temporarily for any of the following reasons—

(i) for the purpose of a temporary statutory provision,

(ii) by reason of some emergency, or,

(iii) if that road is a road subject to a speed limit of 30 m.p.h. or under, by reason of the execution of works, or of any obstruction on the road;

(d) any sign to which this paragraph applies and is either not so fixed as provided in sub-paragraph (a) or is erected in such a manner that it is not illuminated regularly throughout the hours of darkness by a means of internal or external lighting, shall be illuminated by the use of reflecting material in accordance with the provisions of Regulation 18 (3) and (4).

(3) Subject to the provisions of paragraph (7), this paragraph applies to any sign shown in diagrams 501, 504.1 to 510, 512, 513, 516, 517, 520 to 524.1, 528 to 532.1, 533, 537, 538, 543, 544 to [544.3], 555, 556, 564, 564.5 to 566, 567.2, 569.2, 569.3, 601.1, 602, 626.1, 628.1 to 632, 642 (if the diameter of that sign is more than 450 millimetres), 649.1, [649.2], 652 to [654.1], 701 to 712.1, 714, 718.2, 718.3, 727.2, 818 to 819.2, 837.1 to 838.2, 858 to 858.2, 901.1 to 911, 915 to 916.1, 918.1 and 919.1 in construing the following sub-paragraphs—

(a) without prejudice to the next following sub-paragraph, if a sign to which this paragraph applies is erected on a road within 50 metres of any such lamp as is described in sub-paragraph (*c*) of paragraph (2) that sign shall be illuminated by a means of internal or external lighting as is therein provided unless it is erected temporarily for such a reason as is therein specified;

(*b*) any sign to which this paragraph applies which is erected in such a manner that it is not illuminated regularly throughout the hours of darkness by a means of internal or external lighting, shall be illuminated by the use of reflecting material as provided by paragraph (2) (*d*).

(4) Any sign shown in diagrams 515, 539 to 542.2, 545, 548 to 552, 554, 554.1, 557 to 559, 562, 569, 569.1, 569.4, 574, 577, 578, 580, 633 to 635, 642 (if the diameter of that sign is 450 millimetres or less), 646, 647, 655, 713, 715 to 718.1, 719 to 727, 728 to 737.1, 746.2, 754 to 757, 760, 761, 801, 806 to 806.3, 808.1, 808.3, 811 to [812.2, 812.5 and 812.6], 819.3 to 825, 827, 828.2, 830 to 832.2, 838.3, 838.4, 854 to 856, 861 to 863, 912, 917, 920 and 925 may be illuminated by a means of internal or external lighting, but if not so illuminated throughout the hours of darkness, shall be illuminated by the use of reflecting material in accordance with the provisions of Regulation 18 (3) and (4).

(5) The signs shown in diagrams [557.1] 603, 604 and 814, shall be illuminated throughout the hours of darkness by a means of internal or external lighting.

(6) The sign shown in diagram 828.1 shall be illuminated by an intermittent light flashing at a rate of not less than 54 nor more than 90 flashes per minute during such times only as it is necessary that the sign shall be illuminated for the purpose of indicating the information shown in diagram 828.1.

(7) Where a sign to which any of the foregoing paragraphs applies is placed on or near a road for the purpose of conveying a warning or information from time to time to vehicular traffic, or in connection with a statutory prohibition, restriction or requirement which relates to such traffic but does not apply at all times, that sign shall be illuminated in accordance with such of the foregoing provisions of this Regulation as apply to it but only during such times as, for the said purpose or in the said connection, it is necessary that the sign shall be visible from a reasonable distance to drivers of approaching motor vehicles, any other provision of this Regulation to the contrary notwithstanding.

(8) Subject to the foregoing paragraphs of this Regulation and to Regulation 19, any sign shown in a diagram in Schedule 1 may be illuminated by a means of internal or external lighting and where, subject as aforesaid, the means of lighting any such sign is external, then that means of lighting shall be either fitted to the sign or to the structure on which it is mounted or otherwise specially provided.

[Regulation 15 is printed as amended by SI 1982 No 1879, SI 1983 No 1088, and SI 1984 No 966.]

16. Where a sign shown in a diagram in Schedule 1 (not being a sign consisting of a plate) is illuminated by a means of lighting in accordance with the provisions of Regulation 15 and a plate shown in a diagram in that Schedule is used in conjunction with that sign, the said plate shall, unless the means of lighting provided for the illumination of the sign adequately illuminates the plate, be illuminated, during such times as the sign is illuminated, by a means of lighting and that means of lighting shall accord with that one of the methods of lighting, namely, internal or external adopted for the illumination of the sign.

*　　*　　*

18. Illumination of signs by reflecting material

(1) Nothing in this Regulation shall apply to the signs shown in diagrams 536, 560, 561 and 828.1.

(2) Subject to the provisions of Regulation 15 and paragraph (1) above any sign shown in a diagram in Schedule 1 shall be illuminated by the use of reflecting material in accordance with the following provisions of this Regulation.

(3) Subject to paragraph (4) where reflecting material is used on any sign shown in a diagram in Schedule 1 it shall be of the same colour as that of, and extend throughout, that part of the sign to which it is applied:

Provided that no reflecting material shall be applied to—

(a) any part of a sign coloured black, or

(b) any part of the sign shown in diagram 605.1 which is coloured fluorescent yellow unless the reflecting material is applied to that part in horizontal strips each such strip being 3 millimetres wide, spaced at intervals of 6 millimetres from each other, the centre of the sign being located at a point in one such interval equidistant from the strips so spaced.

In this paragraph the word 'part', in relation to a sign, means any part of the surface of that sign uniformly coloured and bounded by parts of a different colour.

(4) (a) Where in accordance with the last paragraph, different colours of reflecting material are used next to one another on the same sign being a traffic sign to which this paragraph applies in accordance with the next following sub-paragraph, a gap of not more than 20 millimetres in width may be left between the different colours of reflecting material.

(b) This paragraph applies only to traffic signs which being circular in shape have a diameter of at least 1.2 metres, being triangular in shape have a height of at least 1.2 metres along the perpendicular from apex to base, or being rectangular in shape have a side which is at least 1.2 metres in length.

*   *   *

SECTION IV

Traffic Signs shown in Schedule 2

20. Road markings

(1) Subject to the provisions of these Regulations, a traffic sign consisting of a line or mark on a road (in these Regulations referred to as a 'road marking') for conveying to traffic on roads a warning, a requirement or information of the description specified under a diagram (other than diagrams 1003 and 1013.1) in Schedule 2 shall be of the size and type shown in the diagram relating to that warning, requirement or information.

(2) In any diagram in Schedule 2, the dimensions indicated in brackets against dimensions not so indicated may be treated as an alternative to the last mentioned dimensions.

(3) Where the circumstances so require, the indication given by any of the signs shown in the diagrams in Schedule 2 shall or may be varied as hereinafter provided in this paragraph:—

(a) any indication given by such a sign may be varied in the respect (if any) in which it is shown below the diagram relating to that sign that the indication may be varied;

(*b*) in the sign shown in diagram 1035 route numbers place names and the direction in which any arrow-head points shall be varied and interchangeable to accord with the circumstances but the words 'turn left', 'ahead' or 'turn right' shall not appear as a part of the said sign.

21. Particular road markings

A road marking for conveying to vehicular traffic the requirement specified in paragraph (2) of the next succeeding Regulation shall be of the size and type shown in diagram 1003.

22.—(1) For the purposes of this Regulation—

'minor road' means a road at a road junction on which road there are placed the transverse lines shown in diagram 1003;

'major road' means the road at a road junction into which road there emerges vehicular traffic from a minor road.

(2) Except as provided by the next following paragraph, the requirement conveyed by the said transverse lines, whether or not they are used in conjunction with the sign shown in diagram 602, shall be that no vehicle shall proceed past such one of those lines as is nearest to the major road into that road in such a manner or at such a time as is likely to cause danger to the driver of any other vehicle on the major road or as to necessitate the driver of any such other vehicle to change its speed or course in order to avoid an accident with the first-mentioned vehicle.

(3) Whenever the said transverse lines are used in conjunction with the sign shown in diagram 602 and that sign is at the same time used in combination with the sign shown in diagram 602.1 at a level crossing where a road is crossed by a railway then the said requirement shall be that no vehicle shall proceed past such one of those lines as is nearest to the said level crossing in such a manner or at such a time as is likely to cause the driver of any railway vehicle to change its speed to avoid collision with the vehicle first above-mentioned in this paragraph.

23.—(1) A road marking for conveying the requirements specified in the next succeeding paragraph and the warning specified in paragraph (5) shall be of the size and type shown in diagram 1013.1.

(2) The requirements conveyed by the road marking mentioned in the last preceding paragraph shall be that—

(*a*) subject to the provisions of paragraph (3), no vehicle shall stop on any length of road along which the marking has been placed at any point between the two ends of the marking; and

(*b*) subject to the provisions of paragraph (4), every vehicle proceeding on any length of road along which the marking has been so placed that, as viewed in the direction of travel of the vehicle, the continuous line is on the left of a dotted line or of another continuous line, shall be so driven as to keep the first-mentioned continuous line on the right hand or off side of the vehicle.

(3) Nothing in sub-paragraph (*a*) of the last preceding paragraph shall apply—

(*a*) so as to prevent a vehicle stopping on any length of road so long as may be necessary—

   (i) to enable a person to board or alight from the vehicle,

  (ii) to enable goods to be loaded on to or to be unloaded from the vehicle, or

 (iii) to enable the vehicle, if it cannot be used for such purpose without stopping on that length of road, to be used in connection with any building operation or demolition, the removal of any obstruction to traffic, the maintenance, improvement or reconstruction of that length of road, or the laying, erection, alteration or repair in or near to that length of road of any sewer or of any main, pipe or apparatus for the supply of gas, water or electricity, or of any telegraphic line as defined in the Telegraph Act 1878,

so, however, that no vehicle shall be enabled by virtue of this sub-paragraph to stop for any of the purposes at (i), (ii) or (iii) above on a part of that length of road, not being a lay-by or a road verge, if it is reasonably practicable to stop the vehicle for that purpose on a part of that length of road, being a lay-by or a road verge;

(b) to a vehicle used for fire brigade, ambulance or police purposes;

(c) to a pedal bicycle not having a sidecar attached thereto, whether additional means of propulsion by mechanical power are attached to the bicycle or not;

(d) to a vehicle stopping in any case where the person in control of the vehicle is required by law to stop, or is obliged to do so in order to avoid an accident, or is prevented from proceeding by circumstances outside his control; or

(e) to anything done with the permission of a police constable in uniform or in accordance with the direction of a traffic warden.

(4) Nothing in sub-paragraph (b) of paragraph (2) shall apply so as to prevent a vehicle crossing or straddling the continuous line first mentioned in that sub-paragraph for the purpose of obtaining access to any other road joining the length of road along which the line is placed or to land or premises situated on or adjacent to the said length of road or if it is necessary to do so—

(a) in order to pass a stationary vehicle, or owing to circumstances outside the control of the driver or in order to avoid an accident, or

(b) for the purposes of complying with any direction of a police constable in uniform or a traffic warden.

(5) The warning conveyed by the road marking mentioned in paragraph (1) shall be that no vehicle while travelling next to a dotted line placed on the left, as viewed in the direction of travel of the vehicle, of a continuous line should cross or straddle the first mentioned line unless it is seen by the driver of the vehicle to be safe to do so.

[The Telegraph Act 1878, s 2, defines 'telegraphic line' as 'telegraphs, posts, and any work (within the meaning of the Telegraph Act 1863) and also any cables, apparatus, pneumatic or other tube, pipe, or thing whatsoever used for the purpose of transmitting telegraphic messages or maintaining telegraphic communication, and includes any portion of a telegraphic line as defined by this Act'. In the definition of 'telegraphic line' the words from 'and also' to 'communication' have been repealed by the British Telecommunications Act 1981, s 89 (1), and Sched 6, Part I. The Telegraph Act 1863, s 3, defines 'telegraph' as 'a wire or wires used for the purpose of telegraphic communication, with any casing, coating, tube, or pipe inclosing the same, and any apparatus connected therewith for the purpose of telegraphic communication'; 'post' as 'a post, pole, standard, stay, strut, or other above-ground contrivance for carrying, suspending, or supporting a telegraph'; and 'work' as including telegraphs and posts.]

24. Colour of road markings

(1) Except as otherwise provided by this Regulation, the road markings shown in the diagrams in Schedule 2 shall be white.

(2) Road markings shown in diagrams 1016.1 to 1021, 1027.1 and 1043 to 1045 shall be yellow.

(3) In the road markings shown in the diagrams 1025.1 and 1025.3 the line shown therein as coloured yellow and having a width of 200 or 300 millimetres shall be yellow.

(4) The road markings shown in diagrams 1025 and 1025.2 and when displaying the word 'Taxis' in diagram 1028.1 shall be yellow in the following but in no other circumstances, that is to say, where those markings are placed in a part of the carriageway which is subject to restrictions on waiting or on waiting, loading and unloading for at least 8 hours during the period from 7 a.m. to 7 p.m. on at least 4 days, none of them being a Sunday, in any week by all vehicles, other than stage and express carriages in the case of the markings shown in diagrams 1025 or 1025.2 and other than hackney carriages in the case of the marking shown in diagram 1028.1.

(5) Road markings shown in diagram 1055 consisting of marks arranged in transverse lines may be either white or silver or light grey in colour.

(6) In this Regulation, 'hackney carriage' has the same meaning as in the Vehicles (Excise) Act 1971.

[*The term 'hackney carriage' is defined in the Vehicles (Excise) Act 1971, s 38 (1), as meaning: 'a mechanically propelled vehicle standing or plying for hire, and includes any mechanically propelled vehicle let for hire by a person whose trade it is to sell mechanically propelled vehicles or to let mechanically propelled vehicles for hire, so however that for the purpose of this definition a letting under a hire-purchase agreement (as defined in section 1 of the Hire-Purchase Act 1965 or section 1 of the Hire-Purchase (Scotland) Act 1965) shall not be treated as a letting for hire'. This definition was substituted and definitions of 'conditional sale agreement', 'hire agreement' and 'hire-purchase agreement' were added to s 38 (1) with effect from 19 May 1985 (see the Consumer Credit Act 1974 (Commencement No 8) Order 1983 (SI 1983 No 1551) by the Consumer Credit Act 1974, s 192, Sched 4, para 32. Under the new definition, 'hackney carriage' means a mechanically propelled vehicle standing or plying for hire and includes any mechanically propelled vehicle bailed or (in Scotland) hired under a hire agreement by a person whose trade it is to sell such vehicles or bail or hire them under hire agreements. For these purposes, 'hire agreement' means an agreement for the bailment or (in Scotland) the hiring of a vehicle which is not a hire-purchase agreement. A 'hire purchase agreement' is an agreement, other than a conditional sale agreement, under which—(a) a vehicle is bailed or (in Scotland) hired in return for periodical payments by the person to whom it is bailed or hired, and (b) the property in the vehicle will pass to that person if the terms of the agreement are complied with and one or more of the following occurs—(i) the exercise of an option to purchase by that person, (ii) the doing of any other specified act by any party to the agreement, and/ or (iii) the happening of any other specified event. A 'conditional sale agreement' is an agreement for the sale of a vehicle under which the purchase price or part of it is payable by instalments, and the property in the vehicle is to remain in the seller (notwithstanding that the buyer is to be in possession of the vehicle) until such conditions as may be specified in the agreement are fulfilled.*]

25. Use on road markings of reflecting material and studs with reflectors

(1) (a) The road markings shown in diagrams 1011 to 1014 shall be illuminated with reflecting material, and

(b) studs incorporating reflectors and spaced so as to form a single line of studs at intervals of not less than 3·6 nor more than 4·4 metres apart shall be fitted between the two lines constituting the marking shown in diagram 1013.1 unless that marking—

    (i) is placed on any automatic railway level crossing, or

(ii) is placed on a length of the road falling within a distance of 90 metres measured from the transverse stop line provided in association with any such crossing and in conformity with diagram 1001, or

(iii) is so placed that the continuous lines shown in diagram 1013.1 are more than 175 millimetres apart and are separated by an area of cross-hatching so shown.

(c) Where the marking shown in diagram 1013.1 is placed as described in any of the cases in sub-paragraph (b) (i) to (iii) above, then such studs as aforesaid and so spaced as aforesaid shall be fitted either within the width of each of the said two lines or between them.

In this paragraph the expression 'automatic railway level crossing' means an automatic half-barrier level crossing, and an automatic open crossing (R) as both those crossings are defined for the purposes of Regulation 11 (2) and includes a level crossing which is the same as an automatic open crossing (R) except that the operation of the light signals is monitored at or near the crossing by the driver of the train instead of remotely from the crossing.

(2) Subject to the foregoing provisions of this Regulation, any road marking may be illuminated with reflecting material and studs incorporating reflectors may be fitted to the markings shown in diagrams 1003.4 to 1012.1, 1025.2, 1025.3 and 1040 to 1042 in such a manner that any such stud shall not be fitted to any mark coloured white and forming part of any of the markings so shown as aforesaid but shall be applied to the surface of the carriageway in the gap between any two such marks:

Provided that in the case of the markings shown in diagram 1011 or 1012.1, the said studs shall, if fitted, be applied to the surface of the carriageway at the side of and adjacent to the line shown in the diagram.

[(2A) The road markings shown in diagram 1060 including the permitted variants shall be illuminated with reflecting material.]

(3) Reflectors incorporated in studs shall be white except that in the case of reflectors fitted to the markings shown in diagrams 1009 to 1012.1, 1025.2, 1025.3, 1041 and 1042 they may be—

(a) red where the near side edge of a carriageway is indicated to drivers of approaching motor vehicles, or when fitted to the markings shown in diagrams 1041 and 1042 to indicate the offside edge of a carriageway.

(b) amber to indicate the offside edge of a carriageway which is contiguous to a central reservation or which carries traffic in one direction only, and

(c) green when fitted to the markings shown in diagrams 1009, 1010, 1025.2 and 1025.3 where the edge of any part of the carriageway available for through traffic at a road junction, a lay-by or a parking place is so indicated as aforesaid.

In this Regulation 'central reservation' means any provision made in a road (not being the provision of a street refuge) for dividing the road for the safety or guidance of vehicular traffic.

[Regulation 25 is printed as amended by SI 1983 No 1088.]

*   *   *

27. Certain temporary signs

(1) Notwithstanding the provisions of Regulation 9 and subject to the succeeding paragraphs of this Regulation, signs placed temporarily on or near a road—

(a) for conveying to traffic—

(i) information as respects deviations of, or alternative traffic routes,

(ii) information as respects the route which may conveniently be followed on the occasion of a sports meeting, exhibition or other public gathering, in each case attracting a considerable volume of traffic,

(iii) information as to the date from which works are to be executed on or near a road, or

[(iv) information or warnings as to the avoidance of any temporary hazards occasioned by works being executed on or near a road, by adverse weather conditions or other natural causes, by the failure of street lighting or by malfunction of or damage to any apparatus, equipment, or facility used in connection with the road or any thing situated on near or under it or by damage to the road itself.]

(b) for conveying to vehicular traffic any prohibition, restriction or requirement of a description required for the purposes of a temporary statutory provision; or

(c) pending the erection of any permanent sign prescribed by these Regulations, for conveying to traffic the indication which such a permanent sign indicates,

may be of such size, colour and type as is specified in the following provisions of this Regulation.

(2) Every such sign placed as aforesaid (hereinafter referred to as a 'temporary sign') shall be of a shape which—

(a) is rectangular;

(b) is rectangular, but with the corners rounded; or

(c) is rectangular, but with one end pointed.

(3) Every temporary sign shall be of such size as is necessary to accommodate the wording, numerals, arrows or chevrons and any symbol taken from any diagram shown in Schedule 1 appropriate to the purpose for which the sign is placed as aforesaid and to accommodate any arms, badge, device, words or letters incorporated in the sign in accordance with the provisions of paragraph (6).

(4) Every letter and numeral incorporated in a temporary sign other than any letter incorporated in the sign in accordance with the provisions of paragraph (6) shall be not less than 40 nor more than 250 millimetres in height, and every arrow so incorporated shall be not less than 250 nor more than 500 millimetres in length except that where an arrow is incorporated in the index part of a sign with a pointed end such arrow shall be not less than 100 nor more than 200 millimetres in length.

(5) Every letter, numeral, arrow, chevron or symbol incorporated in a temporary sign shall be—

(a) black on a background of white, or yellow; or

(b) white on a blue background[; or]

[(c) if the sign conveys information or warnings as to the avoidance of any temporary hazards such as are mentioned in paragraph (1)(a)(iv) above, white on a red background.]

(6) There may be incorporated in, or attached to, a temporary sign the arms, badge or other device of a highway authority, police authority or an organisation representative of road users, or words or letters indicating the highway authority, or that the sign is a police sign.

(7) No sign shall by virtue of this Regulation convey to traffic any information, warning, requirement, restriction or prohibition of a description which can be so con-

veyed either by a sign shown in a diagram in Part I, Part II, or Part IV of Schedule 1 or by a sign so shown used in combination with or in conjunction with another sign shown in such a diagram.

[Regulation 27 is printed as amended by SI 1982 No 1879.]

*   *   *

31.—(1) Light signals may be used for the control of vehicular traffic and shall be of the size, colour and type prescribed by paragraph (2), by paragraph (3) or by paragraph 2(4).

(2) The size, colour and type of light signals prescribed by this paragraph shall be as follows:—

(*a*) three lights shall be used, one red, one amber and one green;

(*b*) the lamps showing the coloured lights aforesaid shall be arranged vertically, the lamp showing a red light being the uppermost and that showing a green light the lowermost;

(*c*) each lamp shall be separately illuminated and the effective diameter of the lens thereof shall be not less than 195 nor more than 220 millimetres unless the lens is a lens of the kind shown in diagram 3001 when instead the said diameter may be not less than 290 nor more than 310 millimetres;

(*d*) the height of the centre of the amber lens from the surface of the carriageway in the immediate vicinity shall be in the case of signals placed at the side of the carriageway or on a street refuge not less than 2·4 nor more than 4 metres and in the case of signals placed elsewhere and over the carriageway not less than 6·1 nor more than 9 metres;

(*e*) the centres of adjacent lenses shall be not less than 305 nor more than 360 millimetres apart;

(*f*) no lettering shall be used upon the lenses or in connection with a light signal;

(*g*) the sequence of the lights shown for the purpose of controlling vehicular traffic shall be as follows:—
  (i) red,
  (ii) amber and red together,
  (iii) green,
  (iv) amber.

(3) The size, colour and type of light signals prescribed by this paragraph shall be as follows:—

(*a*) Four lamps each showing an intermittent red light shall be used.

(*b*) The lamps shall be so fitted as to enclose a rectangular area bounded by the one pair of sides extending horizontally and terminating as to each side in the centres of each pair of lenses (in these Regulations called 'the horizontal pairs') and by the other pair of sides extending vertically in relation to the ground and terminating as to each side in the centres of each pair of lenses (in these Regulations called 'the vertical pairs').

(*c*) When the four lamps are erected beside the carriageway, the distance between the centres of the lenses for each of the horizontal pairs shall be not less than 945 nor more than 955 millimetres and for each of the vertical pairs shall be not less than 695 nor more than 705 millimetres in accordance with the arrangement shown in diagram 6032.

(*d*) When the four lamps are erected over the carriageway, the distance between the said centres for each of the horizontal pairs shall be not less than 1395 nor more than 1405 millimetres and for each of the vertical pairs not less than 545 nor more than 555 millimetres in accordance with the arrangement shown in diagram 6031.

(e) Subject to the provisions of the next following sub-paragraph, each lamp shall be separately illuminated and the effective diameter of the lens thereof shall be not less than 120 nor more than 130 millimetres.

(f) When the signal is operated, each lamp shall show its intermittent red light at a rate of flashing of not less than 60 nor more than 90 flashes per minute, and in such a manner that the lights of one of the vertical pairs are always shown when the lights of the other vertical pair are not shown.

(g) The height of the centres of the lenses comprising the lower of the horizontal pairs from the surface of the carriageway in the immediate vicinity shall be in the case of signals placed at the side of the carriageway not less than 1·8 nor more than 3·2 metres and in the case of signals placed over the carriageway not less than 5·8 nor more than 6·8 metres.

(h) No lettering of any kind shall be used upon any of the lenses.

(4) The size, colour and type of light signals prescribed by this paragraph shall be as follows:—

(a) two lamps each showing an intermittent red light and one lamp showing a steady amber light shall be used;

(b) the lamps showing an intermittent red light shall be arranged horizontally so that there is a distance of not less than 585 nor more than 665 millimetres between the centres of the lenses of the lamps;

(c) the lamp showing the amber light shall be placed below the red lenses in such a position that a vertical line passing through the centre of the lamp is horizontally equidistant from the vertical lines passing through the centre of each red lens and that the vertical distance between a horizontal line passing through the centres of the red lenses is not less than 235 nor more than 345 millimetres;

(d) each lamp shall be separately illuminated and the effective diameter of the lens thereof shall be not less than 195 nor more than 220 millimetres;

(e) when the lamps showing an intermittent red light are operated, each such lamp shall show a red light at a rate of flashing of not less than 60 nor more than 90 flashes per minute, and in such a manner that the light of one lamp is always shown at a time when the light of the other lamp is not shown;

(f) the height of the centre of the amber lens from the surface of the carrriageway in the immediate vicinity shall be in the case of signals placed at the side of the carriageway or on a street refuge not less than 2·4 nor more than 4 metres and in the case of signals placed elsewhere and over the carriageway not less than 6·1 nor more than 9 metres;

(g) the lenses shall be provided with a rectangular backing board having an overall width of not less than 1·3 metres and extending not less than 300 millimetres above the centre of each of the red lenses and not less than 300 millimetres below the centre of the amber lens, which board shall be coloured black, save for a white border having a width of not less than 80 nor more than 100 millimetres on the side from which the lamps show;

(h) the sequence of the signal lights under this paragraph shown for the purpose of controlling vehicular traffic shall be amber followed by red;

(i) no lettering of any kind shall appear on any of the lenses.

(5) Light signals prescribed by paragraph (4) may be surmounted by a cross of the size, colour and type shown in diagrams 542 and 542.1.

32.—(1) Subject to the next following paragraph, a lens or lenses of the size and colour shown in diagram 3001 in Schedule 3, which, when illuminated, shows a green arrow—

(a) may be substituted for the lens showing the green light in the light signals referred to in Regulation 31 (2) in any of the methods shown in diagrams 3003, 3005, 3006 and 3011 in the said Schedule;

(b) may be affixed to the light signals referred to in Regulation 31 (2) or to those signals as altered in accordance with the preceding sub-paragraph in any of the methods shown in diagram 3002 and diagrams 3004 to 3011 in the said Schedule.

In this paragraph, the substitution authorised in sub-paragraph (a) thereof in the method shown in the said diagram 3011 shall be treated as having been effected by means of the upper arrow shown in that diagram, the lower arrow shown therein being treated as affixed in accordance with sub-paragraphs (b) thereof.

(2) When a lens is, or lenses are, so affixed as provided in paragraph (1) (b) and any one lens so affixed is of the larger of the two sizes specified in diagram 3001 in the said Schedule, the distance between the centre of that lens and the centre of any other lens affixed next in position immediately above, below or to the side of that first mentioned lens shall be not less than 415 nor more than 440 millimetres.

(3) The direction in which the arrow shown in diagram 3003 in the said Schedule points may be varied so as to be—

(a) a direction which lies straight upright, or

(b) a direction which lies at any angle between 90 degrees either to the left or to the right of the said upright direction.

(4) The direction in which any arrow shown in any of the diagrams 3002, 3004 to 3006, 3009 and 3010 in the said Schedule points may be varied so as to be—

(a) a direction which lies straight upright, or

(b) a direction which lies between the direction shown in the diagram showing that arrow and the said upright direction.

(5) The direction in which the upper arrow shown in diagram 3007 of the said Schedule points may be varied so as to be a direction which lies at any angle from the upright position shown to an angle of 45 degrees to the left and the direction in which the upper arrow shown in diagram 3008 in that Schedule points may be so varied as aforesaid to an angle of 45 degrees to the right.

(6) The direction in which the lower arrow shown in each of the said diagrams 3007 and 3008 points may be varied so as to be a direction which lies at any angle from the position shown in each such diagram respectively to an angle of 45 degrees towards the upright position as shown for the upper arrow in each such diagram.

(7) When both arrows shown in diagram 3011 of the said Schedule are illuminated and extinguished simultaneously the direction in which the upper arrow shown in that diagram points may be varied so as to be a direction which lies at any angle from the position so shown for that arrow to an angle of 45 degrees to the right passing through an arc of 135 degrees and the direction in which the lower arrow so shown points may be varied so as to be a direction which lies at any angle from the position

so shown for that arrow to an angle of 45 degrees towards the upright position or alternatively so as to be a direction lying at any angle from a position in which that arrow faces in the opposite direction from that so shown to an angle 45 degrees towards the upright position.

(8) When both arrows shown in the said diagram 3011 are illuminated and extinguished independently of each other, the direction of each such arrow may be varied so as to be a direction which lies at any angle between 90 degrees either to the left or to the right of the upright position.

33. Portable light signals for control of vehicular traffic

(1) Portable light signals may be used for the control of vehicular traffic in the circumstances specified at (a) to (c) of this paragraph—

[(a) on a length of road having no junction along its length with any other road carrying vehicular traffic to or from it and where the width of the carriageway of that length of road is temporarily restricted so that it will carry only one line of traffic,]

(b) at a level crossing where a road is crossed by a railway when work in relation to that crossing is being carried out, or

(c) during the progress of temporary schemes of traffic control, if the signals are being operated and maintained by, and under the regular supervision of, the police or have been erected at a site approved in writing by the highway authority.

[(2) Such light signals shall comply with—

(a) the provisions of Regulation 31(2)(a), (b), (c), (f) and (g), or if appropriate, those provisions as varied by Regulation 32(1), and

(b) the provisions of Regulation 31(2)(e), or if appropriate, those provisions as varied by Regulation 32(2) as if for '305' there appeared '270'.]

[Regulation 33 is printed as amended by SI 1982 No 1879.]

34. Significance of light signals

(1) The significance of the light signals prescribed by Regulation 31 (2) or by Regulation 33 shall be as follows:—

(a) except as provided in the next following sub-paragraph, the red signal shall convey the prohibition that vehicular traffic shall not proceed beyond the stop line on the carriageway provided in conjunction with the signals or, if that line is not for the time being visible or there is no stop line, beyond the post or other structure on or in which the primary signals are mounted;

(b) on an occasion when a vehicle is being used for fire brigade, ambulance or police purposes and the observance of the prohibition conveyed by the red signal as provided by the last preceding sub-paragraph would be likely to hinder the use of that vehicle for the purpose for which it is being used on that occasion, then the said sub-paragraph shall not apply to that vehicle; but instead the prohibition conveyed to that vehicle by the red signal shall be that that vehicle shall not proceed beyond the stop line, or as the case may be as provided by the said sub-paragraph, beyond the said post or other structure in such a manner or at such a time—

   (i) as is likely to cause danger to the driver of any other vehicle proceeding on or from another road or on or from another part of the same road in accordance with the indications of the light signals operating there in association with the said red signal or as to necessitate the driver of any other such vehicle to change its speed or course in order to avoid an accident, or

(ii) in the case of any traffic which is not vehicular, as is likely to cause danger to that traffic proceeding on or from another road or on or from another part of the same road;

(c) the amber-with-red signal shall be taken to denote an impending change in the indication given by the signals from red to green but shall not alter the prohibition conveyed by the red signal;

(d) the green signal shall indicate that vehicular traffic may pass the signals and proceed straight on or to the left or to the right;

(e) the amber signal shall, when shown alone, convey the prohibition that vehicular traffic shall not proceed beyond the stop line or, if that line is not for the time being visible or there is no stop line, beyond the said post or other structure, except in the case of any vehicle which when the signal first appears is so close to the said line, post or structure that it cannot safely be stopped before passing the line, post or structure.

(2) The significance of the light signals prescribed by Regulation 31 (2) as varied in accordance with the provisions of Regulation 32, shall be as follows:—

(a) subject as provided in sub-paragraph (d) of this paragraph, the red signal shall convey the prohibition that vehicular traffic shall not proceed beyond the stop line on the carriageway provided in conjunction with the signals or if the stop line is not for the time being visible or there is no stop line, beyond the post or other structure on or in which the primary signals are mounted, except that when a vehicle is being used on such an occasion as is specified in paragraph (1) (b), the foregoing prohibition prescribed by this sub-paragraph shall not then apply to that vehicle but instead the prohibition conveyed to it on that occasion by the red signal shall be the same as that provided by paragraph (1) (b) in relation to the vehicle mentioned in that paragraph;

(b) subject as provided in sub-paragraph (d) of this paragraph, the amber-with-red signal shall denote an impending change in the indication given by the signals from red to green (where a green signal is provided) or from red to a green arrow or arrows but shall not alter the prohibition conveyed by the red signal;

(c) the green signal (where a green signal is provided) shall indicate that vehicular traffic may pass the signals and proceed straight on or to the left or to the right;

(d) any green arrow during such time as it is illuminated shall indicate that vehicular traffic may pass the signals and proceed in the direction indicated by the arrow notwithstanding any other indication given by the signals;

(e) the amber signal shall, when shown alone, convey the prohibition that vehicular traffic shall not proceed beyond the stop line, or if the stop line is not for the time being visible or there is no stop line, beyond the said post or other structure, except in the case of any vehicle which when the signal first appears is so close to the said line, post or structure that it cannot safely be stopped before passing the line, post or structure.

(3) Vehicular traffic passing any light signals in accordance with the foregoing provisions of this Regulation shall proceed with due regard to the safety of other users of the road and subject to the direction of any police constable in uniform or other duly authorised person who may be engaged in the regulation of traffic.

(4) The significance of the light signals prescribed by Regulation 31 (3) shall be

that the intermittent red lights when displayed at the side of the carriageway convey the prohibition that vehicular traffic shall not proceed beyond those lights and when displayed over the carriageway so as to operate in relation to vehicular traffic proceeding in the traffic lane (as defined by Regulation 36 (1)) situated immediately beneath them, the said lights convey the prohibition that such vehicular traffic as aforesaid shall not proceed beyond those lights:

Provided that this paragraph shall not apply to a vehicle when it is being used on such an occasion as is specified in Regulation 34 (1) (b); and for that vehicle when it is being so used, the intermittent red lights whether so displayed at the side of or over the carriageway shall have no significance.

(5) The significance of the light signals prescribed by Regulation 31 (4) shall be as follows:—

(a) the amber signal shall convey the prohibition that vehicular traffic shall not proceed beyond the stop line of the carriageway provided in conjunction with the signal or, if that line is not for the time being visible or there is no stop line beyond the post or other structure on or in which the primary signals are mounted, except in the case of any vehicle which when the signal first appears is so close to the said post or structure, that it cannot safely be stopped before passing the post or structure; and

(b) the intermittent red signals shall convey the prohibition that vehicular traffic shall not proceed beyond the stop line on the carriageway provided in conjunction with the signals or, if that line is not for the time being visible or there is no stop line, beyond the said post or structure.

(6) In this Regulation,

(a) the expression 'Stop line' means the road marking shown in diagram 1001 placed on the carriageway in conjunction with light signals being either primary signals alone, or secondary signals alone or both primary and secondary signals;

(b) any reference to light signals, to the signals or to a signal of a particular colour, is, where secondary signals have been erected as well as primary signals, a reference to the light signals, signals or particular signal displayed by both the primary signals and the secondary signals or by either the primary signals operating without the secondary signals, or by the secondary signals operating without the primary signals;

(c) the expression 'primary signals' means light signals erected on or near the carriageway of a road and sited in the vicinity of either one end or both ends of the stop line or, if there is no stop line, sited at either or both edges of the carriageway or part of that carriageway which is in use by the traffic approaching and controlled by the signals; and

(d) the expression 'secondary signals' means light signals erected on or near the carriageway facing approaching traffic in the same direction as the primary signals but sited beyond those signals as viewed from the direction of travel of such traffic.

*   *   *

36. Light signals for lane control of vehicular traffic

(1) In this Regulation the expression 'traffic lane' means, in relation to a road, a part of the carriageway having as a boundary which separates it from another such part, a road marking of the type shown either in diagram 1004, 1005, 1007 or 1013.1.

(2) Light signals placed above the carriageway and facing the direction of the on-coming vehicular traffic may be used for the control of that traffic proceeding along the traffic lane over and in relation to which those signals have been so placed and, subject to the provisions of this Regulation, shall be of the size, colour and type shown in diagrams [5001 to 5004].

(3) The height of the centre of each such signal from the surface of the carriageway in the immediate vicinity shall be not less than 5.5 metres or more than 9 metres.

(4) The said signals shall be so designed that—

(a) the red cross shown in diagrams 5003 and 5004 (hereinafter referred to as 'the red cross') can be internally illuminated in such a manner as to show a steady red light,

(b) the white arrow shown in diagrams 5001 and 5002 (hereinafter referred to as 'the white downward arrow') can be internally illuminated by a steady white light, and

(c) whenever the red cross is illuminated above a traffic lane, the white downward arrow above that traffic lane is not also then illuminated and whenever the white downward arrow is illuminated above that same lane, the red cross is not also then illuminated.

(5) The significance of the light signals prescribed by this Regulation shall be—

(a) the red cross conveys to vehicular traffic proceeding in the traffic lane above and in relation to which it is displayed the prohibition that such traffic shall not proceed beneath or beyond the red cross in the said traffic lane in the direction opposite to that in which the red cross faces until that prohibition is cancelled by a display over that traffic lane of the white downward arrow or by the display over that traffic lane or beside the carriageway of the traffic sign shown in diagram 6001 or of a traffic sign bearing the legend 'End of lane control'; and

(b) the white downward arrow conveys to such traffic proceeding in the traffic lane above and in relation to which it is displayed the information that that traffic may proceed or continue so to do in the said lane beneath or beyond the said arrow and in the direction opposite to that in which that arrow faces.

[Regulation 36 is printed as amended by SI 1982 No 1879.]

*   *   *

PART II

GENERAL DIRECTIONS

*   *   *

5. Without prejudice to [section 77 of the Road Traffic Regulation Act 1984]—

(1) whenever a sign shown in diagram 734.7 or in any of the diagrams 837.1 to 838.2 is to be placed for the first time at any given site on or near a primary route, that sign shall not be so placed unless the site shall have first been approved in writing by or on behalf of the Secretary of State; and

(2) whenever the sign shown in diagram 601.1 is to be placed for the first time at any given site on or near any road whatsoever, that sign shall not be so placed unless the site shall have first been so approved as aforesaid, except that if the said site shall already have been duly so approved for placing the sign shown in diagram 601 in

Schedule 1 to the Regulations of 1964, its replacement by the sign shown in diagram 601.1 shall be treated as a placing otherwise than for the first time for the purposes of this sub-paragraph.

[Direction 5 is printed as amended by the Road Traffic Regulation Act 1984, s 144 (1), and Sched 10, para 2.]

*   *   *

10. The traffic signs shown in the diagrams whose numbers appear in column 1 of the table set out in this paragraph shall not be used on a road unless so used in conjunction with the road markings shown in the diagrams whose numbers appear in column 2 of that table opposite to the number in column 1 to which they relate:

Provided that the provisions of this paragraph requiring the use of the signs shown in diagrams 601.1, 602, 611.1 and 650 in conjunction with a road marking shall not apply during the execution of works on a road in the vicinity of the place where any of those signs is erected, if those works necessitate the temporary removal of that marking, and shall not apply if any of those signs is erected only temporarily in connection with the execution of works on a road.

TABLE

Column 1 Sign diagram number	Column 2 Road marking diagram number
601.1	both 1002.1 and 1022
602	both 1003 and 1023
611.1	[if used in conjunction with diagram 602, 1003.4; in any other case both 1003.3 and 1003.4]
650	either 1025.1 or 1025.3
653	both 1048 and 1049
654	both 1048 and 1049
[625.3	1057]
[654.1	both 1049 varied to a width of 150 millimetres, and 1057

Any reference in this paragraph and in the next following paragraph to a traffic sign shown in diagram 601.1 and to the number of that diagram in the said table shall be treated as a reference until the [31st December 1982] inclusive of that date to any sign which can be treated as if prescribed by the Regulations until that date if it is a sign of the type shown in the diagram numbered 601 in Schedule 1 to the Traffic Signs Regulations 1964.

References in this paragraph to the road marking shown in diagram number 1002.1 specified in column 2 of the table above include, until the 31st December 1983 inclusive of that date, references to any road marking which can be treated until that date as if prescribed by the Regulations if it is a sign of the type shown in diagram 1002 in Schedule 2 to the Regulations of 1975.

[Direction 10 is printed as amended by SI 1982 No 1880.]

11.—(1) The sign shown in diagram 501 shall not be used unless used either in combination with a plate of the type shown in diagram 502 and in conjunction with the sign shown in diagram 601.1 or in combination with a plate of the type shown in diagram 503 and in conjunction with the sign shown in diagram 602.

(2) The sign shown in diagram 545 shall not be used unless used in combination with any of the following, that is to say, with a plate of the type shown in diagram 546 to 547.3, or the traffic sign (warning lights) prescribed by Regulation 37 (2) of the Regulations.

(3) The traffic signs shown in the diagrams whose numbers appear in column 1 of the table set out at the end of this paragraph shall not be used unless used in combination with a plate of the type shown in the diagrams whose numbers appear in column 2 of that table opposite to the number in column 1 to which they relate.

(4) Where the indications given by any of the signs shown in diagrams 530, 532.1 and 629 to 629.2 are varied in accordance with Regulation 12 (1) (*a*) of the Regulations, the sign whose indications shall have been so varied shall not be used displaying the permitted variant unless used in combination with another sign of the same type whose indications have not been so varied and which gives the indications prescribed in the relevant diagram without the permitted variant.

[When the signs shown in the diagrams specified in this paragraph are incorporated as symbols displayed by other signs incorporating them and the indications given by those symbols are so varied, this paragraph shall apply to those other signs incorporating the varied symbols in the same way as it applied to the said signs so symbolised.]

TABLE

Column 1 Sign diagram number	Column 2 Plate diagram number
533	either 534.1 or 534.2 or 535.1
544.2	547.4
562	either 537.3 or 563
617	either 618 or 618.1
632	either 570 or 645
[557.1	557.2, 557.3 or 557.4]

[Direction 11 is printed as amended by SI 1982 No 1880 and SI 1983 No 1086.]

12. A plate of the type shown in diagrams 502, 503, 511, 518, 519, 519.1, 525 to 527, 534.1, 534.2, 535.1, 537.1 to 537.4, 546, 547.1 to 547.4, 553, 556.3, 556.4, [557.2, 557.3, 557.4] 563, 564.1, 570 to 573, 575, 579, 602.1, 607, 608, 618, 618.1, 619.3,

619.4, 620, 620.1, 622.3, 625.2, 627, 636.1, 642.1, 643 to 645, 656, 656.1, 660.2, 662, 802.1 to 805, 807, 812.3, 812.4 and 817.1 shall not be used unless used in combination with the signs which are specified beneath the diagrams showing the plate.

[Direction 12 is printed as amended by SI 1983 No 1086.]

*   *   *

18.—(1) Signs shown in diagrams 603 and 604 may be used only where one-way working is necessary owing to a temporary closure to vehicular traffic of a width of the carriageway of a road.

(2) The signs shown in diagrams 615 and 811 shall not be used unless used in conjunction with one another and shall not be used at all in conjunction with the signs shown in diagrams 603 or 604.

(3) The signs shown in diagrams 634 and 635 may be used only by a constable in uniform or a person acting under the instructions or authority of the chief officer of police for the police area in which the signs are to be placed.

19. The sign shown in diagram 569.2 or 569.3 may be placed on or near a road only in connection with works involving an alteration in the layout of the carriageway or involving the removal of or change in the road markings or other traffic signs placed on or near a road at cross roads or other junctions (including in the case of the sign shown in the diagram 569.3 an automatic railway level crossing within the meaning of Regulation 25 (1) of the Regulations), and shall be retained for not more than 3 months from the date of the completion of those works.

20. Signs shown in diagrams 830, 830.1, 831 and 832 (except when varied to contain the words 'weight check') may be used only in connection with a traffic census the taking of which on a road has been approved by the highway authority for that road, by the chief officer of police of the police area in which the road is situate, and by or on behalf of the Secretary of State.

*   *   *

24.—(1) The road marking shown in diagram 1001 shall not be placed on a road unless it is so placed for use in conjunction with the light signals prescribed by paragraph (2) or paragraph (4) of Regulation 31 of the Regulations or with the light signals prescribed by the said paragraph (2) as varied in accordance with Regulation 32 of the Regulations or unless it is so placed at a site where vehicular traffic is from time to time controlled by the police.

(2) Where both primary and secondary signals within the meaning of Regulation 34 (6) of the Regulations have been erected, the reference in sub-paragraph (1) above to light signals prescribed by the said paragraph (2) or paragraph (4) of Regulation 31 or by the said paragraph 2 as so varied as aforesaid shall be construed as a reference to both the primary and the secondary signals or if either the primary or secondary signals are not operating, to the primary signals operating alone or to the secondary signals operating alone as the case may be.

25. The road markings shown in diagrams 1002.1 and 1022 shall not be placed on a road unless they are so placed for use in conjunction with the sign shown in diagram 601.1 or until the [31st December 1982] inclusive of that date, with any sign which can be treated as if prescribed by the Regulations until that date if it is a sign of the type shown in the diagram numbered 601 in Schedule 1 to the Traffic Signs Regulations 1964; and the road marking shown in diagram 1003.4 shall not be so placed as aforesaid unless it is placed for use in conjunction with the sign shown in diagram 611.1.

[Direction 25 is printed as amended by SI 1982 No 1880.]

*   *   *

30.—(1) The road markings shown in diagram 1023 shall not be placed on a road unless so placed for use in conjunction with the road marking shown in diagram 1003.

(2) The road markings shown in diagrams 1025.1 and 1025.3 shall not be placed on a road unless so placed for use in conjunction with at least one sign of the type shown in diagram 650 which shall have been erected on or near the same side of the road as that on which the marking is placed.

(3) The road marking shown in diagram 1048 shall not be placed on a road unless so placed for use in conjunction with the marking shown in diagram 1049 and either the traffic sign shown in diagram 653 or that shown in diagram 654; and the marking shown in diagram 1049 shall not be placed on a road unless so placed for use in conjunction with the marking shown in diagram 1048 and either the sign shown in diagram 653 or that shown in diagram 654.

[(4) No road marking of a kind shown in diagrams 1003, 1023 or 1049 when varied in size to conform with any of the smaller alternative dimensions prescribed for it shall be placed on the carriageway except for use in conjunction with the marking shown in diagram 1057 and also with one or more of the signs shown in diagrams 625, 625.3, 654.1 or 815.]

[(5) No roadmarking of the kind shown in diagram 1009 when varied in size to conform with the smallest alternative dimensions prescribed for it shall be placed on the carriageway except to mark the junction of a cycle track and another road, in conjunction with road markings of the smallest alternative dimensions prescribed for diagrams 1003 and 1023.]

[(6) No roadmarking of a kind shown in diagram 1057 shall be placed on a road except in conjunction with at least one of the signs shown in diagrams 625, 625.3, 654.1 or 815 erected along that road.]

[(7) The road markings shown in diagrams 1058 or 1059 shall not be placed on a road unless so placed for use in conjunction with at least one road marking of the kind shown in diagram 1057.]

[Direction 30 is printed as amended by SI 1982 No 1880.]

*   *   *

34.—(1) Light signals such as are prescribed by Regulations 31 to 33, 35, 36, 37 (2), 38 and 39 of the Regulations may be placed on or near a road only if the following conditions are satisfied, that is to say—

(*a*) the said signals are so placed that they face the stream of traffic to which they are intended to convey respectively the warning, information, requirements, restrictions or prohibitions prescribed by the Regulations;

(*b*) the apparatus (including the content of all instructions stored in, or executable by it) used in connection with the said signals is of a type which has been approved in writing by or on behalf of the Secretary of State; and

(c) if the light signals are light signals prescribed by Regulation 31 (4) of the Regulations and are to be erected at or near a level crossing (where a road is crossed by a railway) otherwise than in pursuance of an Order made by the Secretary of State under section 66 of the British Transport Commission Act 1957 (which empowers the Secretary of State to authorise special arrangements at public level crossings), [an] Order so made under section 124 of the Transport Act 1968 (British Railways Board's obligations at level crossings with roads other than public carriage roads), [or of an order under section 1 of the Level Crossings Act 1983 (which empowers the Secretary of State to provide for the protection of those using the level crossing)] the site for, and the number and disposition of, those signals shall first have been approved in writing by or on behalf of the Secretary of State after consideration of such plans for the site and such other information as he may require for the purposes of his function in this condition.

(2) If, after any light signals such as are mentioned in sub-paragraph (1) of this paragraph have been placed on or near a road, the apparatus used in connection with the said signals is altered so as to enable any further instructions to be stored in, or made executable by, the apparatus, the said signals shall not be further used unless that alteration is of a type which has been approved in writing by or on behalf of the Secretary of State.

(3) The light signals prescribed by Regulation 31 (2) and (4) of the Regulations or those light signals as varied in accordance with Regulation 32 thereof shall not be used unless used in conjunction with the road marking shown in diagram 1001, except that this sub-paragraph shall not apply while works which necessitate the temporary removal of that road marking are being executed on a road in the vicinity of the place where the said light signals are erected.

(4) The containers enclosing the lamps of each of the kinds of light signals mentioned in sub-paragraph (1) of this paragraph shall be coloured black, except that if those containers enclose lamps of the light signals prescribed by Regulation 31 (3), 36, 37 (2) or 39 of the Regulations, they may be coloured grey instead of black.

(5) Any of the kinds of light signals mentioned in sub-paragraph (1) of this paragraph other than the signals prescribed by Regulation 35 of the Regulations may be mounted with a backing board and if so mounted, the backing board shall be coloured black and may have a white border not less than 85 nor more than 95 millimetres in width in the case of signals prescribed by Regulation 31 (4) of the Regulations and not less than 45 nor more than 55 millimetres in width in the case of the other kinds of light signals which may be so mounted.

(6) Without prejudice to the next following sub-paragraph, where light signals prescribed by any of the Regulations specified in sub-paragraph (1) of this paragraph are mounted on a post specially provided for the purpose, that part of the post which extends above ground level shall be coloured grey and may have one white band not less than 140 nor more than 160 millimetres in depth, the lower edge of the band being not less than 1.5 nor more than 1.7 metres above the level of the surface of the ground in the immediate vicinity.

(7) In the case of light signals prescribed by Regulation 33 of the Regulations, instead of being mounted on a post coloured in accordance with the provisions of the last preceding sub-paragraph, they may be mounted on either a post coloured yellow (but having no such white band as therein specified) or, alternatively on a tripod coloured yellow.

[Direction 34 is printed as amended by SI 1984 No 966 (the word '[an]' has been added editorially in para 1 (c) following that amendment).]

*   *   *

36.—(1) The back of any sign shown in a diagram in Schedule 1, other than a sign in diagram 569.1, of any backing board or other fitting provided for the assembly of such a sign, including any container enclosing apparatus for the illumination of that sign, shall be coloured—

(*a*) black, if the sign is mounted on the same post as that on which light signals prescribed by Regulation 31 (2) of the Regulations or those signals as varied by Regulation 32 thereof, or prescribed by Regulation 33 of the Regulations are mounted, and

(*b*) grey in any other case except that information about sites for placing the sign may be indicated on the back of the sign in characters not exceeding 15 millimetres in height.

(2) The back of a sign of the type shown in diagram 569.1 in Schedule 1 shall be coloured either grey or white.

[(3) The containers enclosing the road danger lamps prescribed by Regulation 40 shall be coloured yellow.]

[Direction 36 is printed as amended by SI 1982 No 1880.]

*   *   *

42. At least one road marking of the kind shown in diagram 1014 shall be placed for use in conjunction with a road marking of the kind shown in diagram 1013.1 on the length of carriageway which extends backwards from the commencement of any continuous line marked on the carriageway as a part of the last mentioned road marking so shown, such commencement being viewed in the direction of travel of a vehicle driven so as to have and keep that continuous line on the right hand or offside thereof in accordance with Regulation 23 (2) (*b*) of the Regulations, and if more than one road marking of the kind first above-mentioned is placed on the said length of carriageway then those road markings shall be so spaced apart that one follows in *[sic]* in line in front of the other.

43. Nothing in these Directions shall be taken to limit the power of the Secretary of State acting as the appropriate Minister by any special Direction to dispense with, add to or modify any of the requirements of these Directions in their application to any particular case.

PART III
GENERAL CITATION AND COMMENCEMENT

*   *   *

The Transport Act 1981 (Commencement No 2) Order 1981

(SI 1981 No 1617)

[In relation to the commencement of the provisions of the Transport Act 1981 which are relevant to this work, attention is drawn to s 31. (The Transport Act 1981 (Commencement No 1) Order 1981 (SI 1981 No 1331) brought s 35 (in part) and one entry in Part III of Sched 12 into operation on 12 October 1981; the Transport Act 1981 (Commencement No 3) Order 1982 (SI 1982 No 300) brought s 23 (6) and (7) (and s 30 (1) so far as it relates to those provisions) into operation on 29 March 1982; the Transport Act 1981 (Commencement) (No 4) Order 1982 (SI 1982 No 310) brought the remaining parts of s 35 and another entry in Part III of Sched 12 into operation on 1 April 1982; the Transport Act 1981 (Commencement No 5) Order 1982 (SI 1982 No 866) brought s 23 (and s 30 (1) so far as it relates to s 23) into operation on 1 October 1982 and 1 February 1983; the Transport Act 1981 (Commencement No 10) Order 1983 (SI 1983 No 930) brought Sched 6, para 10, to the Act into operation on 2 August 1983; the Transport Act 1981 (Commencement No 11) Order 1983 (SI 1983 No 1089) brought s 32 of and Sched 10 to the Act into operation on 25 August 1983 and also effected the repeal of the Road Traffic Act 1974, s 17 (see Sched 12, Part III, to the 1981 Act); the text of none of these provisions is set out in Volume 2 of this work.)]

*   *   *

2. The 1st December 1981 is hereby appointed as the day on which the provisions of the Transport Act 1981 specified in column (2) of the Table below, which relate to the subject matter specified in column (3) of that Table, come into force.

TABLE

Item Number	(2) Provisions of the Transport Act 1981	(3) Subject matter of provisions
1	Section 21	Offender escaping consequences of endorsable offence by deception.
2	Section 22	Seizure of licence required to be produced in Court.
3	Section 26	Increase of penalty for failure to stop etc.
4	Section 27	Compulsory wearing of seat belts.
5	Section 30— (a) subsection (1), in so far as it relates to— (i) section 22, (ii) section 26, and (iii) subsection (3) in so far as it is commenced by this Order; (b) subsection (2) in so far as it relates to section 21; and (c) subsection (3) in so far as it relates to item 6 in this Table.	Interpretation of Part IV and consequential and minor amendments.
6	Schedule 9 in so far as it consists of— (a) paragraph 14; (b) paragraph 18, sub-paragraph (b) in so far as it relates to section 33A and sub-paragraph (c) in so far as it relates to section 33A; and (c) paragraph 22.	Consequential and minor amendments of Road Traffic Act 1972 etc.

The Transport Act 1981 (Commencement No 6) Order 1982

(SI 1982 No 1341)

1. *[Omitted.]*

2. The 31st January 1983 is hereby appointed as the day on which section 28 of the Transport Act 1981 and section 30(1) of that Act so far as it relates to the said section 28 come into force.

The Transport Act 1981 (Commencement No 7) Order 1982

(SI 1982 No 1451)

1. *[Omitted.]*

2. The 1st November 1982 is hereby appointed as the day on which the following provisions of the Transport Act 1981 come into force, namely—

Section 19,
Section 20,
Schedule 7,
Schedule 9, paragraphs 2, 4, 5, 6, 7, 8, 9, 10, 11, 13 and 15,
Schedule 12, Part III, the items relating to sections 93(3) and (5) and 177(2) of the Road Traffic Act 1972.
Section 30(1) and (2) so far as it relates to the above provisions.

The Transport Act 1981 (Commencement No 8) Order 1982

(SI 1982 No 1803)

1. *[Omitted.]*

2. The 20th December 1982 is appointed as the day on which paragraph 12 of Schedule 9 to the Transport Act 1981 comes into force save that—

(*a*) the substitution provided for by that paragraph is not brought into force in so far as section 101(7) of the Road Traffic Act 1972 relates to sections 5(1), 6(1) and 9(3) of that Act; and

(*b*) section 101(7A) of the Road Traffic Act 1972 as provided by that paragraph is not brought into force so far as it relates to section 5(1), 6(1)(*a*) and 8(7) of that Act.

[As to Sched 9, para 12, see further SI 1983 No 576, below.]

The Transport Act 1981 (Commencement No 9) Order 1983

(SI 1983 No 576)

1. *[Omitted.]*

2. The 6th May 1983 is appointed as the day on which the provisions of the Transport Act 1981 specified in Article 3 below come into force.

3. The provisions referred to in Article 2 above are:—

Section 24;

Section 25;

Section 30(1) so far as it relates to sections 24 and 25;

Schedule 8;

Schedule 9, paragraphs 1, 3, 12 (save in so far as brought into force by the Transport Act 1981 (Commencement No 8) Order 1982 *[SI 1982 No 1803]*, 17, 18 (save in so far as brought into force by the Transport Act 1981 (Commencement No 2) Order 1981 *[1981 No 1617]*, 19, 20, 21, 23, 24 and 25; and

Schedule 12, the repeals relating to sections 89, 90 and 189 of, and paragraph 1 of Part V of Schedule 4 to, the Road Traffic Act 1972.

The Transport Act 1982 (Commencement No 1) Order 1982

(SI 1982 No 1561)

[The Transport Act 1982, ss 53 to 56 and para 18 (except sub-para (a)) of Sched 5 came into force on the date the Act received the royal assent (i.e. 28 October 1982); see s 76(3). The rest of the provisions of the Act are to come into operation on dates appointed for the purpose; see s 76(2) and (4). (The Transport Act 1982 (Commencement No 2) Order 1982 (SI 1982 No 1804) brought ss 1 to 7, 64, 67 and 71 into operation on 20 December 1982; but s 64 does not apply to offences committed before that date.) The Transport Act 1982 (Commencement No 5) Order 1984 (SI 1984 No 175) brought s 52, Sched 4, Sched 5, para 6, and Sched 6 (so far as it relates to the Transport Act 1968) into operation on 1 June 1984, subject to transitional provisions set out in the order.]

1. *[Omitted.]*

2. The 1st November 1982 is hereby appointed as the day on which the following provisions of the Transport Act 1982 come into force, namely:—

Sections 16, 58, 60, 61, 68, 70 and 72 (so far as it relates to sections 53 and 54).

Schedule 5, paragraphs 25 and 26;

Schedule 6 insofar as it relates to section 72(2) and (4) of the Road Traffic Regulation Act 1967.

The Transport Act 1982 (Commencement No 3) Order 1983

(SI 1983 No 276)

1. *[Omitted.]*

2. The 1st April 1983 is hereby appointed as the day on which the Transport Act 1982, Schedule 5, paragraph 10(*b*) (minor and consequential amendments about certificate of conformity) comes into force.

3. The 11th April 1983 is hereby appointed as the day on which the Transport Act, section 57 (authorisation of head-worn appliances for use on motor cycles), section 63 (amendment of certain penalties) and section 65 (marking of builder's skips) comes into force.

The Transport Act 1982 (Commencement No 4) Order 1983

(SI 1983 No 577)

1. *[Omitted.]*

2. The 6th May 1983 is hereby appointed as the day on which the Transport Act 1982, section 59 (specimens of breath for breath tests etc.) and paragraph 13 of Schedule 5 (minor and consequential amendments) come into force.

The Various Trunk Roads (Prohibition of Waiting) (Clearways) Order 1963

(SI 1963 No 1172)

* * *

3. Interpretation

(1) In this Order the following expressions have the meanings hereby respectively assigned to them:—

'the Act of [1984]' means the [Road Traffic Regulation Act 1984];

'main carriageway,' in relation to a trunk road, means any carriageway of that road used primarily by through traffic anmd excludes any lay-by;

'lay-by,' in relation to a main carriageway of a trunk road, means any area intended for use for the waiting of vehicles, lying at a side of the road and bounded partly by a traffic sign consisting of a yellow dotted line on the road, or of a white dotted line and the words 'lay-by' on the road, authorised by the [Secretary of State for Transport] under subsection (2) of [section 64 of the Road Traffic Regulation Act 1984], and partly by the outer edge of that carriageway on the same side of the road as that on which the sign is placed;

'verge' means any part of a road which is not a carriageway.

(2) [The Interpretation Act 1978] shall apply for the interpretation of this Order as it applies for the interpretation of an Act of Parliament and as if for the purposes of [section 17] of that Act this Order were an Act of Parliament and the Orders revoked by Article 2 were Acts of Parliament thereby repealed.

[Article 3 is printed as amended by the Road Traffic Regulation Act 1967, Sched 8, para 2, the Interpretation Act 1978, s 17 (2), the Minister of Transport Order 1979 (SI 1979 No 571), the Transfer of Functions (Transport) Order 1981 (SI 1981 No 238), and the Road Traffic Regulation Act 1984, s 144 (1), and Sched 10, para 2.]

4. Prohibition of waiting on main carriageways

Save as provided in Article 5 of this Order no person shall, except upon the direction or with the permission of a police constable in uniform, cause or permit any vehicle to wait on any of those main carriageways forming part of trunk roads which are specified in Schedule 1 to this Order.

5. Exceptions to Article 4

Nothing in Article 4 of this Order shall apply—

(*a*) so as to prevent a vehicle waiting on any main carriageway specified in Schedule 1 to this Order for so long as may be necessary to enable the vehicle, if it cannot be used for such purpose without waiting on that carriageway, to be used in connection with any building operation or demolition, the removal of any obstruction or potential obstruction to traffic, the maintenance, improvement or reconstruction of the road comprising that carriageway, or the erection, laying, placing, maintenance, testing, alteration, repair or removal of any structure, works, or apparatus in, on, under or over that road;

(b) to a vehicle being used for fire brigade, ambulance or police purposes;

(c) to a vehicle being used for the purposes of delivering or collecting postal packets as defined in section 87 of the Post Office Act 1953;

(d) so as to prevent a vehicle being used by or on behalf of a local authority from waiting on any main carriageway specified in Schedule 1 to this Order for so long as may be necessary to enable the vehicle, if it cannot be used for such a purpose without waiting on that carriageway to be used for the purpose of the collection of household refuse from, or the clearing of cesspools at, premises situated on or adjacent to the road comprising that carriageway;

(e) to a vehicle waiting on any main carriageway specified in Schedule 1 to this Order while any gate or other barrier at the entrance to premises to which the vehicle requires access or from which it has emerged is opened or closed, if it is not reasonably practicable for the vehicle to wait otherwise than on that carriageway while such gate or barrier is being opened or closed;

(f) to a vehicle waiting in any case where the person in control of the vehicle:—
  (i) is required by law to stop;
  (ii) is obliged to do so in order to avoid accident: or
  (iii) is prevented from proceeding by circumstances outside his control and it is not reasonably practicable for him to drive or move the vehicle to a place not on any main carriageway specified in Schedule 1 to this Order.

6. Restriction of waiting on verges, etc

No person shall cause or permit any vehicle to wait on any verge or lay-by immediately adjacent to a main carriageway specified in Schedule 1 to this Order for the purpose of selling goods from that vehicle unless the goods are immediately delivered at or taken into premises adjacent to the vehicle from which sale is effected.

*　　*　　*

The Vehicle and Driving Licences Records (Evidence) Regulations 1970

(SI 1970 No 1997)

*   *   *

3. Matters prescribed for [s 182(3)] of the Act

The following matters are prescribed for the purposes of [section 182 (3) of the Road Traffic Act 1972]—

(1) in connection with the licensing of drivers under [Part III of the Road Traffic Act 1972]—

   (*a*) a document being, forming part of, or submitted in connection with, an application for a driving licence;

   (*b*) a driving licence;

   (*c*) a certificate of competence to drive;

   (*d*) the conviction of an offence specified in Part I or Part II of Schedule [4 to the Road Traffic Act 1972] of any person or any order made by the Court as a result of any such conviction;

(2) in connection with the licensing and registration of mechanically propelled vehicles under the [Vehicles (Excise) Act 1971]—

   (*a*) a document being, forming part of, or submitted in connection with, an application for—

      (i) a vehicle licence;

      (ii) a trade licence;

      (iii) a repayment of duty under [section 17 of the 1971 Act] or the recovery of underpayments or overpayments of duty under [section 30] of that Act;

   (*b*) a vehicle licence, trade licence, registration book or registration mark;

   (*c*) a document containing a declaration and particulars such as are prescribed under the [1971] Act in relation to vehicles exempted from duty under that Act;

   (*d*) the conviction of an offence under the [1971] Act of any person;

(3) in connection with the examination of a goods vehicle under regulations under [section 45 of the Road Traffic Act 1972]—

   (*a*) an application for an examination of a vehicle under the said regulations;

   (*b*) a notifiable alteration made to a vehicle and required by the said regulations to be notified to the [Secretary of State for Transport];

   (*c*) a plating certificate, goods vehicle test certificate, notification of the refusal of a goods vehicle test certificate, Ministry plate, Ministry test date disc or certificate of temporary exemption.

[Regulation 3 is printed as amended by the Vehicles (Excise) Act 1971, Sched 7, para 11, the Road Traffic Act 1972, Sched 10, para 3, the Minister of Transport Order 1979 (SI 1979 No 751) and the Transfer of Functions (Transport) Order 1981 (SI 1981 No 238).

For the regulations under s 45 of the Road Traffic Act 1972, see the Goods Vehicles (Plating and Testing) Regulations 1982 (SI 1982 No 1478).]

*   *   *

The Vehicle Licences (Duration and Rate of Duty) Order 1980

(SI 1980 No 1183)

* * *

2. Interpretation and application

(1) In this Order 'the Act of 1971' means the Vehicles (Excise) Act 1971.

(2) This Order shall, save in the case of licences for periods of seven consecutive days, apply only to vehicle licences issued to run from 1st October 1980 or from the beginning of any subsequent month.

3. Commencement and duration of licences

Vehicle licences (other than licences for one calendar year) may be taken out—

(a) in the case of any vehicle licence, for any period of twelve months running from the beginning of the month in which the licence first has effect;

(b) in the case of any vehicle the annual rate of duty applicable to which exceeds £18, for any period of six months running from the beginning of the month in which the licence first has effect;

(c) in the case of a goods vehicle which is authorised to be used on roads by virtue of an order made under section 42 (1) of the Road Traffic Act 1972, and the unladen weight of which exceeds eleven tons, for any period of seven consecutive days.

4. Rate of duty

The duty payable on a vehicle licence for a vehicle of any description shall—

(a) if the licence is taken out for a period of twelve months, be paid at the annual rate of duty applicable to vehicles of that description under section 1 of the Act of 1971;

(b) if the licence is taken out for a period of six months, be paid at a rate equal to one half of the said annual rate plus ten per cent, of that amount;

(c) if the licence is taken out for a period of seven consecutive days, be paid at a rate equal to one fifty-second of the said annual rate plus ten per cent of that amount;

and in computing the rate of duty in accordance with paragraph (b) or paragraph (c) above, any fraction of 5p shall be treated as 5p if it exceeds 2.5p and shall otherwise be disregarded.

* * *

The 'Zebra' Pedestrian Crossings Regulations 1971

(SI 1971 No 1524)

ARRANGEMENT OF REGULATIONS

PART 1
GENERAL

PART II
MARKS, SIGNS AND OTHER PARTICULARS AS RESPECTS ZEBRA CROSSINGS

PART III
REGULATIONS GOVERNING USE OF ZEBRA CROSSINGS AND ZEBRA CONTROLLED AREAS

SCHEDULES

PART I
GENERAL

*　　*　　*

3. Interpretation

(1) In these Regulations, unless the context otherwise requires, the following expressions have the meanings hereby respectively assigned to them:—

'the appropriate Secretary of State' means, in relation to a crossing established on a road in England excluding Monmouthshire, the [Secretary of State for

Transport], in relation to a crossing established on a road in Scotland, the Secretary of State for Scotland, and, in relation to a crossing established on a road in Wales or Monmouthshire, the Secretary of State for Wales;

'appropriate authority' means, in relation to a crossing on a trunk road, the appropriate Secretary of State, and in relation to any other crossing the local authority in whose scheme submitted and approved under [section 23 of the Road Traffic Regulation Act 1984] the crossing is for the time being included;

'carriageway' does not include that part of any road which consists of a street refuge or central reservation, whether within the limits of a crossing or not;

'central reservation' means any provision, not consisting of a street refuge, made in a road for separating one part of the carriageway of that road from another part of that carriageway for the safety or guidance of vehicular traffic using that road;

'crossing' means a crossing for foot passengers established either—

(a) by a local authority in accordance with the provisions for the time being in force of a scheme submitted and approved under [section 23 of the Road Traffic Regulation Act 1984], or

(b) in the case of a trunk road, by the appropriate Secretary of State in the discharge of the duty imposed on him by [section 24 of the Road Traffic Regulation Act 1984]; but does not include a 'Pelican' crossing within the meaning of the 'Pelican' Pedestrian Crossings Regulations 1969 [SI 1969 No 888];

'dual-carriageway road' means a length of road on which a part of the carriageway thereof is separated from another part thereof by a central reservation;

'give-way line' has the meaning assigned to it by paragraph 2 of Schedule 3;

'one-way street' means any road in which the driving of all vehicles otherwise than in one direction is prohibited at all times;

'stud' means a mark or device on the carriageway, whether or not projecting above the surface thereof;

'zebra controlled area' means, in relation to a zebra crossing, the area of the carriageway in the vicinity of the crossing and lying on both sides of the crossing or only one side of the crossing, being an area the presence and limits of which are indicated in accordance with Schedule 3;

'zebra crossing' means a crossing the presence and limits of which are indicated in accordance with the provisions of Schedule 2;

'uncontrolled zebra crossing' means a zebra crossing at which traffic is not for the time being controlled by a police constable in uniform or by a traffic warden.

(2) Any reference in these Regulations to a numbered Regulation or Schedule is a reference to the Regulation or Schedule bearing that number in these Regulations except where otherwise expressly provided.

(3) Any reference in these Regulations to any enactment shall be construed as a reference to that enactment as amended by any subsequent enactment.

(4) The [Interpretation Act 1978] shall apply for the interpretation of these Regulations as it applies for the interpretation of an Act of Parliament, and as if for the purposes of [section 17] of that Act these Regulations were an Act of Parliament and the Regulations revoked by Regulation 2 were Acts of Parliament thereby repealed.

[Regulation 3 is printed as amended by the Interpretation Act 1978, s 17 (2), the Minister of

Transport Order 1979 (SI 1979 No 571), the Transfer of Functions (Transport) Order 1981 (SI 1981 No 238), and the Road Traffic Regulation Act 1984, s 144 (1), and Sched 10, para 2.]

PART II

MARKS, SIGNS AND OTHER PARTICULARS AS RESPECTS ZEBRA CROSSINGS

4. Zebra crossings

(1) The provisions of Part I of Schedule 2 shall have effect for regulating the manner in which the presence and limits of a crossing are to be indicated by marks or studs on the carriageway for the purpose of constituting it a zebra crossing.

(2) The provisions of Part II of Schedule 2 shall have effect as respects the size, colour and type of the traffic signs which are to be placed at or near a crossing for the purpose of constituting it a zebra crossing.

5. Zebra controlled areas and give-way lines

(1) Subject to paragraph (3) of this Regulation, the provisions of Schedule 3 shall have effect as respects the size, colour and type of the traffic signs which shall be placed in the vicinity of a zebra crossing for the purpose of constituting a zebra controlled area in relation to that crossing and of indicating the presence and limits of that area.

(2) A give-way line (included among the said signs) shall, where provided, also convey to vehicular traffic proceeding towards a zebra crossing the position at or before which a driver of a vehicle should stop it for the purpose of complying with Regulation 8.

(3) Where the appropriate authority is satisfied in relation to a particular area of carriageway in the vicinity of a zebra crossing that, by reason of the layout of, or character of, the roads in the vicinity of the crossing, the application of such a prohibition as is mentioned in Regulation 10 or 12 to that particular area or the constitution of that particular area as a zebra controlled area by the placing of traffic signs in accordance with Schedule 3 would be impracticable, it shall not be necessary for that area to be constituted a zebra controlled area but, if by virtue of this paragraph it is proposed that no area, on either side of the limits of a zebra crossing (not on a trunk road), is to be constituted a zebra controlled area by the 30th November 1973, a notice in writing shall be sent by the appropriate authority before that date to the appropriate Secretary of State stating the reasons why it is proposed that no such area should be so constituted.

6. Variations in dimensions shown in Schedule 3

Any variations in a dimension specified in the diagram in Schedule 3 or otherwise specified in that Schedule shall be treated as permitted by these Regulations if the variation—

(a) in the case of a dimension of 300 millimetres or more, does not exceed 20% of that dimension; or

(b) in the case of a dimension of less than 300 millimetres, where the actual dimension exceeds the dimension so specified, does not exceed 30% of the dimension so specified, and where the actual dimension is less than the dimension so specified, does not exceed 10% of the dimension so specified.

*   *   *

PART III

Regulations governing use of Zebra Crossings and Zebra Controlled Areas

8. Precedence of pedestrians over vehicles

Every foot passenger on the carriageway within the limits of an uncontrolled zebra crossing shall have precedence within those limits over any vehicle and the driver of the vehicle shall accord such precedence to the foot passenger, if the foot passenger is on the carriageway within those limits before the vehicle or any part thereof has come on to the carriageway within those limits.

For the purpose of this Regulation, in the case of such a crossing on which there is a street refuge or central reservation the parts of the crossing which are situated on each side of the street refuge or central reservation as the case may be shall each be treated as a separate crossing.

9. Prohibition against the waiting of vehicles and pedestrians on zebra crossings

(1) The driver of a vehicle shall not cause the vehicle or any part thereof to stop within the limits of a zebra crossing unless either he is prevented from proceeding by circumstances beyond his control or it is necessary for him to stop in order to avoid an accident.

(2) No foot passenger shall remain on the carriageway within the limits of a zebra crossing longer than is necessary for the purpose of passing over the crossing with reasonable despatch.

Prohibition against overtaking at zebra crossings

10. The driver of a vehicle while it or any part of it is in a zebra controlled area and it is proceeding towards the limits of an uncontrolled zebra crossing in relation to which that area is indicated (which vehicle is in this and the next succeeding Regulation referred to as 'the approaching vehicle') shall not cause the vehicle, or any part of it—

(a) to pass ahead of the foremost part of another moving motor vehicle, being a vehicle proceeding in the same direction wholly or partly within that area, or

(b) subject to the next succeeding Regulation, to pass ahead of the foremost part of a stationary vehicle on the same side of the crossing as the approaching vehicle, which stationary vehicle is stopped for the purpose of complying with Regulation 8.

For the purposes of this Regulation—

(i) the reference to another moving motor vehicle is, in a case where only one other motor vehicle is proceeding in the same direction in a zebra controlled area, a reference to that vehicle, and, in a case where more than one other motor vehicle is so proceeding, a reference to such one of those vehicles as is nearest to the limits of the crossing;

(ii) the reference to a stationary vehicle is, in a case where only one other vehicle is stopped for the purpose of complying with Regulation 8, a reference to that vehicle and, in a case where more than one other vehicle is stopped for the purpose of complying with that Regulation, a reference to such one of those vehicles as is nearest to the limits of the crossing.

11.—(1) For the purposes of this Regulation, in the case of an uncontrolled zebra crossing, which is on a road, being a one-way street, and on which there is a street refuge or central reservation, the parts of the crossing which are situated on each side of the street refuge or central reservation as the case may be shall each be treated as a separate crossing.

(2) Nothing in paragraph (*b*) of the last preceding Regulation shall apply so as to prevent the approaching vehicle from passing ahead of the foremost part of a stationary vehicle within the meaning of that paragraph, if the stationary vehicle is stopped for the purpose of complying with Regulation 8 in relation to an uncontrolled zebra crossing which by virtue of this Regulation is treated as a separate crossing from the uncontrolled zebra crossing towards the limits of which the approaching vehicle is proceeding.

Prohibition on stopping in areas adjacent to zebra crossings

12.—(1) For the purposes of this Regulation and the next two following Regulations, the expression 'vehicle' shall not include a pedal bicycle not having a sidecar attached thereto, whether additional means of propulsion by mechanical power are attached to the bicycle or not.

(2) Save as provided in Regulations 14 and 15, the driver of a vehicle shall not cause the vehicle or any part thereof to stop in a zebra controlled area.

*   *   *

14. A vehicle shall not by Regulation 12 or 13 be prevented from stopping in any length of road on any side thereof—

(*a*) if the driver has stopped for the purpose of complying with Regulation 8 or Regulation 10 (*b*);

(*b*) if the driver is prevented from proceeding by circumstances beyond his control or it is necessary for him to stop in order to avoid an accident; or

(*c*) for so long as may be necessary to enable the vehicle, if it cannot be used for such purpose without stopping in that length of road, to be used for fire brigade, ambulance or police purposes or in connection with any building operation, demolition or excavation, the removal of any obstruction to traffic, the maintenance, improvement or reconstruction of that length of road, or the laying, erection, alteration, repair or cleaning in or near to that length of road of any traffic sign or sewer or of any main, pipe or apparatus for the supply of gas, water or electricity, or of any telegraph or telephone wires, cables, posts or supports.

15. A vehicle shall not by Regulation 12 be prevented from stopping in a zebra controlled area—

(*a*) if the vehicle is stopped for the purpose of making a left or right turn;

(*b*) if the vehicle is a public service vehicle, being a stage carriage or an express carriage being used otherwise than on an excursion or tour within the meaning of section 159 (1) of the Transport Act 1968, and the vehicle is waiting, after having proceeded past the zebra crossing in relation to which the zebra controlled area is indicated, for the purpose of enabling persons to board or alight from the vehicle.

[The Transport Act 1968, s 159 (1) (as amended by the Transport Act 1980, s 43 (1), and Sched 5, Part II; see reg 3 (3) of these regulations), defines 'excursion or tour' as meaning 'a stage or express carriage service on which the passengers travel together on a journey, with or without breaks, from one or more places to one or more other places and back'.]

SCHEDULE 1

Regulations Revoked

*　　　*　　　*

SCHEDULE 2

Manner of Indicating Presence and Limits of Zebra Crossings

PART I

Studs and Marks

1.—(1) Every crossing and its limits shall be indicated by two lines of studs placed across the carriageway in accordance with wthe following provisions of this paragraph.

(2) Each line formed by the outside edges of the studs shall be so separated from the other line so formed that no point on one line shall be less than 2·4 metres nor more than 5 metres or such greater distance (not being more than 10·1 metres) as the appropriate Secretary of State may authorise in writing in the case of any particular crossing from the nearest point on the other line:

Provided that the preceding provisions of this sub-paragraph shall be regarded as having been complied with in the case of any crossing which for the most part complies with those provisions notwithstanding that those provisions may not be so complied with as respects the distance from one or more points on one line to the nearest point on the other line, so long as the general indication of the lines is not thereby materially impaired.

(3) The studs of which each line is constituted shall be so placed that the distance from the centre of any one stud to the centre of the next stud in the line is not less than 250 millimetres nor more than 715 millimetres, and a distance of not more than 1·3 metres is left between the edge of the carriageway at either end of the line and the centre of the stud nearest thereto:

Provided that the preceding provisions of this sub-paragraph shall be regarded as having been complied with in the case of any line where most of the studs constituting it comply with those provisions notwithstanding that those provisions may not be complied with as respects one or more such studs, so long as the general indication of the line is not thereby materially impaired.

(4) Studs shall not be fitted with reflecting lenses and shall be—

(*a*) white, silver or light grey in colour;

(*b*) square or circular in plan, the sides of a square stud not being less than 95 millimetres nor more than 110 millimetres in length and the diameter of a circular stud not being less than 95 millimetres nor more than 110 millimetres, and

(*c*) so fixed that they do not project more than 16 millimetres above the carriageway at their highest points nor more than 7 millimetres at their edges.

2. A crossing or its limits shall not be deemed to have ceased to be indicated in accordance with the preceding provisions of this Part of this Schedule by reason only of the discoloration or temporary removal or displacement of one or more studs in any line so long as the general indication of the line is not thereby materially impaired.

3. Without derogation from the provisions of the preceding paragraphs of this Part of this Schedule, every crossing shall be further indicated in accordance with the following provisions of this Part and of Part II of this Schedule.

4.—(1) The carriageway shall be marked within the limits of every such crossing with a pattern of alternate black and white stripes:

Provided that where the colour of the surface of the carriageway provides a reasonable contrast with the colour of white that surface may itself be utilised for providing stripes which would otherwise be required to be black.

(2) Every stripe shall—

(a) extend along the carriageway from one line formed by the inside edges of the studs or from a part of the crossing which is not more than 155 millimetres from that line to the other line so formed or to a part of the crossing which is not more than 155 millimetres from that line; and

(b) be of a width of not less than 500 millimetres or of such smaller width not being less than 380 millimetres as in the case of any particular crossing the appropriate authority may consider necessary having regard to the layout of the carriageway and, in the case of the first stripe at each end of the crossing, not more than 1·3 metres, or in the case of any other stripe, not more than 715 millimetres or of such greater width not being more than 840 millimetres as in the case of any particular crossing the appropriate authority may consider necessary having regard to the layout of the carriageway.

(3) The preceding provisions of this paragraph shall be regarded as having been complied with in the case of any crossing which for the most part complies with those provisions notwithstanding that those provisions may not be complied with as respects one or more stripes and a crossing shall not be deemed to have ceased to be indicated in accordance with those provisions by reason only of the imperfection, discoloration or partial displacement of one or more of the stripes, so long as the general appearance of the pattern of stripes is not materially impaired.

PART II

Traffic Signs

1. The traffic signs which are to be placed at or near a crossing for the purpose of constituting it and indicating it as a zebra crossing shall consist of globes in relation to which the following provisions in this Part of this Schedule are complied with.

2.—(1) At or near each end of every crossing there shall be placed, and in the case of a crossing on which there is a street refuge or central reservation there may be placed on the refuge or reservation, in accordance with the following provisions of this paragraph globes mounted on posts or brackets.

(2) Globes shall be—

(a) yellow in colour;

(b) not less than 275 millimetres nor more than 335 millimetres in diameter; and

(c) so mounted that the height of the lowest part of the globe is not less than 2·1 metres nor more than 3·1 metres above the surface of the ground in the immediate vicinity.

(3) Globes shall be illuminated by a flashing light or, where the appropriate Secretary of State so authorises in writing in the case of any particular crossing, by a constant light.

(4) Where globes are mounted on or attached to posts specially provided for the purpose, every such post shall, in so far as it extends above ground level, be coloured black and white in alternate horizontal bands, the lowest band visible to approaching

traffic being coloured black and not less than 275 millimetres nor more than 1 metre in width and each other band being not less than 275 millimetres nor more than 335 millimetres in width:

Provided that nothing in this sub-paragraph shall apply to any container fixed on any such post which encloses the apparatus for providing the illumination of a globe.

3. A crossing shall not be deemed to have ceased to be indicated in accordance with the preceding provisions of this Part of this Schedule by reason only of—

   (*a*) the imperfection, discoloration or disfigurement of any of the globes, posts or brackets; or

   (*b*) the failure of the illumination of any of the globes:

      Provided that this sub-paragraph shall not apply unless at least one globe is illuminated in accordance with the provisions of sub-paragraph (3) of the last preceding paragraph.

SCHEDULE 3

MANNER OF INDICATING ZEBRA CONTROLLED AREA AND PROVISION AS TO PLACING OF GIVEWAY LINE

PART I

Traffic Signs

1. Subject to the provisions of Regulation 5 (3), the traffic signs which are to be placed on a road in the vicinity of a zebra crossing for the purpose of constituting a zebra controlled area lying on both sides of the limits of the crossing or on only one side of such limits and indicating the presence and limits of such an area shall consist of a pattern of lines of the size and type shown in the diagram in Part II of this Schedule and so placed as hereinafter provided.

2. A pattern of lines shall, subject as hereinafter provided, consist of:—

   (*a*) a transverse white broken line (hereinafter referred to as a 'give-way line') placed on the carriageway 1 metre from and parallel to the nearer line of studs indicating the limits of the crossing and shall extend across the carriageway in the manner indicated in the said diagram; and

   (*b*) two or more longitudinal white broken lines (hereinafter referred to as 'zig-zag lines') placed on the carriageway or, where the road is a dual-carriageway road, on each part of the carriageway, each zig-zag line containing not less than 8 nor more than 18 marks and extending away from the crossing at a point 150 millimetres from the nearest part of the give-way line on the same side of the crossing to a point 150 millimetres from the nearest part of a terminal line of the size and type shown in the said diagram (hereinafter referred to as a 'terminal line').

3. Where the appropriate authority is satisfied in relation to a particular area of carriageway in the vicinity of a zebra crossing that by reason of the layout of, or character of, the roads in the vicinity of the crossing it would be impracticable to lay the pattern of lines as shown in the diagram in Part II of this Schedule and in accordance with the preceding paragraph any of the following variations as respects the pattern shall be permitted—

   (*a*) the number of marks contained in each zig-zag line may be reduced from 8 to not less than 2;

(b) a mark contained in a zig-zag line may be varied in length so as to extend for a distance not less than 1 metre and less than 2 metres, but where such a variation is made as respects a mark each other mark in each zig-zag line shall be of the same or substantially the same length as that mark, so however that the number of marks in each zig-zag line shall not be more than 8 nor less than 2.

4. The angle of the give-way line (if any) in relation to and its distance from the nearer line of studs indicating the limits of a crossing may be varied, if the appropriate authority is satisfied that such variation is necessary having regard to the angle of the crossing in relation to the edge of the carriageway at the place where the crossing is situated.

5. Where by reason of Regulation 5 (3) an area of carriageway in the vicinity of a zebra crossing is not constituted a zebra controlled area by the placing of a pattern of lines as provided in the foregoing provisions of this Schedule, a give-way line shall nevertheless be placed on the carriageway as previously provided in this Schedule unless the appropriate authority is satisfied that by reason of the position of that crossing it is impracticable so to place the line.

6. Each mark contained in a give-way line or in a zig-zag line and each terminal line may be illuminated by the use of reflecting material.

7. A zebra controlled area or its limits shall not be deemed to have ceased to be indicated in accordance with the provisions of this Schedule by reason only of the imperfection, discoloration or partial displacement of either a terminal line or one or more of the marks comprised in a give-way line or a zig-zag line, so long as the general indication of any such line is not thereby materially impaired.

Section C

European Community Regulations

Regulation No 543/69/EEC of the Council
of 25 March 1969

on the harmonisation of certain social legislation
relating to road transport

[The text of this regulation is printed as amended by:
 Regulation No 514/72/EEC (OJ No L 67/1, 20.3.72, p 124) (28 February 1972);
 Regulation No 515/72/EEC (OJ No L 67/11, 20.3.72, p 134) (28 February 1972);
 Regulation No 2827/77/EEC (OJ No L 334, 24.12.77, p 1) (1 January 1978); and
 Regulation No 2829/77/EEC (OJ No L 334, 24.12.77, p 11) (12 December 1977).
The dates referred to above are the dates on which the regulations took effect.]

THE COUNCIL OF THE EUROPEAN COMMUNITIES,

Having regard to the Treaty establishing the European Economic Community, and in particular Article 75 thereof;

Having regard to the Council Decision of 13 May 1965 *[OJ No 88, 24.5.1965, p 1500/65]* on the harmonisation of certain provisions affecting competition in transport by rail, road and inland waterway, and in particular Section III thereof;

Having regard to the proposal from the Commission;

Having regard to the Opinion of the European Parliament;

Having regard to the Opinion of the Economic and Social Committee;

Whereas, in the case of road transport, it is a matter of some urgency to bring into operation the social legislation referred to in the above-mentioned Decision; whereas it is also desirable to take account as far as possible of the needs deriving from the prescribed approximation of such provisions as between the three modes of transport;

Whereas for this purpose priority should be given to necessary measures which deal with manning, driving time and rest periods;

Whereas the provisions of the Regulation dealing with working conditions cannot be allowed to prejudice the right of the two sides of industry to lay down, by collective bargaining or otherwise, provisions more favourable to workers; whereas, in order not only to promote social progress but also to improve road safety, each Member State must retain the right to adopt certain appropriate measures; whereas, accordingly, the Commission must keep the development of the situation in Member States under review and submit reports thereon to the Council at regular intervals so that any adaptation of the Regulation to the developments thus noted may be effected;

Whereas provision must be made for this Regulation to be applied uniformly to all carriage in vehicles circulating within the territory of Member States, whether such vehicles are registered in a Member State or in a third country;

Whereas certain transport operations may be exempted from the application of this Regulation;

Whereas it is desirable to lay down provisions concerning the minimum ages for drivers engaged in the carriage of goods or of passengers—bearing in mind here certain vocational training requirements—and concerning also the minimum age for drivers' mates and conductors;

Whereas for journeys exceeding a certain distance and for certain vehicles, it is necessary to lay down manning requirements; whereas it is desirable that undertakings should be left free to choose between arranging for the presence of two drivers on board the vehicle and arranging for relief drivers;

Whereas, with regard to driving periods, it is desirable to set limits on continuous driving time and on daily driving time, but without prejudice to any national rules whereby drivers are prohibited from driving for longer than they can with complete safety;

Whereas, with regard to driving periods, it is nevertheless desirable to provide that the requirements laid down in the Regulation be brought into operation only by stages whereas for this purpose there must be transitional provisions, laying down the rules to be applied during an initial two-year stage; whereas it is nevertheless desirable, for reasons of road safety and other reasons, to provide that, from the entry into force of this Regulation, more restrictive provisions should be applied to certain long and heavy vehicles;

Whereas, with regard to rest periods, it is desirable to lay down the minimum duration of and other conditions governing the daily and weekly rest periods of crew members;

Whereas it is desirable, in order to make it possible to check that the provisions of this Regulation are being observed, that each member of the crew be required to have an individual control book; whereas, however, in the case of crews of vehicles used for regular services, a copy of the timetable and an extract from the undertaking's duty roster may replace the individual control book;

Whereas it is desirable to provide for the replacement, wherever possible, of the individual control book by mechanical recording equipment; whereas, for this purpose, it is desirable that the technical characteristics and the methods of using such equipment should be settled at Community level within a set time limit;

Whereas, in order that this Regulation may be applied and that compliance therewith may be checked, it is appropriate for Member States to give each other assistance;

Whereas it is desirable, in order to enable undertakings to adjust their operations so as to conform to the provisions of this Regulation, that during an initial phase such provisions should apply only to international transport between Member States and that their application should be extended in a second phase to all the transport operations referred to in this Regulation;

HAS ADOPTED THIS REGULATION:

SECTION I

DEFINITIONS

Article 1

In this Regulation:

1. 'carriage by road' means any journey by road of a vehicle, whether laden or not, used for the carriage of passengers or goods;

2. 'vehicles' means motor vehicles, tractors, trailers and semi-trailers, defined as follows:

    (*a*) 'motor vehicle': any mechanically self-propelled vehicle circulating on the road, other than a vehicle running on rails, and normally used for carrying passengers or goods;

(b) 'tractor': any mechanically self-propelled vehicle circulating on the road, other than a vehicle running on rails, and specially designed to pull, push or move trailers, semi-trailers, implements or machines;

(c) 'trailer': any vehicle designed to be coupled to a motor vehicle or a tractor;

(d) 'semi-trailer': a trailer without a front axle coupled in such a way that a substantial part of its weight and of the weight of its load is borne by the tractor or motor vehicle;

3. 'crew member' means the driver, driver's mate, and conductor, defined as follows:

(a) 'driver': any person who drives the vehicle even for a short period, or who is carried in the vehicle in order to be available for driving if necessary;

(b) 'driver's mate': any person accompanying the driver of a vehicle in order to assist him in certain manoeuvres and habitually taking an effective part in the transport operations, but not being a driver within the meaning of (a);

(c) 'conductor': any person who accompanies the driver of a vehicle used for the carriage of passengers and has the particular duty of issuing and checking tickets;

4. 'week' means any period of seven consecutive days;

5. 'daily rest period' means any uninterrupted period of at least eight hours during which the crew members may freely dispose of their time and are entirely free to move about as they please;

6. (a) 'regular goods services' means transport services operated at specified intervals along specified routes, goods being loaded and unloaded at predetermined stopping points;

(b) 'regular passenger services' means the services defined in Article 1 of Regulation (EEC) No 117/66;

7. 'permissible maximum weight' means the maximum authorised operating weight of the vehicle fully laden.

[The term 'regular passenger services' is defined in art 1 of Regulation No 117/66/EEC (OJ No 147, 9.8.1966, p 2699/66) as 'services which provide for the carriage of passengers at specified intervals along specified routes, passengers being taken up and set down at predetermined stopping points'.]

SECTION II

Scope

[Article 2

1. This Regulation applies to carriage by road by means of vehicles registered in a Member State or in a third country for any journey made within the Community.

2. However, as from January 1, 1978:
— the European Agreement concerning the Work of Crews of Vehicles Engaged in International Road Transport (AETR) shall apply to international road transport operations to and/or from third countries which are contracting parties to that Agreement, or in transit through such countries, for the whole of the journey where such operations are effected by vehicles registered in a Member State or in one of the said third countries;

— transport operations to and/or from a third country effected by vehicles registered in a third country which is not a contracting party to the Agreement shall be subject to the Agreement for any journey made within the Community.]

[Article 2 was substituted by Council Regulation No 2829/77/EEC.]

Article 3

The Community shall enter into any negotiations with third countries which may prove necessary for the purpose of implementing this Regulation.

Article 4

This Regulation shall not apply to carriage by:

1. vehicles which in construction and equipment are suitable for carrying not more than nine persons including the driver and are intended for that purpose;

2. vehicles used for the carriage of goods, the permissible maximum weight of which, including any trailer or semi-trailer, does not exceed 3·5 metric tons;

3. vehicles used for the carriage of passengers on regular services where the route covered by the service in question does not exceed 50 km;

[4. vehicles used by the police, gendarmerie, armed forces, fire brigades, civil defence, drainage or flood prevention authorities, water, gas or electricity services, highway authorities and refuse collection, telegraph or telephone services, by the postal authorities for the carriage of mail, by radio or television services or for the detection of radio or television transmitters or receivers, or vehicles which are used by other public authorities for public services and which are not in competition with professional road hauliers;

5. vehicles used for the carriage of sick or injured persons and for carrying rescue material, and any other specialized vehicles used for medical purposes;]

6. tractors with a maximum authorised speed not exceeding 30 kilometres per hour;

[7. tractors and other machines used exclusively for local agricultural and forestry work;

8. vehicles used to transport circus and fun-fair equipment;

9. specialized breakdown vehicles.]

[Article 4 is printed as amended by Regulation No 515/72/EEC, and Regulation No 2827/77/ EEC.]

SECTION III

CREW

Article 5

1. The minimum ages for drivers engaged in the carriage of goods shall be as follows:

(*a*) for vehicles, including, where appropriate, trailers or semi-trailers, having a permissible maximum weight of not more than 7·5 metric tons, eighteen years;

(*b*) for other vehicles:
    — twenty-one years, or

— eighteen years, provided the person concerned holds a certificate of professional competence recognised by one of the Member States confirming that he has completed a training course for drivers of vehicles intended for the carriage of goods by road. The Council shall, on a proposal from the Commission, lay down the minimum level of such training by 1 April 1970 at the latest.

Where, in accordance with Article 6, there are two drivers, one of the drivers shall have reached the age of twenty-one years.

2. Any driver engaged in the carriage of passengers shall have reached the age of twenty-one years, and meet one of the following conditions:

(a) he must have worked for at least one year in the carriage of goods as a driver of vehicles with a permissible maximum weight exceeding 3·5 metric tons;

(b) he must have worked for at least one year as a driver of vehicles used to provide the passenger services referred to in Article 4 (3);

(c) he must hold a certificate of professional competence recognised by one of the Member States confirming that he has completed a training course for drivers of vehicles intended for the carriage of passengers by road. The Council shall, on a proposal from the Commission, lay down the minimum level of such training by 1 April 1970 at the latest.

3. The minimum age for drivers' mates and conductors shall be eighteen years.

4. Where any driver engaged in the carriage of passengers has reached the age of twenty-one years he shall be exempt from the conditions laid down in paragraph 2 (a), (b) and (c):

— for an indefinite period if he has carried on that occupation for at least one year prior to 1 October 1970.

5. Each Member State may, as regards those persons residing within its territory who on 1 October 1970 already hold the requisite driving licence, suspend application of the rules laid down in paragraphs 1 and 2 in respect of carriage within its own territory.

6. Each Member State may, as regards those persons residing within its territory who on 1 October 1970 are already employed as driver's mate or conductor, suspend application of the provisions of paragraph 3 in respect of carriage within its own territory.

[7. In the case of internal transport operations carried out within a radius of 50 kilometres from the place where the vehicle is based, including municipalities the centre of which is situated within that radius, Member States may reduce the minimum age for drivers' mates to 16 years, on condition that this is for purposes of vocational training and subject to the limits imposed by their internal law on employment matters.]

[Article 5 is printed as amended by Regulation No 515/72/EEC.]

Article 6

[1.] Where a driver is engaged in carriage by:

(a) a motor vehicle or tractor with more than one trailer or semi-trailer;

(b) a motor vehicle or tractor with one trailer or semi-trailer where this combination is used for the carriage of passengers and the permissible maximum weight of the trailer or semi-trailer exceeds 5 metric tons;

(c) a motor vehicle or tractor with one trailer or semi-trailer where this combination is used for the carriage of goods and the permissible maximum weight of such combination exceeds 20 metric tons;

and the distance to be covered between two consecutive daily rest periods exceeds 450 km, that driver shall from the beginning of the journey be accompanied by another driver or shall, on reaching the 450th km, be relieved by another driver.

[2. Paragraph 1 shall not apply where in these vehicles there is in use recording equipment as provided for in Article 1 or in Article 20 (1) of Council Regulation (EEC) No 1463/70 of 20 July 1970 on the introduction of recording equipment in road transport, as last amended by Regulation (EEC) No 2828/77.

[*Article 6 is printed as amended by Regulation No 2827/77/EEC.*]

SECTION IV
DRIVING PERIODS

Article 7

1. No period of continuous driving shall exceed four hours.

Any driving period interrupted by breaks which do not at least satisfy the conditions laid down in paragraphs (1) and (2) of Article 8 shall be deemed to be continuous.

2. The total period of driving time between two consecutive daily rest periods (hereinafter called the 'daily driving period') shall not exceed 8 hours.

3. In the case of drivers of vehicles other than the vehicles referred to in Article 6 the daily driving period may, by way of derogation from paragraph 2, be extended, not more than twice in any one week, to nine hours.

4. The driving period may in no case exceed forty-eight hours in any one week or ninety-two hours in any two consecutive weeks.

Article 8

1. For drivers referred to in Article 6, driving shall be interrupted for a period of not less than one hour at the end of the first four-hour period of continuous driving.

This break may be replaced by two breaks of not less than thirty minutes each, spaced out over the daily driving period in such a way that the first subparagraph of Article 7 (1) is complied with.

2. For drivers of vehicles other than the vehicles referred to in Article 6, driving shall be interrupted for a period of not less than thirty consecutive minutes at the end of the period referred to in the first subparagraph of Article 7 (1).

This break may be replaced by two breaks of not less than twenty minutes each or by three breaks of not less than fifteen minutes each, which may all be spaced out over the driving period referred to in the first subparagraph of Article 7 (1) or may in part fall within that period and in part immediately follow it.

3. During the breaks referred to in paragraphs 1 and 2 of this Article, the driver shall not perform any activity covered by Article 14 (2) (c) or (d).

4. If the vehicle is manned by two drivers, the requirements of paragraphs 1 and 2 of this Article shall be deemed to be met if the driver who is having his break does not perform any activity covered by Article 14 (3) (b).

Articles 9, 10 [*Deleted.*]

SECTION V

[Rest Periods]

Article 11

1. Every crew member engaged in the carriage of goods shall have had a daily rest period of not less than eleven consecutive hours during the twenty-four-hour period preceding any time when he is performing any activity covered by Article 14(2) (c) or (d).

The daily rest period referred to in the preceding subparagraph may be reduced to nine hours, not more than twice in any one week, when such rest is taken at the place where the crew is based (where the vehicle is based), or to eight hours, not more than twice in any one week, when such rest is taken elsewhere than at the place where the crew is based (where the vehicle is based).

2. Every crew member engaged in the carriage of passengers shall have had, during the twenty-four-hour period preceding any time when he is performing any activity covered by Article 14 (2) (c) or (d):
- — a daily rest period of not less than ten consecutive hours, which shall not be reduced during the week, or
- — a daily rest period of not less than eleven consecutive hours, which may be reduced twice a week to ten consecutive hours and twice a week to nine consecutive hours provided that the transport operation includes a scheduled break of not less than four hours' uninterrupted duration or two breaks of not less than two hours' uninterrupted duration and that during such breaks the crew member concerned does not perform any activity covered by Article 14 (2) (c) or (d) or any other work in a professional capacity.

The individual control book provided for in Article 14 shall contain particulars showing which daily rest system is being followed during the week in question by every crew member engaged in the carriage of passengers.

3. Where the vehicle is manned by two drivers and has no bunk enabling the crew members not performing any activity to lie down comfortably, each crew member shall have had a daily rest period of not less than ten consecutive hours during the twenty-seven-hour period preceding any time when he is performing any activity covered by Article 14 (2) (c) or (d).

4. Where the vehicle is manned by two drivers and has a bunk enabling crew members not performing any activity to lie down comfortably, each crew member shall have had a daily rest period of not less than eight consecutive hours during the thirty-hour period preceding any time when he is performing any of the activities covered by Article 14 (2) (c) or (d).

5. The daily rest period shall be taken outside the vehicle. However, if the vehicle has a bunk the rest period may be taken on that bunk provided that the vehicle is stationary.

6. Any reductions in the duration of the daily rest period made by virtue of the exceptions provided for in paragraphs 1 and 2 shall be compensated.

[Article 11a

Where a crew member engaged in the carriage of goods or passengers accompanies a vehicle which is transported by ferryboat or train, the daily rest period may be interrupted not more than once, provided the following conditions are fulfilled:

— that part of the daily rest period spent on land may be taken before or after the portion of the daily rest period taken on board the ferryboat or the train,

— the period between the two portions of the daily rest period must be as short as possible and may on no account exceed one hour before embarkation or after disembarkation, customs formalities being included in the embarkation or disembarkation operations,

— during both portions of the rest period the crew member must have access to a bunk or couchette,

— where a daily rest period is interrupted in this way, it shall be increased by two hours,

— any time spent on board a ferryboat or a train and not counted as part of the daily rest period shall be regarded as a break defined in Article 8.]

[Article 11a was inserted by Regulation No 2827/77/EEC.]

[Article 12

1. In addition to the daily rest periods referred to in Article 11, every crew member shall have a weekly rest period of not less than 29 consecutive hours, which shall be immediately preceded or followed by a daily rest period.

2. The rest period referred to in paragraph 1 may be reduced to not less than 24 consecutive hours provided that a rest period equivalent to the reduction is granted to the crew member concerned during the same week.

3. However, during the period between 1 April and 30 September, the weekly rest period referred to in paragraph 1 hereof may be replaced, for crew members of vehicles used for the international road transport of passengers, by a rest period of not less than 60 consecutive hours to be taken in full before the expiry of a period not exceeding 14 consecutive days. This rest period must be immediately preceded or followed by a daily rest period conforming to the provisions of Article 11.

Subparagraph 1 shall not apply to crew members of vehicles assigned to regular passenger services.]

[Article 12 was substituted by Regulation No 2827/77/EEC.]

[SECTION Va

PROHIBITION OF CERTAIN TYPES OF PAYMENT]

[The heading 'Section Va' was inserted by Regulation No 2827/77/EEC.]

[Article 12a

Payments to wage-earning crew members, even in the form of bonuses or wage supplements, related to distances travelled and/or the amount of goods carried shall be prohibited, unless these payments are of such a kind as not to endanger road safety.]

[Article 12a was inserted by Regulation No 2827/77/EEC.]

SECTION VI
EXCEPTIONS

Article 13

[1. Each Member State may apply higher minima or lower maxima than those laid down in Article 5 and Articles 7 to 12 and may refrain from applying Article 6 (2).]

2. From the date of entry into force of this Regulation, the Commission shall, every other year, submit to the Council a report on the development of the situation in the fields covered by this Regulation.

[Article 13 is printed as amended by Regulation No 2827/77/EEC.]

[Article 13a

Provided that road safety is not thereby jeopardized, the driver may, in case of danger, in circumstances outside his control, to render assistance, or as a result of a breakdown, and to the extent necessary to ensure the safety of persons, of the vehicle or of its load, and to enable him to reach a suitable stopping place or, according to circumstances, the end of his journey, depart from the provisions of Articles 6, 7 (2) and (4), and 11. The driver shall indicate the nature and reasons for such departure in the individual control book, or on the record sheet of the recording equipment.]

[Article 13a was inserted by Council Regulation No 514/72/EEC.]

SECTION VII
CONTROL PROCEDURES AND PENALTIES

Article 14

[1. Crew members of a vehicle not assigned to a regular service shall carry an individual control book conforming to the model in the Annex to this Regulation. That Annex forms an integral part of this Regulation.

However, in the case of drivers of vehicles registered in a third country which is not a party to the AETR Agreement, the Commission shall, on the application of a Member State, approve a control book of a model different from the model shown in the Annex, on condition that such model does not differ in essential points from the model laid down by the Community.

The Commission shall notify the other Member States accordingly.]

2. Members of the crew shall from day to day enter in the daily sheets of the individual control book details of the following periods:

(a) under the symbol 🛏 : daily rest periods;

(b) under the symbol 🏃 : breaks from work of not less than fifteen minutes;

(c) under the symbol 🗝 : driving periods;

(d) under the symbol ▨ : other periods of attendance at work.

3. Each Member State may prescribe, in respect of individual control books issued in its territory, that the periods covered by paragraph 2 (d) should be subdivided so as to show separately:

(*a*) under the symbol ▨ :

> — waiting time, that is to say the period during which crew members must be at their place of work only for the purpose of answering any calls to carry out or resume any of the duties covered by paragraph 2 (*c*) or by subparagraph (*b*) of this paragraph;
> — time spent beside the driver while the vehicle is on the move;
> — time spent on a bunk while the vehicle is on the move;

(*b*) under the symbol ⚒ : all other working periods.

[4. Any Member State may take the necessary measures to exempt crew members of vehicles registered in its territory carrying out internal transport operations from having to enter in the daily sheets of the individual control book any period of time covered by paragraph 2 which can be suitably recorded by means of recording equipment fitted on the vehicle and approved in accordance with Article 20 of Council Regulation (EEC) No 1463/70 of 20 July 1970 on the introduction of recording equipment in road transport, without prejudice to the implementation of that Regulation as a whole with effect from the dates laid down in Articles 4 and 20 thereof.

Information thus recorded shall be shown in the weekly report in the individual control book.]

5. When crew members subject to the provisions of paragraph 4 are engaged in an international transport operation, the periods of time thus recorded covering the seven previous days shall, in so far as they have not been entered in the weekly report in accordance with the second subparagraph of paragraph 4, be shown in the daily sheets of the individual control book.

6. Crew members shall produce the individual control book whenever required to do so by any authorised inspecting officer.

7. All undertakings shall keep a register of the individual books, which shall show the name of each crew member to whom a book is issued, an acknowledgement of receipt by the crew member, the number of the book, its date of issue and the date of the last daily sheet completed. It shall be produced at the request of any authorised inspecting officer.

8. All completed individual books shall be kept by the undertaking for at least one year.

9. Member States shall take all necessary measures concerning the issue and control of the books.

[*Article 14 is printed as amended by Regulation No 514/72/EEC, and Regulation No 515/72/ EEC.*]

[Article 14a

[1.] In the case of internal goods transport operations carried out within a radius of 50 kilometres from the place where the vehicle is based, including municipalities the centre of which is situated within that radius, Member States may:

(*a*) after consulting the Commission, grant exemption

> (i) from Articles 7 (1) and 8. The daily driving period must, however, include sufficient breaks to ensure that the periods laid down in Article 8 (1) and (2) are observed and that, in each case, there is a break of at least 30 minutes or two breaks of not less than 15 minutes each;

(ii) as regards the transport of harvest produce and in respect of not more than thirty days in any year, from Article 11 (1), provided that a daily rest period of not less than 10 consecutive hours is observed and that the reduction in the daily rest period is made good by a corresponding additional rest period to be taken immediately before or after the weekly rest period;

(iii) in respect of the transport of milk from farm to dairy [and vice versa],

— from Article 11 (1), provided that a daily rest period of not less than 8 consecutive hours is observed and that a break in driving of not less than 4 consecutive hours is taken in the course of the day, during which the crew member does not perform any activity covered by subparagraph (c) or (d) of Article 14 (2) or any other work in a professional capacity;

— from Article 12, provided that the maximum driving permitted during the period intended for the weekly rest is not more than twice two hours.

(b) until the compulsory installation, of the recording equipment provided for in Article 1 of Regulation (EEC) No 1463/70, grant exemption from Article 14, provided:

— that the vehicles in question are fitted with recording equipment conforming to article 20 of that Regulation; or

— that Member States, after consulting the Commission, take appropriate measures to keep an effective check on compliance with the provisions applicable to such transport operations such as will ensure that standards of employee protection and road safety are not impaired.

[2. Member States may, after consulting the Commission, grant exemptions from this Regulation for the following national transport operations and uses:

(a) use of vehicles which are constructed and equipped to carry not more than 15 persons including the driver;

(b) use of vehicles undergoing local road tests for purposes of repair or maintenance;

(c) transport of live animals from farms to local markets and vice versa, and transport of animal carcases or waste not intended for human consumption.

3. Member States may, after authorization by the Commission, grant exemptions from this Regulation for the following national transport operations and uses:

(a) use of specialized vehicles for local markets, for door-to-door selling, for mobile banking, exchange or savings transactions, for purposes of worship, for the lending of books, records or cassettes, for cultural events or mobile exhibitions;

(b) transport of milk from the farm to the dairy and vice versa.

In adopting these measures the Commission may specify the conditions and arrangements for their application which it deems necessary.

4. To enable transport services to provide assistance to the population of particular areas during temporary emergencies, Member States may grant temporary exemptions from Sections IV and V for national transport. They shall forthwith notify the measures they have taken to the Commission, which may amend or annul them.

5. Where an exemption from this Regulation is granted, Member States shall take appropriate measures at the same time to keep an effective check on such transport so as to ensure that standards of social protection and road safety are not impaired.]]

[Article 14a was inserted by Regulation No 515/72/EEC and is printed as amended by Regulation No 2827/77/EEC.]

Article 15

1. All operators of regular services shall draw up a service timetable and a duty roster.

2. The duty roster shall show, in respect of each crew member, the name, date of birth, place where based and the schedule, which shall have been laid down in advance, for the various periods of time covered by Article 14 (2) and (3).

3. The duty roster shall include all the particulars specified in paragraph 2 for a minimum period covering both the current week and the weeks immediately preceding and following that week.

4. The duty roster shall be signed by the head of the undertaking or by a person authorised to represent him.

5. Each crew member assigned to a regular service shall carry an extract from the duty roster and a copy of the service timetable.

Article 16

The Council shall, on a proposal from the Commission and by 31 December 1969 at the latest, determine the technical characteristics of mechanical recording equipment to replace, as far as possible, the individual control book prescribed by Article 14. At the same time, it shall, on a proposal from the Commission, determine the details concerning the approval, use and inspection of such recording equipment. At the same time, the Council shall fix the dates from which vehicles—taking separately those brought into service for the first time and all other vehicles—shall be fitted with the above-mentioned mechanical recording equipment.

Article 17

1. Each year the Commission shall present to the Council a general report on the implementation of this Regulation by Member States.

2. In order to enable the Commission to draw up the report referred to in paragraph 1, Member States shall communicate annually to the Commission the necessary information, using a standard form of report to be drawn up by the Commission after consulting the Member States.

Article 18

1. Member States shall, in due time and after consulting the Commission, adopt such laws, regulations or administrative provisions as may be necessary for the implementation of this Regulation. Such measures shall cover, inter alia, the organisation of, procedure for and means of control and the penalties to be imposed in case of breach.

2. Member States shall assist each other in applying the provisions of this Regulation and checking compliance therewith.

3. If it is brought to the notice of the competent authorities of a Member State that a breach of the provisions of this Regulation has been committed by a crew member of a vehicle registered in another Member State, those authorities may notify the authorities of the State where the vehicle is registered of such breach. The competent authorities shall send each other all the information in their possession concerning the penalties imposed for such breaches.

SECTION VIII

Final Provisions

Article 19

1. This Regulation shall enter into force on 1 April 1969.

2. From 1 October 1969, this Regulation shall apply to international transport operations between Member States.

3. From 1 October 1970, this Regulation shall apply to all transport operations, covered by Article 2 of this Regulation.

4. *[Spent.]*

[Article 19 is printed as amended by Regulation No 514/72/EEC.]

This Regulation shall be binding in its entirety and directly applicable in all Member States.

ANNEX

Individual Control Book

*   *   *

Regulation No 1463/70/EEC of the Council

of 20 July 1970

on the introduction of recording equipment in road transport

[The text of this regulation is printed as amended by:
  Regulation No 1787/73/EEC (OJ No L 181, 4.7.73, p 1) (25 June 1973); and
  Regulation No 2828/77/EEC (OJ No L 334, 24.12.77, p 5) (1 January 1978).
The dates referred to above are the dates on which the regulations took effect.
  The text as printed has also been corrected in accordance with a corrigendum to the main regula-
tions which was published at OJ No L 110, 27.4.73, p 39.]

THE COUNCIL OF THE EUROPEAN COMMUNITIES,

Having regard to the Treaty establishing the European Economic Community, and in particular Article 75 thereof;

Having regard to Council Regulation (EEC) No 543/69 of 25 March 1969 on the harmonisation of certain social legislation relating to road transport, and in particular Article 16 thereof;

Having regard to the proposal from the Commission;

Having regard to the Opinion of the European Parliament;

Having regard to the Opinion of the Economic and Social Committee;

Whereas Article 16 of Regulation (EEC) No 543/69 provides for the determination of the technical characteristics of recording equipment to replace as far as possible the individual control book and for the determination at the same time of the details concerning the approval, use and testing of such equipment and the dates from which vehicles are to be fitted with such equipment;

Whereas in the current state of technical knowledge it is possible to envisage the development and production of types of recording equipment capable of replacing entirely the individual control book while ensuring that an effective check is kept on all periods of time referred to in Regulation (EEC) No 543/69 concerning the activities and rest of the crews of vehicles;

Whereas a certain period of time will be needed to develop and produce recording equipment and to set up the services necessary for the installation, repair and testing of such equipment; whereas it is furthermore appropriate to provide for installation to be staggered over a certain period of time in order to maintain stability on the market, while giving priority to installation in vehicles which enter into service for the first time on or after a certain date and to installation in vehicles used for the carriage of dangerous goods;

Whereas the obligation to introduce such recording equipment can be imposed only for vehicles registered in Member States; whereas furthermore certain of such vehicles may, without giving rise to difficulty, be excluded from the scope of this Regulation;

Whereas, in order to ensure effective checking, the equipment must be reliable in operation, easy to use and designed in such a way as to minimise any possibility of fraudulent use; whereas to this end recording equipment should in particular be capable of providing, on separate sheets for each crew member and in a sufficiently precise and easily readable form, recorded details of the various periods of time;

Whereas automatic recording of other details of a vehicle's journey, such as speed and distance covered, will contribute significantly to road safety and will encourage sensible driving of the vehicle; whereas, consequently, it appears appropriate to provide for the equipment also to record those details;

Whereas, in certain Member States, there are as yet no rules concerning recording equipment in motor vehicles and whereas among the other Member States rules differ; whereas such omissions and differences are liable to hinder the free circulation of motor vehicles within the Community and to bring about distortions in the conditions of competition;

Whereas to remedy this situation it is necessary to lay down sufficiently detailed Community standards for construction and installation; whereas, in order to avoid any impediment to the registration of vehicles fitted with such recording equipment or any impediment to their entry into service or use, or to such equipment being used throughout the territory of the Member States, it is necessary to provide for an EEC approval procedure;

Whereas, in order to ensure that recording equipment functions reliably and correctly, it is advisable to lay down uniform requirements for the periodic checks and inspections to which the equipment is to be subject after installation;

Whereas, in order to achieve the aims hereinbefore mentioned of keeping a check on work and rest periods, it is necessary that employers and crew members be responsible for seeing that the equipment functions correctly and that they perform with due care the operations prescribed;

Whereas, in the interests of road safety and of keeping a more effective check on compliance with the provisions of Regulation (EEC) No 543/69 it is appropriate to lay down transitional provisions for the period preceding the compulsory introduction of recording equipment, so as to enable each Member State, in respect of vehicles registered in its territory, either to bring forward the dates specified in this Regulation for the installation of recording equipment complying with its terms, or to prescribe the use of recording equipment conforming to a type which has received national approval;

Whereas exercise by a Member State of the latter option is compatible with the measures provided for in Article 14 (4) and (5) of Regulation (EEC) No 543/69; whereas, in the interests of economy, it is desirable to avoid replacing too soon recording equipment conforming to a type which has received national approval and, therefore, the date from which the vehicles concerned must be fitted with recording equipment complying with the terms of this Regulation should be deferred for a certain time;

HAS ADOPTED THIS REGULATION:

CHAPTER I

PRINCIPLES AND SCOPE

Article 1

Recording equipment within the meaning of this Regulation shall, as regards construction, installation, use and testing, comply with the requirements of this Regulation and of Annexes I and II thereto, which shall form an integral part of this Regulation.

Article 2

For the purposes of this Regulation the definitions set out in Article 1 of Regulation (EEC) No 543/69 shall apply.

Article 3

[1.] Recording equipment shall be installed and used in vehicles used for the carriage for passengers or goods by road and registered in a Member State, with the exception of the vehicles referred to in Article 4 of Regulation (EEC) No 543/69 and of vehicles used for the carriage of passengers on regular services where the route covered by the service in question exceeds 50 kilometres.

[2. However, after consulting the Commission, Member States may exempt from the application of this Regulation vehicles mentioned in Article 14a (2) of Regulation (EEC) No 543/69.]

[3. Member States may, after authorisation from the Commission, exempt from the application of this Regulation vehicles mentioned in Article 14a (3) (a) of Regulation (EEC) No 543/69.]

[Article 3 is printed as amended by Regulation No 2828/77/EEC.]

[Article 4

1. Without prejudice to the provisions of Annex VII, Point III, paragraph 4 of the Act of Accession, with effect from 1 January 1975 the installation and use of recording equipment shall be compulsory:

 (a) at the time of their entry into service for vehicles registered for the first time on or after that date;

 (b) whatever the date of their registration, for vehicles used for the carriage of dangerous goods.

2. With effect from 1 January 1978 the installation and use of recording equipment shall be compulsory for other vehicles.

3. However the date referred to in paragraph 2 shall be deferred to 1 July 1979 for vehicles used exclusively for the domestic carriage of goods, other than dangerous goods,

> — which are engaged in transport operations within a radius of 50 kilometres of the vehicle's depot, including local administrative areas the centres of which are within this radius, or
> — which have a maximum authorized weight, inclusive of trailers or semi-trailers, of not more than six tonnes or a payload of not more than 3·5 tonnes.]

[Article 4 was substituted by Regulation No 2828/77/EEC.]

[Article 5

Articles 14 and 15 of Regulation (EEC) No 543/69 shall not apply to crew members of vehicles using recording equipment conforming to the provisions of Annexes I and II to the present Regulation.]

[Article 5 was substituted by Regulation No 2828/77/EEC.]

CHAPTER II

TYPE APPROVAL

Article 6

Applications for EEC approval of a type of recording equipment or of a model record sheet shall be submitted, accompanied by the appropriate specifications, by the manufacturer or his agent to a Member State. No application in respect of any one type of recording equipment or of any one model record sheet may be submitted to more than one Member State.

Article 7

A Member State shall grant EEC approval to any type of recording equipment or to any model record sheet which conforms to the requirements laid down in Annex I to this Regulation, provided the Member State is in a position to check that production models conform to the approved prototype.

[Any modifications or additions to an approved model must receive additional EEC type-approval from the Member State which granted the original EEC type-approval.]

[Article 7 is printed as amended by Regulation No 2828/77/EEC.]

Article 8

1. Member States shall issue to the applicant an EEC approval mark, which shall conform to the model shown in Annex II, for each type of recording equipment or model record sheet which they approve pursuant to Article 7.

2. The Commission may, by means of a Regulation, assign to Luxembourg a special number for the EEC approval mark referred to in the preceding paragraph to replace the letter assigned to that country under paragraph 1 of Chapter I of Annex II, in order to ensure harmony with any international agreements to which Luxembourg may become a party.

Article 9

The competent authorities of the Member State to which the application for type approval has been submitted shall, in respect of each type of recording equipment or model record sheet which they approve or refuse to approve, either send within one month to the authorities of the other Member States a copy of the approval certificate accompanied by copies of the relevant specifications, or, if it is the case, notify those authorities that approval has been refused; in cases of refusal they shall communicate the reasons for their decision.

[Article 10

1. If a Member State which has granted EEC type-approval as provided for in Article 7 finds that certain recording equipment or record sheets bearing the EEC type-approval mark which it has issued do not conform to the prototype which it has approved, it shall take the necessary measures to ensure that production models conform to the approved prototype. The measures taken may, if necessary, extend to withdrawal of EEC type-approval.

2. A Member State which has granted EEC type-approval shall withdraw such approval if the recording equipment or record sheet which has been approved is not in conformity with this Regulation or its Annexes or displays in use any general defect which makes it unsuitable for the purpose for which it is intended.

3. If a Member State which has granted EEC type-approval is notified by another Member State of one of the cases referred to in paragraphs 1 and 2, it shall also, after consulting the latter Member State, take the steps laid down in those paragraphs, subject to the implementation of paragraph 5.

4. A Member State which ascertains that one of the cases referred to in paragraph 2 has arisen may forbid the placing on the market and putting into service of the recording equipment or record sheets until further notice. The same applies in the cases mentioned in paragraph 1 with respect to recording equipment or record sheets which have been exempted from EEC initial verification, if the manufacturer, after due warning, does not bring the equipment into line with the approved model or with the requirements of this Regulation.

In any event, the competent authorities of the Member States shall notify one another and the Commission, within one month, of any withdrawal of EEC type-approval or of any other measures taken pursuant to paragraphs 1, 2 and 3 and shall specify the reasons for such action.

5. If a Member State which has granted EEC type-approval disputes the existence of any of the cases specified in paragraphs 1 or 2 notified to it, the Member States concerned shall endeavour to settle the dispute and the Commission shall be kept informed.

If talks between the Member States have not resulted in agreement within four months of the date of the notification referred to in paragraph 3 above, the Commission, after consulting experts from all Member States and having considered all the relevant factors, eg economic and technical factors, shall within six months adopt a decision which shall be communicated to the Member States concerned and at the same time to the other Member States. The Commission shall lay down in each instance the time limit for implementation of its decision.]

[Article 10 was substituted by Regulation No 2828/77/EEC.]

Article 11

[1. An applicant for EEC type-approval of a model record sheet shall state on his application the type or types of recording equipment on which the sheet in question is designed to be used and shall provide suitable equipment of such type or types for the purpose of testing the sheet.]

2. The competent authorities of each Member State shall indicate on the approval certificate for the model record sheet the type or types of recording equipment on which that model sheet may be used.

[Article 11 is printed as amended by Regulation No 2828/77/EEC.]

Article 12

No Member State may refuse to register any vehicle fitted with recording equipment, or prohibit the entry into service or use of such vehicle for any reason connected with the fact that the vehicle is fitted with such equipment, if the equipment bears the EEC approval mark referred to in Article 8 and the installation plaque referred to in Article 14.

Article 13

All decisions pursuant to this Regulation refusing or withdrawing approval of a type of recording equipment or model record sheet shall specify in detail the reasons on which they are based. A decision shall be communicated to the party concerned, who shall at the same time be informed of the remedies available to him under the laws of the Member States and of the time-limits for the exercise of such remedies.

CHAPTER III
Installation and Inspection

Article 14

[1. Recording equipment may be installed or repaired only by fitters or workshops approved by the competent authorities of Member States for that purpose after the latter, should they so desire, have heard the views of the manufacturers concerned.]

Approved fitters or workshops may also be authorised to undertake, if necessary concurrently with the competent authorities of the Member States, checking on installation and subsequent inspection of recording equipment.

2. The approved fitter or workshop shall place a special mark on the seals which it affixes. The competent authorities of each Member State shall maintain a register of the marks used.

3. The competent authorities of the Member States shall send each other their lists of approved fitters or workshops and also copies of the marks used.

4. For the purpose of certifying that installation of recording equipment took place in accordance with the requirements of this Regulation an installation plaque affixed as provided in Annex I shall be used.

[Article 14 is printed as amended by Regulation No 2828/77/EEC.]

CHAPTER IV
Use of Equipment

Article 15

The employer and crew members shall be responsible for seeing that the equipment functions correctly and that the seals remain intact. Any operation or interference resulting in falsified readings or recordings shall be prohibited. The seals may be broken only in case of absolute necessity, which will have to be duly proved.

Article 16

1. The employer shall issue a sufficient number of record sheets to crew members, bearing in mind the fact that these sheets are personal in character, the length of the period of service and the possible need to replace sheets which are damaged, or have been taken by an authorised inspecting officer. The employer shall issue to crew members only sheets of an approved model suitable for use in the equipment installed in the vehicle.

[2. The employer shall retain record sheets for a period of at least one year after their use; the sheets for each crew member shall be produced or handed over at the request of any authorised inspecting officer.]

[Article 16 is printed as amended by Regulation No 2828/77/EEC.]

Article 17

1. Crew members shall not use dirty or damaged record sheets. The sheets shall be adequately protected on this account. In case of damage to a sheet bearing recordings, the crew members shall attach the damaged sheet to the spare sheet used to replace it.

2. Crew members shall see that the equipment is kept running continuously from the time when they take over the vehicle until they are relieved from their responsibility for it. [In particular:

— they shall ensure that the time recorded on the sheet agrees with the official time in the country of registration of the vehicle;

— they shall operate the switch mechanisms enabling the following periods of time to be recorded separately and distinctly:

    (a) driving time,

    (b) other periods of work and of attendance at work,

    (c) breaks from work and rest periods.

The periods of time referred to in (b) may be recorded separately on the record sheet;

— they shall make the necessary changes to the record sheet in the case of a crew of several members so that the information referred to in Chapter II (1), (2) and (3) of Annex I is recorded on the record sheet of the crew member who is actually driving.]

When the crew members are away from the vehicle and therefore unable to operate the equipment fitted to the vehicle themselves, the various periods of time shall, whether manually, by automatic recording or otherwise, be entered on the sheet in a legible manner and without the sheets being dirtied.

Where the preceding subparagraph applies, crew members shall ensure that the entry marking the beginning of a period of time is made at the beginning of the period to which the entry relates.

3. Each crew member shall enter the following information on his record sheet:

(a) on beginning to use the sheet—his surname and first name;

(b) the date and place where use of the sheet begins and the date and place where such use ends;

(c) the registration number of each vehicle to which he is assigned, both at the start of the first journey recorded on the sheet and then, in the event of a change of vehicle, during use of the sheet;

(d) the odometer reading:

— at the start of the first journey recorded on the sheet;

    . . .

— at the end of the last journey recorded on the sheet;

— in the event of a change of vehicle during a working day (reading on the vehicle to which he was assigned and reading on the vehicle to which he is to be assigned);

(e) the time of any change of vehicle.

[4. The equipment shall be so designed that it is possible for an authorised inspecting officer, if necessary after opening the equipment, to read the recordings relating to the nine hours preceding the time of the check without permanently deforming, damaging or soiling the sheet.

The equipment shall, furthermore, be so designed that it is possible, without opening the case, to verify that recordings are being made.]

5. Crew members must be able to produce on request by any authorised inspecting officer a record sheet or sheets giving full details of all relevant periods for not less than the [seven] days preceding the time when the check is made.

6. Any Member State may take the necessary measures to reduce the period specified in the preceding paragraph to a minimum of two days for crew members of vehicles registered in its territory engaging in national transport operations.

[Article 17 is printed as amended by Regulation No 2828/77/EEC.]

Article 18

1. In the event of breakdown or faulty operation of the equipment, the employer shall have it repaired by approved fitters or workshops, at the latest as soon as the vehicle has returned to the premises of the undertaking.

If the vehicle is unable to return to the premises within a period of one week counting from the day of the breakdown or of the discovery of defective operation, the repair shall be carried out en route.

Measures taken by Member States pursuant to [Article 23] may give the competent authorities power to prohibit the use of the vehicle in cases where breakdown or faulty operation has not been put right as provided in the foregoing subparagraphs.

2. While the equipment is unserviceable or operating defectively, crew members shall mark on the record sheet or sheets, or on a temporary sheet to be attached to the record sheet, all information for the various periods of time which is not recorded correctly by the equipment.

[Article 18 is printed as amended by Regulation No 2828/77/EEC.]

CHAPTER V

Transitional Provisions

Article 19

Any Member State may, for vehicles registered in its territory, bring forward the operative dates laid down in Article 4.

Article 20

1. Without prejudice to the provisions of Article 14 (4) and (5) of Regulation (EEC) No 543/69, any Member State may, for vehicles registered in its territory, prescribe during the period preceding the compulsory introduction of the recording equipment provided for in Article 4 of the present Regulation, the installation and use of recording equipment of a type which has received national approval.

2. By way of derogation from the provisions of Article 4 (2) of this Regulation, the installation and use of recording equipment conforming to the provisions of Annexes I and II to this Regulation shall become compulsory only from 1 January 1980 for vehicles fitted with recording equipment of the type permitted under paragraph 1 of this Article.

[3. By way of derogation from Article 4 (1) (*b*), the installation and use of recording equipment conforming to Annexes I and II to this Regulation shall be compulsory only from 1 January 1980 for vehicles registered before 1 January 1975 and fitted before that date with recording equipment of the type permitted under paragraph 1 of this Article. For the new Member States the date of 1 January 1975 shall be replaced by the date of 1 January 1976.]

[Article 20 is printed as amended by Regulation No 1787/73/EEC.]

CHAPTER VI
FINAL PROVISIONS

[Article 21

The amendments necessary to adapt the Annexes to this Regulation to technical progress shall be adopted in accordance with the procedure laid down in Article 22.]

[Article 21 was inserted by Regulation No 2828/77/EEC.]

[Article 22

1. A Committee for the adaptation of this Regulation to technical progress (hereinafter called 'the Committee') is hereby set up; it shall consist of representatives of the Member States, and a representative of the Commission shall be chairman.

2. The Committee shall adopt its own rules of procedure.

3. Where the procedure laid down in this Article is to be followed, the matter shall be referred to the Committee by the chairman, either on his own initiative or at the request of the representative of a Member State.

4. The Commission representative shall submit to the Committee a draft of the measures to be taken. The Committee shall give its opinion on that draft within a time limit set by the chairman having regard to the urgency of the matter. Opinions shall be delivered by a majority of 41 votes, the votes of the Member States being weighted as provided for in Article 148 (2) of the Treaty. The chairman shall not vote.

5. (*a*) The Commission shall adopt the envisaged measures where they are in accordance with the opinion of the Committee.

   (*b*) Where the measures envisaged are not in accordance with the opinion of the Committee or if no opinion is delivered, the Commission shall without delay submit to the Council a proposal on the measures to be taken. The Council shall act by a qualified majority.

   (*c*) If the Council has not acted within three months of the proposal being submitted to it, the proposed measures shall be adopted by the Commission.]

[Article 22 was inserted by Regulation No 2828/77/EEC.]

Article [23]

1. Member States shall, in good time and after consulting the Commission, adopt such laws, regulations or administrative provisions as may be necessary for the implementation of this Regulation.

Such measures shall cover, inter alia, the reorganisation of, procedure for, and means of carrying out, checks on compliance and the penalties to be imposed in case of breach.

2. Member States shall assist each other in applying the provisions of this Regulation and in checking compliance therewith.

3. If it is brought to the notice of the competent authorities of a Member State that

a breach of the provisions of this Regulation has been committed by a crew member of a vehicle registered in another Member State, those authorities may notify the authorities of the State where the vehicle is registered of such breach. The competent authorities shall send each other all the information in their possession concerning the penalties imposed for such breaches.

[Article 23, originally art 21, was renumbered by Regulation No 2828/77/EEC.]

This Regulation shall be binding in its entirety and directly applicable in all Member States.

ANNEX 1

REQUIREMENTS FOR CONSTRUCTION
TESTING, INSTALLATION AND INSPECTION

I DEFINITIONS

In this Annex:

(a) Recording equipment means:
[equipment intended for installation in road vehicles] to show and record automatically or semi-automatically details of the movement of those vehicles and of certain working periods of their crews.

(b) Record sheet means:
a sheet designed to accept and retain recorded data, to be placed in the recording equipment and on which the marking devices of the latter inscribe a continuous record of the information to be recorded.

(c) The constant of the recording equipment means:
the numerical characteristic giving the value of the input signal required to show and record a distance travelled of 1 kilometre; this constant must be expressed either in revolutions per kilometre ($k = \ldots$ rev/km), or in impulses per kilometre ($k = \ldots$ imp/km).

(d) Characteristic coefficient of the vehicle means:
the numerical characteristic giving the value of the output signal emitted by the part of the vehicle linking it with the recording equipment (gearbox output shaft or axle) while the vehicle travels a distance of one measured kilometre under normal test conditions (see [Chapter VI (4)] of this Annex). The characteristic coefficient is expressed either in revolutions per kilometre ($w = \ldots$ rev/km) or in impulses per kilometre ($w = \ldots$ imp/km).

(e) Effective circumference of wheel tyres means:
the average of the distances travelled by the several wheels moving the vehicle (driving wheels) in the course of one complete rotation. The measurement of these distances must be made under normal test conditions (see [Chapter VI (4)] of this Annex) and is expressed in the form: $l = \ldots$ mm.

II GENERAL CHARACTERISTICS AND FUNCTIONS OF RECORDING EQUIPMENT

The equipment must be able to record the following:

(1) distance travelled by the vehicle;

(2) speed of the vehicle;

(3) driving time;

(4) other periods of work or of attendance at work by the crew member or members;

(5) breaks from work and daily rest periods;

(6) opening of the case containing the record sheet.

For vehicles used by a crew consisting of more than one member the equipment must be capable of recording simultaneously but distinctly and on separate sheets details for two separate crew members of the periods listed under (3), (4) and (5). If the crew consists of more than two members, priority must be given to recording periods for those who are employed as drivers.

III   Construction Requirements for Recording Equipment

(a) General points

1. Recording equipment shall include the following:

    1.1 Visual instruments showing:
- distance travelled (distance recorder);
- speed (speedometer);
- time (clock);

    1.2 Recording instruments comprising:
- a recorder of the distance travelled;
- a speed recorder;
- one or more time recorders satisfying the requirements laid down in Chapter III (c) 4.

    1.3 A marking device showing on the record sheet each opening of the case containing that sheet.

2. Any inclusion in the equipment of devices additional to those listed above must not interfere with the proper operation of the mandatory devices or with the reading of them.

    The equipment must be submitted for approval complete with any such additional devices.

3. *Materials*

    3.1 All the constituent parts of the recording equipment must be made of materials with sufficient stability and mechanical strength and stable electrical and magnetic characteristics;

    [3.2 Any modification in a constituent part of the equipment or in the nature of the materials used for its manufacture must, before being generally applied in manufacture, be submitted for approval to the authority which granted type-approval for the equipment.]

4. *Measurement of distance travelled*

    The distances travelled may be measured and recorded either:
- so as to include both forward and reverse movement; or
- so as to include only forward movement.

Any recording of reversing movements must on no account affect the clarity and accuracy of the other recordings.

5. *Measurement of speed*

    5.1 The range of speed measurement shall be as stated in the type approval certificate.

5.2 The natural frequency and the damping of the measuring device must be such that the instruments showing and recording the speed can, within the range of the measurement, follow acceleration changes of up to 2m/s^2, within the limits of accepted tolerances.

6. *Measurement of time* (clock)

6.1 The control of the mechanism for resetting the clock must be located inside a case containing the record sheet; each opening of that case must be automatically recorded on the record sheet.

6.2 If the forward movement mechanism of the record sheet is controlled by the clock, the period during which the latter will run correctly after being fully wound must be greater by at least 10% than the recording period corresponding to the maximum sheet-load of the equipment.

If the forward movement mechanism of the sheet is controlled by the movement of the vehicle, the clock must be capable of running correctly without rewinding for at least one week.

6.3 . . .

7. *Lighting and Protection*

7.1 The visual instruments of the equipment must be provided with adequate non-dazzling lighting;

7.2 For normal conditions of use, all the internal parts of the equipment must be protected against damp and dust. In addition they must be made proof against tampering by means of casings capable of being sealed.

(b) Visual instruments

1. *Distance travelled indicator* (distance recorder)

1.1 The value of the smallest grading on the instrument showing distance travelled must be 0·1 kilometres. [Figures showing hectometres must be clearly distinguishable from those showing whole kilometres.]

[1.2 The figures on the distance recorder must be clearly legible and must have an apparent height of at least 4 mm.]

1.3 The distance recorder must be capable of reading up to at least 99 999·9 kilometres.

2. *Speed indicator* (speedometer)

2.1 Within the range of measurement, the speed scale must be uniformly graduated by 1, 2, 5 or 10 kilometres per hour. The value of a speed graduation (space between two successive marks) must not exceed 10% of the maximum speed shown on the scale.

2.2 The range indicated beyond that measured need not be marked by figures.

2.3 The length of each space on the scale representing a speed difference of 10 kilometres per hour must not be less than 10 millimetres.

2.4 On an indicator with a needle, the distance between the needle and the instrument face must not exceed 3 millimetres.

[3. *Time indicator* (clock)

The time indicator must be visible from outside the equipment and give a clear, plain and unambiguous reading.]

(c) Recording instruments

1. *General points*

    1.1 All equipment, whatever the form of the record sheet (strip or disc), must be provided with a mark enabling the record sheet to be inserted correctly, in such a way as to ensure that the time shown by the clock and the time-marking on the sheet correspond . . .

    [1.2 The mechanism moving the record sheet must be such as to ensure that the latter moves without play and can be freely inserted and removed.]

    1.3 For record sheets in disc form, the forward movement device must be controlled by the clock mechanism. In this case, the rotating movement of the sheet must be continuous and uniform, with a minimum speed of 7 millimetres per hour measured at the inner border of the ring marking the edge of the speed recording area.

    In equipment of the strip type, where the forward movement device of the sheets is controlled by the clock mechanism the speed of rectilinear forward movement must be at least 10 millimetres per hour.

    1.4 Recording of the distance travelled, of the speed of the vehicle and of any opening of the case containing the record sheet or sheets must be automatic.

2. *Recording distance travelled*

    2.1 Every kilometre of distance travelled must be represented on the record by a variation of at least 1 millimetre on the corresponding co-ordinate.

    2.2 Even at speeds reaching the upper limit of the range of measurement, the record of distances must still be clearly legible.

3. *Recording speed*

    3.1 Whatever the form of the record sheet, the speed recording stylus must normally move in a straight line and at right angles to the direction of travel of the record sheet. However, the movement of the stylus may be curvilinear, provided the following conditions are satisfied:

    — the trace drawn by the stylus must be perpendicular to the average circumference (in the case of sheets in disc form) or to the axis (in the case of sheets in strip form) of the area reserved for speed recording.

    [— the ratio between the radius of curvature of the trace drawn by the stylus and the width of the area reserved for speed recording must be not less than 2·4 to 1 whatever the form of the record sheet.]

    — the markings on the time-scale must cross the recording area in a curve of the same radius as the trace drawn by the stylus. The spaces between the markings on the time-scale must represent a period not exceeding one hour.

    3.2 Each variation in speed of 10 kilometres per hour must be represented on the record by a variation of at least 1·5 millimetres on the corresponding co-ordinate.

4. *Recording time*

    [4.1 Recording equipment must be so constructed that it is possible, through the operation where necessary of a switch device, to record automatically and separately four periods of time as indicated in Article 17 including a possible separation of category (b) into two periods of time.]

4.2 It must be possible, from the characteristics of the traces, their relative positions and if necessary the signs laid down in Regulation (EEC) No 543/69, to distinguish clearly between the various periods of time. The various periods of time should be differentiated from one another on the record by differences in the thickness of the relevant traces, or by any other system of at least equal effectiveness from the point of view of legibility and ease of interpretation of the record.

4.3 In the case of vehicles with a crew consisting of more than one member, the recordings provided for in paragraph 4.1 must be made on two separate sheets, each sheet being allocated to one crew member. In this case, the forward movement of the separate sheets must be effected either by a single mechanism or by separate synchronised mechanisms.

(d) Closing device

1. The case containing the record sheet or sheets and the control of the mechanism for resetting the clock must be provided with a lock.

2. Each opening of the case containing the record sheet or sheets and the control of the mechanism for resetting the clock must be automatically recorded on the sheet or sheets.

(e) Markings

[1. The following markings must appear on the instrument face of the equipment:
  — close to the figure shown by the distance recorder, the unit of measurement of distance, indicated by the abbreviation 'km',
  — near the speed scale, the marking 'km/h',
  — the measurement range of the speedometer in the form 'V_{min}... km/h. V_{max}... km/h'. This marking is not necessary if it is shown on the descriptive plaque of the equipment.

However, these requirements shall not apply to recording equipment approved before the entry into force of this Regulation.]

2. The descriptive plaque must be built into the equipment and must show the following markings, which must be visible on the equipment when installed:
  — name and address of the manufacturer of the equipment;
  — manufacturer's number and year of construction;
  — approval mark for the equipment type;
  — the constant of the equipment ... in the form 'k = ...rev/km' or 'k = ...imp/km';
  — optionally, the range of speed measurement, in the form indicated in point 1 above.
  [— should the sensitivity of the instrument to the angle of inclination be capable of affecting the readings given by the equipment beyond the permitted tolerances, the permissible angle expressed as:

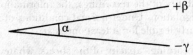

where α is the angle measured from the horizontal position of the front face (fitted the right way up) of the equipment for which the instrument is calibrated, while β and γ represent respectively the maximum permissible upward and downward deviations from the angle of calibration α.]

(f) Maximum tolerances (visual and recording instruments)

1. *On the test bench before installation*

   [(a) distance travelled: 1% more or less than the real distance, where that distance is at least 1 kilometre]

   [(b) speed 3 km/h more or less than the real speed]

   (c) time:
   ± two minutes per day with a maximum of ten minutes per seven days in cases where the running period of the clock after rewinding is not less than that period.

2. *On installation*

   [(a) distance travelled: 2% more or less than the real distance, where that distance is at least 1 kilometre]

   [(b) speed: 4 km/h more or less than the real speed]

   (c) time:
   ± two minutes per day or
   ± ten minutes per seven days.

3. *In use*

   [(a) distance travelled: 4% more or less than the real distance, where that distance is at least 1 kilometre]

   [(b) speed 6 km/h more or less than the real speed.]

   (c) time:
   ± two minutes per day or
   ± ten minutes per seven days.

4. The maximum tolerances set out in paragraphs 1, 2 and 3 above are valid for temperatures between 0 and 40°C, temperatures being taken in close proximity to the equipment.

5. Measurement of the maximum tolerances set out in paragraphs 2 and 3 above shall take place under the conditions laid down in Chapter VI.

IV   RECORD SHEETS

(a) General points

[1. The record sheets must be such that they do not impede the normal functioning of the instrument and that the records which they contain are indelible and easily legible and identifiable.]

[The record sheets must retain their dimensions and any records made on them under normal conditions of humidity and temperature.] In addition it must be possible to write on the sheets, without damaging them and without affecting the legibility of the recordings, the information referred to in Article 17 (3) of this Regulation. Under normal conditions of storage, the recordings must remain clearly legible for at least one year.

2. The minimum recording capacity of the sheets, whatever their form, must be twenty-four hours.

If several discs are linked together to increase the continuous recording capacity which can be achieved without intervention by staff, the links between the various discs must be made in such a way that there are no breaks in or overlapping of recordings at the point of transfer from one disc to another.

(b) Recording areas and their graduation

1. The record sheets shall include the following recording areas:
   — an area exclusively reserved for data relating to speed:
   — an area exclusively reserved for data relating to distance travelled;
   — one or more areas for data relating to driving time, to other periods of work and attendance at work, to breaks from work and to rest periods.

2. The area for recording speed must be scaled off in divisions of 20 kilometres per hour or less. The speed corresponding to each marking on the scale must be shown in figures against that marking. The symbol 'km/h' must be shown at least once within the area. The last marking on the scale must coincide with the upper limit of the range of measurement.

3. The area for recording distance travelled must be set out in such a way that the number of kilometres travelled may be read without difficulty.

4. The area or areas reserved for recording the periods referred to in 1 above must be so marked that it is possible to distinguish clearly between the various periods of time.

(c) Information to be printed on the record sheets

Each sheet must bear, in printed form, the following information:
— name and address or trade name of the manufacturer:
— approval mark for the model of the sheet;
— approval mark for the type or types of equipment in which the sheet may be used;
— upper limit of the speed measurement range, printed in kilometres per hour.

By way of minimal additional requirements, each sheet must bear, in printed form, a time-scale graduated in such a way that the time may be read directly at intervals of fifteen minutes while each five minute interval may be determined without difficulty.

(d) Free space for hand written insertions

A free space must be provided on the sheets such that employees may as a minimum write in the following details:
— surname and first name of crew member;
— date and place where use of the sheet begins and date and place where such use ends;
— the registration number or numbers of the vehicle or vehicles to which the crew member is assigned during the use of the sheet;
— odometer readings from the vehicle or vehicles to which the crew member is assigned during the use of the sheet;
— the time at which any change of vehicle takes place.

V INSTALLATION OF RECORDING EQUIPMENT

1. Recording equipment must be positioned in the vehicle in such a way that the driver has a clear view from his seat of speedometer, distance recorder and clock while at the same time all parts of those instruments, including driving parts, are protected against accidental damage.

2. It must be possible to adapt the constant of the recording equipment to the characteristic coefficient of the vehicle by means of a suitable device, to be known as an adaptor.

Vehicles with two or more rear axle ratios must be fitted with a switch device whereby these various ratios may be automatically brought into line with the ratio for which the equipment has been adapted to the vehicle.

3. After the equipment has been checked on installation, an installation plaque shall be affixed to the vehicle beside the equipment or on the equipment itself and in such a way as to be clearly visible.

[After every inspection by an approved fitter or workshop requiring a change in the setting of the installation itself, a new plaque must be affixed in place of the previous one.]

[The plaque must show at least the following details:]
— name, address or trade name of the approved fitter or workshop;
— characteristic coefficient of the vehicle . . . in the form 'w = ... rev/km' or 'w = ... imp/km';
— effective circumference of the wheel tyres in the form 'l = ... mm';
— the dates on which the characteristic coefficient of the vehicle was determined and the effective measured circumference of the wheel tyres.

4. *Sealing*

The following parts must be sealed:

[(a) the installation plaque, unless it is attached in such a way that it cannot be removed without the markings thereon being destroyed;]

(b) the two ends of the link between the recording equipment proper and the vehicle;

(c) the adaptor and the point of its insertion into the circuit;

(d) the switch mechanism for vehicles with two or more axle ratios;

(e) the links joining the adaptor and the switch mechanism to the rest of the equipment;

(f) the casings required under Chapter III (a) 7.2

In particular cases, further seals may be required on approval of the equipment type and a note of the positioning of these seals must be made on the approval certificate.

Only the seals mentioned in (b), (c) and (f) may be removed in cases of emergency: for each occasion that these seals are broken a written statement giving the reasons for such action must be prepared and made available to the competent authority.

[VI   Checks and Inspections

The Member States shall nominate the bodies which shall carry out the checks and inspections.

1. *Certification of new or repaired instruments*

Every individual device, whether new or repaired, shall be certified in respect of its correct operation and the accuracy of its readings and recordings, within the limits laid down in Chapter III (f) 1, by means of sealing in accordance with Chapter V (4) (f).

For this purpose the Member States may stipulate an initial verification, consisting of a check on and confirmation of the conformity of a new or repaired device with the type-approved model and/or with the requirements of the Regulation and its Annexes, or may delegate the power or certify to the manufacturers or to their authorized agents.

2. *Installation*

When being fitted to a vehicle, the equipment and the whole installation must comply with the provisions relating to maximum tolerances laid down in Chapter III (f) 2.

The inspection tests shall be carried out by the approved fitter or workshop on his or its responsibility.

3. *Periodic inspections*

(a) Periodic inspections of the equipment fitted to vehicles shall take place at least every two years and may be carried out in conjunction with roadworthiness tests of vehicles.

These inspections shall include the following checks:
— that the equipment is working correctly,
— that the equipment carries the type-approval mark,
— that the installation plaque is affixed,
— that the seals on the equipment and on the other parts of the installation are intact,
— the actual circumference of the tyres.

(b) An inspection to ensure compliance with the provision of Chapter III (f) 3 on the maximum tolerances in use shall be carried out at least once every six years, although each Member State may stipulate a shorter interval for such inspections in respect of vehicles registered in its territory. Such inspections must include replacement of the installation plaque.

4. *Measurement of errors*

The measurement of errors on installation and during use shall be carried out under the following conditions, which are to be regarded as constituting standard test conditions:

— vehicle unladen, in normal running order.
— tyre pressures in accordance with the manufacturer's instructions,
— tyre wear within the limits allowed by law,
— movement of the vehicle: the vehicle must proceed, driven by its own engine, in a straight line and on a level surface, at a speed of 50 ± 5 km/h; provided that it is of comparable accuracy, the test may also be carried out on an appropriate test bench.]

[*Annex I is printed as corrected in the corrigendum (OJ No L 110, 27.4.73, p 39, and as amended by Regulation No 2828/77/EEC.*

The Passenger and Goods Vehicles (Recording Equipment) (Amendment) Regulations 1984 (SI 1984 No 144 and correction slip dated February 1984), reg 3(2) provide that nothing in para 3(a) or (b) of Chapter VI of Annex I of this regulation (as amended and as read with the Community Road Transport Rules (Exemption) Regulations 1978 (SI 1978 No 1158))—

'shall require an inspection of recording equipment installed in a vehicle to be carried out—
(*a*) before the expiry of the period of three months beginning with the coming into operation of these Regulations; or
(*a*) where the vehicle is subject to an annual test [as defined] and the equipment was installed before 13th June 1983, before the annual test of the vehicle next following the expiry of that period and the relevant period [as defined]'.

The 1984 regulations came into operation on 13 March 1984 (reg 1) and reg 3(3) defined the terms 'annual inspection' and 'relevant period' for the purposes of reg 3(2) above as follows:

'annual test' means an annual test required by regulations under section 43 or 45 of the Road Traffic Act 1972;

'relevant period' means—

(a) in the case of an inspection required by the said paragraph 3(a), the period of two years;

(a) in the case of an inspection required by the said paragraph 3(b), the period of six years,

beginning (in either case) with the date shown on the installation plaque affixed to the vehicle.]

ANNEX II

APPROVAL MARK AND CERTIFICATE

*   *   *

Section D

International Agreements

Agreement on the International Carriage of Passengers by Road by means of Occasional Coach and Bus Services (ASOR)

[THE CONTRACTING PARTIES]

Desiring to promote the development of international transport and especially to facilitate the organization and operation thereof;

Whereas some international carriage of passengers by road by means of occasional coach and bus services are liberalised as far as the European Economic Community is concerned by Council Regulation No 117/66/EEC of 28 July 1966 on the introduction of common rules for the international carriage of passengers by coach and bus *[OJ L 147, 9.8.1966, p 2688/66]* and by Regulation (EEC) No 1016/68 of the Commission of 9 July 1968 prescribing the model control documents referred to in Articles 6 and 9 of Council Regulation No 117/66/EEC *[OJ L 173, 22.7.1968, p 8]*;

Whereas in addition, the European Conference of Ministers of Transport (ECMT) adopted on 16 December 1969 resolution No 20 concerning the formulation of general rules for international coach and bus transport *[volume of ECMT resolutions, 1969, p 67; volume of ECMT resolutions, 1971, p 133]* which also concerns the liberalisation of some international carriage of passengers by road by means of occasional coach and bus services;

Whereas it is desirable to provide for harmonised liberalisation measures for occasional international services for passengers by road and to simplify inspection procedures by introducing a single document;

Whereas it is desirable to assign some administrative tasks concerned with the Agreement to the Secretariat of the European Conference of Ministers of Transport;

Have decided to establish uniform rules for the international carriage of passengers by road by means of occasional coach and bus services,

AND . . . HAVE AGREED AS FOLLOWS:

SECTION I

SCOPE AND DEFINITIONS

Article 1

1. This Agreement shall apply:

(a) to the international carriage of passengers by road by means of occasional services effected:
 — between the territories of two Contracting Parties, or
 — starting and finishing in the territory of the same Contracting Party,

and, should the need arise during such services, in transit through the territory of another Contracting Party or through the territory of a non-contracting State, and
 — using vehicles registered in the territory of a Contracting Party which by virtue of their construction and their equipment, are suitable for carrying more than nine persons, including the driver, and are intended for that purpose;

697

(b) to unladen journeys of the vehicles concerned with these services.

2. For the purpose of this Agreement, international services are understood to be services which cross the territory of at least two Contracting Parties.

3. For the purposes of this Agreement, the term 'territory of a Contracting Party' covers, as far as the European Economic Community is concerned, those territories where the Treaty establishing that Community is applied and under the conditions laid down in that Treaty.

Article 2

1. For the purposes of this Agreement, occasional services shall mean services falling neither within the definition of a regular service in Article 3 nor within the definition of a shuttle service in Article 4. They include:

(a) closed-door tours, that is to say services whereby the same vehicle is used to carry the same group of passengers throughout the journey and to bring them back to the place of departure;

(b) services which make the outward journey laden and the return journey unladen;

(c) all other services.

2. Save for exemptions authorised by the competent authorities of the Contracting Party concerned, in the course of occasional services no passenger may be taken up or set down during the journey. Such services may be operated with some degree of frequency without thereby ceasing to be occasional services.

Article 3

1. For the purposes of this Agreement regular services shall mean services which provide for the carriage of passengers according to a specified frequency and along specified routes, whereby passengers may be taken up or set down at pre-determined stopping points. Regular services can be subject to the obligation to respect previously established timetables and tariffs.

2. For the purposes of this Agreement, services, by whomsoever organised, which provide for the carriage of specified categories of passengers to the exclusion of other passengers, in so far as such services are operated under the conditions set out in paragraph 1, shall also be considered to be regular services. Such services, in particular those providing for the carriage of workers to and from their place of work or of school children to and from school, are called 'special regular services'.

3. The fact that a service may be varied according to the needs of those concerned shall not affect its classification as a regular service.

Article 4

1. For the purposes of this Agreement, shuttle services shall mean services whereby, by means of repeated outward and return journeys, previously formed groups of passengers are carried from a single place of departure to a single destination. Each group, consisting of the passengers who made the outward journey, shall be carried back to the place of departure on a later journey.

Place of departure and destination shall mean respectively the place where the journey begins and the place where the journey ends, together with, in each case, the surrounding locality.

2. In the course of shuttle services, no passenger may be taken up or set down during the journey.

3. The first return journey and the last outward journey in a series of shuttles shall be made unladen.

4. However, the classification of a transport operation as a shuttle service shall not be affected by the fact that, with the agreement of the competent authorities in the Contracting Party or Parties concerned:

— passengers, notwithstanding the provisions of paragraph 1, make the return journey with another group,

— passengers, notwithstanding the provisions of paragraph 2, are taken up or set down along the way,

— the first outward journey and the last return journey of the series of shuttles are, notwithstanding the provisions of paragraph 3, made unladen.

SECTION II
LIBERALISATION MEASURES

Article 5

1. The occasional services referred to in Article 2 (1) (*a*) and (*b*) shall be exempted from the need for any transport authorisation on the territory of any Contracting Party other than that in which the vehicle is registered.

2. The occasional services referred to in Article 2 (1) (*c*) shall be exempted from the need for any transport authorisation on the territory of any Contracting Party other than that in which the vehicle is registered where they are characterised by the following:

— the outward journey is made unladen and all the passengers are taken up in the same place, and

— the passengers:

(*a*) — constitute groups, in the territory of a non-Contracting Party or a Contracting Party other than that in which the vehicle is registered or that where the passengers are taken up, formed under contracts of carriage made before their arrival in the territory of the latter Contracting Party, and

— are carried in the territory of the Contracting Party in which the vehicle is registered; or

(*b*) — have been previously brought, by the same carrier in the circumstances provided for under Article 2 (1) (*b*), into the territory of the Contracting Party where they are taken up again and carried into the territory of the Contracting Party in which the vehicle is registered; or

(*c*) — have been invited to travel into the territory of another Contracting Party, the cost of transport being borne by the person issuing the invitation. Such passengers must constitute a homogeneous group, which has not been formed solely with a view to undertaking that particular journey and which is brought into the territory of the Contracting Party where the vehicle is registered.

3. In so far as the conditions laid down in paragraph 2 are not satisfied, in the case of occasional services referred to in Article 2 (1) (*c*), such services may be made subject to a transport authorisation in the territory of the Contracting Party concerned.

SECTION III
Control Document

Article 6

Carriers operating occasional services within the meaning of this Agreement shall, whenever required to do so by any authorised inspecting officer, produce a passenger waybill which forms part of a control document issued by the competent authorities in the Contracting Party where the vehicle is registered or by any duly authorised agency. This control document shall replace the existing control documents.

Article 7

1. The control document referred to in Article 6 shall consist of detachable passenger waybills in duplicate in books of 25. The control document shall conform to the model shown in the Annex to this Agreement. This Annex shall form an integral part of the Agreement.

2. Each book and its component passenger waybills shall bear a number. The passenger waybills shall also be numbered consecutively, running from 1 to 25.

3. The wording on the cover of the book and that on the passenger waybills shall be printed in the official language or several official languages of the Member State of the European Economic Community or of any other Contracting Party in which the vehicle used is registered.

Article 8

1. The book referred to in Article 7 shall be made out in the name of the carrier; it shall not be transferable.

2. The top copy of the passenger waybill shall be kept on the vehicle throughout the journey to which it refers.

3. The carrier shall be reponsible for seeing that passenger waybills are duly and correctly completed.

Article 9

1. The passenger waybill shall be completed in duplicate by the carrier for each journey before the start of the journey.

2. For the purpose of providing the names of passengers, the carrier may use a list already completed on a separate sheet, which shall be firmly stuck in the place provided for it under item No 6 in the passenger waybill. The carrier's stamp or, where appropriate, the carrier's signature or that of the driver of the vehicle shall be placed across both the list and the passenger waybill.

3. For the services involving an outward journey unladen referred to in Article 5 (2) of this Agreement, the list of passengers may be completed as provided in paragraph 2 at the time when the passengers are taken up.

Article 10

The competent authorities in two or more Contracting Parties may agree bilaterally or multilaterally that the list of passengers under item No 6 of the passenger waybill need not be drawn up. In that case, the number of passengers must be shown.

Article 11

1. A model with stiff green covers and containing the text of the model cover page recto verso of the control document shown in the Annex to this Agreement in each official language of all the Contracting Parties must be kept on the vehicle.

2. The following shall be printed on the front cover of the model in capital letters and in the official language or several official languages of the State in which the vehicle used is registered:

'Text of the model control document in Danish, Dutch, English, Finnish, French, German, Greek, Italian, Norwegian, Portuguese, Spanish, Swedish and Turkish'.

3. This model shall be produced whenever required by any authorised inspecting officer.

Article 12

Notwithstanding the provisions of Article 6, control documents used for occasional services before the entry into force of this Agreement may be used for two years after the entry into force of the said Agreement pursuant to Article 18 (2).

SECTION IV

GENERAL AND FINAL PROVISIONS

Articles 13, 14 *[Omitted.]*

Article 15

The provisions of Articles 5 and 6 shall not be applied to the extent that Agreements or other arrangements in force or to be concluded between two or more Contracting Parties provide for more liberal treatment. The terms 'Agreements or other arrangements in force between two or more Contracting Parties' shall cover, as far as the European Economic Community is concerned, the Agreements and other arrangements which have been concluded by the Member States of that Community.

Articles 16, 17 *[Omitted.]*

Article 18

1. *[Omitted.]*

2. This Agreement shall enter into force, when five Contracting Parties including the European Economic Community have approved or ratified it, on the first day of the third month following the date on which the fifth instrument of approval or ratification is deposited.

3. This Agreement shall enter into force, for each Contracting Party which approves or ratifies it after the entry into force provided for under paragraph 2, on the first day of the third month following the date on which the Contracting Party concerned has deposited its instrument of approval or ratification with the ECMT Secretariat.

4. The provisions of Section II and III of this Agreement shall apply seven months after the entry into force of the Agreement as specified in paragraphs 2 and 3 respectively.

Articles 19–21 *[Omitted.]*

ANNEX

(green-coloured paper: DIN A4 = 29·7 x 21 cm)

(Front cover — recto)

> (To be worded in the official language or several of the official
> languages of the State where the vehicle is registered)

State in which the control document is issued — Distinguishing sign of the country —	Competent authority or duly authorized agency	Book No ....

BOOK OF PASSENGER WAYBILLS

for the international carriage of passengers by road by means of occasional coach and bus services
established pursuant to:

— **ASOR (Agreement on the International Carriage of Passengers by Road by means of Occasional Coach and Bus Services) and**

— **Regulation No 117/66/EEC (Council Regulation on the introduction of common rules for the international carriage of passengers by coach and bus)**

Name and first name of carrier or trade name: ....

....

Address: ....

....

....
(Place and date of issue of book)   (Signature and stamp of the authority or agency issuing the book)

(green-coloured paper: DIN A4 = 29·7 x 21 cm)

(Flyleaf of the book of waybills — recto)

(To be worded in the official language or several of the official
languages of the State where the vehicle is registered)

IMPORTANT NOTICE

I. TRANSPORT WITHIN THE JURISDICTION OF ASOR

Pursuant to Article 5 (1) and (2) of ASOR, the following shall be exempted from the need for any transport authorization on the territory of any Contracting Party other than that in which the vehicle is registered:

(a) certain occasional international services carried out by means of a vehicle registered in the territory of a Contracting Party:
 — between the territories of the Contracting Parties, or
 — starting and finishing in the territory of the same Contracting Party,
 and, should the need arise, during such services, in transit through the territory of another Contracting Party or through the territory of a non-contracting State.

(b) unladen journeys of the vehicles concerned with these services.

The occasional services covered by the above provisions are as follows:

A. closed-door tours, i.e. services whereby the same vehicle is used to carry the same group of passengers throughout the journey and to bring them back to the place of departure, this place being situated on the territory of the Contracting Party where the vehicle is registered,

B. services which make the outward journey laden and the return journey unladen,

C. services where the outward journey is made unladen and where:

 — all the passengers are taken up in the same place to be carried into the territory in which the vehicle is registered, and

 — the passengers:

 C.1. constitute groups in the territory either of a non-Contracting Party or of a Contracting Party other than that in which the vehicle is registered or than that where the passengers are taken up, formed under contracts of carriage made before their arrival on the territory of the latter Contracting Party, or

 C.2. have been previously brought, by the same carrier, on a service referred to in B above, into the territory of the Contracting Party where they are taken up again, or

 C.3. have been invited to travel into the territory of another Contracting Party, the cost of transport being borne by the person issuing the invitation. Such passengers must constitute a homogeneous group, which has not been formed solely with a view to undertaking that particular journey.

II. TRANSPORT WITHIN THE JURISDICTION OF REGULATION No 117/66/EEC

Pursuant to Article 5 (1) and (2) of Council Regulation No 117/66/EEC of 28 July 1966, certain international occasional services whose place of departure is in the territory of a Member State and whose destination is in the territory of the same or another Member State and which are operated using a vehicle registered in a Member State other than the State where the vehicle is registered. For journeys in transit over the territory of an ASOR Contracting Party other than the Community, the ASOR provisions apply.

The occasional services covered by this provision are as follows:

A. closed-door tours, i.e. services whereby the same vehicle is used to carry the same group of passengers throughout the journey and to bring them back to the place of departure,

B. services which make the outward journey laden and the return journey unladen,

C. services where the outward journey is made unladen, provided that all the passengers are taken up in the same place and that the passengers:

 C.1. constitute groups formed under contracts of carriage made before their arrival in the country where they are to be taken up, or

 C.2. have been previously brought by the same carrier, on a service referred to in B above, into the country where such passengers are taken up again and carried out of that country, or

 C.3. have been invited to travel to another Member State, the cost of transport being borne by the person issuing the invitation. Such passengers must constitute a homogeneous group, which has not been formed solely with a view to undertaking that particular journey.

III. COMMON PROVISIONS APPLICABLE TO ALL INTERNATIONAL SERVICES WITHIN THE SCOPE OF ASOR OR REGULATION No 117/66/EEC

1. For each journey carried out as an occasional service the carrier must complete a passenger waybill in duplicate, before the start of the journey.

 For the purpose of providing the names of passengers, the carrier may use a list already completed on a separate sheet, which must be firmly stuck in the place provided for it under item No 6 in the passenger waybill. The carrier's stamp or, where appropriate, the carrier's signature or that of the driver of the vehicle must be placed across both the list and the passenger waybill.

 For services where the outward journey is made unladen, the list of passengers may be completed as provided above at the time when the passengers are taken up.

 The top copy of the passenger waybill must be kept on board the vehicle throughout the journey and be produced whenever required by any authorized inspecting officer.

2. A model with stiff green covers and containing the text of the model cover page recto/verso, in each official language of all the Contracting Parties to ASOR, must be kept on the vehicle.

3. For services where the outward journey is made unladen, referred to in C, the carrier must attach the following supporting documents to the passenger waybill:

 — in cases mentioned under C.1: the copy of the contract of carriage in so far as some countries require it, or any other equivalent document which establishes the essential data of this contract (especially place, country and date of conclusion, place, country and date when passengers are taken up, place and country of destination);

 — in the case of services falling within C.2.: the passenger waybill which accompanied the vehicle during the corresponding journey made by the carrier outward laden/return unladen in order to bring the passengers into the territory either of the Contracting Party or the EEC Member State where they are taken up again;

 — in the case of services falling within C.3: the letter of invitation from the person issuing the invitation or a photocopy thereof.

4. Occasional services not falling within points I and II may be made subject to transport authorization on the territory of the Contracting Party or of the Member State of the EEC concerned. For these services, a cross must be placed in the appropriate box, under point 4D of the waybill, showing whether a transport authorization is or is not required. If a transport authorization is required it must be attached to the waybill. If no transport authorization is required justification must be given.

5. In the course of occasional services no passenger may be taken up or set down during the journey, save for exemption authorized by the competent authorities. This authorization must also be attached.

6. The carrier is responsible for seeing that passenger waybills are duly and correctly completed. They shall be completed in block letters and in indelible ink.

7. The book of waybills is not transferable.

(Flyleaf of the book of waybills – verso)

(To be worded in the official language or several of the official
languages of the State of registration of the vehicle)

Explanation of symbols used in the passenger waybill and instructions on how to fill it in

#		
1	Registration No	Number of passenger seats available
2		Name and first name of carrier, or trade name, and address
3		Name of driver or drivers

Type of service

4		
A Closed-door tour	**B** Outward journey laden – return journey unladen	= Locality where passengers are set down and distinguishing sign of the country
C Outward journey unladen in order to take up a group of passengers and transport them to the country of vehicle registration	**C1**	
	C2	See 'Important Notice'
○ – Locality where passengers are taken up and distinguishing sign of the country	**C3**	
◉ – Locality where passengers are set down and distinguishing sign of the country		
D Another occasional service (particulars)	– The required authorization is attached	
	– Authorization not required because _____	

Itinerary

5		Daily stages			
Dates	**from**	**to**		Km	Km	Customs
	Locality, and distinguishing sign of the country		Use of vehicle (Indicate the number of kilometres in the relevant column)		Frontier crossing points
	from	**to**	laden	unladen	

Passenger list (surnames and initials)

6	1	22	43
	2	23	44
	3	24	45
	21	42	63

(Passenger waybill – recto)   (Green coloured paper – DIN A4 = 29·7 x 21 cm)

Book No ....

Waybill No ....

(To be worded in the official language or several of the official languages of the State of vehicle registration)

(State in which the document is issued) — Distinguishing sign of the country

1

2

3

> 1 ....
> 2 ....
> 3 ....

Type of service (put a cross in the appropriate box and add the required supplementary information)

A

B

4

C Outward journey unladen in order to take up a group of passengers and transport them to the country of vehicle registration.

C1 The passengers were assembled, under a contract of carriage made on .... with .... (travel agency, association, etc.). They arrive(d) on ....

☐ in the territory of the Contracting Party where they are to be taken up,

☐ in the Member State of the EEC where they are to be taken up (for EEC vehicles only),

☐ copy of the contract of carriage or equivalent document (cf. Important Notice under III.3) is attached.

C2 previously brought by the same carrier on a service referred to in B, to the country where they are to be taken up again.

The passenger waybill for the previous outward laden journey and unladen return journey is attached.

C3 invited to travel to ....

Cost of transport being borne by the person issuing the invitation and the passengers constitute a homogeneous group which has not been formed solely with a view to undertaking that particular journey. The letter of invitation (or a photocopy thereof) is attached.

D Another occasional service (particulars):

_____

☐ – The required authorization is attached

☐ – Authorization not required because ....

Itinerary

Dates	from	to	Km	Km	Customs
5					
		Total	+	=	

(Passenger waybill – verso)

1	22	43
2	23	44
3	24	45
4	25	46
5	26	47
6	27	48
7	28	49
8	29	50
9	30	51
10	31	52
11	32	53
12	33	54
13	34	55
14	35	56
15	36	57
16	37	58
17	38	59
18	39	60
19	40	61
20	41	62
21	42	63

6

Date of completion of waybill | Signature of carrier

7

Unforeseen changes

8

Control stamps
if any

9

SIGNATURES

[The Agreement was signed in Dublin on 26 May 1982 on behalf of:

the Council of the European Communities
Austria
Finland
Norway
Portugal
Spain
Sweden
Switzerland
Turkey

Regulation No 56/83/EEC imposed responsibility for the implementation of ASOR on the Member States of the European Communities. The ASOR was approved on behalf of the European Communities by Decision No 82/505/EEC and entered into force within the Community on 1 December 1983; see the Road Transport (International Passenger Services) Regulations 1984 (SI 1984 No 748), reg 2(1)(b).]

Declaration by the Contracting Parties on the Application of the Agreement

The Contracting Parties agree that the liberalisation measures provided under Article 5 (2) of the Agreement shall only be enforceable between the Contracting Parties who apply the provisions of the European Agreement concerning the work of crews of vehicles engaged in International Road Transport (AETR) from 1 July 1970, or equivalent conditions to those provided under the AETR, to the occasional services governed by this Agreement.

Each Contracting Party which intends, for the reasons set out above, to adopt measures for the non-application or the suspension of the liberalisation provisions under Article 5 (2) of the Agreement, declares itself ready to consult the relevant Contracting Party before the possible adoption of these measures.

———

Declaration by the European Economic Community Concerning Article 5 of the Agreement

With regard to Article 5, the European Economic Community declares that the liberalisation measures laid down for the entry of an unladen vehicle into another Contracting Party with a view to taking up passengers for the return journey to the territory of the Contracting Party where the vehicle is registered shall only apply, where the return to the territory of the European Economic Community is concerned, to return journeys to the Member State in which the vehicle used is registered.

*   *   *

European Agreement concerning the Work of Crews of Vehicles engaged in International Road Transport (AETR)

(Cmnd 7401)

[The text of this agreement is printed as amended by amendments published as Cmnd 9037 (which took effect on 3 August 1983).]

THE CONTRACTING PARTIES,

Being desirous of promoting the development and improvement of the international transport of passengers and goods by road,

Convinced of the need to increase the safety of road traffic, to make regulations governing certain conditions of employment in international road transport in accordance with the principles of the International Labour Organisation, and jointly to adopt certain measures to ensure the observance of those regulations,

HAVE AGREED AS FOLLOWS:

Article 1: Definitions

For the purposes of this Agreement

(a) 'vehicle' means any motor vehicle or trailer; this term includes any combination of vehicles;

(b) 'motor vehicle' means any self-propelled road vehicle which is normally used for carrying persons or goods by road or for drawing, on the road, vehicles used for the carriage of persons or goods; this term does not include agricultural tractors;

(c) 'trailer' means any vehicle designed to be drawn by a motor vehicle and includes semi-trailers;

(d) 'semi-trailer' means any trailer designed to be coupled to a motor vehicle in such a way that part of it rests on the motor vehicle and that a substantial part of its weight and of the weight of its load is borne by the motor vehicle;

(e) 'combination of vehicles' means coupled vehicles which travel on the road as a unit;

(f) 'permissible maximum weight' means the maximum weight of the laden vehicle declared permissible by the competent authority of the State in which the vehicle is registered;

(g) 'road transport' ['carriage by road'] means
    (i) any journey by road of a vehicle, whether laden or not, intended for the carriage of passengers and having more than eight seats in addition to the driver's seat;
    (ii) any journey by road of a vehicle, whether laden or not, intended for the carriage of goods;
    (iii) any journey which involves both a journey as defined in either (i) or (ii)

of this definition and immediately before or after the said journey, the conveyance of the vehicle by sea, rail, air or inland waterway;

(*h*) 'international road transport' ['international carriage by road'] means road transport which involves the crossing of at least one frontier;

(*i*) 'regular passenger services' means services for the transport of passengers at specified intervals on specified routes; such services may take up or set down passengers at predetermined stopping points.

Terms of carriage covering in particular operating schedules (timetable, frequency), tariffs and the obligation to carry shall be specified in operating rules or equivalent documents approved by the competent public authorities of the Contracting Parties and published by the carrier before they are put into effect, in so far as such terms are not already laid down in laws and regulations or in administrative provisions.

Any service by whatever person organized catering only for specific categories of passengers to the exclusion of others, such as a service for the carriage of workers to and from their place of work and of schoolchildren to and from school, shall also be treated as a regular service in so far as it complies with the conditions set out in the first sub-paragraph of this definition.

(*j*) 'driver' means any person, whether wage-earning or not, who drives the vehicle even for a short period, or who is carried on the vehicle in order to be available for driving if necessary;

(*k*) 'crew member' means the driver or either of the following, whether wage-earning or not

    (i) a driver's mate, *i.e.* any person accompanying the driver in order to assist him in certain manoeuvres and habitually taking an effective part in the transport operations, though not a driver in the sense of paragraph (*j*) of this article;

    (ii) a conductor, *i.e.* any person who accompanies the driver of a vehicle engaged in the carriage of passengers and is responsible in particular for the issue or checking of tickets or other documents entitling passengers to travel on the vehicle;

(*l*) 'week' means any period of seven consecutive days;

(*m*) 'daily rest period' means any uninterrupted period in accordance with article 6 of this Agreement during which a crew member may freely dispose of his time;

(*n*) 'off-duty period' means any uninterrupted period of at least fifteen minutes, other than the daily rest period, during which a crew member may freely dispose of his time:

(*o*) 'occupational activities' means the activities represented by items 6, 7 and 7a in the daily sheet of the individual control book shown in the annex to this Agreement.

[*In art 1, the square brackets used in the definitions of 'road transport' and 'international road transport' occur in the text of the agreement and (unlike the use of square brackets elsewhere in this work) do not denote amendments to the text.*

The Annex to the agreement is not reproduced. Items 6, 7 and 7a in the daily sheet of the individual control book (referred to in the definition of 'occupational activities') concern driving periods, periods of occupational activities other than driving, and actual work other than driving, respectively.

On depositing their instruments of accession to or ratification of this agreement, the governments of Belgium, Denmark, France, Luxembourg, the Netherlands and the United Kingdom each made the following declaration: 'Transport operations between Member States of the European Economic

Community shall be regarded as national transport operations within the meaning of the AETR in so far as such operations do not pass in transit through the territory of a third State which is a contracting party to the AETR'. (cf art 2(2) of Council Regulation (EEC) 2829/77).]

Article 2: Scope

1. This Agreement shall apply in the territory of each Contracting Party to all international road transport performed by any vehicle registered in the territory of the said Contracting Party or in the territory of any other Contracting Party.

2. Nevertheless,

(a) if, in the course of an international road transport operation one or more crew members do not leave the national territory in which they normally exercise their occupational activities, the Contracting Party for that territory shall be free not to apply to him or them the provisions of this Agreement;

(b) unless the Contracting Parties whose territory is used agree otherwise, this Agreement shall not apply to the international road transport of goods performed by a vehicle having a permissible maximum weight not exceeding 3·5 tons;

(c) two Contracting Parties with adjoining territories may agree that the provisions of the domestic laws and regulations of the State in which the vehicle is registered and the provisions of arbitral awards and collective agreements in force in that State shall alone be applicabsle to international road transport confined to their two territories if the vehicle concerned:

    — does not while in one of those territories travel beyond a zone contiguous to the frontier and defined by agreement between the two Contracting Parties as a *frontalier* zone, or

    — crosses one of those territories in transit only;

(d) Contracting Parties may agree that the provisions of the domestic laws and regulations of the State in which the vehicle is registered and the provisions of arbitral awards and collective agreements in force in that State shall alone be applicable to certain international road transport operations confined to their territories and covering a distance of less than 100 km from the point of departure to the point of arrival of a vehicle, and to regular passenger services.

[Agreements to be reached with third countries under art 2(2) will be concluded, on behalf of Member States of the EEC, by the Community; see Council Regulation (EEC) 2829/77, art 3.]

Article 3: Application of some provisions of the Agreement to road transport performed by vehicles registered in the territories of non-contracting States

1. Each Contracting Party shall apply in its territory, in respect of international road transport performed by any vehicle registered in the territory of a State which is not a Contracting Party to this Agreement, [provisions not less strict than those laid down in articles 5, 6, 7, 8, 9, 10, 11, in article 12 paragraphs 1, 2, 6 and 7 and in article 12*bis* of this Agreement].

2. However, any Contracting Party shall be free not to apply the provisions of paragraph 1 of this article

(a) to the international carriage of goods by road by a vehicle whose permissible maximum weight does not exceed 3·5 tons.

(b) to international road transport confined to its territory and to the territory of an adjoining State which is not a Contracting Party to this Agreement if the vehicle concerned does not while in its territory travel beyond a zone contiguous to the frontier and defined as a *frontalier* zone or if it crosses its territory in transit only.

[Article 3 is printed as amended by Cmnd 9037.

The measures provided for under art 3(2) will be adopted by the Council of the European Communities on a proposal from the Commission; see Council Regulation (EEC) 2829/77, art 3.]

Article 4: General principles

1. In all international road transport to which this Agreement applies, the undertaking and crew members shall observe in the matter of rest periods, driving periods and manning, the rules laid down by domestic laws and regulations in the district of the State in which the crew member normally exercises his occupational activities and by arbitral awards or collective agreements in force in that district: the rest periods and driving periods shall be calculated in conformity with the said laws and regulations, arbitral awards or collective agreements. In so far as the rules thus applicable are not at least as strict as the provisions of articles 6, 7, 8, 9, 10 and 11 of this Agreement the latter provisions shall be observed.

2. Except by special agreement between the Contracting Parties concerned or except to the extent that pursuant to article 2, paragraph 2, of this Agreement certain provisions of this Agreement are not applied, no Contracting Party shall enforce observance of the provisions of its domestic laws and regulations regarding the matters dealt with in this Agreement by undertakings of another Contracting Party, or by crew members of vehicles registered by another Contracting Party, in cases where the said provisions are stricter than those of this Agreement.

[When signing the agreement, the Contracting Parties agreed the following statement on art 4 which was set out in the Protocol of Signature to the agreement:

'The provisions of article 4, paragraph 1, shall not be construed as rendering applicable, outside the State in which the vehicle performing the transport operation is registered, any prohibition of traffic on certain days or at certain hours which may apply in that State to certain categories of vehicles. The provisions of article 4, paragraph 2, shall not be construed as preventing a Contracting Party from enforcing in its territory the provisions of its domestic laws and regulations which prohibit certain categories of vehicle traffic on certain days or at certain hours.

'Every Contracting Party which, being a Party to af special agreement as referred to in article 4, paragraph 2, of this Agreement, authorizes international transport operations beginning and ending in the territories of the Parties to the said special agreement by vehicles registered in the territory of a State which, being a Contracting Party to this Agreement, is not a Party to the said special agreement may make it a condition for the conclusion of bilateral or multilateral agreements authorizing such transport operations that the crews performing those operations shall, in the territories of States Parties to the said special agreement, comply with the provisions of the said special agreement.']*

Article 5: Conditions to be fulfilled by drivers

1. The minimum age of drivers engaged in the international road transport of goods shall be:

(a) for vehicles of a permissible maximum weight not exceeding 7·5 tons, 18 years;

(b) for other vehicles:

    (i) 21 years, or

    (ii) 18 years where the person concerned holds a certificate of professional competence recognized by the Contracting Party in whose territory the vehicle is registered and confirming the completion of a training course for drivers of vehicles intended for the carriage of goods by road. However, in the case of drivers whose age is less than 21 years any Contracting Party may:

— prohibit them from driving such vehicles in its territory even if they hold the certificate aforesaid; or

— restrict permission to drive such vehicles to those who hold certificates which it recognizes as having been issued after the completion of a training course for drivers of vehicles intended for the carriage of goods by road equivalent to the course prescribed by its own domestic laws and regulations.

2. If under the provisions of article 10 of this Agreement two drivers are required to be on board, one of the drivers shall have reached the age of 21 years.

3. Drivers engaged in the international road transport of passengers shall have reached the age of 21 years.

4. Drivers of vehicles shall be responsible and trustworthy. They shall possess sufficient experience and the qualifications essential to thet performance of the services required.

[In relation to art 5, the Government of Spain (on depositing its instrument of accession) has stated that it 'avails itself of the first of the options provided for in article 5, paragraph 1 (b) (ii) of the agreement whereby persons whose age is less than 21 years may be prohibited from driving in its territory vehicles of a permissible maximum weight exceeding 7.5 tons'.]

Article 6: Daily rest period

1. (a) Except in the cases referred to in paragraphs 3 and 4 of this article, every crew member assigned to the international road transport of goods shall have had a daily rest period of not less than eleven consecutive hours in the period of twenty-four hours preceding any time when he is exercising one of his occupational activities.

(b) The daily rest period referred to in sub-paragraph (a) of this paragraph may, not more than twice in the course of any one week, be reduced to not less than nine consecutive hours provided that the rest period can be taken at the crew member's normal place of residence; or not more than twice in the course of any one week, to not less than eight consecutive hours in cases where for operational reasons the rest period cannot be taken at the crew member's normal place of residence.

2. (a) Except in the cases referred to in paragraphs 3 and 4 of this article, every crew member assigned to the international road transport of passengers shall have had, in the period of twenty-four hours preceding any time when he is exercising one of his occupational activities, either:

(i) a daily rest period of not less than ten consecutive hours, which shall not be reduced during the week; or

(ii) a daily rest period of not less than eleven consecutive hours, which may be reduced twice a week to not less than ten consecutive hours and twice a week to not less than nine consecutive hours, provided that in the latter two cases the transport operation shall include a scheduled break of not less than four consecutive hours, or two scheduled breaks each of not less than two consecutive hours and that during these breaks the crew member shall neither exercise any of his operational activities nor perform any other work as an occupation.

(b) The individual control book referred to in article 12 of this Agreement shall contain particulars showing the daily rest system applied during the current week to the crew member assigned to the international road transport of passengers.

3. If the vehicle is manned by two drivers and has no bunk enabling crew members to lie down comfortably, each crew member shall have had a daily rest period of not less than ten consecutive hours during the period of twenty-seven hours preceding any time when he is exercising one of his occupational activities.

4. If the vehicle is manned by two drivers and has a bunk enabling crew members to lie down comfortably, each crew member shall have had a daily rest period of not less than eight consecutive hours during the period of thirty hours preceding any time when he is exercising one of his occupational activities.

5. The rest periods specified in this article shall be taken outside the vehicle; however, if the vehicle has a bunk enabling crew members to lie down comfortably, the rest periods may be taken on that bunk provided that the vehicle is stationary.

[Article 6*bis*: Interruption of the daily rest period in the course of combined transport operations

Where a crew member engaged in the carriage of goods or passengers accompanies a vehicle which is transported by ferryboat or train, the daily rest period may be interrupted not more than once, provided the following conditions are fulfilled:

(a) that part of the daily rest period spent on land may be taken before or after the portion of the daily rest period taken on board the ferryboat or the train,

(b) the period between the two portions of the daily rest period must be as short as possible and may on no account exceed one hour before embarkation or after disembarkation, customs formalities being included in the embarkation or disembarkation operations,

(c) during both portions of the rest period the crew member must have access to a bunk or couchette.

(d) where a daily rest period is interrupted in this way, it shall be increased by two hours,

(e) any time spent on board a ferryboat or a train and not counted as part of the daily rest period shall be regarded as a break as defined in article 8.]

[Article 6bis was inserted by Cmnd 9037.]

Article 7: Daily driving period, maximum weekly and fortnightly driving period

1. The total driving time between two consecutive daily rest periods as prescribed by article 6 of this Agreement, which driving time is hereinafter referred to as the 'daily driving period', shall not exceed eight hours.

2. In the case of drivers of vehicles other than vehicles as referred to in article 10 of this Agreement the daily driving period may, by derogation from the provisions of paragraph 1 of this article, be extended to nine hours not more than twice in one week.

3. The driving time may not exceed forty-eight hours in one week or ninety-two hours in one fortnight.

Article 8: Maximum continuous driving periods

1. (*a*) No continuous driving period shall exceed four hours except where the driver cannot reach a convenient stopping place or his destination; in such a case the driving period may be extended by not more than thirty minutes, provided that the use of this option does not result in a breach of the provisions of article 7 of this Agreement.

(*b*) Any driving period which is interrupted only by breaks not meeting at least the provisions of paragraph 2 or paragraph 3 of this article shall be deemed to be continuous.

2. (*a*) For drivers of vehicles as referred to in article 10 of this Agreement, driving shall be interrupted for not less than one hour at the end of the period referred to in paragraph 1 of this article.

(*b*) This break may be replaced by two uninterrupted breaks of not less than thirty minutes each, spaced out over the daily driving period in such a way that the provisions of paragraph 1 of this article are complied with.

3. (*a*) For drivers of vehicles other than vehicles as referred to in article 10 of this Agreement, and where the daily driving period does not exceed eight hours, driving shall be interrupted for not less than thirty consecutive minutes at the end of the period referred to in paragraph 1 of this article.

(*b*) This break may be replaced by two uninterrupted breaks of not less than twenty minutes each or by three uninterrupted breaks of not less than fifteen minutes each, which may all be spaced out over the driving period referred to in paragraph 1 of this article or may in part fall within that period and in part immediately follow it.

(*c*) If the daily driving period exceeds eight hours the driver shall be required to discontinue driving during not less than two uninterrupted periods of thirty minutes.

4. During breaks as referred to in paragraphs 2 or 3 of this article the driver shall not engage in any occupational activity other than supervision of the vehicle and its load. However, if the vehicle is manned by two drivers the requirements of paragraphs 2 or 3 of this article shall be deemed to be met if the driver who is having his break does not engage in any of the activities falling under item 7a in the daily sheet of the individual control book referred to in article 12 of this Agreement.

[The reference in art 8, para 4, to item 7a in the daily sheet of the individual control book is to the item concerning actual work other than driving. (The individual control book is set out in the Annex to this agreement which is not reproduced in this work.)]

Article 9: Weekly rest period

1. In addition to the daily rest periods referred to in article 6 of this Agreement, every crew member shall have a weekly rest period of not less than twenty-four consecutive hours which shall be immediately preceded or followed by a daily rest period conforming to the provisions of the said article 6.

2. (*a*) However, during the period from 1 April to 30 September inclusive the weekly rest period referred to in paragraph 1 of this article may be replaced, for crew members of vehicles used for the international road transport of passengers, by a rest period of not less than sixty consecutive hours to be taken in full before the expiry of any maximum period of fourteen consecutive days. This rest period shall be immediately preceded or followed by a daily rest period conforming to the provisions of article 6 of this Agreement.

(*b*) The provisions of this paragraph shall not apply to crew members of vehicles used on regular passenger services.

Article 10: Manning

[Subject to the provisions of article 12*bis* paragraph 2 of this Agreement, in the case of]

(*a*) a combination of vehicles including more than one trailer or semi-trailer; or of

(*b*) a combination of vehicles used for the carriage of passengers where the permissible maximum weight of the trailer or semi-trailer exceeds 5 metric tons; or of

(*c*) a combination of vehicles used for the carriage of goods where the permissible maximum weight of the combination of vehicles exceeds 20 metric tons,

the driver shall be accompanied by another driver from the start of the journey, or be replaced by another driver after 450 km, if the distance to be travelled between two consecutive daily rest periods exceeds 450 km.

[Article 10 is printed as amended by Cmnd 9037.]

Article 11: Exceptional cases

Provided that there is no detriment to road safety, the driver may depart from the provisions of articles 6, 7, 8 and 10 of this Agreement in case of danger, in case of *force majeure*, to render aid, or as a result of a breakdown, to the extent necessary to ensure the safety of persons, of the vehicle or of its load and to enable him to reach a suitable stopping place or, according to circumstances, the end of his journey. The driver [shall record in the individual control book or in the case mentioned in article 12*bis*, as appropriate, in the record sheet and/or in the other control documents envisaged under paragraph 1 of that article, the nature of and] reason for his departure from those provisions.

[Article 11 is printed as amended by Cmnd 9037.]

Article 12: Individual control book

1. Every driver or driver's mate shall enter in an individual control book, as the day proceeds, a record of his occupational activities and rest periods. He shall keep the book with him and produce it whenever required by the control authorities.

2. The specifications with which the control book must comply and the requirements to be met in keeping the records are set out in the annex to this Agreement.

3. The Contracting Parties shall take all necessary measures concerning the issue and control of individual control books, and, in particular, measures required to prevent the simultaneous use of two such books by the same crew member.

4. Every undertaking shall keep a register of the individual control books it uses; the register shall show at least the name of the driver or driver's mate to whom the book is issued, the driver's or driver's mate's signature in the margin, the number of the book, the date of issue to the driver or driver's mate and the date of the last daily sheet completed by the driver or driver's mate before final return of the control book to the undertaking after use.

5. Undertakings shall keep the used books for a period of not less than twelve months after the date of the last entry and shall produce them together with the registers of issue, at the request of the control authorities.

6. At the beginning of an international road transport operation every driver or driver's mate shall have with him an individual control book conforming to the specifications in the annex to this Agreement, in which the data relating to the seven days preceding that on which the transport operation begins shall be entered. However, if domestic laws and regulations of the State where the driver or driver's mate exercises his occupational activities do not prescribe the obligation to use an individual control book conforming to the specifications in the annex to this Agreement for road transport operations which are not international, it will suffice if the data relating to the 'uninterrupted rest period before coming on duty' and the 'daily driving periods' during the seven days concerned appear against items 12 and 13 of the daily sheets or in the weekly report of the individual control book conforming to the specifications in the annex to this Agreement.

7. It shall be open to any Contracting Party, in the case of a vehicle registered in a State which is not a Contracting Party to this Agreement, merely to require, in lieu of an individual control book conforming to the specifications in the annex to this Agreement, papers made out in the same form as the daily sheets of the said book.

[The references in art 12, para 6, to 'items 12 and 13 of the daily sheets . . . of the individual control book' relate to the total duration of the rest period before going on duty and to the driving period, respectively. (The Annex to the agreement which sets out the individual control book is not reproduced.)

On signing the agreement, the Contracting Parties agreed the following statement which was set out in the Protocol of Signature to the agreement: 'The undersigned undertake to discuss after the Agreement has entered into force the insertion therein, by means of an amendment, of a clause providing for the use of a control device of approved type which when placed on the vehicle would so far as possible replace the individual control book'.]

[Article 12*bis*: Control device

1. If a Contracting Party describes or authorises the installation and use on vehicles registered in its territory of a mechanical control device, such device may give rise to complete or partial exemption from the filling in of the individual control book mentioned in article 12, under the following conditions:

- (*a*) The control device must be of a type either approved or recognised by one of the Contracting Parties;
- (*b*) If the crew includes more than one person and if the recording is not made on separate sheets but on only one sheet, this must show clearly the part of the recording corresponding to each of the persons;
- (*c*) If the device provides for the recording of crew members' driving times, times spent performing occupational activities other than driving, and rest periods as well as vehicle speeds and distance covered, the keeping of the individual control book may be entirely dispensed with;
- (*d*) If the device provides only for recording driving time, time during which the vehicle is stationary, speed and distance covered, the exemption will only be partial and limited to the entries in the daily sheets of the said control book, the crew members being obliged to complete daily the appropriate columns of a weekly report conforming to the model sheet (*e*) appearing in the annex to the Agreement;
- (*e*) If the normal and appropriate use of a control device installed on a vehicle is not possible, each crew member shall enter by hand, using the appropriate graphic representation, the details corresponding to his occupational activities

and rest periods on a record sheet, or on a daily sheet conforming to the model sheet (*c*) appearing in the annex to the Agreement;

(*f*) When, by reason of their being away from the vehicle, the crew members are unable to make use of the device, they shall insert by hand, using the appropriate graphic representation, in the record sheet or a daily sheet conforming to the model sheet (*c*) envisaged in the annex to this Agreement, the various times corresponding to their occupational activities while they were away;

(*g*) The crew members must always have available, and be able to present for inspection, as appropriate, the record sheets and/or the other control documents filled in as provided under (*c*), (*d*), (*e*) and (*f*) of this paragraph, relating to the previous seven days;

(*h*) The crew members must ensure that the control device be activated and handled correctly and that, in case of malfunctioning, it be repaired as soon as possible.

2. If the control device within the meaning of paragraph 1 is installed and used on a vehicle registered in the territory of one of the Contracting Parties, the application of the provisions of article 10 of this Agreement to that vehicle shall not be required by the other Contracting Parties.

3. Undertakings shall keep, as appropriate, the record sheets and/or the other control documents filled in as provided under (*c*), (*d*) and (*e*) of paragraph 1 of this Article, for a period of not less than twelve months after the date of the last entry and shall produce them at the request of the control authorities.]

[Article 12bis was inserted by Cmnd 9037.]

Articles 13–26 [*Not reproduced.*]

* * *

SIGNATURES

[The following States have signed and ratified the agreement:

Austria
Belgium
Federal Republic of Germany (including West Berlin)
France
Luxembourg
the Netherlands
Norway
Portugal
Sweden and
the United Kingdom (including the Isle of Man)

The following States which signed the agreement have not yet ratified it (ratification being required under art 16, para 2):

Italy
Poland and
Switzerland

The agreement came into operation, in accordance with art 16, para 4, on 5 January 1976; it came into operation in the United Kingdom on 18 August 1978.

On signature of the agreement, the Contracting States agreed the following declaration which was set out in the Protocol of Signature to the agreement: 'The Contracting Parties declare that this Agreement is without prejudice to such provisions as may, if appropriate, subsequently be drawn up in the matter of the duration and spread-over of work.']

ACCESSIONS

[The following countries have acceded to the agreement:

> *Czechoslovakia*
> *Democratic Republic of Germany*
> *Denmark*
> *Greece*
> *Spain*
> *Union of Soviet Socialist Republics and*
> *Yugoslavia]*

ANNEX
INDIVIDUAL CONTROL BOOK
* * *

PROTOCOL OF SIGNATURE
* * *